EXAMPLES & EXPLANATIONS

Property

ASPEN PUBLISHERS

EXAMPLES & EXPLANATIONS

Property

Third Edition

Barlow Burke

John S. Myers & Alvina Reckman Myers Scholar
and Professor of Law
American University
Washington College of Law

Joseph Snoe

Professor of Law
Samford University
Cumberland School of Law

Wolters Kluwer
Law & Business

AUSTIN   BOSTON   CHICAGO   NEW YORK   THE NETHERLANDS

Aspen Publishers
Attn: Permissions Department
76 Ninth Avenue, 7th Floor
New York, NY   10011-5201

To contact Customer Care, e-mail customer.care@aspenpublishers.com,
call 1-800-234-1660, fax 1-800-901-9075, or mail correspondence to:

Aspen Publishers
Attn: Order Department
PO Box 990
Frederick, MD 21705

Printed in the United States of America.

1 2 3 4 5 6 7 8 9 0

ISBN 978-0-7355-7031-3

Library of Congress Cataloging-in-Publication Data
Burke, D. Barlow, 1941-
    Property : examples & explanations / Barlow Burke, Joseph Snoe. — 3rd ed.
        p. cm.
    Includes index.
    ISBN 978-0-7355-7031-3 (perfectbound)
    1. Property — United States — Cases. 2. Property — United States — Problems, exercises,
etc. I. Snoe, Joseph A. II. Title.

    KF560.B87 2008
    346.7304 — dc22

                                                                    2007049420

About Wolters Kluwer Law & Business

Wolters Kluwer Law & Business is a leading provider of research information and workflow solutions in key specialty areas. The strengths of the individual brands of Aspen Publishers, CCH, Kluwer Law International and Loislaw are aligned within Wolters Kluwer Law & Business to provide comprehensive, in-depth solutions and expert-authored content for the legal, professional and education markets.

CCH was founded in 1913 and has served more than four generations of business professionals and their clients. The CCH products in the Wolters Kluwer Law & Business group are highly regarded electronic and print resources for legal, securities, antitrust and trade regulation, government contracting, banking, pension, payroll, employment and labor, and health-care reimbursement and compliance professionals.

Aspen Publishers is a leading information provider for attorneys, business professionals and law students. Written by preeminent authorities, Aspen products offer analytical and practical information in a range of specialty practice areas from securities law and intellectual property to mergers and acquisitions and pension/benefits. Aspen's trusted legal education resources provide professors and students with high-quality, up-to-date and effective resources for successful instruction and study in all areas of the law.

Kluwer Law International supplies the global business community with comprehensive English-language international legal information. Legal practitioners, corporate counsel and business executives around the world rely on the Kluwer Law International journals, loose-leafs, books and electronic products for authoritative information in many areas of international legal practice.

Loislaw is a premier provider of digitized legal content to small law firm practitioners of various specializations. Loislaw provides attorneys with the ability to quickly and efficiently find the necessary legal information they need, when and where they need it, by facilitating access to primary law as well as state-specific law, records, forms and treatises.

Wolters Kluwer Law & Business, a unit of Wolters Kluwer, is headquartered in New York and Riverwoods, Illinois. Wolters Kluwer is a leading multinational publisher and information services company.

Summary of Contents

PART I. POSSESSION, PERSONAL PROPERTY, AND ADVERSE POSSESSION

PART II. COMMON LAW ESTATES AND INTERESTS IN REAL PROPERTY

PART III. THE LAW OF LANDLORD AND TENANT

PART IV. TRANSFERS OF LAND

PART V. PRIVATE LAND USE CONTROLS

PART VI. PUBLIC LAND USE CONTROLS

Contents

Contents

Contents

PART II. COMMON LAW ESTATES AND INTERESTS IN REAL PROPERTY

Contents

Contents

PART III. THE LAW OF LANDLORD AND TENANT

Contents

Chapter 20   Premises Liability of Landlords   333

Chapter 21   The Holdover Tenant and Concluding Comments   341

PART IV. TRANSFERS OF LAND

Chapter 22   The Sales Contract   351

Contents

Contents

PART V. PRIVATE LAND USE CONTROLS

Contents

Chapter 29 Assignability, Scope, and Termination of Easements 507

Chapter 30 Real Covenants and Equitable Servitudes: Running with the Land 527

PART VI. PUBLIC LAND USE CONTROLS

Contents

Preface

Property, the study of the rights and duties among persons with respect to objects, land, and other assets, is perhaps the least intuitive of all the required courses taught during the first year of law school. The course blends a mixture of abstract relationships and concrete rules, at once a remnant of laws introduced in bygone centuries and a dynamic reflection of changes occurring today.

Property: Examples & Explanations discusses the fundamental definitions, rules, and concepts covered in Property courses. Most of this book's readers will be first-year students either preparing for class, supplementing class discussion, or studying for examinations. We aim to make the book useful at each of these stages of your semester. It will help bring the course materials into focus and provide the many perspectives to help you "think like a lawyer."

Each chapter contains an introductory overview that supplements (but does not supplant) your daily class assignments and aids in your review for examinations. Each overview provides a clear and accessible exposition of the fundamentals of the law of property, with the object of helping someone focusing on the subject for the first time.

Each chapter also includes a series of Examples that test your understanding of the material and your ability to apply the law to specific problems. We recommend that you think about, analyze, and write answers to as many Examples as you can. Writing out your responses is good practice for writing final examinations. It also forces you to analyze the facts and the law, evaluating possible solutions and ramifications of each choice you make. Alternatively, you might discuss each Example with a study partner or study group, gaining insight from the discussion.

Following the Examples in each chapter are Explanations that give our solutions. The Explanations discuss majority and minority rules and offer insights not readily grasped in class discussions or in the introductory overviews of the chapters themselves. Some Explanations will help you identify your weak areas; others will reinforce your conclusions and analysis. We have strived to make each Explanation a stepping stone on the path to success in your property course.

The Third Edition incorporates new developments in property law, such as the increasingly important role that trusts play in estate planning, the role of summary procedure in defining the landlord-tenant relationship, the continuing importance of the Restatement (Third) of Property in the law of mortgages and servitudes, the increasing sales of homes by owners, lateral and subjacent support of neighboring lands, securing easements for cable networks, and the effect of recent Supreme Court cases on takings jurisprudence.

There are no exhaustive citations of authority in this book. What citations are used in the text or in our Explanations we consider helpful either to orient the student reader to casebook materials or to indicate basic writings and leading cases in the field.

We enjoy our magnificent subject and want students to grasp its fundamental rules and concepts, all the while enjoying their experience.

B.B.
J.S.

January 2008

Acknowledgments

Barlow Burke acknowledges the helpful and patient research of five research assistants, Les Anderson, Athena Cheng, Stephanie Quaranta, Rachel Rueben, and Meryl Eschen Mills, while they were law students. He also acknowledges with appreciation the financial support, over several summers, of the Washington College of Law, American University. Joseph Snoe appreciates Diane Wade, Judy McAlister, and Tracy Luke for their help with the manuscript. He also thanks the Cumberland School of Law, Samford University, for its financial support.

We are both grateful for the guidance of the several anonymous reviewers of this manuscript provided by Aspen Publishers, the many comments of students and professors on the first two editions, and for the editorial work of Carol McGeehan, Jessica Barmack, Eric Holt, John Lyman, Vincent Nordhaus, Sarah Zobel, and Margaret Rehberger at Aspen — all gave their professional best. Aside from the above, we acknowledge our limitations, inevitable and otherwise, in attempting to pull so diverse a subject within the covers of one book, and look forward to the diverse suggestions of readers for the improvement of this third edition.

B.B.
J.S.

Property

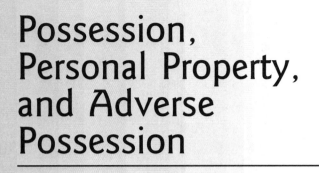

Possession, Personal Property, and Adverse Possession

PART I

CHAPTER 1

The Law of Property

INTRODUCTION

Some courses on property law begin with the analysis of cases — sometimes they concern the acquisition of personal property, sometimes wild animals; and sometimes they introduce the subject with a U.S. Supreme Court case concerning the Fifth Amendment's takings clause or with a case about Native American claims to property that throws our own American system into perspective. Historical and philosophical readings about property law's development might also be used to gain perspective.

Different perspectives on the institution or the idea of property have been around for a long time. These perspectives have long been controversial. Plato and Aristotle disagreed as to property's role in society. Since that time, property has been viewed variously as the product of one's labor (John Locke), as an extension of one's will (Georg W. F. Hegel), as the product of a person's settled expectations (Jeremy Bentham), and as the foundation of capitalism and class conflict (Karl Marx). Anthropologists, psychologists, and social scientists from many disciplines have more recently taken a turn at assessing its function. If there ever was an idea that held society in a love-hate relationship, it is property; it is something that society lives with uneasily, but cannot live without. The Ten Commandments do not protect property, but do forbid the stealing of it. Neither does our federal Constitution endorse a right to property, but provides that the state may not take it without due process or payment of just compensation. Property rights have long been regulated, and are not absolute.

In the first year of law school, property is studied along with the two other wide-ranging areas of private and commercial law, the law of torts and the law of contracts. The three subjects are studied in separate classes, but even though the signs on the classroom doors are different, this curricular separation should not lead you to the conclusion that the three subjects are entirely distinct. They are not. They are constantly intersecting. Property and torts, for example, have in common an historic origin in the cause of action for trespass, and often a substantive statement of a rule of property law begins or ends with the phrase "absent an agreement to the contrary" — meaning that persons involved are free to make a contract providing what the rule does not. In particular, the law of landlord and tenant (pertaining to leases) is a recently developed combination of contract and property law. Property, contract, and tort doctrines constantly arise and intersect in any law practice.

The subject matter of a course on property typically covers several topics. There may be a roadmap to your course in contracts, but with property there is no *one* roadmap; instead, there are at least six roadmaps. Thus, to the beginning student, the course's subject matter may seem huge. Personal property, common law estates and concurrent interests, landlord and tenant, real estate transactions, easements and covenants, and public land use regulation are the topics most frequently mapped in the first-year course on property.

Although some of these subjects will be unfamiliar if you are reading this during your first semester or quarter of law study, once you delve into each of them you will quickly realize that each has its origins in a different historical era of our legal system's development. The economic and social context in which the rules of each arose shaped it in different ways: Each developed in spurts and at different times. For example, common law estates developed rapidly in the late middle ages, while the law of landlord and tenant developed most quickly over the past several decades. Our legal system's rules for real estate transactions developed in response first to the system of estates, then to the development of the executory contract in the eighteenth century, and finally to American modifications in the English system designed to suit our own needs. The law of easements and covenants developed rapidly in the nineteenth century in response to the industrialization and urbanization then taking place. Our system of land use regulation developed gradually over the last century, but did so more rapidly during some decades — the 1920s, the 1950s, and the 1970s — than during others.

Add to this variety of origins the many intersections of property law with that of torts and contracts, and the teaching and study of property law becomes a challenge of a different dimension than is encountered in the latter subjects. As the topics change, beginning students need to treat each change as if it were the start of a new course, steeping themselves in both the context and the body of rules and doctrines governing each new topic.

Putting the various contexts you study into perspective should help you realize that the study of property is often the study of **tenures** — using an old-fashioned word for the study of the many ways in which property may be possessed or held — rather than the study of property itself. Thus the study of property is of the various interests that define the rights of its holder and of the documents conveying various interests in property and defining how it may be used, kept, or sold. It is also the study of deeds, leases, and the various other documents that purport to create or transfer it or an interest in it.

Over the course of history people have wanted property of various kinds and in so many guises that one has to conclude that there is something basic and human at work in its creation and protection. Not every society has used a law of property during its development. China is an example of one that did not. However, there is a correlation between the development of some democratic, nontotalitarian societies and the degree of protection given property; one can't be said to cause the other, but they coexist well.

Property is not a thing wanted for itself, and property law is not about one person's relationship to a thing. Instead, it is about relationships between and among persons with regard to a thing. Put in a more humane way, property is derived from our wanting to be involved with others. Property permits one person to exclude another from using a thing; to use it himself; to gain rents, profits, or income from it; to sell it; or to give it by will to one relative and not another. All this is possible only when one's relationship to property is clear insofar as others are bound to respect it.

Property law is a series of rules defining a person's relationship to a thing that others must respect. The former is called an owner. The primary right of an owner is the right to exclude others from using or profiting from a thing. If the thing is movable, the thing becomes **personal property**. Land and the improvements on it become **real property**. The study of property generally includes both personal and real property, with a touch of intellectual property.

Defining property as a three-way relationship (owner to thing, others to thing, others to owner) requires that the legal rules pertaining to it have widespread support. Support in this sense is the result of an appeal to the terms of a legal rule, its underlying policies and historical precedent, the judicial procedures in which the rule was formed, and the philosophy of law or jurisprudence underlying all of these.

Property law is the creation of society, useful to make society function, and not a product of natural law, although most would also say that property supports and enhances a person's identity and that a person's acquisitiveness is as close to a natural instinct as one can come.

COMMON LAW CASES

Property law is largely **state law**. If the case concerned property, it typically arose in a state court. Each of our states, territories, and the District of Columbia, with the exception of Louisiana, adopted for its legal system the common law of England in all of the jurisdictional, decisional, and analytical senses in which that phrase is used. So property law is typically state law, as opposed to federal law. As in the law of torts or contracts, courts often speak of the New York, the Pennsylvania, or the California rule. Such references make the point that, technically, it is too facile to speak of a law of property — instead, each state in our country has its own law. Even when a federal court decides a case involving property, it uses the law of the state whose law applies and, in the absence of a federal constitutional or statutory issue, must follow state court precedent.

A party who felt the trial court erred as to matter of law or finding of fact can appeal to an appeals or appellate court to review the challenged matter. Most cases reproduced in casebooks are appellate cases. Usually seven to nine judges sit together on a state's intermediate or highest appellate court, the latter typically called the state's supreme court or court of appeals.

An appellate opinion has four parts. First, there is a statement of the facts of the case. These are facts found as such by the jury or, in a nonjury matter, by the judge sitting as a fact-finder in the trial court, and accepted as such by the appellate court. In an appeal from the trial court's decision, the facts are not retried, unless they are so unreasonable that the record of the case in the trial court does not provide any basis for them. So facts recited in an appellate opinion typically accept the factual determinations of the trial court.

Second, there is a statement of the legal issues involved in the case, followed, third, by a statement of the rule(s) resolving the issues and applying the rules to the facts. This third portion may be brief, but sometimes is lengthened into a fourth part of the opinion. There the judge articulates a rationale for the rule — perhaps a public policy underlying it, and an explanation as to why it is fair to apply it to the case at hand; how it promotes ethical behavior in attorneys, litigants, or the public at large; or how it might be efficiently administered or used in the future. Articulating a rationale usually involves the application (or not) of cases with precedential value for the court. The judge here may explain what aspect of the facts is particularly important to the decision or what is not being decided (see below, dicta) in order to throw the decision itself into relief. Finally, the judge writing the opinion gives the holding and the decision in the case.

The cases in casebooks are selected for their facts and details, their analysis, their influence, or their widespread acceptance. They may have more than one opinion — they may produce a (1) majority opinion, in which most of the judges on the court agree on the statement of the law, the analysis, and the result — the judgment or other remedy given in the case; (2) a dissenting opinion, with which some but not most of the judges agree; or (3) a concurring opinion, in which some judges agree with the majority's result, but not with some other aspect of their opinion. If there is more than one, the comparisons and contrasts between them may produce interesting statements as to the law, analysis, or remedies involved.

The cases studied may not represent the law of the state in which you eventually will practice law, but not all judicial opinions are created equal. There are at least two reasons for this. First, the United States' more than 50 common law systems have produced many fine judges and attorneys but, yesterday as today, some were and are more famous than others — Kent, Story, Shaw, Cooley, Holmes, and Cardozo, to name a few. Their influence goes beyond the borders of their states. Second, the **precedential rules** of authority — looking first to a judge's own state or jurisdiction, then for similar cases in other jurisdictions, then to secondary (or noncase) authorities such as law reviews and legal treatises — produce a tendency to make the law of many jurisdictions into one uniform body of law, and many opinions into works of considerable scholarship.

Amid the secondary authorities, some of the more formal organized methods of legal expression, backed by large sectors of the legal profession, also re-enforce this tendency to uniformity. First, there are the American Law Institute's **Restatements of the Law**. Its first Restatement of the Law, Property, was published in 1944. Restatements of the Law (Second), Property, have been published more recently: for Landlord and Tenant in 1977, for Security (Mortgages) in 1996, and for Servitudes (Easements and Covenants) in 1998. Other property subjects are in draft. Restatements are secondary authorities publishing their drafters' versions of the rules of law taken from decided cases, although not always the rule settled by a majority of cases deciding a particular issue. Sometimes drafters prefer what they see as a trend in the decided cases and extract their rule from the cases they see as representing that trend, rather than a rule representing the law established in a majority of states. Sometimes there is no majority; sometimes the law is unsettled or open. Whatever approach the Restatement takes, its decision is influential and its text will disclose the reasons and the authorities behind its choice.

Second, the Commissioners on **Uniform State Laws** have published Model Laws for adoption by American jurisdictions. The Uniform Commercial Code that you study in contracts class is the most successful of these laws. The Uniform Landlord Tenant Act, the Uniform Land Transactions Act, and the Uniform Probate Code are examples that have been influential, if not widely or completely adopted, in the law of property. Such laws may codify, modify, or repeal common law rules and, like the Restatements, may be cited by judges deciding common law cases as embodying a legal rule.

Third, there are **treatises** with discussions of the law attempting to make sense of disparate decisions and statutes. The *American Law of Property* (1952) is a collection of essays by (mostly) law professors specializing in the law of property. *Thompson on Real Property* (1994) is a more recent collection of such essays. Roger Cunningham, William Stoebuck, and Dale Whitman, *The Law of Property* (2d ed. 1993), is an excellent one-volume treatise. More specialized treatises, such as Raymond Brown, *Personal Property* (3d ed. 1975); Jon Bruce & James Ely, *Easements and Licenses in Land* (rev. ed. 1995); and Daniel Mandelker, *Land Use Law* (5th ed. 2003), perform the same function within narrower limits. Although there are many excellent treatments on common law estates and interests in the previously mentioned works, John Makdisi & Daniel Bogart, *Estates in Land and Future Interests* (5th ed. 2007), is an excellent workbook on a subject some students find challenging.

CASE ANALYSIS

Much law is gleaned from the analysis of cases. Case analysis is an essential skill for attorneys. If the case is concerned with the substantive law of property, the case is probably one involving a common law rule — i.e., a rule formulated by judges for cases that they heard and decided. Case law or **common law** rules are established by court decisions, as opposed to those made by legislatures enacting a statute. A judge deciding a case tries to resolve the issues in the case by following or drawing from prior decisions by judges in his or her jurisdiction. This doctrine of precedent is unique to the common law as opposed to civil law or code systems of law used in other countries.

The **doctrine of precedent** (or stare decisis) is fundamental to case analysis. It rests on the idea that people in similar situations should receive similar treatment at the hands of a court. Similar cases should be decided in a similar way so that people are treated as equally and fairly as possible, and so that people not in court who find themselves in a situation similar to one that a court has decided may predict what the law will be if and when they go to court. A judicial decision, published or reported in an opinion, not only binds the parties to the litigation that produced it, but also has predictive value for others.

An opinion has predictive value only when another court is bound to follow it. At the state level, this means that the opinion of a state Supreme Court binds itself and all courts lower in the judicial hierarchy of the state, thus binding any intermediate appellate court and all trial courts. A trial court decision, at the other end of that hierarchy, is not binding outside the county or municipality in which the court sits, although it may be **persuasive authority**.

The root idea is that of providing equality for persons in similar situations. Deciding who is in a similar situation — not an identical situation (that almost never happens) — involves analysis of a reported case. Appellate or reported cases may be distinguished — i.e., read narrowly to avoid their applications — or applied — i.e., read for similarities.

Distinguishing case precedent is often necessary because courts have no control over who brings a case to court. In formulating and enacting a regulation or a statute, a legislature or an administrative agency might consider all the possible or predictable situations to which its work product might apply and draft a regulation or statute encompassing them; a court has no such opportunity. If a judge in an opinion writes more generally about the law than the facts of the case require, that part of the opinion will be considered *obiter dictum* — Latin for a statement "made in passing" — or **dicta**. Dicta may be included to explain a decision, or to limit its applicability to the facts found at trial — particularly when the facts were contested at trial. While not binding as legal precedent, dicta may be a persuasive authority even so.

Lots of cases, with lots of rules, may eventually form a body of law encompassing most aspects of a subject (some attorneys refer to rules synthesized from many cases as legal **doctrine** — but such terms of art have various and variable meanings). From many cases, a synthesis of the law may emerge. Producing this synthesis is a form of inductive reasoning — deriving a general rule from the individual cases. The generalization takes place using the materials the judge finds at hand — case(s), statute(s), and secondary authorities. If necessary (nothing else being available), even one case might be generalized for use in an opinion in another case.

Application of a case to another situation is a process of making analogies between the case and the situation at hand. It is often arranged in an opinion as a syllogism, a form of deductive reasoning, as in the following:

(1) Possession of land is necessary to bring an action of trespass.
(2) Alex has possession of land.
(3) Alex may bring an action of trespass.

Here the first proposition (1) is a major or general premise or rule, (2) is a minor or factual premise, and (3) is a conclusion, permitting a general rule to be applied to a particular situation.

The reasoning found in judicial opinions is either deductive or inductive — not unlike the forms of reasoning in other modes of expression. Analysis of any one opinion involves separating it into its parts and extracting its reasoning, but this task is complicated by the use of citation to cases and other authorities as it proceeds, by the judge's doing two or more things at once, and by the opinion's haphazard or blurry organization, as in the following opinion written for illustrative purposes by one of the authors.

1. The Law of Property

(The facts in this opinion have been taken from the opening chapter of James Fenimore Cooper's novel *The Pioneers*, published in 1826.)

Alex Hunter, Plaintiff v. **Mo Montour**, Defendant

in the Supreme Court of the State of Grace

LEARNED, J., delivered the opinion of the Court.

The plaintiff, Alex Hunter, was deer hunting in unposted woods in the unincorporated portions of Green County. After spying a large buck, Hunter's son, accompanying him, accidentally tripped and discharged his rifle, grazing the buck's flank and startling it. Hunter aimed at the startled animal, fired and hit it, not where Hunter aimed, but as the buck started and jumped, putting a bullet in its lungs. As a result of being thus fatally hit, the deer ran onto the land of Owen Owner, who held it and reached for a hunting knife. Just as Owen was about to plunge the knife into the buck, it leaped up a final time and was just about to run into the roadway abutting Owen's land when the passing defendant, Mo Montour, seeing the commotion of all this pursuit, brought his automobile to a halt and sprang from it. The defendant Montour then fired a pistol into the buck's head and seized it, carrying it off from the side of the road.

The plaintiff Hunter brought a complaint sounding in trespass[1] against the defendant Montour in order to recover the buck or its value. The defendant Montour moved to dismiss the case, but this motion was denied and it was tried before Judge George Judd, sitting in the Circuit Court of Green County. The Circuit Court jury rendered a verdict for the plaintiff and Judge Judd gave judgment accordingly. The defendant appealed to this court. We now reverse.

Trespass is an action brought for the taking of personal property. It involves carrying off the goods of another. Its first element is a showing that the "goods" in question are in the plaintiff's possession. Spying the buck by the plaintiff's son, for example, did not amount to possession because the son's spying the animal shows neither an intent to possess it nor an act of possession. Both are essential to sustain the plaintiff's complaint. That the buck was unintentionally and slightly wounded adds nothing to the plaintiff's case. However, the plaintiff's fatally wounding it is a different matter. If accomplished intentionally, it shows that the plaintiff did intend to kill the buck and, if pursuit ensues, the pursuit itself might be the functional equivalent of taking actual possession of the buck.

---

1. The phrase "sounding in trespass" may itself seem strange. It is lawyer talk, and means that the theory on which Hunter brought his lawsuit was trespass. Every course in law school is full of such talk, and getting comfortable with it will permit you to do what lawyers do with much of their time — talk about law.

Here, however, the wound was accidental, and so the ensuing pursuit proved nothing.

Owner by seizing the buck all but possessed it; but even here, when the animal is still capable of bolting as a wild animal might be expected to do, it is just as likely to regain its natural liberty as lose it. The defendant, seemingly on Owner's behalf, raises another claim: that Owner in any event has a better right to the buck than does the plaintiff. This other claim is to the animal, as one on Owner's land: A landowner has a right to start wild animals naturally on their land, *ratione soli.*[2] However, here the animal was not naturally on Owner's land, having been pursued there by the plaintiff Hunter. Moreover, if the buck bolted onto the land of a neighbor, instead of going onto the roadway, Owner's right to it would likely end when Owner began his trespass onto the neighboring land — although this result would be stronger if the neighbor's land was posted, warning off hunters and trespassers. So Owner's claim to the animal by the landowner's right fails. In any event, this is not an argument open to the defendant to make. Owner is no part of this litigation and his rights may be asserted in a future case. The defendant must win this one on his own merits, not on the weakness of the plaintiff's.

Under the law of this state, it is an open and unsettled question as to whether the defendant interfered with the plaintiff's or Owner's hunt. This court need not resolve this issue, however, as the defendant, firing a fatal wound showing his intent to take the buck, was also the first to actually seize the animal. He there has its possession to a degree that trumps the plaintiff's, and so the plaintiff's right to bring an action of trespass.

The plaintiff's complaint is dismissed. Judgment reversed.

LIVINGOOD, J., dissenting. I respectfully dissent. If the plaintiff's pursuit was an active one and the defendant had notice of it, I see no reason in law or policy why the defendant should be privileged to interfere with the plaintiff's hunt. The plaintiff's activity is a lawful one, the land through which it was pursued was unposted, and the plaintiff was in full view of the defendant when seizing the buck. The defendant's interference is to me an event highly likely to result in a breach of the peace, even if it occurred by the side of a public road and did not disturb the rights of an abutting owner.

It might be said that the rule of actual possession laid down by the majority will give the law a crispness and ease of administration that is highly desirable where the public must know the rules of the hunt, but to my mind, the certainty of the law is in no way diminished if a pursuit in

---

2. A Latin phrase meaning "on account or with reference to the soil." That is, the ownership of the soil is the basis for the right to start hunting there, just as a landowner owns a bee hive on his or her land. The law is full of such strange words and phrases, so keep your law dictionary handy: lawyers, judges, and professors will freely use terms that you as a lawyer will be embarrassed not to know.

plain view of the defendant of a fatally wounded animal is found the equivalent of actual possession. The aim is the capture of the buck, and the animal must first be pursued in order to be captured; otherwise, hunters will go at it with ever more powerful rifles and guns, endangering us all. Finding a constructive possession in pursuit such as this will surely result in the capture of the buck, without the defendant firing an additional shot. That the additional shot prevented the buck from running onto a public roadway points out that, at the kill, the plaintiff had just as much right to be there as did the defendant.

Finally, if this suit fails as a proposition pled under the law of possession and property, I foresee it refiled as a tort suit in which the quantum of possession required may well be less and in which the plaintiff might well succeed. This being so, it seems to me that the law of property should conform itself to the expectations of the jury below.

I would affirm their verdict and the ensuing judgment of Judge Judd.

Examples

1. Is the *Hunter* opinion binding on the courts of another state deciding a case with similar facts? Would it matter whether the other court was a trial or an appellate court?

2. After Hunter v. Montour is decided, Owen Owner sues Mo Montour for the buck that the result in the *Hunter* opinion permitted him to keep. May Owen do so?

3. Suppose that Owner's land abutted not a road, but Larry Lander's land, and the buck escaped Owner and ran onto Larry's land. Would the *Hunter* opinion prevent Owner from pursuing the buck there?

Explanations

1. The *Hunter* opinion is not binding on the courts of any other jurisdiction. It does not matter whether the other court is a trial court or an appellate court. The *Hunter* opinion is binding as legal precedent on all state courts in the State of Grace. The opinion is useful in other states, however, as persuasive authority. A judge in another state may read the opinion for its logic and reasoning, and may decide to agree with the *Hunter* opinion and adopt its reasoning as the judge's own.

2. Yes. Owen Owner's rights, including the right to sue, are unaffected by a lawsuit to which he was not made a party. If the court never gained jurisdiction over Owner, its judgment does not bind him. As the facts are stated in the opinion, for example, it is unclear whether Owen's lands were posted, and so it is also unclear whether Mo and Alex were

trespassers at the time of the hunt and the kill. Whether Mo was a trespasser would affect his rights to the buck. Moreover, the effect of any trespass, if found, would make the case sufficiently different from the precedent established in the *Hunter* opinion, so even if found to be binding on the court in which Owner sues, it need not control the outcome of Owner's suit.

3. Once Owen Owner joins the hunt, as the opinion suggested in dicta, his trespass on the land of another might well prevent him from obtaining legal possession of the buck. The discussion in *Hunter* as to Owner is dicta, and while persuasive authority to courts in the state of Grace, it is still merely persuasive and not binding authority. Moreover, the *Hunter* dicta may not apply to Owner's situation perfectly. For example, Owen might be asserting not only his right to hunt, but also his right to take game from his own lands and, by extension of that right, to take game found on his land that, when pursued there, went elsewhere. If Larry's land were posted, that might prevent Mo and Alex from starting their hunt there, but might not prevent Owen from continuing an ongoing hunt there, pursuing an already wounded animal. So Owen Owner's position is distinguishable from Alex and Mo's: Owner is participating in a hunt that started rightfully, while Alex and Mo's hunt was tainted, with regard to Owner's rights, from the moment they entered the boundaries of Owner's land. Property rights are relative to the rights of other people, particular people finding themselves in a context laden with facts. However, if Larry Lander's land were posted — i.e., had signs saying "No trespassing or hunting: Keep out" — the posting would affect Owner's rights.

CHAPTER 2

Personal Property and Possession

INTRODUCTIONS AND DEFINITIONS

Property falls into two binary categories: real property and personal property. (Intellectual property has some aspects of both.) **Real property**, **real estate**, or **realty** refers to land and the improvements attached to the land. Buildings, fences, and dams, for example, are included with land as real property. **Personal property** or **personalty** is all property other than real property. Automobiles, books, tables, clothes, computers, and corporate stock are examples of personal property.

A **fixture** is personalty that has been permanently attached to real property, but that could be removed. A dishwasher installed into a kitchen cabinet is a fixture, for example. Fixtures' hybrid nature subjects them to rules applicable to personal property and sometimes to rules applicable to real property.

Property may change character. For example, trees and crops in the field are real property. When cut or harvested, the cut trees become personal property. Cut trees turned into lumber are personal property, but once incorporated into a building become real property.

Personal property may be tangible personal property or intangible personal property. **Tangible personal property** includes property of a physical nature. You can see it and touch it. Examples include automobiles, books, clothing, lumber, jewelry, paintings, furniture, and coins. Intangible personal property includes assets that cannot be touched or seen but that have value nonetheless. Examples include stock in corporations, bonds, patents, copyrights, notes or accounts receivable, goodwill, and contract rights. Intangible personal property often is represented by a writing — tangible property — but the asset itself — a patent, corporate stock, or a note receivable — is an intangible asset. Recently recognized intangible assets are the rights of publicity and privacy that prohibit others from using a person's name, face, or other attribute of that person for commercial purposes without permission.

POSSESSION, RELATIVITY OF TITLE, AND FIRST-IN-TIME

As discussed in Chapter 1, the word "property" has multiple connotations. It may be the thing itself; or it may define relationships and priorities, rights, and obligations among persons with respect to a thing. The study of the relationships among persons with respect to personal property is helpful in understanding three basic concepts: possession, relativity of title, and first-in-time.

Possession is the controlling or holding of personal property, with or without a claim of ownership. It has two elements: (1) an intent to possess on the part of the possessor, and (2) his or her actual controlling or holding the property. As to the second element, control is the key. Both the intent and the control elements must be present to acquire the rights of a possessor. Possession need not be actual possession. More on this topic will follow.

A court's definition of possession can vary according to the type of litigation in which it is used as well as the ends the judge sees it serving. Thus, for example, possession can be good against all except those with a better right, sufficient to permit a person to recover possession of an item of personal property, or sufficient to recover damages for its injury or destruction. A court will manipulate the two elements of possession according to the needs of the case.

Possession is basic to our law of personal property. Because proving ownership is so difficult and burdensome, we rely on possession as a surrogate for ownership and title. You probably own a wristwatch, for example, but how would you prove it if you were asked to do so?

Relativity of title is the idea that a person can have a relatively better title or right to possession than another, while simultaneously having a right inferior to yet another person. This doctrine is necessary because, in a common law system, few acquire a perfect title. That would require that the person acquiring title litigate its relative strength against all other persons who have, or might conceivably have, any right or interest. Thus, an attorney speaks of a relatively better right to possession, or of a superior title or right.

One way of prioritizing several individuals' rights is accomplished by a rule of **first-in-time, first-in-right**, establishing a priority of rights based on the time of acquiring the right in question. Under such a rule, all other things being equal, the chronologically first possessor has the better title.

However, all things are not always equal. So a rule of priority based on time is not always the way the law arranges several rights in personalty. Sometimes subsequent possessors prevail over prior possessors: A good faith purchaser and adverse possessor can acquire title superior to those who came into possession before they did. In contrast, persons taking their interests from a thief acquire no title to the thing: Title from a thief is a void title.

ACTUAL POSSESSION AND THE FOX CASE

This chapter will discuss wild animal cases, using them as the prototypes for problems in other areas of property law. Hunters of wild game provide a seemingly endless number of situations in which one or the other elements of possession is present — or missing. Whether a hunter has taken "possession" of an animal is the issue here.

The leading case in American law is Pierson v. Post, 3 Cai. Rptr. 175 (N.Y. Sup. Ct. 1805). Post was hunting on a beach. While he was in pursuit of a fox, Pierson intervened, shot the fox being chased by Post, and carried the animal off.

Post sued Pierson, and won in the lower or trial court. Pierson appealed. Post lost on appeal because he did not physically seize the animal before another (the original defendant and appellant Pierson) shot and carried it off. So the second element of possession (called **occupancy** in parts of this opinion) was not present. Without it, the plaintiff does not have a sufficient interest in the thing sued for to warrant the court's hearing his complaint.

Pierson involved a rule of possession formulated so that the first hunter to capture a fox wins. This is a rule of first-in-time, first-in-right. It is into this rule of priority in time, reworded for the situation of two or more claimants for the same thing, that the concept of possession fits — as in, first-to-possess, first-in-right.

However, the hunter's race for the fox is without a fixed starting line — that is, without a starting line that all the racers share. So we have Post, huffing and puffing over a distance longer than Pierson's, but Pierson wins. Put this way, the outcome hardly seems fair. Post expends considerably more effort and labor, and still he loses! Why? One answer is that there are no rules about the permissible gear that a hunter can use — more precisely, no restrictions on gear. One hunter can carry a high-powered rifle, another a pistol. Why is this? One answer might be that the courts think it is a bad idea for the law to have such restrictions; they might be taken for an attempt to make one set of laws for the hunter rich enough to afford the rifle, and another for the hunter using the cheaper pistol. Another answer might be that the cheaper pistol can be more skillfully and accurately used than the more expensive rifle — and the outcome of the hunt may change accordingly.

Yet another answer might be one of necessity — if the law is to devise a rule for a race without a common starting line, then the end of the race is all that matters because it is all the court has to work with. Add to that the majority opinion's own justifications — wanting a rule that keeps the peace, damps down litigation, and is clear and easy to administer — and you have the justifications for the majority's decision.

Another version of the holding found in Pierson v. Post is in the opinion's discussion of several writers of legal treatises; that is, close pursuit after a **mortal wounding** gives a hunter a right to possession of the fox that is superior to another hunter's intervention. In the hypothetical opinion Hunter v. Montour in Chapter 1, Alex Hunter had the same argument in his favor, and it was no more successful for him than it was for Post. A "mortal wound" is one that, (1) on an objective basis, is likely to prove fatal to the animal — it will, given time, "deprive the fox of his natural liberty" — and (2) shows subjectively a "manifest intention" to seize the animal — that the pursuer intended to follow the hunt with a kill and is not just out for the enjoyment of the chase. Again, as with mere pursuit, intention alone will not do — or else Owen Owner would have won the hypothetical lawsuit whose opinion you read earlier. Instead, the intention must be manifest, or clearly shown by the wound. With this discussion of wounding, the court shows the two elements of possession coming together. In a sense, a mortal wounding is constructive possession of the animal.

The Pierson v. Post holding accepts as public policy that killing foxes is a socially useful enterprise. The dissenting judge in *Pierson* elaborates on this idea by saying that killing foxes saves chickens or, more precisely, protects the activities of chicken farmers. Look for public policy reasons to adopt a rule of law in controversies you study in Property and other courses.

The underlying ideas of both the majority and the dissenting opinions are not far apart, except that dissent would define possession in order to protect Post's pursuit of the fox. For both the majority and the dissent, the underlying rationale for the case drives the definition of "possession." Both the majority's rule of capture and the dissent's rule of pursuit are means to the same end — as are the ideas of "possession" and its kin, "constructive possession."

Constructive Possession

Constructive possession denotes possession that has the same effect in law as actual possession, although it is not actual possession in fact.[1] The dissent in

---

1. The word "constructive" means "established by construing the facts of a case so that the facts give rise to an inference of [whatever — here, possession]." Attorneys also speak of constructive bailments, conversion, delivery, fraud, and larceny; and that is just a limited sample of constructive legal concepts, limited to the course on real property. You will encounter the same word in other areas of law as well.

Pierson argued in effect that Post's pursuit put him in constructive possession of the fox, in that it gave him a right to possession that was not yet actual possession. In the context of natural resources law, constructive possession has also proven useful: The owners of land with unextracted oil, gas, or other minerals lying beneath its surface might not be in actual possession of those minerals, but they are often said to be in prior constructive possession of them. Hence, the legal maxim is that whoever owns the surface also owns to the depths of the earth.

The *Pierson* opinion says that prior cases involving hunters were decided under some type of regulation or statute, or involved litigation between hunters and the owners of private land on which the hunter captured the wild animal and in which the landowner usually prevailed. These factors are all potentially limiting facts in this case.

An English version of *Pierson* is the case of Young v. Hichens, 115 Eng. Rep. 228 (Queen's Bench, 1844). The plaintiff, from his boat, had enclosed a very large quantity of mackerel worth £2000 sterling in his net 140 fathoms long, drawn in a semicircle completely around the fish, with the exception of a space five to seven fathoms wide. Before the plaintiff could completely encircle the fish using a second net, the defendant's boat rowed through the gap, enclosed the fish, and captured them.

The court gave judgment for the defendant, except that the defendant had to pay a nominal amount for damage to the plaintiff's net: The court held that the plaintiff had not yet taken actual possession; neither did the plaintiff have constructive possession, because "all but reducing to possession" is not the same as possession. Were it otherwise, the plaintiff would be able to allege that he had a property interest sufficient to protect the fish in an action of conversion or trespass.

CUSTOM

In the Hunter v. Montour opinion you read in the first chapter, the hunt began on unposted lands. The traditional rule in many regions of this country is that when a landowner has not otherwise notified hunters with "no hunting" signs, hunters are free to roam unimproved lands in search of game: by **custom**, sometimes by statute, unposted land becomes fair game, and entry upon it is not a trespass to land.

Pierson may also have been decided in a way that most hunters in the locale might have found offensive. Judge Livingston suggests by dissenting that Post's hotfooted pursuit may have given him possession of the animal pursued according to the custom of local hunters. Used in this way, custom is another basis for awarding possession, custom being a use or practice long adopted by acquiescence, having the force of law. The majority of the court chose to ignore this basis. For example, the custom might be that the first hunter to put a bullet into an animal has the right to pursue it and reduce it to possession. Or, the custom might be that the hunter eventually taking possession of an animal must split the animal with the first shooter, so that the possessor and the shooter share the spoils. However, whatever the form of the custom, unless the first wound produced is a mortal wounding, it will typically not be seen by other hunters, who (assuming they recognize the custom) then will not know whether to observe it.

Customs are market- or locale-specific. For example, among hunters pursuing wild animals with a bow and arrow, the custom like the ones described may be somewhat more workable — an animal with an arrow sticking out of its body may be assumed to be an animal that is being pursued. In addition, in the whaling industry the use of harpoons makes the custom still easier to observe.

One court, Ghen v. Rich, discussing a segment of the nineteenth-century whaling industry, suggested that the custom of any group or industry should be recognized only under certain circumstances, to wit:

- when its application is limited to the industry and limited to those working in it,
- when the custom is recognized by the whole industry (or fishery in Ghen),
- when the custom "requires in the first taker the only act of appropriation that is possible" (e.g., the whale in Ghen, once harpooned and dead, quickly sinks to the ocean floor),
- when the custom is necessary to the survival of the industry, and
- when the custom "works well in practice."

Although custom dictated the result in Ghen, not many customs are likely to survive all these tests. In this sense, when setting out so many tests, the Ghen opinion really represents a triumph of the common law over custom in our legal system. Why is the court so suspicious of custom? A first answer might be that the custom of the industry will be formulated for the benefit of the industry, not for society as a whole. Second, although of benefit to an industry, a custom might be dangerous to those employed in it and the courts should consider that as well. Third, the custom can be wasteful of the resource; some of the whales in the Cape Cod finback fishery "floated out to sea" and were "never recovered." Finally, a custom can lead to overinvestment in technology — the bomb-lance here. A bigger bomb-lance, with a rope attached to a bigger boat, could have meant immediate capture of the whale, but at what cost? The rule of capture taken from Pierson v. Post might lead to both waste and overinvestment.

In Ghen, the custom along Cape Cod's whaling areas required specially made equipment. Whaling ships elsewhere, using a harpoon with a rope attached to strike the whale, required a different custom. Herman Melville's novel *Moby-Dick*, chapter 89, describes various rules in the industry. Those other customs, untested in court, were not given the force of law; no custom should be imposed on wider regions or for a longer time than its use coincides with the law's needs.

THE DOCTRINE OF CUSTOM GIVING ACCESS

Custom has not just been used in cases involving the creation of property by capture; it has also been used to create a common law right of access to certain types of real property. When, for example, a beach has been considered accessible to persons in a locale, their access may be said to arise by custom. A custom giving rise to access must be long-continued, uninterrupted, and reasonably asserted as a right. It is an inheritance from English common law, used to permit a local population to cut peat from a certain bog, use a certain spring for drinking water, or harvest timber for firewood in a certain forest, although the customary right to take away a substance will be more limited than the landowner's right to do so. Limitations for domestic or personal uses were often customary, and assertions of the custom in excess of that were regarded as unreasonable.

Blackstone said that the access must be so long continued "that the mind of man runs not to the contrary." In the United States, the custom must typically have been exercised from the beginning of the state's existence within the Union and uninterrupted thereafter. However long, this is known as the doctrine's antiquity requirement. See State ex rel. Haman v. Fox, 594 P.2d 1093 (Idaho 1979) (finding 60 years insufficient). The state was created subject to the preexisting custom, and so the persons benefiting from the custom have a right prior to any power of the state. As the examples from England have indicated, the custom must also be certain and reasonable as to place, subject matter, and persons benefiting from it.

NATURAL RESOURCES AND OTHER CONCERNS

First to possess, first in right, and rules of capture have proven useful to attorneys in at least two other contexts — in the law of natural resources and in water law. As to natural resources, a surface owner also owns the minerals underneath, such as coal or gold. Two minerals — oil and gas — are found in "pools" and flow through the ground to points of low pressure, much as water does. The first driller to tap and produce oil or natural gas from a pool underlying the lands of several owners has acquired possession of the resource brought to the surface, even though it may drain the pool under the other's lands. Whereas lateral drilling is a trespass, drilling straight down from one's surface is not, no matter that it is conducted close to a surface boundary line. Because this first-in-time rule resulted in inefficient over-production of oil and gas, today state statutes and regulations allocate common pools of an oil or gas resource. In actions against lateral drillers, trespass and conversion are permitted.

WATER LAW

The second use of a rule of first-in-time, first-in-right, in the context of natural resources concerns water. Water rights can be divided into rights to surface water (lakes, rivers, and streams) and those to underground or groundwater.

(a) Surface Water Courses

First-in-time applies to the acquisition of surface **water in a water course** — in a stream, creek, or river with a steady or seasonal flow — but the application of the rule differs in different parts of the country. Roughly divided, the water-rich eastern states are known as **riparian states**. Each person with land abutting a water course may take water from it for any **reasonable use**. Many riparian states limit the use of the water to benefit the land parcel abutting the surface water. In times of scarcity, a riparian landowner cannot use the water to benefit his nonriparian lands. Likewise, some riparian states limit the use of water to the surrounding watershed, so that the riparian user returns the water to the water course from whence it came.

Because water is scarcer in western states, water is allocated based on **prior appropriation**. While initially developed by custom and common law, prior appropriation allocations are controlled by state statute today. Under a prior appropriation system, the first person to make beneficial use of water gains a vested right to continue that use. The only way to prove a first-in-time allocation is to file an administrative action with the state water agency or engineer. The first person to file has the first priority; the second person to file has the second priority, and so on. A water right allocated in this manner entitles its holder to divert a set amount of water (often measured in "acre feet"), at a certain location, in a certain ditch, and for a defined use. In many ways, once allocated, water is treated like personal property the right to use it can be transferred, it can be moved out of the watershed, and it is treated separately from the land on which it is used. In a drought, persons with lower priorities may be prohibited from using any water until those whose claims have higher priority have satisfied their needs.

(b) Groundwater

Groundwater (subsurface water) can be classified into two categories. Groundwater that flows in a channel is called an underground stream. The rules on use of water from underground streams follow the same rules applied to surface water.

The second type of groundwater is water not in a channel. These are known as **percolating waters**. As with oil and natural gas, the owner of the property had an absolute right to withdraw percolating water and use it as he willed, either on the land or elsewhere. The absolute rule has often been supplanted by a **reasonable use doctrine**, also known as the American rule. Under the reasonable use doctrine, the water must be used solely on the overlying land if use elsewhere would cause hardship to other landowners with access to the common underground pool of water.

Some states follow a rule that dispenses with first-in-time and allocates the water equally to all owners of land overlying the common pool. The equal sharing is based on land acreage owned, not a per-owner equality. This is known as the **correlative rights doctrine**.

The Restatement Second of Property § 858 combines these approaches and allows a person to withdraw and use percolating groundwater unless the withdrawal unreasonably harms neighboring lands by lowering the water table or decreasing the water pressure; exceeds the landowner's reasonable share of the water; or reduces the level of surface lakes, harming users of the lakes.

As water becomes a scarce resource, state and local laws will become more technical and sophisticated. Even riparian states increasingly regulate its use.

ACTIONABLE INTERFERENCE

Keeble v. Hickeringill, 103 Eng. Rep. 1127, 11 Mod. 74 (Queen's Bench 1707), involved a decoy pond for ducks. Plaintiff Keeble brought an action against the defendant for discharging guns with the object of frightening the ducks away from the plaintiff's pond. The jury found for the plaintiff and awarded him £20 sterling. On appeal, defendant argued that there was no cause of action to redress the actions of which the plaintiff complained since the plaintiff did not own the ducks. Rejecting this argument, the appellate court held that the plaintiff had a cause of action. The court stated that "the true reason [for this holding] is that this action is not brought to recover damage for loss of the fowl, but for the disturbance" of the plaintiff's taking possession of them.

The opinion of Judge Holt in 103 Eng. Rep. makes three points. First, the plaintiff is a tradesman, using the decoy pond in a lawful manner for his business; second, the defendant, even as a competitor of the plaintiff, was acting illegally; and third, the general welfare is best served by promoting the social goal of providing ducks for English dinner tables. The first two points are related and do not depend necessarily on who owns land or who owns the ducks. The issue for lawyers reading the case is whether the earlier ones are preconditions (e.g., having a trade to protect, or being a competing tradesman) for a plaintiff's bringing and winning this action. If so, they discuss factors limiting the pool of future plaintiffs in these actions. If, however, the third paragraph is the dispositive one, then it makes no difference whether the plaintiff is a tradesman. Whether the three points are equally crucial to the holding, or whether the last point is "where the judge is going" and so controls all others, depends on whether you take a formalistic or a functional approach to the law of this case. An attorney must learn to treat the case both ways, both as a way of defining possession and as a method of achieving some greater social good.

Compare *Keeble* with Pierson v. Post. Post's hunt in Pierson v. Post was ostensibly for sport, while the plaintiff in *Keeble* had improved the pond for his particular purposes and was hunting ducks there as his trade or business. The court recognizes that certain types of activity in competition with another business are acceptable while others are not, even though the end result of each may be to cause one competitor to be no longer able to conduct his business profitably (or at all). The stark example given by the court is that one person may (and is even encouraged to) set up a new school to compete with an established school, even if the new school recruits faculty and students such that the old school must close. In contrast, the court deems it impermissible (in fact, do not ever advise anyone to do this) to "lie in the way with his guns, and fright the boys from going to school, [so that] their parents would not let them go thither."

In contrast to Post, who was hunting on "wild lands," Keeble was in possession of Minott's Meadow, where his pond was. Thus, Keeble was in possession ratione soli — a term meaning that the owner of land has sufficient possession of the wild animals on the land to start a hunt for them, as well as the right to pursue them while on that land. Possession ratione soli is a specific instance of constructive possession — again, not actual possession, but a type of possession treated as if it were actual possession, in other words, a legal fiction. This is the rationale for the case as reported in 11 Mod. 74, a case report available and cited by the majority in *Pierson*, and on the basis of which the majority distinguished the *Keeble* case. Why would a judge treat a situation as if it were enough like another situation that both should be handled in the same way by the law? In this instance, the judge might wish to deter poaching and to discourage the trespasses of hunters on private land.

The Eng. Rptr. opinion concludes that "decoy ponds and decoy ducks have been used . . . whereby the markets of the nation may be furnished." Whether the case involves ducks or venison, the opinions in both *Keeble* and *Pierson* define "possession" in such a way as to get animals to market. To do that, constructive possession suffices for the plaintiff in *Keeble*, while actual possession is required in *Pierson*.

MISAPPROPRIATION

Taking possession of an already existing object of personalty is not the only way to acquire the thing as property. A person might invent or create a thing, and be entitled to obtain a patent or copyright under federal law, or a right to sue to prevent its misappropriation generally. See International News Service v. Associated Press, 248 U.S. 215 (1918) (holding that as between two competing news services, the systematic misappropriation of "hot news" stories by one competitor (the INS) was sufficient to justify an injunction against the INS until the commercial value of the stories dissipated). The opinion's **doctrine of misappropriation** has been used and discussed in many judicial opinions. See National Basketball Ass'n, Inc. v. Motorola, Inc., 105 F.3d 841 (2d Cir. 1997) (discussing and confirming the doctrine for a "sports score" reporting service). So when a plaintiff has by substantial investment created an intangible thing of value not protected by patent, copyright, or other intellectual property law, and the defendant appropriates the intangible at little cost so that the plaintiff is injured and plaintiff's continued use of the intangible is jeopardized, an action for misappropriation will lie. Some courts are hostile to the doctrine because copying many things results in useful competition and lower prices, and often respects the limits of existing patent and copyright statutes. See Cheney Brothers v. Doris Silk Co., 35 F.2d 279 (2d Cir. 1929) (refusing to use misappropriation doctrine against dress-design copiers).

Examples

Post–*Pierson* Problems

1. Assume the facts of Pierson v. Post: Post chasing the fox with hounds leading the way.
   (a) Suppose further that the record at the trial in Pierson v. Post proved that Post's hunt was interrupted by nightfall, and he camped and slept while his dogs continued to pursue the fox overnight. Post

resumed the hunt in the morning, and thereafter the facts of *Pierson* are the same as reported in the opinion. Pierson happened by as Post closed in on the fox, and Pierson killed the fox before Post did. Would this proof change the outcome of the case?

(b) Suppose that the record at the trial in Pierson v. Post proved that Pierson saw Post running after the fox, and just as Post closed in on the animal, Pierson muttered, "That no-good Post can't have that fox," and that, just after saying that, Pierson shot the fox and carried it off right under Post's nose. Would this proof change the outcome of the case?

(c) Suppose Pierson captured and caged the fox. A week later the fox escaped the cage. The next day Post killed the fox. Pierson sues for damages. What result?

(d) Suppose Pierson captured and caged the fox. Under cover of darkness, Post then entered Pierson's land and took the fox from the cage. Pierson discovered what happened and sued Post to recover the fox. What result?

(e) What types of pursuit — short of actually resulting in possession — do you think might give rise to a judicial finding of possession?

Custom-Made Law

2. (a) Ghen is a whaler pursuing a finback whale off Cape Cod. He shoots a bomb-lance and hits the whale, which instantly dies of the wound. The whale (as whales do when dying) sinks and two days later is discovered on a beach by Ellis, who sells it to Rich. Who owns the whale? See Ghen v. Rich, 8 F. 159 (D. Mass. 1881).

(b) Why wouldn't the *Ghen* court decide its case just on the basis of the law as stated in *Pierson*? (And why wasn't *Pierson* decided according to the custom of hunters, as Judge Livingston suggested in his dissent in Pierson v. Post?)

(c) The *Ghen* opinion states: "Neither the respondent (Rich) nor Ellis knew the whale had been killed by [Ghen], but they knew or might have known, if they had wished, that it had been shot and killed with a bomb-lance, by some person engaged in this species of business." What do you think might have been the effect of this trial court finding in *Ghen* on a case like *Pierson*?

Ownership of Fish in a Creek

3. A manufacturing company discharges chemicals from its plant into a nearby creek, causing a fish kill. The state attorney general's office sues the company for the value of the fish, alleging a property interest in the fish. In this suit, what result and why?

Oil Depletion

4. Who has possession of the empty underground space left after mining or after the extraction of oil or gas from a cavity in the earth? If oil or gas was injected into the cavity, would the surface owner have a trespass action against the injecting party?

Running Interference

5. Today, almost all states have enacted hunter harassment statutes, making it at least a misdemeanor to interfere intentionally with lawful hunting, and including in the definition of "interference" actions that are intended to affect the natural behavior of a hunted wild animal. What is the likely effect of such a statute on the outcome in *Pierson*?

Explanations

Post–*Pierson* Problems

1. (a) No. The only difference is the interruption in Post's hunt — and, if anything, that interruption seems to give the result in favor of Pierson more, rather than less, support. Post would likely argue that his dogs carried on the hunt for him, so the hunt never really was interrupted, and that the dogs put Post in constructive pursuit all the while. But pursuit is not possession.

   (b) It might. With this additional proof, Pierson's intent is not to seize the fox, but to deprive Post of it. A court that considers the subjective intent or an objective manifestation of spite or maliciousness might rule in Post's favor, or more specifically might rule against Pierson because of Pierson's bad conduct. Alternatively, a court may conclude Pierson does not have the requisite intent to possess that the law requires for legal possession — i.e., two requirements are necessary for possession: intents to possess and to control. Control by itself is not enough. Other courts may not look to Pierson's motives but may conclude his action of picking up the fox exhibited the requisite intent to possess and control.

   (c) Post owes no damages. An escaped wild animal is deemed to have returned to nature and once more belongs to no one. There are exceptions. If the animal is not native to the area such that a reasonable person would gather that the animal belonged to someone, the original owner remains the owner. A person seeing a kangaroo hopping though the streets of San Francisco, for example, should expect that the kangaroo belongs to someone. Second, under the doctrine of *animus revertendi*, a person does not lose his interest in an animal that has the habit of returning to its owner's property.

This usually applies to domesticated animals, and is easy to apply to cats, dogs, horses, and cattle. The doctrine is less predictable for traditionally wild animals such as deer and raccoons.

(d) Easy question. Post must return the fox. Pierson's property interest in the fox remains in full force as long as the fox is caged. Post's unlocking the cage is a wrongful interference with Pierson's rightful possession. It might even be larceny — the carrying away of chattel in the possession of another. Post's trespass onto Pierson's land, moreover, factors against Post. The law frowns on trespassers, with the result that trespassers usually lose out to landowners.

(e) It might be a pursuit (1) halted by an interference that gives rise to tort liability; or (2) halted by a person like Pierson, but whose actions also violate the hunting regulations of the state; or (3) halted by a person who commits a crime or violates some other public policy by interfering. That is, the interference by an outside party might be of such a nature as to render his activity illegal, tainting his acts from the start and so focusing the court's attention on the actions of the intermeddler, rather than the rights of the plaintiff claiming possession. As indicated in dicta in Pierson v. Post, use of traps or nets or wounding such that escape is highly improbable might constitute constructive possession, which results in possession being in the owner of the traps or nets, or whoever did the wounding.

Custom-Made Law

2. (a) Ghen inflicted a mortal wound and so arguably has constructive possession of the whale at that point, even though he did not actually seize the whale. See Ghen v. Rich, 8 F. 159 (D. Mass. 1881) (reaching this result on another ground). The trial judge in *Ghen* reported: "The usage on Cape Cod, for many years, has been that the person who kills a whale in the manner and under the circumstances described, owns it. . . ." The custom of the industry as quoted is the ground on which *Ghen* was decided.

(b) The court could have followed Pierson v. Post, but the holding would have upset an entire industry that had operated successfully under the custom of awarding the whale to the person whose iron holds the whale, with a finder receiving a salvage (a reward). The judge limited the custom-as-law holding to cases where the custom had been recognized and acquiesced in for many years, and that undoing the custom may destroy the industry. It also helped that the finder received a salvage for finding the whale and notifying the whaler. Why wasn't Pierson v. Post decided by custom? The dissent in *Pierson* wanted to do just that. One argument may be that the custom should be limited to issues unique to an industry, and Pierson and Post were not professional fox hunters. It may be that this custom was not essential to the survival of fox-hunting businesses, even if there was one at the time, or that fox hunting was not critical to the economy of the region. It may be that no one presented evidence as to what the custom was in the area. It may be that, as the majority stressed, the first to kill (or take actual possession) is easier to apply in practice. The custom of hunters, moreover, may not be in the best interests of the wider society — farmers, families, and so on.

(c) The judges in *Pierson*, relying on *Ghen*, might have said that while in pursuit Post was in constructive possession of the fox for purposes of protecting his right to hunt that fox. If so, the court would have ruled in favor of Post this time. More likely, the majority in *Pierson* would have distinguished *Ghen* on the grounds that in *Ghen* the plaintiff killed the whale. Mere pursuit of a whale conferred no benefit. Pierson's majority opinion, in (nonbinding) dicta, said that intercepting an animal (fox or whale) so as to deprive it of its natural liberty and make its escape impossible may be considered possession. Using this logic, harpooning and killing a whale is much like "intercepting" it, but not sighting and chasing it.

Ownership of Fish in a Creek

3. A state government may have sufficient "possession" of wild animals to regulate the hunting of them. Geer v. Conn., 161 U.S. 519 (1896). Yet this possession is for regulatory rather than hunting purposes, and so may be insufficient to justify the state's bringing an action based on ownership of the fish. Commonwealth v. Agway, Inc., 232 A.2d 69 (Pa. Super. Ct. 1967). The state might be authorized by statute to do so, and this case shows the need for statutes governing water pollution and protection of wild animals, fish, and fowl.

Oil Depletion

4. The surface owner regains "possession" of the mined-out space after the minerals have been extracted. It may be a trespass, therefore, when already captured oil or gas is pumped back into the cavity for storage. Another thought, following the rule of wild animals, is that the oil has returned to its natural state (given its "natural liberty" again, if you will), and thus is owned by the first landowner to pump it back out. In that case, the injecting party does not have sufficient possession of it to commit a trespass with it — or, put another way, the surface owner could claim ownership by drilling for the oil himself. Compare Hammonds v. Central Kentucky Natural Gas Co., 75 S.W.2d 204, 206 (Ky. 1934) (holding that the injecting party does not have possession after the injection),

with Texas American Energy Corp. v. Citizens Fidelity Bk. & Tr. Co., 736 S.W.2d 25 (Ky. 1987) (overruling *Hammonds*). *Hammonds* is not the law in the major oil-producing states.

Running Interference

5. Two outcomes seem reasonable here. First, the purpose behind these statutes may be to resolve disputes between hunters and nonhunters (environmentalists and animal rights advocates), so that disputes between two hunters, such as is presented in Pierson v. Post, would be unaffected and the outcome the same as under the common law. Second, and more broadly, Post would win if the effect of such a statute was to extend the unlawful interference policy in *Keeble* to the facts of *Pierson*. Pierson's actions may reasonably be argued to have influenced the behavior of the hunted animal, and so the statutory definition of interference is met and the statute applies. The policy behind these harassment statutes further argues that the "interference" cause of action recognized in *Keeble* should be extended to the facts of *Pierson* and that the factual distinctions between the two cases — e.g., between sportsmen and commercial hunters — should be ignored today. Viewed in the light of the policy and provisions of these statutes, the plaintiffs in both cases should be seen as having a "possession" sufficient to bring their actions.

Law of Finders
and Prior Possessors

As noted in the first two chapters, possession is important in determining rights to things. Although familiar sayings such as "possession is nine-tenths of the law" and "finders keepers, losers weepers" are inaccurate as statements of the law, they do echo the law's recognition that a person in possession of a thing has greater rights to that thing than do most other persons.

The study of finders of personal property (property other than real property) serves many purposes. For one, the concept is easy: Someone lost something; someone else found it; now who owns it? More importantly, some black-letter rules have evolved when the original or true owner cannot be found, for then the finder and the owner of the place of the find (the *locus in quo*) may each claim possession.

The study of finders law gives you the opportunity to apply the rules and rethink the law. How should a court resolve issues pertaining to finders? Should it try to fit the facts into a box of the existing rules to determine who has the superior right to the thing? Or should the court determine who prevails based on instrumental goals — i.e., considerations other than black-letter rules? Or should the court simply say, "Finders win"? The common law holds that a finder of lost property has greater rights to the found property than the entire world except the true owner. The rule is often stated, "The title of the finder is good as against the whole world but the true owner." See Raymond A. Brown, *The Law of Personal Property* 25 (3d ed. 1975). If the true owner is located, the true owner can recover the lost property. The goal of the common law here is to facilitate the return of lost property to its true owner. Many times, however, the issue is who gets the property if the true owner never surfaces.

A finder of lost property is a person who (1) takes control of the lost property and (2) has the intent to maintain possession of the property. To illustrate, three children, Andy, Brad, and Charlie, are playing. Andy finds a bag weighty enough to be tossed. Andy tosses the bag to Brad. As Brad catches the bag, the bag breaks open and money spills on the ground. Charlie snatches up the money. To which child would you give the money, assuming the true owner cannot be located?

One answer, of course, is to say the boys are acting in unison and thus should split the money equally. Another is to say Andy took control of the bag with the intent to possess it, and thus he should get the money since the money was in the bag. A third option gives the money to Charlie since it was Charlie who took control over the money with the intent to possess it. Brad, it seems, never had the requisite control or intent to possess. The issue may turn on whether you feel Andy ever had actual control or, more likely, any intent to possess the bag or the money. See Keron v. Cashman, 33 A.1055 (N.J. 1896).

Let's explore the practical application of the general rule that a finder of lost property has greater rights to the property than the entire world except the true or rightful owner. First, the easy case: TO (true owner) loses her watch; F1 finds the watch. F1 lays the watch on a table surrounded by a group of people. While F1 is standing there, F2 picks up the watch. F1 demands F2 return the watch. F2 refuses. Which of the two has the right to leave with the watch? Answer: F1. F1 has greater rights to the watch than the entire world except the rightful owner. F2's only argument is that F1 is not the true owner, but that argument does F2 no good. F1 as finder has greater rights to the watch than does F2 and all other persons except the true owner.

The result is a good one as a practical matter since it would be very difficult for a person to prove he or she owns that which he or she possesses. For example, you probably do not carry "proof" that you own your casebook, your laptop, or your backpack.

Now a more difficult scenario: TO loses her watch; F1 finds the watch. A week later F1 loses the watch in the park. Four days later F2 walks into a room, with F1 present, and announces that she found a watch in the park. F1 asks if the watch has certain characteristics. The watch does. F1 claims the watch. F2 does not want to give the watch to F1. Question: Who should get the watch? F1 or F2?

The answer is F1 has greater rights to the watch than the whole world except the rightful owner, and thus F1 gets the watch. F1 and F2 are both finders. The common law rule as stated does not anticipate our scenario. The rule must be modified to say a finder of lost property has greater rights to the found property than the whole world except the rightful owner, a prior or rightful possessor, or a person holding through the rightful owner or rightful possessor. F2 has greater rights than everyone except TO and F1. Once F1 appears, however, F1 gets the watch.

CONVERSION, REPLEVIN, AND TROVER

Generally, a finder will return found property to the rightful owner if the rightful owner appears. But what happens if the finder, a borrower, or another person to whom the property has been entrusted refuses to return the property, has sold or given it to another person, or has modified the property such that it may not be acceptable to the true owner? When a person wrongfully exerts control over an asset inconsistent with the true owner's rights to the property, that person has engaged in an act of conversion.

Conversion is a common law action for the tort of using another's property as one's own. The true owner or rightful possessor can recover the property. The action or remedy to recover the asset itself (plus money damages for injury to the asset) is called **replevin**. Alternatively, the rightful owner or rightful possessor can seek monetary damages for the asset. The action for monetary compensation for conversion of personal property is called **trover**. In effect, trover is a forced sale. A person who is compensated pursuant to a trover action loses his rights to have the asset returned. The decision whether to seek trover (compensation) or replevin (the return of the property) lies with the true owner or rightful possessor, not with the present possessor.

ARMORY v. DELAMIRIE

Most casebooks introduce finders through the brief opinion in the case of Armory v. Delamirie, 1 Str. 505, 7 Term R. 396 (King's Bench, 1722). There a chimney sweep found a piece of jewelry and delivered it to a goldsmith's shop for an appraisal. The goldsmith's apprentice removed the stone and then refused to return it to the sweep. The jewelry's appraisal without the stone was for three half-pence. The goldsmith offered the sweep that sum of money for the jewelry, but the sweep refused to accept and brought an action in trover — for the value of the jewelry — against the goldsmith.

The *Armory* court held that "the finder of a jewel, though he does not by such finding acquire an absolute property or ownership, yet he has such a property as will enable him to keep it against all but the rightful owner, and consequently may maintain trover." 7 Term R. at 398. In this holding, the term "prior possessor" might be substituted for the word "finder" — and the rightful or true owner then stands for any person whose possession is prior to that of the litigating parties.

The sweep wins this case because he is the prior possessor of the jewel. He could have stolen it from the house whose chimney he last cleaned and, still, as against the goldsmith, he would be the prior possessor, even though the rule of law is that "a thief's title is void" against the true owner's. Anderson v. Gouldberg, 53 N.W. 636 (Minn. 1892) (a replevin action for stolen logs); and see Gissel v. State, 727 P.2d 1153, 1156 (Idaho 1986) (stating, "[m]ere possession alone is sufficient to sustain a trespasser's cause of action for conversion against all but the true owner," over a strong dissent that a thief should receive no reward for her crime). In the litigation here, the goldsmith is the greater wrongdoer, even assuming that the sweep was a thief.

EXTENSIONS OF THE *ARMORY* RULE — AND A RIGHT OF SUBROGATION

Suppose that the jewel's true owner found out about the facts and outcome in *Armory* and brought a lawsuit against the goldsmith. What might be the theory of such a suit? It might be brought for conversion. Why? Because the goldsmith treated the jewel as his own when refusing to return it, as he was bound to do. And because the goldsmith does not have the jewel itself anymore, the suit will have to be brought for trover rather than replevin. The complaint says, in essence, "You converted it, you bought it." In this suit, the court applying the rule in *Armory* will give judgment for the owner. By paying the judgment, the losing party — here, the goldsmith — acquires the rights in the jewel upon which the owner based his suit — i.e., the right to sue for the conversion of the jewel perpetrated by the goldsmith.

This goldsmith's acquisition of the true owner's rights is an example of the doctrine of **subrogation**. The owner had a right to sue, sued, and by winning transferred her rights to the defendant goldsmith. Subrogation is a succession to another's right or claim. It puts another in the place of a person originally holding the claim, substituting the former for the latter.

Suppose further that the smith uses the right acquired by subrogation to sue the chimney sweep. In this second suit, the smith is here attempting to put the parties back *status quo ante*.[1] Because (1) the smith now holds some of the rights of the owner, and (2) that owner is the holder of a right to the jewel prior in time to the sweep, the judgment should be given to the smith. Up to now, the smith has run the risk that the sweep will take the money from the *Armory* suit and move beyond the jurisdiction of the court. It is better for the smith to bear that risk than it is for the owner to do so, but now things can be put right by returning the money to the smith. The law should do so.

---

1. This Latin phrase means "the state of affairs at a previous time" and Latinists might say that it should read *status in quo ante*.

LOST PROPERTY, MISLAID PROPERTY, ABANDONED PROPERTY, AND TREASURE TROVE

The law of finders discussed to this point has a semblance of rationality. Unfortunately, judges over the centuries have complicated the analysis so that someone other than the finder may get the found property. Often the courts look at various factors to determine who keeps found property.

The most typical disputes occur between the finder of the property and the owner of the land or building where the property was found. Courts have categorized ways the true owner was separated from his property. Without overruling *Armory*, over time judges began to characterize found property as lost property, mislaid property, abandoned property, or treasure trove.

Lost property — property the true owner unintentionally and unknowingly drops or loses — belongs to the finder (unless and until the true owner is located). **Mislaid property** — property the true owner intentionally placed in a given location and then left, or intentionally left intending to return for it later — belongs to the owner of the *locus in quo* (unless and until the true owner is located). The idea is that the possessor of the real estate on which the property is found is in a better position to give the found property back to the true owner if the true owner comes back looking for it. Judges created this second category — mislaid property — to justify giving the found property to the possessor of the *locus in quo* in an attempt to preserve the true owner's rights.

To illustrate, a finder finds a watch with a broken watchband in a shop. If the true owner's watchband broke and the watch fell to the ground, then the watch is lost property. The finder keeps the watch. On the other hand, if the true owner put the watch on a table after discovering the watchband was broken and left without picking up the watch, the property is characterized as mislaid property and the owner of the shop keeps the watch.

The difficulty with this approach is that the only person who truly knows whether the object was lost or mislaid is the true owner, who never appears. If the true owner appears and claims the watch, the ownership issue as between the finder and the owner of the *locus in quo* is moot.

The judicial inquiry becomes only slightly more complex when two more categories are introduced. **Abandoned property** is property the true owner intentionally and voluntarily relinquished, with the intent no longer to own the object, and without transferring his rights to another person. Like possession, abandonment has two elements: an act of abandonment, and the intent to abandon. It is not presumed, but must be proven. The mere passage of time gives rise to no presumption of abandonment. Abandoned property belongs to the finder.

The finder also keeps **treasure trove**, which is gold, silver, and, in some jurisdictions, currency, intentionally concealed or underground, with indications it has been so long concealed that the true owner has long since died.

Treasure trove carries a sense of antiquity. In England, treasure trove belongs to the crown; in the United States, treasure trove goes to the finder.

OTHER CONSIDERATIONS

Some courts find other factors to be important. These remaining factors carve out exceptions to the general rule that the finder keeps found property. The exceptions favor employers and owners of the locus in quo. For example, courts disfavor trespassers. Therefore, a trespasser who finds lost property, abandoned property, or treasure trove will lose out to the landowner (unless the trespass is "trivial").

Similarly, a finder who is on premises for a limited purpose must relinquish any found property to the landowner. In an abstract way, the finder does not have permission to find things, and so is acting outside the scope of his authorized entry.

Many cases have held that employees are acting for the benefit of their employers and therefore must give all found items to their employers (mislaid objects still go to the owner of the locus in quo). Other courts require the employee to turn over the object to the employer only when the employee found the object in a place not open to the public. Hotel staff, for example, are often required to give objects found in guest rooms to the hotel; many courts would rule in favor of the hotel employee if the employee found the object in a public area such as a lobby, however.

Even visitors may lose out to the owner of the property. In addition to the lost/mislaid dichotomy discussed earlier, many judges will award even lost property (as well as mislaid property) to the owner of the premises if the object was found in a private place, such as a private office, rather than in a public part of the premises.

Items found in a residence belong to the owner or renter of the residence, assuming the owner or renter lives there. In Hannah v. Peel, 1 K.B. 509 (1945), the finder prevailed even though the item was found in a residence because (a) the owner had never used the house as his residence and (b) the current tenant, the British Royal Artillery, did not use the house as a residence either.

Another analytical distinction that results in a landowner rather than a finder getting possession of found property centers on whether the found object was embedded in the soil or was on the surface of the property. Objects embedded in the soil belong to the property owner and not to the finder, even if the object is foreign to the native soil. See, e.g., Goddard v. Winchell, 52 N.W. 1124 (Iowa 1892) (aerolite/meteorite), and Allred v. Biegel, 219 S.W.2d 665 (Mo. App. 1949) (ancient Indian canoe). Objects found on the *surface* might stay with the finder subject to all the earlier rules that award found property to the owners of the premises or others (mislaid property, private place, residence, limited purpose access, employee). While a few states even award treasure trove embedded in the soil to the landowner, many courts modify the embedded/surface dichotomy to award treasure trove to the finder unless the finder is a trespasser.

INSTRUMENTAL VIEW

As a policy matter, should labels of lost, mislaid, abandoned, or treasure trove; or the happenstance of where the property was found; or who found it dictate who should get ownership rights of found property? Many commentators think not, and favor an instrumental view that asks what conduct or goals should be encouraged. All, for example, agree that any rule should facilitate the return of the property to the rightful owner. You can argue that giving the finder the property encourages disclosure; otherwise, the finder may not disclose to anyone that he found the property. The same instrumental goal of returning the found object to its rightful owner also justifies giving the found object to the owner of the premises. The true owner is more likely to return to the premises where the object was lost than he is to happen upon the finder of the object. The premises owner, moreover, must store and care for the found object in case the true owner returns to claim it. As an exercise in evaluating laws, list the reasons why the finder should keep the found object and the reasons why the premises owner should get it. Once you have your lists, draft what you think would be the best statute on this subject.

LEGISLATION

About 20 states have statutes addressing this issue. Many are patterned on statutes regarding estrays.[2] Some simply modify common law or provide that finders keep the property if the true owner cannot be found. Others require a finder to report the find to the local police department. The police will take custody of the found object. After a period of time, if the true owner does not claim the property, the finder may claim not just possession but title to the property as his own. Statutes transferring the title to the property are particularly useful when adapted, as some states have, for the situation of pets adopted through a local animal shelter. Some statutes provide that the true owner either pays a reward based on the value of the property to the finder, or else reimburses the finder for the costs and expenses of keeping the property.

---

2. A legal term for strayed, domesticated farm animals.

Examples

I Know the Owner

1. Would the result in Armory v. Delamirie be the same if the true owner were known? Assume the same facts as *Armory* except that the chimney sweep found the jewel outside the Pickering home. The chimney sweep sues the goldsmith as before. As a defense, the goldsmith proves the jewel belongs to someone other than the sweep. What result?

The Oil Painting Caper

2. Owen purchases an expensive painting to hang in his home. Owen thereafter gives the painting to Seth, his son, with a letter saying, "if and when you don't have a place to hang it, I want it back." Owen keeps the bill of sale for the painting. Seth moves to a studio apartment with no place to hang the painting. Seth consigns it to an art dealer for sale. Ted steals the painting from the dealer. Ted sells the painting to Ben. The police recover the painting from Ben. Who should the police give the painting to? Clue: Who has the right to present possession of the painting?

Cash Preserves

3. In 1970 Charles buried $25,000 in coins and paper money in tin cans and glass jars in his backyard. It was commonly known that Charles did not trust banks and hid money on his property. Charles died in 1990. All his property passed to his son Ozzie. Ozzie sold the land to David in 2000. Later David hired Ellison to tear down and replace a garage. In removing the garage Ellison found the tin cans and glass jars containing the $25,000.
   (a) Ozzie, David, and Ellison all claim the $25,000. Who prevails?
   (b) Was the money lost, mislaid, abandoned, or treasure trove?
   (c) Assume Ozzie cannot be found. Who gets the cash: David or Ellison?

Finders Keepers

4. Omar collects stamps. A decade or so ago he purchased a set of stamps for $150,000. Last year Omar donated a dresser to charity. Pete bought the dresser for $30. Pete found the stamps in the dresser and advertised them for sale in a nationally circulated stamp catalog. Omar saw the ad and demanded the stamps be returned to him. Pete refused. Omar sued. Pete defended by arguing, "Finders keepers, losers weepers."
   (a) Is Omar's action one for replevin or one for trover?
   (b) As a judge, how would you rule on Pete's "finders keepers, losers weepers" argument?

Plane Old Money

5. Central Bank repossessed an airplane when the owner defaulted on a loan. Four months later Central Bank took the plane to Lindner Aviation for its annual inspection. Lindner Aviation conducted its business in a hanger leased from the City Airport. Benjamin, an employee of Lindner Aviation, inspected the plane. As part of the inspection Benjamin removed panels from the wings. Although these panels are supposed to be removed annually at the inspection, a couple of screws were rusted into place. Benjamin used a drill to remove the rusted screws and panels. Inside the left wing, Benjamin discovered two packets of $20 bills with mint dates primarily in the 1950s. The bills totaled $80,000.
   (a) As between Benjamin and Lindner Aviation, who gets the $80,000?
   (b) As between the prevailing party in (a) and City Airport, who gets the money?
   (c) As between the prevailing party in (b) and Central Bank, who gets the money?
   (d) As between the prevailing party in (c) and the previous owner of the airplane (who defaulted on the loan to Central Bank), who gets the money?

The Horsey Set-To

6. Abel is training Opal's racehorse. Under Abel's tutelage, the horse loses several races and Abel becomes indebted to Ben. Abel then comes into possession of the title certificate to the horse from the jockey club, and seeing that it has Opal's name forged on it, Abel sells the property to Ben in exchange for a release from the debt. Ben then endorses the certificate and sells the horse to Cory, another trainer. Cory transfers an interest in the horse to Dan and starts racing it again, on his own and Cory's behalf. The horse wins several races and Opal, watching one of these races, recognizes the horse as her own. What advice would you give Opal?

Explanations

I Know the Owner

1. The case of Jeffries v. The Great Western R.R. Co., 119 Eng. Rep. 680 (Queen's Bench 1856), was a trover action for the value of "trucks" or railroad cars. It held that the outcome would be the same as in *Armory*. The rationale of *Jeffries* was that a defendant in a prior possession case should win (if at all) on the strength of his own claim to the chattel, not because someone else, not before the court, has a better claim than the plaintiff. Objecting to the defendant's doing otherwise is known as the *jus tertii*

defense. In other words, a party should litigate on the strengths of his own claim, not on the weakness of another's.

The Oil Painting Caper

2. The police should give the painting to Owen, as Owen has the present right to possession. Seth, his son, was given the painting subject to a condition that he return it upon the happening of a certain event. That event occurred. Seth's consignment to the dealer attempted to give the dealer a power (to sell) that Seth did not have. A thief has void title — i.e., no title, and cannot transfer good title — so Ted acquires no rights at all by his theft, and Ben consequently acquires no rights from Ted.

Cash Preserves

3. (a) Ozzie gets the money. He inherited all of George's property, including the money and the land. He is the rightful owner of the money and prevails over David, the current landowner, and Ellison, the finder.

   David's main argument is that by selling him the land, Ozzie included everything buried on the property. The money and land, however, are separate assets. The sale of one is not the sale of the other. See Ritz v. Selma United Methodist Church, 467 N.W.2d 266, 269 (Iowa 1991). David loses. Any right Ellison might have is subject to the rights of Ozzie, the rightful owner.

   (b) The money was not lost because Charles intentionally placed the money in the ground. The fact that the money is in cans and jars is some indication of that; the value of the money is further indication that it has not been abandoned. The money lacks the feel of antiquity. That it has been hidden so long and that the true owner is not discoverable are the hallmarks of treasure trove. The only characterization that comes close is that the money was mislaid — intentionally placed in the ground and the whereabouts forgotten, or at least not told to Ozzie.

   (c) This Example is based loosely on Corliss v. Wenner, 34 P.3d 1100 (Idaho App. 2001). Ellison must argue that the money was lost, abandoned, or treasure trove since David as owner of the premises wins if the money was mislaid. As discussed in (b), the money was mislaid. Mislaid property goes to the owner of the land. Hence David, the landowner, gets the cash. David, moreover, could persuade a court that Ellison was on David's land for a limited purpose, which limited purpose did not include finding and claiming the money. Anything Ellison found in or on David's land belongs to David. Finally, David could argue the money was embedded in the soil and not on the surface. Embedded objects belong to the owner of the soil rather than to the finder. David gets the money if Ozzie is not located.

Finders Keepers

4. (a) Omar brought an action for replevin to obtain possession of personal property wrongfully detained by another.

   (b) Under the holding of Armory v. Delamirie, Pete had greater ownership rights against the whole world except the true owner. Once Omar proves he is the true owner, he wins and Pete loses. The sale or contribution of the dresser to the charity was not a gift of the stamps inside. Finders keepers, losers weepers is not the law. See Gantor v. Kapiloff, 516 A.2d 611, 613-614 (Md. App. 1986).

Plane Old Money

5. (a) The Example is based on Benjamin v. Lindner Aviation, Inc., 534 N.W.2d 400 (Iowa 1995). Using the labels and categories, Benjamin is the finder, but as he is an employee in a place solely because of his employment, a court likely would award the money to his employer, Lindner Aviation. From an instrumental view, if a court finds that the true owner may return, it may award the money to Lindner Aviation as being the easiest for the true owner to locate.

   On the other hand, giving the money to Benjamin rewards honesty and encourages people to publicize their findings. Despite the instrumental view, most courts would characterize the find as one by an employee and award the money to Lindner Aviation.

   (b) As between Lindner Aviation and City Airport, Lindner Aviation prevails. Although City Airport owned the land and hanger, Lindner Aviation had legal possession. While courts often speak in terms of the owner of the locus in quo, the legal possessor — the tenant in this case — keeps the money.

   (c) As between Lindner Aviation and Central Bank, the issue is whether the packets of money were "lost" or "mislaid." The packets do not have the taint of antiquity to be treasure trove. While debatable, it does not seem the money is abandoned. The very circumstance of its being $20 bills placed in packets that ended up inside the wing of an airplane suggests that someone intentionally placed the money there. Therefore, the money was mislaid and not lost. Mislaid property belongs to the owner of the place where the money was found.

   The money was found in an airplane owned by the Central Bank, even though the plane was in a hanger under Lindner Aviation's control. Central Bank wins.

   (d) As between Central Bank and the owner of the plane before Central Bank foreclosed, Central Bank as current owner of the plane prevails. The only chance the previous owner has is to show he was the true owner of the money. Merely owning the plane at one time avails him nothing unless there is evidence he owned the money before it was placed in the wing.

The Horsey Set-To

6. Opal may elect to sue any one of the successive convertors of her property — Abel, Ben, or Cory and Dan — in trover, probably making this election depending on the value of the horse at the time of each conversion. While Opal may obtain a judgment against each separately, only one of these judgments may be satisfied. Otherwise Opal would wind up overcompensated. So once one of them is satisfied, none of the others may be, on the theory of the forced sale: Opal will then have exchanged the title to the horse for whatever one of the possible defendants pays. See Baram v. Farugia, 606 F.2d 42 (3d Cir. 1979). Presumably a winning horse is worth more, so the suit should be against Cory and Dan. What if Opal sues them in trover, obtains a judgment against both, but Cory is judgment proof and Dan flees the jurisdiction, both sending the certificate for the horse back to Opal. May Opal then sue Abel? Yes. If Opal elects not to take the horse back, Opal doesn't have to do so, and this time the theory of her case will be based on a bailment — the bailee might re-deliver the horse, but when he cannot, he is strictly liable for his failure or refusal. What is the measure of damages for this failure? Does it include lost profits, or is it limited to the value of the horse when the bailee converted Opal's right to it? Some cases say the former, but the latter is the traditional measure of damages.

Bailments

At this point, we turn from a discussion of the means of acquiring possession to one on the methods of transferring the right to possession. Bailment, gift, and sale are the three methods of transferring an object of personal property. This chapter considers bailments. Gifts and sales are introduced in the next two chapters.

DEFINITIONS

A **bailment** is the transfer and delivery by an owner or prior possessor (the **bailor**) of possession of personal property to another (the **bailee**):

(1) whose purpose in holding possession is often for safekeeping or for some other purpose more limited than dealing with the object or chattel as would its owner, and

(2) where the return of the object or chattel in the same, or substantially the same, undamaged condition is contemplated.

This transfer of possession of property for a limited purpose, once accomplished, requires the transferee or bailee to redeliver the property to the transferor or bailor. Once that purpose is accomplished, a failure to redeliver renders the bailee strictly liable. A bailment results in the rightful possession of personal property by a person not its owner.

4. Bailments

Bailments affect everyday life. When a person rents a car or parks it in a commercial parking lot, a bailment arises. When you leave your clothes at the cleaner's or your film at the photo shop, a bailment is created. Even borrowing a book from a friend gives rise to a bailment.

Bailments are common in commercial transactions. For banks, pawnbrokers, common carriers, warehouses, and hotels, bailments are at the heart of their businesses. Some commercial bailments, as with warehouses, are treated in detail in the Uniform Commercial Code, Article 7. Thus bailments represent a pervasive form of transfer transaction, arising frequently and in many commercial and noncommercial contexts.

A bailment is the result of a contract or agreement, express or implied, or the conduct of the parties — or some combination of agreement and conduct. Some jurisdictions require an express agreement of some type to create a bailment, but also may imply agreements and bailments from conduct. Identifying a bailment requires, then, that you look not only at the parties' agreement, but also at their conduct — if only as evidence of their implementation of an implied agreement. More generally, then, a bailment may be regarded as the implementation of a contract, as a transfer of property, or as some sui generis hybrid of both contract and property law.

Because the subject of any bailment is personal property, regarding bailments as an area of the law of property takes the most realistic view, they being typically established because of some property interest of the bailor in an object. Bailments typically also are limited to tangible personal property, but this term includes pieces of paper representing rights in other things. It is now well settled that securities, bonds, and negotiable instruments may be held in a bailment as well. Whether intellectual property may be held in a bailment is a controversial subject.

The general rules governing bailments are predicated on the absence of a specific agreement that may supersede or vary those rules. In other words, the rules are implied by law in the absence of an agreement to the contrary. In this view, bailments may be founded upon either an express or an implied agreement.

A bailment requires a delivery of possession — without delivery there is no bailment. No particular ceremony is necessary; however, there are three types of delivery. It may be actual, constructive, or symbolic. With an **actual delivery** of an object, the object is physically handed over to the bailee. A **constructive delivery** occurs when one gives the keys to a safe deposit box or to a heavy or bulky object, such as a bureau or chest of drawers, to the transferee; this transfers control of the object without actually delivering it, and is the gist of a constructive delivery. A **symbolic delivery** is the receipt by the bailee of a thing symbolizing the object of the bailment. While this may be something associated with the object, a symbolic delivery usually means transfer by use of a written instrument.

44

In addition to delivery, a bailment requires the bailee's **acceptance** of the delivered property. Like the delivery element, acceptance might not be actual. Constructive acceptance is found when a person comes into possession of an object by mistake or takes possession of it when it is left or lost by its owner.

Without an actual delivery and acceptance, some courts refer generally to the possibility of a constructive bailment without identifying the missing element. A **constructive bailment** arises when possession of personal property is acquired and retained under circumstances in which the recipient should keep it safely and return it to its owner. Shamrock Hilton Hotel v. Caranas, 488 S.W.2d 151 (Tex. App. Ct. 1972) (involving a purse left in a hotel dining room and found by a hotel employee). In *Caranas*, there was no intentional delivery of the purse, but the court found that a constructive bailment arose because the hotel patron would expect that, if found, the misplaced purse would be retained and kept safe for her eventual return. Thus, where there is evidence that the bailee received and accepted the object, but not that the bailor intended to deliver it, a constructive bailment arises for purposes of allocating the loss or damage to the object upon its misdelivery.

OVERVIEW OF NEGLIGENCE AND STRICT LIABILITY

Some of the following material discusses when a bailee is strictly liable and when it is liable only for negligence. **Strict liability** means an actor is liable for damages, notwithstanding any actions he took or failed to take. **Negligence**, on the other hand, demands the actor be at fault. Negligence depends on state law creating (1) a duty or standard of care, and (2) the defendant's action or inaction breaching that duty and so falling short of the applicable standard of care. If the actor's conduct falls below the applicable standard of care, the actor is negligent.

For the defendant to be liable for his negligence, however, the negligence must be the cause of a plaintiff's injuries. Thus injury or damage is the third element of a negligence action. In addition, the defendant's negligence must be the proximate or legal cause of the plaintiff's injury. The proximate or legal cause considerations are matters of law, including whether the legal system believes a defendant should be liable in circumstances of the case. Finally, the plaintiff must suffer actual damages. An actor's "standard of care" varies based on the circumstances and is often a determination by a jury or trier of fact as to how a "reasonable person" should act under the circumstances. As this discussion indicates, it is easier for a plaintiff to win a strict liability case than it is to win a negligence case.

SPECIALIZED BAILMENT ISSUES

(a) Pledges

Some bailments have more specialized uses. A **pledge** is a bailment to secure a debt or obligation of the bailor. It is a bailment for security. The transfer of possession need not be made to the pledgee (the creditor or obligee). Instead, it can be to a third party.

(b) Park-and-Lock Cases

One tricky area of bailments is distinguishing a bailment from a lease or license. Identifying a transaction as a bailment — instead of a lease, say — is an important step for the alleged bailor because of the duty placed on the bailee to redeliver the chattel. A failure to redeliver raises a presumption that the bailee negligently handled the chattel in her care.

Take, for example, a parking lot that requires that you pull a ticket to lift a gate at entry, choose the space in which to park, and lock your car so that it cannot be moved by the management. If parking the car in the lot constitutes a bailment, the parking lot operator becomes a bailee, and with it comes the responsibility to care for the car. If the lot operator merely gives the car owner a license to use space to park his car, no bailment results and the car remains under the owner's control. If the space is leased for a definite period of time, the car remains under the control of the car owner, and no bailment exists.

Such a park-and-lock arrangement would have at one time created no bailment. Control over the car, coupled perhaps with an exculpatory clause on the ticket, negated the delivery requirement for a bailment. A license to use the parking space was instead created, or if you paid a fee at entry, perhaps a lease was found. Today a park-and-lock arrangement in some jurisdictions creates a bailment. See Allen v. Hyatt Regency–Nashville Hotel, 668 S.W.2d 286 (Tenn. 1984) (holding that a bailment was created when a car owner parked and locked his car in an indoor multistory garage operated in conjunction with a hotel).[1]

Peeling away the facts in *Allen* shows the difficulties with these cases. What if the lot were outdoors (in a setting in which the operator has less control over the parking spaces)? What if it were not associated with a hotel? The owner of an open park-and-lock lot, in which each space has a separate meter, is an unlikely bailee. See Rhodes v. Pioneer Parking

---

1. Absent a statute, an innkeeper was strictly liable at common law for his guests' personal safety and property.

Lot, Inc., 501 S.W.2d 569 (Tenn. 1973). A license or a lease is a more likely characterization of the arrangement in such a parking lot.

The New Jersey Supreme Court has ruled that the traditional elements of a bailment are inadequate for the enclosed park-and-lock lot cases and has found that a parking lot owner has a duty of reasonable care under all the circumstances of a case and that when the parked car is damaged upon its owner's return, there is a presumption of negligence by the owner of an enclosed lot because (1) the owner is in the best position to absorb and spread the risk of damage; (2) the car owner's expectation is that he will reclaim the car in the condition he left it; and (3) were it otherwise, the owner's proof of negligence while he was away "imposes a difficult, if not insurmountable, burden" on him. See McGlynn v. Parking Authority of City of Newark, 432 A.2d 99 (N.J. 1981).

Even when a bailment is recognized in a transaction, identifying the subject of the bailment may provide further problems. In a jurisdiction in which park-and-lock parking creates a bailment, the bailee will be liable for any vandalism that damages the exterior of the parked car, but might still argue that no bailment was created as to valuables found in — and stolen from — its glove compartment. The ground for this argument is that valuables might be expected to be found in, say, a safe deposit box in a bank, but not in the glove compartment of a car. There are exceptions, however. The operator of a parking garage in a well-known tourist location, such as the French Quarter of New Orleans, may be held to know that tourists carry valuables in the trunks of their cars.

(c) Safe Deposit Boxes

The same preliminary issues occur when a person rents a safe deposit box at a bank: Is the renting of the box a bailment, license, or lease? Despite the use of the word "rent" in transaction, courts usually find a bailment has occurred. The box remains under the bank's control.

MISDELIVERY OF BAILED PROPERTY

(a) Strict Liability and Negligence

The relationship between bailor and bailee gives rise to a standard of care and liability for the misdelivery or misredelivery of the object. Causes of action involving bailments are styled in their complaints in either contract or tort. For misdelivery of the bailed object, the bailee is strictly liable in tort, absent a special agreement or a statute. So a bailee is liable even if the bailee is not at fault for the misdelivery. An important example of a statute absolving a bailee from strict liability for misdelivery is found in the Uniform Commercial Code sections applicable to warehouse operators. UCC § 7-404 (imposing no duty if reasonable commercial standards are used by the warehouseman). Otherwise, the bailee is strictly liable for a misdelivery of the chattel. In some states, a rule of strict liability has been replaced by a presumption of negligence—i.e., by a rule that says that unless the bailee can account for the loss of the bailed item in some nonnegligent way, a presumption arises that its loss was the result of the bailee's negligence.

(b) Burden of Proof

The burden of proof in a negligence case of misdelivery is on the bailee—who is generally the defendant in such cases—to show that he did not act in a negligent manner. This asks the bailee to prove a negative—that he was not negligent—and this is a very difficult task.

This burden of proof is assigned to the bailee for five reasons. First, the bailee knows the history of the bailment best. Second, the bailee has the right to sue thieves and converters of the chattel. Third, the bailee is in the best position to take steps to secure (the recovery of) the chattel. Fourth, the risk of damage or misdelivery is best borne by the bailee, since it can spread the risk in its charges to its customers. Fifth, and finally, the assignment serves to prevent the bailee from engaging in fraudulent misdeliveries or other acts. Many of these justifications also justify the imposition of strict liability on the bailee. To some extent, then, the assignment of this burden to the bailee serves as a stand-in or surrogate for strict liability.

Even if the bailee shows that it took reasonable care, a failure to take steps to secure the recovery of the chattel would render it liable, unless it shows that the steps would have been futile.

If a bailee deviates from the terms of the bailment, it will have to show that the deviation makes no difference to the loss or damage. Examples arise when the bailee takes a different route than instructed, or when the bailee entrusts the goods to a third party without authority, or where the chattel is stored elsewhere than as authorized. The deviating bailee in effect becomes the insurer of the goods and strict liability follows, unless it can show that the deviation was harmless.

(c) What Must Be Redelivered

Generally it is obvious what property must be returned to the bailor. The issue in some cases, however, is what must be delivered back to the bailor. Consider the following four examples: First, a deposit of money in a bank.

Here the same bills are not expected back, so no bailment arises; rather, a debtor-creditor relationship arises between the bank and its depositor.

Second, consider the deposit of grain into a silo or a grain elevator for its operator to hold for delivery to a railroad. Here the depositor expects that a similar quality of grain will be given over or back, but not the exact grains deposited. If the silo operator goes bankrupt, will the depositor have a lien on the silo's contents in order to recover the value of the grain? Does the lien suffice as a remedy for the depositor? The purpose of the bailment sometimes determines its presence or absence.

Third, a herd of cattle is put in the care of a farmer. Only if all the animals perished in the hands of the transferee would a court find this to be a bailment. The herd can be expected to suffer attrition if it is mostly bulls, but not so if it is mostly cows. Some courts might hold that the herd as a whole is the subject of a bailment, but that there is no bailment of the individual animals in it.

Fourth, consider seed delivered to a farmer by a merchant. There is no bailment when the merchant expects a mature crop in return. If bailor and bailee expect a change in the basic nature of the chattel, there is no bailment. But what if a transferee delivers grapes and expects to get wine back, delivers apples and expects cider, or delivers leather and expects shoes? That the bailed property is due back in some altered state is no reason not to find a bailment, unless there is some type of "net yield" clause in the agreement, in which case the bailee might keep the excess over the agreed-upon yield and the transaction might be seen as a partial sale of the property.

WHEN BAILED PROPERTY IS LOST OR DAMAGED

The bailee is liable not only for misdeliveries, but also if the bailed goods are lost or damaged. Strict liability does not apply in lost or damaged property cases. The bailee is liable only in negligence.

The **standard of care** traditionally required of the bailee varies with the degree of reward or benefit the bailee receives. A three-pronged rule is used, as follows:

(1) When the benefit of the bailment to the bailee is slight, the care required of the bailee is slight; the bailee is liable only for **gross negligence**. This is typically a **gratuitous bailment** such as a person taking care of an object for a friend or neighbor, or one created by a mistake. Ordinarily, a finder is such a bailee.

(2) If the bailment benefits both bailor and bailee mutually and is equally beneficial to both, the standard of care imposed on the bailee rises and the bailee is liable for negligence and has a duty of reasonable

care under the circumstances. Leaving an item in a packet with the desk clerk of a hotel was found in one case to be a bailment benefiting both the bailor (the guest) and the bailee (the hotel). *Peet v. Roth Hotel Co.*, 253 N.W. 546 (Minn. 1934); *Shamrock Hilton Hotel v. Caranas*, 488 S.W.2d 151 (Tex. App. Ct. 1972) (involving a purse left in a hotel dining room and found by a busboy). In *Caranas*, for example, leaving the purse unattended on the floor might not create a bailment, but the subsequent assumption of its possession by an employee does — and its subsequent disappearance from the hostess's desk will make the hotel liable for a misdelivery.

(3) Finally, if the bailment benefits the bailee, as with a borrowed object, the bailee's standard of care rises again and the merest neglect or any damage renders the bailee liable. This higher standard of care also applies to certain commercial bailees such as transport companies and repair shops.

This three-pronged standard was first developed in an early American legal treatise by Joseph Story in his *Commentaries on the Law of Bailments*. It was well received at its inception because it offered the American bar a refined view of older contract-based English and American cases and also incorporated into those older cases then-emerging theories of negligence. Story believed that the duty imposed on a gratuitous bailee could not be the same as that imposed when a consideration was paid. The gratuitous bailee was only liable because of actual performance by the bailee and subsequent reliance by the bailor — in other words, a type of detriment consideration established the bailment.

Story's views have not gone unchallenged. Many courts take a contractual view of bailments because they regard Story's approach as too mechanical. Others think that the focus on the rewards inherent in a bailment excludes an examination of the propriety of the parties' conduct. Still others see this skewed focus, but also perceive a need for one modern general rule that fits ubiquitously all types of bailments; they think that Story's incorporation of negligence law into bailment law did not go far enough. Thus, some courts have abandoned this three-pronged standard of care. They have done so either expressly or with opinions that tend to combine or blur Story's several standards. These courts adopt, expressly or in fact, a rule of reasonable care under the circumstances (including as a circumstance the degree of benefit received by the bailee), making a bailee's liability dependent on the exercise of such reasonable care. This reasonable-care rule juxtaposes the risk and the bailee's conduct; the relationship between the risk and the conduct determines how much care is reasonable under the circumstances.

Nevertheless, Story's three-pronged standard remains the traditional and widely used method of analysis for a bailment where the issue is the standard of care to be applied.

Examples

Honor Among Thieves

1. Armas steals a valuable wristwatch from its true owner and then takes it to Burrell's shop for repairs. Clayton sees the watch on Burrell's shop counter and takes it. Can Burrell replevy the watch from Clayton?

Parking Lot Tribulation

2. During the early evening hours, Darrell parks his car in an attended parking lot. He gives the keys to the attendant, who asks him how long it will be before Darrell returns. Darrell says that he will return at midnight, two hours after the lot closes. The attendant moves the car into a space visible from the booth and Darrell pays the parking fee for the hours up to closing. The attendant says that at closing he will put the keys to Darrell's car under the floor mat. Darrell nods to the effect that he has heard the attendant, but when he returns at midnight, his car has vanished. Darrell sues the parking lot owner for conversion of the vehicle. In this suit, what result and why?

High-Priced Free Parking

3. Florence went shopping. On the way, she stopped at a drive-through sandwich shop. After paying for her food, Florence put her wallet on the passenger seat. Florence parked her car at Barney's Clothes, Inc., which maintains a free parking lot for its customers. An attendant tends the lot. At the request of the parking lot attendant, Florence left her keys with him. When Florence left her car to go shopping, she inadvertently left the wallet on the car seat.

    When trying to pay for a new outfit, Florence missed her wallet and immediately returned to her car. Neither she, the attendant, nor the police could find Florence's wallet. The wallet contained $350. Florence sues Barney's Clothes for the value of the wallet but mainly for the $350. Who prevails?

Borne Away Bearer Bonds

4. A messenger employed by Stock & Co., a corporate securities brokerage firm, is instructed to deliver some bearer or demand bonds of Harmony Company to Bond Brothers, Inc., another securities firm. The messenger is given the bearer bonds of Harman, Inc., instead of those for Harmony Company. He carries the Harman bonds to Bond Brothers. He enters the Bond Brothers' office, approaches the receiving teller's window, rings the bell, deposits the bonds in a secure box to the side of the window,

turns away, and returns to Stock & Co. An employee of Bond Brothers quickly notices the mistake, calls "Stock" through the window, and is approached by a man who says, "Yes, stock." The employee hands the Harman bonds to the man, who takes them and vanishes. Has a bailment for the bonds been created at Bond Brothers' office?

Organ Solo

5. The biotechnology industry is in part founded on the use of other people's body parts. Is a bailment created when a diseased organ is removed surgically from a patient by a doctor and later used in research that produces valuable medicine?

Are My Pictures Back?

6. Is a photography laboratory that accepts undeveloped film for processing into prints or slides a bailee of the film? Is this a bailment where the same thing, or a different chattel, is expected back? If there is a bailment, is the lab liable for the value of the film or the value of the prints? Can the fine print on the box of film or the receipt for the film exculpate or limit the liability of the lab?

Orlando Wright

7. Aron delivers Orlando's jewelry for cleaning by Ben. Once cleaned, Orlando calls for the jewelry and demands possession. Must Ben deliver them to Orlando?

Explanations

Honor Among Thieves

1. Yes. The issue is whether the bailee of a thief acquires the right to sue third-party wrongdoers. The orderly conduct of bailments requires that although the thief has no possessory right to transfer, Clayton should not be able to set up a weakness in the transfer from Armas to Burrell as a defense. That would be deciding the suit on the basis of Clayton's *jus tertii* defense — rarely a good idea.

Parking Lot Tribulation

2. The transfer of the keys, as well as the moving of the car by the attendant to a space selected by the attendant, suggests that there is a bailment.

Assuming the attendant was acting within the scope of his employment, the crucial question is whether there was a constructive redelivery of the car. Because the action of the attendant made possible the theft, the rule of strict liability or the presumption of negligence should apply. See System Auto Parks & Garages v. Am. Economy Ins. Co., 411 N.E.2d 163 (Ind. App. Ct. 1980).

High-Priced Free Parking

3. This Example derives from Swarth v. Barney's Clothes, Inc., 242 N.Y.S.2d 922 (1963). Barney's Clothes wins. Barney's was bailee of the automobile under the facts, but it does not necessarily follow that Barney's was bailee of the wallet. The elements of the bailment are actual physical control with intent to possess—i.e., delivery and acceptance. Assuming the wallet was "delivered," there was no acceptance or intent to possess. A wallet is not usually possessed by the operator of the parking lot, and the attendant had no notice of the wallet. No bailment of the wallet; thus no liability under the bailment rules.

Borne Away Bearer Bonds

4. These are the facts of Cowen v. Pressprich 192 N.Y.S. 242 (N.Y. Sup. Ct. App. Term), rev., 194 N.Y.S. 926 (1922). The intermediate appeals court first held that a bailment was created. It was at first an involuntary or gratuitous one, to which only the slightest duty attached. When the Bond Brothers employee picked up the Harman bonds, however, it became a voluntary one, and a duty of reasonable care attached. Not having seen the messenger from Stock & Co., the Bond Brothers employee should have required identification, sent the bonds back using its own employees, or called Stock & Co. to check the identity of the messenger. Instead, the court said, when Bond Brothers undertook to redeliver the bonds, it took the risk of misdelivery upon itself, and so should pay damages for its conversion of the bonds. The intermediate appeals court opinion in *Cowen* was issued over a strong dissent.

On further appeal, the state's highest appellate court adopted the lower court dissenter's analysis based on the fact that Bond Brothers took possession by mistake, and promptly noticed and honestly tried to remedy the mistake, without any intent to interfere with the plaintiff's ownership of the bonds and by an action consistent with the plaintiff's ownership. The highest appellate court concluded that Bond Brothers never accepted delivery and hence did not take on the responsibilities of a bailee. Because no bailment was created in Bond Brothers, Bond Brothers was not strictly liable for misdelivery of the Harmon bonds.

Organ Solo

5. Several issues arise. Many are discussed in Moore v. Board of Regents of the University of California, 793 P.2d 479 (Cal. 1990) (finding a breach of fiduciary duty and no patient consent, but not conversion). The first is whether a human organ can be the object of a bailment by the donor. Many courts and statutes frown on treating the human body as an object to be bought and sold in commerce. Many states refuse to recognize the organ as personal property; hence the bailment rules would not apply.

   If the bailment rules do apply, the issue turns on whether the patient intended to give the organ to the surgeon for any purpose or for a limited purpose of destroying it according to law, whether the patient abandoned or released all interest in the organ, or whether the patient retained a property interest in the organ. Since there is no evidence that the patient intended to deliver the organ to the surgeon for research purposes, if the state permits a bailment in this situation, a finding of bailment — or at least constructive bailment — and conversion seems appropriate.

Are My Pictures Back?

6. The laboratory is a bailee. In the end, it does not matter. The photos to be returned can be traced to the original film, which distinguishes this case from one of fungible goods. The lab is liable for the price of the film. This may be a case where the lab can limit its liability. Some courts may not allow a bailee to limit its liability for its own negligence, however. This Explanation also assumes the laboratory has no reason to know of any "special circumstances" about this film's importance. See Carr v. Hoosier Photo Labs, 441 N.E.2d 450 (Ind. 1982) (holding, first, that it was a bailment to return the film, though in a new form; second, that the photographer accepted the terms of the exculpatory provision on both the box of film and the receipt for the film given by the lab; and third, that the provision was neither unconscionable nor void). Carr involved an experienced amateur photographer, also an attorney with a business law practice, who took a European trip and brought back 18 rolls of exposed film for processing to a major film manufacturer's lab. Four of the rolls were lost and never accounted for. The photographer won a $13.60 judgment for the value of the film, but lost a lower court's award of $1000 for the value of his prints to him.

Orlando Wright

7. Yes, when Orlando provides proof of ownership. Older cases might add that Orlando should obtain a court order mandating that Ben deliver the

jewelry to him. See Hentz v. The Idaho, 93 U.S. 575 (1876). In either event, delivery of the jewelry to the true or rightful owner should justify their later non-delivery to the bailor. Acceptance of the bailment should not estop the bailee from inquiring into the right of the bailor. Acceptance raises only a rebuttable presumption of the bailor's right. An otherwise silent bailment agreement implicitly provides that the bailee will restore or re-deliver the goods, deliver them at the direction of the bailee, or else account for their delivery. The bailee accounts for the goods when he delivers them to one whose rights are superior to the bailor's. A rule of judicial economy justifies this result. The defense of *jus tertii* is best seen only as a defense that someone other than a defendant has a better right so that the defendant might keep the property himself; it is not intended to deny the true owner his rights.

CHAPTER 5

Good-Faith or Bona Fide Purchasers

Chapter 4, on bailments, explained that the bailee (possessor of the property belonging to another) is obligated to redeliver the property to the bailor or to the rightful or true owner. This chapter deals with the rights of the true owner against a third party if the bailee wrongfully sells the object to the third party. It also addresses the rights of the true owner against good-faith third-party purchasers who purchased from thieves or other persons with voidable title. From the good-faith purchaser's perspective, the issue is the risk she takes that she must return a purchased item to the true owner.

A **good-faith** or **bona fide purchaser** (BFP) of personal or real property is a person who buys honestly and without notice of any conflicting claim on the property bought, whether or not the purchaser is negligent. For example, if Bert buys a television set from Andy, intentionally giving Andy a bad check, and later sells the television to Peter, Peter may inquire about the identity of the former owner and be told that Bert has forgotten who that was. When Peter does not insist on finding out who the former owner is, he still qualifies as a BFP, even though, had he insisted, he would have learned of Bert's fraud. Bert can give a better right to the television than he had.

This situation provides one example of one of two exceptions to the maxim that no one acquires greater rights in an object than one's vendor has to transfer. The first exception is for **good-faith purchasers** and the second is for **entrustments**. Both apply only in some limited, but important, situations. They are important because, as in the example in the previous paragraph, when and if one of the two exceptions applies, a transferee can transfer more rights to property than he has.

VOIDABLE TITLE AND BONA FIDE PURCHASERS

At early common law, the law favored owners over all persons. A person could transfer only the rights he enjoyed; he could not transfer more rights than he had. Under this approach, a good-faith purchaser who bought an item from someone who did not have good title to it would return the item to the rightful owner without compensation. If the seller could not be found, the bona fide purchaser would be out his money too.

The rule that a person cannot transfer better title than he has is still the rule in cases where the transferor has a void title. **Void title** means no title. A bailee, for example, has no title, and generally cannot transfer good title (but see *entrustment, infra*). A thief has no title. A person buying stolen goods can be forced to relinquish the goods to the rightful owner.

When commercial markets developed, good-faith purchasers needed protection. It would stymie market trade if every seller had to document all owners in his chain of title for every item sold. The first exception to the general rule occurs when the true owner is tricked by fraud or misrepresentation into voluntarily parting with title. The bad check in the Bert and Peter example is one such case. In another, the fraud or misrepresentation might happen because the dishonest purchaser misrepresented his identity. For example, the wrongdoer may negotiate a purchase by convincing the true owner he is wealthy when he is not, or he may trick the true owner into signing a document that transfers title, the true owner thinking the document is another instrument.

The courts label the title in these cases **voidable title**. The title is voidable in that the true owner can rescind the transaction and get the property back. Voidable title in the wrongdoer is good until the true owner rescinds, at which time the wrongdoer's title becomes void. If, however, the wrongdoer sells the object to a BFP — a person who pays fair value without notice the wrongdoer does not have good title — the BFP receives good title and will prevail even against the original owner. Thus, while the true owner can void the title of the wrongdoer, the true owner cannot void the title of the BFP.

The reason the wrongdoer can transfer good title has nothing to do with the wrongdoer. The courts, faced with two innocent parties having to suffer a loss, lay the loss at the feet of the true owner since she was the one who helped create the situation by transferring title to the wrongdoer. Of the two innocent parties, the innocent person who most easily could have prevented the problem or misunderstanding must suffer the loss. The true owner still has recourse against the wrongdoer, if she can find him.

As a reminder, the BFP prevails only if the true owner transfers title to the wrongdoer. A thief cannot transfer good title, even to a good-faith purchaser.

Moreover, only a BFP wins in this situation. A BFP must actually act in good faith — she must act in good faith and without notice the wrongdoer did not have good title. In addition, the BFP must pay valuable consideration. If she signed a note or IOU or has not made payment, she has not yet suffered a loss. Hence she needs no protection. She has no obligation to pay. A donee — a recipient of a gift or a person who inherits from the wrongdoer — is not a purchaser and is not protected under this rule. The price paid by the BFP must provide adequate consideration, not necessarily fair market value, as long as the price is not so inadequate as to warrant a conclusion the purchase was not bona fide.

THE UCC AND BONA FIDE PURCHASERS

The following section of the Uniform Commercial Code (UCC), adopted in some form in all states but Louisiana, has been very influential in the law concerning bona fide purchasers.

UCC § 2-403 (1962). (1) purchaser of goods acquires all title which his transferor had or had power to transfer except that a purchaser of a limited interest acquires rights only to the extent of the interest purchased. A person with voidable title has power to transfer a good title to a good faith purchaser for value. When goods have been delivered under a transaction of purchase the purchaser has such power even though (a) the transferor was deceived as to the identity of the purchaser, or (b) the delivery was in exchange for a check which is later dishonored, or (c) it was agreed that the transaction was to be a "cash sale", or (d) the delivery was procured through fraud punishable as larcenous under the criminal law.

The first sentence in subsection (1) states that no vendor can transfer a better title than he or she has. It also restates, by implication, the void title rule, to the effect that a vendor with a void title cannot transfer any title at all. Subsection (1)'s second sentence expressly restates the voidable title rule, and so gives the true owner the power to revoke a transfer of goods in the hands of the transferee, while also giving that transferee the power to render it absolute by himself transferring it to a BFP. A voidable title is defective, but not wholly so. Instead, it is a title subject to a right of rescission in the transferor or the true owner of the object.

The UCC's bona fide purchaser is a person who acquires title (1) in a transaction in which a fair market value of the object is the consideration, (2) with an honest belief that he was acquiring title to the object, and (3) under circumstances that would not lead him to think otherwise. These requirements are not unusual; they merely restate the law as it existed prior to, and made as a result of, the UCC. The first requirement means again that a donee would not qualify as a BFP; some new and separate consideration must be given by the purchaser. The second requirement means that the transaction must be complete before the purchaser has knowledge — actual or implied — of the true owner's claim. The third requirement has been expanded under the UCC to require a purchaser to investigate the title offered with due diligence. See, e.g., Porter v. Wertz, 416 N.Y.S.2d 254 (N.Y. App. Div. 1979), affirmed, 421 N.E.2d 500 (N.Y. 1981) (involving the sale of a painting, and requiring that the gallery purchasing it investigate the title of its transferor, but without providing guidelines for that investigation). Such due diligence is important when the personalty is expensive — as with works of art or racehorses.

The UCC states that a person is not prevented from becoming a bona fide purchaser "even though . . . the transferor was deceived as to the identity of the purchaser. . . ." UCC § 2-403(1)(a). What is deceptive is seen from the transferor's point of view. However, the intent of the UCC might be said to protect bona fide purchasers from both elegant and crude deceptions. The drafters' comment on this section says generally that it is specifically aimed at protecting the bona fide purchaser in situations "troublesome under prior law" (without ever saying what the trouble was). UCC § 2-403, Comment 1 (1962).

If the UCC does abolish the distinctions of prior law, the con artists and rogues of the world might then extract a voidable title from owners — not to protect themselves, but to protect those of their transferees who pay value and can show bona fide ownership. Thus, whether the con artist uses face-to-face impersonation, the mail, the fax machine, or other means of deception should not matter. However, under this provision of the UCC, a theft accomplished by fraud and not by misrepresentation still leaves the thief with a void title.

ENTRUSTMENT

Under common law, a bailee did not have title and could not transfer good title to a good-faith purchaser. Recognizing that commerce would operate best if purchasers were assured they could keep objects they bought from merchants, first courts and then the UCC stepped forward to protect people who purchased from "merchants." UCC § 2-403 provides:

> (2) Any entrusting of possession of goods to a merchant who deals in goods of that kind gives him power to transfer all rights of the entruster to a buyer in ordinary course of business.
> (3) "Entrusting" includes any delivery and any acquiescence in retention of possession regardless of any condition expressed between

the parties to the delivery or acquiescence and regardless of whether the procurement of the entrusting or the possessor's disposition of the goods have been such as to be larcenous under the criminal law.

In this statutory exception to the void title rule, when a chattel's owner delivers it to a bailee who is a merchant, and the bailee wrongfully sells the chattel to a person who buys it "in the ordinary course" of the bailee's business, the owner is estopped to deny the title of the purchaser. See Zendman v. Harry Winston, Inc., 111 N.E.2d 871 (N.Y. 1953). This exception is intended to keep trade and commerce with merchants humming by safeguarding purchasers' rights to what they think they have bought.

The definition of "entrustment" expressly states that the merchant can transfer good title to a purchaser in the ordinary course of business, regardless of any agreement between the entrusting person and the "entrustee." A former owner or possessor may not raise or assert objections to the subsequent extraordinary transfer, based on what the person dealing with an entrustee could not know. To illustrate, a person takes a diamond necklace to a jeweler solely to have the necklace appraised. The jeweler sells the necklace to a customer who happened to see it in the shop. UCC § 2-403 protects the purchaser who bought from a merchant in the ordinary course of the merchant's business. The necklace's original owner's only remedy is against the merchant for damages.

A "buyer in the ordinary course of business" is "a person who in good faith and without knowledge that the sale to him is in violation of the ownership rights or security interest of a third party in the goods buys in ordinary course from a person in the business of selling goods of that kind." See UCC § 2-201(9) (1962). Excluded from this definition is a pawnbroker, who is governed usually by special state statutes and regulations. Thus, while a buyer in the ordinary course of business may also be a BFP, the phrase limits the inquiry into a purchaser's bona fides to the sales transaction.

Examples

Broaching the Brooch

1. Joan, the owner of a valuable brooch, transfers it to TCo, a trust company, to hold in trust for Bess. A trust involves TCo's retention of the legal title, while Bess as the so-called beneficiary of the trust has the right to use it (the so-called equitable interest). Before giving it to Bess, however, TCo mistakenly sells the brooch to Pete, a bona fide purchaser. Does Pete get to keep the brooch?

A Man of Wealth and Fame

2. Odetta meets Ricardo. Odetta is induced by Ricardo's false representation that he is JR (a man of wealth and good reputation), so that Odetta parts

with possession of a jewel. Ricardo sells the jewel to BFP, a bona fide purchaser. In a suit between Odetta and BFP, what result and why?

The Trusting Entruster

3. (a) Oprah purchases an expensive painting to hang in her home. Oprah thereafter gives the painting to Dan, an art dealer and conservator, for cleaning. A week later, Bridget sees the painting hanging in Dan's gallery and showroom and purchases it from Dan for a fair price and without any actual knowledge that Dan does not own it. Who now owns the painting?

   (b) Same facts, except that Bridget sees the painting in Dan's conservator shop, rather than in Dan's gallery. Bridget purchases as before. Who owns the painting?

   (c) Same facts as in (a), except that Bridget is another art dealer and owner of an art gallery. Should another merchant have the benefit of the UCC's entrustment provision, or is it just a "consumer statute"?

Stolen Goods

4. (a) Olive removes her brooch during dinner at a restaurant. When Olive is distracted, Rolfe picks up the brooch and walks away with it. Rolfe sells the brooch to Benny, a good-faith purchaser. In Olive v. Benny, who prevails?

   (b) Same facts as in (a), except Rolfe sells the brooch to Benny, a good-faith purchaser who sees the brooch in Rolfe's jewelry store. Who prevails between Olive and Benny?

Explanations

Broaching the Brooch

1. Yes. Joan intended to split the title into a legal and an equitable component, so the title in TCo's hands was voidable (one that Joan could rescind to prevent TCo from misusing it), so, if as stated, Pete was in fact a bona fide purchaser, Pete's ownership now trumps Joan's. Bess still has a remedy: she has the right to sue TCo for a breach of TCo's fiduciary duty as a trustee, measuring damages by the lost value of the brooch, but no right to replevin the brooch from Pete.

A Man of Wealth and Fame

2. Odetta intended to deal with Ricardo and, even though Ricardo posed as JR, Odetta transferred the jewel to him. Odetta assumed the risk that Ricardo was not JR when she could have checked the facts and the representation made, but did not do so. If she had checked and discovered that

Ricardo was not JR, then she would have had a right to rescind. Ricardo had a voidable ownership or a title that ripened into absolute title once in the hands of a BFP. Moreover, as between Odetta and BFP, Odetta had the ability to prevent the problem, and did not do so. On the equities of the situation, judgment for BFP. See Phelps v. McQuade, 115 N.E. 441 (N.Y. 1917). Although mistaken as to the identity of the purchaser, the owner's primary intent was to sell the chattel to the person he met face to face.

The Trusting Entruster

3. (a) Bridget owns the painting because she has dealt with a merchant to whom the painting has been "entrusted" — i.e., transferred to a "merchant who deals in art work." Although the painting was given to Dan for a limited purpose (this transfer creates a bailment), its hanging in the gallery of an art dealer gives Bridget the undisputed impression that Dan deals, in the ordinary course of his business, in works of art of a similar type. So under UCC § 2-403(2), Dan has authority to transfer absolute ownership of the painting to Bridget.

   (b) Oprah does. With the change in the location of the painting, the doctrine of entrustment is not available to Bridget. Bridget's seeing the painting in the shop would not give her the impression that Dan has the authority to sell it. Bridget might then be tempted to fall back on the argument that Dan has a voidable title, not a void one, and then on proof that she is a bona fide purchaser. Although Bridget gives every indication of being a bona fide purchaser, the transfer by Dan defrauds Oprah and gives Bridget only a void title, one that can never ripen into absolute ownership for Bridget.

   (c) A good question. There is authority that because the Code is not clear on this, the provision's protection should also extend to other merchants. Mattek v. Malofsky, 165 N.W.2d 406 (Wis. 1969) (so long as the merchant has observed reasonable commercial standards of care in the acquisition).

Stolen Goods

4. (a) Olive wins. Rolfe had no title. His title is void and he cannot transfer good title.

   (b) Olive still wins. Rolfe had void title, not voidable title. Rolfe stole the brooch. Olive did not entrust it to him, so Benny cannot rely on UCC § 2-403.

Gifts

Gifts play an important role in life and law. We saw in Chapter 5 that a donee — the recipient of a gift — cannot be a bona fide or good-faith purchaser because she is not a "purchaser." Similarly, real estate recording acts do not protect donees the way they protect good-faith purchasers and creditors. However, many uses of common law estates and interests, discussed later in this book, begin with a gift or a bequest.

A **gift** is a noncontractual, gratuitous transfer of property. It is made without legal consideration. If there is consideration, the law of gifts does not apply. A transfer for consideration is a sale, and the law of contracts applies.

There are two types of gifts: first, a gift between living persons is called an **inter vivos gift**; second, a gift made on account of a donor's impending death is called a **gift causa mortis**. A transfer of property by will after a person's death is called a **devise** or **bequest** and not a gift.

INTER VIVOS GIFTS

An **inter vivos gift** is a gift between living persons. For an inter vivos gift to be effective between the giver (the donor) and the recipient (the donee), the donee must show three things: first, a clear and convincing intent in the donor to transfer the object to the donee (donative intent); second, the donor in most cases must actually deliver the object to the donee; and third, the donee must accept the object. Thus, the donor's **donative intent**, plus physical **delivery** and **acceptance**, are the three elements required for a valid gift.

(a) Donative Intent

For a gift to be effective the donor must intend to make the gift. Mere delivery is not a gift. The delivery, after all, may have been part of a loan, or a bailment. Courts are suspicious of the claim that a gift was made, and will scrutinize the facts of a transfer to ensure that the donor had the requisite intent. Indeed, the donor's intent controls the gift, and an otherwise silent deed of gift is construed in the donor's favor — unlike a bill of sale, whose terms are construed in favor of the transferee or buyer. The donee also bears the burden of proof to show that the donor had the donative intent. The evidentiary standard for a showing of donative intent — i.e., clear and convincing evidence — is high. Often, vague terms evidence a transfer of an object, as when someone says, "Take charge of this." It will be up to the alleged donee to show that a gift was intended. Thus the law's suspicion about gifts is soundly grounded in a skeptic's view that a person would not freely give away property.

Having the intent to make an oral gift and delivery of that gift usually occur simultaneously, but not always. If someone lends a book to a friend, but later discovers that he has two copies of it and says that the friend can keep the loaned copy, the donative gift exists; proving that a gift of the book was intended will be very difficult, however, its delivery and the intent to deliver it being shown to exist at different times. Certainly the lender's statement that the friend can keep the book is evidence of a donative intent; while evidence after the time of delivery is admissible, it is not as convincing as evidence of intent at the time of delivery. On the other hand, when a donor says, "I'll give you the book next week," and does so, the evidence of intent shows an upcoming delivery and acceptance that next week by the donee will complete the gift transaction. The latter transaction has completed the elements of the gift in a typical, nonsuspicious chain of events. In a third transaction, when the donor says, "I'll give the book to you, friend, if I find out that I have a second copy of it," there is no gift until there has been a delivery. A gift cannot be subject to a condition precedent (an act or event that must occur or not occur before the gift will be made or become effective).

Note that if the donor makes a gift of a book because he thought he had two copies of it and discovers after delivering the book that he did *not* have two copies of it, he cannot demand the book back. The gift was complete — and irrevocable — when the gift was accepted by the donee. Even if the donor says that having a spare copy is a condition of the gift, that condition will not survive the donee's acceptance. An oral condition on a gift is invalid on the acceptance or completion of the gift. The difficulties of proof, and the temptation the donor might feel to make up conditions after the fact, are simply too great. The law's treatment of gifts is, after all, rooted in its distaste for perjury.

(b) Delivery

Delivery is a necessary element of a gift. Delivery is, usually, the actual physical delivery of the object. An agreement that a donor will transfer, and another receive, an object is insufficient for a delivery. A promise to make a gift is unenforceable by the donee, and the donor can decide not to make the gift (revoke the promise) any time before delivery. The law otherwise would be saying that, as a matter of contract law, an offer and acceptance without consideration constitute an enforceable contract. Similarly, a gift may be accomplished by the donor's first executing a deed of gift, expressing a present intent to give, and then delivering the deed to the donee; the gift is complete once the deed is delivered, but not before.

When physical delivery is impossible (the chattel is large or heavy) or impractical (it is in the hands of a third party, or in a bailee's possession), physical delivery is not required and courts have shown a willingness to recognize other types of delivery. In such circumstances, the delivery element may be satisfied by a symbolic delivery. A **symbolic delivery** occurs when the thing delivered stands in the place of the property. Symbolic delivery occurs, for example, when a picture of a large chest of drawers is delivered to the donee; that would be a symbolic delivery of the chest. Another example involves the delivery of one item, along with a written inventory of similar items: The one in such a situation stands for the many. A symbolic delivery in these situations may be either representational (in the former situation) or representative (in the latter). Generally, a sale deed or deed of gift stands for the thing itself; likewise, a corporate share certificate stands for the interest in the entity.

A delivery may also be **constructive**. The property itself is not transferred, but something giving access to and control over it is. Examples involve giving the keys to an automobile or the keys to a safe deposit box to the donee. Here a constructive delivery gives the donee access, or the means of exercising possession and control, over the chattel. Other examples of this type of delivery occur when the donee is already in possession, or has possession in some other capacity, as a bailee or employee. Actual delivery would be a fruitless action, one that most persons would not think worth taking.

Still another example of constructive delivery involves lost chattel, the donor giving instructions to the donee as to how to go about finding it; upon its recovery by the donee, the chattel has been constructively delivered. Likewise, a donor's revealing the hiding place of chattel is also its constructive delivery.

Intent and delivery are separate elements. Clear evidence of the donor's intention is needed to complete the gift. Although physical delivery is evidence of the intent to make the gift, delivery is only one bit of evidence and not a conclusive substitute for evidence of intent: It is too easy to obtain the keys to a chest, or a car, and claim it was the subject of a gift. This is particularly true when the donor is in ill health, is dying, or is otherwise unable to put his or her hands on the chattel at the moment. Constructive delivery only emphasizes that the rationale for the concept of delivery is to have the donor relinquish possession and control over the chattel.

(c) Acceptance

For a completed gift, the recipient must accept the gift. Although a donee may refuse or reject a gift, acceptance is generally presumed from the benefit received by the donee; thus, acceptance has not been the subject of much reported litigation. Without evidence to show rejection, there is no rejection. The presumption of acceptance is a rebuttable one. No one is required to accept whatever "gift" someone else thinks would be to his or her benefit. Property may not be forced on the unwilling.

GIFTS CAUSA MORTIS

A *gift causa mortis* is made when the donor has an apprehension or expectation of his or her own impending death and delivers the chattel with the intention that control over the subject of the gift takes effect immediately, but becomes absolute only upon the donor's death. Jewelry is often the subject of gifts causa mortis.

The expectation of death required is subjective; an objective or reasonable expectation is not required. Whether or not the expectation of death is present is a question of fact. The illness, disease, or peril prompting the expectation must be objectively present, however. A threatened assassination, minor surgery, and a perilous journey or enterprise undertaken voluntarily have all traditionally been found insufficient.

The donor must have a present intention to deliver absolute ownership of the property in the future, at death; an attempt by the donor to reserve control over the property until death invalidates this type of gift. Such an attempt would result in a gift (if recognized) that was subject to a condition precedent, and invalid as such. There is a presumption that a gift made while death is impending is a gift causa mortis, rather than a gift inter vivos. This presumption is rebuttable by proof of the donor's intention to part unconditionally with the property given.

The title of the donee causa mortis is not absolute until the donor is dead. Death must result from the same illness, disease, or peril producing the donor's initial expectation, not some other illness or event, although it is not necessary that the sole cause of the donor's death be the same as that causing the donor's expectation of death.

Meanwhile, the donee is the donor's bailee. Gifts causa mortis are revocable. In some jurisdictions, revocation is automatic if and when the donor recovers from the illness, accident, or other event that made death seem likely. Recovery is seen as a determinable event.[1] In some jurisdictions, however, a gift causa mortis is revoked only if the donor affirmatively revokes the gift after recovery. An automatically revoked gift causa mortis belongs to the donor as though no gift causa mortis had ever been made. The gift is not thereafter revived by a relapse or another, equally grave, illness. To illustrate, if just before heart surgery Mother gives her wedding ring to her youngest daughter at her bedside, and Mother survives surgery, Mother gets her wedding ring back. If Mother a month later dies from a heart attack or any other reason, Mother's wedding ring passes according to her will or the canons of descent, and her youngest daughter has no superior claim to the ring because Mother at one time made the ring the subject of a gift causa mortis.

A person cannot make a gift causa mortis to escape the claims of creditors. Gifts causa mortis are subject to the claims of creditors when other assets of the donor are insufficient to repay the debts. Whether such gifts are subject to marital rights is generally a matter for state probate codes and statutes — and generalizations about this subject are hazardous. Real estate may not be the subject of a gift causa mortis.

The gift causa mortis is the functional equivalent of a devise (a transfer of property by will). Every state has enacted elaborate requirements in a Statute of Wills that must be fulfilled to give effect to a will or testamentary transfer. The gift causa mortis is thus an extraordinary power and, being in derogation of the jurisdiction's Statute of Wills, is not favored. A high standard of proof — that of clear and convincing evidence — is generally required to uphold such gifts. Courts are also likely to strictly construe statutes and cases upholding such gifts. As with inter vivos gifts, the judicial rationale for strictly construing the elements of this type of gift has to do with the evidentiary problems associated with them. In the instance of gifts causa mortis, however, the evidentiary problems are acute because the donor is dead.

---

1. A determinable event (or condition subsequent) automatically terminates the donee's ownership and returns title to the donor without any action on the donor's part.

Examples

Dresser Delivery

1. Is the giving of the keys to a dresser a symbolic or a constructive delivery?

Revocation and Donative Intent

2. Owen executes an otherwise valid deed of gift. The deed contains a power to revoke. Does the power to revoke indicate a lack of donative intent sufficient to invalidate the gift?

Christmas Carol

3. (a) In September, Lee hands Peter a signed paper promising that Lee will give Peter 10,000 shares of Profit Corporation as a Christmas present. Lee dies in November, devising all his "stock and bonds" to Carol. Carol and Peter both claim the Profit Corporation stock. Who gets the stock?

   (b) In September Lee transfers 10,000 shares of Profit Corporation stock to Peter, with the qualification that Lee (the grantor) will receive all dividends paid by Profit Corporation on the stock on or before Christmas. Lee dies in November, devising all his "stock and bonds" to Carol. Carol and Peter both claim the Profit Corporation stock. Who gets the stock?

The Uncashed Check

4. Odysseus writes and signs a check to Don, drawn on Odysseus' checking account, but dies before Don cashes it. Does Don have a right to cash the check?

Suicide and the Gift Causa Mortis

5. Ollie, contemplating suicide because of recent business and personal problems, executes a deed of gift of the contents of her safe deposit box to Del. Is suicide a life-threatening illness justifying a gift causa mortis?

War

6. Fred is a member of the armed forces and is about to go to war. Is he contemplating death in the way required to make a gift causa mortis?

Explanations

Dresser Delivery

1. Giving the keys may be a symbolic delivery of the piece of furniture, but could be a constructive delivery of the contents of the dresser, found in the drawers. These two concepts are easily confused, but both are useful means for courts to uphold a gift when there is sufficient evidence of donative intent but no actual delivery.

Revocation and Donative Intent

2. No. If the deed adequately indicates a present donative intent — i.e., an intent at the time Owen delivered the deed to make a gift — the gift is good. The donee owns the property. Owen made the gift with a qualification, and retains the right to demand that the property be returned to him. The gift was complete and belongs to the donee until and unless Owen affirmatively revokes.

   Some courts refuse to enforce revocation clauses as a matter of public policy. See dicta in Gruen v. Gruen, 496 N.E.2d 869 (N.Y. 1986) ("Once the gift is made it is irrevocable . . . and the donor is not an owner.") As you will learn, revocable trusts are common. A revocable trust arises when a grantor transfers property to a person (the trustee) to hold for the benefit of a third party (the beneficiary). The grantor can retain the right to revoke the trust and get the property back. If the revocable trust is permissible, the revocable gift should be permissible. The only reason to differentiate between the two is that revocation rights in a trust usually are in writing, whereas many gifts are oral.

Christmas Carol

3. (a) Carol wins. Lee's promise is unenforceable because Peter gave no consideration. When Lee died, he was the legal owner and the stock passed according to his will.
   (b) Peter keeps the stock. The gift in September was a present gift, with a present intent to make a gift, delivery, and acceptance. Lee's retaining the income for four months does not make the gift incomplete.

The Uncashed Check

4. No. The donor could have stopped payment on the check any time before it was cashed, and the donor's death revoked the authority of the bank to cash it, so the gift was incomplete because of the donor's retention of a power to revoke the gift. The donor could have cashed a check and given

the donee the money. The check is not a deed of gift, and the power to cash it is not the same as a gift. See Woo v. Smart, 442 S.E.2d 690 (Va. 1994) (holding that the delivery of a check is an incomplete assignment of the funds on account).

Suicide and the Gift Causa Mortis

5. A person contemplating suicide has traditionally not been regarded as being in imminent peril of death sufficient to justify an exception to the Statute of Wills, so older authorities would answer this query in the negative. A suicide is traditionally an insane act. A few more recent cases reason that mental illness is just as pressing a backdrop for a gift causa mortis as physical illness; they hold that the contemplation of a suicide should be treated as one in contemplation of death. Scherer v. Hyland, 380 A.2d 696 (N.J. 1977). The analogy between a person facing major surgery (being allowed to make a gift causa mortis) and a suicide makes it difficult to deny a suicide donative power. The recent view is that some mental illnesses (e.g., depression) are accompanied by an irresistible urge to commit suicide, putting a person in contemplation of death. More generally, it might be said that if a jurisdiction recognizes (as most do) that a suicide may have testamentary capacity, a suicide's will becoming valid on that account, it should also be possible for a suicide to make a gift causa mortis.

War

6. A person about to go to war is not facing an imminent peril giving rise to an expectation of death. There are, however, English cases to the contrary.

Accession, Confusion, and Fixtures

In this chapter we will discuss three methods of transferring title to personal property that operate by law — meaning that they operate regardless of the intent of the parties involved in the transfer — as opposed to agreement, and so may involve involuntary and non-consensual transfers.

ACCESSION

Accession is the addition of labor to a chattel of another person that, even without the other's consent, so changes the chattel that its title is transferred to the laborer. The idea for this type of non-consensual transfer first arose as a defense to an action for replevin. Older cases suggest that it is the physical identity of the chattel that had to change to make the defense good, but later the addition of value to a chattel was sufficient as well, so that the title to the chattel, after the addition of the laborer, lies with the claimant who contributed the most to a chattel's final identity or value. In this calculation, it is the fair market value that matters, not some subjective value to either the original possession or the laborer. Thus using bricks to build a wall, or planks to make a boat, or making timber into lumber, or lumber into two-by-fours, barrel staves, or some other specialized wood product; or making thread into cloth, or cloth into an article of clothing; or gems into jewels, or into jewelry — all have the potential to transfer the title to the thing labored over.

In these examples, however, notice that the thing cannot be returned to its original state without losing most or all of its value, so that the response to a defense of accession, in the context of a replevin action, might be that whatever was added might be removed without damage. Automobile tires, for example, are integral to the running of the auto, but by the same token can be removed without damage to it. A closer case might be posed by an auto mechanic who installed a new engine. Its removal might also be possible, but unless it is of the finest quality when one of lesser quality would do, its accession is likely.

A claimant contributing a chattel to a more valuable one and so denied replevin is left with an action for trover and conversion.

CONFUSION

Confusion is a sub-set of accession generally involving only one type of chattel. It is the intermingling of two or more items of personalty so that the rights in each of the items are no longer distinguishable. Typically this mingling occurs with fluids or fungible items, such as natural gas, oil, minerals, grains, or timber. Once mingled, each prior possessor is entitled to receive back a pro rata share of the whole, measured by each possessor's contribution. If such a division is not possible, then each receives back an equal share, unless one of the contributors intentional or negligently intermingled the items, in which case that contributor either has the burden of proving what his or her share was, or, failing that, loses that share entirely.

Confusion is a doctrine that is sparingly used — that is, it is used only when necessary — and is as much a rule of evidence as one of substantive law. It imposes loss, not on the innocent, but on the intentional or negligent party — or more generally, on the one whose actions suppress the more precise identification of property. When a windfall accrues to an innocent party, this result is as close to justice as the evidence permits.

FIXTURES

Some chattels are permanently or (because of their weight) so firmly attached to the real property on which they are located that the law calls them **fixtures**. A fixture is a form of chattel or personal property that, while retaining a separate identity, is so connected to the real property that the law considers it a part of the realty. In this sense, a fixture is the accession of personalty onto realty. A furnace is commonly thought of as a fixture in a house. Other common fixtures in a house would be a dishwasher, light fixtures, bathtubs, and toilets. A fixture thus stands on the definitional border between personal property and real property.

A fixture has three elements, all of which are essential. First, the former chattel must be annexed to the realty. **Annexation** means attachment to the realty. It may be either actual or constructive. In older cases, this is the most important of all three elements.

Second, it must be adapted or applied to a particular use or purpose beyond itself and made a part of some larger component of or function on the realty. Parts of a heating or cooling system are examples. This second, **adaptation** factor has sometimes been absorbed into the first, by a doctrine of constructive annexation. Under this doctrine, although not physically annexed, the item at issue is taken to be essential to the functioning of the property, as a rolling pin might be found essential to the operation of a steel mill, or type is essential to the operation of a printing press. Sometimes this doctrine is codified as the "economic unit" or industrial plant doctrine. In some jurisdictions, this second aspect of the elements of a fixture has tended to drop away.

Third, there must be an **intention to annex** it to the realty. Whose intention controls is the question here. In many American decisions, intention is the most important — perhaps the most confused — element of the three-prong test for a fixture. The most cited, leading American case on the subject, Teaff v. Hewitt, 1 Ohio St. 511 (1853), uses the intent of the annexor, actual or inferred from a combination of several factors: the nature of the chattel annexed, the relation and situation of the annexor, the method of annexation, and the purpose or use of the chattel. The element of intention does not refer to the annexor's subjective mental state; instead, it is the objective intention of a reasonable person acting within the facts and circumstances of the transaction(s) in dispute.

Thus, the law of fixtures is context-specific. A theater seat is a fixture, whereas a living room chair is not. A pipe organ is a fixture in a church, but not in a house unless its removal would cause substantial destruction. A woodstove may not be a fixture in an urban residence (where other means of heating are available), but might be in a cabin in the north woods. An air conditioner may well be a fixture in Tucson, but not in Seattle.

What difference does it make that a former chattel is called a fixture? The consequences can be seen in two situations, the first involving vendors and purchasers of the underlying real property. Absent an agreement to the contrary, a fixture is automatically transferred to the next grantee of the realty. This transfer occurs, then, when the contract of sale and the deed to the real property are silent on the matter. It is said to happen "by operation of law." The best advice for the parties to such a transfer is to agree what will and will not pass with the title to the realty. Otherwise, what a vendor of property might consider personal property may, upon transfer to a purchaser, become a fixture. If an item is expressly bargained over, and the vendor is given an express right to remove it in a contract of sale, the vendor has a license to enter the property and do so within a reasonable time. In the vendor/purchaser context, that reasonable time is likely to be measured by the executory period, during which the contract is outstanding and the deed to the property is not yet delivered. After that time, the vendor is deemed to have waived his right of removal.

A second situation occurs when the real property is used as security for repayment of a loan (in a word, "mortgaged"), a lien is enforced against the realty for nonpayment of the mortgage loan, and the secured property is sold to satisfy the debt (in a "foreclosure" action to enforce the lien). The issue arising in this context is whether the lien applies to a particular piece of equipment or attached chattel, thus made subject to the sale. The answer depends on whether the law regards the disputed chattel as a fixture. Here, again, it is best to regard the issue as context-specific: The chattel alleged to be a fixture, but not necessary to lend its value to the property in order to repay the debt, will likely not be found a fixture. On the other hand, the chattel necessary to provide security or to attract purchasers to the forced sale of the property will likely be regarded as a fixture.

In both of these situations, it is the intention of the annexor that counts. Relative to the vendor-purchaser and mortgagor-mortgagee situation, the actions or intent of a remote annexor will provide disinterested evidence. In the mortgage situation, use of the annexor's intent makes irrelevant the subjective intent of the mortgagor not to include the chattel within the items providing security for the loan. The annexor's intent may truly have been to exclude the item from the security, but once the loan is not repaid and the lien asserted, the temptation will be to widen that exclusion. The use of annexor's intent also makes irrelevant whether the chattel was annexed before or after the mortgage documents were executed. It is not the mortgagor-mortgagee bargain that turns the chattel into a fixture — it is the annexor's intent to do so. (While this may give the mortgagee more security than it bargained for, one might say that it bargained for a functioning piece of property as security — and that use of the annexor's intent avoids the property damage to that security attendant on removal of the chattel.) Once no longer annexed, a fixture resumes its former status as an item of personal property.

Examples

Button It Up

1. Do shirt buttons accede to the shirt?

Silas's Silo

2. Farmer Fred stores his wheat in Silas's silo, awaiting sale. Silas converts Fred's wheat, along with the wheat of two other farmers. Fred sues Silas in replevin, Silas responds to Fred's complaint by saying that giving Fred

a judgment would be a windfall to him and that all the farmers must sue at once. Is Silas's defense a good one?

Range Removal

3. Vendors executed a contract of sale to sell their house, but had another house on the real property they sold. The second house was rented to a tenant. The contract reserved the right to remove a gas range from the vendor's house. Can the vendors remove an identical stove from the rental house?

Farm Fixture

4. The Farmers and Mechanics Bank holds a mortgage on Fred's farm in a semi-arid region of the country. The farm's fields are watered by a standard irrigation system that has three components: first, lightweight and portable gated pipes of various lengths and diameters, with gates or windows on one side that can be opened or closed and thus regulate the flow of water onto a field; second, riser pipes permanently connecting the gated pipes to underground water pipes buried under the fields; and third, the underground water pipes attached to the water supply. Fred defaults on the repayment of the mortgage loan, and the bank forecloses. At the sale of the farm, will the gated pipes be included in the real property and sold as a fixture?

Explanations

Button It Up

1. Yes. They are necessary to its function and are easily valued, and removal would destroy the function of the final and dominant chattel. The owner of the materials is not entitled to the new chattel because, were it otherwise, the law would work a penalty on labor and discourage engaging in a useful trade, and so a transfer of title is preferable to some type of joint ownership of the final chattel. Still, context matters, and a tailor's financier loaning money on his inventory of clothing is more likely to win a case based on accession when the opposite party is another creditor, like the tailor's button supplier. Why? Because the former made a bargain to have a functioning article of clothing; the latter did not.

Silas's Silo

2. Yes, it is a good defense, even if Silas was an intentional convertor of Fred's wheat. The other farmers can be regarded as co-owners of the wheat in the silo and thus are indispensable parties to Fred's suit.

See Mucha v. King, 792 F.2d, 602, 613 (7th Cir. 1986) (providing an example of the sparing use of the doctrine of confusion).

Range Removal

3. No. The rental house was presumably sold as a unit, not in discrete parts. What seems important to the purchasers about the rental house is that it is an economic unit for collecting rent money. What is a fixture in one setting (e.g., the main house) may not be so in another (e.g., the rental unit). Here the reservation of the right to remove the stove in the main house is presumed to be exclusive unless the vendors reserve further items in the contract. In this instance, they did not do so.

Farm Fixture

4. No. The gated pipes are portable, are used in the various lengths and diameters needed for irrigation, and can be easily removed without damage to the underground and riser pipes. The irrigation system being a standard one, the gated pipes probably have a resale value once removed and, unless necessary for the bank to recoup its loan amount outstanding at the time of Fred's default, are unlikely to be included within the farm's real property. It is also possible that the risers could be attached to sprinklers, hoses, and other devices, and so the fields could be irrigated in other ways and without the use of the gated pipes. With all these features, these pipes are not fixtures. See Wyoming State Farm Loan Bd. v. Farm Credit Sys. Capital Corp., 759 P.2d 1230 (Wyo. 1988). In contrast, the underground water pipes are part of the realty, or at least fixtures, and will remain with the farm. The riser pipes are a closer issue. If they are permanently attached to the underground water pipes, they likely will be found to be fixtures passing with the farm.

CHAPTER 8

Adverse Possession

The preceding chapters dealt mainly with personal property. This chapter introduces a legal process to gain title to either real or personal property.

INTRODUCTION

Adverse possession is a process through which a person who uses property for a statutorily determined period of time becomes the owner of the property and defeats all rights of its true or rightful owner, even if the latter had legal or record title. Thus a person in possession can take ownership of property through adverse possession by using property long and visibly enough, as would its true owner.

Every state has enacted an adverse possession statute. Each state's statute sets out the number of years the adverse possessor must use the property before its true owner will be prohibited from ejecting the adverse possessor. After that period of time, a trespasser becomes the owner and his subsequent purchasers, heirs, and descendants succeed to his rights. The former legal or record owner has no further rights to the property and cannot claim damages for his or her loss.

Adverse possession statutes are the successors of statutes of limitations for the common law cause of action in ejectment. If the true owner of property fails to sue a trespasser on it within the period of time allotted for bringing ejectment, the trespasser thereafter acquires its title. The possessor acquiring title in this way may or may not believe the property was his—such a belief, or its absence, does not matter. Put another way, the main rule of adverse possession may be expressed in the same way as the rule in Armory v. Delamirie: a possessor of property may protect his possession against everyone in the world but the true owner.

The adverse possessor obtains an original title to property, although in some states it may not be marketable until so established in court. His title, in other words, is not derived from its former owner's.

The number of years an adverse possessor must use the property, also known as the **statute of limitations period**, the limitations period, or the statutory period, varies widely among the several states, and may vary within a state depending on whether the adverse possessor has a faulty deed (known as "**color of title**") or bought the property at a tax sale. In Iowa, for example, the statutory period is 40 years without color of title, but only 10 years with color of title. Texas has shorter statute of limitations periods: ten years without color of title and three years under color of title. California and Idaho have five-year statutes of limitations for use both with color of title and without color of title. Most states fall between these extremes, requiring between 7 and 30 years for the statute to run.

Although all authorities, courts, and legislatures embrace the idea of adverse possession, they do not agree on why we allow adverse possession and on the underlying rationale for adverse possession.

There are several traditional rationales. First, adverse possession *punishes* true owners who sit on their rights for too long. "You snooze, you lose." True owners are encouraged to monitor their property. This rationale deals with the abandoning owner; it was most useful in the nineteenth century, when pioneers traveled from region to region, never intending to return to their origins and abandoning land in the process. Our society is more comfortable if someone uses and lays claim to property. Rights must be asserted, or lost.

Second, adverse possession laws *reward* the person who uses, works on, or improves property for a long time, becoming in the process known in the community as its owner. In this vein, some state statutes require the adverse possessor to improve, cultivate, or enclose the claimed property for the statutory period.

Beyond these punishment or reward rationales, a third rationale views the elements of adverse possession as *evidentiary* tools. Evidence decays as time passes, and stale claims to property should be barred. Another evidentiary function is to confirm lost grants or otherwise correct conveyancing mistakes and oversights. Landowners, moreover, are not required by law to record deeds and other documents affecting real property. Thus long and visible possession and use becomes a substitute for documentary proof of a lost or misplaced deed. And some deeds are invalid for technical reasons. The person signing a deed may not have authority to do so; its drafter may have described the property incorrectly; or the possessor may have received the property as an oral or parol gift, ineffective because real property transfers must be in writing under the Statute of Frauds. With the passage of time, adverse possession laws eliminate these problems.

Fourth, adverse possession laws serve a *structural* purpose, facilitating the efficient transfer of property. Land, in particular, does not wear out. A purchaser or other possessor of property should be free from potential ownership claims originating decades earlier when the putative legal owner has not indicated she even knows or cares that she owns the property. Courts in many contexts begin with a premise that no person should be forced to "buy a lawsuit." Adverse possession serves to quiet titles, reinforce the reliability of land records, and allow transferability of land at lower cost than would otherwise be possible. To some, including Professor Henry Ballantine, the integrity and reliability of the deed records alone justifies denying relief to long unenforced claims.

Finally, adverse possession preserves the *status quo*. As O.W. Holmes wrote, "Man, like a tree in the cleft of a rock, gradually shapes his roots to his surroundings, and when the roots have grown to a certain size, can't be displaced without cutting at his life." When ejecting the adverse possessor would result in more of a loss than the true owner would gain, there is no longer any point in denying the adverse possessor title. The true owner might even at that point regard regaining possession as a windfall that he could sell back to the adverse possessor. Adverse possession thus renders trespass efficient and is akin to the idea of an efficient breach in the law of contracts.

Adverse possession cases concerning land fall into two broad categories. In one, the adverse possessor claims a parcel of land completely unrelated to any other land the adverse possessor owns or claims. The second category concerns boundary disputes, where neighboring landowners dispute who has the right to a strip of land used by one party but included within the legal description of another. Despite the potentially different concerns applicable in each of these two categories, courts resort to the same statute and common law principles in resolving both, but may use the elements of adverse possession differently.

ELEMENTS OF ADVERSE POSSESSION

How did statutes of limitations for ejectment become adverse possession laws? To some degree, courts assumed that possession drew title along with it. The burden of proof to show that possession ripened into title required the adverse possessor to prove that the true owner was without title, and he could only meet this burden by showing what he had done with the land or property since his entry onto it. As we will see, the date of that entry is important in this area of the law — it is the date on which the true owner first had a cause of action in trespass or ejectment against the adverse possessor.

Evaluating his claim, a court considers not only the elements contained in its state's adverse possession statutes, but invariably also several judicially developed elements to determine whether the adverse possessor "adversely possesses" the property. These judicially created elements — which began as a judicial gloss on the state statutes — are often redundant and require many determinations of fact. Thus, to assert a successful adverse possession claim, an adverse possessor must show that the adverse possession met each of the following common law elements:

1. Actual
2. Open and notorious
3. Exclusive
4. Hostile or adverse
5. Continuous

In addition, some courts add other elements, by common law or by statute, including the following:

6. Claim of title or claim of right
7. Good faith or bad faith
8. Improvement, cultivation, or enclosure
9. Payment of property taxes

While some courts list claim of right or claim of title as separate elements and require either good faith or, conversely, bad faith as a separate element, commentators seem to agree these are subsets of the hostility element (hostile or adverse).

An adverse possessor must satisfy each required element to prevail. Courts apply a checklist approach. Failure to satisfy even one element defeats the action. In analyzing a case for the following elements, note that the same acts may satisfy several elements. As a general guideline, an adverse possessor who acts with respect to the property as would an owner of similar property in the community for the period of limitations usually satisfies each element.

(a) Actual Possession

An adverse possessor must be in **actual possession** of the property. Actual possession serves several purposes. It gives notice to the true owner and others who come to the property that the adverse possessor is using the property. It also indicates that the adverse possessor may be claiming the property and has ousted all other persons. Finally, on the date of the adverse possessor's entry, it acts as a trigger for the true owner's cause of action in ejectment or trespass, so that the limitations period can start running.

What constitutes actual possession is a function of the type of property involved, where the property is located, and what uses of the property would be expected in the community. A person does not have to live on the property though, in most cases, the adverse possessor does live on or adjacent to the claimed property. In one early, leading case, the adverse possessor lived across the street from the lot he claimed, stepping onto it as needed to sell the right to dig sand and gravel to some, refusing it to others. These actions were confirmed by several witnesses at trial. His adverse possession claim was successful. See Ewing v. Burnet, 36 U.S. 41 (1837). Building a house, farming, fencing, even cutting timber or hunting and fishing in the right situations may constitute actual possession. While paying taxes helps establish actual possession, unless the state law requires payment of taxes as an essential element, an adverse possessor is not required to pay taxes and, in fact, may claim adverse possession even though the legal owner pays the taxes. Selling the land, mortgaging it, or renting it to others could constitute possession.

Generally, an adverse possessor gains ownership of only so much of a tract of property as the adverse possessor actually occupies. The adverse possessor bears the burden of proving the boundaries to the land used adversely. The true owner continues to own any unoccupied land.

However, an exception to this rule occurs when the adverse possessor claims the land under **color of title**. A person enters under color of title when he claims ownership pursuant to a written document, usually a deed, purporting to transfer the property to him, but the document is defective in some manner. Thus a faulty deed, or a deed from someone not owning the property, or owning a part or fractional share of the property, or a sheriff's tax sale deed that is defective because some part of the sale was improperly conducted does not convey legal title to the purchaser, but does clothe the purchaser with color of title.

Having color of title benefits the adverse possessor in two ways. First, as noted earlier, many state statutes reduce significantly the statute of limitations period for persons taking possession of property with color of title. In North Carolina, for example, the 20-year period is reduced to 7 years if an adverse possessor has color of title. Second, the adverse possessor with color of title who successfully proves an adverse possession claim based on actual possession of a part of the tract described in the document constituting color of title is deemed to be in **constructive possession** of the whole tract.

Example 1: Wally owns Blackacre, a 500-acre parcel of heavily wooded land in Arkansas. Wally sells and deeds Blackacre to Edwin, who lives in St. Louis. Five years later, Wally dies. Wally's daughter, Serena, believing she inherited Blackacre, sells and deeds Blackacre to Judy. The deed to Judy does not convey good title to Judy since Serena did not own Blackacre. The faulty deed to Judy, however, is color of title. Judy clears 5 of the 500 acres and uses the 5 acres as her residence. Judy lives there for the statutory period. Because Judy has color of title, she has adversely possessed the entire 500 acres described in her deed, not just the 5 acres she actually possessed.

An exception to the constructive ownership by color of title rule is that the true owner's actual possession of a part of the described land negates the constructive possession and the adverse possession is limited to the land actually possessed. As explained by the U.S. Supreme Court in Deputron v. Young, 134 U.S. 241, 255 (1890) (applying Nebraska law), "Where the rightful owner is in the actual occupancy of a part of his tract, he is in the constructive and legal possession and seisin of the whole, unless he is disseised by actual occupation and dispossession; and where the possession is mixed, the legal seisin is according to the legal title, so that in the case at bar there could be no constructive possession on the part of the defendant or his grantors, even if that might exist if he had had actual possession of a part, and no one had been in possession of the remainder."

Example 2: Assume the facts in Example 1 above except that shortly after buying Blackacre Edwin moves to Arkansas, clears out five acres of Blackacre, and lives there. Edwin remains unaware that Judy is residing on another five acres of Blackacre. After the limitations period has passed, Judy may claim only the five acres actually possessed.

Constructive possession benefits the adverse possessor in a variety of transfer situations. An adverse possessor occupying one lot has constructive possession of several lots conveyed separately if all lots are enclosed as a unit. Likewise, constructive possession reaches several lots conveyed in one document even if the lots are separately described in the deed. If the deed describes multiple lots — some occupied, others not — constructive possession even extends to lots that do not adjoin the occupied land.

(b) Open and Notorious Possession

Open and notorious possession means the adverse possessor's use of the property is so visible and apparent it gives notice to the true owner that someone may be asserting an adverse claim to the land. The adverse possessor's use must be of such character under the circumstances as would indicate to a reasonably attentive owner that someone else might be claiming the property. Except where one co-owner of property tries to take property from another co-owner, the adverse possessor is not required to give actual notice to the true owner. If he has actual knowledge, however, the open and notorious element is met even though no one else has reason to know of the adverse claim. Buildings, fences, crops, or animals might constitute an open and notorious presence. Fences or crops — enclosure or cultivation — are sometimes statutory requirements as well.

(c) Exclusive Possession

Exclusive possession means that the adverse possessor holds the land to the exclusion of the true owner. Possession cannot be exclusive, moreover, if two or more adverse possessors use the property adverse to each other's ownership. If, however, one adverse possessor has a superior legal right — by holding under color of title or having entered the property first, for example — the adverse possessor with the superior right may oust the other adverse possessor and continue possession, the statutory period running from the time the senior adverse possessor initially occupied the property. As any prior possessor may, the first adverse possessor may eject or oust subsequent adverse possessors even though the senior adverse possessor has not occupied the property for the statutory period. Some states, on the other hand, hold that exclusive possession means exactly what it implies — that only one person can claim adverse possession.

Exclusive possession does not mean only one person can ever gain title by adverse possession. Most states permit persons acting in concert to adversely possess property.

(d) Hostile or Adverse Possession

There are three theories as to what constitutes hostile or adverse possession.

(1) The Majority or Objective View

Hostile or *adverse possession* in most states means simply that the adverse possessor uses the occupied property without the true owner's permission, and inconsistent with the true owner's legal rights. A person entering property with the true owner's permission cannot claim adverse possession. A tenant leasing the property for more than the statutory period, for example, cannot claim ownership, since her possession was never hostile. The fact that the true owner gave permission to an adverse possessor already on the premises might not destroy the hostility element, however, if the possessor intends to remain on the property with or without the true owner's permission.

If a person enters onto the property with permission, or his occupation is consistent with the true owner's title, the possessor's continued stay could become hostile, but the hostility claim must be unequivocal. In most cases a tenant or co-owner must give actual notice to the true owner or engage in some act that clearly brings home the fact that the possessor is claiming full ownership as against the landlord or co-owner. Arguably, a tenant refusing to vacate property after a lease ends and denying any continuing obligation to pay rent may exhibit the hostility element. In some states, however, the tenant must vacate the property and then re-enter to begin the running of the statute of limitations.

(2) The Minority, Bad Faith, or Intentional Trespass View

Some courts deem important the adverse possessor's subjective intent, and look to the possessor's state of mind. The issue, particularly acute in boundary disputes, is whether the possessor's subjective intent is relevant. Courts and commentators favoring the objective view discussed previously agree that a possessor using land on his neighbor's property under the mistaken belief as to the exact location of the boundary line can adversely possess the land as long as he claims the strip used as his own.

A small minority of jurisdictions hold that mistaken possession does not constitute hostility. These courts find no hostility if the adverse possessor intended to claim only the property described in his deed, and was on neighboring land under the mistaken belief that the land was described in his deed. The subtle difference between the possessor's intending to claim the property whether or not described in the possessor's deed and not intending to claim unless the disputed strip was contained in the possessor's deed, to be determined after the statutory period has run, tempts the possessor, who may never have thought about it, to lie. Because of this, and because most courts conclude that if the rule were otherwise, only bad-faith adverse possessors could win and good-faith purchasers would typically lose, most but not all courts conclude that the possessor's intent is irrelevant.

(3) Good Faith View

In a few cases courts have required the adverse possessor in a boundary dispute to be on his neighbor's land in good faith, actually believing it to be included in his deed description. Only if the adverse possessor is on the neighboring land mistakenly thinking the neighboring land is included in his deed will the adverse possessor be able to satisfy the hostile and adverse possession element. As with the bad-faith discussion above, however, most courts hold the possessor's good faith irrelevant.

Some analysts believe the confusion on subjective intent and mistaken belief derives from the similarity of the labels "color of title," "claim of title," and "claim of right." A claim of right or of title is synonymous with hostility, but a "claim of title" often is confused with "color of title."

As discussed earlier, color of title only means a possessor claims the property pursuant to a faulty document.

(e) Continuous Possession

To satisfy the statute of limitations for adverse possession, a claimant must be in **continuous possession** for the entire limitations period. Continuous does not mean uninterrupted. It does not mean the person must be on the property 24 hours a day, or even every day. The possessor must use the property as would a true owner under the circumstances. Intermittent use usually does not constitute continuous possession, but seasonal use may be continuous, as in the use of a hunting cabin during hunting seasons, or the cutting of timber when appropriate. In one interesting case, a court held that two prison sentences of four and nine months each did not interrupt the possessor's continuity of possession. See Helton v. Cook, 219 S.E. 2d 505 (N.C. App. 1975).

You may have noticed that the elements of adverse possession are redundant, in that one fact might be used to evaluate more than one element. For example, when a claimant's use of land slowly and incrementally increases over time, only when the use becomes open and notorious will the statutory period start to run. Here the elements of actual, continuous, and open and notorious possession intersect. This intersection is particularly likely in boundary disputes.

The continuity element focuses on the adverse possessor's time on the property, rather than on how long the true owner has been dispossessed. If an adverse possessor abandons the property, and a second adverse possessor independently enters into possession, the statute of limitations starts anew. If an adverse possessor leaves the property with the intent to return and returns to find a new adverse possessor on the property, the returning possessor can eject the second adverse possessor and continue the running of the statute.

PRIVITY AND TACKING

The adverse possessor gains an interest in the property even though he has occupied the property for less than the time necessary to gain title and is subject to an ejectment proceeding by the true owner. An adverse possessor may eject other trespassers and adverse possessors even before the statute of limitations runs, as long as the adverse possessor entered the property first.

The adverse possessor, moreover, may sell or give his interest to another person. The purchaser or donee succeeds to the adverse possessor's attributes, including the time the first possessor occupied the property. This adding of time the first possessor used the property to the time the second possessor used the property is called **tacking**. The relationship necessary to allow tacking is called privity. **Privity** occurs by contract of sale, gift, will, or other inheritance (intestate succession).

DISABILITIES AND TOLLING THE RUNNING OF THE STATUTE OF LIMITATIONS

Many states provide that the statute of limitations for an adverse possession claim will not run against a true owner who is under a **disability** when the adverse possession commences. States consider various conditions or situations to be disabilities. Infants (minors) and the mentally ill generally are deemed disabled. Other common groups include persons in prisons, those in military service, or those who are absent from the state.

If a true owner of property is under a disability, the statute of limitations will not run against him or her until the disability is removed. Meanwhile the statute is said to be **tolled**. To illustrate, if a statute provides for a ten-year statute of limitations, the state law deems a minor to be under a disability until the minor reaches age 21, and the true owner is 15 years old when the adverse possession begins, the statute of limitation is tolled and does not begin to run until the true owner turns 21. In this example, therefore, the statute is tolled for six years and the true owner has until he or she turns 31 to bring an ejectment action against the adverse possessor. Some statutes reduce the limitations period following a period of disability (but the person under a disability has at least the standard limitation period to bring suit).

Some guiding principles seem common to most states. First, the disability must exist on the date of the adverse possessor's entry onto the land. A disability that arises after the adverse possession begins will not toll the running of the statute. To illustrate, if an adverse possession begins in year one, and in year two the true owner is sentenced to 20 years in the state penitentiary, the statute is not tolled. If the true owner had been sentenced in year one and the possession began in year two, however, the statute would be tolled until the true owner was released from prison.

Second, there is no tacking of disabilities, although when the true owner is under more than one disability, the one of most benefit to him may be elected. If a true owner under a disability when the adverse possession begins falls under a second disability during the time of the adverse possession, the statute is tolled only during the continuance of the first disability. For example, if the true owner is 15 when the possession begins, and is sentenced to prison for ten years when he is 19, the statute is tolled until he reaches majority (say, age 21), and will run against him after that date even though he still is in prison.

Third, a person taking from or through the true owner under a disability generally can take advantage of the tolling statute to the same extent as the person with the disability, except that the disability is deemed to end on the day of the sale or gift. The logic behind this rule is as follows. Without the rule, if the statute ran against the new owner from the first day the adverse possessor entered onto the property, the person under a disability might not ever be able to sell the property because the property might immediately vest in the adverse possessor. Or, from the new owner's perspective, he could lose all rights in the property before having an opportunity to discover and eject an adverse possessor.

TEMPORAL AND PHYSICAL SEVERANCE AND ADVERSE POSSESSION

Adverse possession laws protect persons who have a future interest in property. Land ownership can be divided temporally — i.e., by time. In a simple scenario, O, the true owner, may transfer property to A to use during A's life, and give to B the right to possess the property after A dies. A is said to be the life tenant in this example. B is called the remainderman. The general rule is that the statute does not begin to run against a person having a future interest until the future interest becomes possessory. In the life tenant–remainderman scenario, the remainderman has no right to possess or use the property until A dies. If an adverse possessor enters the property after the ownership has been divided in time between the life tenant and the remainderman, he can divest only the life tenant and the statute does not begin to run against the remainderman until A, the life tenant, dies, and B, the remainderman, gains the right to possession. If the adverse possessor enters the property before O, the original owner, makes the transfer to A and B, however, the statute runs against both the life tenant and the remainderman.

Likewise, land ownership can be divided vertically — into air rights, surface rights, and subsurface (typically mineral) rights. If minerals have been sold separately from the right to use the surface, and thereafter an adverse possessor enters the property, he can divest only the holder of the surface rights — unless he opens a mine, at which point he starts to run the statutory period against the person holding the mineral rights. If the adverse possessor enters the property before the surface and the mineral rights are severed, however, the statute runs against both the surface and the mineral owner.

In one famous case, Marengo Cave Co. v. Ross, 10 N.E.2d 917 (Ind. 1937), the discoverer of a spectacular cave, owning the land where the cave's mouth was located, mistakenly believed that the whole cave was located under his land. It wasn't, and the owner of the land whose surface lay adjacent and partly above the cave sued the discoverer's successors in title, but only after the cave's users had, over a period of 50 years, improved its accessibility and made extensive efforts to turn it into a profitable tourist destination. Ross, the adjacent owner, sued Marengo, the current operator of the enterprise, to quiet title to that portion of the cave under his land. A court-ordered survey disclosed that the cave was indeed under Ross's land. The court held that Marengo's possession "tacked" onto that of prior operators of the cave. It also held that the use was actual, hostile, and continuous, but not exclusive and open and notorious, even though even Ross had occasionally toured the cave, buying a ticket to do so.

As to the open and notorious element, you might argue that the development of the cave enterprise, exploiting the cave as its true owner would, is sufficient. On the other hand, the underground nature of the cave might not give Ross notice that his rights are being used. Ross could not locate the cave without entering it, which he could not do without a court order. Just as when a miner exceeds the extent of his mineral rights when extending a mine under land he does not own, there is something secret and fraudulent about the trespass. Either argument is reasonable, but the *Marengo Cave* court chose the second.

PERSONAL PROPERTY AND ADVERSE POSSESSION

Where personal property is concerned, does the application of the law of adverse possession make sense? In early cases concerning domesticated animals, it was used, but the animals were often taken out of their original locale, to places where their true owners were very unlikely to find them. In such cases, and also when chattels were fraudulently concealed, the rule was that the statute of limitation was tolled.

Additionally, as to some of adverse possession's elements — actual possession, exclusivity, hostility, and continuity — the law worked reasonably well. But what about other elements such as open and notorious possession? With personalty, that presents a problem. A person can wear his or her wristwatch, but who will notice? Under such circumstances, is it sensible to let the limitations period run out in the usual fashion?

These questions are the more pressing because the statutes of limitations for personality — for actions of trover, conversion and replevin — are shorter (typically between four and eight years) than similar ones for realty. So these questions have been a source of debate, and two rules have developed to answer them. The first, traditional rule is that the statute of limitations for actions for personality does not start to run until the action "accrues" — that is a lawyer's way of saying that the last element of the cause of action is in place. So, for example, when a work of art disappears and then reappears on the wall of a purchaser, the cause of action to recover it does not accrue until its true owner discovers its whereabouts and makes a demand for its return. This gives the purchaser an opportunity to return it, but upon refusing to do so, the true owner's action is complete — the demand and refusal being the last element in it. This "demand and refusal" rule means that a possessor runs the statute from the date of the refusal and that the statute was tolled beforehand. See Solomon R. Guggenhein Fdn. v. Lubell, 569 N.E. 426 (N.Y. 1991).

The second rule is the rule of due diligence. Here, after the personalty disappears, the true owner may toll the statute for the period of time that he or she searches diligently for it, but if the search is discontinued, the statute runs. The true owner bears the burden of proof on the issue of diligence. Meanwhile, the cause of action does not accrue until the true owner discovers, or by the exercise of reasonable diligence should discover, the facts which will permit the action to accrue. See O'Keeffe v. Snyder, 416 A.2d 862 (N.J. 1980). Discovery of the facts is here the key; no demand is necessary.

Both the "demand and refusal" and the "due diligence" rule have advantages and disadvantages. They both, rather than modifying the elements of adverse possession, focus on when the statute of limitations starts and stops. Consider, for example, a cause of action in replevin: its elements are (1) the loss of personalty, (2) the plaintiff's right to it up to the time of the action, and (3) a demand for and a refusal to return it. The due diligence rule's focus is on the second element; the demand and refusal's rule is (obviously) on the third element, and differs in the extent to which the court is willing to prefer the rights of the true owner over its present possessor. The demand and refusal rule is easier to apply and consistent with the traditional preference of the common law for a true owner's rights. The due diligence rule is more flexible, considers the disadvantage at which possessors find themselves showing adverse possession, and allows the true owner to show how much she valued the chattel. Yet both rules attempt to inhibit the fencing or thievery of personalty (if in different ways), and both are fact-based enough to take account of the many ways in which the true owner might be "diligent" in searching for lost chattel.

Examples

Hunting Lodge

1. Arthur obtains a defective tax deed to a section of land on which he constructs a hunting cabin. When the cabin is destroyed by fire several years later, Arthur rebuilds it on a cement foundation, clears the acreage around the cabin, plants grass, and posts a sign along a nearby road indicating an access road to the cabin. Arthur occupies the cabin during

hunting seasons and occasional other weekends over the course of the limitations period, but never resides there or attempts to keep others off the land around the cabin. He never otherwise improved the land or posted it against other hunters, but he did pay the taxes, and sold the scrub timber on the land for pulpwood. Has Arthur acquired adverse possession?

Timing Is Everything

2. In a state with a 20-year statute of limitation, Alie enters and begins adversely possessing Blackacre. Nineteen years later, trespasser Tom destroys Blackacre's crops. May the record owner of Blackacre (the true owner, or TO) sue Tom for damages to Blackacre on the day after the statutory period ends in favor of Alie?

Interim Transfer

3. Ten years ago Adam entered and began adversely possessing TO's Whiteacre, located in a state with a 20-year statute of limitations for adverse possession. This year, Adam deeds Whiteacre to Xeno, a bona fide purchaser. What estate does Xeno obtain?

It's Yours? Really?

4. A quarter century ago Angie entered, immediately began adversely possessing TO's Brownacre, and held until two years ago. TO now arrives and tells Angie it is TO's land. Angie says she is sorry; she thought it was her land and didn't know it belonged to TO. In a state with a 20-year statute of limitations, does Angie own Brownacre?

With Your Kind Permission

5. TO tells Andy, "Stay as long as you need a place." Andy does and, after the statutory period has passed, sues TO in order to establish adverse possession. Will Andy's claim succeed?

One Farm, Two Deeds

6. Amy gives Brad a deed to Amy's farm. Amy then gives Charlie a similar deed to the same farm (except, of course, for the name of the grantee — here, Charlie). Brad starts to cut timber on the farm. Charlie moves into the farmhouse and farms the fields. Both Brad and Charlie continue in this way for the limitations period. Charlie then sues Amy and Brad for adverse possession of the land described in the deed from Amy. What result and why?

Dispossessing Future Estate Holders

7. (a) AP enters Blackacre adversely. TO holds a life estate in Blackacre, remainder to Bobbie and her heirs. The prescriptive period in the jurisdiction is ten years. Eleven years later, TO dies and Bobbie brings suit to oust AP. In this suit, what result and why?

   (b) AP enters Blackacre adversely. TO, the true owner of Blackacre, then dies and leaves a will devising a life estate in Blackacre to Angelina, remainder to Bobbie and her heirs. The statue of limitations period in the jurisdiction is ten years. Eleven years later, Angelina dies and Bobbie brings suit to oust AP. In this suit, what result and why?

Calculating Time in Possession

8. Owen owns Blackacre. In a state with a 20-year statue of limitations Ayn begins adversely possessing Blackacre. After satisfying all the elements for adverse possession for 10 years, she leaves Blackacre (and the state). Hearing Ayn has moved, Bessie moves onto Blackacre adversely and stays for the next 15 years. Then Owen sues Bessie in ejectment, claiming he owns Blackacre and Bessie is a trespasser. What result and why?

This Land Is My Land

9. Assume a 20-year statute of limitations in the following Examples:

   (a) In 1985, Odie, the true owner, is ousted from Blackacre's possession by Arthur, who in 1990 is ousted by Betty, who in 1995 is ousted by Cory, who in 2000 is ousted by Dan. Who has title to Blackacre in 2011?

   (b) If, in 2002, Cory had sued Dan in ejectment to regain possession, what result?

   (c) What result if Dan had sued Cory for damages in polluting the soil on Blackacre's wheat fields?

   (d) Ossie is disseised by Addy in 1980. Addy is in possession until 2005. In that year, Ossie sells to Ben and Ben then sues Addy in ejectment. In this suit, what result and why?

   (e) Same facts as in (d) except Ossie sells to Ben in 1995, and Ben sues in 1995, What result?

   (f) Same facts as in (e) except Ben waits until 2005 to bring his ejectment action. What result?

Disabled Advice

10. O is insane when ousted by *A* in 1990. *A* is in adverse possession from 1990 to 2005 when O, in a lucid moment, conveys the property to his insane son S. Assuming a 20-year statute of limitations, what would you advise O to do?

Bad Fences Make Bad Neighbors

11. A fence is mistakenly constructed between Arden's and Ben's lots 20 feet into Ben's property, and for ten years Arden uses the extra 20 feet as his own. Ben then constructs an improvement on his land on his side of the fence and, during the construction, tears down the fence to get construction equipment onto the land and around his new improvements. After the construction, the fence is rebuilt, but in a different place, ten feet from the boundary indicated in the record title. Another ten years pass, with Arden and Ben fully using the land on their respective sides of the new fence. In a state with a 20-year limitations period, Arden sues Ben for adverse possession of the 20 feet now in dispute. What result?

Intent on Ownership

12. Twenty-one years ago, the true owner, Owen, left Blackacre. Annie told two persons that she was the new owner, and was in adverse possession thereafter for 20 years. Annie's witnesses are dead and, upon Owen's return, Owen sues Annie for ejectment. Annie's defense is her adverse possession. Assuming a 20-year statute of limitations, what result and why?

Step Neighbors

13. The New Jersey adverse possession provision at the time of the dispute in Mannillo v. Gorski, 255 A.2d 258 (N.J. 1969), stated: "Every person having any right or title of entry into real estate shall make such entry within 20 years next after the accrual of such right or title of entry, or be barred therefrom thereafter." In the summer of 1946 Gorski made certain additions and changes to their house. Among the improvements were a concrete stoop with steps on the west side of the house for use in connection with a side door, and a concrete walk from the steps to the end of the house. The concrete walk was the same width as the steps. The steps and concrete walk encroached 15 inches upon their neighbors' (the Mannillos') land. The Mannillos brought an action in 1968 for an injunction to stop the continuing trespass. Gorski countered for a declaratory action that she owned the 15-inch strip by adverse possession. Gorski did not know that the steps and walk encroached on the Mannillos' property until shortly before trial.

    (a) Does the New Jersey adverse possession statute provide that an adverse possessor, such as Gorski, prevails by using the property for 20 years; or does it provide that the record or true owners, such as the Mannillos, lose all rights to eject anyone who has been in possession for 20 years?

    (b) Was Gorski's possession actual?

    (c) Was Gorski's possession open and notorious?

(d) Was Gorski's possession hostile and adverse? Could the fact that Gorski did not know the steps encroached on the Mannillos' property affect your answer?

(e) Was Gorski's possession exclusive?

(f) Was Gorski's possession continuous for 20 years?

(g) If the Mannillos prevail, should the court force them to sell the disputed land to Gorski? If Gorski prevails, should the court order her to pay the Mannillos for the disputed land?

(h) The platform, steps, and walk were in place and visible when the Mannillos bought their property. A survey at the time should have discovered the encroachment. Should either of these facts affect your analysis of this dispute?

Marengo More

14. Consider the more difficult issues and arguments in the case of Marengo Cave Co. v. Ross, discussed in the text to this Chapter.

(a) Was Marengo's possession exclusive?

(b) If Ross prevails, should a court make him reimburse Marengo for improvements made to the cave?

(c) If Ross prevails, should the court force Ross to sell his part of the cave to Marengo? If Marengo prevails, should the court force Marengo to pay Ross for the portion of the cave under Ross's land? Restated, is the correct solution to this case — whether adverse possession is proved or not — that the court should order Marengo to pay Ross for the portion of the cave under Ross's land, or should the court rule completely in one party's favor and let the parties negotiate?

Tack and Toll Time

15. The state in which you practice has a ten-year statute of limitations period for adverse possession claims. The state also authorizes an extension of the statute of limitations period if the true owner is under a disability. It allows possessors in privity to tack holding periods for purposes of the adverse possession statute. The state's disability provision reads as follows:

> Tolling for Disabilities (1) If a person entitled to bring an action is, at the time the cause of action accrues, either under the age of 20 years; or insane; or imprisoned on a criminal charge, the action may be commenced within 2 years after the disability ceases, except that where the disability is due to insanity or imprisonment, the limitation period prescribed in this chapter may not be extended for more than 5 years. (2) Subsection (1) does not shorten a limitation period otherwise prescribed. (3) A disability does not exist, for the purposes of this section, unless it existed when the cause of action accrues. (4) When two or more disabilities coexist at the time the cause of action accrues, the two-year period specified in subsection (1) does not begin until they all are removed.

Assume for the following Examples that the adverse possessor has met the actual, open and notorious, hostile and adverse, exclusive, and continuous elements of adverse possession.

(a) Bryan, born December 1, 1989, inherits property on July 1, 1995, when he is five years old. Poe enters upon the property on January 1, 2000, claiming it as her own. When does Poe gain title by adverse possession?

(b) Same as (a) except Bryan was convicted of robbery and sentenced to prison on July 1, 2008, when he was 18. He served four years, and was released on July 1, 2012. When does Poe gain title by adverse possession?

(c) Same as (a) except on January 1, 2005, when Bryan is 15, Bryan (by his trustee) sells the property to Michelle, who turned 18 on January 1, 2005. When does Poe gain title by adverse possession?

(d) Same as (c) except Bryan sold the property to Michelle on July 1, 2010. When does Poe gain title by adverse possession?

(e) Lance was 18 when he inherited property on January 1, 2000, while serving in the armed forces. Poe enters on the property on July 1, 2001, claiming it as her own. On January 1, 2001, Lance dies in an automobile accident, leaving the property to his one-year-old son, Kevin (born July 1, 1999). When does Poe gain title by adverse possession?

(f) Same as (e) except Poe sold the property to Ed Verse on January 1, 2004, giving him a deed for the property. When does Ed Verse gain title by adverse possession?

(g) Same as (f) except the state statute reduces the limitation period to five years if the adverse possessor has color of title. When does Ed Verse gain title by adverse possession?

Explanations

Hunting Lodge

1. Yes. Arthur used the property as would a true owner. A true owner using the property as a hunting lodge would not clear the land or necessarily fence in the land. The posting of the directions to the cabin, the road to the cabin, and the cabin itself are open enough possession to give notice to the true owner. Holding pursuant to the tax deed satisfies the adverse and hostile element. Even though Arthur does not reside on the land, his use as would a true owner of a hunting cabin, especially as reinforced by the presence of the road and the cabin itself, is enough to satisfy the continuing possession element. Arthur had exclusive possession. The faulty tax deed is a color of title, so any problems Arthur may have in establishing exactly how much of the

property he used at all—much less continuously for the limitations period—are overcome since Arthur is deemed to be in constructive possession of all the land described in the tax deed. Some states require payment of property taxes to claim by adverse possession; most states do not. Either way, Arthur is okay because he paid them. See Monroe v. Rawlings, 49 N.W.2d 55 (Mich. 1951).

Timing Is Everything

2. Yes, depending on the state. Once the title to Blackacre is transferred to Alie, TO no longer has any right to sue Alie in ejectment to recover possession and title. However, that does not necessarily mean that rights against trespassers such as Tom that arise before the limitations period runs end as well. See 10 *Thompson on Real Property*, § 87.03, at p. 86 (David Thomas, ed., 1994) (indicating that in some states the owner's suit will lie). On the other hand, in some states the title acquired by adverse possession relates back to the date of the adverse possessor's entry and, when this rule is given its broadest effect, the TO might now be held to have no right to sue Tom.

Interim Transfer

3. Xeno acquires all of the right, title, and estate that Adam had. Thus, Xeno can tack her own possessory right onto Adam's ten years of adverse possession, so that Xeno can acquire title by adverse possession in ten more years in a state with a twenty-year statute of limitations.

It's Yours? Really?

4. Yes. The post-limitations period admission is irrelevant to the passage of title to Angie by adverse possession. The statute is a statute of repose. Once perfected, title by adverse possession is as good as any title, and nothing said by the claimant will divest it. Adverse possession creates a new title, not just a defense to the former owner's title. Land transfers are subject to the Statute of Frauds, which requires a writing to transfer title. For Angie to return Brownacre to TO, she must execute a deed. An oral statement is inadequate to transfer title. While Angie's possession was not consciously hostile to TO, she was on the property other than with TO's permission, and that is all the hostility most states require.

With Your Kind Permission

5. No. TO's permission immunizes his holdings from Andy's claim. Andy's possession must be hostile and adverse to TO's ownership. TO can stop Andy's claim dead by showing that Andy had permission to take possession (as a tenant with a lease has permission to do so).

One Farm, Two Deeds

6. Judgment for Charlie as to the farmland. Charlie has color of title and constructive possession of the land described in the deed as to Amy. Constructive possession, however, must give way to Brad's actual possession of the forest: Both Brad and Charlie have constructive adverse possession of the whole farm — fields and forests — against Amy. Against each other, however, the doctrine of color of title does not resolve the dispute. The second deed to Charlie does not annul the first; indeed, the usual rule is "first in time, first in right," so that Brad's deed would control, except for lands in Charlie's actual adverse possession. Thus, Charlie gets the farmland; Brad gets the timberland and any land not used by either. Land in constructive adverse possession must, in other words, bear some reasonable relationship to land actually possessed. See 3 Am. L. Prop. § 15.11, at 820 (James Casner, ed., 1952).

Dispossessing Future Estate Holders

7. (a) Judgment for Bobbie. You will study future interests later in the course. Return to this Example after studying future interests. TO holds a life estate, which means he owns Blackacre as long as he lives. Once he dies, Blackacre automatically passes to Bobbie. The adverse possessor takes the true owner as she finds her. Thus, AP ran the statute for the full limitations period, but only against TO, the holder of the life estate, not against Bobbie. AP owns Blackacre as long as TO lives. Once Bobbie's remainder vests in possession at TO's death, AP in effect has to run the statute against Bobbie all over again. So no matter that the adverse possessor fully and efficiently used the land during the life tenant's tenure for the full limitations period, title is not transferred to the adverse user in this instance. No amount of honest labor will be rewarded by transferring Bobbie's title to AP, because Bobbie is not the sleeping owner the law means to penalize. Both theories of adverse possession cannot be satisfied in this instance.

   (b) This time, judgment for AP. The adverse possession began at a time when TO held Blackacre in fee simple absolute (TO owned it potentially forever), so the statute continued to run against all persons, including Bobbie, who had interests in Blackacre originating in TO's ownership. When TO died and left Blackacre partly to Angelina (life estate) and to Bobbie (remainder after Angelina's death), each took subject to AP's rights already established in the property. AP successfully acquires the fee simple absolute that TO held at the time of AP's entry.

Calculating Time in Possession

8. Judgment for Owen. Bessie is not in privity with Ayn and therefore cannot tack Ayn's time to Bessie's possession period. The statute of limitations for Bessie began running when she entered onto Blackacre in late 1990. Owen, although a true owner sleeping on his rights for more than the statutory period, still prevails over the adverse user, who has not herself been in possession and satisfied the elements of adverse possession for the statutory period. This result shows that the "sleeping owner" statute of limitation rationale is not as important as the reward theory in these circumstances.

This Land Is My Land

9. (a) Odie still owns Blackacre because no one adverse possessor has run the statute for the required 20 years. Dan held it the longest, 11 years, but still fell short of the required 20 years. For the successive disseisers, one must be in possession for the statutory period to oust the true owner thereafter. None of the disseisers can tack preceding possessors' time on the land since they were not in privity. If Betty had sold or willed her rights to Cory, and Cory had deeded or willed her rights to Dan, Dan could tack both Betty's and Cory's times of possession and prevail, but that's not what happened.

(b) Judgment for Cory. The prior possessor has a right to possession superior to the right of a later adverse possessor, even if the latter is satisfying all the elements required for adverse possession up to the time of the suit. Adverse possession is a method of transferring title after the statute has run, not an exception to the doctrine of relativity of title. The prior adverse user has a right superior to any successors, assuming she can prove that she did not abandon the property. Cory can eject Dan, but does not have the title yet. Does Cory get credit for Dan's possession? This is an open question.

(c) Judgment for Dan. Dan has a separate interest in the wheat crop, assuming that he planted it and intends to harvest it, no matter that Cory has a right of prior possession. Protecting the crop presents an issue separate from the prior right to possession of the soil. Here Dan seeks not possession, but damages.

(d) Judgment for Addy, who has acquired (assuming that proper proof is presented in this suit) Ossie's title by adverse possession, so that, in 2005, Ossie had no rights to transfer to Ben. Ben cannot acquire more than his vendor had to give and so acquires nothing. Ben is not without a remedy, as he likely has a suit against Ossie for failing to convey good title.

(e) Ben prevails. He acquired all of Ossie's rights as legal owner. The statute of limitations has not run on Addy's adverse possession, so Ben can eject her.

(f) Addy wins. Ben waited too long to sue. He has 20 years to bring suit. The statute of limitations is measured by the time the adverse possessor is in possession, not by the time a record title owner has title.

Disabled Advice

10. Absent some special statutory provision on this problem that adjusts the time a person can bring suit once a disability is removed, your advice to O should be to sue A in his son's name before 2025, when the limitations period will run in A's favor in a majority of states. The statute of limitations is tolled while O is insane since insanity is a disability. We do not tack disabilities, however. Only the disabilities in effect at the time the adverse possessor entered the land toll the statute. Though O's son S was insane when taking his interest, the statute of limitations begins running in A's favor as soon as the title is transferred to S: S's disability does not stop or toll the statute's running.

Bad Fences Make Bad Neighbors

11. Ben's construction interrupted the prescriptive period. Judgment for Ben. See Mendonca v. Cities Service Oil Co., 237 N.E.2d 16 (Mass. 1968). For certain the limitations period was disrupted as to ten feet. An argument could be made that Arden used ten feet continuously for the entire 20-year period. A better argument can be made, however, that if Arden was truly claiming adversely he would have challenged Ben's taking down the fence and using the ten feet. Having failed to assert his rights in a situation where the true owner would have challenged Ben's actions, Arden lost his adverse claim to the entire 20 feet and started the limitations period anew as to the remaining ten feet after the fence was back up. The degree of the intrusion matters. Ben reclaimed half the challenged land unopposed, not just a relatively small fraction of it.

Intent on Ownership

12. Judgment for Annie in states adopting the objective view of hostility, and for Owen in states requiring subjective good faith on the adverse possessor's part. Actually, this problem is really an argument for the majority rule. Annie's possession (if she can prove it), regardless of what she told people about it, should control. Adverse possession cases often turn as much on matters of proof as on questions of law. Annie, for example, may not be able to prove when she took possession, or that she took hostilely, because her main witnesses are not able to testify. In practice, adverse possessors entitled to have a title decreed theirs should actively pursue a judgment saying so. At a minimum, witnesses'

affidavits at the beginning and at the end of the limitations period and a record of the possession over the required length of time should be made and kept.

Step Neighbors

13. The Example is based on Mannillo v. Gorski, 255 A.2d 258 (N.J. 1969), reversing 241 A.2d 276 (N.J. Super. Ct. Ch. Div. 1968). The case appears in several Property casebooks.

    (a) The New Jersey adverse possession statute provides that the record or true owners, such as the Mannillos, lose all rights to eject anyone who has been in possession for 20 years. The statute says anyone having a right to enter can bring suit, in this case for ejectment. The person with the right to enter is the legal owner, in our case the Mannillos. According to the statute the true owner can bring the action as soon as the action accrues, which is as soon as the Gorskis' stoop, steps, and walk encroach onto the Mannillos' land. The statute says if the person with the right to bring the action fails to bring the action within 20 years after the cause of action accrues, the true owner is barred from ever bringing the suit. Since the legal owner cannot bring a suit to oust or eject the trespasser after the statute of limitations has run, the trespasser in effect and legally has the right to the property.

    (b) Gorski's possession was actual. She claims only the land where her stoop, steps, and walk sit.

    (c) A critical issue in the opinion in Mannillo was whether Gorski's possession was open and notorious. Although the stoop, steps, and walk were visible (and in all likelihood walked on by Mannillo at times), the New Jersey Supreme Court concluded the encroachment onto the Mannillo property was not open and notorious. Beginning with an assertion that the foundation of adverse possession is the failure of the true owner to commence an action for the recovery of the land involved, the court concluded the possessor's use must be of such character

    > as to put an ordinarily prudent person on notice that the land is in actual possession of another. . . . Generally, where possession of the land is clear and unequivocal and to such an extent as to be immediately visible, the owner may be presumed to have knowledge of the adverse occupancy. . . . However, when the encroachment of an adjoining owner is of a small area and the fact of an intrusion is not clearly and self-evidently apparent to the naked eye but requires an on-site survey for certain disclosure as in urban sections where the division line is only infrequently delineated by any monuments, natural or artificial, such a presumption is fallacious and unjustified. . . . Accordingly, we

hereby hold that no presumption of knowledge arises from a minor encroachment along a common boundary. In such a case, only where the true owner has actual knowledge thereof may it be said that the possession is open and notorious.

While the New Jersey court's approach is sensible in urban settings, it causes enough practical problems that most other states have not expressly adopted the "minor encroachment" rule. One troubling issue that arises, for example, is what constitutes a minor encroachment and what a major encroachment. In a later case, a New Jersey trial court and the supreme court disagreed over whether a strip of land one foot wide and 152 feet long was a minor or a major encroachment ("minor encroachment," ruled the supreme court). The rule also makes more difficult determining whether long-used property may be claimed by adverse possession when prior owners' knowledge is unknown. Another issue, as discussed in Explanation (h), below, is whether a survey taken when Mannillo purchased the property should have given Mannillo actual, inquiry, or constructive notice. Because Gorski's possession was not open and notorious under the New Jersey approach, Gorski's adverse possession claim fails no matter how she fares under the other elements.

(d) A major issue in *Mannillo* was whether an entry and continuance under the mistaken belief that the possessor has legal title to the land in dispute exhibits the requisite hostile and adverse possession to sustain an adverse possession claim. Until this case, New Jersey held adverse possession could not be bottomed on mistake. In *Mannillo*, New Jersey held that the adverse possessor's intent is irrelevant.

New Jersey's former rule, called the "Maine Doctrine," requires as an essential element of adverse possession that the adverse possessor intend to claim the property whether or not his deed describes the land, and whether or not it is eventually determined he had no right to enter upon the property. "If, on the other hand, a party through ignorance, inadvertence, or mistake occupies up to a given fence beyond his actual boundary, because he believes it to be the true line, but has no intention to claim title to that extent if it should be ascertained that the fence was on his neighbor's land, an indispensable element of adverse possession is wanting. In such a case the intent to claim title exists only upon the condition that the fence is on the true line. The intention is not absolute, but provisional, and the possession is not adverse." 255 A.2d at 261. Thus the Maine Doctrine favors a person with hostile ambitions and disfavors an honest but mistaken person. A minority of states continue to adhere to the Maine Doctrine. If New Jersey had not disclaimed the Maine Doctrine in *Mannillo*, Gorski would not have satisfied the hostile and adverse element, and thus could not avail herself of the adverse possession statute.

In *Mannillo*, however, New Jersey aligned itself with the vast majority of states and commentators that adhere to the Connecticut Doctrine that the possessor's mental state is immaterial. Besides treating intentional wrongdoers better than honest possessors, the Maine Doctrine encourages dishonesty at trial. A person who knows she might prevail if she testifies that she intended to claim the disputed property but definitely loses if she says she used the property by mistake will be tempted to testify that she intended to claim the property as her own even though it was not described in her deed. We disfavor laws that encourage dishonesty and lying. The Connecticut Doctrine, on the other hand, posits an objective rule that the very nature of the entry and possession of the property is an assertion of an adverse and hostile possession when that possession is without the consent of the true owner. Adopting the more objective Connecticut Doctrine, the New Jersey Supreme Court concluded that Gorski satisfied the hostile and adverse element. In the end, it was a short-lived victory, since the court held that Gorski's possession was not open and notorious. See Explanation (c), supra.

(e) Gorski's possession was exclusive. Even though guests and invitees used the stoop, steps, and walk (including, presumably, the Mannillos when they visited Gorski), Gorski was the only one to claim possession. You might have noticed that although Gorski used a small portion of the Mannillos' lot, the Mannillos resided on the biggest portion of the lot, used the lot daily, and used it more intensely than Gorski. Only by treating the one lot as two pieces of property can Gorski be deemed to be in exclusive possession. Courts in fact do treat a portion of the property as separate property for determining exclusivity. This type of treatment was also an issue in Explanation 14, supra, in *Marengo Cave*, the court there refusing to sever the surface from the cave.

(f) Gorski's possession was continuous for more than 20 years. The stoop, steps, and walk were in place from 1946 until 1968, which exceeds 20 years. It is the possessor's use and possession of the land that must exist during the limitations period. It also does not matter that the Mannillos had owned their house for only 15 years (since 1953). The time the possession was adverse to the Mannillos' predecessor in interest (their seller) is deemed to run against the Mannillos.

(g) The general rule is that the successful adverse possessor does not have to compensate the former owner and that the true owners are not required to sell to trespassers. Some commentators have criticized the all-or-nothing approach, arguing that adverse possessors — especially in boundary disputes — should have a right to purchase the land, but not to take the land without payment. Some states, through betterment statutes (discussed in Explanation 14), force the true owner in some cases to elect to pay for improvements made in good faith by an innocent improver or to sell the property to the innocent improver. It seems unfair to require Mannillo to compensate Gorski since Mannillo cannot benefit in the slightest from the stoop, steps, and walk. The New Jersey court held that since its holding could result in undue hardship in boundary disputes, "if the innocent trespasser of a small portion of land adjoining a boundary line cannot without great expense remove or eliminate the encroachment, or such removal or elimination is impractical or could be accomplished only with great hardship, the true owner may be forced to convey the land so occupied upon payment of the fair value thereof without regard to whether the true owner had notice of the encroachment at its inception" where "no serious damage would be done to the remaining land as, for instance, by rendering the balance of the parcel unusable or no longer capable of being built upon by reason of zoning or other restrictions." 255 A.2d at 264.

(h) Although it may be tempting to consider the pre-existing condition because the Mannillos got what they expected when they bought the home and the surprise discovery is more of a psychological windfall than a loss of expectations, adverse possession and trespass laws do not take into account the fact that the encroachment existed at the time the true owner bought the property. Nonetheless, under New Jersey's minor encroachment rule, a survey may have given the Mannillos actual notice of the encumbrance, thus making Gorski's possession open and notorious. Even if the survey did not give the Mannillos actual notice because, hypothetically, they did not look at the survey and no one told them of the problem, a court might conclude a reasonable person should have known what the survey shows and treat the Mannillos as having **constructive notice** or that they should have asked about the survey results (known as **inquiry notice**). Unfortunately for Gorski, treating the survey as giving the Mannillos notice of any type would not have helped her since the Mannillos purchased (and thus would have received notice) in 1953. The case was filed in 1968, so only 14 or 15 years had elapsed, preventing Gorski's adverse possession from meeting the 20-year requirement.

Marengo More

14. (a) The subterranean nature of the cave complicates the exclusive possession question. First, the public's touring the cave does not

destroy Marengo's exclusive possession. All members of the public entering the cave entered with Marengo's permission (use was "through" Marengo). Marengo was not just one member of the general public; he was the only one claiming the cave as owner. All others respected his claim. Second, although Marengo personally claimed the property for only eight years and his predecessors claimed before him, Marengo's claim is still exclusive since he is in privity with the others in his chain of title claiming exclusive possession. The sale from person to person constituted privity of contract for purposes of allowing Marengo to "tack" his predecessors' attributes to his, and claim their activities as his own. Marengo was in exclusive control of the cave.

The only other issue is whether Ross's use of the surface land defeats Marengo's otherwise exclusive possession. The issue turns on whether a court will "sever" the surface use from the cave use. A landowner, for example, can divide one parcel into multiple lots. Likewise, a landowner can sever the mineral rights from the surface rights, or sever ownership rights based on time. To illustrate, if Ross owned 160 acres and actually occupied the southern 80 acres while Marengo farmed the northern 25 acres for the requisite 20-year statute of limitations, a court would "conceptually sever" the northern 25 acres from the remaining acres. The court would envision Ross as actually occupying 80 acres and constructively possessing 55 acres as title holder. The court would view Marengo as actually possessing 25 acres. The court would allow Marengo to claim exclusive possession of the northern 25 acres, and Marengo could claim the 25 acres under adverse possession.

The issue then becomes whether a court would sever the cave from the surface. If not, Marengo did not exclusively possess the property, since he and Ross claimed the same property. The court in *Marengo* refused to sever the two. Under the court's approach, a person who owns land owns it from the surface to the center of the earth. The true owner (Ross, in our case) can sell or transfer the subsurface rights, and could have sold the cave, thereby severing the cave from the surface. If Ross or a predecessor had sold the cave, Marengo could have adversely possessed as against the cave owner. But since Ross did not sell, his possession of the surface was constructive possession of all the subsurface areas. Contrast this court's rationale with *Mannillo* in Explanation 13(e) above.

Supporting the *Marengo* court's conclusion, a person adversely possessing the surface for the limitations period becomes owner of the whole property, not just the surface. If oil, gas, coal, or some other mineral is found beneath the land, the adverse possessor becomes owner of the minerals. The converse would not hold true, however. If Marengo was found to have satisfied all the elements of adverse possession as to the cave, and no one had occupied the surface during the limitations period, a court probably would have limited Marengo's ownership rights to the cave and would refuse to extend his ownership to the surface. Since Marengo did not exclusively possess the land, Marengo's adverse possession claim fails no matter how he fares under the other elements.

(b) There is no single correct answer. Ross as legal owner of the property succeeds to all improvements attached to the land (**rule of accession**). If the legal owner sues the adverse possessor/trespasser for profits attributable to the illegal use of the property, courts allow the trespasser to offset any profits owed by the value of the improvements. A few courts of equity might even require the legal owner to pay the reasonable value of good-faith improvements to an innocent improver on the theory that the true owner otherwise would receive an unjust enrichment. About two-thirds of the states have enacted **"betterment"** or **"innocent improver" statutes** allowing some relief to an innocent improver who improves the property in a good-faith belief that she owns the property. Although state statutes vary, most give the true owner the option of paying the value of improvements to the innocent improver or of offering to sell the land to the innocent improver. Other states do not force the true owner to sell or purchase, but authorize an equitable lien placed on the property so that the innocent improver receives part of any future sales proceeds (should the property ever be sold).

(c) In general, courts resolve the immediate issue and will not force a prevailing adverse possessor to purchase the interest, nor require a prevailing true owner to sell. Some commentators have criticized this all-or-nothing approach, arguing that the adverse possessor, especially in a boundary dispute, should have the right to purchase the interest but not to take it without payment. Some states force the true owner through betterment statutes to elect to pay for improvements made in good faith by the innocent improver or to sell the property to the innocent improver. See Explanation (g), supra.

Tack and Toll Time

15. (a) Poe would gain title by adverse possession on December 1, 2011. Under the statute, the earliest Poe could gain title by adverse possession would be January 1, 2010. Bryan, a minor or infant under the statute until he turns 20, cannot be dispossessed until two years after his disability ceases. Bryan turns 20 on December 1, 2009. Two years later is December 1, 2011.

(b) Poe would gain title by adverse possession on December 1, 2011, the same time she would have possessed had Bryan not gone to prison. Provision (3) of the state statute, as do all or virtually all state statutes, provides that a disability does not exist for purposes of adverse possession unless it existed when the cause of action accrued. Bryan's only disability when the action accrued — when Poe entered onto the land — was his age. Bryan's going to prison does not toll the running of the limitation period.

(c) Poe gains title by adverse possession on January 1, 2010. Under the statute the earliest Addie Poe could gain title would be January 1, 2010. The statute provides that a person is entitled to an additional two years after the disability ends to bring an action. The "person entitled to bring an action" includes Bryan and any person taking through Bryan, including his estate should he die, his successors, devisees, or heirs, including in our Example the purchaser, Michelle. Bryan's disability ceased on January 1, 2005. Two years later is January 1, 2007, which is earlier than if Bryan had no disability. The statute sensibly provides that the two-year extension rule cannot shorten a limitation period otherwise prescribed. The prescribed period ends on January 1, 2010. Poe gains title then. The limitation period does not begin anew when ownership changes hands. Michelle has only five years to bring an action to eject Poe, not twenty years.

(d) If Bryan sold to Michelle on July 1, 2010, Poe gains title on December 1, 2011. Again, the earliest Poe could claim title by adverse possession is January 1, 2010. Since Bryan's disability ended on December 1, 2009, he and any person claiming through him, including Michelle, have until November 30, 2011, to bring an action to eject Addie Poe. Michelle bought after January 1, 2010, but bought while Bryan (and, through Bryan, Michelle) had almost a year and a half to bring an action. Michelle must bring an action before December 1, 2011. The statute continues to run against Michelle, however. The limitations period does not begin anew when Michelle purchases the land from Bryan.

(e) Poe gains title by adverse possession on July 1, 2010, the earliest day possible under the statute. Lance had one disability when he acquired the land: being under age 20. Note that the statute does not include being in the military or being out of state as a qualifying disability. Lance dies in 2001. His disability ends on that date. The two-year extension would not benefit Lance or Kevin. The main issue is whether Kevin can toll the statute because he was a minor or an infant both when Lance acquired the land and when Lance devised the land to him. Unfortunately for Kevin, he was not a "person entitled to bring an action at the time the action accrued."

Kevin could not bring suit, and in fact had no right to the land at all, until the land passed to him under Lance's will. Despite his age, therefore, Kevin may lose all rights to eject Poe on July 1, 2010, when Kevin just turns 11. Let's hope Kevin's parent, legal guardian, or trustee looks out for his interest!

(f) Ed Verse gains title by adverse possession on July 1, 2010. Ed Verse is able to "tack" the time Poe was on the land. Poe sold the land to Ed Verse, and thus was in "privity" with Ed Verse, so he succeeds to her attributes, including time she adversely possessed the property.

(g) Ed Verse would gain title by adverse possession on July 1, 2010. This is tricky. Under the analysis in Explanation (f), above, the latest Ed Verse would gain ownership would be July 1, 2010. The shorter limitation period for holding under color of title should benefit rather than hurt Ed Verse. Under the color of title provision, Ed Verse, acquiring the property on January 1, 2004, normally would gain title by adverse possession on January 1, 2009. If Ed Verse could tack Addie Poe's time, he would have acquired title on July 1, 2005. Ed Verse cannot tack Poe's time, however, since either the statute would provide the five-year period begins when the adverse possessor receives color of title, or a court would require the adverse possessor to satisfy the complete five years under color of title. Otherwise, an adverse possessor not under color of title could deed her property to a person qualifying for the shorter limitation period before the true owner files suit (and maybe arrange for that person to deed the land back to her). Because Ed Verse enters under the color of title statute rather than the general adverse possession statute, he enters for purposes of the color of title statute when Kevin is the owner and when Kevin is a minor or infant. So Kevin would be able to toll the statute until he reaches 20, plus two years, or until July 1, 2021. Since Ed Verse prevails sooner under the ten-year general limitation period — whether or not he has color of title — by tacking Poe's time and avoiding a tolling of the running of the limitation period due to Kevin's disability, Ed Verse would rely on the general limitation period and gain title by adverse possession on July 1, 2010.

PART II

Common Law Estates and Interests in Real Property

Common Law Estates and Present Interests

Real property can be divided up several ways. O, owning 100 acres of real property, might transfer 50 acres to A and the other 50 acres to B. Alternatively, O might sell the surface rights to A and the mineral rights to B. If he wanted, O could transfer the management rights to A (a trustee of a trust, for example) and the income and profits interest to B (a beneficiary of the trust, for example). The next few chapters develop a fourth method of dividing up ownership: over time. O, for example, might transfer acreage to A for a period of time (say, 10 years) and then give it to B for the rest of the time, or might give it to A "for life" (this is known as a life estate, meaning it lasts as long as A lives, and no longer) and then give it to B for the rest of the time, meaning that B will wind up, after A dies, owning the property in perpetuity. In other words, property can be divided physically, but may also be divided along a timeline.

Studying estates and present and future interests requires more than reading for and attending class. You should work problems outside of class. In addition to the Examples in this book, you can find more practice problems in John Makdisi and Daniel Bogart, *Estates in Land and Future Interests* (5th ed. 2007), and Linda H. Edwards, *Estates in Land and Future Interests: A Step-By-Step Guide* (2d ed. 2005).

SOME HISTORY

In 1066, the battle of Hastings set English legal history on its present course: a Norman archer shot the Anglo-Saxon king, Harold, in the eye socket, killing him and leading to the conquest of England by William I, the Conqueror. After the battle, William parceled out the countryside to his knights; what he gave them was a use right, or **tenure**—the right to hold.

William initially parceled out lands for limited periods of time, usually for the life of a particular knight. The knights, once in possession of their holdings, quickly became interested in the rights of their families and children to continue to hold the land after their deaths. They were actually interested in two rights: the right to transfer or dispose of their property by will after death (**testamentary power**, or **devisability**) and the right to dispose of their land during their lifetimes (a **power to alienate**, or **alienability**). Like William, the knights were also interested in setting up a line of successors who could hold tenure, accounting for spouses, children, and grandchildren: It was and is still possible today to create interests in property that are split along a timeline running successively from the present into the future. Such a split in ownership is one of the features of our common law interests and estates, created first for England's nobility but available to all of us today.

Split ownership—fragmented over time—involves a transferor's or testator's desire to control the ownership of property after the transfer or, in the case of a will, after the testator's death (a **testator** is a person dying and leaving a will, a/k/a a **decedent**; and whatever property is transferred by will is often referred to as a **decedent's estate**, administered by an **executor**). Most devices for transfers and wills discussed in this chapter were either formulated for testators interested in such control or by their children, heirs, and transferees resisting that control. The history of common law estates may be seen as a series of intergenerational conflicts, as well as a series of devices designed to achieve that age-old aim of the propertied classes, tax avoidance.

ESTATES AND INTERESTS

The study of estates and interests is, for the beginner, one of concepts and vocabulary. We'll begin by defining and distinguishing "estates" and "interests." Interests are either present or not: they refer to when ownership begins — either now, or anytime in the future. So interests are either current or **present interests** — ones that become vested and possessory at the moment of their creation — or **future interests**, for which an owner must wait until some future time to obtain possession of property.[1] While ownership of a future interest in property, being without the right to immediate possession, in effect means the future interest owner gets no present enjoyment or

---

1. Later chapters explore concurrent interests, in which more than one person shares present or future possessory rights in property.

economic benefit (other than appreciation in value) from owning the land, the future interest is an ownership interest nonetheless. **Estates** further classify interests and refer to when and how ownership ends. All estates are interests in land. Hence estates are a subset of interests. Thus, in classifying estates and interests, it is said that "Owen has a present interest (or future interest, as the case may be), held in an estate known as a. . . ." You will spend the best part of the next several chapters learning to fill in that last blank. This task will require constant study — cramming the subject won't suffice.

ESTATES: SOME FUNDAMENTAL FRAGMENTS

Fragmentation of ownership interests over time is the basic concept under-lying present and future interests. The human mind, particularly that of judges in early England, wanted to visualize ownership of property for all time. Moreover, land was considered to last forever. An oft-used diagram shows a dot representing today and a line extending to infinity to identify all estates in property from today to infinity:

●————————————————————→ ∞

A **fee simple absolute** is what we think of as complete ownership, lasting until the end of time. Its owner can enjoy the property, transfer it away by sale or gift during his life, or devise it (by will) at his death. If he dies without a will and still owning the property, the property passes to his descendants, usually family members, designated in a state statute known generally as the Canons of Descent or the Intestacy Statute. The above diagram illustrates the fee simple absolute.

The diagram indicates that beginning at the present, the dot, on the facts known today, all persons who can use or possess the property from now to infinity must get their rights from or through the fee simple absolute owner. Obviously the owner cannot personally use the property until infinity. Human mortality precludes that. The owner, however, controls who gets the property from now until infinity. The owner during his life or at his death will pass the right to control use and possession to others.

A common transfer is from the property owner (O) to A for life, remainder to B. This grant would be diagrammed:

A has a present interest, held in a life estate.
B has a future interest, a (vested) remainder, held in a fee simple absolute.

If O had granted A a life estate and not stipulated what happens after A dies, the law stipulates the property will revert back to O (or O's later designee) at A's death. The timeline would look like this:

A has a present interest, held in a life estate.

O has a future interest, a reversion, held in a fee simple absolute. That is, once A dies, the property reverts to O, and O again has a fee simple absolute, and once more is free to possess the property or designate who will.

There are four core estates, categorized based on the potential longevity or duration of the possessory interests.

Estate	Duration
Fee Simple	Forever (Infinity)
Fee Tail (fee simple conditional)	Until original grantee's lineage dies out
Life Estate, or Term for Life	For the life of the grantee
Term of Years	Fixed period measured in years, months, or days

The first three estates for historical reasons are known as **freehold estates**. As you can see, this category of estates, or types of tenure, has nothing to do with how they begin; the key is that they have different ways of ending. Freehold estates have inherent in them a right to possession that will be protected by the common law causes of action relating to land. Trespass, trespass to try title, and ejectment are examples. Possession of a freehold estate is denoted by a special word: *seisin*—pronounced "seez-in." So lawyers say, "land must always be seised of some person" or "O has seisin." Seisin is a word that falls strangely on modern ears, in part because we moderns emphasize record or legal title to land, in contrast to the intimate connection between title, possession, physical contact with the land, and responsiveness to civil government that seisin invokes.

The fourth estate listed here, the term of years, along with the periodic tenancy, the tenancy at will, and their documentary cousin, the leasehold, are all known as **nonfreehold estates.** Historically and today, a nonfreehold estate is a less complete form of ownership than a freehold estate. An apartment rental, for example, is a nonfreehold estate.

THE IMPORTANCE OF TERMS — AND SOME MORE TERMS

Much of the study of estates is the study of nomenclature, or labels. Therefore it is important to master precise labels. There are differences among fee simple absolute, fee simple determinable, fee simple subject to a condition subsequent, and fee simple subject to an executory limitation. Do not label a reversion a reversionary interest, because you will only confuse yourself and other people. First, know the wording used to create each estate. There may be seemingly subtle differences in wording to distinguish different estates. There is a big difference, for example, between a grant to "Jill and her heirs" (fee simple absolute) and one to "Jill and the heirs of her body" (fee tail or fee simple conditional). Next, know the characteristics of each estate. The one on which you need to concentrate refers to its **termination**. A fee simple absolute ends at infinity; a life estate lasts only for the life of some person. Learn how estates end — either naturally or by a condition subsequent. A **condition subsequent** is the occurrence or nonoccurrence of an event that can cut short an estate. Finally, know whether and in what ways the estate or interest holder can transfer the interest. Property is **devisable** if the owner can transfer ownership by a will — a testamentary transfer. Property is **descendible** or **inheritable** if the property can pass by the state's intestacy statute to "heirs" if the owner dies without a will. Property is **alienable**, **assignable**, or **transferable** if the owner can sell or give it away during his lifetime — an *inter vivos* transfer. Most estates and interests are devisable, inheritable, and alienable to some extent today, but there are exceptions.

(a) Fee Simple Absolute

A **fee simple absolute** is an estate with an infinite or perpetual duration. A person owning a fee simple interest theoretically can possess the property forever. There is no inherent end to the ownership. The owner may sell or give the property away, devise it by will, or die without a will and have the property go by operation of law under the canons of descent to his "descendants." Hence a fee simple absolute is alienable (transferable or assignable), devisable, and descendible.

The language traditionally used to create a fee simple absolute is **"to A and his heirs."** Today the phrase "to A" also transfers a fee simple absolute, as do phrases such has "to A, his heirs and assigns." The phrase "to A and his heirs" is rife with historical influences. In the eleventh century in England, the king granted life estates to his soldiers — later dukes and knights. He prized personal loyalty above all, and rewarded it with land. But that loyalty had to be tested and affirmed anew with each generation, and so the land reverted to the king at death. Over time, the dukes and knights were allowed to pass property along to male heirs. The right to alienate it was recognized by the Statute *Quia Emptores* (Latin for "concerning purchasers") in 1290.[2]

---

2. Throughout this book, you'll notice common law forms of action and procedures based initially on late-thirteenth-century statutes. Many are the result of the work of Edward I, known as a law reformer in his day and to this day. These are not statutes in the modern

Because the life estate was the dominant estate for more than 100 years, courts interpreted transfers "to A" as life estates. That is, when in doubt whether the grantor meant to transfer a life estate or a fee simple absolute, English courts 1000 years ago would find a grant to be a life estate. The reverse is true today. Either by statute or judicial decision, a person transferring property today is deemed to transfer his or her entire interest in the property unless the words of grant or other evidence indicate that the grantor intended to transfer a lesser interest. Today a grant from O to A would transfer a fee simple absolute to A. And today the traditional words used to create a fee simple absolute are still "to A and his heirs" or "to A and her heirs." A's heirs get absolutely nothing from this transfer. Only A gets the property. Diagramming the grant:

$$\underbrace{\text{to } A}_{\text{words of purchase}} \qquad \underbrace{\text{and his heirs}}_{\text{words of limitation}}$$

The critical language to determine who owns the estate are the **words of purchase**. Property transferred "to A" belongs to A. They denote who takes the estate. Property transferred "to A and his heirs" still belongs solely to A. Property "to A's heirs" goes to A's heirs today (most of the time — more on this later). The remaining language, "and his heirs," are **words of a limitation**. They tell experienced lawyers what was granted, that the grantor intended the estate to be one greater than a life estate, and that the estate lasts in perpetuity — i.e., that the grantor transferred a fee simple absolute.

(b) Life Estate

The life estate — as the name implies — means the owner owns the property for life. As discussed earlier, the life estate is the oldest type of freehold estate. So the life tenant (the holder of a life estate) has seisin. Its duration is measured by someone's life. It is alienable inter vivos by the life tenant, for a term lasting so long as the measuring life, but it is generally neither devisable nor descendible. So the life tenant can transfer this estate to others, with the caveat that, no one being able to transfer more than he has to begin with, the third party's right to continue using the property ends with the original life tenant's life.

---

sense — they are the product of "the King sitting in Parliament" with his nobles, and so are more like executive orders issued with the consent of the nobles. That the King "sat" was a reference to seisin. We today say that a legislature "sits" in the state capital, and that each county has a seat — a county seat — from which its government comes. In the same way, all power was "seated" in the King and by delegation from him, to his courts, thus enabled to sit in judgment in his name.

(1) Attributes of Life Estate

There is no traditional usage of words required to create a life estate. Thus, "to *A* for her natural life," "to *A* during her lifetime," "to *A* for the term of her life," and "to *A* for life" all create a life estate. It may also be implied. As long as it lasts, its holder may use the property, collecting all the rents and profits generated from it. He may use the property as would its owner, except that he must not destroy the value of successive future interests.

> *Example 1:* Owen transfers Blackacre "to B when *A* dies." *A* has a present interest, held in a life estate, implied from the words of limitation "when *A* dies." When *A* dies, B has a future interest, a remainder following the life estate. No words of art are necessary to create a life estate, and it may be implied from the words of the transfer.

A life estate can be measured by the transferor's life, the transferee's life, or the life of a third person. Thus O's conveyance "to *A* for O's life" might be a means of conferring lifetime benefits on *A* when O wants the property to benefit someone else after his death.

Usually the life tenant is also a person whose death terminates the interest. Thus if O transfers Blackacre "to *A* for life," *A* owns the property until *A* dies, at which time O, or some other person holding the reversion through O, owns the property again. In some situations, however, the owner of the life estate and the person whose life determines the duration of the life estate are different people. For example, assume *A*, the owner of a life estate, transfers her life estate to B. B now owns a life estate; B's ownership ends not on B's death, however, but on *A*'s death. B's interest is called a **life estate pur autre vie** A — that is, a life estate measured by the life of another person, *A* in this example.

B's life estate pur autre vie is alienable just as *A*'s life estate was alienable. In addition, since B may die before *A*, B's life estate pur autre vie is devisable and descendible. Since *A* cannot transfer more than she owned, B's interest in Blackacre will terminate immediately upon *A*'s death, even if B is still alive. The same result can be achieved in one step rather than two, as in the following example:

> *Example 2:* Owen transfers Blackacre "to *A* for the life of B." *A* dies while B is still alive. *A*'s estate is a present interest that continues, for the rest of B's life — and so is, to that extent, both devisable and descendible.

The words "to *A*" are words of purchase or words indicating who gets the property. The words "for . . . life" are words of limitation or words indicating that the transferee — in the example, *A* — gets a life estate, and the words "pur autre vie" indicate that *A* gets a life estate measured by the life of B. B takes nothing by way of this transfer.

(2) Marketability Problems

In practice, life estates are difficult to market. Lenders may be reluctant to take property held as a life estate for security for a loan for fear the life tenant may die before the loan is repaid. Purchasers who wish to improve the property likely will not purchase a life estate and invest millions of dollars in constructing improvements since they would lose the improvements and land as soon as the life tenant dies. There are other problems with life estates, so much so that England no longer recognizes the *legal* life estate (the *equitable* life estate — one held in trust — is recognized). The legal life estate continues to be recognized in the United States.

Why? A transferor may want to impose duties on the life tenant, want to avoid the fees and costs involved in administering a trust for property, want to preserve the property in its present use, or may not wish to lease it when the leasehold value (because of the marketability problems discussed in the previous paragraph) does not reflect its full market value. There may be reasons driven by the federal and state estate tax codes as well: since by definition it expires on the life tenant's death, it will not go into the life tenant's decedent's estate and thus be subject to estate taxes. Income taxes might figure in the transferor's calculations too: when the transferor wants to carve out a future interest for a charity, and obtain a charitable deduction for the value of that interest, creating a life estate will allow the transferor or his family to enjoy the property meanwhile.

(3) Conflicts Between Life Tenants and Remaindermen

Besides the lender and sales problems discussed above, legal life estates create problems between the holder of the legal life estate and the person who owns the property once the life estate ends (the original grantor who has a *reversion*, or a third party who has a *remainder*). Often a life tenant will want to use the property in a manner contrary to what the future interest holder would. Some rules have evolved to resolve these conflicts.

First, logically enough, the holder of the life estate can exclude others from the property, including any holder of a future interest (either a reversion or a remainder). That is, a life tenant has a cause of action in trespass against all intruders, and so may recover damages to the land against the trespasser.

Example 1: Owen transfers Blackacre "to *A* for life." *T* trespasses on Blackacre. *A* successfully sues *T* and obtains judgment, but when it comes time for the court to measure *A*'s damages, *T* argues that the damages should only be measured by the life estate, not the value of the full fee simple absolute. *A* counters that such measurement would give *T* a windfall, allowing him to escape full liability for the trespass. The traditional view here is that T is right, and that doing otherwise would give A the windfall, and that Owen could join the suit if he chose.

Second, the life tenant keeps all the income, rents, and profits from the use of the land during the life estate.

Example 2: Owen transfers Blackacre "to A for life." A leases Black-acre — a farm — to B in April. B plants wheat on the farm. A dies. B enters Blackacre to harvest the wheat. O sues B in trespass. In this suit, what result? Judgment for B. B is not trespassing; he is merely recovering the source of income that made his lease desirable. The crop was not intended as a permanent improvement to Blackacre. B can harvest the crop because that's what A would have done.[3]

Third, a life tenant has obligations. The life tenant must keep the premises in ordinary repair, must pay taxes, must pay the interest on any mortgage for all the property, and in some jurisdictions must pay insurance premiums. A life tenant is not entitled to contribution or reimbursement from the future interest holder for these expenses. The repairs required to be made are ordinary repairs only. The life tenant is not obligated to improve the property; to repair extraordinary damages caused by storms, earthquakes, fires, etc. (but it may be his duty to repair damages from ordinary wear and tear). Likewise, a tenant who constructs improvements on the land cannot seek partial payment from future interest holders. We take this up in detail later in this chapter in the discussion of the cause of action for waste.

As for mortgages and notes secured by the property and outstanding when the life tenant takes his estate, the life tenant is responsible for the interest payments but not for the principal of any loan secured by the property. A life tenant who pays the principal on a mortgage can seek contribution[4] from the future interest holder.

Example 3: O transfers Blackacre "to A for life" when Blackacre has a 30-year mortgage on it, and the mortgage still has 25 years worth of payments on it. A, age 80, pays off this mortgage. When A seeks contribution from O, the holder of the future interest, a reversion, O answers that he never

---

3. The common law has a word for the crop — it was an "emblement," a product of the soil. The result in the trespass suit would be different if the harvest was of a vineyard or orchard — the fruit of which was of permanent value to Blackacre and so not an emblement. Most of our jurisdictions recognize the law of emblements. Although sometimes courts have been urged to do so when a lessee improves realty with a building, the principles behind the law of emblements have not been applied so as to include improvements to realty generally.

4. Here is a word that should send you to your law dictionary. Contribution is a cause of action for reimbursing a life tenant who does more than fulfill her obligations. It also governs the relationships between persons with interests in the same property. We will meet it again when discussing the relationships between holders of concurrent interests.

would have paid the mortgage off, couldn't have afforded to do so, and fully expected, considering A's advanced age, to be making the mortgage payments as they fell due. O's answer is the right one — A can recover what O will have saved by not having made the payments, discounted to the present value of those savings, but that recovery is not the full pay-off price of the mortgage.

Although some states require the life tenant to insure buildings on the land, most do not. In these states, a life tenant who insures the building anyway cannot seek reimbursement from the future interest holder. Some states hold a life tenant may keep any insurance proceeds received on any claim made against the policy, while other states hold the life tenant and the remaindermen must split any insurance proceeds according to the relative values of each person's interest (which can be calculated using actuarial tables).

Example 4: O transfers Blackacre "to A for life." A, knowing that he must pass the property on to the holder of a future interest, purchases a fire insurance policy on Blackacre. A fire destroys Blackacre and A dies in the fire. The insurer refuses to pay the claim on the policy made by the administrator of A's decedent's estate since interest of the insured ends with the death of the life tenant. Is this refusal justified? Of course not. The law of insurance and the law of estates are distinct branches of the law, and the administrator is not concerned with the insured's estate, but his contractual rights under the policy.

Further, a life tenant has a duty to pay real property taxes. This duty includes an obligation to buy the property at a tax sale. This makes sense: if the life tenant has the duty to pay taxes, then he has the duty to remedy the situation when the taxes fall into default and the local government seeks to sell the property to satisfy that default. Moreover, if the government makes a special assessment against the property for permanent improvements, such as streets, sidewalks, sewers, and so on, most states hold the life tenant and the remainderman liable for each person's proportionate share (again based on relative values of each person's interest).

Example 5: Arnie holds a life estate in Blackacre. He defaults on a special assessment due and unpaid for so long that the taxing authorities seize Blackacre and sell it for non-payment. After notifying Bernice, the future interest holder, Arnie bids at the tax sale and obtains title. He then gives Bernice a second notice that she should pay a part of the assessment permanently benefiting her remainder. Bernice refuses. What advice would you give Arnie at this point? You might tell him that his acquisition of the tax title in his own name could be construed as an ouster and start the statute of limitations for adverse possession running against Bernice's interest. An ouster notice might get Bernice to pay.

(4) Life Estate or Fee Simple

When a nonlawyer prepares a will, deed, or other transfer document, sometimes the issue of whether a transferor or grantor intended to give the transferee a fee simple absolute, a life estate, or some nonfreehold estate arises. A court trying this issue will first read the plain language of the document, attempting to ascertain the grantor or testator's intent. When that doesn't work, often the court resorts to rules of construction. **Rules of construction** are not laws, but are accepted suppositions that can be rebutted by evidence. One rule of construction is that the testator intended to give away all her property through her will. An interpretation that disposes of all the testator's property in the will rather than resorting to the state's intestacy statute is favored. A corollary of the first rule is that a partial intestacy is disfavored. Another rule of construction is that a grantor or testator conveys her full interest in the property unless the intent to pass a lesser estate is clearly expressed or necessarily implied by the terms of the deed or will. Thus "to A, Blackacre to be used as her home for so long as she desires," might be held a life estate, while "to A while the property is unsold" might not. What's the difference? The reference to the termination of A's estate in an event outside of his control in the latter instance makes it likely that what was transferred was some type of defeasible estate. Likewise, "to A for the time he keeps the property up" refers to only one of the attributes of a life tenant's rights and duties, and so probably is something less.

Example: O transfers Blackacre "to A from the first of May, 2007, he having the privilege of moving out anytime." Although this might be a lease of some type, it is clearly dependent on making use of the property and is most likely a life estate, A's being able to use it being dependent on his being alive. We might also say that this life estate is subject to early termination if he moves out, but if we construe toward the higher estate, the life estate is that estate.

(c) Fee Tail and Fee Simple Conditional

The fee tail and fee simple conditional are related estates — in fact, one replaced the other and both are created by the same language: "**to A and the heirs of his body**." Initially these words created a **fee simple conditional**. Its holder had a fee simple absolute when he first had an heir. At the time, "heir" meant a male heir, the system of inheritance then in use being *primogeniture*, or inheritance limited to the eldest son. Before the birth of a son, the holder of the fee simple conditional had a fee simple conditioned on the birth of an heir. If its holder died without an heir, the property reverted back to the grantor. By the Statute *De Donis Conditionalibus* (1285), the fee simple conditional was changed into a fee tail, and thereafter, when O conveyed "to A and the heirs of his body," a fee tail, inheritable to the last member of the grantee's family line, was established. And a younger son inherited and became the heir if his elder brother died before inheriting. South Carolina is the only jurisdiction recognizing the fee simple conditional today.

Can you think of a family still using a line of succession dictated by primogeniture? If you are thinking of the English royal family, the House of Windsor, you have probably the most famous example of the use of the fee tail in the world. Daughters don't inherit the English throne unless there is no son — which is how the current Queen Elizabeth II came to sit (seisin, again) on her throne.

Desiring to maintain large estates as a unit for generations so as to preserve a family's wealth and social standing, a grantor might have created a fee tail. The **fee tail** in effect was a series of life estates. A enjoyed a life estate; on A's death the property automatically passed by primogeniture to A's eldest son for his life; on his death the property passed to that son's eldest; and so on until the family line ended (died **"without issue"** is the traditional phrase for this event), at which point the property reverted back to the grantor (or more likely to one of the grantor's heirs). The ending of the grantee's bloodline is called **failure of issue**. The fee tail thus thinks in dynastic, not individual, terms.

Today a fee tail is a freehold estate in which there is a fixed line of succession limited to the heirs of the body of a grantee or devisee, by which the regular, default rules of succession are cut off. So, in the transfer "to A and the heirs of his body," the words "to A" are words of purchase, and the phrase "and the heirs of his body" are words of limitation — sometimes called in this instance **"words of procreation."** Down through the generations, each generation of A's heirs (still defined by the words of purchase in the original transfer, deed, or will, or by descent) has a life estate. For example, at common law, a fee tail could be a **"fee tail special"** — e.g., "to A and the heirs of her body by her husband Ben" — or **"fee tails male"** or **"fee tail female"** — e.g., "to A" and the male (or female) heirs of his body.

> **Example:** O transfers Blackacre "to A and the issue of his body." What estate is created by these words? It is not a fee tail because no words of limitation are used indicating inheritance, so it is a life estate measured by two generations of A's family.

Likewise, "to A and his offspring" or "to A and his seed" are insufficient to produce a fee tail. Today the law construes the words of a grant against a finding that an estate is entailed.

So fee tails, like life estates, are not devisable or generally inheritable because the property passes from one generation to the next under the terms of the fee tail grant. The fee tail, when used in conjunction with a principle of primogeniture, served to preserve the largest English estates intact rather than to split them up among the children of the nobility. It was also early used to return land transferred to a child to the family's estate should the line of that child die out. This second use of the estate was particularly useful in transfers of land to a second or third son, who normally would not inherit the family's main estate under the system of primogeniture. (During the time the estate was first created, mortality rates due to war, disease, and the limited ability of farmers to produce enough food were such that it took on average a minimum of four children in a family to ensure the continuation of a family dynasty.)

Today all but four states have abolished the fee tail by statute, many doing so in the early nineteenth century. States still recognizing the estate are three New England states (Maine, Massachusetts, and Rhode Island) and Delaware. In these four states, the holder of the fee tail can break the entail or **disentail** the property simply by conveying his interest in fee simple absolute to a third party, who takes it in fee simple absolute. Often the beneficiaries of disentailing are creditors of the estate holder, and often the third party is the entailed owner's attorney, who serves as strawman, or someone bound to convey it right back in fee simple absolute. In all other states, the fee tail is abolished by statute.[5] The statutes abolishing it result in one of several configurations of estates: the most common of those has either the first grantee taking a fee simple absolute, or else a life estate after which the heirs of his body take a fee simple absolute. Only about seven states use the second configuration. A few states preserve the fee tail for one generation.

Fee tails, even where authorized, are seldom used. More than that, the use of the fee tail was unusual even at common law, because grantors and testators often did not want to take the chance that after their children and grandchildren, there would be a failure of issue. Better to have used the conveyance "to A and his heirs" or some variation or to split the fee into more acceptable present and future interests.

WASTE

(a) Voluntary, Permissive, and Ameliorating Waste

Ever since at least the middle of the thirteenth century, "*waste*" of property by a life tenant has been an actionable injury for a remainderman or reversioner,

---

5. Often these statutes simply said something like "the estate in fee tail is abolished." Thus, to know whether the statute applies, one must know the words necessary to create the estate in the first place.

with damages the traditional remedy. The Statutes of Marlborough (1267) and of Gloucester (1278) confirmed its use and expanded its remedies — particularly to the use of injunctions — in English courts. Waste is a cause of action for substantial injury to these future interests caused by the life tenant. Under English common law, a life tenant was obligated to deliver the property in essentially the same condition or use as when the life tenant took possession. So waste occurs when the possessory life tenant permanently impairs the property's condition or value to the future interest holder's detriment. In general, it involves the abuse, alteration, or destruction of realty by a person not a trespasser and not holding a fee simple absolute.[6] The future interest holder has standing to enjoin waste.

A grant or transfer can be made "to A for life, without impeachment for waste," meaning that the holder of the life estate is immune from suit by the future interest holder.

Waste falls into several categories. **Affirmative** or **voluntary waste** occurs when the life tenant actively changes the property's use or condition, usually in a way that substantially decreases the property's value. A court will enjoin affirmative waste. A second category of waste, **permissive waste**, is akin to nonfeasance — the life tenant fails to prevent some harm to the property. For example, one court found that not making normal repairs to a water pump that resulted in dead lawn, shrubs, and trees was permissive waste. See Kimbrough v. Reed, 130 Idaho 512, 943 P.2d 1232 (1997). The life tenant was required to pay damages to the remainderman. The law of permissive waste evolved to become the duties discussed earlier: to make ordinary repairs, to pay interest on debt, to pay taxes and assessments, and in some jurisdictions to pay insurance premiums. A variation of affirmative waste is **meliorating** or **ameliorating waste**. In England, the law of waste was strict: A life tenant could not stop growing crops and begin grazing cattle, for example, even if it made the property more productive or valuable. Even changing crops may have been waste. Courts in the United States have allowed reasonable changes in use and condition. For example, in Melms v. Pabst Brewing Company, 79 N.W. 738 (Wis. 1899), a life tenant owned a stately mansion in the midst of a brewery complex. Over time other commercial activities encroached on the mansion to the point at which it was no longer suitable for use as a residence, and not efficiently convertible to commercial purposes. The court held under the circumstances that demolishing the mansion and replacing it with a commercial building would not be waste. In effect, meliorating waste is non-compensable waste. In evaluating whether it will be permitted, courts look at the life tenant's expected remaining life, the need for change, and the good faith of the life tenant and future interest holder in proposing or opposing the change.

---

6. Waste is used to regulate two other relationships in the law of real property — the landlord-tenant and the mortgagor-mortgagee relationship.

(b) Open Mines Doctrine

The open mines doctrine sets out rules applicable to natural resources, particularly minerals. Under the **open mines doctrine**, a life tenant may mine and remove minerals (and keep the profits) if the grantor had opened the mines or began the mining and removal before he granted the life estate. The presumption is the grantor intended the life tenant to continue using the property as the grantor had been using it. That same presumption swayed courts to conclude, unless the future interest holder consented, that the life tenant could not begin or conduct mining operations if no mining took place before the life estate began. While England applied the same rule to timber cutting, American courts in some cases allow timber cutting using the ameliorative waste analysis.

(c) Economic Waste

A variation on waste is economic waste. **Economic waste** occurs when the income from property is insufficient to pay the expenses the life tenant has a duty to pay: ordinary maintenance, real estate taxes, interest on mortgages, and in some jurisdictions insurance. Economic waste does not mean the property is not being used for its highest and best use, only that it does not pay for its own upkeep. The life tenant — and in some cases the remainderman — can bring an action to sell the property if economic waste occurs.

In Baker v. Weedon, 262 So. 2d 641 (Miss. 1972), Anna Weedon, the life tenant, suffered personal economic distress and wished to sell land (her life estate interest and the remainder interest) and put the money in a trust so she could use the income from the trust to pay for her personal living expenses. The court held that economic waste does not mean the life tenant personally would be better off financially, or that a court can act when a life tenant needs to sell (not just her interest but the remainderman's as well) for economic reasons. Only if the income from the property is insufficient to "pay taxes and maintain the property" could a court order a sale. The property in that case generated just enough money each year to pay the taxes and maintenance. Hence the court found no economic waste.

DEFEASIBLE FEE SIMPLE ESTATES

The three freehold estates developed to this point — fee simple absolute, life estate, and fee tail (and the fee simple conditional) — are subject to several variations, particularly of the fee simple absolute, that may be prematurely terminated by a condition subsequent. A **condition subsequent** is an event whose occurrence or nonoccurrence will terminate the estate. Once the condition subsequent occurs, the estate holder's interest ends and the property either reverts to the original grantor or passes to a third party.

Example: Armas transfers Blackacre "to Britney and her heirs, but if Britney sells alcohol on Blackacre, then to Carrie." Armas has transferred a fee simple to Britney but it is not a fee simple absolute since Britney may lose all her interest in Blackacre if she sells alcohol on Blackacre.

The example illustrates the concept of a defeasible estate. A life estate may also be defeasible, but most defeasible estates are defeasible fee simples. Three distinct defeasible fees have evolved, each with its own label and characteristics. Britney's estate in the above example is called a fee simple subject to an executory limitation. If the property were to return to Armas, the grantor, Britney's interest would be called a fee simple subject to a condition subsequent. The grant could have been worded differently to create a fee simple determinable.

(a) Fee Simple Determinable

A *fee simple determinable* is an estate that would be a fee simple absolute but for a provision in the transfer document that states that the estate shall *automatically* end on the happening of an event or nonevent. It is the creation of American courts and is the "youngest" fee simple, often used as a form of private land use control. An example is "to A and her heirs so long as the property is used for church purposes," or "to A and his heirs unless liquor is sold on the property." Although it is sometimes said that no words of art are necessary to create such estates and that the transferor's intent controls, the words typically employed to create a fee simple determinable are "so long as," "during," "while," "unless," and "until." All these words, with the phrases that follow, are words of limitation, indicating a fee simple determinable.

The significant difference between a fee simple absolute and a fee simple determinable is that while both potentially have an infinite or perpetual duration, the fee simple determinable might terminate automatically if the condition subsequent occurs. Historically a grantor could not provide that the property would pass to a third party if the condition subsequent eventuated and the fee simple determinable ended. The only option was to have the property return to the original grantor (or his heirs if the original grantor was dead). The chance that the property might return to the grantor if the condition subsequent happened is called the **possibility of reverter**. In sum, absent words to the contrary, a fee simple determinable is a present possessory estate followed by a possibility of reverter in the grantor. Sometimes the possibility of reverter is expressed in the deed or will creating the fee simple determinable; if not expressed it will be implied as part of the nature of a fee simple determinable.

Example 1: In a state recognizing the fee simple conditional, if O conveys "to A and the heirs of her body," what estate is created before the birth of an heir? A has a present interest, held in a fee simple determinable. In the context, this estate's words of limitation might read, "to A until the birth of an heir," making A's fee simple a determinable one, followed by a future interest held in a possibility of reverter by O.

Example 2: Armas deeds Blackacre to Britney "so long as Britney does not sell alcohol on Blackacre." Britney owns a fee simple determinable estate in Blackacre that could last forever. However, if Britney sells alcohol on Blackacre, the property automatically returns to the grantor, Armas.

(b) Fee Simple Subject to a Condition Subsequent

Closely related to the fee simple determinable is the **fee simple subject to a condition subsequent**. The holder of a fee simple subject to a condition subsequent may hold it forever, but could lose it entirely if the condition subsequent occurs. The difference between a fee simple determinable and a fee simple subject to a condition subsequent is that the fee simple determinable ends automatically upon the happening of the condition subsequent, whereas the grantor of a fee simple subject to a condition subsequent must assert his right of entry (also called "right of reentry" or "power of termination"). Until the grantor exercises his power of termination, the holder of the fee simple subject to a condition subsequent continues to own the property.

The fee simple subject to a condition subsequent usually can be identified by some of the following language in the granting instrument: "provided that," "but if," "on the condition that," or "provided, however." Compare these phrases with the one used to create a fee simple determinable.

Example 1: Armas transfers Blackacre "to Britney; provided, however, if Britney sells alcohol on Blackacre, then Armas may re-enter and retake the land." Britney owns a fee simple subject to a condition subsequent in Blackacre. Her interest may last forever. If she sells alcohol on Blackacre, however, Armas can elect to take back the property.

As is the case with the fee simple determinable, the only person who can retake the property on the event of the condition subsequent is the grantor or his heirs. The grantor's right to retake the property is called the **right of entry** or **of reentry**, or the **power of termination**.

Example 2: Alex conveys Blackacre "to Betty provided that she is not married." This was an invalid condition, thought to restrain a person's right to marriage, and void as a matter of public policy. On the other hand, "to Betty so long as she remains unmarried" is valid as an attempt to support Betty until her marriage. So a limitation on marriage was valid, but a condition was not. Limitations might be, "to Betty so long as she remains a widow," or "to Bart while he remains my widower." Both create a determinable life estate. See Restatement of Property § 108 (1936). That is, that remarriage might terminate the life estate early is no bar to its still being a life estate.

Some commentators have been highly critical of this distinction. See Olin Browder, "Conditions and Limitations on Marriage," 39 Mich. L. Rev. 1288 (1941). Such a distinction has some evidentiary value. But how much? It has also provoked statutes in some states prohibiting conditions on marriage or remarriage. California, Georgia, and Indiana have such statutes. Often, however, these statutes explicitly do not reach limitations in support of marriage.

There are some different legal consequences between a fee simple determinable and a fee simple subject to a condition subsequent. First, title automatically reverts to the holder of the possibility of reverter on the broken condition, so the owner of the fee simple determinable loses all interest in the property immediately. Once title reverts, it is too late for a waiver. A new deed is required to undo the effect of the broken condition. On the other hand, since the holder of a right of entry does not automatically gain immediate possession upon a broken condition, the holder may waive any transgression. In that case the owner of the fee simple subject to a condition subsequent continues owning the land.

Second, unless modified by statute (which many states have done), the running of the statute of limitations for adverse possession starts at different times. The adverse possession statute starts running against the holder of a possibility of reverter on the day the condition subsequent happens. In contrast, since the owner of a fee simple subject to a condition subsequent continues owning the property even if the designated event occurs, the adverse possession limitations period does not begin to run until the holder of the right of entry exercises that right. A few states by judicial decision or by statute equate the two estates for adverse possession purposes and begin the running of the statute of limitations as soon as the condition occurs. Finally, while most states have adopted a uniform rule on the assignability of possibilities of reverter and rights of entry — either both are assignable or neither is — in a few states the possibility of reverter is transferable, while the right of reentry is not.

Commentators have long urged that the two estates be consolidated by statute and that the remaining differences are too small to warrant continuing both. The critics contend that despite the fact that the fee simple determinable has an automatic termination feature and the fee simple subject to a condition subsequent does not, a reentry is never automatic. To them the view that O turns up and A gives up possession is simply unrealistic. Further, as a matter of policy, any exercise of O's rights ought to be judicially supervised in any event, no matter what words the grantor uses.

Some state legislatures have responded to the problems that possibilities of reverter and rights of reentry create for conveyancing attorneys by enacting statutes that limit their duration to a period of 20 or 30 years. These interests must be asserted within the statutory time period or else be forever barred. A few courts have done the same thing without waiting for their legislatures by limiting the life of a possibility of reverter or right of reentry to a reasonable length of time. See, e.g., Mildram v. Town of Wells, 611 A.2d 84 (Me. 1992) (holding that not asserting a right of reentry for 82 years vested the holder of the present interest with a fee simple absolute). Other courts have found, based on the language used by the drafter, that the future interest was personal to the grantor or transferor and not intended to be alienable, devisable, or descendible for the benefit of his or her heirs.

(c) Distinguishing a Fee Simple Determinable From a Fee Simple Subject to a Condition Subsequent From a Covenant

At times it may be critical to determine whether a given grant is a fee simple determinable or a fee simple subject to a condition subsequent. If properly drafted, the determination is easy. A grant using the words "as long as," "so long as," "during," "while," "unless," or "until" creates a fee simple determinable. A grant using the words "provided that," "provided, however," "but if," or "on condition that" creates a fee simple subject to a condition subsequent. Problems arise when the grant uses words from both categories or the grant is otherwise ambiguous.

A court will try to ascertain the grantor's intent as expressed in the document as a whole. Courts disfavor forfeitures, however. Consequently, when in doubt, as a matter of construction, a court more likely will construe a grant as a fee simple subject to a condition subsequent rather than as a fee simple determinable because the fee simple subject to a condition subsequent allows the possessor to continue ownership until the holder of the right of reentry (power of termination) acts to retake the property.

In some cases a court may interpret the qualification to the title as not being a divesting condition at all, but instead a covenant. A **covenant** is a promise to do or not do some act. A grantor may seek injunctive relief or damages for a breach of a covenant, but the owner of the fee simple will not forfeit ownership. In some cases a court may even interpret limiting language as **precatory language** (giving rise to an unenforceable suggestion, expectation, or intention) instead of as a condition or a covenant.

(d) Fee Simple Subject to an Executory Limitation

One shared characteristic of the fee simple determinable and the fee simple subject to a condition subsequent is that only the original grantor or his heirs can hold the future interest (the possibility of reverter or the right of reentry). For more than 200 years in England, a grant could not divest a defeasible fee in favor of a third party. The grantor had to retain a future interest for himself. Finally, by the Statute of Uses enacted in 1536, grantors could pass future interests following a defeasible fee simple to a third party. After more than 200 years of judges and lawyers repeating the mantra "only the grantor can have a future interest following a defeasible fee," the English legal community settled on a new label for the expanded rights.

The same granting language that would create either a fee simple determinable or a fee simple subject to a condition subsequent creates a **fee simple subject to an executory limitation**. (also known as a fee simple on executory limitation). Only one label for the possessory interest was coined, not two. The new label given to the future interest to a third party following a fee simple subject to an executory limitation is the **executory interest**.

Example 1: Armas transfers Blackacre "to Britney as long as Britney does not sell alcohol on Blackacre." Britney's present possessory interest is held in a fee simple determinable. Armas's future interest is a possibility of reverter.

Example 2: Abe transfers Blackacre "to Betty so long as Betty does not marry Charlie." Betty's interest is again a present possessory one, held in a fee simple determinable, with language indicating a limitation, not a condition, on marriage. See the prior discussion in this Chapter on the fee simple subject to a condition subsequent. Even viewed as a condition, it is not a general restraint on marriage, just a condition on a particular marriage, and what few cases American courts have decided on this issue, have upheld the limitation as valid.

Example 3: Armas transfers Blackacre "to Britney as long as Britney does not sell alcohol on Blackacre, then to Carl and his heirs." Britney's estate is a fee simple subject to an executory limitation. Carl's future interest is an executory interest (technically a *shifting* executory interest, as will be discussed in Chapter 10).

CLASSIFYING ESTATES IN FEE SIMPLE — A FLOWCHART

If an estate is alienable, devisable, and descendible, then ask yourself the following questions, in the order presented in the following flowchart:

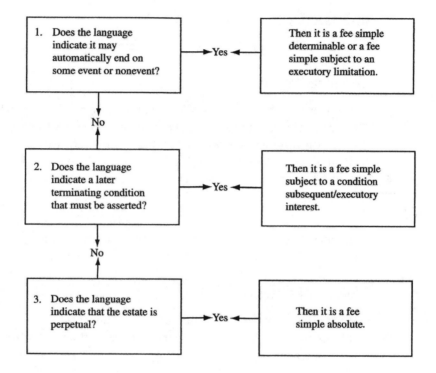

Examples

A Present and a Future Estate

1. (a) O, having full ownership, conveys Blackacre "to A for ten years." What is A's estate?
   (b) What is O's interest?
   (c) What estate will A and O have in ten years?

Words of Purchase and Limitation

2. In the following conveyances, does A hold an estate in fee simple absolute?
   (a) O conveys "to A."
   (b) O conveys "to A and his heirs."
   (c) O conveys "to A and his heirs, but if A dies, to B and his heirs."

No Issue

3. O conveys "to A and his bodily heirs, but if A dies without issue, to B and his heirs." A has a daughter, C, who predeceases A. This may occur, for example, if a farmer, Orville, dies, leaving his farm to his eldest son, "Arnold, and his bodily heirs, but if Arnold dies without issue, to Bart and his heirs." What estates are created?

An Estate for Joint Lives

4. O conveys "to A and B for the lives of A and B." When does the estate end?

Insurance Proceeds

5. O conveys Blackacre "to Larry for life, remainder to Freda and her heirs." Larry the life tenant insures Blackacre against fire for $100,000. Improvements on Blackacre are worth $75,000. They burn to the ground. Larry claims the proceeds of the policy. Freda appears and claims the bulk of the proceeds. Can she do so successfully?

She Meant Well

6. O writes, "I give my house and lot to you for your residence. Don't sell it. Let your sister have the rest of my property." What estate is transferred?

A Slew of Estates

7. What estates are created in the following transfers?
   (a) O conveys "to A and his heirs so long as the property is used as a residence."
   (b) O conveys "to A and her heirs, on the express condition that Blackacre be used only for residential purposes, but if it ceases to be used for such purposes, then O and her heirs shall have the right to reenter."
   (c) O conveys "to A, provided that the estate granted shall cease and determine if liquor is sold, used, or stored on the premises."
   (d) O conveys "to A and his heirs, it being my wish and purpose in making this conveyance that the property be used for residential purposes."
   (e) O conveys "to A and his heirs, provided further that O and A agree and promise that the property shall only be used for residential purposes."
   (f) O conveys Blackacre "to A so long as he wishes to live on the property."
   (g) O conveys Blackacre "to A so long as he cares for me during my life."

(h) O conveys Blackacre "to A, provided that he lives on the property, but if he does not live there, then to O."

(i) O conveys "to A for life, then if B graduates from law school, to B and her heirs so long as the land is used for a law office." What interests do the parties have before B graduates from law school?

(j) What interest do the parties have when B graduates from law school?

(k) O conveys "to A so long as the property is used as a residence solely, provided, however, that if it is not so used, the estate shall cease and revert to B and his heirs, who have the right to repossess the property." What estate does A have?

Defeating Devises

8. O conveys "to A and her heirs, but in case she does not sell or devise it by the time of her death, then to B and his heirs." What estates are created in this transfer?

Explanations

A Present and a Future Estate

1. (a) A has a term of years or a leasehold, a nonfreehold estate. It is a present possessory estate.

   (b) Just after the conveyance, O has a reversion in fee simple absolute. It is a future interest (currently nonpossessory). See infra Chapter 10.

   (c) After a term of years ends, A no longer has any interest in Blackacre. O will possess, among estates, the grandest of them all — a freehold held in fee simple absolute, which is what we think of when we say that a person has "ownership" of real property.

Words of Purchase and Limitation

2. (a) Yes. Today A holds an estate in fee simple absolute. The words of purchase are "to A" and the words of limitations are supplied by the canon of construction that a fee simple absolute is preferred, unless the language of the deed or will indicates the grantor or testator meant to transfer a lesser estate.

   (b) Yes. Although other words might be used, "to A and his heirs" are the recommended words to create a fee simple absolute.

   (c) No. A's estate is something less. The words of purchase are the same, but the words of limitation are "and his heirs, but if A dies to B and his heirs," and indicate that the grantor intends that descendibility and devisability not be part of A's estate; thus no fee simple absolute was intended. A holds a life estate. See Mark Reutlinger, Wills, Trusts, and Estates: Essential Terms and Concepts 92 (1993).

No Issue

3. "*A* and his bodily heirs" is interpreted to mean the same as "*A* and the heirs of his body." Hence *A* has a fee tail (or fee simple conditional), where it is recognized.

    Since *A* has a child, *C*, who predeceased him, it matters how the jurisdiction handles the failure of issue. If the state is one of the few that retains the fee tail, the land would belong to *A* as long as he lived, then to *A*'s eldest child as long as he lived, then to his eldest child as long as he lived, until *A*'s bloodline ended, at which point the land would go to B (or his heirs). In the Example, *A*'s line died with him and his daughter, *C*; so on *A*'s death B would get a fee simple absolute estate in the farm.

    States that have abolished the fee simple conditional and the fee tail have interpreted language that historically created one of the two estates in two different ways. The majority of states treat the "and the heirs of his body" and "and his bodily heirs" language as words of limitation indicating a fee simple absolute — i.e., just like "and his heirs." In those states, *A* received a fee simple absolute, and B got nothing.

    In other states *A* has a life estate and if he dies with children living at his death (or grandchildren if no surviving child) the child (or grandchild) takes the land in fee simple absolute. If *A* dies without issue, the property passes to B in fee simple absolute.

    Which interpretation applies makes a big difference in the Example since *A* died without a surviving child (*C* predeceased *A*). In the first instance *A* owns the farm in fee simple absolute and can devise it in his will or it passes to his heirs (siblings, cousins, etc.). In the second instance, *A*'s interest in the farm ends on *A*'s death and B owns the farm in fee simple absolute.

An Estate for Joint Lives

4. The estate ends either (1) when the first of A and B dies, or (2) when the last of the two dies. The intent of the transferor or grantor, O, controls the choice. That choice involves either construing the greatest estate granted by the transferor or freeing the title of this life estate at the earliest possible time and vesting the transferor's reversion. Thus, policies of either presuming the words of conveyance against the grantor or freeing up the alienability of the title conflict here. The transferor's intent should control. If there were added to this conveyance a "remainder to the survivor of them in fee simple absolute," the length of the life estate would be clear. (This remainder would, as we will see, be a contingent remainder, lacking as it does ascertainability of the identity of the survivor until the

death of either *A* or *B*.) See 1 *American Law of Property* § 2.15, at 128 (James Casner, ed., 1952).

Insurance Proceeds

5. Some courts hold that a life tenant has no duty to insure the property. If Larry has no duty under a state's law to insure the improvements, then the proceeds should be wholly his, and some courts have so held. There may be insurance law questions as to what Larry can insure, but Freda as the holder of the remainder has no standing to raise those questions. (The moral here is for the present and future interest holders to get together and purchase insurance, making sure that everyone's interest is adequately covered — or for the person creating the tenancy to impose the duty to insure specially on the tenant.) See 1 *American Law of Property* § 2.23, at 159 (James Casner, ed., 1952).

She Meant Well

6. Several aspects of this language are relevant. The "for your residence" language may indicate a life estate; dead people don't need a house. Similarly, the "don't sell it" language perhaps negates the alienability aspect of a fee simple absolute. On the other hand, perhaps the drafter intended merely to reenforce and define the purpose of the writing — to provide a residence for the transferee — i.e., precatory language. The restraints on use and alienability on the holder of the estate may be consistent with either a fee simple absolute or a life estate. If the court finds it to be a fee simple, the court will independently review the "don't sell it" language to decide whether the restraint is an unreasonable restraint on the alienability of land. Still, perhaps the "rest of my property" language indicates a future interest to follow a life tenancy in the house and lot. If this is a lay drafter, however, one cannot put too much store in such a person's knowledge of future interests. Also relevant to a determination of the issue of how to define the estate are the other provisions of the transfer. Is the sister otherwise well provided for by the "rest of my property" language? As things stand, the jurisdiction's statutes preferring the larger estate, such as a fee simple, most likely will control. See White v. Brown, 559 S.W.2d 938 (Tenn. 1977), discussed and distinguished in Williams v. Estate of Williams, 865 S.W.2d 3 (Tenn. 1993).

A Slew of Estates

7. (a) *A* has a present interest in fee simple determinable, followed by 0's future interest, a possibility of reverter, held in fee simple absolute.

See Thomas Bergin & Paul Haskell, *Preface to Estates in Land* 48 (2d ed. 1984).

(b) *A* has a present interest in fee simple subject to a condition subsequent. *O*'s future interest is a right of reentry or a power of termination. If, after the terminating event is described, the last clause were to read instead "B and his heirs shall have the right to reenter," *A* would hold a fee simple subject to an executory limitation, and B would hold an executory interest in fee simple absolute.

(c) This is a conveyance with words indicating a fee simple determinable (the "cease and determine" phrase, indicating an automatic shift of the fee simple back to grantor *O*) and with words indicating a fee simple subject to a condition subsequent (the "provided that" language). In this ambiguous grant, the modern canon of construction, that the grantor is presumed to have conveyed whatever interest and estate he held becomes a preference for finding the larger estate in the grantee; this preference helps construe the conveyance as a present interest in *A*, held in fee simple subject to a condition subsequent, *O*'s retaining a right of reentry at the moment of the conveyance.

(d) *A* has a fee simple absolute. The additional language is precatory language, indicating *O*'s desire, but is neither a condition nor a covenant, and therefore is unenforceable.

(e) *A* has a fee simple absolute. The language neither makes the interest into a fee simple determinable nor subjects it to a condition subsequent. Rather, the promise is a covenant to use the property as a residence; when he does not, the breach of this promise subjects *A* to contract remedies (e.g., damages or an injunction). The difference between a condition and a covenant is that breach of a condition results in a forfeiture of the property while the owner retains ownership when a covenant is breached, but may be subject to monetary damages or, more likely, an injunction.

(f) This conveyance creates either a determinable life estate or a fee simple determinable in *A*. A court will try to ascertain the grantor's intent based on the surrounding facts and circumstances. Today a court would tend to find that *O* transferred the fee simple determinable, the larger estate, to *A*, the grantee. If the grant is a fee simple determinable, *O* retains a possibility of reverter. If, on the other hand, the grant is a determinable life estate, *O* has a reversion, getting Blackacre back when *A* ceases living on Blackacre and no later than *A*'s death. If *A*'s interest is a fee simple determinable and *A* continued to live on the property up to his death, *A* has satisfied the condition and, as a result, at the moment of death he holds the property in fee simple absolute. Some good it will do him! This result will, however, benefit his heirs or assigns.

(g) *A's* interest is tied to the transferor's (*O's*) life, so it is a life estate, but is it measured by *O's* or *A's* life? If a court is to construe the doubtful case toward the higher estate, then a court should require a clear express of intent otherwise, and that clear intent does not appear to be present here. *A* has a life estate, measured by his life.

(h) *A* has a fee simple subject to a condition subsequent. It is not subject to an executory limitation. Such a limitation would require that the reentry be made by a third party. The drafting, however, is extremely sloppy: Instead of "then to *O*," better to have said that "*O* has the power to terminate *A*'s interest and the right to reenter the property." This makes plain that the termination is not automatic and that *O* must do something, through either self-help or at law, to reenter. See 1 *American Law of Property* § 4.6, at 417 (James Casner, ed., 1952).

(i) *A* has a life estate, *B* has remainder (a contingent remainder since *B* must satisfy a contingency — graduating from law school — to take after *A* dies). Because it is possible *A* may die before *B* graduates, *O* the grantor retains a reversion. *O* also has a possibility of reverter, but as a matter of tradition, lawyers only mention the first interest *O* holds, the reversion.

(j) *B*'s remainder interest is no longer contingent. It is a vested remainder in fee simple determinable. Contingent and vested remainders are developed more fully in the next chapter. Since *B*'s remainder is vested, *O*'s reversion has ended, but *O*'s future interest, the possibility of reverter, remains. Thus, *B* has a vested remainder in fee simple determinable, and *O* has a possibility of reverter. See 1 *American Law of Property* § 4.12, at 427 (James Casner, ed., 1952).

(k) *A* has a fee simple subject to an executory limitation. The language is ambiguous, indicating either a fee or a life estate. The preference for the larger estate permits this language to be construed as a fee simple subject to an executory limitation. *B* has an executory interest (in the next chapter we learn that *B* has a *shifting* executory interest).

Defeating Devises

8. The power to sell or devise, sometimes a power to "consume" or "appoint," is known as a power of appointment. This power is used when the life estate is to be used for the support and maintenance of the life tenant, whose needs may become greater with time. In a substantial minority of states, the presence of this power expands what might be a present interest held in a life estate into a fee simple absolute. This in turn means that the following future interest was void at early common law and in our early cases. "No fee on a fee," said the early lawyers. On the other hand, this future interest might well be a shifting executory interest (of this, more in Chapter 10). Early American cases and commentators,

notably Chancellor James Kent of New York, took the view that the executory interest was void, not just once the power of appointment was exercised, but from the moment of the transfer and as a matter of law. See Jackson v. Robins, 16 Johns 537 (N.Y. 1819), discussed in 4 Kent's Comm. *535. Oliver Wendell Holmes, Jr., commenting on Kent's view, criticized it, saying that there was no logical reason for it, adding that if the drafter had conveyed "to A for life, with A having the power to sell or devise the property, remainder to B," the remainder would be valid. John Chipman Gray, then Professor of Law at Harvard Law School and the author of the first casebook on Property, agreed with Holmes, as did Lewis Simes's treatise on Future Interests. See Fox v. Snow, 76 A.2d 877 (N.J. 1950) (Vanderbilt, C.J., dissenting and reviewing the controversy among these notables of American law). It might be best said that if the executory interest is invalid, it is invalid because it is repugnant to the preceding interest as a matter of construction, not a matter of law. Why would the transferor wish the executory interest to follow an alienable and devisable estate? The question is even harder to answer once it has been sold or devised. So a fee simple absolute might be created from the beginning. See Woodlief v. Clay, 71 S.W.2d 600, 603 (Tex. App. 1934). The broader the power of appointment, the more likely it is that a court will embrace the minority rule as a matter of construing the transferor's intent.

CHAPTER 10

FUTURE INTERESTS

INTRODUCTION

The previous chapter introduced present interests and estates, and, to a lesser extent, future interests. An estate held in fee simple absolute, for example, is perpetual ownership or ownership until the end of time. A fee simple absolute can be diagrammed on a timeline as follows:

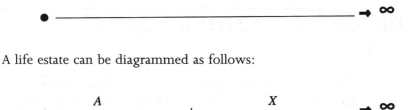

A life estate can be diagrammed as follows:

where *A* has a life estate. X has either a remainder in fee simple absolute or a reversion, depending on who X is.

Perhaps the most important feature of these two diagrams is the ∞ symbol at the end of each timeline. From the earliest years of English and American common law, judges and lawyers classify interests and estates by visualizing who controlled ownership of land from the moment of the effectiveness of a deed, will, or other instrument until infinity. If a person owned a life estate, their legal minds wanted to know who (or whose heirs or assigns) took possession once the life estate ended. To illustrate, Orville transfers Blackacre to Andrew for life. Andrew has a life estate or, more fully described, Andrew has a present interest held in a life estate. Because he transferred less than his full interest in Blackacre and will take back possession of Blackacre once Andrew dies, Orville has a future interest, a reversion. A reversion is a future interest since the holder does not have a present possessory right to the land. Orville has a present property right, but the possession is deferred until a later time. Nothing else being said, Orville holds that reversion in fee simple absolute.

Example: Orville leases Blackacre "to Alfred for ten years." Once again, Orville has a reversion, just as a landlord might have a reversion after an apartment lease terminates. The difference between this example and the preceding text is that Alfred has a nonfreehold estate — and the difference between a freehold and a nonfreehold is that the former has seisin, and the latter does not. But the common law lawyer always had to account for the seisin — it always had to be somewhere — so the lawyer spoke of Orville's reversion being subject to Alfred's lease, but treated the reversion as established at the moment of the lease's effectiveness.

Some commentators thus say that the nonfreehold estate rides piggyback on the reversion, and both the lease and the reversion are treated as running concurrently. This piggyback rule eliminates later confusion. See John Makdisi and Daniel Bogart, *Estates in Land and Future Interests*, 50 (5th ed. 2007).

DISTINGUISHING PRESENT INTERESTS AND FUTURE INTERESTS

A person's interest in property has two analytical components. First, the interest is either a present interest or a future interest. Second, the interest is held in some type of estate. For shorthand purposes, lawyers normally think and classify future interests into those held by the transferor or grantor, and those held by a third party, meaning someone other than the transferor or grantor. A reversion is an example of the first category, and a remainder is an example of the second.

Example: Orville transfers Blackacre to Andrew for life, then to Becky for life, then to Carrie. Andrew owns a present interest held in a life estate. It is a present possessory interest, meaning Andrew can use Blackacre and exclude all others, including Orville, Becky, and Carrie from Blackacre. Since here Becky also holds a life estate as a future interest, it is unwise to shorten the label of Andrew's interest in Blackacre to just a "life estate" or to assume its present interest component.

Becky has a "future interest, a vested remainder held in a life estate." So don't just say Becky has a "vested remainder in a life estate" (more about vested remainders later). The term "vested remainder" indicates a future interest, a particular future interest with its own legal attributes.

Carrie too has a future interest, her interest being a "future interest held in fee simple absolute." Becky and Carrie currently own property interests in Blackacre, but cannot use the property — they are not entitled to possession until a later date, so they merely have future *possessory* interests. Once Andrew dies, Becky's interest becomes a present possessory interest — she will have a "present interest held in a life estate." Until both Andrew and Becky die, Carrie's interest remains a vested remainder in fee simple absolute. Once Andrew and Becky die, Carrie's possessory interest then becomes a fee simple absolute.

FUTURE INTERESTS RETAINED BY THE GRANTOR OR TRANSFEROR

The future interest (currently owned interest that becomes possessory at a future date) retained by the transferor (or his heirs or assigns) are the reversion, the possibility of reverter, and the right of reentry (the last a/k/a "right of entry" and "power of termination").

These three interests were introduced in the previous chapter. The **reversion** is retained by the transferor or grantor when he transfers an interest less than the one he owns to another. It follows a life estate, fee tail, or term of years.

Example: Orville transfers Blackacre to Andrew for life. Andrew has a present possessory interest in life estate in Blackacre. Orville has a reversion. Orville gets possession of Blackacre when Andrew dies.

As discussed in Chapter 9, the **possibility of reverter** is a future interest held by a transferor or grantor who transfers a fee simple determinable. The **right of reentry** follows the fee simple subject to a condition subsequent.

Once classified, a future interest thereafter has the same name: If the transferor dies or assigns his future interest to a third party, the name of the future interest remains the same. Thus, if O transfers a reversion in Blackacre to A, A's interest is a reversion.

Sorting and classifying future interests in your own mind is best accomplished by moving from the particular to the general in a process of elimination — ask whether the words used in the transfer are those preceding a possibility of reverter, a right of reentry, and if the answer to this questions is in the negative, then consider whether the future interest in the transferor or grantor is a reversion.

FUTURE INTERESTS IN THIRD-PARTY TRANSFEREES

Future interests in transferees can be divided into three fundamental types:

1. Vested remainders
2. Contingent remainders
3. Executory interests

Each of these types can be further sub-divided into more precise sub-categories.

(a) Remainders

A remainder is a future interest that "remains" after interests and estates prior to it terminate or fail. That's an alliterative but misleading definition, since the full definition of a remainder is multidimensional. It must be created, simultaneously and in the same instrument of transfer — either a will, deed, or other document — after one or more prior possessory interests. It is created in a person other than the transferor — some third party — or a legal entity. (The same future interest retained by the grantor is a reversion.)

Example 1: Owen transfers Blackacre to Abe for life, then to the Nature Conservancy. Is the remainder valid? Yes. A remainder may be created for a charity.

Example 2: Ozzie transfers Blackacre to Abby for life, then to Elvis Presley. Is the remainder valid? No. A remainder must be created in a person in existence now or in the future.

Example 3: Ollie transfers Blackacre to Alex for life. Ollie then transfers all her interest in Blackacre to Becky. What is Becky's interest? It is a future interest, a reversion, because that was what Ollie had originally, and the reversion once classified in Ollie's hands, remains a reversion in any subsequent transfer. A remainder must be created in the same transfer document as the life estate, and here it was not.

A remainder follows a prior interest that is not held a fee simple absolute. A remainder follows the natural termination of a prior interest or estate; a remainder does not divest or cut short a prior estate. So a future interest following a fee simple absolute cannot be a remainder since such a fee simple has a potentially infinite duration and so cannot terminate naturally. A remainder can, however, follow an estate held in a fee tail. In the words of Professor Joseph Warren, a remainder "is patient."

A remainder is also "successive" — its owner takes possession immediately following the natural ending of the prior interest or estate, with no gap in time between possessions. It often immediately follows a life estate. So a transfer to "A for life, then to B and her heirs," gives B a remainder, held in fee simple absolute, but "to A for life, then to B and her heirs after A's funeral" does not create a remainder in B since there is a gap in time or some waiting period between the natural termination of A's life estate and the start of B's right to possess. B owns an interest (called an executory interest), but it is not a remainder. This is another way to classify a future interest as a remainder: it is not an executory interest. On this topic, more later.

Declaring that a person has a remainder merely says he owns a future interest, an interest that may become possessory sometime in the future. As previously emphasized, the term "remainder" in and of itself does not say what estate that future interest is held in: The estate may be a life estate, a fee simple absolute, a term of years, a fee tail, a fee simple subject to condition subsequent, a fee simple determinable, or a fee simple subject to an executory limitation.

Example: Orville transfers Blackacre to Andrew for life, then to Becky. Andrew has a present possessory interest held in a life estate. Becky has a remainder. She takes possession of Blackacre immediately following the natural termination of Andrew's life estate, which occurs at Andrew's death. What estate — how long will Becky get to possess Blackacre — does Becky get? While the grant was silent on how long Becky will own Blackacre, the rules of construction favoring a fee simple interest over a life estate mean Becky's estate is a fee simple absolute. Thus, Becky's interest in Blackacre at the time of the grant is a remainder, held in fee simple absolute. Once Andrew dies, Becky's interest becomes a present interest, held in fee simple absolute. That is, future interests can become present ones, but once classified, an estate of whatever type stays the same.

(b) Executory Interests

An **executory interest** is a future interest in a third party (again, someone not the transferor) that divests or cuts short a prior estate. Unlike a remainder, it is not patient. It typically follows an interest held in some type of defeasible fee simple. Although similar to a possibility of reverter and a right of reentry (which are interests in the grantor that follow, respectively, an estate held in a fee simple determinable and a fee simple subject to a condition subsequent), an executory interest is an interest following a defeasible fee if the property passes to a *third party* instead of to the grantor. The fee simple divested in favor of the third party is called a **fee simple subject to an executory limitation**.

Example 1: Orville transfers Blackacre to Andrew and his heirs, but if Andrew does not graduate from law school by age 30, then to Becky. Andrew's estate is a present interest, held in a fee simple subject to an executory limitation, and Becky has a future interest, an executory interest held in fee simple absolute.

Orville's transfer shifts the fee simple estate from Andrew to Becky. Becky's interest is not patiently awaiting the natural termination of Andrew's interest — so it cannot be a remainder; instead, it awaits the occurrence of some event that might or might not happen.

Example 2: Orville transfers Blackacre to Andrew for life, then to Becky and her heirs if she graduates from law school, whether her graduation occurs before or after Andrew's death. Becky's interest is still an executory interest, but if her interest becomes possessory "before Andrews's death" it shifts the fee as in the prior example, but if it becomes possessory "after Andrew's death," it springs from a reversion held by Orville in order to capture the seisin after Andrew's death.

Thus, as will appear later in this chapter, an executory interest can be either a **springing** or **shifting** executory interest. But neither type can be a remainder. Remainders and executory interests are mutually exclusive types of future interests — which is why we present a short introduction to executory interests at this point, before further categorizing remainders for you.

Now that you know a little about remainders and executory interests, try the following Example:

Example 3: Owen transfers Blackacre to Abby for life so long as she farms Blackacre, but if she does not farm it, to Becky. What is Becky's interest? It is a remainder — that is, it succeeds the life estate, becoming possessory at Abby's death. It can also succeed sooner — upon Abby's not farming Blackacre — but that earlier termination does not turn Becky's interest into an executory one. It would if the earlier termination were the only possible way Becky's interest could end, but it is not. Abby's life estate being a determinable one does not prevent Becky's interest from being a remainder.

The following chart summarizes present estates, words normally used in the creating the estate, and names of the future interests held either by the grantor or by third persons:

Estates in Real Property, with Future Interests

Freehold Estates		Future Interest	
(Typical wording in italics in second column, followed by future interests in the two right-hand columns)		Grantor	Third Person
Fee Simple			
Absolute	*"to A"* *"to A and her heirs"*	None	None
Determinable/Subject to an Executory Limitation	*"to A so long as . . ."* *"while . . ."* *"during . . ."* *"unless . . ."* *"until . . ."*	Possibility of Reverter	Executory Interest
Subject to a Condition Subsequent/Executory Limitation	*"to A provided that . . ."* *"on condition . . ."* *"but if . . ."*	Right of Reentry	Executory Interest
Fee Tail	*"to A and the heirs of his body"*	Reversion	Remainder
Life Estate	*"to A for life"*	Reversion	Remainder
			Executory Interest

Non-Freehold Estate		Future Interest	
Term of years	*"to A for _____ years"*	Reversion	Remainder

VESTED AND CONTINGENT REMAINDERS

Remainders in land can be either vested or contingent. These two sub-categories of remainders are mutually exclusive. A **vested remainder** is one that (a) is owned by an ascertained person or persons and (b) is not subject to a condition precedent. A **contingent remainder** is one where either the owner is unascertained or possession of the property is subject to a condition precedent (a contingency).

Because they are already possessory, all present interests, whether a life estate, fee simple absolute, fee simple determinable, fee simple subject to a condition subsequent, or a fee simple subject to an executory limitation, are vested. In addition, all future interests in the *grantor* (or his later assigns or heirs) are deemed vested even if the interests become vested only upon the happening of a contingency. Distinguishing between vested and contingent interests, therefore, becomes critical only with regard to remainders and executory interests — i.e., future interests in third parties.

To review, a vested remainder is given to an ascertained person and is not subject to a condition precedent. The vested remainder becomes possessory upon the natural termination of the immediately preceding estate. It follows any freehold estate. A contingent remainder is a remainder that either is given to an unascertained person or is subject to a condition precedent. Executory interests, because they cut short a prior estate and thus do not follow a natural termination of the prior estate, are contingent interests (but not contingent remainders).

(a) Ascertained Persons

Assuming no condition precedent, a remainder is vested if it is given to an ascertained person and contingent if it is given to an unascertained person. A person is ascertained if he or she can be specifically determined at the time a transfer or devise is effective.[1] One foolproof way to have an ascertained person is to name the person. Thus a remainder to "Paul Property" or to "my son, Paul Property" would be vested (assuming no condition precedent) because Paul Property is an ascertained person. In discussing interests and estates, lawyers reduce a transfer to its essentials: an ascertained person is by convention designated by a letter. Thus a gift to "*A*" is a gift to an ascertained person.

There is some difficulty, though not much, when a transferee is identified by a label or description. If the description can apply to only one person or individually identifiable persons, the persons are ascertained. If further developments are necessary before a specific individual can be pinpointed, the recipient is an unascertained person. The most common unascertained persons are unborn persons. For example, if Orville dies, his will devising Blackacre to his daughter, Andrea, for life and then to Andrea's first-born child, but she has no child, the remainder to Andrea's first-born child is to an unascertained person.

Example 1: O conveys to A for life, then to B and his heirs. Both A and B are ascertained persons.

Example 2: O conveys to A for life, then to B's children. B is childless. The remainder to B's children is to a group of unascertained persons. Therefore, B's children have a contingent remainder.

---

1. Thus a deed or deed of gift is effective at the time of its execution and delivery. A will or devise is effective at the time of the death of the decedent — lawyer's shorthand for this is "a will speaks at death."

Example 3: O conveys to A for life, remainder to B's heirs. B is married to C and has one son, D. Since B's heirs can be definitely identified only when B dies but B is still alive, the grant to B's heirs is a gift to unascertained persons. No living person can have heirs. The remainder is a contingent remainder. Once B dies, B's heirs can be identified; they are then ascertained persons. Since there is no condition precedent they have a vested remainder in fee simple to take possession on A's death.

Example 4: O conveys to his son, A, for life, and then to A's children (O's grandchildren). A is alive. A has three children (B, C, and D). B, C, and D are ascertained persons. The gift to "A's children" is a class gift. When one person in the class is identified, the class is vested. Nonetheless, as will be developed more fully later, for a very important purpose — applying the Rule Against Perpetuities — a gift to a class that is vested but subject to more people being added to the class will be treated as a contingent remainder until the class "closes" (i.e., all persons who might take are ascertained).

Example 5: O conveys to A for life, then to A's widow. A is married to B. A's widow is an unascertained person. As facts develop, B and A's widow may be different people. B may expect to be A's widow, but she may predecease A, or she may divorce A. A's widow has a contingent remainder. B has an expectation only, which is not a recognizable property interest.

(b) No Condition Precedent

A vested remainder has no condition precedent. A remainder with a condition precedent is a contingent remainder. A **condition precedent** is an event (condition) that must occur (or fail to occur, depending on how it is worded) *before* an interest becomes vested (for a remainder) or possessory (for an executory interest). To illustrate, if O conveys Blackacre to A for life, and then to B if B becomes a lawyer before A dies, the requirement that B become a lawyer before A dies is the condition precedent. It must occur before B's contingent remainder becomes a vested remainder. That it is also a condition subsequent so far as A's interest is concerned is no bar to that interest being a life estate and to its being a conditional precedent to B's interest. So a condition precedent must be contrasted with a condition subsequent that terminates a possessory or vested interest. The fee simple determinable, fee simple subject to a condition subsequent, and fee simple subject to an executory limitation all incorporate a condition subsequent. The holder can be divested if the condition subsequent occurs. A condition divesting a fee simple on executory limitation and giving possession to an executory interest is both a condition subsequent and a condition precedent. Since a remainder by definition follows the natural termination of a life estate or other freehold, a condition before a remainderman can take can only be a condition precedent.

Example 1: O conveys to *A* for life, but if A goes bankrupt, to B and her heirs. *A*'s life estate is subject to a condition subsequent that is also a condition precedent to B's future interest, held in remainder, and classified as a contingent remainder because it has a condition precedent.

Example 2: O conveys Blackacre to *A*, but if B marries before *A* dies, to B. What is *A*'s estate? It is a fee simple subject to an executory limitation. It is a fee simple with a condition subsequent. B's marriage before *A* dies also is the condition precedent to make B's executory interest possessory.

INTERPRETING TRANSFERS WITH CONDITIONS PRECEDENT AND CONDITIONS SUBSEQUENT

When interpreting grants, read them in the order written, usually interpreting up to a comma or semicolon. The order in which a grant is written can change the type of interest created and whether any remainder created is vested or contingent. Consider the following examples.

Example 1: O conveys Blackacre to *A* for life, then if B survives *A*, to B and her heirs. B's interest is a remainder since it follows the natural termination of *A*'s life estate. For B to take possession, however, B must outlive *A*. The survivorship requirement[2] is a condition precedent. B has a contingent remainder. In the actual conveyance the drafter should provide who takes if the condition precedent is not satisfied. Since no provision was made, O (or O's heirs) as the holder of the reversion takes Blackacre on *A*'s death if *A* survives B.

Example 2: O conveys to *A* for life, and when *A* dies, to B and her heirs. What interests and estates are involved? *A* has a present interest, held in a life estate. B's interest is a remainder since it follows the natural termination of *A*'s life estate. B has a vested remainder, held in a fee simple absolute. The words "and when *A* dies" is not a condition precedent—they are merely words of limitation just as the words "for life" are. A life estate naturally terminates on the death of the life tenant. The natural termination of a life estate is neither a condition precedent nor a condition subsequent.

Example 3: O conveys to *A* for life, then to *A*'s surviving spouse and her heirs. What is the spouse's interest? It is a contingent remainder because survivorship is an express condition precedent to taking the interest.

---

2. In contrast, in a conveyance "to A for life, then to B and her heirs" there is no survivorship requirement — that is, B need not survive A to take the remainder. Unless explicit, no survivorship requirement is implied for a future interest.

Example 4: O conveys Blackacre to A for life, then to B and his heirs, but if B does not survive A, then to C and his heirs. A has a present interest, held in a life estate. B's interest is a vested remainder since the interest follows the natural termination of the preceding life estate and there is no condition precedent. There is a condition subsequent, however. B's interest, therefore, is a vested remainder, subject to divestment, held in fee simple absolute. Compare Example 1 above, where essentially the same grant was labeled a contingent remainder. The difference in the two is the order in which the grant was written. In Example 1 the condition came first and was a condition precedent; here it came after the interest was vested and is a condition subsequent. C does not have a remainder because a condition must divest or cut short B's vested remainder before C can possess Blackacre. C, therefore, has an executory interest in Blackacre.

Example 5: O conveys Blackacre to A for life, remainder to B's children. B is alive and has two children, C and D. A has a life estate. B's two children, C and D, have vested remainders subject to open (more on subject to open later). B's children's interest follows the natural termination of the preceding life estate and there is no condition precedent (B's children do not have to survive A). Hence the children's interest is vested. Their interests are subject to partial divestment (subject to open), however, if B has another child, who when born would share in the grant.

Example 6: O conveys to A for life, remainder to B's children who attain age 18. B is alive and has one child, C, who is ten years old. B's children, including C and any later-born children, have a remainder. It is a contingent remainder because to take Blackacre the child or children must reach age 18. Reaching age 18 is the condition precedent. Until C or some other child of B reaches age 18, the interest remains a contingent remainder in fee simple absolute. Since O did not make a provision as to what happens to Blackacre if none of B's children attains age 18, O retains a reversion.

Example 7: O conveys to A for life, then if B murders C and burns his house down, to B and his heirs. If the transfer — or a devise for that matter — is intended to induce an illegal act — here murder and arson — then the inducing language is stricken. B's interest is a vested remainder, held in fee simple absolute.

ALTERNATIVE CONTINGENT REMAINDERS

Whenever a grantor fragments ownership rights into present and future interests, parties must be able to identify an owner for all periods of time and all events and contingencies. Of special importance, a grant of a contingent remainder should include a determination of who takes if the condition precedent fails to develop. There are two main options. First, explicitly or by default if the grantor makes no provision, the grantor retains a reversion. Second, the grantor may provide that another person take if the contingency fails, creating an alternative contingent remainder. An alternative contingent remainder results where one of two named persons takes to the exclusion of the other, depending on whether or not a condition precedent occurs.

Example 1: O conveys Blackacre to A for life, then to B if B attains the age of 21; but if B does not attain age 21, to O. A's interest is a life estate. B, an ascertained person, has a contingent remainder because she must live to age 21. If B does not attain age 21, O at A's death once more owns the property. O therefore has a reversion.

Example 2: O conveys Blackacre to A for life, then to B if B attains age 21. B is 15. Same result here as in Example 1. A's interest is a life estate, B has a contingent remainder, O has a reversion. O has a reversion since he transferred less than his full interest. The grantor retains a reversion when he transfers a life estate followed by a contingent remainder. If B turns 21 during A's life, B's contingent remainder becomes a vested remainder and O's reversion disappears. If A dies before B attains age 21, O once more owns Blackacre, subject to a (springing) executory interest in B if and when B attains age 21 (more on executory interests later in this chapter).[3]

Example 3: O conveys Blackacre to A and then to B if B reaches 21, but if B does not attain age 21, then to C. A has a life estate. B and C have alternative contingent remainders. O has a reversion. If B attains age 21, B gets Blackacre on A's death and C gets nothing. Alternatively, if B dies before turning 21, B loses her interest and C gets Blackacre on A's death. If A dies before B turns 21 but while B is still alive, O gets back Blackacre until either B celebrates her twenty-first birthday, in which case B gets Blackacre, or B dies before reaching 21, in which case C gets Blackacre.[4]

---

3. In a few jurisdictions, a contingent remainderman must satisfy the contingency before the prior estate ends; otherwise, the contingent remainder is destroyed. This Rule of the Destructibility of Contingent Remainders is developed more fully in Chapter 11. If B's contingent remainder is destroyed, O gets Blackacre back as a fee simple absolute (which is also why there must a reversion after alternative contingent remainders).
4. If the Rule of the Destructibility of Contingent Remainders applied, and A died before B reached age 21, both B's and C's alternative contingent remainders would be destroyed.

WHY WE DISTINGUISH VESTED AND CONTINGENT REMAINDERS

We distinguish vested remainders from contingent remainders for several reasons, many only of historical importance in most jurisdictions. For example, at one time a person could assign and devise vested remainders but not contingent remainders. Today both vested and contingent remainders are assignable and devisable. In addition, persons holding vested remainders had rights to prevent waste by the present possessor. Finally, some special rules destroyed contingent remainders or rendered them void. The Rule of Destructibility of Contingent Remainders (mentioned in footnotes in this chapter), the Rule in Shelley's Case, the Doctrine of Worthier Title, and the Rule Against Perpetuities are the common judicially created rules developed to terminate contingent remainders. These rules, to the extent they remain in force, do not apply to vested remainders. We delve into these rules more in Chapter 11 and discuss the Rule Against Perpetuities in Chapter 12.

EXECUTORY INTERESTS

For centuries the only future interests allowed to third parties were remainders. In particular, a grantor could not create a defeasible fee (fee simple determinable or fee simple subject to a condition subsequent) in one party and the equivalent of a possibility of reverter or power of termination (right of reentry) in a third party. That is no longer the case. Since the Statute of Uses in 1536, a grantor can create interests other than remainders in third parties. These future interests are called executory interests.

Recall that remainders must take effect on the natural ending of the prior estate. There can be no gap in seisin after the prior estate ends and the next vested interest commences. Thus, a conveyance "to *A* for life, then to B one year after *A*'s death" cannot be a remainder, and prior to 1536 was void. One type of executory interest recognized today, the **springing executory interest**, can occur after a gap in time. This interest divests or cuts short the grantor's fee simple. Its most common uses are transfers following a gap in time. Thus the conveyance from O "to *A* one year after O's death" is enforceable as a springing executory interest. A similar interest is created when O conveys "to *A* and his heirs twenty years after the date of this deed" and in "to *A* for life, then one year after *A*'s death to B and her heirs." The last example contains a present interest in *A*, held in a life estate, and followed by a future interest, a reversion, in O, held in fee simple subject to an executory interest in B, held in fee simple absolute. Why isn't O's interest a leasehold for a year?

Because the gap-filling reversion is intended to fill a gap in seisin. Recall that the common law assumption was that seisin always had to be somewhere, and a lease being a nonfreehold estate, does not carry seisin along with it. And because *O's* estate is not a life estate, not a fee tail or fee simple absolute (it has a definite duration and termination date), it was, by process of elimination, a fee simple subject to a condition subsequent.

Related to the no-gap-in-time rule was an early rule that a grantor could not convey an interest in property to be effective at some time in the future.

Example 1: Grandpa deeds Blackacre to Junior when he graduates from law school. Today this is a valid transfer. Junior's interest is not a remainder since it does not follow the natural termination of a prior estate; it is a springing executory interest, springing from the grantor. Until Junior graduates, Grandpa continues to hold his estate, subject to the defeasance inherent in Junior's interest springing from his. Grandpa's interest is a reversion.[5]

A second characteristic of remainders is that the holder of a remainder takes possession only after the natural termination of the prior estate. Any proposed interest in a third party that takes effect only when the preceding interest is cut short pursuant to a condition subsequent is not a remainder. Prior to the Statute of Uses in 1536, transfers to third parties following a fee simple determinable or fee simple subject to a condition subsequent were void. No "shifting" of the seisin to a third party (a stranger to the deed) was allowed. These transfers, resulting in **shifting executory interests**, have been allowed since 1536. What is called a fee simple determinable or fee simple subject to a condition subsequent when the grantor retakes the property once the condition subsequent occurs is called a **fee simple subject to an executory limitation** when a third party takes the property on the happening of the condition subsequent. The third party's interest following the fee simple subject to an executory limitation is called the **shifting executory interest**.

Example 2: O conveys Blackacre to A for life, then to B and her heirs, but if A uses Blackacre for commercial purposes, then Blackacre is to go immediately to B and her heirs. A has a present interest, held in a life estate subject to an executory limitation, followed by B's two futures interests, a vested remainder and a shifting executory interest. The first future interest awaits the natural termination of the life estate, and the second cuts it short. Why would O arrange the interests this way? To avoid a gap-filling reversion

---

5. Because (again) an executory interest holder was in early cases not permitted a cause of action in waste, some American courts held that Grandpa's interest was a leasehold instead of an executory interest. Why? These courts were fearful that Grandpa might "milk" the property in the meanwhile, and tenants were subject to waste actions.

previously discussed, during which anyone holding that reversion might "milk" Blackacre after *A* uses it for some commercial purpose but while *A* remains alive.

In a will, a similar devise might be "to *A* for life, remainder to B and his heirs, but if *A* is survived by a child alive at the time of his *A*'s death, then to such child or children and their heirs" when *A* has one child C, C's interest is a shifting executory interest, not a remainder. This devise let's you see some estate planning possibilities for using two future interests instead of one.

In planning a conveyance or a devise, lawyers have to ask many "what if" questions. Consider the following examples.

Example 3: O conveys to *A* and his heirs, but if *A* dies without issue, to B and her heirs. This creates a present interest in *A*, held in a fee simple subject to an executory limitation, with B's interest being a shifting executory interest.

But wait a minute! Did the lawyer ask about *A*'s issue? What about them? Isn't one implication of the conveyance that O intended them to obtain some interest? Some (not most, but some) courts have, depending on the surrounding circumstances, said yes and implied a remainder in *A*'s issue. Yes, remainders have been implied. (They are useful devices.) Thus the prior conveyance reads as follows:

Example 4: O conveys to *A* for life, remainder to *A*'s issue, but if *A* dies without issue, to B and her heirs. The remainder is a contingent one (having issue being a condition precedent), held in a fee simple subject to an executory limitation, and B's interest is a shifting executory interest.

No different legal consequences exist between shifting executory interests and springing executory interests. The only difference is that the *springing* executory interest divests the transferor, whereas the *shifting* executory interest divests a transferee (grantee).

Example 5: O transfers Blackacre to *A* as long as Blackacre is used for farming; then it reverts to O. *A*'s is a present interest, held in a fee simple determinable. O has a future interest, a possibility of reverter.

Example 6: O transfers Blackacre to *A* as long as Blackacre is used for farming, then to B and his heirs. *A* has a present interest, held in a fee simple subject to an executory limitation. B has a shifting executory interest.

Example 7: O transfers Blackacre to B to take effect if and when B agrees to farm Blackacre. O has a present interest, held in a fee simple subject to an executory limitation. B has a springing executory interest.

VARIATIONS ON VESTED REMAINDERS

Vested remainders are remainders in which the holders are ascertained persons and no condition precedent exists. There are some analytical variations of vested remainders. Their very variety shows you that courts have a preference for construing a remainder as vested rather than contingent.

(a) Indefeasibly Vested Remainder

The **indefeasibly vested remainder** is a remainder with no condition subsequent and is not a class gift subject to open. A gift "to A for life, remainder to B and her heirs" illustrates the indefeasibly vested remainder. B has a future interest, a vested remainder held in fee simple absolute. B's vested remainder is certain to become possessory. Her interest cannot be divested; she need not worry about any class gift complications.

(b) Vested Remainder Subject to Divestment

Because of the canon of construction disfavoring contingent remainders, courts favor vesting remainders as soon as possible. Thus a vested remainder may be subject to divestment before it becomes a possessory. These remainders are **vested remainders subject to divestment**. The key to distinguishing a vested remainder subject to divestment from a contingent remainder is whether the determinative condition is a condition precedent (so the remainder is a contingent remainder) or a condition subsequent (so the remainder is a vested remainder subject to divestment). The following examples clarify the distinction:

Example 1: O conveys Blackacre to A for life, then to B and her heirs. B has an indefeasibly vested remainder held in fee simple absolute.

Example 2: O conveys Blackacre to A for life, then to B and her heirs if B attains age 21, but if B does not attain age 21, to C and his heirs. B has a contingent remainder held in fee simple absolute, the condition precedent being B's attaining age 21. C has an alternative contingent remainder. O has a reversion.

Example 3: O conveys Blackacre to A for life, then to B and her heirs; but if B does not attain age 21, to C and his heirs. B has a vested remainder subject to divestment held in fee simple absolute. B's interest is vested because the divesting condition occurs after the clause granting B her interest; it is a condition subsequent. Contrast this with Example 2, where the condition is part of the grant itself, and is a condition precedent. Because B's interest is a vested remainder that may be divested or cut short, C's interest cannot be a contingent remainder. C's interest ripens into possession only if B's interest is divested. Hence C has a shifting executory interest in fee simple absolute.

Example 4: O conveys Blackacre to A for life, then to B and her heirs; but if B stops farming Blackacre, to C and his heirs. B has a vested remainder held in fee simple subject to an executory limitation. B's remainder is not subject to a condition precedent and so is not a contingent remainder. Further, B's vested remainder is not subject to divestment before B takes possession (i.e., while it is still a vested remainder); therefore, it is incorrect to label it a vested remainder subject to divestment. Her interest is a future interest, a vested remainder; her estate will be a fee simple subject to an executory limitation. Contrast this Example with Example 3 and Example 5. C has a shifting executory interest.

Example 5: O conveys Blackacre to A for life, then to B and her heirs, but if A ceases to farm Blackacre, to C and her heirs. Since B's interest may be divested before she takes possession (i.e., B's vested remainder may be divested while it is still a vested remainder), B has a vested remainder subject to divestment in fee simple absolute. B's interest is vested and not contingent because the grant as written, read in the order written up to the comma, says "A for life, then to B," the language creating a vested remainder. Her vested remainder is subject to divestment before she takes possession. Therefore, her interest is a vested remainder subject to divestment in fee simple absolute. C owns a shifting executory interest since she can take only if B's interest is divested.

(c) Vested Remainder Subject to Open

A common estate-planning device is for a testator (or a decedent) to leave property to a child for life, then to the testator's grandchildren (the life tenant's children), even if none then are born. For example, Owen may devise Blackacre to "my son, Albert, for life, then to Albert's children." The remainder to Albert's children is a **class gift** since it is to a group of persons identified by description rather than by names. Albert may or may not have any children. Assuming Albert has two children when Owen died, the two children have vested remainders since their interest follows the natural termination of their father's life estate and there is no condition precedent; but it is not an indefeasibly vested remainder. Albert may have more children who, when born, will share in the grant to "Albert's children." Albert's living children's remainder in Blackacre is vested — they will have a shared right to possession of Blackacre on Albert's death — but that vested remainder is subject to partial divestment in favor of later-born siblings. Hence we label the children's interest a **vested remainder subject to open**, indicating others can enter the described class; or, synonymously, a **vested remainder subject to partial divestment**, indicating the vested members of the class may lose some interest in the property.

(1) Class Closing Physiologically or Naturally

For practical reasons, at some point the class of persons who will share in a class gift must *close* (no more persons can enter the class even if later born). Two rules have evolved. First, a *class closes physiologically* or it closes *naturally* whenever biologically no one else can be born into the class.

Example: O dies, devising Blackacre "to my wife, Edna, for life, then to my son Franklin's children." Franklin has one child, Greta. Greta has a vested remainder subject to open. If Franklin has a second child, Harold, Harold shares equally with Greta in the vested remainder subject to open. If Franklin has a third and a fourth child they, too, would share in the vested remainder subject to open. Once Franklin dies, however, or more precisely nine months after Franklin dies, Franklin can have no more children. The class is complete with however many children are then born. Assuming Franklin dies with two children, Greta and Harold, in the class, the two children will be co-owners of Blackacre, with no chance Franklin will have another child.[6]

(2) Class Closing by Rule of Convenience

A class also may close by the rule of convenience. The **rule of convenience** states that a class closes whenever any member of the class can demand possession or distribution. The class does not necessarily close when a person is identified and satisfies any condition precedent, but only when some member of the class can demand possession. A vested member can demand possession usually no sooner than the natural termination of the preceding life estate, or term for years, or until the divesting condition occurs in a fee simple subject to an executory limitation. Living persons — including those born within nine months — who are identifiable members of a class when the class closes by convenience, but who have not satisfied any condition precedent, may still share in the property if they later satisfy the condition precedent. In other words, the class closing rules merely circumscribe the persons who

---

6. For purpose of class closing — and also for the Rule Against Perpetuities — acceptable procreation techniques are limited to those used two centuries ago. Frozen embryos and cloning are not as yet possibilities in class closing and Rule Against Perpetuities applications.

might take; it does not limit the number of persons who are in the class to those already vested.

Example 1: O's will devises Blackacre to W for life, then to A's children who attain age 21. A has two children: K (age 8) and L (age 5). K and L have contingent remainders, contingent on attaining age 21. The class of A's children remains open to any after-born children of A.

Example 2: When K is age 15 and L is age 12, A has another child, M. The three children (K, L and M) have contingent remainders. The class is still open for A's children who may be born later.

Example 3: K reaches age 21, and now has a vested remainder subject to open. The class does not close physiologically since A is still alive and can have more children. Likewise, the class is not closed by the rule of convenience since K, although vested, cannot demand possession of Blackacre until W's life estate ends.

Example 4: Continuing the facts of Example 3, A has a fourth child, N. N has a contingent remainder and shares ownership of Blackacre as long as N attains age 21.

Example 5: K dies at age 23. K is still vested. The condition precedent is attaining age 21. There is no condition precedent requiring any of A's children to survive the life tenant, W. K's devisee or heir will take K's share of Blackacre on W's death.

Example 6: W dies when L is 21, M is 9, and N is 2. A is still alive. The class of "A's children" closes pursuant to the rule of convenience since K and L have satisfied the condition precedent — attaining age 21 — and K's and L's devisees or heirs can demand possession of Blackacre as soon as W's life estate ends, which it did when she died. While the class closes, the class is "A's children," not "A's children who have attained age 21." Thus M and N are still members of the class and will be vested if and when they attain age 21.

Example 7: Two years after the events in Example 6, A has a fifth child, X. X is A's child, and just as cute as were K, L, M, and N. However, X was born after the class of A's children closed and so will not share in Blackacre. The rule of convenience sometimes is unfair, but nonetheless makes land more alienable and marketable. Without it, A's children could not sell Blackacre until A dies since A may have another child at any time.

Example 8: N dies in car wreck at age 18. N will not attain age 21, and thus neither N's devisees nor heirs will own any share of Blackacre.

Blackacre will be co-owned in equal shares by K's devisee, L, and M (age 27 at N's death).

In sum, classifying remainders is best undertaken by asking, first, whether it has a condition precedent. If so, the remainder is contingent. If not, ask whether there is some defeasing condition subsequent attached to the remainder. If so, the remainder is vested subject to divestment. If not, ask whether there is one person ascertained and certain to take the remainder, no matter how soon or however the prior interest ends. If so, the remainder is vested subject to open or partial divestment. If he answer to all these questions is negative, then remainder is a vested remainder.

Examples

Reversion Review

1. Consider which of the following conveyances creates a reversion:
   (a) O (the holder of a fee simple absolute) conveys Blackacre "to A for life."
   (b) O conveys Blackacre "to A for life, but if B marries C, then to C and his heirs so long as B and C use the property as a residence."
   (c) O conveys Blackacre "to A for life" and A transfers "to C for C's life."

A Has a Life Estate

2. Identify the interests created by the following transfers: O conveys Blackacre "to A for life . . .
   (a) "then to B and his heirs."
   (b) "then to B's children." B is childless at the time of the conveyance.
   (c) "remainder to B's heirs." B is alive.
   (d) "but when A dies, to B and his heirs."
   (e) "then if B survives A, to B and his heirs."
   (f) "then to B if B survives A, but if B does not survive A, to C and his heirs."
   (g) "then to B for life, then to C and his heirs."
   (h) "then to B and his heirs, but if B does not survive A, then to C and his heirs."

B Has a Vested Remainder

3. Identify the interests created by each of the following transfers in which O transfers Whiteacre . . .
   (a) "to A for life, then to B for life, then to C and her heirs."
   (b) "to A for life, then to B for life, then if C survives A and B, to C and her heirs."

(c) "to A for life, then to B for life, then when A and B die, to C and her heirs."

More Future Interests

4. Identify who has what interest in what estate in the following: transfers of Brownacre from O . . .
    (a) "to A for life, remainder to B's children." B is alive and has two children, C and D.
    (b) "to A for life, remainder to B's children who attain age 18." B is alive and has one 10 year old child.
    (c) "to A for life, remainder to B's heirs." B is divorced and has one child, C (age 10).
    (d) "to A for life, remainder to B if she graduates from law school; if not, to C."

Minor Gift

5. (a) O conveys Blackacre "to my son A for life, then to his children who reach 21." A has two children, B (age 8) and C (age 13). What interests and estates do B and C have?
    (b) If C were to die after reaching 21 while A is alive, who owns what then?
    (c) Assuming the facts in (a), A dies, leaving B (then age 10) and C (age 15). What interests and estates are created at A's death?
    (d) What happens six years later, when B is 16 and C is 21 years old?

A Class Gift

6. Edna owned a 100-acre farm at her death. Her will provided that the farm went to her sister, Faye, for life; at Faye's death, the farm passed to Faye's son, George, for life; it then went to George's children who survive George. George has one child, Trudy.
    (a) What interests do the respective parties have at Edna's death?
    (b) George has a second child, Sam. Does Sam have an interest in the farm?
    (c) Faye dies. A year later George has a third child, Robert. A month after Robert is born, Trudy dies, her only heir being her father, George. Who owns what interests in the farm?
    (d) George dies, survived by Sam and Robert. Who has what interests in the farm?

A Final Go

7. Identify the interests and estates created in the following conveyances:
    (a) O conveys Blackacre "to my daughter A for life, then to my grandchild B and his heirs, but if any issue of my grandchild B survive A, then to those surviving issue."

(b) Same facts as in (a). B dies, survived by his wife, C, and his child, D. B's will devises his interest to his wife, C.
(c) Same facts as in (a) and (b). A dies.
(d) O conveys Whiteacre "to A for life, remainder to B and her heirs, but if B marries C, then to C and his heirs."
(e) O conveys Whiteacre "to A for life, then to B and his heirs, but if B sells alcohol on Whiteacre, then to C and her heirs."
(f) O conveys "to A for 99 years if he lives so long, then to B and his heirs."
(g) O conveys "to A for life, then one day after A is buried, to Bentham and his heirs."
(h) O conveys "to A for life, then if B survives A, to B and his heirs, but if B does not survive A, to C and his heirs."

Explanations

Reversion Review

1. (a) O has a reversion, even though it is not stated in the grant itself. O transferred less than his full interest in Blackacre. What O retains is a reversion to take possession as soon as A's life estate ends.
   (b) O has a reversion until B marries C. If A dies before B marries C, O retakes possession of Blackacre. Once B marries C, O's reversion ends. O still has an interest, but it is not a reversion. O's interest is a future interest, a possibility of reverter, that follows C's fee simple determinable.
   (c) Both O and A have revisions. O has a reversion upon the end of A's life estate. A has a reversion upon the end of C's life estate if A outlives C.

A Has a Life Estate

2. A has present interest held in a life estate, and then . . .
   (a) B has a vested remainder. There is no implied condition that B survive A. If B dies before A, upon A's death B's heirs or devisees take both possession and the remainder.
   (b) B's children have a contingent remainder because they are not yet born. They are unascertained persons until born. O has a reversion in case B has no children. When a child of B is born, then that child will be said to have a vested remainder subject to partial divestment or "subject to open" (upon the birth of that child's siblings, when that second child, and each subsequent sibling, will partially divest his or her older siblings, gradually and pro rata reducing their share of the property). This is an example of the law's preference to classify remainders as vested.
   (c) B's heirs have a contingent remainder. No one is an heir of a living person — one may only be an heir apparent — a putative heir maybe, a hopeful heir certainly, but not legally an heir until the death of B, at

which time the remainder becomes vested. If this conveyance were contained in B's will, the remainder would be vested because B's heirs are known at her death. A will, remember, is effective or "speaks" for this purpose at death, no matter how long before the fact it was executed.

(d) B has a vested remainder in fee simple absolute. The words "but when A dies" do no more than indicate when A's present interest will naturally terminate. The words are not a condition precedent to the remainder.

(e) While A is alive, B's estate is a contingent remainder. The condition of survivorship is express and is a condition precedent. Unless clearly expressed as a condition precedent, surviving the life tenant is not a condition to taking a remainder. In this case, however, O expressly conditioned the vesting of the remainder on B's surviving the life tenant, A. O keeps a reversion in case B does not survive A.

(f) When the words "but if B does not survive A, to C and his heirs" are added to this conveyance shown in (e) above, B's and C's remainders are both contingent; they are alternative contingent remainders, meaning that the condition precedent attached to one interest is the opposite of the condition attached to the other. At the time of the termination of the life estate, one of the two conditions will be satisfied and so one of the two remainders will become vested. While the remainders are both contingent, O would retain a reversion in fee simple absolute. Alternative contingent remainders were much used in England during the age of Queen Elizabeth I to ensure that when two sons were alive at the conveyance, if the elder son and heir were to die before his parents, the family property would devolve on the younger.

(g) B has a vested remainder in life estate. It is vested even though B may die before A's life estate ends. The reason B might never actually possess Blackacre is that her estate ends on her death, which may occur prematurely; surviving A is not a condition precedent to the grant but an end to her estate. C has vested remainder in fee simple absolute. C takes possession of Blackacre after both A and B die.

(h) B has a vested remainder subject to divestment in fee simple absolute. The survivorship condition is a condition subsequent, not a condition precedent. Since C can take only if B's vested remainder is cut short or divested, C cannot have a contingent remainder. C has a shifting executory interest in fee. If B dies before A, then B's interest is extinguished and C takes.

B Has a Vested Remainder

3. A has a present interest held in a life estate, and then . . .
   (a) B has a vested remainder in life estate (or for life). Remainders designate the interest is a future interest. What estate is held is a different

query. Here B's future interest is a life estate or an estate held for life. C has a vested remainder as well, his being a vested remainder in fee simple absolute.

(b) B has a vested remainder held in a life estate. C's remainder is now subject to a condition precedent — C's surviving both A and B. Thus C has a contingent reminder in fee simple absolute. O has reversion in case C fails to survive A and B.

(c) B has a vested remainder in life estate (or for life). C has a vested remainder in fee simple absolute. The clause "then when A and B die" states the law as to when a remainder takes possession: Life estates end at the death of the life tenant and remainders take immediately thereafter. It is not a condition to C's taking. C (or her heirs or devisees) will possess Whiteacre after A and B die.

More Future Interests

4. A has a present interest held in a life estate, and then . . .

(a) The two children, C and D, have a vested remainder subject to open in fee simple absolute (or, alternatively labeled, a vested remainder subject to partial divestment). If B has more children, the after-born or adopted children will share in the remainder with C and D. B's age is irrelevant to this classification.

(b) B's 10-year-old child has a contingent remainder in fee simple absolute, contingent on attaining age 18. O has a reversion in fee simple absolute to take effect on A's death if either B's son dies before he reaches 18 (and B has no more children who have attained age 18 by A's death), or B's son is still a minor. Once B's son turns 18 he will have a vested remainder subject to open in fee simple absolute.

(c) Assuming B is alive, B's heirs have a contingent remainder: Only decedents have heirs, so B's heirs are unascertained. C may have an expectation, but no interest yet; C may be an heir apparent but is not an heir until B dies (and C survives B). O has a reversion in fee simple absolute. If, on the other hand, B is dead, B's heirs (may be only C on the facts) are ascertained and have a vested remainder in fee simple absolute.

(d) B has a contingent remainder, contingent on B's graduating from law school. C also has a contingent remainder, contingent on B's not graduating from law school. B's and C's remainders here are alternative contingent remainders, one taking if there is a graduation, the other if there is none. If both remainders are contingent, the logic of the common law dictates that O has a reversion in case the life tenant, A, should die before B dies or before B graduates from law school.

Minor Gift

5. (a) B and C, then ages 8 and 13, respectively, have a contingent remainder, being subject to a condition precedent (their reaching the age of 21). O has a reversion.

   (b) When C reaches 21, the remainder vests as to C, so C has a vested remainder subject to open (subject to partial divestment) upon B's reaching 21. C's heirs or devisees would take his interest in this vested remainder subject to open. B is included in the class of A's children but still holds a contingent remainder since B at age 16 has not reached 21 yet.

   (c) Assuming the Rule of Destructibility of Contingent Remainders is not the law in this jurisdiction (the Rule is discussed the next chapter), O's reversion becomes the present interest at the time of A's death, held in fee simple subject to an executory limitation. A's children, B and C, hold a springing executory interest. This interest is indestructible and inheritable (and alienable, too).

   (d) Six years later, once C turns 21, C's springing executory interest divests O's reversion. C or C's heirs hold in fee simple subject to partial divestment by B when B reaches 21.

A Class Gift

6. (a) Faye has a life estate. George has a vested remainder in a life estate. Trudy has a contingent remainder, the condition precedent being her surviving her father, George. Edna has a reversion in case George dies with no child surviving him. This question was intentionally written with names instead of letters so you can practice word problems, but if it is easier for you to visualize, rewrite the problem using letters: E conveys to F for life, then to G for life, then to G's children who survive him.

   (b) Yes. Sam is "George's child" so Sam has a contingent remainder, the same as Trudy.

   (c) George has a present interest held in a life estate, it becoming a present possessory estate when Faye's life estate ended. Sam and Robert still have contingent remainders, contingent on surviving their father. Neither Trudy's heirs nor her devisees have any interest since Trudy did not satisfy the condition precedent of surviving her father. Edna's heirs or devisees (we need more facts to know for sure which) have a reversion in case none of George's children survives him.

   (d) Robert and Sam own the farm in fee simple absolute. They will own the farm in equal proportions as tenants in common (tenants in common are covered later).

A Final Go

7. (a) *A* has a present interest held in a life estate; B has a vested remainder subject to divestment in fee simple absolute. B's children who survive *A* have a shifting executory interest. There is no condition precedent to B's remainder so it is a vested remainder, but B may be divested of his interest if a child of his survives *A* (whether or not they survive B); so B has a vested remainder subject to divestment in fee simple absolute. B's issue who survive *A* have a shifting executory interest.

(b) *A* has a present interest held in a life estate. C has inherited B's vested remainder subject to divestment in fee simple. B's surviving issue, D, has a shifting executory interest in fee simple absolute.

(c) After *A*'s death, C's vested remainder is divested. When D survives *A*, D's shifting executory interest shifts the fee simple held by B's heir, C, to D. So D owns Blackacre in fee simple absolute. Modern canons make the words "and his heirs" unnecessary.

(d) *A* has present interest held in a life estate. B has a vested remainder subject to divestment in fee simple absolute. C would have a shifting executory interest in fee simple absolute if C married B.

(e) *A* has present interest held in a life estate. B has a vested remainder in fee simple subject to an executory limitation. It is not a vested remainder subject to divestment since B must sell alcohol on Whiteacre to be divested, and this cannot occur until after B takes possession. Hence B's interest cannot be divested while it is still a vested remainder. C has a shifting executory interest.

(f) *A* owns a determinable term of years. B has a shifting executory interest in fee simple absolute. *A*'s interest has a definite maximum term, but can be cut short by his death before the end of the term. It is not a life estate even though in all likelihood *A* will die before the 99 years have passed.

(g) *A* has present interest held in a life estate. O has a reversion. Bentham has a springing executory interest (springing from O, not *A*). At common law, Bentham's estate was void because there was a gap in seisin. No one could be buried before his or her death, unless he or she was buried alive — a possibility the law did not admit. Today the gap in seisin, as well as the shift in seisin, is permitted and Bentham's estate is a springing executory interest, held in fee simple absolute.

(h) *A*'s life estate is followed by two alternative contingent remainders in fee simple absolute in B and C, respectively, and followed further by a reversion in O. The condition determining who will take the property is whether B survives *A*. If B survives *A*, B gets a fee simple absolute interest in the property. If B does not survive A, the property goes to C in fee simple absolute. O has a reversion even though one of the remainders, B or C, has to take. This is because at common law a life estate terminated by forfeiture before the death of A if the life tenant was found to be a traitor or disloyal to the king.

Special Rules of Construction

Several rules of law or construction have developed to decrease the control that grantors, testators, and other transferors have over real property over time, and later on, to increase the alienability of property. They were developed in, and inherited by our legal system from, English law. Most states no longer follow many of them, but some do and in some instances, understanding them is necessary to see the extent to which they are and are not followed. This chapter covers these rules, except for the Rule Against Perpetuities, which is discussed in Chapter 12.

THE RULE OF DESTRUCTIBILITY OF CONTINGENT REMAINDERS

In England during the fourteenth and fifteenth centuries, seisin had to be continuous. It could not ever be in abeyance, for if it was to be, the lord of the manor could not know who was responsible for the land within his domain. So lawyers and judges were troubled when a life tenant died and the holders of a remainder were not yet ascertained, or when a named contingent remainder holder had not satisfied the condition precedent. Early examples generally involved the naming of heirs.

Example 1: Owen conveys Blackacre to Alex for life, remainder to Ben's heirs. Ben is alive. A living person's heirs are unascertained (common law lawyers said that "no living person has heirs"), so the remainder was contingent. If Alex died before Ben, then, the remainder had not vested, being that seisin had not rested on anyone — a nightmare in the feudal system since no one was responsible for paying taxes and providing soldiers for the King.

In addition, because the common method of transfer was by enfeoffment with livery of seisin, judges came to require that all transfers had to take place at once. A vested remainder relaxed this requirement, and the judges regarded the remainder as being capable of taking possession when and if the prior freehold estate ended — at which time seisin passed instantly to the remainderman. A contingent remainder required a further relaxation of the rule that seisin had to be continuous. And the judges balked — and wouldn't do it. Given the choice between having the property revert back to the grantor until the remainderman satisfied the condition precedent or voiding the contingent remainder, the judges chose to void the contingent remainders that were still contingent when the preceding life estate ended. A remainder, they said, had to vest at or before it came into possession.

Thus the **rule of destructibility of contingent remainders** states that a contingent remainder is destroyed if it has not vested at or before the termination of all preceding life estates.

Example 2: O conveys Blackacre to A for life, then to A's children who attain age 21. A dies when A's only child, C, is age 15. Since C's remainder is not vested (i.e., it is still contingent on C turning 21) upon or before the end of A's life estate, according to the rule of destructibility of contingent remainders, C's contingent remainder is destroyed. It is void. O (or O's heir or devisee takes Blackacre by way of a reversion. Put differently, in this case, the rule prefers the reversion over waiting for the remainder to free itself of uncertainty.

Example 3: O conveys Blackacre to A for life, then to B for life, then to A's children who attain age 21. B dies when A's only child, C, is 15. C's contingent remainder is not destroyed since C's remainder does not need to be vested until A's life estate ends.

Example 4: Same facts as in Example 2 except A rather than B dies when C is 15. C's contingent remainder is not destroyed since B has possession after A dies. Only if both A's and B's life estates end before C turns 21 would C's contingent remainder be destroyed.

The rule of destructibility of contingent remainders has its limits. First, the rule applies only to contingent remainders in real property. It does not apply to personal property. Thus, the rule does not apply to transfers of artwork, stocks, bonds, furniture, and other personal property. Second, it does not apply to equitable interests — i.e., interests held in trust. Thus a transfer of real property to a trustee in trust to benefit A for life, then to B if B attains age 21, will continue to be valid even if A dies before B turns 21. Third, it applies only to contingent remainders. It does not destroy executory interests. In fact, a major impetus for the development of executory interests as legally cognizable ownership vehicles was to circumvent the rule of destructibility of contingent remainders. Finally, the rule is simply not a factor in the vast majority of states. Only a few states retain it.

Judges worked hard to contain the rule, since it often thwarted a transferor's intent.

Example 5: Ted devises Blackacre to Alex for life, then to Ben's children. After Ted dies, Alex dies the next day when Ben was already dead, but when Ben's wife was pregnant with Ben's later-born child Charlie. Charlie was allowed to take the remainder. A person ascertained within the period of gestation preserved the remainder that would otherwise be destroyed by the rule of destructibility of contingent remainders.

Example 6: O transfers Blackacre to "A for A's life or five years, whichever is greater, then to B if B attains age 21" at a time when B is 16. B's contingent remainder will not be destroyed since A or his heir or devisee will own the land for at least five years, long enough for B to turn 21. That is, the rule of destructibility of contingent remainders can be avoided by structuring the transfer of property as a grant of a term of years rather than as a life estate since a term of years is a nonfreehold estate and not a freehold estate.

Example 7: O conveys Blackacre to A for life, remainder to T (a trustee) in trust for the life of B, remainder to B's children who survive B and their heirs. T's interest is a remainder to preserve contingent remainders in the surviving children. This devise was the creation of a great seventeenth century English conveyancer by the name of Orlando Bridgeman (who also argued the case creating the Rule against Perpetuities discussed in Chapter 12). T's remainder was a vested one that would last until the second remainder vested too, and as the next section discusses, T's remainder was also not subject to the merger rule, so it was doubly bullet-proofed against destruction.

As mentioned in the last example, there are other ways contingent remainders can be destroyed or voided. The merger rule, explained next, is one such way.

THE MERGER RULE

The basic idea of the merger rule is simple. If a person holding a life estate acquires a vested remainder in the same property, instead of saying he owns a life estate and the vested remainder in the same property, we say the two estates "merge" into one larger estate, the fee simple absolute.

Example 1: Owen conveys Blackacre to Abby for life, remainder to Buzzy. If Abby acquires Buzzy's future interest, a remainder, it makes no sense to call Abby's interests other than a present one, held in fee simple absolute. The lesser estate, Abby's life estate, is thus merged into Buzzy's fee simple absolute.

The common law went further, however, as in the following example.

Example 2: Owen conveys Blackacre to Abby for life, remainder to Buzzy for life when he attains the age of 21, remainder to Charlie and his heirs. Abby's acquires Charlie's remainder when Buzzy is 16. Because the doctrine of merger applies only to vested interests, the merger of two successive vested interests was held to destroy intervening contingent ones. So Buzzy's contingent remainder was destroyed because he could not take the seisin at the time he needed to — the date of Abby's acquisition of Charlie's interest. Buzzy's interest could not be vested at the termination, through merger, of the prior estate.

There is nothing inerrant about the result in this example. It's just the law, and one reason that some commentators regard the merger rule as a component of the rule of destructibility of contingent remainders. So a further statement of the **merger rule** would read, "If a *vested* life estate and the next succeeding *vested* estate come to be owned by the same person, the two estates are merged into one." So there are consequences flowing from the merger rule when a contingent remainder intervenes between the two vested estates, and important exceptions to its operation. First, as the example pointed out, if a person owning a life estate acquires a vested remainder that follows a contingent remainder held by some other person, the life estate and the vested remainder merge, destroying the contingent remainder. The rule works the other way too. So if a person holding a vested remainder that immediately follows another person's contingent remainder in the same property acquires the possessory life estate that immediately precedes the contingent remainder, the life estate and vested remainder merge, destroying the contingent remainder. That simplifies the title, but at the expense of the holder of the contingent remainder.

For the two vested interests to merge to destroy an intervening contingent remainder, the two vested estates must be acquired at different times. Two vested interests acquired in the same document do not destroy intervening contingent remainders.

Example 3: O conveys Blackacre to A for life, then to B for life if B attains age 21, then to C. B is age 15. A has a present interest held in a life estate, B has a contingent remainder held in a life estate, and C has a vested remainder held in fee simple absolute. No merger occurs because A and C are different people. B's contingent remainder is good.

Example 4: Same facts as in Example 3, except two years later A buys C's vested remainder. A now owns a (vested) life estate and a vested remainder in the same property, the two vested interests having been acquired at separate times. The two vested interests merge, the lesser life estate is merged into the greater fee simple absolute, destroying B's contingent remainder in life estate. A then owns Blackacre in fee simple absolute. The same result follows if C had acquired A's life estate — that is, the lesser life estate can be absorbed into the greater fee simple absolute.

Example 5: O conveys Whiteacre to A for life, then to B for life if she attains age 21 (B is 14), then to C if C attains age 21 (C is 5). Three years later A acquires C's interest. After the acquisition, A has a present interest held in a life estate and a contingent remainder held in fee simple (contingent on C's attaining age 21). B's intervening interest is a contingent remainder held in a life estate. A's two estates do not merge since A has one vested estate and one contingent estate. A person must own two *vested* estates for the two to merge. B's contingent remainder remains valid. O's had a reversion all along.

Example 6: O conveys Brownacre to A for life, then to B for life, then to C if C attains age 21 (C is 14). A has a present interest held in a life estate, B has a vested remainder in life estate, C has a contingent remainder in fee simple absolute, and O has a reversion (in case C does not reach 21). Two years later B acquires A's life estate. Since B now owns two vested interests, the two interests merge into one possessory life estate for the longer of A's or B's life. The merger does not destroy C's contingent remainder, however, since C's interest follows the two vested estates and is not an intervening estate.

Example 7: O conveys Redacre to A for life, then to B for life, then to C. A has a present interest held in a life estate, B has a vested remainder in a life estate, C has a vested remainder in fee simple absolute. Two years later A acquires C's vested remainder. A has a vested life estate and a vested remainder in fee simple absolute, but the two estates do not merge to destroy B's intervening interest since B's remainder in life estate is vested and not contingent.

Example 8:   O conveys Greenacre to A for life, then to B for life if she attains age 21, then to A. A has a present interest held in a life estate and a vested remainder in fee simple absolute. In between A's two vested estates is B's contingent remainder in a life estate. A's two vested estates do not merge to destroy B's contingent remainder since the three estates were created in the same document.

Example 9:   O conveys Redacre in a deed with a warranty of title, to A for life, remainder to B if she attains age 21. O, still holding a reversion held in fee simple absolute, acquires the life estate. Some courts will, when O's conveyance was made with a warranty of title, hold that O is estopped from participating in any merger of interests.

Illinois courts have used the estoppel idea in the last example. Whatever. It is arguable that the title O warranted included only a remainder subject to merger, not an indestructible remainder. What do you think?

Still another limitation on the merger rule dealing with reversion occurs when O devises property to A for life, then to A's first child to attain the age of 21. When the devise is effective, at O's death, if A is O's only heir, A also has a reversion. Does the life estate and the reversion merge? Many courts have said no. To hold otherwise would defeat the O's intent too much. The merger doctrine does not apply. The merger rule is generally a rule of law, but there are limits.

FORFEITURE

Still another way that a contingent remainder might be destroyed was by its being subject to forfeiture. If O conveyed Blackacre to A for life, remainder to B if B attained age 21, and when B was 16, A's life estate was forfeited for treason or some other crime, or A committed waste on Blackacre and the remedy was forfeiture (as often it was in the early cases), the contingent remainder was destroyed. Today A might forfeit his property used in a drug transaction, and the same rules would apply: the contingent remainder would be destroyed.

THE RULE IN SHELLEY'S CASE

The **Rule in Shelley's Case** is simply stated: When a devise or conveyance transfers a freehold estate to a person and in the same instrument also transfers a remainder to that same person's heirs or the heirs of his body, and both estates are either legal or equitable, both are considered to be held by the first-named freeholder, either for life, in fee simple absolute, or in fee tail. In short, it provides that a remainder in a freehold in favor of the preceding life tenant's heirs is held by the life tenant from the devise or conveyance's effective date. Stated this way, the rule can be seen to depend on the merger rule and a preference for vested remainders. See Wolf v. Shelley, 1 Co. Rep. 93b (1581) (Lord Edward Coke reporting the case). This rule is usually broken down into three requirements: (1) a freehold estate given to a first transferee, (2) a remainder limited to the heirs of the first transferee in the same instrument, and (3) a freehold and a remainder of the same quality — i.e., either being both legal or equitable in nature.

Thus if O conveys "to A for life, remainder to A's heirs," by operation of law, A comes into ownership of both the life estate (under the terms of the conveyance) and the remainder in his heirs. Early cases using the rule interpreted this remainder as meaning ". . . then to A and his heirs." The words creating the remainder ("remainder to A's heirs") are all construed in this case as words of limitation, thus construing these words toward the fee simple absolute. Thus, too, by operation of law, the courts changed the contingent remainder into a vested remainder — and the full conveyance into "to A for life, remainder to A and his heirs." Pursuant to the merger rule previously discussed, A's two estates merged. A then holds his merged interests in fee simple absolute.

The rule is a rule of law, not a canon of construction for ascertaining the transferor's intent. See Perrin v. Blake, 96 Eng. Rep. 392 (K.B. 1769) (Lord Mansfield, J., holding the rule a canon of construction), reversed, 98 Eng. Rep. 355 (Ex. Chamber, 1770) (Blackstone, J., holding the rule one of law — a holding that he later embedded in his famous treatise, much read by early American lawyers). The grantor's intent makes no difference to the question of whether the rule in Shelley's case applies. Today many call the rule an anachronism, but many defend it still as a means of rendering land alienable sooner.

The remainder to A's heirs need not follow the first freehold estate directly; there may be an intervening estate, as when O conveys "to A for life, remainder to B for life, remainder to A's heirs and their heirs." Under the rule, A holds both the present interest in the life estate and a future interest, the vested remainder held in fee simple absolute. The same result would occur if a condition precedent were added to the remainder to A's heirs, as where the words "if the land is still used as a farm" were added to the conveyance. That the remainder is not vested makes no difference. The rule applies to both vested and contingent remainders.

In some cases the Rule in Shelley's Case gives A two interests in property, but not the complete ownership of the property in fee simple absolute. This is so because the Merger Rule will not operate if there is an intervening estate created by the same document or if the remainder is a contingent remainder. Only when there is no impediment to merger will

A wind up with a fee simple absolute. In other words, all the Rule in Shelley's Case does is transform a grant to "*A*'s heirs" to a grant "to *A*" if *A* also receives a freehold estate (usually a life estate) in the same document. Once that transformation is done, whether the Merger Rule applies depends on the Merger Rule guidelines.

The Rule in Shelley's Case has been abolished by statute in well over 40 states. Where wholly abolished, a conveyance to *A* for life, then to *A*'s heirs, creates the following interests: a life estate in *A*, a contingent remainder in *A*'s heirs, and a reversion in *O*. Some states have partially abolished the Rule: for example, Indiana abolishes it for trusts, but not for wills, and Oregon and New Hampshire abolish it for wills, but not for non-testamentary trusts. So the statutes may require a close reading. The Rule is still the law in Colorado, Delaware, and Washington.

Moreover, many statutes abolishing the rule provide simply that "the Rule in Shelley's Case is hereby abolished." Reading such a statute, you are no better off if you do not know what the rule is in the first place — hence your need to know it. In some states the rule has been abolished only prospectively, meaning that it still controls conveyances made before the effective date of the abolition statute.

The rule applies to transfers of real property but not usually to personalty. If *O* deeds his farm equipment to *A* for life, remainder to *A*'s heirs, the Rule does not apply in all but about a dozen states. Where it does not apply, the interests created take effective as written. What if *O* deeds Blackacre and its farm equipment to *A* for life, remainder to *A*'s heirs? Maybe the Rule should apply — and the equipment are transferred as trade fixtures (fixtures not otherwise fixtures but necessary to the operation of Blackacre).

Example 1: *O* conveys Blackacre to *A* for life and then to *A*'s heirs. *O* intended for *A* to have a life estate followed by a contingent remainder in fee simple in *A*'s heirs (contingent on *A*'s heirs being identified at *A*'s death). Notwithstanding *O*'s intent, the Rule in Shelley's Case converts the contingent remainder in *A*'s heirs to a vested remainder in *A*. Since *A* owns a life estate and the immediately following vested interest, pursuant to the merger rule, *A*'s two interests merge into a fee simple absolute.

Example 2: *O* conveys Whiteacre to *A* for life, then to B for life, then to *A*'s heirs. The Rule in Shelley's case converts the contingent remainder in *A*'s heirs to a vested remainder in *A*. *A*'s heirs have no interest. Even though *A* owns a (vested) life estate and a vested remainder, the two estates do not merge because there is an intervening vested remainder in life estate in B. Merger would not apply even if B's interest were a contingent remainder since the interests were all created in the same document. The intervening estate delays full application of the Rule. Meanwhile *A* can convey a fee simple subject to B's life estate. B meanwhile can have a cause of action in waste if needed against *A* as a life tenant.

Example 3:   O conveys Greenacre to *A* for life, then to *B*'s heirs. The Rule in Shelley's Case does not apply since *B* received no other interest in the grant. Therefore, *B*'s heirs have a contingent remainder in fee simple absolute, contingent on being identified at *B*'s death.

Example 4:   O conveys Brownacre to *A* for life, then to *A*'s heirs if the land is used for a farm at *A*'s death, and, if not, to *B* and her heirs. The Rule in Shelley's Case transforms the contingent remainder in *A*'s heirs to a contingent remainder in *A*, contingent on Brownacre being farmed at *A*'s death. No merger results because *A* must own two vested estates for merger, and here he owns one vested estate (the life estate) and one contingent estate (the contingent remainder). Contrast this result with that in Example 1, where the contingent remainder was transformed into a vested remainder. The reason for the different result is that the Rule in Shelley's Case merely converts a grant "to *A*'s heirs" to one "to *A*." Rewritten, the grant in Example 1 is to "*A* for life, remainder to *A*" — the contingency of being an heir disappears automatically. In this Example, on the other hand, if rewritten after application of the Rule in Shelley's Case, the grant is "to *A* for life, then to *A* if the land is used as a farm at *A*'s death" — the contingency remains.

Example 5:   O conveys Blackacre to *A* for life, then to *A*'s children, but if *A* has no children, to *A*'s heirs. The Rule does not apply here because the remainders are alternate contingent remainders — courts tend to require the precise formula of a life estate in *A* and a remainder in *A*'s heirs in order to apply the Rule — and the application of the Rule is delayed again by the intervening estate. How long delayed? If *A* has no children at his death, he can, in his will, devise a fee simple absolute.

Example 6:   O conveys Redacre to Amy for life, then to Amy's heirs, excluding her sisters Bea and Carlotta. The Rule does not apply because any limitation on the class of heirs renders it inapplicable. Likewise, a conveyance to Abby for life, then to Abby's heirs and Beatrice, would render the Rule inapplicable.

Example 7:   O conveys Whiteacre to *A* for life, remainder to *A*'s heirs and their heirs. The Rule applies, because to hold otherwise would turn a rule of law into a canon of construction.

THE DOCTRINE OF WORTHIER TITLE

When O conveys "to *A* for life, then to O's heirs" or "to *A* for life, then to my heirs," the conveyance is somewhat similar to the prototypical conveyance involved in the Rule in Shelley's Case. As with the Rule, the transferor was either attempting to avoid taxes due the King on the descent of property or was looking to narrow the rights of creditors to *A*'s life estate. The courts responded in a similar fashion. They voided *O*'s remainder and held that instead *O* has a reversion. Thus the **Doctrine of Worthier Title** states that when there is a conveyance or devise to a person, with a remainder or executory interest to the grantor's heirs (not heirs of the grantor's body), no future interest is created in the grantor's heirs; rather, the grantor retains a reversion. Once deemed to hold the reversion, *O* can transfer it again and, being a vested interest, it can be subjected to levy and sale by *O*'s creditors. This doctrine applies to real, personal, legal, and equitable property. The Doctrine is in effect a prohibition against remainders in a transferor's heirs. Traditionally and today, it applies to conveyances of real property, but because it is a rule of construction and not a rule of law, it applies to personal property as well.

Why is the reversion "worthier" than a remainder? First, because a reversion is always vested — and thus the Doctrine is an example of a preference for vested interests. Second, because it promotes the alienability of property. And third, because descent at common law was worthier than a devise.

That third rationale seems strange today. At common law it made sense because descent was a taxable event, the devise using a remainder to *O*'s heirs was an estate tax dodge, and devises were not possible until the Statute of Wills in 1540. Today the Doctrine is widely applied only to inter vivos transactions — to deeds and similar instruments of transfer. The Doctrine's so-called wills branch (applying it to devises) is not much used, being abolished by statute or judicial decision in about 30 states. Where abolished, a devise from *O* "to *A* for life, then to *O*'s heirs" will be enforced as written. Probate and decedent's estates lawyers have pushed for this abolition, because future interests in unascertained persons is inconvenient and often more expensive, making the settling of decedents' estates that much more difficult.

The Doctrine of Worthier Title continues to apply to deeds in many states. It started as a rule of law, restated in Chancellor James Kent's Commentaries on American Law and thereby embedded in the law of many states. Today it survives only as a rule of construction, to which the grantor's intent is relevant, and not as a rule of law. As a rule of construction, a gift over to *O*'s heirs creates a rebuttable presumption that *O* did not in fact intend the gift over to take and intended instead that the grantor retain the reversion. The grantor's heirs have no interest, only the hope or expectation that they will inherit if the grantor does not sell or devise it to others. After Kent restated the Doctrine, it went largely unchallenged until the case of Doctor v. Hughes, 12 N.E. 221 (N.Y. 1919) (a leading case, with an opinion by Cardozo, J., changing the Doctrine from a rule of law into one of construction, and rendering it a rebuttable presumption, in a state that later abolished it).

The presumption can be rebutted. The use of a word other than one commonly meaning "heirs" in the limitation is one way to rebut the presumption. O's conveying "to A for life, remainder to those persons who would be my heirs at A's death" does the trick, changing the common meaning of the word just enough. So does "to A for life, remainder to my heirs, the latter persons to take as purchasers," as does "to my children" or "to my issue."

The doctrine has been abolished in about 30 states (including, California, Illinois, and New York). Even where abolished by statute, the statute's express language may not provide for its retroactive effect (affecting documents drafted before abolishment). When the state statute is silent on the issue of retroactivity, a court may refuse to abolish the doctrine retroactively. In order to avoid running afoul of the Doctrine of Worthier Title, a drafter should specifically name the person to whom the transferor intends property to go.

Example 1: O conveys to T (a trustee) in trust for O for O's life, remainder to O's heirs. The Doctrine applies because it contains no limitation on the type of prior estate; it could be a fee tail, a term for years, or more typically a life estate, and unlike the Rule in Shelley's Case, the prior estate and the remainder need not be of the same quality — the two need not be both legal or equitable.

Example 2: O conveys to A and his heirs, but if A dies without children surviving him, then to O's heirs and their heirs. The Doctrine applies, but with a twist. O's future interest is an executory interest, so since the Doctrine is a canon of construction, the courts construe the conveyance as saying, "to A and his heirs so long as A has surviving children," giving O a possibility of reverter. The Doctrine's inter vivos branch — its application to deeds and other conveyances — may mean that O has a possibility of reverter or a right of reentry as well as a reversion.

Example 3: O conveys to the heirs of the grantor. O intended no reversion and the Doctrine, being a canon of construction, does not apply.

Courts have tended to strictly construe the Doctrine. Thus in a conveyance to A for life, then to O's lineal heirs, or to A for life, then to O's heirs living at A's death, courts would not apply the Doctrine. In the first example, the Doctrine requires that the common law class of heirs be included, and in the second example, since heirs are determined at the transferor's death, the common law class is again absent: the second example uses the word heirs in a sense that makes them not common law heirs at all. A similar conveyance is, to A for life, then to O's heirs in equal shares. Here the

Doctrine would not apply because heirs generally take, under the canons of descent, in representational shares — in law Latin, per stirpes, not per capita: that is, when one of Grandma's children are deceased, a grandchild takes the share of the deceased parent and does not take in her own right. Likewise, when O conveys to A for life, then to B and her heirs, when B is in fact the sole heir of O, the Doctrine would not apply: B takes the remainder by way of words of purchase, not descent or limitation, so the Doctrine is inapplicable.

Examples

The Rule of Destructibility of Contingent Remainders

1. Unless stated otherwise, assume that the state recognizes the Rule of Destructibility of Contingent Remainders.
   (a) O conveys Blackacre to "my son A for life, then to his children who reach 21." A has two children, B (age 8) and C (age 13). What interests and estates do B and C have?
   (b) Same facts as in (a). A dies when B is 10 and C is 15. Who owns what interests in Blackacre?
   (c) Same facts as in (a). A dies when B is 19 and C is 23. Who owns what interests in Blackacre?
   (d) Same facts as in (b), except the state does not recognize the Rule of Destructibility of Contingent Remainders. Who owns what interests in Blackacre?

The Rule in Shelley's Case

2. (a) O conveys "to A for ten years, then to A's heirs." Does the Rule in Shelley's Case apply?
   (b) O conveys "to A for life, and then two days after A's death, to A's heirs." Does the Rule in Shelley's Case apply?
   (c) O conveys "to A for life, and on A's death, to A's children." Does the Rule in Shelley's Case apply?
   (d) O conveys "to A for life, then to B for ten years, then to A's heirs." Does the Rule in Shelley's Case apply?

The Doctrine of Worthier Title

3. (a) O conveys Blackacre "to A for life, then to O's next of kin." Does the Doctrine of Worthier Title apply?
   (b) O conveys "to A for life, then to B and her heirs," where B is an heir of A. Does the doctrine apply?
   (c) O conveys "to A for life, but if A does not live on Blackacre, to the heirs of O." Does the doctrine apply?

Explanations

The Rule of Destructibility of Contingent Remainders

1. (a) *A*'s interest is a present one, held in a life estate. *A*'s children, alive and after-born, have a contingent remainder, contingent on their attaining age 21. O has a reversion. The Rule of Destructibility is not implicated while *A* is alive.

    (b) Pursuant to the Rule of Destructibility of Contingent Remainders, the contingent remainders to B and C are destroyed. O owns Blackacre.

    (c) C owns Blackacre subject to partial divestment if B reaches 21. Once C turns 21, *A*'s children's interest becomes a vested remainder subject to open. The Rule of Destructibility of Contingent Remainders does not destroy any type of vested remainder.

    (d) Because of the reversion, O owns Blackacre. O's present interest is held in a fee simple subject to an executory limitation. B and C own springing executory interests.

The Rule in Shelley's Case

2. (a) No. *A* does not hold a *freehold* estate, as the rule requires. Instead *A* holds a nonfreehold estate, a term of years. So a variance in wording produces a different legal result, so be alert to — for example, O transferring "to *A* for 99 years should *A* live so long, remainder to *A*'s heirs" is a way to avoid the Rule in Shelley's Case: This is a term of years, rather than a life estate, followed by a remainder in *A*'s heirs.

    (b) No. The heirs' interest here is a springing executory interest, not a remainder. The rule applies to remainders, not to executory interests. *A* has a life estate; O has reversion in fee simple subject to an executory limitation, O's reversion to become possessory when *A*'s life estate ends. *A*'s heirs have a springing executory interest. *A*'s heirs' interest is not a remainder since it does not immediately follow the prior life estate; it follows O's fee simple and it must cut short the fee simple to become possessory. Historically, the fact that the Rule in Shelley's case does not destroy executory interests was the impetus for creating executory interests in the first place.

    (c) Still no. The remainder in "*A*'s children" is not the same as "*A*'s heirs" even though children constitute a major category of "heirs." The Rule in Shelley's Case applies only to "heirs," not to "children" or "issue" or even to "persons who would be my heirs." From these three Examples you see how attorneys avoid the impact of the rule. There are other ways to avoid the Rule in Shelley's Case. For example, the use of two instruments — one to the life tenant, another to the heirs of the tenant — will avoid the rule since the Rule in Shelley's

Case requires the interest to be created in the same document. Or, either the life tenant's or the heirs' interest can be put in trust, making it an equitable interest, so that the requirement that both interests be either legal or equitable is not satisfied and so (again) the rule does not apply. The Rule in Shelley's Case may be avoided by leaving the remainder to the life tenant's widow or widower, for example, or to named heirs. This would conform to the typical estate plan of many people and still avoid the rule with a slight change in the wording of the transfer. When the rule is so easily avoided, it becomes a trap for the unwary. For some, this argues also for the Rule's abolition.

(d) Yes. The document purported to create a life estate in *A* and a remainder in *A*'s heirs. Thus the remainder becomes a vested remainder in *A*. *A* then owns both a life estate and a vested remainder in fee simple absolute. The two interests do not merge to form a fee simple absolute, however. The merger rule demands the two vested interests be acquired at different times; merger will be allowed to destroy an intervening interest only when the intervening interest is contingent. Here *A* received both interests in the same document, and B's term of years is vested. So there was no merger in this case.

The Doctrine of Worthier Title

3. (a) Yes, the words "next of kin" are sufficiently close to "heirs" to render the doctrine applicable since the Doctrine today is a canon of construction, not a rule of law.

   (b) No, the limitation must use just the term "heirs" or its equivalent.

   (c) An older, shortened statement of the Doctrine is that a "limitation over to an heir is void." Why? Because an heir cannot be a purchaser, meaning that the word heirs cannot be words of purchase under the Doctrine. So an executory interest is arguably just as much "a limitation over" as a remainder, so the Doctrine of Worthier Title transforms the executory interests in O's heirs to a right of reentry in O. But James Casner, an eminent authority on future interests, has disagreed. See James Casner & Barton Leach, *Property* 343 (2d ed. 1969). Professor Casner, like many traditionalists, strictly construed the Doctrine. It was fully formed by the time executory interests became established, so a strict construction of the Doctrine required that executory interests be excluded from its reach.

CHAPTER 12

The Rule Against Perpetuities

THE RULE AGAINST PERPETUITIES

You must master the present and future estate rules discussed in the previous chapters before applying the Rule Against Perpetuities (RAP). Applying the Rule may turn on events not immediately apparent, involve your imagining the deaths of many, and results in voiding future interests that "vest too remotely." The classic statement of the Rule, formulated by Professor John Chipman Gray,[1] *The Rule Against Perpetuities*, § 201 (4th ed. 1942) in its totality, provides:

> No interest is good unless it must vest, if at all, not later than twenty-one years after some life in being at the creation of the interest.

The Rule voids some future interests. It invalidates an interest not meeting its requirements. Professor Gray used the word "good" to point out that the interest conforming to the Rule is not invalid at its creation, but is instead "good." The Rule balances the marketability and alienability of land against the legitimate reasons a grantor may have for controlling who owns property after the grantor has died. In general, it permits a person to control ownership of property for one generation beyond those persons alive and

---

1. Gray (1839-1915) graduated from law school in 1861, served in the Civil War, and then entered practice in Boston. He began teaching law in 1869, was an early advocate of the case method and was the author of the first property casebook. He practiced and taught until he retired. His law firm survives to this day.

known to the grantor. It applies to both inter vivos transfers by deed and to testamentary transfers or devises by will.

The Rule Against Perpetuities, at common law, has always been and is a judicially created rule. As a judge proceeds to use the Rule, he or she may seem to you to have two personalities. At first, the judge will interpret the deed or will to establish who owns what interests and estates, according to the instrument. Here the judge attempts to carry out the transferor's intent, resorting to the canons of construction as necessary, and to apply the other rules of law studied in the prior two chapters in order to determine who has vested interests and who has contingent interests. But the Rule is, at the last, not one of intent, but is instead a rule of law. As Professor Gray said, it is not a canon of construction, but a peremptory rule of law. So, as analysis proceeds, a judge's demeanor shifts from that of trying to carry out the transferor's intent to that of seeking any possibility that any part of the transfer violates the Rule. In this stage, the judge need find only one possible scenario, no matter how remote the possibility, in which the intended transfer violates the Rule to void an interest.

THREE STEPS USING THE RULE

The use of the Rule requires a judge or a lawyer to take three and possibly four steps.

Step One. This Rule prevents the creation of certain contingent future interests. This means that it voids the interest ab initio — from the moment of its creation. The first task in using the Rule is to classify the future interest challenged under the Rule and to determine whether or not a future interest is subject to it. As one Hindu sage said, "Before we bring the heavens down, let us sit and think a little."

The Rule applies (unlike the Rule of Destructibility for Contingent Remainders) to both legal and equitable interests in real property. Indeed, much of the litigation concerning it takes place amid the law of trusts, although charitable trusts are exempted from the Rule as being public entities.

A gift to charity, followed immediately by a second charitable gift, is also not subject to the Rule. For example, O's gift "to the local School Board, but if the land is not used for school purposes, then the land is to shift over to the local Red Cross," creates a second gift (of the Red Cross's executory interest) to which the Rule does not apply. The purpose of this exemption is to encourage charitable giving, but it is often authorized and therefore circumscribed by a state statute, so research is often necessary to determine its scope.

Likewise, the state and its subdivisions are not subject to the Rule.

In carrying out this first step, the following chart is useful in identifying those interests that are subject to the Rule:

Subject to RAP	Not Subject to RAP
Contingent remainders	Vested remainders[2]
Vested remainders subject to open	Vested remainder subject to defeasance
Executory interests	Reversions
	Possibilities of reverter
	Rights of reentry

All of the foregoing are future interests. From classifying interests as this chart does, the law has drawn three conclusions about the Rule. (1) All interests vested at its creation (vested remainders subject to open being the exception) satisfy the Rule. Thus the Rule will not void any *present possessory interests* in third parties holding a life estate, fee tail, term of years, fee simple absolute, fee simple subject to a condition subsequent, fee simple determinable, or fee simple subject to an executory limitation. It may void those estates when and if they are in a contingent remainder, however. (2) As you see also in the chart above, the Rule will not void *future interests* in third persons if the interests are vested immediately upon creation. Hence the Rule will not void vested remainders (except for some vested remainders subject to open). (3) Because all future interests in the grantor are vested, the Rule will not void reversions, possibilities of reverter, and rights of reentry. It is possible however, to have a present interest subject to open or subject to partial divestment — and that interest too would be subject to the Rule.

Professor Gray's formulation of the Rule uses the phrase "unless it [the challenged interest] must vest." "Vest" is one of the more difficult abstractions in the law. In this regard, the Rule is concerned with the time within which such an estate vests (in the case of remainders, which must **vest in interest**) or become possessory (in the case of executory interests, which must **vest in possession**).[3] This time is the "**perpetuity period**," or in Professor

---

2. It is sometimes said that the Rule does not apply to indefeasibly vested remainders. This statement is more like a legal conclusion that there is a person alive at the time of the effective date of the instrument, who is able to provide a measuring life and by whom one is able to prove that the remainder will vest, or not, within the period permitted by the Rule. The person vesting the interest provides, in other words, the validating life required under the Rule.

3. Recall that a remainder is vested when all recipients are ascertained and all contingencies (conditions precedent) have been satisfied. At that point the remainder is said to be vested in interest. The vested remainder remains a future interest and the holder of a vested remainder will not have the right to possess the property until all preceding estates have ended. There is no direct relationship between being vested in interest and having the right of possession, which may occur decades after the remainder is vested in interest. A remainder can vest in interest without being currently possessory. In contrast, a person owning an executory interest will see his interest become vested and possessory at the same moment. An executory interest is said to become vested in possession. In most cases the difference between vested in interest and vested in possession will not affect your analysis.

Gray's formulation of the Rule quoted previously, "lives in being plus twenty one years, plus period of gestation" — in that order. If O devises "to A if A is living 20 years after my death" and A survives O, the devise is valid because the survivorship contingency in the springing executory interest subject to the Rule will be resolved within the period allowed by the Rule. The perpetuity period is not at all concerned with the duration of the challenged interest — that is irrelevant to the Rule. After all, the fee simple absolute can last indefinitely, but as such is not affected by the Rule. The Rule is concerned only with interests, not estates. Put another way, the Rule is concerned not with how some interest might end (that is of concern when classifying any estate), but with when they might possibly begin.

So the Rule is concerned with the postponement of either vesting or coming into possession of those future interests to which the Rule applies. Contingencies in such interests must be resolved within the perpetuity period. That resolution must be evident at the time of the initial creation of the interest. Thus the Rule's requirement is initial certainty of vesting or possession within the perpetuity period. Courts do not, under the Rule, await the unfolding of events, the way they do if the Doctrine of Destructibility of Contingent Remainders is involved. Under the Rule, in order for such an interest to be valid, there cannot be *any* possible chain of events that would permit the challenged interest not to vest in either interest or possession beyond the perpetuity period.

So the perpetuity period is not a set one; rather, it is measured by a life (one among the many) "in being" or living at the effective date of the document in which the interest challenged under the Rule appears, plus 21 years, plus actual periods of gestation.

Example 1: Owen devises Blackacre "to my grandchildren twenty one years after my death." This interest is valid under the Rule. The twenty one year period does not, for purposes of the Rule, have to be preceded by a measuring life. The interest is vested or not within the twenty one year component of the perpetuity period.

Example 2: Ozzie conveys Blackacre "to A for life, remainder to A's children who survive 21 years and 9 months after A's death." This conveyance's contingent remainder is invalid under the Rule as vesting too remotely. A period of gestation is thus not automatically part of the perpetuity period.

Example 3: Ollie devises Blackacre "to A for life, remainder to such of A's children who attain the age of 21." A survives O. "Children" is under the Rule construed to mean "children whenever born." If no child of A is alive at O's death or no child of A has reached 21 by then, the remainder is a contingent one; if a child has reached 21, then the remainder is vested subject to open. In either case, the Rule applies, but in both instances, the remainder is valid under the Rule because it will "vest" or not within the perpetuity period since all children of *A* must be conceived within his lifetime or so born (allowing for post-death gestation) within the period of the Rule.

Step Two. The second analytical task is to assemble the pool of candidates of measuring lives. From it, we can later pick and choose in order to test for the proof showing whether the interest is (again, in Gray's formulation of the Rule) "will vest or fail to vest," within the perpetuities period. If O devises "to such of my lineal descendants living 20 years after my death," the Rule applies to the descendants' springing executory interest and it is valid, not because of the 20 year survivorship contingency, but only because all those who will share in the devise will be identified within the perpetuity period.

This pool consists of those persons who (1) can either affect the vesting or taking possession of the challenged interest—that is, who will either make it happen, or who stand ready to receive its benefits, or who (2) is connected in some way to the transaction. The latter is in some ways a broader definition, as we will see later in this chapter. There is in fact some scholarly disagreement over the extent of that pool. For example, some authorities would include the transferor in the pool—others would not. This pool thus includes all those who can control the termination of the preceding estate or can meet, or not, any precondition to vest in the challenged interest itself. Keep in mind, though, that this pool has, as a precondition to membership, being alive at the effective date of the instrument—i.e., being a life in being.

A member of the pool does not have to be a devisee or a transferee under the document searched for measuring lives (although each certainly qualifies for membership). He or she can also be the survivor of a group. Indeed, a measuring life need not even be mentioned in the document. The person only needs to be linked or connected in some way to the transactions mentioned in the document. Although there is some dispute about this, having "casual connection" to the vesting or taking possession, is how the test for membership is often stated.

There are three limitations on the size of the pool. First, it must only contain a reasonable number of members; excluded are persons who all can affect vesting or taking possession in the same way when they constitute an unreasonably large group. Second, excluded are persons with the same impact on vesting or taking possession, if all of them cannot be reasonably ascertained within the perpetuities period. Third, and finally, excluded are persons whose lives have redundant impacts on the vesting or taking possession of the challenged interest.

Example 1: Owen conveys "to *A* provided that the property is used for a dry goods store, but if not, Owen and his heirs shall have the right to repurchase within six months of its ceasing to be used for said store." Is this interest option to repurchase violative of the Rule? Yes. It violates The Rule. The option is treated like a future interest, springing or shifting the fee simple like an executory interest. It can be specifically performed. Recent RAP cases often involve options to purchase because, since the 1950s, land prices have risen more than option prices, making the options worth enforcing and defending against.

Example 2: Ozzie conveys "to Acme Corporation an option to purchase Blackacre when its appraised value is greater than $1,000,000 an acre." Is the option to purchase held by a "life in being"? No. Although Acme Corporation is a legal entity with many useful purposes in our legal system, it is not a "life in being." Such a life must be that of a natural person. So the perpetuity period as to the option, is 21 years, measured in gross, and because the possibility exists that the appraised value won't rise this much over the perpetuity period, the interest is invalid. Ozzie could also become the validating life, but he might die the day after the conveyance, leaving the option to be exercised 22 years later, so with him, the interest is also invalid.

Thus has the Rule Against Perpetuities has been used to void options to purchase in commercial transactions. However, the second Example partly — the parts involving the rise in acreage prices and Ozzie's death — gets us ahead of ourselves. It involves step three.

Step Three. Having assembled the pool, the next analytical task is to find, from among all the measuring lives (plural), a **validating life** (singular). That is, the search now is for a person who must necessarily vest or take possession of the interest when the prior interest ends. If there is a valid life in being — just one, among the many whose lives are connected to the document in which the challenged interest appears — then the interest itself is valid under the Rule. Interests valid under the Rule will have a measuring life and invalid interests have none. Thus the search for a measuring life is in effect the search for the answer to the question of whether an interest is destroyed by the Rule, or not.

In this step a judge tests each member of the pool's qualifications. The goal is to find that one person for whom there exists no invalidating chain of possible events occurring after the effective date of the document. Find one such, and the interest is valid. This search is a matter of imagining what might happen to move the vesting or taking possession of the challenged interest, beyond the period permitted by the Rule. It is the "what-might-happen" method of proof, illustrated below in the problems.

Only one person need be identified to validate the interest, and conversely only one possible chain of events after the effective date of the document is sufficient to invalidate a person's qualifications to be the validating life. Showing that such a chain of events exists, is the proof required to invalidate a challenged interest. Showing that there is no such chain, proves the validity of the interest. In sum, one of the measuring lives may become the validating life.

Step Four. This step applies only when the challenged interest is found void under the Rule. Then the original transfer instrument must be revised by striking out the challenged interest and any contingency that is a precondition or condition precedent to it.

Example 1: Owen conveys "to Abby for life, then to such of Abby's children then living." Step one: The remainder is contingent, so subject to the Rule. Abby is a life in being — i.e., alive at the effective date of the conveyance, so there is no need for the 21 year period of the Rule (Abby being the validating life) since the remainder will vest or fail at the end of Abby's life.

Example 2: Ollie devises property "to A for life, then to my grandchildren who shall reach the age of 21." Step one: Is the Rule applicable to the remainder? Yes, because it is a contingent remainder. Step two: Who are the lives in being? Ollie's children. Step three: Will they procreate or die within the period allowed? Yes. So no step four rewriting is needed. Here you might ask whether the condition precedent — that is, the thing making the Rule applicable to the interest — will occur, if it occurs at all, within 21 years following the death of the measuring and validating life or lives. So here the more specific question is, will Ollie's last grandchild reach 21 within 21 years of the death of Ollie's last surviving child? The answer is yes and the remainder interest is valid under the Rule.

AN UPDATED RULE

Based on the foregoing discussion, it is appropriate to restate in plainer, modern English the Rule. Here are two updated versions:

> Any interest, other than one in the testator, grantor, or transferor, is invalid when it might (1) vest or fail to vest as a remainder, or (2) become possessory, or not, as an executory interest at a time more distant than 21 years after a life in being at the effective date of the transferor's instrument.

> No contingent remainder, executory interest, or vested remainder subject to open is valid at its creation unless it is then so created as to (1) become vested in

possession, become vested in interest, or become a vested remainder in a class no longer subject to possible partial divestment, or (2) fail by its own terms, not later than 21 years after a life in being at the time of its creation. For purposes of this Rule, the time of creation shall be the date of (1) the delivery of an inter vivos deed or (2) the death of the testator for an interest created by will, or (3) a trust's becoming irrevocable.

INTERESTS AFFECTED AND CLASS GIFTS

Step three often involves a problem concerning class gifts. The Rule Against Perpetuities has always applied to class gifts. They are considered to be, for purposes of the Rule, nonvested interests. **Vested remainders subject to open** are grants to more than one person (a class gift), where the recipients are identified by description rather than named, and/or at times must satisfy a condition precedent. As soon as one person in the class is identified and satisfies any condition precedent, that person's interest becomes vested. The interests of the remaining people in the class may still be contingent, however.

All persons receiving a class gift must pass muster under the Rule or no member's interest can be good. Professor Dukeminier called this special rule "the all-or-nothing rule." Instead of holding the class is vested if any one of the class members becomes vested, or holding that the interest of any member in the class whose interest is sure to vest (or sure to fail to vest) within the perpetuity period is valid even if other members' or prospective members' interests are not, the Rule demands each and every person in the class be certain to vest (or certain to fail to vest) within the perpetuity period. No class gift can be partly valid and partly void. If even one *potential* member of the class can be identified or envisioned who will not vest (or fail to vest) within the required period, the grant to the entire class fails and is void. We discuss class gifts in more detail later.

Example 1:   O conveys Blackacre "to A for life, then to B's children who attain age 35." B is alive and has one child, C, age 6. In taking step one, we know that A has a present (for purposes of the rule, vested) possessory interest, held in a life estate — so not subject to the Rule; B's children (C and any child born to B in the future) have a contingent remainder, contingent on being identified and on attaining age 35 — so subject to the Rule. O has a reversion — not subject to the Rule. Thus the contingent remainder to B's children is subject to the Rule. Step two: Note the contingent remainder to B's children is a class gift. All of B's children (living and potential children) are members of the class; each child to take must reach age 35. C is alive and we will know whether C reaches age 35 on or before his death, but the test is not whether one member will vest or fail to vest within the time period, or whether one member of the class is a "life in being," or whether we can envision one scenario where all members vest or fail to vest in time. Under step three, the test is, can we imagine or dream up one scenario, however improbable, in which we will not know within 21 years of all lives in being whether a member of the class will vest or fail to vest? Yes, we can. We can envision a chain of events where we will not know within 21 years of a life in being whether all of B's children either will or will not reach age 35. B could have another child, X, not a life in being at the creation of the contingent remainder. O, A, B, and C (all the relevant lives in being) could die soon after X is born. Since X is not even one year old when all relevant lives in being die, and so we will not know in 21 years whether X reaches age 35, the contingent remainder to B's children who attain age 35 violates the Rule and is, therefore, void. B's children's interest is struck from the grant. Under step four, after the Rule is applied to the original conveyance, A has a life estate, O has a reversion.

Example 2:   O conveys Whiteacre "to A for life, then to B's children in fee simple, provided if any of B's children fail to attain 35 that child's interest passes to B's surviving children." B is alive and has one child, C, age 6. As in Example 1, A has a present, vested and possessory interest held in a life estate, so not subject to the Rule. C has a vested remainder, subject to open (partial divestment) if A has more children, and subject to complete divestment if C does not reach age 35 — and subject to the Rule. Attaining age 35 is a *condition subsequent* potentially divesting a child's interest; it is not a *condition precedent* to taking an interest. Since we will know at B's death who B's children are (B cannot have a child after his death),[4] B's children's interest will vest no later than B's death. At that point, B's children will have a vested remainder subject to an executory limitation. Thus the remainder to B's children is valid under the Rule. While the conveyances in Examples 1 and 2 may be alternative wordings to achieve the transferor's intent, the conveyance in Example 2 succeeds while the one in Example 1 fails to accomplish the transferor's goals. The original transfer in Example 2, before applying the Rule, divests the vested interest of any child who does not attain age 35. Any divested interest passes to B's surviving children, if any, who therefore have a shifting executory interest in any divested interest. The shifting executory interest is subject to the Rule. It fails to satisfy the Rule. The reasoning: After every life in being (O, A, B, and C) dies, we still might not know if any of B's children's executory interests will vest in possession within 21 years of the last to die. The executory interests are void and must be deleted from the grant. Step four is now required. After deleting the offending language,

---

4. Recall that a child in gestation is considered born for purposes of the Rule.

the conveyance reads, "to A for life, then to B's children in fee simple." A has a life estate; B's children have a vested remainder in fee simple absolute. The divesting condition disappears.

The Rule Against Perpetuities is best mastered by working practice problems. In addition to the examples in this chapter, you can find more practice problems in John Makdisi and Daniel Bogart, *Estates in Land and Future Interests: Problems and Answers*, 5th ed. (Aspen 2007).

INTERESTS DEPENDENT ON AN EVENT

The Rule Against Perpetuities is likely to invalidate interests in one of three scenarios. The first is when a contingent interest (contingent remainder, executory interest, or vested remainder subject to open) depends on the occurrence or nonoccurrence of an event to vest. Unless the event must be accomplished by a life in being, during a life in being's life, or within a definite period of time less than 21 years, in all likelihood any interest dependent on the occurrence or nonoccurrence of an event will violate the rule, no matter how improbable the chances we will not know one way or the other within the perpetuities period. When a condition is an event or act, look for a life in being — known again in step three as the validating life — who must accomplish the act, or in whose life (or no longer than 21 years after that person's life ends) the event will occur or forever be unable to occur. If there is a validating life, the contingent remainder or executory interest will be good. If there is no validating life, the future interest most likely will be invalid.

    Example 1: O conveys Blackacre "to A for life, then to B and his heirs if A is given a Christian burial." Step one determines each person's interest as intended by the grantor. A has a present, vested, and possessory interest held in a life estate, O has a reversion. Neither is subject to the Rule. B, however, has a springing executory interest. (B does not have a contingent remainder since it does not follow immediately after A's life estate ends; there is a break between the time A dies and the time A is buried — or so we hope. Blackacre returns to O in that interim period.) Only B's springing executory interest is subject to the Rule.

    Step two applies the Rule to B's springing executory interest. The odds against A's either receiving or not receiving a Christian burial within 21 years of his death (and O's and B's deaths since they are lives in being also) are infinitesimal. Unfortunately, the Rule's step three is not a rule of logical proof (nor a rule of common sense). A judge can imagine a scenario in which A dies and his body is not discovered until 21 years after all lives in being have died, or in which the undertaker failed to act in the requisite time; and A is given a Christian burial more than 21 years after all lives in being have died. All it takes is one scenario in which it is uncertain whether the interest vests within the perpetuities period. In this case B's springing executory interest violates the Rule and is invalid.

Once an interest is invalid under the Rule, judges in step four literally draw a line through the invalid part of the conveyance. So a line would be drawn through "then to B and his heirs if A is given a Christian burial." What remains is "to A for life," with an unstated and implied reversion in O.

Example 2: O conveys Whiteacre "to Local School District so long as Whiteacre is used for a school, then to A and her heirs." Step one determines each party's interest before applying the Rule. Local School District has a fee simple subject to an executory limitation. A has a shifting executory interest. Local School District's fee simple subject to an executory limitation is a present, vested, and possessory interest and is not subject to the Rule. A's shifting executory interest is subject to the Rule, however. Having determined that, steps two and three apply the Rule as stringently as possible. Since Local School District may use Whiteacre for a school for a time lasting at least 21 years after all lives in being have died, the Rule voids A's executory interest because there is no validating life. Drawing a line through "then to A and her heirs" leaves a grant "to Local School District so long as Whiteacre is used for a school." After applying the Rule, Local School District has a fee simple determinable. O has a possibility of reverter (which is again not subject to the Rule).

Example 3: O conveys Brownacre "to Local School District; but if Local School District ceases to use Blackacre for a school, to A and his heirs." The analysis parallels Example 2, but with a twist. Before applying the Rule, Local School District has a fee simple subject to an executory limitation. A has a shifting executory interest. Since Local School District may use Brownacre well beyond the perpetuity period, A's executory interest violates the Rule and thus is void. Drawing a line through "but if Local School District ceases to use Brownacre for a school, to A and his heirs" leaves a grant "to Local School District." Local School District has a fee simple absolute. Neither A nor O has any interest in Brownacre. Contrast this with the result in Example 2.

Not all events can occur past the perpetuities period. If a life in being must be the one to satisfy the condition, the condition or event must happen no later than that person's death.

Example 4: O conveys Greenacre "to A and his heirs, but if A sells alcohol on Greenacre, to B and her heirs." Step one is to determine each person's interest as intended by the grantor. A has a fee simple subject to an executory limitation, an interest not subject to the Rule. B has a shifting executory interest that is subject to it. Step two applies the Rule. B's shifting executory interest is good since either A will sell alcohol on Greenacre during his life (in which case B gets Greenacre) or A will not sell alcohol on Greenacre during his life (in which case A can devise Greenacre or his heirs get it, and B gets nothing). Under step three, A's is the validating life because the condition must occur, "if at all" (the phrase used in Gray's formulation of the Rule) during A's lifetime. If the grant were changed to read "to A and his heirs, but if alcohol is ever served on Greenacre, to B and her heirs," the Rule would void B's interests since alcohol may not be sold on Greenacre until at least 21 years after all lives in being have died.

Example 5: A Property professor funds a trust with $10,000, to be paid to the first person in her current Property class who becomes a U.S. senator. The trustees have legal title and each person in the class — used in two senses here since the gift is a "class gift" — has an opportunity to claim the $10,000 by becoming a U.S. senator. Every student in the current class is a validating life. Since we will know at least by the death of the last student in the class whether any one became a U.S. senator, the gift is valid under the Rule. The probability that any student in the class will become a senator is irrelevant; only the certainty that we can tell one way or the other during the lives in being matters.

Example 6: Contrast Example 5 with these facts: A Property professor funds a trust with $10,000 to be paid to the first student to become a U.S. senator who was ever or will ever be enrolled in her Property classes during her teaching career. This is a present vested interest subject to open, so the Rule applies, but there is no validating life. It is possible that a person, X, may be born a year after the trust is established, thus not a life in being, and enroll in the professor's Property class 25 years later. Then at least 21 years after the last of the professor and all her Property students who were lives in being at the creation of the trust died, student X, who was not a life in being, may be elected U.S. senator, or may live another 50 years without holding any office. Since we might not know at the end of the perpetuities period whether anyone was vested, the interest is invalid. The Property professor gets her money back.

GRANTEES IDENTIFIED BY DESCRIPTION RATHER THAN NAMED

A second scenario that raises Rule Against Perpetuities concerns occurs when a measuring life or a recipient of a contingent remainder or executory interests is described by a label rather than a name. The rub comes because a person who was not a life in being at the creation of the interest can fit the description. The most troublesome situation arises when some person already seems to fit the description, and likely will be the person to fit the description, but a remote chance exists that some other person ultimately might be the one described. A famous example in this category is the unborn widow — or, as some today might call it, the Anna Nicole Smith example.[5]

Unborn Widow Example: O conveys Blackacre "to A for life, then to A's widow, if any, for life, then to A's issue then living." This is an understandable grant, especially if A is married at the time of the grant. Unfortunately, A's current spouse may not be A's widow, and the person who will be A's widow may not even be a life in being at the creation of the interest. A, for example, may divorce or become widowed himself, and many years later may marry someone who had not been born at the time of the original grant. Step one determines each person's interest as intended by the grantor. A has a present, vested, and possessory interest held in a life estate not subject to the Rule; A's widow has a contingent remainder in a life estate, contingent on being identified, and we must wait until A's death to identify A's widow, "A's issue then living" is also a contingent remainder, contingent on being alive when A's widow dies.

Step two applies the Rule. A's widow's contingent remainder is valid under the Rule. A's widow will be identified immediately upon A's death, and once identified her interest is vested. A is the validating life for his widow's interest. A was a life in being at the creation of the interests so A's widow's interest will be vested well within the perpetuity period. If A dies without a widow, that fact is known at A's death also.

The contingent remainder in A's issue then living at A's widow's death, on the other hand, fails to satisfy the Rule. A's issue then living must satisfy two contingencies. First, A's children must be identified, which they will be by A's death (or nine months thereafter), so that causes no RAP problem. Second, the children must survive A's widow. A's widow is not a validating life since she might not have been a life in being at the creation of the interest. Under step three, it is possible to imagine that A will divorce his current spouse, then 30 years later A will marry a woman who was not born when the interest was created. All of A's children by his prior marriage and his first wife may die. A and his new spouse may have children, also not lives

---

5. When Anna Nicole Smith married Howard Marshall in 1994, she was 63 years younger than he was on the date of his marriage. Such marriages do not happen very often — but their frequency is irrelevant to the Rule. Such a marriage could happen and when they do, the Rule assumes that the Howard Marshalls of this world are fertile — an assumption known often as the "fertile octogenarian" rule — and might conceive a child on the wedding night and die the next day. See Marshall v. Marshall, 126 Sup. Ct. 1735 (2006).

in being at the creation of the children's contingent remainder. *A* dies, leaving a widow and children, none of whom were lives in being at the creation of the children's contingent remainder. *A*'s widow easily might live another 21-plus years, so it is possible we will not know within the perpetuity period which of *A*'s children survive *A*'s widow. *A*'s children's contingent interest, therefore, is invalid under the Rule.

Drawing a line through "then to *A*'s children then living," the remaining grant as rewritten reads, "to *A* for life, then to *A*'s widow, if any, for life." *A* has a present interest held in a life estate, *A*'s widow has a contingent remainder held in a life estate, and *O* has a reversion not subject to the Rule.

This example also shows that the use of the word children, without specifying that the children must be alive and vest at the termination of some valid interest, is likely to run afoul of the Rule.

A similar situation may occur where, for example, *O* conveys "to *A* for life, then to *A*'s children for life, then to the principal of City High School." The grant to the City High School principal is invalid. Labels such as husband, wife, widow, mayor, minister, president, and so on, present similar difficulties under the Rule. When testing interests held by a person identified by or following an interest held by a person identified by a descriptive label, separate the possible ultimate recipient from the identifiable person currently wearing the label.

ACQUIRING A STEP THREE IMAGINATION

The unborn widow example is but one of several types of daydreams that can void an interest under the Rule. It relies on the assumption that any living person, no matter how old, could marry at any age and then could have a child. An associated assumption is that a child, no matter how young, could have a child. Professor Barton Leach called this second assumption the "precocious toddler rule." Other assumptions result in the following famous flights of imagination:

Example 1: Owen puts some mineral properties he owns on Blackacre into a trust, directing his trustee to "work them until the gravel pits are exhausted, and then to sell them." Because the pits might possibly be worked for a perpetuity period longer than the Rule allows, the trust and all the interests in it are invalid.

Example 2: Ozzie devises Whiteacre "to my relatives who survive the war." Even if the war was going on when Ozzie dies, there is the possibility that it might last longer than the perpetuity period, so that the entire interest of the relatives was invalid under the Rule. This is the "interminable war" example.

Example 3: Ollie devises Brownacre "to my issue living at the distribution of my estate." Under step one, the interest in the issue is a springing executory interest, and so subject to the Rule. The issue living at the time of the distribution are the measuring lives, but all of them might procreate after Ollie's death and then die before the distribution. The interest is invalid. This is the so-called administrative contingency or the "slothful executor" example.

Thus typical conditions and events that run afoul of the Rule are "when a decedent's estate is settled," "when all the gravel is taken from the land," "when my estate is settled," "when a bridge [or building or road] is completed," "as long as used for school purposes" (or church purposes, or park purposes, or lodge purposes), and "after the next President is elected."

INTERGENERATIONAL FAMILY TRANSFERS

Intergenerational family transfers invoke Rule Against Perpetuities scrutiny. The compromise that is the Rule allows a grantor to control ownership of property "from the grave" for persons he knew plus one generation, while not allowing control beyond that generation. Thus the Rule prevents a person from devising property to his children for life, to his grandchildren for life, to his grandchildren's children for life, and so on for centuries. The vesting in interest or possession must occur within or at the end of lives of persons with whom the devisor or transferor dealt face to face. So one key to finding RAP violations is isolating open classes of individuals (classes in which more people can be added, usually by birth). In general, unless the class is subject to a condition precedent other than being born, a class subject to open following a possessory interest will not violate the Rule, but any class gift subject to open held by members of a subsequent generation will violate the Rule.

Example 1: O devises Blackacre "to his son A for life, then to A's children for life, then to A's grandchildren in fee simple." A has no children. Step one determines what interests the testator intended to convey. A owns a present, vested and possessory interest held in a life estate not subject to the Rule; A's children have a contingent remainder held in a life estate, contingent on being born; and A's grandchildren have a contingent remainder held in fee simple absolute, again contingent on being born. Step two applies the Rule to the last two interests, but the contingent remainder to A's children is valid since we will know at *A*'s death whether *A* had any children and who they are. *A* is the validating life for *A*'s children's interest. The class of *A*'s children closes biologically immediately on *A*'s death.[6] The interest in *A*'s grandchildren, on the other hand, violates the Rule. The members of the class can be increased by *A*'s children having children. *A*'s children (or any of them) cannot be validating lives since an after-born child can become a member of the class. In one scenario, for example, *A* could have a child, *X*, who is not a life in being at the creation of the interest. *A* could die suddenly. *X*'s first child may not be born until 21 years after *A* dies. Since under this scenario we will not know whether the interest to *A*'s grandchildren will vest until after the perpetuity period ends, the entire contingent remainder to *A*'s grandchildren fails. The transfer to *A*'s grandchildren fails because the class of persons who can give birth to new members of the class itself can grow to include persons who were not lives in being at the creation of the interest. Finally, as to step four, the will as rewritten after striking out the grandchildren's interest is "to his son *A* for life, then to *A*'s children for life." *A* has a present interest held in a life estate, *A*'s children have a contingent remainder held in a life estate, and O's heirs or devisees have a reversion.

Example 2:   O conveys Whiteacre "to *A* for life, then to *A*'s children for life, then to B's grandchildren." *A* and B are both alive and childless. O intended to give *A* a present interest held in a life estate, *A*'s children a contingent remainder held in a life estate, contingent on *A*'s having children, and a contingent remainder held in fee simple absolute to B's grandchildren, contingent on B's grandchildren being born (no survivorship requirement). Under the Rule, the interests given to *A* and to *A*'s children are valid: as to *A* because he is already vested, and as to *A*'s children because we will know at *A*'s death whether *A* had any children (and who they are). B's grandchildren's contingent remainder, contingent on B's grandchildren being born, violates the Rule, however. The group that can increase the members of the class of B's grandchildren are B's children. Since B is alive she may have one or more children, none of whom would be lives in being at the creation of the interest. Neither B nor B's children are validating lives. B's after-born children could live at least 21 years after the last to die of *A*, B, and O, before procreating any of B's grandchildren. The contingent remainder to B's grandchildren, therefore, is invalid under the Rule since it is possible a grandchild may be born after the perpetuity period has run. By drawing a line through "then to B's grandchildren," the grant is "to *A* for life, then to *A*'s children for life." *A* has life estate, *A*'s children have a vested remainder

---

6. For more on class closings biologically and by the rule of convenience, see supra, Chapter 11.

held in a life estate, and O has a reversion. B's grandchildren have no interest in Whiteacre.

Not all grants to grandchildren are invalid, however. Sometimes a descriptive class can be the validating lives if no after-born person can enter the class. Compare the above Example with the following:

Example 3: O conveys Greenacre "to *A* for life, then to *A*'s children for life, then to *B*'s grandchildren." *A* is alive; *B* is dead, survived by two children, *C* and *D*. As in the prior Example, *A*'s life estate and *A*'s children's contingent remainder are valid under the Rule. Before applying the Rule, *B*'s grandchildren have a contingent remainder in fee simple absolute, contingent on being born. The class of individuals that can procreate and so add more people to the class of *B*'s grandchildren are *B*'s children. In contrast to the prior example, when B herself could have more children, here B, being dead, cannot have any more children. Thus the class of *B*'s children is fixed at two children, C and D, both of whom are lives in being at the creation of the interest. C and D are validating lives. Since we will know whether B had any grandchildren, and who they are, no later than the death of the last to die of C and D, *B*'s grandchildren's contingent remainder will vest at that time if B has any grandchildren, or never vest if B has no grandchildren by that time. The contingent remainder in *B*'s grandchildren is valid.

EFFECT OF CLASS CLOSING RULES

As explained in Chapter 10, classes can close physiologically (naturally or biologically) or by the Rule of Convenience. A class closes *physiologically* whenever no one else can enter the class; usually this means, be born into the class. The preceding three examples illustrate a class closing physiologically. No new child could enter a class when the potential parents and grandparents have died. A class closes pursuant to the **Rule of Convenience** when any member of the class can demand possession of the property. See supra, Chapter 10, for a fuller explanation.

Closing a class does not end the inquiry. Even though a class closes, either physiologically or by the Rule of Convenience, all persons who comprise the class, in addition to being members of the class must be certain to vest (or fail to vest) within the perpetuities period. If just one member of the class is not certain to satisfy the Rule Against Perpetuities, the grant to everyone in the class fails. That bears reiterating: All it takes is one member or hypothetical member of a class to fail to satisfy the Rule Against Perpetuities for the grant to the class to fail, even to those members already vested. This can happen by the class remaining open past the perpetuities period. In addition, it can happen even if the class is closed, if the members cannot satisfy a condition precedent within the perpetuities period.

Example 1: O devises Blackacre "to A for life, then to B's children who attain age 20." B has no children. O intended A to have a life estate and B's children to have a contingent remainder, contingent on attaining age 20. Applying the Rule Against Perpetuities, A's life estate is valid since it is a present interest. Likewise, the contingent remainder to B's children who attain age 20 is good. B is the validating life. The class of B's children — the class is B's children, not B's children who attain age 20 — closes *physiologically* when B dies or, if B is still alive at A's death, by the Rule of Convenience if at least one of B's children has turned 20 by A's death. Or if B never has any children, we will know that by her death. If B has children, after the class closes, all persons who form the class must attain age 20 or definitely fail ever to reach age 20 (by dying prematurely, for example) within 21 years of the last to die of A or B. In this example, since no child can be born to B after she dies, all of B's children will be sure to turn 20 or die before age 20 within 21 years of B's death. Hence, B's children's contingent remainder is valid.

Example 2: O devises Whiteacre "to A for life, then to B's children who attain age 30." B has no children. The only difference between this and the prior example is that in this example B's children must attain age 30. Because of this difference, however, the contingent remainder to B's children fails. B is not a validating life. The class may close when B dies but the contingency of attaining age 30 presents an insurmountable obstacle. B may die the day her youngest child is born, and A may also die that day. In 21 years B's youngest child may be 21, but will still be uncertain whether he or she will attain age 30. RAP does not tolerate uncertainty. B's children's interest fails. Drawing a line through the interest to B's children, A has a life estate, and O's heirs or devisees have a vested remainder in fee simple absolute.

Example 3: Same facts as in Example 2, except B has two children, K, age 33, and L, age 28, when the devise is effective. Before applying the RAP, K has a vested remainder subject to open and L has a contingent remainder, contingent on turning 30. Applying the Rule, the remainder to B's children is invalid. The reason is the class of B's children does not close until either A or B dies. Once the class closes, the last person — living or hypothetical — to enter the class must satisfy the condition precedent within the perpetuities period. An invalidating scenario envisions B having another child, X, and A, B, K, and L die soon after X is born. In that case we won't know for certain within 21 years whether one-year-old X will reach age 30. Hence the gift to the entire class of B's children fails, even though one member already satisfies the condition precedent, and one will or will not do so within a couple of years. Drawing a line through the interest given to B's children, A has a life estate, and O's heirs or devisees have a vested remainder in fee simple absolute.

Example 4: O devises Brownacre to *A* for life, then to *B*'s children who attain age 30. B is dead, survived by K, age 33, L, age 28, and M, age 15. The class is closed physiologically since B, the parent, is dead. Since we will know within 21 years of lives in being (K, L, and M are all lives in being so we will know during their lives in being) which of B's children attain age 30, the vested remainder subject to open is valid.

Example 5: Same facts as in Example 4, except M is age 3. The vested remainder subject to open is still valid. The class is closed physiologically because B is dead, and all three children (K, L, and M) were lives in being at the creation of the interest. So we will know at or before the last of B's children to die whether they attain age 30. B's children themselves are the validating lives. No more children can enter the class. Recall that the perpetuity period is 21 years after all lives in being have died, which includes three-year-old M.

Example 6: Same facts as Example 4, except B is alive and *A* is dead when O's devise becomes effective. The grant to B's children is valid. Since K is age 33 and thus meets the condition precedent, K has a vested interest. A second consequence of K's being vested is that at the end of *A*'s life estate (which never began here since *A* predeceased O), K can demand distribution of her share of Brownacre to own in fee simple subject to partial divestment if her siblings attain age 30. Under the Rule of Convenience, since K can demand distribution, the class of B's children closes. If B has another child, that afterborn child cannot share in Brownacre. Once the class closes, the question becomes whether we are certain to know within 21 years of a life in being if all the members of the class will reach age 30. Since all the members in the class of B's children in this Example are lives in being — and are validating lives since the class is closed — the answer is yes. The grant to B's children is valid.

COMMERCIAL OPTIONS

Early Rule Against Perpetuities issues centered on intergenerational transfers. Interests frequently challenged under the Rule today are options and rights of first refusal. A person may sell land, for example, and stipulate that if the purchaser ever finds a buyer for the property, the original seller has the right to repurchase the land for the price offered by the third party. The seller here has a right of first refusal. It is possible no buyer will be found until after all lives in being have been dead for at least 21 years. Alternatively, a person may acquire an option to purchase land without an outside time limit on the right to exercise the option.

Some commentators dislike extending the Rule to options, favoring instead a more direct inquiry into whether the option is an unreasonable restraint on alienation. Such a restraint is concerned with the duration of an interest. RAP, on the other hand, is concerned not with an interest's duration, but whether or not it vests beyond the perpetuity period. It is not a Rule that voids interests that last too long, but instead voids interests that vest too remotely. Nonetheless, many courts have concluded that an option to purchase is a property interest akin to a springing or shifting executory interest; therefore, they invalidate options to purchase that have no expiration date. Most courts relying on the Rule will not imply a reasonable time period in the agreement, using instead the 21 year period allowed by the Rule. (Recall that the 21 year period of the Rule can come first, and not just succeed the lives in being, when the Rule is applied.) Other courts have refused to extend RAP to options and rights to repurchase.

Example 1: In a state that subjects options to the Rule Against Perpetuities, O gives A the option to purchase Blackacre for $100,000, the option to be good for six months after the State Highway Department completes the Lane Road Bridge over Green River. Since the state may not complete the bridge over Green River within 21 years of any lives in being, the option violates the Rule.

Example 2: In a state that subjects options to the Rule Against Perpetuities, O leases Whiteacre to T for 99 years, giving T, her heirs, successors, and assigns an option to purchase Whiteacre. Since a lease is not subject to the Rule, the option to purchase isn't either. The option is appurtenant to an interest not subject to the Rule and so is not itself subject to it. This makes sense in a modern context too, since the option gives T an incentive to invest in improvements on Whiteacre and in any event promotes the alienability of Whiteacre's title because its exercise, through the doctrine of merger, puts the title previously split between landlord and tenant back together.

Good drafting can save an option or right of first refusal from a RAP challenge. First, drafter can establish a time period of less than 21 years in which the holder of the interest can exercise the option or right. Second, the optionee can be given the sole right to exercise the option or right, specifying that it is not exercisable by the optionee's heirs, assigns or successors. Third, the option or right can be exercisable only by named persons, such as the president of the optionee corporation or other legal entity. Fourth, the option or right can be subject to termination at regular intervals, each of which is within the gross period of the Rule. Finally, the option or right can be explicitly made commercial in nature and governed by commercially reasonable terms and conditions known to the law of contracts, as opposed to real property law.

STATUTORY REFORMS OF THE RULE

The Rule Against Perpetuities in its pure form remains the law in a handful of jurisdictions. Some six states have abolished it. Most of these substituted a statutory provision prohibiting unreasonable restraints on alienation instead. In addition, some states have modified Rule substantially.

(a) The Wait-and-See Doctrine

Wait-and-see means what it says. First, an interest is found — or not — to violate the Rule Against Perpetuities in its common law form. Second, if a violation is found, then the courts await the end of the perpetuity period set up in the instrument — deed, will, or trust — to see what actually are the facts at the end of the period. Courts thus use actual facts, not possible ones, permitting consideration of facts arising after the creation of the challenged interest. With an "actual fact" test to apply, if the interest has vested by then, it is good — if not, it is invalid and a declaration of invalidity is available. Thus, if O devises Blackacre "to A for life, remainder to A's children reaching 25 years of age" and A survives O, but none of his children have attained age 25, we await events as they unfold. If A never has children, if all of the children predecease A, none having lived to 25, the contingent remainder fails under the doctrine. If A dies survived by children ages 1 and 2, the remainder again fails because neither will attain age 25 within the A's life (his is the life in being) plus 21 years. The wait-and-see doctrine was introduced into the law both by statute and judicial decision and has, since the 1960s, reduced the number of reported RAP cases dramatically. About a dozen states today have adopted some form of this doctrine.

(b) The Uniform Statutory Rule Against Perpetuities

A second wave of RAP reform followed the introduction of the wait-and-see doctrine. Twenty two states have adopted a statutory approach set out in the Uniform Statutory Rule Against Perpetuities (USRAP), promulgated in 1986 by the Commissioners on Uniform State Laws, and made part of the Uniform Probate Code. Under USRAP, a court will wait and see what happens instead of imagining one scenario under which the Rule would be violated. If the interest vests (or it becomes certain the interest will never vest) within the waiting period, the interest is valid; otherwise, it is not.

201

Unlike the wait-and-see doctrine, however, the waiting period under USRAP is a definite period of time — usually a period of 90 years — at the end of which the "actual fact" test is applied.

Thus the wait-and-see doctrine and USRAP both use a cumulative approach to reform: the interest that is challenged and found void under the common law RAP, is given a second chance and evaluated under the wait-and-see doctrine in either its basic or USRAP form. Kentucky, Mississippi, New Hampshire, Ohio, Pennsylvania, Rhode Island, and Vermont still use the wait-and-see doctrine in its original form. Many other states that had adopted that form have since switched to the 90 year, USRAP version, finding it easier to apply.

(c) The Cy Pres Doctrine

In a few states, a court will also reform an instrument to validate contingent interests, attempting to carry out the transferor's intent in a way that does not violate the Rule Against Perpetuities. Cy Pres mean "as near as possible" in Latin and so provides a judicially applied rule of construction, not a rule of law. As such, this equitable doctrine is used to construe the transferor's intent so as to save, rather than to destroy, the challenged interest. Unlike the wait-and-see doctrine, it does not typically require that there be a waiting period before the legal effect of a transfer can be ascertained. Under neither the wait-and-see nor cy pres doctrines, the law does not require waiting or reformation of the challenged interest if waiting or reformation would serve no useful purpose. Thus, if O conveys Blackacre "to A for life, remainder to A's child born naturally to A who attains the age of 21" when A is childless and also incapable of conceiving and bearing a child, a declaration that the remainder is void is available at the time of O's death.

THE RULE AND TRUST LAW

Creating a trust separates the legal from the equitable title to property. The trust agreement conveys the legal title of designated real or personal property to a trustee (either a natural person or the trust department of a bank), and the equitable title to a person or persons who benefit from the trust, known as its beneficiaries. A trustee is a fiduciary. Property held in trust is known as trust property, or the *corpus* or *res* of the trust. Property in trust may be added to over time by the person creating the trust — known as the settlor. A trust may be created inter vivos or by will at death. A trust created by will is a matter of public record because a will is probated in a court. But an inter vivos trust need not be a matter of public record — and the resulting privacy is often a motive for using it. Some of the strongest advocates for reforming the common law Rule Against Perpetuities have been the trusts and estates departments of banks and the law firms that counsel them. The express trust is useful to convert wealth and to transfer it from generation to generation. Typically, the res of a trust is stocks, bonds, or other financial instruments. Here the Rule gets in the way.

One method of reform is to abolish the Rule as it applies to trusts. Another is to establish a perpetuity period for trusts that is a fixed number of years — sometimes so long that the trusts permitted as a result are known as "*dynasty trusts*."[7] About one-fourth of the states have modified the Rule to exempt such trusts from the Rule if the power to alienate the trust property is not suspended beyond the new perpetuity period. Some states permit trusts to last a long time (1000 years in Colorado and Utah; 360 years in Florida and Nevada; 150 years in Virginia, Ohio, and a few other states). The Rule in these states still applies to legal estates, but a trustee's retention of legal title has meant that while the beneficiaries of a trust change, the legal title does not. It is in this latter, unchanging title from which numerous attempts to avoid estate taxes spring. Hence the incentive to reform the Rule in order to attract trust business to a state's bank and trust companies.

Estate tax problems aside, there are several reasons for wealthy persons to use trusts. First, trustees are usually sophisticated investors of a trust's assets, swelling their value over the long term. Second, few restraints on the alienation of trust assets by a trustee exist. Third, assets held together grow over time at a rate often exceeding assets without such continuity. Finally, a beneficiary's ability to withdraw some trust assets annually further makes an equitable interest in a trust more like ownership. Factors such as these four spur the use of trusts and Rule's elimination as a bar to their use. Once it was thought the trusts made their beneficiaries lazy. No more!

Examples

Unless otherwise stated, assume the common law Rule of Perpetuities applies to the following Examples.

Grandpa's Class Gift

1. O executed a will six years ago, devising Blackacre to *A* for life, then to *A*'s children for their lives, then to *A*'s grandchildren. At the time, O, *A*, and *A*'s two children (L and M) are alive.

    O dies. *A* died two years before O's death, survived by L, M, and *A*'s newborn daughter, P, and one grandchild, R.

---

7. While best explained in a study of estate and gift taxation, the reform of the Rule, the rise of these trusts, and amendments to the federal estate provisions of the Internal Revenue Code are intertwined in numerous ways. Attempts to tax so-called generation-skipping trusts have occurred alongside RAP reforms.

(a) Who are the lives in being at the creation of the interest?
(b) Are the devised interests valid under the Rule Against Perpetuities?
(c) What result if *A* were alive at *O*'s death?

Another Grandpa Story

2. *O* devises and "to *A* for life, then to *A*'s children for their lives, then to *A*'s grandchildren living at the death of *A*'s last surviving child." At *O*'s death, *A* and his two children, *X* and *Y*, are living. Is the Rule Against Perpetuities violated by this devise?

The Big Event

3. (a) *O* conveys Whiteacre "to *A* and his heirs so long as a commercial use is not made of the property, and, if it is used for a commercial purpose, then to *B* and her heirs." How does this grant fare under a Rule Against Perpetuities analysis?
   (b) What result if *O*'s grant was "to *A* and his heirs; but if used for commercial purposes, to *B* and her heirs?"
   (c) What result if *O*'s grant is to "to *A* and his heirs so long as *A* does not use Whiteacre for commercial purposes, and if *A* uses Whiteacre for a commercial purpose, then to *B* and her heirs?"

RAP Session

4. (a) *O* conveys Blackacre "to *A* for life so long as *A* uses Blackacre as a residence, then to *B* and her heirs, but if liquor is sold there, to *C* and her heirs." Do *B*'s and *C*'s interests violate the Rule Against Perpetuities?
   (b) *O* conveys Brownacre "to *A* for life, then 30 years after *A* dies, to *B* and his heirs." *B* dies, leaving *C* as his heir. Does *B*'s interest violate the Rule Against Perpetuities?
   (c) *O* conveys Whiteacre "to *A* for life, then to *A*'s children for their lives, then to *B*." Is *B*'s future interest valid under the Rule Against Perpetuities?
   (d) *O*, in his will, devises Redacre "to my grandchildren who attain age 21." *O* is survived by his son, *A*, but no grandchildren. Is the grant to *O*'s grandchildren valid?
   (e) *O* while alive conveys Greenacre "to such of my grandchildren who attain 21." *O* has one child, *A*, and one grandchild, *GC*. Is this interest valid under the Rule Against Perpetuities?

Wait and See

5. Assume the following occur in a wait-and-see jurisdiction:
   (a) *O* devises Blackacre to "to *A* for life, remainder to *A*'s child first reaching the age of 25." *A* has no children either at *O*'s death or at

A's death. The remainder to A's child would be void under the common law Rule Against Perpetuities. How does it fare in a jurisdiction with a wait-and-see statute?

(b) What if, in the devise in (a), A's only child is born after the interest is created, and is three years old at A's death? Is the remainder valid in a wait-and-see jurisdiction?

(c) What if A dies survived by his two children, two-year-old B and four-year-old C? B then dies. Is the gift valid in a wait-and-see jurisdiction?

(d) What if, in (c), it was C rather than B who died just after A's death?

(e) On January 1, 2005, O conveys Whiteacre "to A and his heirs so long as a commercial use is not made of the property, and if it is used for a commercial purpose, then to B and her heirs." What result in a wait-and-see jurisdiction?

Explanations

Grandpa's Class Gift

1. (a) A will becomes operational upon the testator's death. Until that time the will can be revoked or amended, and the owner can sell, assign, or gift any property mentioned in the will. The interests, therefore, were created at the time of O's death, rather than when O executed his will six year previously. The lives in being at the time of the death were L, M, P, and R. O and A were both dead and thus not lives in being at the creation of the interests.

(b) Step one is to determine what interests O intended his will to create. Since A is dead, under the will, A's children, L, M, and P, have vested possessory life estates and A's grandchild, R, has vested remainder subject to open in fee simple absolute. The possessory life estates are vested and thus not subject to the Rule Against Perpetuities. The vested remainder subject to open must be tested by the Rule Against Perpetuities since it is a class gift and every member of the class must satisfy the Rule for the class gift to be good: a class gift passes or fails as a unit.

As tested, the class gift to A's grandchildren is good. The validating lives are A's children since we must know at their deaths who their children are. A's children were lives in being at the creation of the interest (i.e., at O's death) and no more children can be born to A and added to the class of A's children. The class of A's grandchildren closes physiologically when the last of A's children dies. Since the class of A's grandchildren closes at the last to die of A's children, the gift to A's grandchildren is good.

(c) R's vested remainder subject to open and any executory interest in future-born A's grandchildren violate the Rule Against Perpetuities if

A is alive at O's death. O intended a life estate in A, a vested remainder subject to open in life estate in A's children, and a vested remainder subject to open in fee simple to R and A's other grandchildren when born. The gift to A is valid since A owns a possessory life estate. The vested remainder subject to open in A's children is valid since the class of A's children closes physiologically and by the Rule of Convenience when A dies, and becomes both possessory and vested immediately upon A's death. A is the validating life.

The vested remainder subject to open in R is invalid, however. An interest is invalid if there is any chance we could not be certain that every possible holder would either be vested or be certain to fail to vest within 21 years of a life in being. In this case, R, L, M, and P could all die suddenly. A could have another child, X. A could die shortly after X is born, and X could live well past 21 years before having any children, or could live a hundred years without having any children. Either way, the class gift to A's children would not be closed until the perpetuity period lapsed.

The interest to R (and A's grandchildren) being invalid, the devise is to A for life, to A's children for life, then to O's heirs or devisees.

Another Grandpa Story

2. The answer is yes, in part. Step One. The remainder to A is vested, so the Rule is inapplicable to it. The remainder to A's children is a vested remainder subject to open in life estate. A's is a validating life — meaning A is alive, no persons who were not lives in being can enter the same class as A (or fit his description), and a class must of logical certainty close at or before A's death or within 21 years of his death — and at his death and no later than his death we will know who his children are. Hence the class of A's children will close and be vested immediately at A's death. A's children's vested remainder subject to open in a life estate is valid under the Rule.

Step two. However, the remainder to A's grandchildren is invalid. The interest is a contingent remainder. The two conditions precedent are the grandchildren being ascertained (which can be done by being born) and surviving until the death of the survivor of A's children. So the Rule applies. For the contingent remainder to A's grandchildren to be valid, we must know for certain which potential grandchildren of A will have died before the last of A's children to die, and which will survive; and we must know these things within 21 years of the lives in being at the creation of the interest. It's possible we will not know them within the perpetuity period.

Step three. The hitch is that there is no validating life, no life in being for which we must know one way or the other before he dies (or 21 years after his death) whether the contingency has occurred or will never occur. Normally, A's children would be the validating lives for A's grandchildren. Unfortunately, in our case "A's children" itself is a class subject to open for after-born children of A, himself a life in being, and also the possible progenitor of more children.

A could have another child, Z, born after O's death; A, X, and Y could then die; 22 years later, Z could have a child, GC (a grandchild of A). GC possibly being born 22 years after all lives in being have died already is an event indicating we will not know within 21 years of a life in being which, if any, of A's grandchildren will survive the last to die of A's children. In addition, Z is not dead yet, and easily could live another 50 years, making it at least 70 years since the last life in being died before we will know if GC survived Z. The Rule does not permit 70 years of uncertainty in this situation.

Step four. As rewritten after invalidating A's grandchildren's interest, O's devise is to A for life, then to A's children for their lives, then to O's heirs or devisees.

The Big Event

3. (a) A has a fee simple subject to an executory limitation and B has a shifting executory interest. A's fee simple subject to an executory interest is a vested possessory interest and not subject to the Rule. The shifting executory interest in B is subject to the Rule, and is invalid under the Rule. The condition subsequent to A's interest, and thus the condition precedent to B's executory interest, is an event, use of the property for commercial purposes. Since Whiteacre may be used for noncommercial purposes for centuries after all relevant lives in being have died, B's shifting executory interest is invalid. Just because the grant mentions two lives in being (A and B) does not mean the condition must occur during their lives. Drawing a line through B's shifting executory interest, the grant reads, "To A and his heirs so long as a commercial use is not made of the property." As rewritten, A has a fee simple determinable. O (or his heirs or devisees) has a possibility of reverter.

   (b) A's interest is a fee simple subject to an executory limitation, and B has a shifting executory interest. A's interest is a present possessory vested interest and thus not subject to the Rule. B's shifting executory interest is invalid under the Rule since the event, using Whiteacre for commercial purposes, may not occur until A and B, the relevant lives in being, have been dead for decades. Drawing a line through B's invalid executory interest, the grant reads, "to A and his heirs." A owns Whiteacre in fee simple absolute. O and B have no interest in Whiteacre. Compare the result in (a).

(c) O intended A to own a fee simple subject to an executory limitation, and B to own a shifting executory interest. A's present possessory interest is vested and not subject to the Rule. B's shifting executory interest dependent on a condition precedent, A's using the land for commercial purposes, is subject to the Rule. In contrast to B's interest in (a) and (b), this time B's interest is good. A is the validating life here. The divesting event by its terms must occur during A's lifetime and A was a life in being at the creation of the interest.

LESSON: When drafting transfers dependent on an event to shift an interest, write the condition so that it can occur only during a life in being at the time the interest is effective — i.e., write it as follows: "to A and her heirs so long as A resides there, then to B and her heirs." This ties the interest to A and limits its force to the length of A's life. It is impossible then for this executory interest to vest only after the lives in being plus 21 years. Stated another way, unless a divesting event must occur during a life in being, the executory interest following a fee simple subject to an executory limitation violates the Rule.

RAP Session

4. (a) B has a vested remainder subject to an executory interest (alternatively, give yourself bonus points if you said B received a vested remainder subject to divestment in fee simple absolute since B may lose her interest if A sells liquor on Blackacre). As a vested interest, it is not subject to the Rule Against Perpetuities. B's interest is valid.

C has a shifting executory interest. It is invalid under the Rule, however. The divesting event, liquor being sold on Blackacre, may occur during A's life estate determinable (if used as a residence), during A's life, or decades after all lives in being have died. This is another "events" type RAP question. Rewriting the grant after striking out C's executory interest, A has a life estate determinable and B has a vested remainder in fee simple absolute. O and C have nothing.

(b) Yes, B's interest violates the Rule. The original grant gave A a life estate, O a reversion in fee simple subject to a springing executory interest, and B a springing executory interest. A's life estate and O's reversion are not subject to the Rule. There is no survivorship requirement for B to take, only the passage of time. An executory interest must vest in possession (rather than just vest in interest) to be valid, however. Unfortunately, the 30 years that must pass after *A*'s life estate ends before the springing executory interest becomes possessory is way too long. *O* and *B* could die about the same time *A* does. If so, 21 years later still no one would be entitled to possession of the executory interest. As rewritten after striking *B*'s springing executory interest, *A* has a life estate, and *O* has a reversion.

(c) *A* has a life estate; *A*'s children have a contingent remainder in life estate, contingent on being ascertained; and *B* has a vested remainder. *A*'s life estate is not subject to the Rule. *A*'s children's contingent remainder is subject to the Rule. *A* is the validating life for a grant to *A*'s children. We will know at *A*'s death who *A*'s children are. Therefore, the contingent remainder in life estate in *A*'s children is good. *B*'s interest is a vested remainder. Unlike executory interests, vested remainders need only be vested in interest not vested in possession. *B*'s vested remainder is good.

(d) Yes, *O*'s grandchildren's interest is valid. The example does not say who owns Redacre until *O*'s grandchildren turn 21, but at any rate *O* intended the grandchildren to have an executory interest. An executory interest must vest in possession within 21 years (or, more precisely, 21 years plus 9 months' gestation period) after all lives in being at the creation of the interest have died. *A* is a validating life since *O*'s grandchildren are the same as *A*'s children, *A* is a life in being, and no other person can enter the class of *O*'s children. Once *A* dies, the class of *O*'s grandchildren closes physiologically. Each member of the class will have either attained age 21 or died before reaching age 21 in the 21 years after *A* dies. The interest to *O*'s grandchildren, therefore, is good.

Note, however, that if *O*'s grandchildren must attain age 22, the gift would be invalid since *A* might die days after his youngest child is born, and 21 years later we still won't know if that child will reach age 22. The Rule would void the interest of that child and every child in the class of *O*'s grandchildren, even those who have already reached age 22.

(e) *O*'s grandchildren would receive a springing executory interest. It is not a vested remainder subject to open since the interest does not follow the natural termination of a life estate or estate for years. It cuts short *O*'s fee simple. What might happen? *A* and *GC* might die soon after the interest is created. *O* might have another child, *B*. *O* then could die, survived by *B*, who was not a life in being. In 21 years we might not know if *B* has any children (if *O* will have any grandchildren, and how many), much less whether all of *O*'s grandchildren will attain age 21. The gift is void. *O* still owns a fee simple absolute. Compare (d).

Wait and See

5. (a) In a "wait-and-see" jurisdiction, we may not know if the contingent remainder in "A's child first reaching the age of 25" is met within the 21-year perpetuities period until 21 years after A dies. No decision can be made either way on O's death. We must wait to see if A has any children during his life. If A dies childless, as in this Example, no one will satisfy the condition precedent. So at this point, whether A's first child is a valid gift or not becomes an irrelevant issue since no one can take. O's reversion becomes a fee simple absolute at A's death. If, instead of using the 21-year perpetuity period, the state adopts a 90-year wait-and-see period, as long as A has a child survive him, no matter the child's age, we wait to see if that child attains age 25.

   (b) In a jurisdiction adopting the common law perpetuity period, the remainder is not valid, because A's life is now the only measuring life. B was not a life in being. When it is clear a three-year-old cannot attain age 25 in the 21-year perpetuity period, the interest is invalid. If, on the other hand, the jurisdiction has adopted a fixed 90-year perpetuity period, we must wait and see if B turns 25 in the 90 years after the interest is created. Assuming B was born within 65 years of O's death, the Rule poses no barrier to B's taking; the condition precedent that he must attain age 25 might, but the Rule does not.

   (c) We must wait and see. The determination of validity cannot be made at O's death or at A's death. The decision is deferred in a "wait-and-see" jurisdiction. B's death is irrelevant. C, at four, is the eldest child and thus stands to be the first of A's children to attain age 25. The Rule is not a barrier to C's taking. If C turns 25, he gets the property.

   (d) B at age two cannot turn 25 in 21 years. In states using the common law perpetuity period, B's interest is invalid. O has a reversion. In states using the 90-year perpetuities period, as long as B was born within 65 years of O's death, which is almost certain, the Rule will not keep B from taking.

   (e) In a wait-and-see jurisdiction using the common law perpetuity period, the parties must wait until 21 years after the last of the relevant lives in being. Here, O, A, and B's being mentioned in the grant would serve as measuring lives. If Whiteacre is used for commercial purposes during the perpetuity period, A is divested and B takes pursuant to the shifting executory interest. If no commercial use is made of the property during that period, B's interest disappears. The condition subsequent to A's interest remains. A continues with a fee simple determinable and O (or his heirs or devisees) has a possibility of reverter. Compare Example 3(a), above.

In a jurisdiction adopting the 90-year rule, the parties must wait 90 years after the interest was created (i.e., from January 1, 2005, until January 1, 2095) to see if the property is used for commercial purposes. If so, B gets Whiteacre. If Whiteacre is used for commercial purposes after 2095, it reverts back to O and his heirs.

Concurrent Ownership

As we have seen, property ownership can be divided up in several ways. A landowner of 100 acres, for example, may give 50 acres to one person and 50 acres to another; the landowner may give one person the whole 100 acres as a life estate and another the remainder; the landowner may sever the surface from the subsurface by granting away the mineral rights; or the landowner may transfer legal title to a trustee with rights to manage and sell the property for the economic benefit of beneficiaries who have the right to income and value appreciation.

Finally, two or more persons may concurrently own the same interest in the same land. There are three major concurrent interests developed in England and recognized in the United States: tenancy in common, joint tenancy with right of survivorship, and tenancy by the entirety. Each may be found in any present or future interest, and may be held in any estate — for life, in fee simple determinable or subject to a condition subsequent, or in fee simple absolute, etc. As we will see, for some purposes, the holders of a concurrent interest must act as a unit — this is the result of the early common law concern that someone or some entity has *seisin*.

TENANCY IN COMMON

The most common form of concurrent ownership is the tenancy in common. Each tenant in common owns a share of one and the same piece of property. The default rule is that each co-tenant has an equal right to possess the whole property and to share equally in rents and appreciation in value. Thus, it is said that their interests are "undivided" — that is, each has *seisin* and the right to possess the whole. In practice, they frequently own varying proportional interests in the land. Tenants in Common (or co-tenants) are presumed to own a property in proportion to the amount each contributed to purchase the property, but this presumption is rebuttable and subject to an agreement to the contrary.

Example 1: A and B rent an apartment or own a condo as tenants in common. A is picked up by the police, and asked if they — the police — can search the apartment unit. A consents, but when the police show up B is home and slams the door in their face. Do the police have a right to enter? No. See Tompkins v. Superior Court, 378 P.2d 113 (1963). For constitutional law Fourth Amendment purposes, consent by A is not consent binding on B. An exclusionary rule for tainted evidence is not just a way of controlling illegal police behavior, it is way of protecting individual constitutional rights — here the undivided right to possession.

Example 2: Suppose that in the prior Example the police had gotten keys from A, and used them, and B wasn't home. During the ensuing search of the unit, illegal drugs were found. Would they be regarded as being in B's possession? Yes, because each tenant has an undivided interest in the unit.

Tenants in common normally share in rents and sales proceeds according to their respective interests. Even if co-tenants own varying interests in property, it does not affect each co-tenant's right to possess the entire property. Thus if A owns a 50% interest and B and C each own a 25% interest in Blackacre, as tenants in common, A would receive 50% of any net rents from the property, but all three would have equal rights of possession.

Concurrent ownership sometimes breeds conflict and disagreement. Common law default rules have evolved to resolve possession, use, profit sharing, and expense contribution issues that may arise when concurrent owners cannot agree.

A person's tenant-in-common interest is assignable (transferable), devisable, and inheritable. Transferees become tenants in common with the remaining tenants in common. A co-tenant can mortgage his interest to secure a loan or can sell his interest, but cannot sell his co-tenants' interests in the property.

Example 3: O transfers Blackacre, a 100-acre farm, to A and B as tenants in common. No more being said in the deed of transfer, A and B each own a 50% undivided interest in the entire 100 acres. Three years later A dies, devising his interest in Blackacre to M. M now owns a 50% interest in Blackacre. B and M are tenants in common.

Example 4: O transfers Whiteacre to *A* and B as tenants in common. A then dies without a will, survived by two children C and D. Without a will, C and D take A's interest under the canons of descent or intestacy, again in equal proportions, so that B owns a 50% interest, and C and D each a 25% interest, in Whiteacre.

Example 5: O transfers Greenacre, along with its farm equipment, to *A* and B as tenants in common. In a majority of states, it is possible to have a tenancy in common in personalty as well as real property.

JOINT TENANCY WITH RIGHT OF SURVIVORSHIP

The joint tenancy with right of survivorship is a form of concurrent ownership with a survivorship element. It is often used as a will substitute. When a joint tenant dies, her interest ends. The last surviving joint tenant owns the property outright, and may sell or devise the property.

Example: Annie and Brady are joint tenants with right of survivorship in Whiteacre. Annie dies, her will devising all her real property to Donna. Donna gets no interest in Whiteacre. Brady is the sole owner. A year later Brady dies, his will devising all his real property to Emmylou. Emmylou owns Whiteacre.

At one time—and still today in many states—a joint tenancy could be created and maintained only if all the tenants shared the four unities:

(1) Unity of Time—The joint tenants' interests must vest at the same time.
(2) Unity of Title—The joint tenants must acquire title in the same deed or will.
(3) Unity of Interest—Each joint tenant must own equal shares of the same estate.
(4) Unity of Possession—Each joint tenant has a right to possession of the whole property.

Historically, a joint tenant could destroy the joint tenancy with right of survivorship by destroying any one of the four unities. That absolute rule is no longer the law either for creating or destroying joint tenancies in many states. An agreement between joint tenants that one tenant have sole possession, for example, does not destroy the unity of possession. Likewise, a court in equity may look to the respective contributions each joint tenant made to acquire the property and divide any sales proceeds in proportion to each joint tenant's respective contribution.

Unity of title is still required in some states, but it has been abolished by statute or judicial opinion in most states, after decades of being circumvented by use of a strawman. A **strawman** is a person who briefly takes legal title for the sole purpose of re-conveying the property back to his grantor. Usually the straw is someone in the lawyer's office, a secretary or a paralegal — someone who can be trusted to re-convey the property.

The process worked this way: A person holding land solely in his own name wanted to own the property as a joint tenant with right of survivorship. He may have wanted to pass the property to his spouse or child outside of probate. The joint tenancy with right of survivorship is a useful tool to avoid the cost and time of probate administration since a decedent's interest in the property ends on his death and the other joint tenant takes the title. Often the property involved is the family residence.

Let's assume the landowner wanted to transfer the family residence to himself and his wife as joint tenants with right of survivorship. The law treated a transfer from a person to himself as a nullity; so either a direct transfer to his spouse or a transfer to himself and his spouse created an interest in the spouse at a different time and under a different title (deed). The landowner could not deed an interest in the property to his spouse as a joint tenant or to himself and his spouse as joint tenants with right of survivorship. A tenancy in common and not a joint tenancy with right of survivorship resulted. The solution was for the landowner to transfer the property to a straw, who immediately deeded the land to the original landowner and his wife as joint tenants with right of survivorship.

Many states have recently concluded that there is no reason to require a straw, especially on transfers between spouses, and allow a direct transfer from one person to himself and another as joint tenants with rights of survivorship, particularly when the other is the spouse.

A joint tenancy does not arise by intestate succession: Two or more persons inheriting the same property become tenants in common. On the other hand, it is possible under proper facts — usually taking the land under a faulty deed naming the co-tenants as joint tenants with right of survivorship — that joint adverse possession could yield a joint tenancy held by two or more adverse possessors.

When two joint tenants die simultaneously, most courts treat half the property as if one tenant survived and the other half as if the other tenant survived — effectively treating the property as a tenancy in common, giving the heirs of each tenant an equal share. When one of two co-tenants murders the other one, the murderer forfeits the right of survivorship, but not his interest. In effect, murder turns the joint tenancy into a tenancy in common.

Since her interest in the joint tenancy ends on her death, a joint tenant cannot devise her interest in a joint tenancy with right of survivorship; nor is her interest inheritable. A joint tenant may, however, transfer or assign her interest *inter vivos*. The assignment ends the joint tenancy at least as to the transferee, who thereafter holds his interest as a tenant in common with the other tenants, who continue to hold their fractional share in a joint tenancy with right of survivorship.

DISTINGUISHING JOINT TENANCIES FROM TENANCIES IN COMMON

Centuries ago in England, the joint tenancy was the default concurrent interest. A transfer from O "to A and B" created a joint tenancy with right of survivorship. English courts were anxious to avoid splitting ownership. It was presumed to be the intent of parties when there was any ambiguity as to whether a document created a tenancy in common or a joint tenancy. The purpose of the presumption was to maintain family estates intact.

Today, however, this presumption is reversed. The tenancy in common is preferred. Statutes in many states provide that a grant to concurrent owners is presumed to be a tenancy in common unless the deed clearly establishes that the grantor intended to create a joint tenancy with right of survivorship. From our earliest times, state legislatures were anxious to encourage widespread ownership of land.

Example: O conveys to a straw S who conveys Blackacre to A and B as trustees for beneficiary C. The common law presumption is still used for equitable ownership by trustees. This encourages efficient administration of trusts and keeps the corpus of the trust in the hands of those originally selected for the longest time.

A major caveat with regard to married couples is in order here. In many states that recognize the tenancy by the entirety (an estate exclusively reserved for married couples — to be developed later in this chapter), a grant to a husband and wife is presumed to create a tenancy by the entireties unless the deed expresses a clear intent to create another interest. In some states that do not recognize the tenancy by the entireties, a grant to a husband and wife is presumed to create a joint tenancy with right of survivorship unless the deed or will clearly manifests intent to create a tenancy in common. In some states that do not recognize the tenancy by the entirety, only married couples can hold property as joint tenants with right of survivorship, but the presumption is that the grant creates a tenancy in common unless the grant evidences a clear intent to create a joint tenancy with a right of survivorship. In the remaining states, a grant to a husband and wife is treated like any other grant to multiple persons, and is presumed to be a tenancy in common unless a clear intent to create another concurrent interest is expressed.

The most popular words to create a joint tenancy with right of survivorship are "to A and B, as joint tenants with a right of survivorship, and not as tenants in common." Some courts will find the requisite intent to create a joint tenancy with right of survivorship in a grant "to A and B as joint tenants," but many courts refuse to find a joint tenancy with right of survivorship unless the deed or will contains words of survivorship. "To A and B jointly" creates a tenancy in common for example, not a joint tenancy with right of survivorship. A specific indication of an intention to establish the right of survivorship, along with a negation of a tenancy in common, is the best course for the conveyancer.

A grant to "A and B as joint tenants, remainder to the survivor of them" creates joint life estates, with a contingent remainder in the survivor. It is not the same as a joint tenancy with right of survivorship, however, and dramatically different legal consequences may follow. As discussed in the next section, any joint tenant can unilaterally "sever" her interest from the joint tenancy and become a tenant in common with the other co-tenants. Severance destroys the survivorship character as to her interest. When she dies, her heir or devisee takes her interest. In contrast, persons holding joint life estates with a contingent remainder cannot unilaterally terminate the survivorship requirement.

SEVERANCE

In some states, when one or more of the four unities of a joint tenancy with right of survivorship is destroyed, the joint tenancy is said to be **severed**. Courts look for some action or relationship that is inconsistent with a person continuing as a joint tenant — or more formally, inconsistent with the four unities — to find a severance. A severance, in short, is the destruction of the four unities. It turns a joint tenancy into a tenancy in common between the severed interest and the remaining joint tenants. The remaining joint tenants continue holding their fractional interests in the property in a joint tenancy with right of survivorship. Thus, when the joint tenancy is created in three or more persons, a unilateral act of one of them leaves the joint tenancy intact as between the remaining tenants, who together then would hold a tenancy in common with the severing tenant.

The most common voluntary severance occurs when one joint tenant unilaterally transfers her interest to another person, as when A, a joint tenant, deeds her interest to a third party. The most common involuntary severance is a foreclosure sale or a sale in bankruptcy proceedings.

Example 1: O, the holder of a fee simple absolute in Blackacre, conveys "to A, B, and C, as joint tenants with right of survivorship." Five years later C conveys to D. The deed to D is a severance of D's interest in the joint tenancy. A and B continue in joint tenancy with each other, but are in a tenancy in common with D, each of the three having a one-third interest in Blackacre. If A dies, leaving a will devising her interest in Blackacre to M, M gets nothing. A's interest ends on her death and B owns a two-thirds interest in Blackacre as a tenant in common with D, who owns a one-third interest.

Example 2:   Same facts as in Example 1, except A and B survive while D dies, leaving a will devising his interest to N. D held an interest as a tenant in common at his death. A tenancy in common is devisable, so N owns a one-third interest in Blackacre. A and B continue to own the remaining two-thirds interest in Blackacre as joint tenants with right of survivorship as between themselves, but as tenants in common with N.

Example 3:   Same facts as in Example 1, except A, B, and D all survive. A sells her interest to L. This severs A's interest from the joint tenancy. Since joint tenancy requires more than one person (and B cannot be in a joint tenancy by herself), the joint tenancy is now a tenancy in common, with B, D, and L as co-tenants.

In a family context, a secret severance is disfavored: one joint tenant may not pass his interest to someone in a younger generation in order to defeat another joint tenant's right of survivorship and to maximize one's bloodline's chances of getting the property. Underlying the joint tenancy is the idea that one should be in a joint tenancy only with people they know and would want to have the property. The chance those expectations may be frustrated is one reason why the law favors the parties hold as tenants in common when the original arrangement is disturbed.

(a) Leases

Courts have disagreed on whether a severance results by one joint tenant's leasing the property to an outsider, or by a joint tenant's granting a mortgage to secure a loan from a financial institution. Courts agree that a short-term lease by one joint tenant does not sever a joint tenancy. However, the lease will end on the death of the leasing joint tenant. The lessee has possessory rights through the lessor joint tenant; when the lessor joint tenant no longer has an interest, the lessee also loses his right of possession. During the term of the lease, non-leasing joint tenants have no cause of action to cancel it. The lease terminates with the death of the leasing co-tenant even though the lessee has no notice in the lease or elsewhere of the extent of the lessor's rights and the lease term has not run its course: the surviving, non-leasing joint tenants do not take subject to the lease. The lessee has, however, a cause of action in damages against the decedent's estate of the leasing joint tenant for the lease's premature termination. Some older cases held that a lease with a long term might work a severance, at least for the term of the lease. More recent cases have concluded that even a long-term lease by one joint tenant will not sever the joint tenancy. Why not? Because, under a principle of "equal dignity," if an intentional act is required to create a joint tenancy, only an intentional act should sever it. By implication, neither does an option to purchase the leasing joint tenant's interest, when contained in the lease, sever the joint tenancy. Lesson to be learned: A lessee should be sure all joint tenants execute a lease.

(b) Mortgages

The vast majority of states are **lien theory states**, meaning a mortgage is security for a loan. Title remains with the debtor. Since legal title remains with the debtor joint tenant, the giving of a mortgage by one joint tenant to secure his personal debt does not sever the joint tenancy. Only if the creditor forecloses on the interest and the interest is sold does a severance occur.

States differ on what happens to the mortgage if the debtor joint tenant dies while the mortgage is outstanding. Conceptually, the mortgage should be worthless since the deceased debtor no longer owns an interest in the property; the creditor's rights depend on the debtor's interest. The deceased joint tenant's interest, moreover, does not pass to the other joint tenants; rather, the interest just ends, similar to a life estate. Some states, by statute or judicial opinion, conclude that the property continues to be subject to the mortgage. Lesson to be learned: Lenders should have all joint tenants sign the mortgage, even if they are not personally liable for the debt.

About a dozen states are known as **title theory states**, where a mortgage conveys legal title to the creditor. The creditor owns the debtor's interest in fee simple determinable, to revert to the debtor when the debt is retired. Some courts, especially a few decades back, viewed the transfer of legal title as destroying at least one of the four unities, and thus severed the debtor's interest from the joint tenancy. While that is still the law in some title theory states, others recognize that the mortgage is a security device, and the debtor remains the true owner. In these states the mortgage, as in the lien theory states, does not sever the joint tenancy.

(c) Judgment Liens

Just as a completed foreclosure of a mortgage will sever a joint tenancy, so also will a levy and sale of a joint tenant's interest sever it. The docketing of the lien, however, does not sever it because the service of a sheriff's writ of execution does not disturb the possessory rights of the joint tenants, so it works no severance. Lesson to be learned: most courts require evidence of a clear intent to sever before finding a severance.

Example: A and B are joint tenants of Blackacre. Together they convey Blackacre in a deed establishing joint life estates in A and B, followed by cross-remainders — one to A, another to B, held in fee simple absolute. Their conveyance provides clear evidence of an intent to sever.

(d) Unilateral and Secret Severances

A joint tenant unilaterally can sever a joint tenancy by transferring her interest to a third party. Sometimes a joint tenant wants to sever her interest from the joint tenancy but continue to maintain her interest in the property as a tenant in common rather than as a joint tenant. In some states the joint tenant must resort to the use of a strawman to sever her interest. A few states from among those that allow the direct creation of a joint tenancy with right of survivorship without the use of a strawman see no reason to prevent the direct severance without using a straw. Some allow direct severance when the other joint tenants are given notification.

Usually direct severance or a deed to a third party is known to others. Attorneys, for example, prepare the document. Often the beneficiaries of the severance — the heirs of the severing joint tenant, for example — are given notice of it in some fashion. Sometimes the severance document is recorded in the public land records of the county. In other words, the unilateral severance is not a matter of complete secrecy — and the notice or the recording may help explain why some cases seem to tolerate it.

The possibility exists, however, that the severance is done secretly and does not come to light until one or the other joint tenant dies. The secret severance opens up the possibility of fraud: A joint tenant may execute a severance deed to himself or to another as a tenant in common without telling anyone else or even recording the deed in the public deed records. If he dies first, a severance will be found to have occurred, with the joint tenant's assignee, devisee, or heir taking the joint tenant's interest as a tenant in common. If he is the survivor, he might destroy the severance document and take the whole of the property. The law does not countenance this ruse. Thus, where courts approve direct severances that do away with the use of strawmen, they more closely scrutinize the completely secret severance. To prevent this fraud on the other joint tenants, some states require either public recording or notification to the other joint tenants.

TENANCY BY THE ENTIRETY

A third form of concurrent ownership is the tenancy by the entirety. The tenancy by the entirety is limited to husbands and wives, who own the property as a unit, not by equal shares. The same four unities necessary to form a joint tenancy with right of survivorship are essential to form a tenancy by the entirety, but in addition, the couple must be married at the time they acquire the property. Thus marriage is the fifth unity required for this type of tenancy. Engaged to be married is insufficient. Hence, a couple buying a home to live in after their marriage will not hold the home in a tenancy by the entirety. Divorce terminates the tenancy by the entirety and a tenancy in common results in most states (a joint tenancy with right of survivorship results in a minority of states).

Like the joint tenancy with right of survivorship, the tenancy by the entirety is characterized by a right of survivorship in the surviving spouse. Unlike in the joint tenancy, one spouse cannot unilaterally sever the tenancy by the entirety. Moreover, neither spouse can seek judicial partition.

About half the states recognize the tenancy by the entirety. In the majority of those, a grant to a husband and wife is presumed to create a tenancy by the entirety unless a different form is indicated in the deed. In other states, a grant to a husband and wife creates a presumption that a tenancy in common is created unless the deed indicates a tenancy by the entirety or joint tenancy with right of survivorship is intended. Parties intending to create a tenancy by the entirety should convey to "H and W, husband and wife, as tenants by the entirety." At one time, a husband and wife owning property as tenancy by the entirety were deemed one — and that one was the husband. He had management rights, rights to the income, and the power to sell. The wife had survivorship rights — even if the husband sold the property, the wife's survivorship rights continued in force; so as a practical matter husbands and wives both signed deeds conveying the property to third parties. A wife relinquished her survivorship rights if she signed the deed.

Since the husband could sell the property, he also could pledge it as security. His creditors, secured and unsecured, could foreclose on the property. A purchaser at foreclosure was entitled to possession of the property, and to all rents and income from the property. If the husband outlived the wife, the purchaser kept the property in fee simple absolute. If the wife survived her husband, she got the property back.

Well over a century ago, states began enacting Married Women's Property Acts (MWPA) giving married women rights to control property. Courts and legislatures applied MWPA to fashion three theories of a modern tenancy by the entirety in all states recognizing this tenancy. Today, in the majority of tenancy-by-the-entirety states, a creditor can foreclose on the tenancy by the entirety property only if both spouses are liable for the underlying debt or both have executed a mortgage. Husband and wife, moreover, must both execute deeds on the sale of the property. In a second group of states, a creditor of one spouse's separate debts may foreclose on the debtor spouse's half interest (the half interest being a fiction, since the couple holds the property as whole) subject to the other spouse's survivorship rights. Thus the creditor can get rents from the property if any are collected, but will lose all rights in the property if the nondebtor spouse outlives the debtor spouse.

Example: H and W, husband and wife, own Blackacre as tenants by the entirety. H abandons W and Blackacre. C, a judgment creditor of H, levies on Blackacre to satisfy the judgment, and purchases H's interest in Blackacre at the judgment sale and then demands half of the fair rental value of Blackacre from W. W refuses. In the second group of states, C must first demand possession and be refused it by W (the common term for this is "ouster"— see below). Only then is C entitled to half Blackacre's rental value.

Finally, in two states — Kentucky and Tennessee — creditors can reach a spouse's survivorship interest, but not the right to current possession and rents. Hence creditors have no interest while both spouses are alive, and will have an interest only if the debtor spouse survives the nondebtor spouse.

RIGHTS AND OBLIGATIONS BETWEEN CO-TENANTS

(a) Possession and Ouster

Each co-tenant (tenant in common, joint tenant, or tenant by the entirety) has the right to possess the entire property. As such, the majority rule is that a co-tenant using the whole property, absent ouster, does not owe rent to the other co-tenants. In a small minority of states, a co-tenant using the property owes a fair rental to the remaining co-tenants.

In the majority of states where a co-tenant owes no rent to his co-tenants for using the property, the rule changes if the occupying tenant ousts the other co-tenants. **Ouster** occurs when the occupying tenant acts to prevent the other co-tenants from using the property. Ouster may occur if the occupying tenant changes the locks or if the occupying tenant makes use of the property in a way that no other use can be made of any part of the property and refuses to make room for another's use. Generally, before the ousted co-tenant can bring an action for ouster, the co-tenant must make a demand for access to the property and be denied access.

(b) Contribution

A co-tenant who expends money for some matter related to the co-owned property may want to be reimbursed for his expenditure. There are three distinct judicial causes of action with which a co-tenant may seek reimbursement from his co-tenants: contribution, an accounting, and a final settlement on sale or partition. A co-tenant may seek **contribution** only after he demands his co-tenants pay for their pro rata share of expenses as discussed below, and they refuse.

(1) Taxes, Interest, and Insurance

Assuming no one is using the property, a co-tenant who pays the annual property taxes, government assessments, or interest on mortgages may seek contribution from the other co-tenants.[1] Taxes and interest are usually known as *carrying charges*. All co-tenants have a duty to pay taxes and interest on mortgages. In a minority of states, property insurance is a carrying charge. Where insurance is a carrying charge, a co-tenant paying insurance premiums can seek contribution. Otherwise, no contribution is allowed for insurance premiums.

If the paying co-tenant is the only co-tenant using the property, no contribution is permitted for carrying charges up to the fair rental value of the property. Because the occupying co-tenant is not obligated to pay rent to her co-tenants, she is responsible for the taxes and interest on the mortgage since she is the principal beneficiary of the payment (plus, it serves as a substitute for the payment of rent). If the occupying co-tenant does pay rent to her co-tenants, she may offset the others' share of the carrying charges against the rent due.

(2) Mortgage Principal

A co-tenant who makes a mortgage principal payment when due or past due may seek contribution from his co-tenants. A co-tenant who prepays the principal of a mortgage, on the other hand, cannot seek contribution, but must wait until the principal payment comes due and payable under the original mortgage.

(3) Repairs and Maintenance

A co-tenant cannot get contribution for repairs, even necessary repairs. While on first blush it would seem best if the paying co-tenant received

---

1. Co-tenants are responsible only for interest on mortgages existing when the concurrent ownership began, or the mortgage secures a debt for which all co-tenants are personally liable. If one co-tenant mortgages the property or her interest in the property, she is solely liable for the interest payment and cannot get contribution.

contribution for necessary repair and maintenance — say, to fix a broken window, replace a roof, or mow the lawn — courts have been reluctant to decide on a case-by-case basis which repairs were necessary, what type of repair (quality and extent) was needed, and how much should have been spent for the repair. Hence courts have concluded that no co-tenant has a duty to make repairs.

>   ***Example:*** A co-tenant in possession pays to repair property and clean up its yard after city officials order him to do so pursuant to a city ordinance. Here contribution would be appropriate if a failure to obey would result in enforcement of the ordinance by seizing the property. Why? Because these repair costs are carrying charges.

(4) Improvements

A co-tenant who improves property cannot compel contribution from his co-tenants. The rationale is that no one has a duty to improve property, and no one who chooses to improve the land should force his co-tenants to contribute. Were it otherwise, rich co-tenants might "improve" poorer co-tenants out of their interest.

(c) An Accounting

Even though a co-tenant cannot seek contribution for repairs and improvements, he may get some reimbursement indirectly in an accounting. An accounting occurs when a co-tenant rents the property to a third party. Even though a co-tenant can solely possess co-owned property and keep any profits generated from that sole possession, once he leases or rents the property to others he must account for any profits and share the net proceeds with his co-tenants. See Statute of Anne, ch. 16, §27 (1705) (adopted by all American states either as part of the common law or by statute).

In an action for an accounting the co-tenant collecting rent payments may offset the costs associated with generating and collecting the rent. So this co-tenant may offset rent revenues by the amount he expended on taxes, interest, mortgage principal, and insurance. In addition, he can offset other expenses, such as advertising, management fees, *actual* amounts spent on repairs or maintenance, and utilities. The co-tenant can offset his monetary outlays only to the extent of any rental income received. So the accounting serves to reduce how much of the rental proceeds the co-tenant must distribute to his co-tenants. Absent an agreement to the contrary, an accounting does not allow him to demand contribution from his co-tenants if expenditures exceed revenues. Notwithstanding this limitation on the accounting, the paying co-tenant can still demand contribution if rent revenues are insufficient to pay the property taxes, interest, and currently payable principal payment on a mortgage.

Example: A, B, and C own raw land as tenants in common. A pays the annual taxes of $3000 and the interest of $5000 on the outstanding mortgage. A rents the land to a local farmer who will cut the grass on the land to use as hay to feed his livestock. The farmer pays A $2000 rental. A can demand B and C each contribute $2000 ($8000 total carrying costs less $2000 rents equals $6000, divided by 3 equals $2000 per co-tenant).

The co-tenant cannot offset the total cost of improvements in an accounting. He can offset only so much of the cost of the improvements as is traceable to an increase in rents received because of the improvements, but no more.

(d) Final Settlement on Sale

If the co-tenants sell the property, either voluntarily or by a judicially ordered partition sale (discussed below), a final settlement takes place. A co-tenant who expended money and has not been reimbursed for taxes, interest, mortgage principal, repairs, maintenance, insurance, and other common expenses associated with owning the property will be reimbursed out of sales proceeds.

Improvements are a special case. A co-tenant who paid for improvements will receive the sales proceeds attributable to the value added by the improvements. The amount paid for the improvement is irrelevant.

Example 1: Adam, who owns a one-third interest in Blackacre as a tenant in common, builds a house on Blackacre for $100,000. Five years later the three co-tenants sell Blackacre for $250,000. The land is worth $75,000; the building is worth $175,000. Adam receives the $175,000 attributable to the building and one-third of $75,000 ($25,000) as his share of the sales proceeds.

Example 2: Maurice, who owns a one-third interest in Whiteacre as a tenant in common, spends $20,000 to install a swimming pool. Two years later the co-tenants sell Whiteacre for $215,000. The land and building are valued at $210,000. The swimming pool added $5000 to the property's value. Maurice receives $5000 for the swimming pool and one-third of the $210,000 ($70,000) for the land and building as his share of the sales proceeds.

Example 3:   Alex and Ben are co-tenants of Blackacre. Alex proposes to sell his interest to Ben. Absent some special relationship, Ben owes Alex no duty to disclose situations affecting Blackacre's value known to Ben but unknown and undiscoverable by Alex. While co-tenants their mutual interest in the property requires that each has a duty to sustain and no injure their concurrent interests, but this duty does not apply when one co-tenant voluntarily undertakes to sell and another to buy an interest in the tenancy.

(e) Tax Sales and Foreclosure Sales

If no co-tenant pays taxes or mortgage payments, the state or the mortgage may seek a judicial sale of the property to pay either the taxes or the mortgage. From such sales, co-tenants may have a right to redeem the property for a short time after the sale. Such rights are alienable and persons to whom co-tenants assign these rights take their assignments as tenants in common. The co-tenants share excess proceeds from these sales as explained above.

If a co-tenant purchases the property at the tax sale or foreclosure sale, the majority rule is that the purchasing co-tenant is deemed to be acting in her capacity as a co-tenant. The remaining co-tenants have the option of remaining co-tenants by contributing their share of the taxes or mortgage. If the other co-tenants choose not to contribute, after a reasonable time the purchasing co-tenant will own the property outright.

In a minority of states, if the other co-tenants have an opportunity to bid at the tax sale or foreclosure sale, the purchasing tenant represents himself and not the co-tenancy. There are exceptions — if the other co-tenants are not adults, if the purchasing co-tenant deceived the other co-tenants into believing he was representing the co-tenancy, or if the purchasing co-tenant intentionally did not pay the taxes or the mortgage because he was in a superior financial position to successfully purchase the property at the forced sale.

(f) Adverse Possession

Since each co-tenant has the right to possess the co-owned property, it is difficult for a co-tenant to adversely possess the property. It can be done, however. To begin running the statute of limitations the co-tenant claiming by adverse possession must give clear notice to the other co-tenants that she is claiming adversely. Usually the notice must be in writing. Mere ouster may not suffice, but ouster combined with acts so inconsistent with a concurrent ownership that co-tenants must be deemed to be on notice of the adverse possession might suffice.

PARTITION

Tenants in common or joint tenants with right of survivorship are not obligated to continue a concurrent ownership and they are not required to sell just their interests to separate themselves from the co-tenancy. Instead, the tenant in common or the joint tenant may petition a court to partition the property. (Neither spouse can seek partition of property held in a tenancy by the entirety.) A partition action is today statutory in nature, although it began as a common law cause of action. See 31 Hen. 8, ch. 1 (1539). There are two distinct categories of partition: partition in kind and partition by sale.

(a) Partition in Kind

Courts favor partition in kind, or physical partition. Why? Because it offers the least upset to the original co-tenancy and it does not force a person to sell who does not wish to do so. (And, in some states, a presumption for a partition is kind is statutory.) In a partition in kind, the court divides the property into parcels of equal value; each co-tenant receives a separate parcel. When fewer than all co-tenants seek partition, they receive separate parcels and the others own the rest of the property as co-owners. If a court cannot partition the property into parcels of equal value, the court may order a money payment from one party to another. This payment is known as **owelty**. Because a partition is seldom likely to involve equally valuable parcels distributed to each tenant, owelty is a common feature in a partition in kind.

(b) Partition by Sale

Partition in kind is not always practicable or advisable. A single-family residence, for example, is not suited to partition in kind. A family emergency might justify a sale. So would a situation in which the objective fair market value exceeds the subjective value of keeping the property, or when the appraisals necessary to justify a partition in king are costly, or the appraisals are unreliable. Other factors, including a large number of co-tenants, the terrain, and the size of the tract, may convince a judge that a partition in kind is inadvisable. The court then may order a **partition by sale**. Judicial discretion in administering this action is generally recognized as a matter of equity, and the rules governing contribution traditionally confine this discretion.

Example: A co-tenancy is created for Blackacre as the result of a decedent's heirs inheriting the property in the course of a probate proceeding.

Here, when the co-tenancy is created involuntarily, partition by sale is more likely if the tenants fall into some dispute over Blackacre's management.

Some states permit a co-tenant to purchase at the sale — others do not. Where permitted, a purchasing co-tenant must pay an equitable amount and that amount is subject to judicial scrutiny. The proceeds of the sale are distributed as in a final accounting and settlement discussed above. Any co-tenant who has not accounted for any rents must do so. Sales proceeds from improvements will be allocated to the improver equal to the *value* of the improvements added to the overall value of the property, and not the *cost* of the improvements.

An agreement between the co-tenants prohibiting judicial partition normally is invalid as a restraint on alienation, but such restrictions will be sustained when limited to a reasonable time. For example, limitations on sale of a residence, embodied in a divorce settlement and prohibiting a co-tenant's filing a partition action, have been found reasonable. Whether a restriction is reasonable may depend on whether the co-tenant wanting partition acquired his or her interest with knowledge of the restriction, the expertise of the co-tenant in possession, or the terms of an agreement on the subject between the parties.

Nonetheless, an agreement to limit access to the judicial process is not to be inferred lightly. Partition is favored by the law and agreements to limit the remedy will be strictly construed. A provision that one of two co-tenants receive the rents and profits from an apartment house, contained in a judicial decree (of divorce, say), is not likely to be found by implication to prohibit a partition action brought by the other tenant. A voluntary contract to the same effect might give rise to such an implication, and the implication might be stronger still if the property were residential.

Examples

Drafting Exercise

1. Now that you know the basic characteristics of all three of the major concurrent interests, please draft the granting clauses in a deed to create a tenancy in common, a joint tenancy with right of survivorship, and a tenancy by the entirety.

Dying to Know What Happened

2. (a) O, the holder of a fee simple absolute in Blackacre, conveys "to A, B, and C as joint tenants with right of survivorship." A year later C conveys all his interest in Blackacre to D. Who has what interest in Blackacre?

(b) *A* dies five years later, devising his interest in Blackacre to E. Who owns what interest in Blackacre?

(c) Three years later B dies, devising his interest in Blackacre to F. Who owns what interest in Blackacre?

Surviving Joint Tenancies

3. O conveys Blackacre "to *A* and B and the survivor of them." What interest or estate is created for *A* and B?

Creating a Tenancy by the Entirety

4. Toby purchased his home when he was single. Now he is married to Veronica and wants to own the home as a tenant by the entirety with Veronica. How would you advise Toby to create the tenancy by the entirety?

On Second Thought

5. Kent and Richard own their law office building as joint tenants with right of survivorship. Kent was recently diagnosed with cancer. He wants to sever the joint tenancy and drafts a deed conveying his interest in the office building to himself as a tenant in common. What is the result of such a conveyance?

Mortgage Business

6. In a jurisdiction that does not clearly adhere to either a lien or a title theory, how would you recommend that a mortgage lender proceed in a loan for the purchase price of a residence whose title is to be held in the name of a husband and wife as joint tenants?

Our Land, His Debt

7. H and *W*, husband and wife, hold title to Blackacre as joint tenants. They separate. H executes a mortgage on Blackacre. A year later H dies. Black-acre is condemned by the state to build a new arena. The state agrees to pay $500,000 for Blackacre. The mortgage ($100,000) is unpaid, but not the subject of a foreclosure. H's executor claims a portion of the condemnation award for his estate. Is this claim valid?

He Did *What?*

8. (a) Anthony and Barlow hold title to Blackacre as joint tenants with right of survivorship. Barlow executes a mortgage in a lien theory state. Barlow defaults on the mortgage loan and the creditor brings a foreclosure action. The court hearing the foreclosure orders that

Blackacre be sold through a judicial sale, conducted as an auction. Barlow shows up at the sale, is the highest bidder for the property, and obtains a decree confirming the title to the property to him in fee simple absolute. Anthony now claims his interest in Blackacre. Barlow sues Anthony to quiet title in fee. What result?

(b) Same facts as in the previous problem, but a third party, not Barlow, obtained title through the foreclosure sale. Would this affect the result?

(c) What result in (a) if Anthony and Barlow had both signed the mortgage, and Barlow was the highest bidder at the foreclosure auction?

Future Interests Intrude

9. (a) O conveys Whiteacre "to A for life, remainder to B and her heirs." A and B cannot agree on the management of Whiteacre and A sues B for partition. What result?

(b) O conveys Blackacre "to A and B as tenants in common for life, remainder to C and her heirs." A and B disagree about the management of Blackacre and A sues B for its partition. May A bring this action?

Contribution and Accounting

10. (a) Shane, a widower, died intestate, survived by his three children: Homer, who lives one mile from Shane's residence; Louise, in Louisiana; and Ken, in Kentucky. Shane's residence passed to his three children under the state's intestacy statute. In what concurrent interest do the three children own the home?

(b) The house sat vacant for four months after Shane's death. Homer looked after the house but did not reside in it. He paid the monthly water and electricity bills totaling $120 for four months, paid a junior high school student $240 over four months to mow the lawn, and paid $90 for the annual termite inspection. Homer sent a check monthly to Mortgage Company in the amount of $1000 ($4000 total in four months). Of the $4000, $1200 was interest, $1800 went against principal of the note, $600 went to property taxes, and $400 went to insurance on the house. Homer asked Louise and Ken to reimburse him. Assuming Ken and Louise do not want to pay anything, but will pay the minimum the law requires, how much will Homer collect from Ken and Louise?

(c) After four months of letting the house sit empty, Homer hired a painter to paint both the exterior and the interior of the house for $4500. He could have a hired a painter for $3600, but felt more comfortable with the one he hired. After the house was painted, Homer paid $90 to advertise the house for rent.

Homer leased the home for $1500 a month. Homes in the neighborhood similar to the house rented for $1800, but Homer was happy to get $1500. Homer continued paying the $1000 each month to Mortgage Company. The tenant paid for the utilities and lawn maintenance.

What are the financial ramifications to Homer, Louise, and Ken after the first month's rental?

(d) After two years, Homer collected enough rental revenues to reimburse himself for expenditures out of his personal funds. In the first month after that he collects $1500 rent and pays Mortgage Company $1000, $120 for the annual termite inspection, and $80 to repair a clogged toilet. What financial consequences to the co-tenants?

(e) A year later the tenant moves out. In the first month there is no revenue on the house, but for outgoing expenses there is only the Mortgage Company's $1000 ($900 carrying charges and $100 insurance premium). Instead of sending Louise and Ken the $1000 a month they had come to expect, Homer sends a letter demanding each contribute $300. Louise does not want to pay and demands to know why she did not receive her $100. Homer, frustrated, files a suit seeking judicial partition. Should the judge order a partition in kind or a partition by sale?

(f) Homer engages a real estate broker, who finds a buyer who purchases the house for $180,000. The broker's commission was $10,800. Other expenses of sale were $4200. To retire the note and mortgage, $15,000 of the sales proceeds were paid directly to Mortgage Company. Homer tells the closing agent that he spent 45 hours on the sale of the house and dedicated 450 hours to managing the property for the benefit of the three co-tenants since their father's death. He figures conservatively his time was worth $20 an hour, for which he has never been compensated, and for which he wanted to be compensated out of the sales proceeds ($900 for time on the sale of the house; $9000 for his labors all those years). How much does each co-tenant get from the sale of the house?

Alimony and Child Support

11. The tenancy by the entirety was established in an era without widespread divorce, and in an era when a person was expected to marry for life. Would it be wise to remove the immunity from levy and sale enjoyed by entireties property when a former spouse seeks to collect support payments — including child support — due from an ex-spouse now remarried and presently holding property in a tenancy with a subsequent spouse? What are the legislative alternatives?

Explanations

Drafting Exercise

1. To create a tenancy in common, you might say that O conveys to "A and B, in equal shares, as tenants in common." For a joint tenancy, say O conveys to "A and B, as joint tenants with full right of survivorship, and not as tenants in common." For a tenancy by the entirety O conveys to "A and B (husband and wife) and to the survivor of them as tenants by the entirety, and not as tenants in common or joint tenants." Some of these suggestions are the product of caution, some make use of a default rule, but the intent in each case is made clear.

Dying to Know What Happened

2. (a) C's deed to D severs the joint tenancy. A and B continue in joint tenancy with each other, but together reform as a tenancy in common with D, each of the three having a one-third interest in Blackacre.

   (b) A's interest in Blackacre ends on his death. He has nothing to devise to E. B, as a joint tenant, gets A's interest. D is a tenant in common and will not increase her ownership. A now owns a two-thirds interest and D owns a one-third interest in Blackacre as tenants in common.

   (c) B died owning her interest as a tenant in common. A tenant in common can devise her interest. Therefore, F owns a two-thirds interest and D owns a one-third interest in Blackacre as tenants in common.

Surviving Joint Tenancies

3. Because a survivorship right is indicated (though not as clearly as it might be), many state courts say that this conveyance creates a joint tenancy with a right of survivorship in A and B. However, some state courts — a minority — hold that A and B have a concurrently held life estate, lasting as long as they both live, followed by a contingent remainder held by the survivor in fee simple absolute. States using the minority rule sometimes do so in order to prevent a partition action that would otherwise defeat the survivorship right. See William Stoebuck & Dale Whitman, The Law of Property § 5.2, at 181 n.39 (3d ed. 2000).

Creating a Tenancy by the Entirety

4. When one party to a proposed joint tenancy already owns the property to be held in the tenancy, the parties should proceed in a two-step transaction. First, Toby should transfer the title to the property to a straw (an intermediary to temporarily hold legal title). Second, the straw should retransfer the title to Toby and Veronica as husband and wife in a tenancy

by the entirety; they then would receive the title with the four unities present at the moment of the tenancy's creation. A straw is used when a jurisdiction does not clearly permit the unilateral creation of a joint tenancy by one of the tenants. The straw serves some function. The formalities of the process bring home to the sole owner the legal significance of what he or she is doing. They also prevent a layperson from accidentally creating a tenancy by the entirety when a tenancy in common was intended.

On Second Thought

5. It depends on the jurisdiction. If a jurisdiction requires a straw for a sole owner to create a joint tenancy in himself and another, then it is also likely to require the use of a straw to end the joint tenancy. Some jurisdictions allowing a person to create a joint tenancy directly without the use of a straw may require a straw for a joint tenancy to sever his interest. In either of these jurisdictions, Kent's deed to himself is ineffective to sever the joint tenancy; and the joint tenancy continues. If, however, the jurisdiction allows a joint tenant unilaterally to sever a joint tenancy, Kent's deed severs the tenancy. This assumes Kent abides by any other requirement the state may impose, such as recording in the public deed records or notifying Richard.

Mortgage Business

6. The simplest and safest method is for both husband and wife to sign both the note and the mortgage.

Our Land, His Debt

7. The executor's claim is not valid. The mortgage, even given without W's consent, works no severance of the joint tenancy in lien theory states and in many title theory states so long as H has the financial ability to repay the loan and eliminate the mortgage. In most states the mortgage is extinguished with H's death (H's estate still is liable on the loan, however; only Blackacre does not serve as security for nonpayment). The survivorship right is still effective on H's death and on H's death W owns Blackacre. As owner of Blackacre she is entitled to the entire condemnation award. The separation does not affect how the title is held. See People v. Nogarr, 330 P.2d 858, 861 (Cal. Dist. Ct. App. 1958). In some title theory states, however, H's mortgage severs the joint tenancy with right of survivorship. In these states H's estate owns a one-half interest in Blackacre as tenant in common and will receive half the condemnation proceeds. The executor can use $100,000 to retire the outstanding note. W keeps her half of the condemnation proceeds.

He Did *What?*

8. (a) Anthony prevails. Barlow will neither win nor quiet the title. The mortgage did not work a severance of the joint tenancy when executed, but when the property was put into foreclosure and beyond Barlow's power to recall, a severance occurred. Thus, when the court ordered that the results of the sale were binding on Barlow, a severance of the joint tenancy had destroyed the survivorship right and Anthony and Barlow became tenants in common. Only Barlow's interest in Blackacre was auctioned. The title obtained in foreclosure was subject to Anthony's rights and, by decree, the court in Barlow's suit will find that Anthony and Barlow hold Blackacre as tenants in common. A deed claiming to give Barlow sole ownership in fee simple absolute may have been color of title for an adverse possession action, but Anthony acted well within any limitations period.

   (b) No. A third party, not Barlow, obtaining title through the foreclosure sale would not affect the result. Anthony and Barlow would still be tenants in common at the point when the court orders the sale. The third party is now a tenant in common with Anthony.

   (c) First, since both parties executed the mortgage, a third party purchasing at a foreclosure sale would own the whole property, not just a one-half interest. The issue is whether Barlow will receive the same favorable treatment allowed a third-party purchaser. In a majority of states Barlow would be deemed to purchase the property on behalf of the joint tenancy. If he had the money to buy at the foreclosure sale he had the money to make the mortgage payments and so he had a duty to make the mortgage payments. Anthony would be allowed to continue as a joint tenant with right of survivorship. In most states Anthony would be required to contribute funds for his share of the purchase price.

   If, however, Anthony and Barlow lived in a state where a joint tenant is treated the same as a third party as long as the other joint tenants have an equal opportunity to bid and there was no indication Barlow engaged in fraudulent conduct or was in a fiduciary relationship with Anthony, Barlow would own Blackacre outright. Any excess sales proceeds over the amount of the mortgage would be divided between the two in a final settlement.

Future Interests Intrude

9. (a) Judgment for B: no partition. A has a present interest held in a life estate; B has a vested remainder held in fee simple absolute. A and B do not have concurrent possessory rights and so neither has a right to bring a partition action against the other.

   (b) Yes. A and B have a concurrent right to possess the life tenancy, so each has a right to bring partition against the other, but only as to the life estate they both hold, and not as to C's remainder. C does not have any concurrent rights to possession with them. Concurrent life tenants may bring partition inter se. An analogous result: If T1 and T2 both hold a joint leasehold, they have a right to partition the lease inter se, but have no such right against their landlord.

Contribution and Accounting

10. (a) A tenancy in common is presumed unless the deed or will stipulates another form. Here there was no deed or will, only a statute. Homer, Louise, and Ken own the residence as tenants in common.

(b) Ken and Louise are obligated to pay carrying charges, which are the interest of $1200, the property taxes of $600, and the mortgage principal reduction payments of $1800. In some states the $400 for insurance is also a carrying charge; in others it is not. The law of the state where the property is located controls the definition of a carrying charge, not the state where the various co-tenants live. Assuming insurance is not a carrying charge, the total of the carrying charges is $3600. The three siblings own equal shares and are equally liable for the carrying charges. Thus Ken and Louise should both contribute $1200 to Homer.

While it seems in fairness the co-tenants should all contribute to pay the reasonable costs of societally acceptable (and even mandated) expenses, a court will not force Louise and Ken to contribute for the yard maintenance, the utilities, the termite inspection, and, in most states, the insurance premiums. An annual termite inspection in some states is mandated by statute, so this may not be an elective expense everywhere. A good argument could be that this should be a carrying charge when it is state mandated and outside the control of any co-tenant. On the other hand, a co-tenant must select the inspector and that may result in a range of costs within the discretion of one co-tenant.

(c) Homer keeps the entire first month's rental of $1500. Under the Statute of Anne, Homer must share net rental proceeds with his co-tenants, Louise and Ken. In an accounting, Homer can reduce the amount to be split with Louise and Ken by the interest ($300), the mortgage principal reduction ($450), and the taxes ($150) (total of $900). In addition, he can offset other expenses related to the rental — insurance ($100), advertising ($90), and painting (repairs and maintenance are not an improvement) ($4500) (total of $4690).

In the accounting the revenues are the actual amount collected, not what *could* have been collected, so rent revenues are $1500, not $1800. Likewise, deductions are actual amounts paid, not what *could* have been negotiated, so it is the full $4500 deductible. The total deductions cannot exceed the gross revenues, however. Thus, even though Homer paid $3990 ($1500−($900 + $4690)) more than he collected, he cannot ask for a contribution for the excess. Homer could have demanded contribution if the rent revenues did not cover the carrying charges, but here they did. Nothing prohibits Homer from requesting Ken and Louise pay their share if Louise and Ken are willing to pay, but he cannot force them to contribute. Expenditures not offsetting revenues are carried forward to offset any excess revenues in the next month, months, or years.

(d) Homer can offset the carrying charges, the insurance premium, and the termite inspection costs (total of $1200). Homer keeps the $1200. He then splits the remaining $300 equally among himself, Louise, and Ken; or $100 to each.

(e) Partition by sale. It's hard to imagine any of the three co-tenants even arguing for a partition in kind. Assuming one does, the judge begins with the presumption that a partition in kind is preferred. But here, where the property is a single-family rental house, the impracticalities of a partition in kind are so great that a partition by sale is an easy decision.

(f) First, no co-tenant is entitled to compensation for representing the co-tenancy unless the co-tenants agree. Therefore, Homer gets no money for his efforts in the sale or for the many years he managed the property. After that, the math is simple. Sales proceeds of $180,000 less the commissions ($10,800), the other fees ($4200), and the mortgage payment ($15,000) leaves $150,000 to be divided among the three co-tenants, or $50,000 each.

Alimony and Child Support

11. There are at least two alternatives. First, legislation might authorize a court to issue a lis pendens (a recorded document in the deed records giving notice of a potential claim against the property) for a tenancy-by-entirety property, so that when the present spouses seek to sell or transfer it, the proceeds of that sale or transfer will be available to support the spouse of the former marriage to the extent of the ex-spouse's interest. This recognizes the continuing usefulness of the tenancy for the subsequent marriage, but only so long as the property itself is needed to support that marriage. This approach might, however, encourage evasion — as when the property is leased under a long-term arrangement, rather than sold outright — and so might be difficult to enforce.

Second, the docketing of a judgment or order for support of the former marriage might convert the tenancy in the subsequent marriage into a tenancy in common for purposes of the lien attachment/execution with regard to the support order. Here, the legislature recognizes the primacy of the first marriage over the second. This alternative is best suited to situations in which an ex-spouse has failed to meet support obligations for children of a former marriage. When the second spouse of the nonsupporting ex-spouse relies on the tenancy, this approach might work a hardship, and might deny the partners of the second marriage a future domicile of equal quality. The choice between these alternatives is perhaps best left to a legislature.

Marital Property

At common law, a spouse was not an heir of his or her husband or wife. By virtue of the marriage, however, each held a life estate in some types of property of the other. These life estates were implied by law, not created by a deed or in a will.

COMMON LAW DOWER

At common law, a wife had a claim in the form of a life estate to a one-third share of all of the real property of which the husband was solely and beneficially seised in fee simple at any time during his marriage. This estate is called *dower*.

Dower is available from the moment of marriage. In early England dower designation of the dower house and lands was a part of the marriage ceremony: This designated property was called "named dower." Originally, the bride's family met with the groom and determined the lands to serve as his bride's house and lands, should she outlive him — hence the term "dowager," meaning a resident of a dower house. Often a large estate had a permanent dower house on its grounds. Kensington Palace in London, for example, is the dower house of the House of Windsor. Dower expanded from that beginning to include a fraction of all the husband's lands — a/k/a "unnamed dower."

Dower is intended to provide economic and social security for a widow, assuring her that she will live as she had become accustomed during her marriage. Originally it permitted her to live in the same locale as during the marriage. Today it permits her to maintain the same social position. In an age of primogeniture, it also provided in some measure for younger sons and daughters, who could continue living with their mother.

Before a husband's death, the wife's dower interests were called **inchoate dower** — not yet a legal estate in the husband's real property, but giving her a basis for suit in case the husband attempted to defeat a later dower claim by a fraudulent conveyance during the marriage.

After the husband's death, dower was termed **choate or consummate dower**. On the basis of it, when the husband in his will provided for the wife less than dower would, she had the right to have the court probating the will survey the husband's property and set aside one-third of each parcel of his land — the dower lands — for her life. Dower is thus a life estate that arises by operation of law.

DOWER REFORM

States are abolishing dower. Where it continues, it is a claim to a one-third or one-half life estate in all of the spouse's real property. Although in most states retaining dower, the wife (and in some states the surviving spouse — dower being extended to husbands as well as wives) has a dower in all lands, unless barred or released, of which the deceased spouse was ever seised during marriage; a few states limit dower to lands held by the decedent spouse at death. In Kentucky a wife has a dower of one-third of the lands the decedent did not own at death and of half the lands held at the husband's death. Moreover, contrary to the trend of most states to abolish dower, Kentucky extends dower to personal property. See Ky. Rev. Stat. Ann. § 392.020 (Michie 1999).

A spouse cannot defeat his spouse's dower by selling or mortgaging the property. Purchasers and lenders thus are best advised to get the dower-owning spouse's signature releasing her dower in the property.

THE ELEMENTS OF DOWER

Today, the first element of a dower claim is a **valid marriage** when the property is owned. A marriage that is annulled or otherwise void ab initio is insufficient. A final decree in divorce may extinguish the dower claim by agreement. If no agreement is reached at divorce or in some other postnuptial agreement, the dower continues, but will not attach to property acquired after the divorce.

The second element is **sole and beneficial seisin** in the deceased spouse of the property at any time during the marriage. Property transferred before the marriage or acquired after the marriage ends cannot be subjected to a dower claim.

Seisin is always in a person holding a present possessory freehold estate. If the deceased spouse was a co-tenant, no dower lies because he or she was not solely seised. If the deceased spouse was a trustee for another, there is no dower in the property held in trust because there was no beneficial seisin. Similar results obtain when the spouse held as a strawman or otherwise held bare legal title. If the spouse, for example, executed a binding contract of sale to sell the property before the marriage, there is no dower in it. That title was held for the purchaser pending the closing and transfer of title.

Example 1:   A husband acquires land in fee simple absolute, subject to an option to buy it held by a third party. The wife's common law dower is also subject to the option since the estate is derivative and cannot outlast its source. A similar result would obtain if the husband took title to land subject to a mortgage during the marriage.

The estate of which the deceased spouse is seised cannot be one that ends at the deceased spouse's death. Dower does not apply to remainders and executory interests since the husband never had seisin in the property. A right of reentry, exercised or exercisable by the time of death, is subject to dower. As to whether a possibility of reverter must be exercised, there is a split in the cases: Some courts do not require exercise because the right of possession given in the possibility of reverter is automatic.

In summary, dower does not apply to a deceased spouse's . . .

1. term for years. It is a nonfreehold estate and has no seisin. It does not matter that the term is 99 or 999 years.
2. life estate. It has seisin, but not inheritability. The purpose of dower is to give the surviving spouse a share of what the deceased's spouse's heirs take, for her security and for the security of younger children of the marriage. The life estate ends at the death of the deceased spouse and the heirs have no further interest in the property to which it applied.
3. joint tenancy. Where the deceased spouse is not the surviving tenant, the latter's right of survivorship prevails over a dower claim.
4. partnership interest in real property. A partnership interest is not subject to common law dower because the interest is regarded as personalty rather than real property. Any restrictions on transfer should be limited to those in the partnership agreement. (Similarly, if the deceased spouse owned shares in a corporation or other legal entity whose sole assets were real property, there would still be no dower, and for the same reason — the shares are personalty.)

241

Dower does apply to a . . .

1. fee simple determinable. Dower attaches, but is subject to the occurrence of the stated condition. Dower rises no higher than the estate to which it attaches (which, as a general rule, also explains why it does not attach to a life estate).
2. fee simple subject to a condition subsequent, or to an executory limitation. Same answer as in the prior paragraph: Dower attaches, but subject to the condition.

Dower applies to legal, rather than equitable, estates. There is no equitable action to protect a dower claim. Dower applies, moreover, whether the spouse held property in fee simple absolute or fee tail. Only in the instance of a fee tail special — i.e., a fee tail limited to the issue of a prior spouse — did dower not apply.

Example 2:   A conveys Blackacre to B in fee simple absolute, B similarly conveys to C, who conveys to D; then A dies, leaving W1 his widow; B dies, leaving widow W2, and C dies, leaving widow W3. Finally, D dies, leaving widow W4. All four widows survive and claim dower. If each widow has a common law dower right, then W1 has 1/3 life interest, W2 has 1/3 of the remaining 2/3s — or 2/9's of Blackacre. Now 1/3 + 2/9s = 5/9s of Blackacre, are already in widows W1 and W2's hands, so W3 has 4/27's and W4 8/81's.

DOWER AND ADVERSE POSSESSION

Property acquired by adverse possession is subject to dower. If the deceased was in the process of adversely possessing property and so was still subject to disseisin or ouster by its true owner, so is the spouse claiming dower: He or she cannot acquire more rights than the deceased spouse had acquired by the time of death.

DOWER AND WASTE

In this country, widows were early permitted by statute to protect their inchoate dower rights with a cause of action in waste, and were protected from suits in waste when clearing uncultivated lands held through dower.

RELEASE OF DOWER

A wife can release dower by signing away her rights. Release of dower claims is necessary, or at least customary where dower has not been repealed, upon the transfer of the property. Buyers and lenders insist wives join in executing deeds with their husbands even if the husband is the sole legal owner of the property. Dower also can be released by a prenuptial or postnuptial agreement. Since dower survives divorce unless the wife (or husband) agrees to release her (or his) rights, a final divorce decree (as opposed to a pending action for one) may and should make express provision to release a spouse's estate from a dower claim by the ex-spouse.

BARRING DOWER

Dower claims can sometimes be barred in two ways. The first way is by putting property into a trust prior to marriage, because dower does not apply to equitable interests. An example of such an interest is a spouse's right to receive the income from a trust. Today this is not a foolproof method of barring dower because it may apply to personal as well as real property — and trust proceeds are regarded as personalty. Second, dower is barred by giving the deceased spouse a life estate in property, with a power of appointment created prior to the marriage. This may be a surer method of barring dower, but it is more inflexible than a trust.

FORCING AN ELECTION

Some states retaining dower stipulate that the surviving spouse must choose between taking her dower or taking under the husband's will (or by inheritance if there is no will). In states that allow a wife to take dower in addition to taking under the deceased husband's will, a husband can force a surviving spouse to elect between her dower rights and her rights under his will.

CURTESY

Dower was a wife's life estate in one-third of her husband's real property at common law. In contrast, at common law a husband received a life estate in all — not just a third — of his wife's real property of which she was seised. This estate arose at the time of the marriage. It lasted until either the husband or the wife died. It was called the **estate by the marital right**, or the estate (in Latin) **jure uxoris** — all this while the wife was entitled only to the equivalent of walking-around money. The husband's estate by marital right was a right of use and occupation — a right to possess the eligible property and use its rents and profits. It carried with it a life tenant's rights and duties and depended on the continued survival of the wife.

At the birth of issue born alive to the husband and wife during their marriage, the husband acquired a life estate measured by his life — called tenancy for life by the **curtesy initiate** (intended to support children and maintain their father in the same economic condition as existed throughout the marriage). So long as the issues of the marriage were born alive, whether or not they survived, the estate *jure uxoris* merged into a larger estate the husband acquired a life estate in the wife's freehold estates inheritable by the children. This estate lasted so long as the marriage did, and was followed by a reversion in the wife, should she outlive her husband. The common law also gave the husband, upon the death of a wife by whom there was a child born, a tenancy for life by the **curtesy consummate** (or curtesy). Thus did curtesy initiate become curtesy consummate, and it continued to the end of the husband's life. Unlike dower, both claims to curtesy by the husband required the birth of issue born to the couple during their marriage; no such requirement attached to a dower claim. So curtesy was, like dower, a life tenancy, except that it applied to both legal and equitable estates of the wife in any lands she held during the marriage. Like dower, it is a derivative estate, but for the husband to claim curtesy, the wife need not have had seisin in the lands claimed; some cases said that "seisin in fact" (bare possession) would suffice.

One of the principal legislative results of the first women's movement, begun at the Seneca Falls Convention in 1848, was the enactment by state legislatures of the Married Women's Property Acts. Courts interpreted the Married Women's Property Acts to have abolished the estate *jure uxoris*. Curtesy soon was abolished. States retaining dower extended dower to husbands so that husbands and wives were treated the same.

Comparing Dower with Curtesy	
Dower	Curtesy
attaches to a fraction	attaches to all
requires seisin in law	requires (actual) seisin in fact
attaches to legal estates	attaches to legal and equitable estates
does not require issue	requires birth of issue

THE MODERN ELECTIVE SHARE

States abandoning dower and curtesy give a surviving spouse an **elective share**, also known as a **statutory share** or **forced share**. At common law, a spouse was not an heir of her husband or his wife. The elective share is a right of the surviving spouse to elect to take as though she were an heir under the state's intestacy statute or under a provision in the elective share statute, or to take under the deceased spouse's will.

The elective share is usually one-third or one-half of the deceased spouse's estate. It is generally one-third of the estate when there are lineal descendants of the decedent, and one-half when there are none. It applies to both real and personal property and to both legal and equitable interests in property, so long as the property is owned by the deceased at death.

The elective share is not self-executing. It provides nothing until the surviving spouse — during probate of the estate or as part of an intestate distribution — files an election to take it after the decedent's death. Typically, the election must be made within nine months of the spouse's death, or within six months after the will is probated, whichever occurs later. The survivor taking the elective share must forego all devises under a decedent's will.

CALCULATING THE AMOUNT OF THE ELECTIVE SHARE

Calculating the amounts of an elective share is complicated. As background, not all of a decedent's property passes by will or by intestate succession (through probate). Much passes outside probate. We have studied tenancy by the entirety and joint tenancy with right of survivorship. Other nonprobate assets include trusts (i.e., one spouse transfers valuable assets to a trustee making himself, his spouse, or a child the beneficiary), life insurance policies, retirement plans, and inter vivos gifts.

An issue is to what extent nonprobate assets should be considered in calculating the elective share. Some states do not consider nonprobate assets; others include only some. The Uniform Probate Code lumps most nonprobate assets into an **augmented estate**, which is the total of the probate estate and a reclaimable estate.

The **reclaimable estate** is comprised of the following:

1. Assets owned by the electing spouse received from the deceased. This prevents the electing spouse from getting a larger share than is due by getting inter vivos gifts, for example, and then electing an intestacy share of what remains in the decedent's estate.

2. Assets held in trust for the spouse that originated with the decedent.
3. Insurance and pension plans of the decedent naming the spouse as beneficiary.
4. Assets held by others, often in a trust, if the decedent had a power of appointment (a right to designate who would receive the income or principal of the trust on a yearly basis or at his death), or had a right to revoke the trust.
5. Assets transferred by the decedent to another where the decedent retained a life estate, possession, or income, or with a right of survivorship. This keeps the decedent spouse from depleting the surviving spouse's share.
6. Any assets gratuitously transferred to anyone within two years of the decedent's death (i.e., gifts). There is a $3000 per donee exception.
7. A 1990 revision to the Uniform Probate Code would bring into the reclaimable estate all the assets held by the surviving spouse, not just those received from the decedent.

The reclaimable estate is added to the probate estate to get the augmented estate. The applicable fraction (normally one-third or one-half) is multiplied against the augmented estate to determine the surviving spouse's elective share. The spouse's elective share is reduced by the assets already in his or her possession, and by the assets passing to the electing spouse outside of probate. That leaves the net elective share, which comes from the decedent's estate.

HOMESTEADS

Some state statutes and state constitutions protect a family's residence or "homestead" against creditors' claims. The homestead exemption protects eligible property from the claims of unsecured creditors and many secured creditors of either spouse. The homestead property cannot be foreclosed on by secured creditors unless the mortgage or lien being foreclosed was given for delineated purposes — a mortgage to purchase or improve the homestead property; a lien for past-due property taxes; a federal tax lien; or as a lien from a property settlement in a divorce, for example.

The main homestead property is the principal residence. The residence is defined as a dwelling and the land on which it is located, the acreage sometimes being limited to a certain area or acreage, or value, or both. Some states protect other assets, such as a car or motorcycle, farm animals, or tools of a trade, but it is the family residence and sometimes one business location that constitutes the major protected asset. Not only is the residence protected against creditors, but purchasers cannot defeat a spouse's homestead rights unless the spouse signs the deed. Hence both spouses are required to sign the deed to a residence even if the house is in the name of only one spouse. In some states a homestead right is not self-executing; there must be a recorded declaration of homestead defining its extent.

The homestead is of limited effectiveness as a shield against the claims of creditors in most states. The homestead exemption is typically limited to a stated value and often that value, adequate when enacted into law, is outmoded and too low. If a residence is worth more than the homestead value, the house gets sold and the creditors can claim the excess value. In other states, however — Texas being the prime example — the homestead exemption can safeguard some valuable assets (200 acres plus improvements for land outside a city; up to 10 acres of land with improvements including the residence and maybe a business in a city).

SEPARATE, MARITAL, AND COMMUNITY PROPERTY

Eight states — Louisiana, Texas, New Mexico, Arizona, California, Nevada, Washington, and Idaho — were founded as community property states, derived from the civil laws of Spain and France, which were brought by early settlers from those countries to these states. Two other states — Wisconsin and Alaska — have chosen to become community property states in recent years. The remaining, common law states, derive their concepts of property ownership from English common law.

In **common law states**, property is owned by the spouse who paid for or inherited it. A person's property is separate from his or her spouse's property. In practice, for most of our history, that meant the husband owned most of the marital assets since he earned income, while the wife cared for the house and children. On divorce the husband got the assets. Common law states developed alimony and support laws to prevent divorced women from becoming destitute. On the death of the husband, he controlled who got his assets, unless dower or the elective share rules protected the widow. Many common law states have passed legislation that mimics those of community property states in cases of divorce. These statutes differ primarily in the extent to which they require a judge to accept either the legal rules classifying or the spouses' designation of property as separate or marital property. To varying degrees, these statutes assume that judges have equitable discretion to divide spousal property upon divorce, no matter which spouse holds title, marriage being in some sense a partnership.

Community property states also view the marital unit as one — a partnership — in which the husband and wife work as a unit for their mutual benefit. Hence, whatever one earns is deemed owned by both. Property bought with the husband's wages, for example, is deemed owned half by the husband

and half by the wife. All property acquired during the marriage is presumed to be community property.

That community property presumption can be rebutted, however. Property acquired before the marriage is **separate property** and belongs to the spouse who owned the property before the marriage. Property acquired during marriage as a gift, an inheritance, or a devise is the separate property of the recipient spouse. In most community property states, a couple can enter into a prenuptial agreement, providing assets purchased with income earned by one party shall remain that person's separate property. This may occur, for example, on second or third marriages, where both spouses have independent sources of income and also likely children by prior marriages.

The biggest divergence among the community property states centers on income earned from separate property. In three community property states (Texas, Louisiana, and Idaho) income from separate property is community property. In the five other states, income from separate property is separate property. Gains from the sale of separate property are separate property and considered a return of the principal asset.

If separate property is commingled with community property (usually this concerns money in bank accounts), the rebuttable presumption is the separate money was spent first and for living expenses rather than for assets. In other words, commingled funds most likely will be found to be community property. To illustrate, if W owns corporate stock as a separate asset and receives dividends from the corporation, in the majority of community property states the money received as dividends remains her separate property (in the minority of community property states the income is community property). If, however, W deposits that money into a joint banking account or any account with both separate funds and community funds in it, unless W kept meticulous records classifying the separate funds and the community funds, the funds will be presumed to be community funds.

The spouses can **transmute** separate property into community property (or vice versa) by agreement — required to be written in most of the eight states, oral in some. Both spouses must agree. One spouse cannot act unilaterally.

Recognizing that some married couples move from common law states to community property states, some community property states say property continues to hold its character as separate or community property, as it had when acquired. Others say all separate property acquired during a marriage is considered to be quasi-community property once the couple moves to a community property state.

Each state has its own rules as to who can manage which assets and which assets creditors can reach. A typical statute may require creditors of only one spouse to exhaust that spouse's separate assets before resorting to the community property. A creditor of one spouse cannot reach the other spouse's separate property. A creditor of both spouses can reach community property, as well as the separate assets of both spouses.

In marriages of any length most assets will be community assets on divorce each spouse is entitled to half the community property. If one spouse has a business, generally that spouse gets the business's assets, and other assets of equal value will be awarded to the other spouse. On death, the deceased spouse may devise his or her half of the community property.

Until 1948, there was a decided federal income tax advantage given to married couples in community property states, but the Internal Revenue Code that year was amended to permit married persons in all states to split their income with their spouse for purposes of income tax liability, hence the category of "married, filing jointly" on IRS Form 1040. Much of the community property system is embodied in the Uniform Marital Property Act, enacted in Wisconsin in a modified form. Its aim is to bridge the gap between common law and community property jurisdictions by providing for shared management of property during the marriage, no matter who holds title to it, and to protect the non-owning spouse if the owner dies first or upon dissolution of the marriage.

ANTE-NUPTIAL AGREEMENTS AND PUTATIVE SPOUSES

Historically courts have been hostile to ante-nuptial agreements, but a Uniform Act — the Uniform Ante-Nuptial Agreement Act — has been adopted in about 20 states in order to change this attitude. So long as the agreement is not solely for the purpose of sexual relations, the scope of such agreements under the Act may include a definition of rights of each spouse in the property of the other, including the disposition of property on death, the elimination or modification of spousal support rights on divorce, inheritance rights, and alienation rights during marriage. An agreement, for example, can disturb the presumption of gifts of property from one spouse to another, leaving the donee spouse with the burden of proof as to the gift and raising the evidentiary standard for proving a gift. When an agreement is annulled, courts often do so because one party did not have legal counsel, or time to consider the agreement's consequences, or for some other procedural deficiency. Full disclosure and time to consider are preconditions to a valid agreement.

Persons who think that they are validly married when they are not are known as **putative spouses**. In most states, marriages must be validly performed by someone with authority to do so, witnessed, etc. State statutory requirements pertain. Only a very few states recognize so-called common law marriages — typically based on lore like "live together for seven years and you are married." In some states putative spouses have been protected by theories of estoppel, implied contract, or unjust enrichment. Where such theories have been successful, they have protected one person in a long-term relationship that ended with the other party to it retaining an unreasonable amount of the property accumulated during the relationship and acquired through the efforts of both parties. Lesson to be learned: Don't count on it! The law everywhere has proceeded on a case-by-case basis, making no progress except by litigation. It might be safer to say that two persons, with support or other rights originating in divorce decrees from prior marriages, don't lose those rights just because they have entered into new co-habitation relationships.

Examples

Dower Power

1. Harry and Wanda marry. Harry acquires Blackacre in fee simple absolute. They divorce. Years later, Harry dies. Does Wanda have a common law dower claim on Blackacre?

Elective Share

2. Darrell holds title in fee simple absolute to Blackacre. Darrell transfers that title to his son Steven for "one dollar ($1.00), love, and affection." Shortly after the transfer, Darrell dies. Is the value of Blackacre subject to the elective share otherwise available to Darrell's spouse, Wynona?

Will Substitutes

3. Does the elective share apply to will substitutes — e.g., gifts causa mortis, gifts to another's bank account, and joint bank accounts?

The Tax Man Cometh

4. H and W, husband and wife, own their residence, Blackacre, as tenants in common. H and W file separate federal income tax returns, as they have done for years. H becomes delinquent in the payment of his taxes. The Internal Revenue Service is authorized by Int. Rev. Code §§ 6321 and 7403 to seize and sell any property in which the delinquent taxpayer has any right, interest, or title. Thus, the IRS seeks to satisfy H's delinquency by asserting its statutory lien on and selling Blackacre. H and W seek to block the sale, saying that under state law the homestead is exempt from such a sale. Are they correct?

Community Property Transmuted?

5. In a community property state, Harvey opens a stock brokerage account, held in trust "for Harvey and Willa as joint tenants, with a right of

survivorship, and not as tenants in common." Willa signs a form consenting to the creation of the trust. Willa dies and her estate asserts a claim against the account as community property. A state statute requires that a "transmutation" (as described above, a civil law term) of community property into separate property is invalid unless an express declaration is made by a spouse whose interest is adversely affected. Is the claim valid?

A Community Effort in Common

6. Larry and Melinda had been married for six years. Larry received a $100,000 year-end bonus at work. He bought $100,000 of Capitol Co. stock. Melinda's grandfather died soon thereafter, leaving Melinda $100,000 in Capitol Co. stock. A year later Capitol Co. sent Larry a dividend check in the amount of $5000. Capitol Co. also sent a $5000 dividend check to Melinda. Larry and Melinda deposited their dividend checks in separate bank accounts (Larry into his account and Melinda into hers). Six months later they divorced.
   (a) Assuming Larry and Melinda live in a common law state, who gets the Capitol Co. stock, and who gets the $10,000 from dividends?
   (b) Assuming Larry and Melinda live in a community property state, who gets the Capitol Co. stock, and who gets the $10,000 from dividends?

Explanations

Dower Power

1. Yes, Wanda has a dower claim. Absent a contrary provision in the divorce decree, dower is not terminated by divorce, and so Wanda's dower claim is not barred, even though it is asserted years after the end of the marriage. This is a rule that was formulated long ago, well before the divorce rate rose so steeply. It indicates the strong attachment of the common law to dower claims.

Elective Share

2. Under the Uniform Probate Code, the value of Blackacre is subject to the elective share otherwise available to Darrell's spouse, Wynona, since it was a gratuitous transfer within two years of Darrell's death. If Darrell's intent in effectuating the transfer is to give S what he would otherwise inherit under Darrell's will, but takes Blackacre out of his estate, the answer should be yes. If, on the other hand, Steven had paid full consideration for the asset, then Darrell's estate would be held harmless and the amount of Wynona's elective share would not be diminished by the transfer.

Will Substitutes

3. Does the elective share apply to will substitutes — e.g., gifts causa mortis, Totten trust bank accounts, and joint bank accounts? This is a generalized way of reiterating the issue in the previous problem. The answer, then, is essentially the same, but with regard to any particular will substitute, the answer will often be a matter of statute and part of the state's probate code. So check the applicable code. When the code is silent, it makes sense to include within the elective share any assets and funds governed by any functional equivalent of a valid will. The intent of the transferor is the same as that of a decedent, and the decedent's estate would be depleted if the use of the substitute robs the estate of its value. The value of the elective share is lost if the value of the substitute is not included in the share's calculation.

The Tax Man Cometh

4. No. A homestead provides an exemption from many debts, but not from tax liens. The IRS may levy on the whole title to property held in co-tenancy by a delinquent taxpayer with a nondelinquent one, so long as the nondelinquent co-tenants receive just compensation for their interest as a result of the IRS sale. See United States v. Rogers, 461 U.S. 677, 698 (1983).

Community Property Transmuted?

5. Yes, there was no express transmutation. The consent form has a narrower purpose and is insufficient. This ends the inquiry. The transfer fails to create a joint tenancy also because it does not meet the four unities to create a joint tenancy with right of survivorship unless the state allows a direct transfer from a person to himself and another as joint tenants rather than using a straw. The property remains community property and Willa's estate gets half the account. Spouses in community property states can hold property as joint tenants with right of survivorship, but the intent to do so must be more formally expressed than was done here.

A Community Effort in Common

6. (a) In a common law state, each marital partner owns separate property. Larry's bonus is his, and his purchase of the stock with his money means he owns the $100,000 worth of stock. The dividends earned from his property are his money. Likewise Melinda's inheritance is hers, and the dividends she receives from her stock are her money. Larry and Melinda each get $100,000 in stock and $5000 in cash.

(b) In a community property state, all income earned by either spouse is community property and belongs equally to both spouses. Larry's bonus, therefore, is community property. The dividends on community property are community property. Gifts and inheritances received by a spouse during a marriage are the separate property of the recipient spouse. Thus the $100,000 in stock Melinda inherited is Melinda's separate property. The community property states differ on the character of the dividends on community property. Some say income earned on separate property is community income; others say income earned on separate property is separate property.

Larry gets $50,000 of Capitol Co. stock and $2500 in cash for his half of the community property. Just as certainly, Melinda gets $150,000 worth of Capitol Co. stock (her $100,000 separate property and her $50,000 share of community property) and $2500 in cash from the community property dividends. In some community property states, Larry and Melinda split the $5000 dividends Melinda received on her separate stock; in other states Melinda gets the entire $5000.

The Law of Landlord and Tenant

PART

III

The Landlord and Tenant Relationship

A *lease* is an agreement whereby the owner of the property (the landlord or lessor) contracts to grant a tenant or lessee exclusive possession of specific real or personal property. It typically is — but need not be — for a definite term and it also is typically given in exchange for rent. (Rent is not necessary for a lease's validity, just as a deed for the conveyance of any interest or estate need not be based on consideration to be valid.) Thus, a lease is either a grant or a contract transferring the right to exclusive possession for an agreed, if indefinite, period of time. The lessor retains a reversion. The property transferred, after being described in detail, is usually known as "the premises."

No particular words of art are necessary to create a lease. Under the provision for real property interests in the Statute of Frauds, states require that a lease with a term longer than one, two, or three years must be in writing. If a lease is for a term exactly one, two, or three years, then it too should be in writing because the executory contract provision of most Statutes will require it. A few states require all leases to be in writing. If the Statute requires that a lease be in writing, so must any agreement modifying or terminating it. The real property recording acts of many states permit the recordation of a lease with a term of more than one year. Recording provides a reason why most leases should, from the lessee's perspective, be in writing.

TYPES OF LEASES

We recognize four distinct types of leases: a term for years, a periodic tenancy, a tenancy at will, and a tenancy at sufferance. The tenancy at sufferance is not a voluntary lease arrangement, but arises when a lessee rightfully in possession pursuant to a lease stays on the property after the lease ends. The other three types of leases are generally voluntary. Remember these four types, because the law is not making new types of leases, and the law applicable to each type has some unique characteristics. Parties to a contract can customize their relationships in ways that the law of property does not permit. This attitude is not outmoded formalism; it is instead a way of making the law accessible and easy to apply, often without hiring a lawyer to do so — shocking as that last idea might be in a law school!

(a) Term for Years

A **term for years** or **tenancy for years** is a tenancy that arises from any lease or rental agreement that expires at the end of a defined period, whether for a day, a week, a month, a year, several years, or 999 years. The emphasis is on the word "term," not "years." A short term for years may be the rental of a hall for a dance or wedding reception, or a beach house for a week. A longer term for years may be a 99-year lease on land on which the lessee intends to construct a building. The common law put not limit on the length of a term for years — and today only some agricultural leases have such a limit and that is imposed by statute.

A term for years, like all leases, is a non-freehold estate. It need not commence when the lease is executed or delivered, but may commence at a time in the future. If it commences more than two or three years in the future, however, it may offend the "executory contract" provision of the Statute of Frauds unless it is in writing. The reversion retained by the landlord is a future interest, arising after the term ends. When the term ends, the reversion's holder takes back possession.

A landlord who grants, demises, and lets "to Tenant for five years" creates a term for years. ("Demise" and "let" are the traditional verbs used to transfer this interest, and "grant" is a verb indicating that a conveyancing document is used to accomplish the transfer.) So, too, is a transfer "to Tenant for 100 years if Tenant so long lives." This is a term for years, but more precisely, a determinable term for years. A fixed maximum term is clearly stated, although this term could end before a century has passed. The fact that it might end earlier is irrelevant for classifying the grant as a term for years: When a maximum term is fixed, the estate granted is not a freehold, but is instead a non-freehold term for years.

The term for years must recite the length of the term. A term for years requires that calendar dates be identified for the first and last days of the lease. The dates can be specified as a date — "November 30, 2010," for example — or based on a familiar day — "until Labor Day 2010," for example — or based on a fixed term — "for six months beginning January 1, 2008" for example. If no date of commencement is given for the term, it may be inferred to begin on the date that the lease is executed by the parties to it, or on the date of its delivery by the landlord to the tenant. So, "to Tenant starting six months from the date of this lease, and thereafter for five years" is sufficient when the lease is dated. Likewise, what can be made certain as a term for years is sufficient, so "to Tenant so long as he rents the property adjoining Blackacre" is sufficient when the lease to the adjoining property is sufficient as a term for years. In this sense, the law refers to the term as a determinate period.

Absent agreement to the contrary, a term for year is inheritable, passing as a "chattel real" or immoveable personalty under the tenant's will. Only when the provisions of the term for years require that the tenant perform personal services will it not be inheritable. (Even an explicit restriction on the tenant's use of the premises will not deny a lease inheritability.) Likewise, if the landlord dies during the term, the executor or administrator of his or her decedent's estate has a duty to recognize the lease's term and provisions.

Absent agreement, a term for year is also alienable, although the assignability of a lease is generally restricted by a clause or covenant in the lease.

An important feature of the term for years is that the tenant need not provide the landlord with notice that she will vacate the premises at the end of the term. Likewise, absent a statute on the subject, neither must the landlord give the tenant a notice to vacate at the end of the term. In both instances, the lease itself provides that notice. The expiration of the term is self-executing and automatic.

A lease failing as a term for years becomes either a periodic tenancy, a tenancy at will, or a license, depending on the particulars of the lease and the case. A **license** is an authorization from an owner to enter premises without liability for trespass; it is revocable at will by the licensor (and presumably by the licensee, too, on a principle of mutuality).

(b) Periodic Tenancy

The **periodic tenancy** is a transfer by which the tenant possesses premises for an indefinite term and in which a periodic rent has been reserved to the landlord. Thus, a periodic tenancy is one that continues or runs from day to day, week to week, month to month, or year to year. If the lease does not stipulate the length of the lease term, the initial term's length will conform to the frequency of the rent payments. Thus, if rent is payable monthly, the parties will be found to have a month-to-month periodic tenancy, and if a lease has a starting date, but no termination date, stated in it, it is a periodic tenancy because by default it is governed by the rental period. It can be terminated only by a notice effective at the end of the period specified in the lease. The periodic tenancy endures until one of the parties gives the notice to end it.

An express notice is required to terminate the periodic tenancy. Generally, unless the lease stipulates a different notice period, either party can terminate a periodic tenancy by giving notice at least equal to the length of the tenancy. To be effective, the notice must state the termination date. A tenant in a periodic tenancy for six months must give six months' notice; one in a month-to-month tenancy must give a month's notice, and so on. Since giving notice to terminate a long-term lease one lease term in advance is impractical and not necessary to protect the parties, periodic tenancies of one year or more can be terminated on six months' notice.

Many states statutorily have relaxed the time requirements when a notice must be given, some to as short a time as seven days for a tenant to terminate a residential lease, or three months to terminate a year-to-year lease. Some states retain the month's notice required for a month-to-month tenancy, but allow the lease, to end a month after the notice is given, even if that date is not the end of the month or the lease period. In these cases, the last month's rent is prorated.

Like the term for years, a periodic tenancy may be created by express agreement. It may also be created by implication, however, as when a term for years with an annual term expires, and the tenant continues to pay rent as it comes due and the landlord continues to accept or collect the rent and does not attempt to reenter the premises. The terms and conditions of the lease for the original term are carried over into the new one.

(c) Tenancy at Will

A **tenancy at will** is a landlord tenant relationship that endures only as long as the parties agree it shall. It continues only by mutual agreement. Its indeterminate term does not, however, affect the tenant's right to exclusive possession and he can protect that possession by suing trespassers. Such a tenancy is not inheritable. It ends at the death of either party. (It might be better to say that death is deemed an exercise of the right to terminate it held by either party — death ending the continuing will necessary for its existence.) It is not transferable or assignable. A transfer of the landlord's title, or an assignment of the tenant's rights, ends it. Even an attempt to assign the tenant's interest has in some cases ended it. It is encountered mostly where the relation of landlord and tenant is an informal one, as where one friend permits another to stay in his or her house. Where it is clear on the face of the agreement that both parties intend to establish this type of tenancy, provisions for notice to terminate and for the payment of rent at intervals do not, standing alone or in concert, create a periodic tenancy.

A tenancy at will may be either express or implied. It has been implied, for example, when a purchaser occupies property pending conveyance of title, or when a lessee occupies under a lease executed by less than all tenants in common.

Either party to it has the right to terminate "at will" and so its term is indeterminate — "to Tenant while she continues her law school studies, paying me as she is able" is neither a term for years nor a periodic tenancy, so by a process of elimination, it must be a tenancy at will. When a tenancy is terminable at the will of one party to it, Lord Coke first suggested that the right to terminate was mutual. (Some courts, however, have disagreed, saying that the evident intention of the parties must be honored.) A conveyance to Tenant "so long as he wishes," or "as long as he pays rent and resides on the premises" might be examples of a tenancy at will, but might also be determinable life estates and, construing toward the higher estate, perhaps the latter is the better view. Early cases found a tenancy at will because the livery of seisin necessary to give rise to a freehold was missing; such a rationale has little force today, so finding that Tenant is a life tenant is preferable.

Such a tenancy will rarely be used in commercial transactions — business people need more certainty that it provides. Even a very broad forfeiture clause in favor of a landlord in a commercial lease will not turn a lease otherwise qualifying as a term for years or periodic tenancy into a tenancy at will. In states where all leases must be in writing to satisfy the Statute of Frauds, not just leases of a duration greater than one, two, or three years, an oral lease by law is a tenancy at will. In several states, all oral leases are presumed to be tenancies at will.

At common law a tenancy at will was terminable at either party's fancy with no notice period required. Most states today require 30 days' notice for a landlord to terminate the lease. Many states by statute require the landlord to give 30 days' notice, and some allow only the tenant to terminate the lease at will. Whether such statutes provide the exclusive means of terminating this type of tenancy has been an issue about which courts have reached different conclusions.

(d) Tenancy at Sufferance

A **tenancy at sufferance** is not a true estate — it is a type of wrongful occupancy. It occurs when a tenant enters into a valid lease of any of the three types mentioned previously and then holds over past the end of the lease term. The tenant's entry onto the premises was rightful, but continuing there is not. When a tenant wrongfully holds over, the landlord may either elect to evict the tenant as a trespasser and recover damages, or consent to the tenant's continued possession and hold him liable for a similar term.

The landlord's election depends on the tenant's holdover being wrongful and nontrivial. The tenant's holding over must be voluntary, for example, and not for reasons out of his control. Similarly, a tenant may leave personal property on the premises after the term so long as what is left does not interfere with the landlord's or new tenant's possession. Further, a delay in vacating, caused by the landlord's failure to provide services, excuses the holdover. These limits are imposed on the holdover doctrine because of its harsh effects on, and the resulting judicial sympathy for, the tenant.

(1) Holdover as Trespasser

If the landlord elects to treat the tenant as a trespasser, she need not give a notice to quit and may oust the tenant at any time. Even though the tenancy by sufferance has no definite term and may be terminated at the will of either party, by statute in some jurisdictions a landlord may oust a holdover only through use of the judicial process, rather than through self-help. Once the landlord elects to treat the tenant as a trespasser, the landlord cannot change his mind and try to extend the lease.

(2) Holdover as Renewing Lease

If the landlord elects to treat the tenant as having renewed the lease on the same or similar conditions and covenants, then the issue turns to the length of the new term. Some courts say the renewed lease will be the same duration as the original lease; others say the lease will last the period covered by one rent payment. For example, if a tenant holds over following a one-year lease, with rent payable monthly, in some states the new lease period would be one year, and in other states it would be one month. Because of the harsh effects of this election on the tenant, no court is likely to hold the tenant to a term longer than one year.

Taking their cue from lease provisions imposing double rent on holdover tenants, many state legislatures have enacted statutes abrogating the rule that a holdover may be treated as a periodic tenant, but imposing a liability for double rent on tenants for each day of a holdover period. Some of these statutes require that the landlord make a demand for double rent before the liability arises, but this matter is not always addressed. Such statutes are intended to mitigate the harshness of the common law doctrine, while still giving tenants ample incentive to vacate.

(3) Holdover in Other Situations

A tenancy at sufferance may also be found when a mortgagor holds over after a foreclosure decree is final, a vendor of property stays in possession after conveying title to a purchaser, or a purchaser or grantee keeps possession after defaulting on a contract to purchase or in disregard of a rightful assertion of a possibility of reverter or right of reentry. This type of tenancy is, after all, more a wrongful occupation than an estate in land.

THE LANDLORD'S DUTY TO DELIVER POSSESSION

The landlord has the duty to convey to the tenant the legal right to take possession of the premises for the term. A further issue is whether the lessor (landlord) must deliver actual possession. Courts differ as to who has the responsibility to oust holdover tenants and trespassers.

For example, assume an incoming law student signs an apartment lease in May, to take effect in August in time for the beginning of classes. The appointed day to move in arrives, and the student opens the door to her apartment only to find the previous tenant still in residence. The prospective law student mentions this disconcerting fact to the landlord, who expresses his awareness and dismay.

The issue now is whose responsibility is it to oust the holdover tenant. The majority rule — the so-called English Rule — places the duty on the lessor (landlord) to oust the holdover tenant and any trespassers on the property at the beginning of the lease. A minority of states adopted the so-called American Rule; it requires the landlord only deliver legal possession, not actual possession. Under the American Rule, the tenant must evict the holdover tenant and any trespassers. The two rules are default rules only; the parties to the lease can contract for or modify either rule. Under either rule, the landlord by implication of law warrants his right to lease and title to the premises.

Example 1: Suppose that Tenant is put into possession, but discovers thereafter that there was a prior lease, does Tenant have to continue to pay rent? Yes. Tenant may not stop paying rent just on discovering the prior lease. The covenant to pay rent is an independent covenant, meaning that the duties it creates continue no matter that the landlord is in default on some other duty. The landlord's warranty of title either rule is only an indemnity agreement (not a guarantee of title by the landlord) so unless the prior lease is asserted, there are no damages yet for which the landlord has a duty to indemnify.

Both the English and the American rule have some rational arguments in its favor. The English Rule requires that the landlord deliver to the tenant not only the right to possession, but actual possession as well. First, this is what most tenants expect; they want to lease property, and do not expect to buy a lawsuit. Second, the landlord will likely know why possession cannot be delivered — why a previous tenant holds over, and if there is any interest paramount to the tenant's. The landlord is likely to be acquainted with the facts necessary to litigate such issues. If the tenant had the burden of litigation, he would find himself relying on the landlord for crucial testimony anyway. Third, the landlord, often in the business of leasing business or residential property, is the one with the experience and expertise in such matters. Fourth and finally, the landlord is often the one best able to bear the risk of holdovers. A tenant under the English Rule has the option of voiding the lease and getting damages caused by the failure of the landlord to deliver actual possession on time, or alternatively to accept possession, abate rent for the time the tenant is denied possession, and collect any damages resulting from her dispossession.

The American Rule holds that the landlord need only deliver the right to possession, not actual possession, to the tenant at the beginning of the lease. First, granting the right to possession is all of the landlord promises to do when the lease is regarded as a conveyance of a term. If the landlord wants to extend a warranty or additional rights to the tenant, the parties should bargain over such matters. Every conveyance or contract can bring on a lawsuit; why should the possibility here be so troubling? Second, the tenant has the burden of litigation all during the term to eject trespassers — why should the rule be different on the first day of the lease? Conversely, the landlord is not responsible if the trespasser damages the premises after the first day of the lease — again, why should the law be different on the first day? The tenant can procure insurance to protect himself against trespassers. Third, the landlord may have expertise dealing with leased premises, but he has no special expertise in predicting which tenants will hold over and in effect become tortfeasors; he should not be responsible for the torts of a holdover tenant unless he contracts for this liability. Finally, the tenant has rights against the trespasser or holdover in trespass. If the landlord is crucial to the litigation, then under modern pleading rules he can be impleaded in the tenant's action.

On balance, which of these rules is better? See Hannan v. Dusch, 153 S.E. 824 (Va. 1930) (adopting the American rule, but including a full discussion of both rules). The English Rule is arguably the better one, particularly for residential leases. It conforms to most tenants' expectations and landlords may otherwise take advantage of a tenant's ignorance of the law. It requires that the landlord bargain for any variation in the rule, rather than the tenant. It requires the landlord to use his legal expertise to evict the holdover. It construes the lease against the landlord — its grantor, probably its drafter, and certainly its beneficiary.

Why, then, did the court in *Hannan* adopt the American rule? The lease involved there was a commercial, long-term lease. It was to last for 15 years. The opinion ignored both the implications of this 15-year term and the commercial use for the premises. Indeed, it makes nothing of either, wanting perhaps a uniform rule for both residential and commercial tenancies. The court noted that the tenant had a summary possession remedy under state law, but valued it so little that he did not assert it.

The tenant is responsible for ousting any trespassers who enter after the tenant takes legal possession (i.e., after the first day of the lease). This likely will not be a problem for the urban apartment house lease, but may occur in a long-term lease of farm- or timberlands.

Example 2: If the lease were for farm land, the American Rule makes more sense because it takes time to grow crops, and only at harvest time will the lessee have income from the lease, so if the this type of land is already leased, holding over to get that income will make the existing lessee want to pay damages to a new tenant rather than vacate. So giving the new tenant the right to sue the old one makes sense.

Example 3: What about retail space in a shopping center? If the existing tenant can make a profit by holding over, that tenant has incentive to hold over. The American Rule is superior because damages are the best remedy — and the existing lessee's old profits versus the new tenant's lost profits will provide the measure of damages. Whether it is efficient to hold over can best be determined by a battle between the two tenants, making the American rule preferable to the English one.

See Matthew J. Heiser, *What's Good for the Goose Isn't Always Good for the Gander: The Inefficiencies of a Single Default Rule for Delivery of Possession of Leasehold Premises,* 38 Col. J. Of Law and Soc. Probs. 171 (2004) (from which these two Examples are drawn).

MORE ON THE HOLDOVER TENANT (MORE LATER TOO)

A **holdover** is a tenant who, having entered rightfully, remains in possession after the end of his or her term, without claiming to be there rightfully. The holdover tenant is a tenant at sufferance. Any sublessee holding over is also a tenant at sufferance. Properly considered, a holdover is not a tenant at all, but, because he or she did not enter wrongfully, neither is he or she a trespasser; so ejectment, not trespass, is the proper action to regain possession. Under the traditional, common law rule, the landlord does not have to provide the holdover with any type of notice to quit, but after a demand for possession is made, the landlord has an election: He may either evict the holdover or else treat him as a tenant for a new term — for the same term as in the original lease — up to one year in length. Some courts use the rental payment period to establish a new periodic tenancy.

This new lease is based more on the landlord's election than it is on any implied agreement. Even when the holdover says that he will not be bound, he is nonetheless bound by the landlord's election. The election is not automatic; the landlord must exercise it, either by accepting rent, by suing for rent, or with a notice that clearly indicates an intent to establish a new lease. The harshness of the holdover doctrine is sometimes justified as a benefit to incoming tenants, assuring them that existing tenants will be quickly out of possession. More likely, it is an incentive for parties to expressly identify an expiration date.

Because of the harshness of obligating the holdover for a new term, courts have held that leaving a few pieces of furniture, retaining the keys, or failing to remove personal property is not a holding over so long as the landlord's repossession is not hindered thereby. The holdover doctrine also does not apply until more than a fraction of a day after the term has elapsed: Black letter law does not recognize the fraction of a day as a holdover. The holding over must also be voluntary. Likewise, if negotiations with an existing tenant for a new lease spill over beyond the term, the landlord cannot treat the tenant as a holdover. The negotiating tenant is usually regarded as a tenant at will Were it otherwise, the landlord would be tempted to drag out the negotiations and the tenant would lose leverage in the negotiations. Holding over will be discussed in more detail in Chapter 21 infra.

Examples

Get a Lease

1. (a) Larry "leases" Blackacre "to Tom, to continue so long as rental payments are made." Is this lease a valid term for years?

   (b) Larry leases Blackacre "to Tom for five years, unless Tom graduates from law school within that time." Is this a valid term for years?

   (c) Larry leases Blackacre "to Tom so long as Tom remains a law student." Is this lease a valid term for years?

   (d) Larry leases a house to Tom, Tom's possession to begin on July 1, for a rent of $500 per month. No term is specified. What type of tenancy is created?

   (e) Same facts as in (d), except that the rent is "at an annual rental of $6000, payable at the rate of $500 per month and due on the first day of each month."

Look at the Time

2. (a) Larry conveys Blackacre "to Tom, starting on July 1, 2008, and ending at midnight on June 30, 2009, and continuing thereafter, year to year." On January 15, 2010, Tom notifies Larry that he will terminate the tenancy and vacate the premises on May 31, 2010. Is this notice effective?

   (b) If Tom does no more, is the notice effective at the end of the next annual period?

   (c) If Lanny leases Blackacre to Tina, month to month, starting on July 1, 2008, is a notice of termination mailed 15 days before the end of the month effective to end the tenancy at the end of that month?

   (d) Would the notice in (c) be effective 45 days later, at the end of the next month, when the initial notice contained the following statement: "Whatever tenancy I hold as of the date of your receipt of this letter, I elect to terminate my tenancy at the end of the next period commencing after the date on which you receive this letter." Is this a clear enough statement of termination?

   (e) Is there an effective notification for a termination in 45 days if Tina hands Lanny the keys to the property, and Tina's notice contains the statement in (d) and, in addition, contains a statement that the landlord "can take possession immediately"?

Get a Lease — Part Two

3. (a) While Larry and Tom are negotiating for a lease, Larry permits Tom to take possession and accepts a weekly rent payment from Tom. What type of tenancy is established?

   (b) Larry leases a store to Tom "with rent payable on demand and computed" according to a fixed ratio of dollars to the volume of goods sold in the store. What type of tenancy is created?

   (c) If a tenancy at will is created when both landlord and tenant have the right to terminate the estate, what is created when only one party has this right?

Holding on to a Holdover

4. (a) Larry leases Blackacre to Tom for a term of years. At the end of the term, Tom would like to vacate the premises but cannot find an alternative lease because of a shortage in the local housing market. Is Tom's holding over a voluntary action?

   (b) What if Tom holds over, but Larry does nothing for two months after the term? What is the legal effect of Larry's silence?

American or English Rules

5. (a) In a state adopting the American Rule, if the landlord and the tenant cannot agree on what cause of action to bring against the holdover — summary possession, trespass, or interference with a contract — who decides?

   (b) In a state adopting the English rule, a landlord sues the holdover for possession, but before the first day of the lease, the new tenant has subleased the property to a third party. The sublease is to begin on the first day of the lease, and the sublessee rescinds the sublease while the landlord's possession action is ongoing. Should the holdover be liable to the new tenant for the profits that would have been realized through the sublet? Can the tenant join the landlord's action? Is the holdover liable to the tenant in a separate action?

Explanations

Get a Lease

1. (a) No. A term for years requires a definite termination date or the ability to ascertain an ending calendar date at the beginning of the lease. The occasion of Tom's death does not satisfy that requirement. Tom's interest is more akin to a determinable life estate, to end if Tom stops making payments; to a month-to-month periodic tenancy, with options to renew; or to a defeasible "perpetual lease." Any person thinking of renting the same premises from Larry could check to see if Tom was alive, but the lack of a definite term counts strongly against finding this document to be a term for years. If Tom were not an individual but instead a corporation, another objection might be made: Because a corporate charter has a potentially perpetual life, the term of this lease would also be potentially perpetual — and the finding that this is a term for years is still less likely. Perpetual leases are not void, but most courts avoid finding one if another interpretation of the lease is available.

   (b) It is a valid term for years. A maximum term of five years is stated, and anyone inspecting the lease can readily determine when it will be safe to let the same premises from Larry.

   (c) No. There is no stated term, and no commencement or termination date, and no way of knowing how long Tom will remain a law student, so no way of determining the term.

   (d) A periodic tenancy from month to month, until terminated by proper notice.

   (e) A periodic tenancy from year to year is established. The annual reservation of the rent establishes the longer of the two periods implied in the lease. The longer reservation of the rent shows that the parties contemplate the year-to-year term. This is the typical result. The reservation of rent clause overrides the rent payable clause.

Look at the Time

2. (a) No, for two reasons. First, this is a periodic tenancy. It cannot be terminated at any time other than the end of the period named in the agreement. Second, the notice provided is not long enough. To end a year-to-year periodic tenancy, a six-month notice is required. The notice given here is 15 days short of that and so is ineffective. This notice should be received by Larry by January 1, 2010.

(b) In most states, the answer is no. An ineffective notice is forever ineffective. After all, the tenant providing the ineffective notice might change his mind about vacating. However, a minority of states answer in the affirmative: The ineffective notice is revived for use in the next period, when it might be effective. The rationale for the majority rule is that a periodic tenant has a duty to provide the landlord with a clear notice of termination, naming the date on which he or she will vacate the premises. If you get to advise Tom in a timely fashion, it is better to advise that Tom give a second notice during 2010, setting out clearly an intent to vacate on June 30, 2011. In any notice, a clear notice is required of the tenant. The rule (that an ineffective notice is forever ineffective, and not revived for use in the next period when it might be effective) forces the tenant to give a second notice, one that clears up any misunderstanding that the landlord might have; it is designed to force the tenant to be clear.

(c) No. Thirty days' notice is required, but the authorities are not uniform. Some states by statute authorize a shorter notice period. In many states the notice would be valid to end the tenancy on July 31. In others, however, the notice is not valid for termination to occur for July 31 either, since the notice does not mention July 31.

(d) When the lease is regarded as a contract, Tina has indicated a clear intention to vacate, so the answer is probably in the affirmative. The issue turns on whether reasonable persons would agree on the termination date. This one seems to pass the test. But it would have been far more sensible to state the termination date.

(e) The court in Worthington v. Moreland Motor Truck Company, 250 P. 30 (Wash. 1926), held this language would be sufficient to provide the landlord with notice ending the lease in 45 days, but indicating that if a date and time of termination were not fixed, the notice might be insufficient. Tina's actual possession ended on the day she turned the keys over; her legal possession continues until the termination date.

Get a Lease — Part Two

3. (a) A tenancy at will. It is not a week-to-week periodic tenancy because the ongoing negotiations indicate that no secure term has yet been fixed: When the negotiations end, the lease for whatever term will commence, and the flexibility required in the negotiations should not be diminished by implying a term for the interim, unless the doctrine of estoppel applies. See Carteri v. Roberts, 73 P. 818 (Cal. 1903) (holding that a month-to-month periodic tenancy is created when a defendant, after notice to the plaintiff, begins to plow the plaintiff's agricultural land while farm lease negotiations between them are pending).

   (b) A tenancy at will. Larry supplies the premises and Tom the sales effort that produces the rent; either can terminate what each brings to this arrangement at will. Since Tom is supplying business and sales skills, it is particularly important that he have the right to terminate — otherwise he would find himself indentured to Larry.

   (c) This problem is often treated by avoidance; that is, many courts hold that when one party has the power to terminate, the other implicitly has such a right as well. Thus, by operation of law, a tenancy at will arises. A principle of mutuality of right (and remedy) supports this result, but in some instances, the intent of the parties is clearly expressed in the agreement to the contrary. What then? One response is to construe the interest as a determinable term for years: A person can only pay rent so long as he or she is alive, so this lease lasts as long as the rent is paid. So when Larry conveys "to Tom for so long as he desires," the interest might possibly last for the rest of Tom's life. Having thus created the possibility of an estate greater than a tenancy at will, that estate or interest is made determinable — i.e., that Tom might end the term sooner. Since checking with Tom provides a way to put future tenants and other transferees of the property on notice of Tom's interest, whatever it is, this result is reasonable. It is akin to a preference for a vested interest and construing toward a higher, or freehold, estate that we have seen in our discussion of common law estates.

   Typically, with a widely used form of conveyance in some regions of the country — e.g., "to Tom for so long as he farms the land" with rents payable as a fixed fraction of the crop — this result is reached to protect a class of farmers or sharecroppers. See Newsom v. Meade, 135 S.E. 604 (W. Va. 1926). If the same sort of transfer is made, but the passive voice is used — e.g., "to Tom while the premises are used for farming," — some courts call the interest a lease and further describe it as a "perpetual one." This must mean that the so-called tenant is running an operation requiring stability and security of possession. Or, put another way, "to Tom while the premises are used for the production of oil and gas." If Tom in the last two examples were to take the interest as an official of a corporation — an entity with perpetual life for a limited business purpose — the lease may more properly be called perpetual, no matter what voice is used in the verbs describing the operation on the premises required to continue and maintain the tenant's interest. Alternatively, the last two transfers create a fee simple determinable, a freehold estate.

Holding on to a Holdover

4. (a) Yes. Although the hardship on Tom is great, this probably is not a holding over that would tempt the courts to excuse the tenant. Tom should have anticipated this problem. The harsh effects of the hold-over doctrine encourage tenants either to settle with landlords on a new lease or to vacate. The doctrine thus benefits all incoming tenants who are, after all, just as affected by a housing shortage as Tom. A different answer may result if Tom could not move for one day because the former tenant in his new place had not vacated, and Tom's remaining on the premises did not inconvenience the landlord or any new tenant waiting for Tom to move. Likewise, not vacating because the tenant suffered a serious illness was involuntary and excused on that account.

(b) The obvious consequence is that the landlord, after a reasonable lapse of time, might be deemed to have consented to a periodic tenancy in most states. There is a time at which the landlord's silence will be deemed consent, but the lapse of two months or so is unlikely to bring about this result. A court's finding an implied election is unlikely, unless the silence lasts an unreasonably long time. See Beach Realty Co. v. City of Wildwood, 144 A. 720 (N.J. 1929) (tenant holding over two months and two days, without any communication from the landlord, is still a tenant at sufferance). This, however, is no reason to advise a landlord in such a way as to encourage her silence in a matter in which the doctrine seeks to encourage communication and clarity: If the landlord passes up opportunities to communicate, that fact might encourage a court to imply an election.

American or English Rules

5. (a) The tenant under the American Rule gets to decide who brings the action for possession, no matter what it is called — summary possession or trespass.

(b) If the landlord's cause of action for possession is for summary possession, then the landlord is interested only in possession and not damages and a cause of action for damages would prolong the landlord's action unduly. If the English rule is adopted for use with a summary possession statute, then the tenant should not be able to join in the landlord's action, but reserves the damages claim for a separate action and trial following the landlord's.

CHAPTER 16

Transfers of the Lease

PRIVITY OF CONTRACT AND PRIVITY OF ESTATE

A landlord and tenant relationship,[1] from the outset, involves both privity of contract and privity of estate. First, the landlord and the tenant are said to be in **privity of contract**. Privity of contract is a relationship existing between both parties to a contract. The lease is a contract. Thus the landlord and the tenant are in privity of contract with respect to the leased premises.

At one time only persons in privity of contract could enforce or be held liable for a contract. This caused problems when a tenant transferred her leasehold to a third party (assignee) and the landlord wanted to collect rent from the assignee who was not a party to the original lease, and hence not in privity of contract with the landlord. The courts resolved this sticky problem by crafting another type of privity — privity of estate.

Landlord and tenant are also in the relationship known as **privity of estate** because both the landlord and the tenant have a mutual, immediate, and simultaneous interest in the leased premises — the tenant having the right to possession for a term, and the landlord having the reversion after the term. See *Restatement, Second, Property*, § 16.1 (1977). Privity of estate permits a landlord to collect rent from the tenant's assignee, even though there is no direct contract between them.

---

1. This chapter uses **landlord** and **lessor** to mean the landowner, **tenant**, **head tenant**, **lessee**, or **sublessor** to indicate the person leasing from the landlord, and **assignee**, **subtenant**, or **sublessee** to indicate the person taking from a tenant.

ASSIGNMENTS AND SUBLEASES

There are two distinct categories of tenant transfers: assignments and subleases. An **assignment** is a transfer of the whole of the unexpired term of the lease. It need not be a transfer of all of the premises. An assignment of a portion of the premises for the unexpired remainder of the term is called an **assignment pro tanto**.

A **sublease** is a partial transfer of less than the full remaining term of the lease. Thus, the subletting tenant (by becoming a sublessor) retains some interest in the term. A sublease is an independent transaction creating a wholly new and distinct landlord-tenant relationship between the sublessor and the sublessee. It has no effect on the original lease — for a court to hold otherwise would be to sanction a unilateral change in an ongoing contract. The sublessee is not bound by the covenant to pay rent in the original lease — the original or head tenant remains bound by it — or by any other covenant in the original lease, also known as the primary or "head" lease.

No particular words of art are required to assign or sublet, but the Statute of Frauds may apply to either category of transfer. A sublease is treated just as a lease would be, and an assignment is subject to the Statute depending on the length of the unexpired term, although the original English Statute required that all assignments be written and that is still required in a few states. Good practice, moreover, requires that assignments and subleases be in writing.

THE TRADITIONAL RULE

The majority and the traditional test for distinguishing between an assignment and a sublease is this: If the original tenant retains an interest in the premises, the transfer from the tenant to the third party is a sublease, but if the original tenant transfers the property for the entire remaining period of the lease, the transfer is an assignment. However, transferring the lease for even one day less than the remaining time of the lease results in a sublease, rather than an assignment. The traditional rule operates regardless of the actual intent of the parties.

Under the traditional rule, the retention of a right of reentry or a possibility of reverter by the original tenant creates a sublease, not an assignment. Likewise, a tenant's right to reenter the premises for a breach of particular covenants in the original lease, in order to preserve that lease, would likely be held to be the right of a sublessor under the traditional rule.

RULE OF INTENT

A minority of jurisdictions have adopted a rule giving effect to the parties' intentions whether they created a sublease or an assignment. See, e.g., Jaber v. Miller, 239 S.W.2d 760 (Ark. 1951), followed in Ernst v. Conditt, 390 S.W.2d 703 (Tenn. App. Ct. 1964). What the parties call what they did — as transferring either a "sublease" or an "assignment" — does not control. Instead, the intent of the parties is ascertained from an interpretation the document as a whole, just as it would be with any other written agreement or contract. This rule gives the parties the right, not to customize their transfer, but to choose whether to use an assignment or a sublease for it. When there is no evidence of the parties' intent in the matter, the traditional rule, once applied regardless of the parties' intent, will likely still be applied as the parties' presumed intent. While the rule of intent brings the law of leases into harmony with the general rules of contract law and interpretation, it provides less certainty in many situations, and perhaps for this reason it has been adopted in only a minority of jurisdictions.

If a tenant with one year remaining on a two-year lease transfers the remaining year of the term to a third party, the tenant has assigned the lease and the third party is the *assignee*. If the tenant transferred the leased premises to a third party only for the summer months while the tenant was on vacation elsewhere, that is a sublease and the third party is a *sublessee*. Similarly, if a tenant leases an apartment and then takes in another person to reside in the second bedroom, that, too, is a sublease of a portion of the premises. Query: Is that the correct classification? Why isn't this considered a fractional assignment of the estate? Some older opinions call it an assignment; more recent ones a sublease.

THE EFFECT OF TENANT TRANSFERS ON PRIVITY

Privity of estate exists between a landlord and a tenant and a landlord and a tenant's assignee, but not between a landlord and a tenant's sublessee. **Privity of contract** exists between a landlord and a tenant, but not between a landlord and a tenant's assignee or a tenant's sublessee. The privity of contract exists between landlord and tenant even after the tenant transfers (either by assignment or subletting) the lease and moves, unless the landlord expressly agrees to substitute the transferee for the tenant, looking only to the transferee for the rent payments and to satisfy all obligations under the lease (known as a **novation**). The landlord's consent to the transfer does not implicitly terminate the privity of contract between the original parties to the lease.

Either the privity of contract or privity of estate can be the basis of a tenant's or assignee's liability for rent. Thus the relationship to the lease agreement itself (privity of contract), or that created by the physical possession of the premises (privity of estate), creates a liability for rent. A landlord may sue for back rent a tenant who has subleased because of privity of contract, and also may sue a tenant's assignee for rent because of privity of estate. The landlord, however, can have only one recovery, judgment, and satisfaction for the rent. Sometimes it is held that the tenant, upon assignment, becomes liable for rent as a surety—someone against whom recovery may be had if the assignee does not pay. A **surety** is a person bound to perform an obligation when another (here, the assignee), who is primarily liable to do so, does not. For example, if the tenant is forced to pay the rent due from an assignee, the tenant may sue the assignee to recover what was paid. This suit is based on a principle of **subrogation**—i.e., the tenant steps into the shoes of the landlord due to rent for purposes of this suit. The tenant in this situation has the burden of litigation—i.e., the burden (not a duty) of enforcing the obligation to pay rent against the assignee.

If and when a tenant's assignee himself assigns the lease to another person, the original assignee thereafter has neither privity of estate nor privity of contract with the landlord. He no longer has a lease relationship—so no privity of contract—and once he moves out, he has nothing on which the landlord may base privity of estate either, although the original assignee remains liable on any past due rents related to his time in possession. Now the second assignee has privity of estate with the landlord, and is liable for rent on that basis. If, on the other hand, the first assignee sublets, there is by definition a gap in time between the end of the new sublessee's term and the landlord's reversion, and because of this gap, the landlord and the new sublessee are not in privity of estate. The sublessee is liable to the assignee for rent, but not to the landlord; however, the assignee and the landlord are still in privity of estate.

REAL COVENANTS

Amid such chains of lease assignments, some particularly important covenants in the primary lease are said to be **real covenants** and to "run with the land." These covenants differ in effect from covenants that are "personal covenants." Real covenants are those whose obligations or burden attaches to the estate or interest of its promisor. A promisor is the person undertaking the obligation to keep the promise contained in the covenant, and may be either a landlord or a tenant. Thus a real covenant will bind any successor of the promisor for the period of time he or she holds the estate of the promisor. Likewise, the promisee's successors also have the right to enforce the benefit of the covenant. The covenant for quiet enjoyment and the covenant to pay rent are important examples of real covenants. As to these covenants, their running provides another basis (in addition to privity of estate and contract) for holding an assignee in possession liable for the obligations in the primary lease.

The requirements for ascertaining whether a covenant is real or personal are very technical, as fully developed in Chapter 30, infra, but in general they involve (1) the **intention** of the original promisor and promisee (here the landlord and the tenant) that they bind successors to the interests of each, (2) **privity of estate** (always present with a chain of assignments between the original landlord and any later assignee in possession), and (3) the requirement that the subject of the covenant **touch and concern** the leasehold premises or land. A restriction on the use of the premises imposed in the lease generally touches and concerns the land, as do the covenant to pay rent, the covenant for quiet enjoyment, a covenant restricting assignments and subleases, a covenant to repair the premises, and a covenant to renew or extend the leasehold's term.

LANDLORD'S CONSENT TO A SUBLEASE OR ASSIGNMENT

In general, leaseholds are freely transferable. Absent a provision in the lease to the contrary, the tenant has the right to alienate his or her interest or estate. A lease silent on the matter of transfer is construed by the courts as permitting a transfer without the landlord's consent.

The tenant's right to sublet or assign may be restricted by an express provision of the lease, however, so long as the provision embodies a reasonable restriction on transfer. Restrictions on alienation by a tenant are valid regardless of the length of the restriction, and justified as a reasonable protection of the landlord's interest and income from the premises. An express restriction on assignment or subletting is strictly construed against the landlord. Often it is said that the restriction on alienation is to be construed against its beneficiary, the landlord — who is typically the drafter of the restriction in any event. The policy of free transferability aside, this provides another contract-based reason for a narrow construction — i.e., that a lease, like any contract or agreement, will be construed against its drafter. Restrictions are rarely implied, although a farm lease has been held inalienable on the basis that the landlord is looking to the personal services of the tenant for rental income.

LANDLORD CONSENT PROVISIONS

A growing number of jurisdictions oblige the landlord to have a commercially reasonable basis for withholding consent to a sublease or assignment when the lease provides that the landlord must approve and give (generally written) consent to any assignment or sublease. This is a so-called **silent consent provision**, the lease being silent on the standards the landlord is to use when considering a request to consent to a sublease or assignment.

In these jurisdictions, the landlord may not arbitrarily refuse to approve a proposed sublessee or assignee and must have a commercially reasonable basis for a refusal. A commercially reasonable basis is a business reason rather than a personal or discriminatory reason, and rather than an excuse to extort more rent. See Kendall v. Ernest Pestana, Inc., 709 P.2d 837 (Cal. 1985) (interpreting a lease provision stating that "there shall be no sublease or assignment without the landlord's consent, holding such consent shall not be unreasonably withheld," and reviewing the reasons for the traditional no-mitigation rule, but adopting the minority rule forbidding unreasonable withholding of consent both as a matter of public policy and as a matter of enforcing an implied covenant of good faith and fair dealing into the lease), noted in 14 Pepp. L. Rev. 81 (1986). The *Pestana* holding is that "where a commercial lease [contains an approval provision, the landlord's] consent may be withheld only where the lessor has a commercially reasonable objection to the assignee or the proposed use." See *Kendall*, 709 P.2d at 849.

There is a trend to adopt the commercially reasonable standard for residential leases, too, as opposed to just commercial ones. Residential tenants are likely to be in greater need of protection than are commercial tenants. Even in jurisdictions that do not imply a commercial reasonable standard for withholding consent, there is a tendency to the standards for reasonable conduct in the original lease. If the proposed assignee or sublessee is as acceptable as the original (or "head") tenant, then the landlord cannot reasonably withhold consent. A landlord acting unreasonably in this context subjects himself to an action for damages by the tenant refused the consent.

The rule requiring the landlord to have a commercially reasonable basis for refusing to consent to the assignment or sublease is justified in several ways. First, it promotes the free transferability or alienation of leases, and furthers the policy of the law of disfavoring restraints on alienation. Second, it arises from an implied covenant of good faith and fair dealing that applies to leases as well as to most agreements or contracts. Third, it carries out the reasonable expectations of the parties.

Assignment and subleasing provisions in commercial leases are among the most fiercely negotiated clauses of a commercial lease. For example, when a jurisdiction's law requires that landlords have a commercially reasonable basis for refusal to consent to a sublease, landlords often insist on the insertion of a "rent recapture" provision in a lease, requiring that the landlord may collect all or part of any appreciation in the rent charged a sublessee. Such provisions are generally found reasonable.

A slight majority of jurisdictions continue to permit the landlord to refuse consent to an assignment or sublease, no matter how suitable the sublessee or assignee appears to be and no matter how unreasonable the landlord's objection. However, in these jurisdictions, the acceptance of rent from the assignee or sublessee by the landlord will be deemed a waiver of a landlord's right to withhold consent. After accepting the rent, the landlord is presumed to know of the transfer and to have consented to it. Likewise, a sublessee or assignee who takes possession and pays the rent under an oral lease may be deemed a periodic tenant.

The lease assigned or sublet without the landlord's consent is not void; rather, it is voidable at the option of the landlord, who may either elect to accept the rent and waive the benefit of the covenant prohibiting transfer without his consent, or else evict the transferee. No automatic forfeiture of the lease is implied. This result follows from the doctrine of independent covenants.

The tenant has several remedies when the landlord acts unreasonably. A suit for damages is the most recognized remedy, but that exposes the tenant to expensive and time-consuming litigation. May a tenant denied consent arbitrarily abandon the lease? Some courts (but not enough to establish a clear trend) have answered this question in the affirmative. The underlying issue is whether, in effect, the adoption of a minority rule throws the burden of finding a transferee on the landlord who unreasonably refuses to consent to an assignment or sublease.

Courts that have addressed the issue ruled in favor a landlord who refused to consent when a tenant, who has a perfectly acceptable assignee waiting in the wings, refuses to let the landlord review that assignee's credentials and consent.

No matter what the rule on the landlord's consent, it is the landlord's duty to clearly provide notice of the landlord's rights to the tenant. Actions under the implied covenant of good faith and fair dealing — particularly as to residential leases — and under state deceptive trade practices acts require no less. But notice alone may not suffice: A secondary issue is whether the landlord and the tenant freely and fairly bargained over the clause. Because many clauses in a long commercial lease may not be bargained over, or may not be bargained over because others are, many courts will strike anti-assignment covenants as being an illegal adhesion contact.

THE RULE OF DUMPOR'S CASE

With a no-assignment-without-consent provision in the lease, once the landlord consents to a first assignment, without reserving a right to consent to future assignments, he is deemed to have waived the right to consent further, and future assignments can be made without consent. This is the Rule of Dumpor's Case, 76 Eng. Rep. 1110 (K.B. 1578), intended to promote the free alienability of the lease. It also, however, typically flies in the face of the expressed intent of the original parties to the lease.

The rule is a trap for the unwary landlord, who may defeat it with a statement that she consents to this particular assignment, rather than to all future ones. The issue is one of forcing one party or the other to be clear about a litigation-breeding silence, and on that ground is consistent with the majority rule adopted by courts for "silent consent" covenants. Many courts, however, accept the rule silently. It might be regarded as an early application (black-lettered) of the doctrine of estoppel. See, e.g., Childs v. Warner Bros. Southern Theatres, Inc., 156 S.E. 923 (N.C. 1931) (collecting the cases). Dumpor's Case does not apply to covenants prohibiting or limiting the right of a tenant to sublease.

TRANSFERS OF THE LANDLORD'S INTEREST

The landlord can sell or assign the leased premises. Any transfer will be subject to any outstanding leases (but see Recording Acts, discussed infra Chapter 27). A transfer of the landlord's reversion is made subject to outstanding leases. This is an application of the rule that a grantor cannot convey more than he or she has. Thus, the transferee does not have an immediate right to possession of premises subject to a lease. After the transfer, the new owner of the property is in privity of estate with the tenant, and all the real covenants (those running with the land) benefit and burden the new owner from that time forward. Thus, the transferee may, and the former landlord or the transferor may not, sue for rent accruing after the transfer. The transferee also has the burden of real covenants and becomes the party primarily liable for them. After transferring the reversion, the landlord's privity of estate with the tenant ends, but his privity of contract does not; thus, absent a release of liability by the tenant, the former landlord remains liable on his personal covenants in the lease, and secondarily liable on its real covenants.

As with the rules governing a tenant's transfers, these rules show that at root the law is protecting the interests of the non-transferring party to the original lease. With assignments and subleases, it is the landlord who is protected; when the landlord transfers the reversion, it is the tenant who has his lease carved out of the reversion. Moreover, none of these rules about transfers are rules of public policy; they are default rules, subject to agreement to the contrary.

Examples

Assignments and Subleases

1. (a) LL leases Blackacre to T. T transfers his interest "to T1 so long as T1 farms the property." Is T1 a sublessee or assignee?

   (b) LL leases Blackacre to T, who transfers his interest to T1 "but if T1 does not pay the rent to LL, T has the right to reenter. . . ." What type of transfer is this?

   (c) LL leases Blackacre to T, who "sublets" his entire interest to T1 and agrees (in a separate document) with LL to remain liable for the rent if T1 does not pay it. What type of transfer is this?

   (d) Same facts as in (c), but T1 learns that T is still liable to LL for T1's unpaid rent. LL then sues T1 directly for the rent. T1 defends, arguing that he has neither privity of estate nor privity of contract with LL and so is not liable for the rent to LL, and that T's liability for T1's unpaid rent implies a right of reentry, re-enforcing the idea that T1 has a sublease. Is T1's defense a good one?

   (e) LL leases a house to T. T "subleases" to T1, using the word "sublease" several times in the course of the T-T1 agreement. The agreement provides that T1 is entitled to possession for T's entire unexpired term. T1 remits the rent payments to T, thinking that he will pass them along to LL, but T does not; instead, he absconds and, six months later, LL notifies T1 that he has not received the rent since T1 took possession. Will T1 have to pay the rent twice, a second time to LL?

Landlord's Consent

2. (a) A lease provision provides that the tenant's interest may be assigned or sublet with the landlord's consent, but if the landlord's consent is not obtained and the tenant transfers his interest, the tenant shall pay the landlord $5000. Is such a provision enforceable?

   (b) A lease contains a prohibition on assignments. Is subleasing prohibited too?

Refusing Consent

3. Assume the following Examples take place in a state that requires a landlord to have a commercially reasonable reason for refusing to consent to an assignment or sublease.

   (a) LL and T execute a commercial lease that prohibits its sublease or assignment. Is this lease provision valid?

(b) LL reserves a right of first refusal to take back the leased premises if LL agrees to accept the same terms as the T offered the proposed assignee or subtenant. Is such a right of first refusal enforceable?

(c) LL and T execute a commercial lease that expressly provides that "LL may withhold consent to any sublease or assignment in its sole and absolute discretion." Is this lease provision valid?

(d) LL and T agree that LL may withhold consent to any sublease or assignment by T, "but only with having a reasonable basis for doing so," and that LL's "decisions in such matters shall be final." T wants to assign its lease to T1, but LL refuses to consent because he does not feel good about T1. Can LL refuse consent?

(e) LL and T execute a lease that provides that T cannot sublease or assign the lease without LL's prior written consent, such consent not to be unreasonably withheld; that T shall give LL notice of any potential sublessee or assignee; and that, "upon T's sublease or assignment of T's leasehold, LL may, at its option, either consent to the sublease or assignment or reenter and repossess the leased premises and terminate all of T's rights under this lease therein." Is this lease provision valid?

(f) LL and T execute a commercial lease that "T may assign the premises with LL's prior written consent." T wants to assign the lease to T1. Must LL have a commercially reasonable reason for refusing to consent to the assignment?

(g) Same facts as in (f). T wants to sublet the premises to T1. The leased premises are in a shopping mall. The landlord considers national chain stores essential to the success of the mall. T, a national chain, wants to sublet the premises to a local resident opening her own business. This would be her first shop. Must T get LL's consent to sublet to T1?

Explanations

Assignments and Subleases

1. (a) T's retention of a possibility of reverter suggests that this is a sublease. See Anderson v. Ries, 24 N.W.2d 717 (Minn. 1946) (holding a transfer to X so long as he is in the armed forces is a sublease). The language used in this transfer is that required for T's retaining a possibility of reverter, a common law estate regarded as a vested one and sufficient to hold that this transfer is a sublease. Classifying a future interest as a contingent one would then change the result.

(b) Recent cases using the traditional rule would find this a sublease as well. It's a close case for many courts, and there are older authorities to the contrary. Even courts using the traditional rule might hold that this is an assignment. The right to reenter is express, but unless the right is asserted, T1 has the same estate as does T. That's good enough for most courts, particularly those using a canon of construction construing the grant liberally and in favor of the transferee. At the start of T1's interest, T is for all practical purposes out of the picture. In fact, the condition sounds like a security device to guarantee the tenant can get the property back if he is forced to pay rent to the landlord. A minority of jurisdictions label this a sublease, the condition subsequent persuading courts there that the estates are not the same. Hence, the right of reentry is inserted between the end of the transferee's estate and the landlord's reversion — this gap prevents privity of estate between LL and T1. Insertion of T into this gap in effect makes T a surety for the rent. All courts agree that the insertion of a reversion creates a sublease, but the late entry of possibilities of reverter and rights of reentry into our system of common law estate left courts free to analogize them to reversions, or not, in these cases.

(c) An assignment. Although T and T1 seemingly intend to make T1 a subtenant, the majority of courts would hold that when the entire interest of a tenant is transferred, an assignment results, no matter what the parties called the transfer. Even courts in states that follow the rule of intent will follow the traditional rule where, as here, evidence of that intent is thin. (Indeed, the rule of intent has in the last half century gains few adherents.)

(d) No. Even though once T pays the rent he could sue T1 for possession and so assert the functional equivalent of a right of reentry, most courts would still follow the rule that a transfer of a tenant's entire interest is an assignment. Further, T's continuing liability is contractual; if a right of reentry is reserved, it should be reserved expressly because the law does not readily imply a new type of estate. Here, one would not be implied from T's payment of T1's rent, on the theory that T and T1 could easily have provided for a right of reentry and did not do so. T1's defense would fail.

(e) The T-T1 agreement is intended to be a sublease, and the rental payments paid to T are consistent with this intention. If, however, the rental payment was made to T without the agreement providing expressly for this, then the sublease analogy starts to break down. The transfer of all of the unexpired term trumps the payment ritual. This argues that the "sublease" is really an assignment — and that is how most courts would classify it. The substance and actions of the parties trump their intent, using the traditional rule, and rejecting the way the parties have styled their transfer as controlling, as courts might find the title of a document less persuasive than its substantive provisions. T1 may thus owe the rent twice, on a theory of privity of estate established between the landlord and an assignee. T1 has an action against T, if he can locate T — not always easy to do.

Landlord's Consent

2. (a) No. Fish v. Robinson, 106 N.E. 1057 (Ohio 1913) (prohibiting the enforcement as a forfeiture or penalty and a violation of the policy proscribing unreasonable restraints on alienation).
   (b) No. Although the cases on the subject are split, the lease should be construed against its beneficiary or drafter and no implication that a prohibition against the lesser act of subletting is included or implied from the express prohibition of the greater or more inclusive act of assigning the tenant's interest. This accords with the weight of authority. The tenant may thus sublease his or her interest.

Refusing Consent

3. (a) Yes. The commercially reasonable refusal standard is an implied covenant and can be overruled by an express provision in the lease. Nothing there holds that the landlord may not, at the start of the lease, bargain for and give the tenant notice (in the lease) of an absolute prohibition on assignments or subleases.
   (b) Yes. See *Restatement, Second, of Property* § 14.2, Comment i (1977). The landlord's willingness to pay the tenant the premium or excess rental the assignee or subtenant would pay eliminates one of the concerns underlying the commercially reasonable standard.
   (c) The provision is valid. If an absolute prohibition is valid (see Explanation 3(a), supra), so should this somewhat lesser prohibition. The provision establishes a standard, the landlord's sole and absolute discretion. The commercial tenant is on notice.
   (d) The express lease provision overrides the implied commercially reasonable standard. The two provisions establishing the standard applicable to the landlord's discretion appear to be inconsistent. A court would try to reconcile the reasonable basis provision against the landlord's final decision provision. Since contracts have an implied covenant of good faith and fair dealing, a court could and should conclude that the landlord must act in good faith in refusing to consent to the assignment. Good faith here would approximate the commercially reasonable standard for refusing to consent.
   (e) The provision is valid in most jurisdictions. The provision provides for forfeiture if the landlord decides it is in his best interest to force the forfeiture. The majority of courts imposing a commercially reasonable standard would interpret the contract as written. Courts in a minority of jurisdictions would hold the provision valid but scrutinize the specific scenario where the dispute arose. The judicial

concern is that a forfeiture provision allows the landlord to reap the benefit of increased rentals otherwise accruing to the tenant. These courts consider the landlord's refusal to consent so the landlord can collect higher rents an abuse of the landlord's power. The context of the leasehold might matter here. A court might strike this provision from a clause in a long-term commercial lease but accept it in a bedroom apartment lease in a private home.

(f) Yes. The lease provides for the landlord's consent to an assignment but does not establish the standard to guide the decision maker. The default rule applies; that requires a commercially valid reason for refusing to consent.

(g) T does not have to get LL's consent. Courts disfavor restraints on alienation and will construe restraints on alienation narrowly. A provision requiring a tenant to get consent before assigning the lease will not be interpreted to require consent to a sublease, even when the lease is essential to the success of a larger enterprise. The lease required the landlord's consent only to an assignment, not to a sublease. See Explanation 2(b).

CHAPTER 17

Waste, Duty to Repair, Destruction of Leased Premises, and Security Deposits

WASTE

A tenant has a duty to his or her landlord not to commit waste. Waste is the unreasonable use of property in which another has an interest and resulting in the destruction, misuse, or neglect of the premises — in the context of the landlord tenant relationship, a substantial injury to the landlord's reversion, this reversion being the interest protected in an action for waste. Waste traditionally involves a change in the physical identity of the premises. There are two principal types of waste: It may be either (1) voluntary and intentional, or (2) permissive. **Voluntary waste** is a direct, willful, or intentional injury to the premises. **Permissive waste** is the result of neglect or omission, such as allowing a structure on the premises to deteriorate or become exposed to injury by the weather; it may be either omissive or commisive.

Traditionally, a tenant's making material or substantial change in the premises was voluntary waste, regardless of the fact that it increased its fair market value. Such an approach has been modified in many jurisdictions to depend on the express or implied intention of the parties, with the result that a reasonable change in the premises — that is, one reasonably necessary to use the property as contemplated in the lease — is now permitted.

The tenant has the duty (implied in every lease) to redeliver the premises to the landlord in the same condition as it was received, wear and tear excepted. This implied covenant to redeliver is the minimum duty that the tenant owes the landlord due to the duty not to commit waste. A tenant's unauthorized changes to the premises' physical condition more likely will be found to constitute waste. This view may not apply, of course, to a long-term leasehold — i.e., to a lease whose term is long enough to amortize or depreciate the value of the tenant's changes, so long as the tenant restores the premises to its original condition.

More generally, the tenant has the duty not to injure the *value* of the landlord's reversion. This duty is subject to two exceptions. First, a tenant may make such changes as are reasonably necessary to use the premises in a way contemplated by the parties to the lease. Sometimes this is stated as a tenant's right to make temporary or minor changes in the premises during the course of the lease, subject to a duty to restore the premises as they were at its beginning. Second, as previously mentioned, a tenant is not liable for damage to the premises caused by wear and tear. However, a tenant is liable for damage resulting from his or her own negligence and, of course, for willful and intentional damage.

The parties are free, of course, to agree that the tenant may use the property "without impeachment for waste," thus waiving the tenant's liability for waste.

THE MEASURE OF DAMAGES FOR WASTE

By statute in some states, the measure of damages for waste is double or triple the amount of the actual damages. See, e.g., 6 Edw. 1, ch. 5, § 1 (1278) (the Statute of Gloucester, imposing triple damages), enacted as D.C. Code § 45-1301 (1976). Injury to freehold estates (the jewels of the common law estate system) by nonfreeholders was the rationale for awards of multiples of the actual damages involved.

FIXTURES

The law of fixtures is an offshoot of the law of waste. As discussed in Chapter 7, a **fixture** is personal property annexed and attached to the premises so as to become real property, not being removable without substantial damage to the premises. Fixtures need not be annexed to the premises, but when they are annexed, they cannot be removed by the tenant at the end of the term.

A fixture has three definitional elements: (1) annexation, either actual or constructive; (2) adaptation of the thing to the use or purpose of the premises to which it is annexed; and (3) an intent to make the thing a permanent feature of the property. An intent to make the thing a permanent feature of the leased premises is the critical element in the United States. If intent is found, a court likely will find constructive annexation, if not actual annexation. In practice, too, the adaptation element has tended to decrease in importance over the years.

The intention of the tenant to annex property to the premises is the traditional test used to determine whether the property is a fixture. Teaff v. Hewitt, 1 Ohio St. 511 (1853). Intention will be inferred from the circumstances, not the tenant's subjective state of mind. In many cases, whether the fixture can be removed without damaging the premises becomes the crucial issue. Because the fixture was personalty and initially the tenant's, there is an inference in these cases that the tenant should be able to remove his property unless the landlord can show that doing so would cause substantial damage to the premises. Thus, the intention and damage elements in the definition of a fixture coexist today in an uneasy tension. If the property cannot be removed from the premises without damaging the leased premises, the property becomes a fixture and remains on the leased property even after the lease ends.

THE DUTY TO REPAIR

At common law the tenant took the leased premises with all its defects. The rule of caveat lessee — tenant beware — applied. The wise tenant inspected the premises for fitness and adequacy of purpose before executing the lease.

Once the tenant took possession, the tenant, not the landlord, had a duty to repair the leased premises. The tenant's duty to repair was sometimes implied from the duty not to commit waste. Generally the tenant had a duty to maintain the premises in its current state but not a duty to rebuild any buildings in case of a building's destruction (unless the tenant destroyed it), or to restore the premises from the effects of wear and tear. The tenant's duty ran from the time he took possession, not from the execution of the lease, and only as to the improvements then in existence. If the premises were to be improved after that time and before the lease move-in date, the tenant had a right to inspect them for fitness and adequacy for the leased purpose. The commercial tenant still has a duty to repair today. The landlord has no duty to repair the leased premises absent an express covenant in the lease.

The residential tenant is responsible for minor repairs. States by judicial opinion and statute, however, have modified the traditional duty to repair in the case of leased residential premises to impose a duty on the landlord to insure the premises meet basic health and safety standards. The landlord, moreover, must maintain the premises in a habitable condition — the so-called warranty of habitability, developed more fully in Chapter 19, infra.

The standards for habitability are often measured by the housing and building codes of the jurisdiction; but, as we will see, some courts have required more of landlords, invoking a rule of reason.

Even under the common law rule imposing the duty to repair on the tenant, the landlord has some duties to repair. (1) The landlord is responsible for the public or common areas of an apartment building — which are, after all, not part of any tenant's leased premises. Halls, entryways, yards, stairs, elevators, common porches, and the roof are examples. (2) Some areas under the landlord's exclusive control are his or hers to repair as well — the furnace room, for example. (3) When the landlord makes a repair, whether or not under a duty to do so, the repair must be performed without negligence. (4) Finally, the landlord may be liable for latent defects of which he or she knew or should have known (and of which the tenant had no knowledge).

Example: Tenant leases a single family house, described by its postal address in the lease. Tenant agrees "to keep the premises in good repair and condition and to return them in as good a condition as received." The landlord insists that Tenant mow the lawn more frequently that Tenant does. Whether Tenant has to or not might turn on the definition of "premises" in the lease. If the house's floor plan were attached to the lease, Tenant probably need not mow more frequently. If the lawn were growing at a record pace due to fertilization due to a leaky underground sewer pipe, there would probably be no duty to fix the pipe — that's no minor repair.

THE DESTRUCTION OF THE PREMISES

(a) Termination of the Lease

At common law, absent a contrary lease agreement, a tenant could not terminate the lease or refuse to pay rent on the destruction of a building or other improvement on the premises. The assumption was that the land was the basis for the lease. See Bunting v. Orendorf, 120 So. 182 (Miss. 1929). That the land was flooded and useless for farming for a season, or that a wildfire swept over it, made no difference. The assumption was fitting when leases were for agricultural purposes and homes had few if any modern conveniences. When improvements are the most valuable component of leased premises, continuing the lease makes little sense when the improvements are destroyed by a storm, fire, or other unforeseen event. Thus most states have changed the law to place the risk of sudden destruction of the premises on the landlord, except where the land itself is the subject of the lease. This is especially true for residential leases. In case of the improvement's substantial destruction, the tenant, but not the landlord, has the option to terminate the lease.

(b) Duty to Rebuild

At common law, absent an agreement in the lease to the contrary, the landlord had no obligation to rebuild after a sudden destruction. The tenant could not terminate the lease, either. The tenant had a duty to maintain and repair the premises, but the common law had no clear rule assigning a duty on the tenant to rebuild destroyed structures. Typically, leased property was agricultural lands and the only improvements were barns and sheds. Even when the tenant was called on to rebuild such structures, the replacement cost, in relation to the value of the lease, fell within the "ordinary repairs" required of tenants.

Imposing a duty on the tenant to rebuild urban property where the land is substantially improved with a building or other structure, and the building's value is substantially more than the value of the underlying land, is inappropriate — as most, but not all, courts have recognized. Courts, moreover, have resisted attempts by landlords to combine a duty to repair and a duty to redeliver the premises at the end of the term in substantially its initial condition to impose a duty on tenants to rebuild destroyed structures.

In some leases, tenants covenant to keep and maintain the premises in the condition that they received them, or to repair the premises. Courts interpret this covenant to be the tenant's duty to make ordinary, incidental, nonstructural repairs, not substantial, major, or structural ones. This interpretation is often an example of courts construing the lease for the benefit of the tenant and against its likely drafter, the landlord.

In some leases, the landlord undertakes to "put" the premises in good condition, but not to "keep" it there. The former implies only a first-day duty, the latter a broader duty continuing throughout the term of the lease. For clarity, to prevent the duty to repair from spilling over into a duty to rebuild after a fire or similar occurrence, the lease should address what happens if the improvements are substantially destroyed in a provision separate from the one that sets out the duty to repair. The landlord, for example, might agree "to put, but not keep" the premises in repair during the term of the lease. The lease could provide the landlord rebuilds, the tenant rebuilds, or the tenant could terminate the lease if the improvements are destroyed.

Example: Landlord leases Brownacre — 100 acres of swampy land — to Tenant for 20 years as a gas storage site. The lease provides that Tenant will "reasonably restore the premises as nearly as possible to their present condition." At the expiration of the term, the cost of cleaning up the land is $1,000,000, but the land has a fair market value for rental purposes is $100,000. Tenant offers Landlord $100,000. Landlord refuses the offer and wants to sue Tenant for $1,000,000. Will you take the case? Not without considering whether to sue in tort or in contract. A suit on the redelivery provision brought in contract might provide Landlord with his million dollars while a tort suit, brought in trespass, might not. Under either theory, the standard of care for the tenant as to the land might be extracted from environmental clean-up statutes.

SECURITY DEPOSITS

Landlords customarily require a cash payment as a **security deposit** to cover damages to the premises by the tenant beyond ordinary wear and tear. Thus, the security deposit secures the tenant's performance of the lease covenants, particularly the covenant not to commit waste. The security deposit payable at the execution of the lease is held by the landlord pending an inspection of the premises at the end of the term. The security deposit is not refundable until the tenant has complied with all covenants of the lease.

Because of the possibility of landlord abuse of this device, particularly wrongful retention at the end of the term, 37 states have limited by statute the landlord's rights in such deposits in various ways. Common statutory restrictions on the landlord's use of security deposits include (1) a maximum dollar amount to be assessed, set typically at not more than one or two months' rent; (2) a requirement that the deposits be held in an escrow account, and not commingled with the landlord's other funds, or held in trust, with a duty to pay interest on them; (3) a procedure for the landlord to account for expenditures (if any) and to return the deposit in whole or in part to the tenant; (4) safeguarding deposits from claims of the landlord's creditors; and (5) multiple damages (usually double or treble damages) and the landlord paying the tenant's attorney's fees when a landlord willfully retains a deposit without accounting for its use. Often these statutes apply only to residential tenancies. California, Colorado, New Jersey, and Texas have particularly detailed legislation in this area. Because of the legislative fear that landlords will simply pocket the security deposit and wait for the departing tenant to sue, courts generally require strict compliance with the procedures imposed on residential landlords by these statutes.

For commercial leases, substitutes for a security deposit are sometimes used — so substituting a letter of credit, a surety bond, or financial collateral of some type provides the landlord with equivalent protection against a tenant's trashing the premises.

Examples

The Injured Tenant

1. A landlord installs carpeting in Tony's apartment. Tony catches his foot in a hole in the carpet, falls, and threatens to sue the landlord for his injuries. Will you take the case?

Building Code Violations

2. A commercial tenant covenants to repair one wall of improved premises during the term of the lease, and does so, but repairs it in such a way that although it is structurally sound, it lacks fire-retardant qualities required by the local building code. Upon discovering this fact, must the tenant redo the repair to comply with the code?

A Burning Issue

3. Larry leases improved premises to Terry, who undertakes in the lease "to restore the premises to the condition in which they were received by me." The premises are totally destroyed by a fire of unknown origin. Larry insists that they be rebuilt as they were received. Must Terry do that?

Last Month's Rent

4. Ted, a tenant, executes a lease with Lisa, a landlord, and provides Lisa with one month's rent as a security deposit to assure the condition of the premises. Can Ted substitute the deposit for the last month's rent?

Explanations

The Injured Tenant

1. You should, but the landlord's duty to install the carpet does not automatically confer a duty to inspect it for defects. That is an issue of negligence, whether the landlord acted reasonably under the circumstances. The relative abilities of both the landlord and the tenant to inspect and the tenant's particular use of the premises will affect the outcome of the case. Premises liability is developed further in Chapter 20, infra.

Building Code Violations

2. Maybe. The duty to repair the wall assigned in the lease is not necessarily the same as the duty to comply with governmental codes. The two duties are related, but the duty to repair involves maintenance of the premises and is particularly related to the tenant's duty to redeliver them in as good

a condition as they were at the start of the lease. Complying with the building code may upgrade the existing facilities. For example, the fire-retardant qualities demanded by the city may require that the tenant spend twice what it would have cost to fix the wall without the fire-retardant materials. Both types of covenants may be found in many leases and both must be consulted before assigning the duty to repair in compliance with codes. Perhaps the landlord is in the best position to be familiar with such codes, due to a longstanding ownership of the premises, or his or her having seen the premises used in different ways, or using it for his or her own purposes. In ruling on the matter, a court likely would consider the length of time remaining on the lease, which party benefits the most from the compliance, and the intent of the parties as can be best ascertained from the lease.

A Burning Issue

3. Some courts would require Terry to rebuild; most would not. A tenant may agree to *restore* the premises at the end of the lease to its first-day condition. Some courts have used this duty to restore as imposing an obligation *to rebuild* the premises after its substantial destruction by a storm or by fire. However, agreeing to restore is different from agreeing to repair or rebuild. The distinction between "repair" and "restore" or between "restore" and "rebuild" is well established in the case law, but not appreciated by the public or many lawyers; the use of such verbal distinctions can ignore the lease's plain meaning, its other provisions, and the surrounding transaction.

The better view is that an obligation to "restore" takes its meaning from the law of waste; that is, it implies a right of the tenant to make temporary or minor changes in the premises during the term of the lease. Such changes may be defined as those that are consistent with the tenant's use, do not affect the structural features of the premises (e.g., the walls, foundation, and so on), can be amortized during the term, and may be removed without material damage to the premises. Under this view, there is no obligation to rebuild after a fire. In any event, such temporary changes must be removed and the premises restored to their original condition at the lease's end. When a fire of unknown origin destroys the premises, the tenant is not at fault and so is not liable in waste — and on this account, will not be liable to "restore" the premises.

If the lease imposed a duty on the tenant to insure the premises and then imposed a duty to apply the proceeds of the insurance claim to the damaged premises, a duty to restore might reasonably be inferred to have been allocated to the tenant. The mere fact that the tenant had taken out a fire insurance policy does not affect the answer — presumably the landlord could have (and in the real world, would have) insured the premises as well. The law pertaining to insurance and the covenants in the lease are two different things.

Last Month's Rent

4. The answer is no. Unless the lease identifies the deposit as the last month's rent, the deposit safeguards the lessor by providing funds in hand to pay for any damages to the leased premises. The tenant has a duty to make ordinary repairs and not to damage the property or commit waste. The security deposit serves as the source of the payments to repair when the tenant fails to fulfill his duty to repair or leave the premises in its original condition, normal wear and tear excepted.

18

Termination and Abandonment of the Lease

Either the landlord or the tenant may wish to terminate the lease prematurely. The landlord may tire of the tenant's complaints, or the tenant's rent may be arrears. The tenant may need or want to move elsewhere. We have already discussed one option open to the tenant — that is, to assign or sublet the premises to a third party. See Chapter 16, supra.

This chapter develops two situations. In the first the landlord wants to evict the tenant for some reason, often for nonpayment of rent, or the tenant has not vacated the premises after the lease ended. In the second the tenant wants to turn the leased premises back to the landlord before the lease ends.

LANDLORD EVICTION OF TENANT IN DEFAULT

A landlord may want to evict a tenant who defaults on a lease covenant, normally for nonpayment of rent, but maybe for violating some other lease term, such as being too rowdy, having pets, or engaging in an illegal activity. Alternatively, the tenant may be a holdover tenant who remains on the premises after the lease ends. The landlord has various options for evicting a tenant in default. We begin with self-help.

SELF-HELP

Eviction by **self-help** takes place when the landlord evicts the defaulting tenant without resort to the judicial process. At one time in England, a landlord could use reasonable force to evict a tenant. No more. First, and most importantly, in no American jurisdiction is a landlord authorized to use excessive force to regain possession of leased premises, no matter what the landlord's rights under the lease. A few states still allow reasonable force, but not many.

In a majority of states today, a landlord can still resort to self-help for retaking possession of the premises if (a) the landlord has a right to repossess the leased premises; and (b) the landlord's exercise of the remedy is peaceable. As liberating as self-help may sound to a landlord, do not become too enamored with it. While self-help is still the rule in a majority of American jurisdictions, the trend is to restrict it, and a growing number of jurisdictions prohibit self-help altogether.

Where self-help without excessive force is permitted, the landlord must have a right to repossess the premises. Otherwise, the tenant has the legal right to possession and any eviction, actual or constructive, is wrongful, subjecting the landlord to liability for trespass and interference with the tenant's quiet enjoyment of the premises. It may also subject the landlord to criminal prosecution for disturbing the peace, breaking and entering, and so forth. The landlord would have a right to possession if the tenant breaches any lease covenant and does not remedy the breach within a reasonable time after notice.

In addition to having a right to repossess, the landlord's self-help eviction must be "peaceable." At one time — and still today in a small number of states — the landlord is allowed to use "reasonable force" to regain possession. Most states that still permit self-help, however, demand that the retaking be peaceable.

States differ on the meaning of "peaceable." For some, no violence is permitted, and the landlord must leave if the tenant puts up any resistance. Some states permit force against objects but not against people. A landlord can force open doors and windows and move furniture and belongings when the tenant is not there, for example. Other states do not permit forcing doors and windows, but do allow the landlord to change the locks. Other jurisdictions say even changing locks is forcible and not peaceable (the theory here is that the lock-out is the equivalent of forcibly keeping the tenant out and is, in any event, often the distraint or unlawful detention of the tenant's personalty). Some say turning off water and utilities is not peaceable. Some say the even the threat of violence is the same thing as violence. In these states, self-help becomes almost illusory. The trend is for states to prohibit self-help in favor of using the judicial process.

Example 1: Landlord evicts Tenant by non-peaceful actions while Tenant is in default of a provision of the lease prohibiting rowdy behavior. Tenant sues Landlord to regain possession of the premises and prevails — otherwise the rule about peaceable actions would be nugatory.

Example 2: Landlord evicts Tenant by non-peaceful actions while Tenant is in default of a provision in the lease prohibiting rowdy behavior. Tenant sues for damages. Landlord prevails: the Landlord cannot trespass on his own property and is taking back his own in repossessing.

Some states will enforce lease provisions giving the landlord the option of self-help. Other states refuse to enforce the self-help provisions, considering them to be against social policy.

EJECTMENT

A landlord can bring a suit in ejectment to oust a defaulting or holdover tenant. Ejectment is the traditional common law cause of action for the recovery of possession or real property and for damages due to the withholding of possession. One problem with the ejectment proceeding is that months or years may pass before a final judgment is reached. While the landlord at that time can seek damages and past due rent from the tenant, the tenant at the end of the process may turn out to be judgment proof. A second problem is that to cover losses suffered while the legal proceedings take place, landlords will try to raise the rents of other tenants and due to market constraints, may not be able to do so. Thus often the landlord would rather have the premises back so she can lease it to another tenant.

SUMMARY POSSESSION STATUTES

Recognizing that the twin extremes of self-help and suits of ejectment were unsatisfactory solutions, all the states have enacted summary eviction procedure statutes, variably called **summary proceedings**, **summary ejectment**, **forcible entry and detainer (a/k/a FED)**, or **summary possession**. The idea is to give the landlord a prompt hearing to evict defaulting tenants. These statutes are a legislative recognition of the doctrine of independent covenants to the extent that the covenant to pay rent is recognized as independent of other covenants in a lease. The landlord gives notice to the tenant to remedy the default or to vacate. States prescribe the number of days the tenant has to cure any default, usually no more than ten. If the tenant does not cure the default or vacate, the landlord can pursue the summary possession procedure, which move quickly. Summary possession suits move to the head of the judicial docket and are often heard in special landlord-tenant courts. Despite their popularity in landlord-tenant cases involving private residential housing cases, summary proceedings are not allowed to evict tenants in federally assisted public housing.

To insure speedy proceedings, some states limit the summary action to nonpayment of rent, with no defenses, offsets, or counterclaims available to the tenant (except a defense the rent was paid). Landlord claims not allowed in summary possession proceedings must be brought in ejectment or other time-consuming civil cases. Other states expand the list of claims the landowner can bring, but this opens up the need for the tenant to rebut, and maybe for each side to conduct discovery. Expanding the options open to the landlord and the defenses available to the tenant prolongs the proceedings, which defeats the purpose of the summary possession actions.

States and judicial opinions, moreover, authorize the tenant to withhold rent in certain circumstances, most notably in residential leases. For example, states have authorized residential tenants to withhold rent if the premises are not habitable. See Chapter 19, infra. Many states allow a tenant to defend again eviction by proving the landlord sought the eviction in retaliation for the tenant's exercising her legal rights. See Uniform Landlord and Tenant Act § 5.101. Each additional defense or safeguard brings with it the potential for further delays in the proceedings.

A check-the-box complaint form, see below, permits the landlord to recover rent due — i.e., back rent, not rent for the time the landlord says that he or she is entitled to possession, not future rent, and not rent due to the anticipatory repudiation of the lease by the tenant. The traditional bargain that the landlord implicitly strikes by bringing a summary possession action is giving up rent or damages in exchange for a quick procedure to regain possession.

18. Termination and Abandonment of the Lease

D.C. Super. Ct., Landlord and Tenant Form 1, 558 A.2d @ LXXXIX-XCII (1989):

SUPERIOR COURT OF THE DISTRICT OF COLUMBIA
CIVIL DIVISION, LANDLORD & TENANT BRANCH

L&T. _____

_____ vs._____

Plaintiff/Landlord   Defendant/Tenant

_____   _____

Address   Address

_____   Washington, D.C._____

                Zip Code   Zip Code

COMPLAINT FOR POSSESSION OF REAL ESTATE

DISTRICT OF COLUMBIA, ss:

☐ _____ being first duly sworn, states: ☐ he or she is the landlord and/or ☐ licensed real estate broker or ☐ the landlord's authorized agent of the house, apartment or office located at_____, Washington, D.C. The property is in the possession of the defendant, who holds it, without right,_____. The landlord seeks possession of the property because:

A. ☐ The tenant failed to pay: $_____, total rent due from _____ to _____: $ _____ late fees; and/or $ _____, other fees (*Specify*) _____. The monthly rent is $ _____. The total amount due to the landlord is $ _____. Notice to quit has been: ☐ served as required by law ☐ waived in writing.

B. ☐ Tenant failed to vacate property after notice to quit expired. (*copy attached*).

C. ☐ For the following reason: (*explain fully*).

_____

_____

    Notice to quit is: ☐ not required   ☐ waived in writing   ☐ either

_____

Therefore, the landlord seeks the Court for:

    ☐ judgment for possession of the property described.

    ☐ judgement for rent, late fees; other fees and costs in the amount of $_____.

    ☐ an order of the Court that all future rent be paid into the Registry of the Court until the case is decided.

Subscribed before me this _____ day of _____,

_____.

_____

Plaintiff/Landlord or Agent

(Notary Seal and Signature here-ed.)

SUMMONS — TO APPEAR IN COURT. YOU ARE HEREBY SUMMONED AND REQUIRED TO APPEAR ON _____, 19 _____ AT 9:00 A.M. PROMPTLY, in Landlord and Tenant Court, Courtroom . . . to answer your landlord's complaint for possession of the premises listed in the above complaint. If you live on the premises and you are not named as a tenant you must come to court if you claim a right to possession of the premises.

IMPORTANT INFORMATION FOR TENANTS — ACT PROMPTLY. WHEN YOU MUST COME TO COURT, ALWAYS BRING THIS COMPLAINT WITH YOU. The form above is a complaint filed by our landlord asking the Court for the right to take back the property you occupy. On the front is the Court date. You must come to Court or you may be evicted. If the landlord seeks a money judgment against you for rent due, and a judgment is entered against you, your wages, bank account, or other property may be attached. When you come to Court, bring your lease, rent receipts, pictures and other papers that may help explain your side. Before you come to Court, you may get your own lawyers, or you can represent yourself. If you wish to have legal advice and you cannot afford a lawyer, contact the Legal Aid Society . . . for more information about where to obtain such help. If you need help to pay the rent, go to the Department of Human Services Center in your neighborhood or when you come to Court ask about Emergency Assistance. Although you are not required to do so, you may enter into an agreement with your landlord to pay the rent, to correct any other problem or to move. Be sure that all promises that either you or the landlord make are in writing before you sign the agreement.

TENANT'S ABANDONMENT AND SURRENDER

Sometimes a tenant wants to end the lease early. In one case a man signed a lease on an apartment in anticipation of his marriage. When the engagement and wedding were canceled, he wanted out of the lease because as a single student he could not afford the apartment. See Sommer v. Kridel, 74 N.J. 446 (1977). What should the tenant do? One option is to assign or sublet the lease. Alternatively, the tenant may surrender the premises back to the landlord or abandon the premises with or without communicating with the landlord.

SURRENDER

The tenant **surrenders** a lease by transferring the lease back to the landlord, with the landlord accepting the return. Many courts require the surrender to be in writing to satisfy the Statute of Frauds if the lease originally had to be written to satisfy the Statute. If the landlord accepts surrender, the tenant is relieved of responsibility for future rent payments. Where the facts indicate the landlord intended to treat the lease as surrendered, a court will find a **surrender by operation by law** even if there is no writing. If a landlord engages in activity so inconsistent with the tenant's continuing obligations under the lease, a court will find surrender by operation by law. A landlord should thus be counseled not to treat the premises as his own if he doesn't want to be found accepting a surrender.

ABANDONMENT

Most complications with mid-lease terminations occur when the tenant abandons the lease with or without notifying the landlord, or the landlord refuses to accept a surrender. Once a tenant abandons the lease, a landlord can elect one of three or four options.

(1) The landlord can treat the lease as continuing, do nothing, and sue the tenant on the covenant to pay rent as the rent falls due.
(2) The landlord can treat the lease as continuing and relet the premises for the tenant's account, reserving the right to sue the tenant for any unpaid balance of the rent.
(3) The landlord can accept the surrender of the lease, and reletting on the landlord's own account.

(4) The landlord can treat the abandonment of the lease as an antici-patory repudiation, suing the tenant for either (a) damages — the difference between the reasonable rental value of the unexpired term and the present value of future rent — or (b) unpaid future rent — the difference between the contract rent and the amount received from a new tenant, both damages and future unpaid rent being recoverable in one judicial proceeding.

Options 1, 2, and 3 provide the most traditional and widely accepted statement of the landlord's options. Options 2 and 3 require careful action — and a paper trail documenting whether the landlord is acting for the tenant or on his own behalf. Option 4 is accepted in some jurisdictions.

(a) Lease Continues — Landlord Does Nothing

The landlord is given this election because the tenant cannot unilaterally terminate the lease. The landlord is within his contractual rights to treat the lease as continuing even if the landlord lets the unit sit empty. The rent is owing and the landlord can collect past due rent. This may entail several successive law suits since the landlord in most jurisdictions can seek only past due rent, not future rents receivable over the remaining term of the lease. As a practical matter, the landlord should not wait until the lease is over to collect since the longer she waits to collect, the greater the chances the tenant has left the jurisdiction, died, or become insolvent.

A few states that by statute permit the landlord to do nothing require the landlord to give notice to the tenant that the landlord is letting the premises lie idle and will sue for the rent as it is due. In jurisdictions without such a statute, failing to provide this notice is seldom found to be an obstacle to collecting rent over the remaining term of the lease. The landlord thus may sit back and sue for the rent from the abandoning tenant, whether the tenant fails to take possession at the beginning of the term, or takes possession and then later abandons. Inevitably, however, the passive landlord runs the risk of the tenant's skipping the jurisdiction or becoming insolvent and judgment proof.

The option to do nothing in its purest form is dying out. Viewing the lease as a contract, courts increasingly impose a duty on the landlord to mitigate her damages, usually by finding a new tenant.

(b) Landlord Relets on Tenant's Behalf

The second option open to the landlord is to treat the lease as continuing and relet the premises on the abandoning tenant's behalf. The tenant remains liable for the difference in rents received and rents owed, and is entitled to any excess rents collected. This option won't be used when the landlord expects to relet for a premium or if the loss of rentals in the months the unit remains empty do not offset the new rent.

In many states the landlord has a duty to mitigate damages when a tenant abandons. The landlord who fails in this duty to mitigate may recover only those future unpaid rents and other damages that she could not have avoided by reletting. Even in states where the landlord does not have a duty to mitigate, the landlord might still relet to get some money from the premises, to help out the tenant, or because the landlord wants the unit occupied.

The duty to mitigate serves several public policies. It is consistent with contract law for the wronged party to a contract to mitigate damages. Moreover, the duty to mitigate encourages landlords to keep leased premises in use and to return them to the rental market as quickly as possible. Finally, it decreases the likelihood of physical damage to the premises through vandalism and neglect.

The tenant often must give the landlord notice of the abandonment before the duty to mitigate is imposed. Until then, the landlord may continue to do nothing. The tenant's merely walking away from the premises could leave the landlord confused about what to do, in part because the landlord's election has its hazards. The tenant may later claim he did not abandon and the landlord trespassed on his property. Alternatively, the landlord's reletting may be found to be an acceptance of the tenant's surrender of the lease, with the consequence that the tenant is traditionally relieved of any obligation to pay any future rent.

Where imposed, a landlord's duty to mitigate is to make reasonable efforts to mitigate. What satisfies the duty to mitigate depends on the facts and circumstances of the situation. Merely listing the premises for rent is insufficient to satisfy the landlord's duty, but it is not clear that the landlord has to move the tenant's premises to the top of its list of vacant apartments and show it first to prospective tenants. The landlord need not attempt to relet using a lease with fewer or more lenient covenants than those imposed on the abandoning tenant or for a use substantially different from the abandoning tenant's use — nor need the landlord relet at a below-market rent.

Courts split on whether the landlord has the burden of proving she mitigated or the tenant has the duty to show the landlord failed to mitigate. Some courts justify putting the burden on the landlord because the proof will be within the landlord's control and this allocation of the burden makes sense on that ground. Putting the burden on the abandoning tenant, on the other hand, may expedite the finding of a new tenant because the abandoning tenant in monitoring the situation may present likely prospects to the landlord as evidence the landlord did not mitigate, and the landlord may accept the new tenant.

(c) Landlord Treats Abandonment as Surrender

A landlord may elect to treat an abandonment as surrender because the premises can be leased for a higher rental, because the landlord sympathizes with the tenant, or because it is not worth the hassle to attempt to hold the tenant liable for the remaining term of the lease. Since some tenants may return and argue the landlord relet on the tenant's behalf, and thus the tenant is entitled to any excess rent collected over the amount the tenant owed on the lease, the landlord should give written notice to the tenant that she is retaking the property or should decisively relet to make clear the landlord is acting for herself and not on the tenant's behalf. Even after giving a notice, the landlord is well advised to relet for a term different than that remaining on the abandoning tenant's lease, changing the leasehold premises slightly, changing the fixtures, or renovating the premises to suit the new tenant. Such actions have been held to show that the landlord acts for herself.

On the other hand, if the landlord intentionally relets on the tenant's account, likely when there is a falling market for rentals, the landlord will not want any reletting activity to be taken as an acceptance of the surrender; instead, the landlord wants this activity to be consistent with standing on the lease's rights. So, to preserve the landlord's rights, the landlord should notify an abandoning tenant in writing that, whether or not the landlord has any duty to relet, she is doing so for the benefit of the tenant and intends to hold the tenant for the difference in rent collected and rent owed. The landlord should keep a separate ledger for the unit so as to prove costs and revenues when necessary.

Some landlords insert a so-called "survival clause" in their leases. Such clauses provide that the landlord may relet without terminating the abandoning tenant's lease. They continue privity of contract as to the rental covenant when privity of estate is terminated. Even with such a clause, courts are likely to hold that the clause only creates a presumption that the landlord did not accept the surrender — and that the facts and circumstances of any reentry may still provide substantial evidence otherwise.

(d) Abandonment as Anticipatory Repudiation

Since the lease mixes contract and conveyancing principles, courts in some jurisdictions let the landlord accept the surrender of the tenant's lease and still sue for rent or damages. The abandonment is viewed as anticipatory repudiation of the lease by the tenant, thus breaching the covenant to pay rent. If the landlord establishes the tenant abandoned the premises for the unexpired term, the landlord can collect an amount equal to the present value of rents due under the lease over either the fair rental value of the lease or the actual rentals of any subsequent lease. Such an election, critics say, gives the landlord an opportunity to increase his damages — not an efficient result. Samuel Williston attacked the doctrine's use on this basis in the landlord-tenant context, urging that the doctrine of independent covenants created no debt to be repudiated until the time for payment of the rent arrived. Proponents of using the doctrine (e.g., Professor Henry Ballentine) thought that Professor Williston did not distinguish between repudiating performance and repudiating the promise to perform — and that repudiating the promise justified use of the anticipatory repudiation doctrine here.

Examples

Peaceable Self-Help

1. (a) In a state in which a landlord's changing the locks has been held to be a forcible entry, is the landlord's entering with a pass key and removing the tenant's goods to a storage facility a forcible entry or a peaceable entry?

   (b) In a state in which locking out the defaulting tenant is not peaceable, may the landlord cut off the utilities?

   (c) When a state legislature prohibits self-help by statute, has it also by implication prohibited the landlord from incorporating a reentry and forfeiture clause into the lease authorizing the landlord to use self-help?

The Duty to Mitigate

2. (a) In a state requiring the landlord to mitigate, can the landlord recover the costs of reletting: advertising the premises, the costs of an agent's time, the brokerage fee, if any, and so forth?

   (b) LL and T enter into a lease that contains both a covenant to pay rent and a provision that permits free assignability and subleasing. How does this provision affect the applicability of a mitigation rule to the lease?

   (c) Should the duty to mitigate be the rule of commercial leases as well as of residential leases?

   (d) Can the duty to mitigate be abrogated in a residential lease by agreement?

Slow Down on Acceleration Clauses

3. In a jurisdiction adopting a rule requiring the landlord to mitigate the abandoning tenant's damages, a landlord inserts a covenant in the lease accelerating the rent for the unexpired term upon the tenant's abandoning the premises. When the tenant asks why this covenant is there, the landlord (or her counsel) replies that it is necessary because the courts

have not held that the doctrine of anticipatory repudiation is available to landlords in the jurisdiction. Acceleration clauses of this type are common, the landlord reports, in mortgage loan documents. How do you evaluate such a response, and how do you reply to it?

Waiting for a Better Tenant

4. In a jurisdiction following the mitigation rule, a shopkeeper approached the landlord and asked if abandoned premises in a shopping center were available for rent. The landlord replied that they were not, and that they had already been relet. This was untrue, but the landlord was then awaiting an appointment with a prospective tenant willing to agree to a higher rent. Four months later, the landlord was successful in renting to a national chain store at a higher rent. Can the landlord charge the abandoning tenant for rent due under its old lease for the four months the store was vacant?

The Abandoning Assignee

5. If the landlord relets on an abandoning tenant's account and as her agent, and the transferee of the tenant's interest defaults and himself abandons, who is responsible for the unexpired term, and for pursuing the transferee?

Explanations

Peaceable Self-Help

1. (a) In the majority of states, any action inconsistent with a tenant's continued possession will be a nonpeaceable eviction and hence a forcible entry.

    (b) It depends on the state. Many states forbid as little as walking through an unlocked door and cutting off utilities without the tenant's consent. Most states would hold this to be peaceable, especially if the utilities can be turned off without confronting the tenant or entering the premises. In fact, most states would allow changing locks; only the most restrictive states prohibit changing locks and turning off utilities.

    (c) Probably the inclusion of a reentry and forfeiture clause, if used to intimidate the tenant resisting self-help, is also a type of force prohibited by the statute, but inclusion of the clause, standing alone, is not a statutory violation. When the clause is used to deter a tenant from asserting a legal right under a statute, and the policy of the state is to deter self-help, then the provision is void under state law.

The Duty to Mitigate

2. (a) Yes. Ordinarily tenants must bear the cost of any reasonable expenses incurred by the landlord in attempting to relet. The rationale for such a result is that if it is clear that the landlord, who, with reasonable diligence, relets at a rent lower than in the original lease, can still recover the difference money, she should recover the attendant transaction costs as well.

   (b) It theoretically could have an effect, but it doesn't. The argument that it should have an effect is that when a tenant has the contractual right to sublease or assign, the tenant should have the duty to use that right to find a new tenant when abandoning the lease. This argument is appealing because the tenant should attempt to minimize both her own damages and disruptions of rent flow to the landlord as much as the landlord should mitigate the tenant's damages. The tenant's having a right to sublet or assign the lease is a plausible reason not to impose a duty on the landlord at all. After all, the landlord has no continuous duty to seek new tenants and here such a duty does not appear to have been party of the parties' initial bargain.

   The tenant's right to assign or sublet does not relieve the landlord of her independent duty to mitigate damages, however. The reasons given in the overview — landlord is in the business of leasing, even the wronged party should mitigate damages he can avoid (often labeled the doctrine of avoidable consequences), the landlord's best interest is to keep units occupied, productive, and not subject to waste — for imposing the duty to mitigate on the landlord remain even if the tenant can sublet or assign the lease. A tenant has some incentive to find a new tenant. A tenant can start searching for a new tenant to take over the lease the day the tenant vacates, whereas the landlord often must wait until the tenant abandons before seeking a new tenant, so that the unit will be vacant at least a month in most cases if the landlord must find a new tenant.

   (c) Yes. There is no policy reason why the holding should not be applicable to commercial leases. Some states require mitigation in commercial as well as residential leases. Some limit as a matter of policy the duty to residential leases. Others, as a matter of statutory construction, limit the duty to mitigate to residential leases if the state legislated the mitigation rule in a law similar to the Model Residential Landlord-Tenant Code or the Uniform Residential Landlord and Tenant Act, but has no similar legislation for commercial leases. About half the states do not require mitigation for residential or commercial leases.

   (d) Probably not. The duty to mitigate is based on public policy that recognizes the landlord's superior knowledge in the residential rental market and superior bargaining position because the landlord can hand the tenant a preprinted lease on a take-it-or-leave-it basis. In that instance the landlord's duty to mitigate should be nonwaivable in a residential lease. A court's ruling may depend on whether the abrogation was a bargained-for provision, or whether it was a provision in an adhesion lease.

Slow Down on Acceleration Clauses

3. Rent acceleration clauses are common in older leases. Their use in loan documents is no reason to use them in leases. The loan is disbursed and must be repaid, but a lease is the landlord's transfer of the use of the premises continuously over the term and after abandoning, the tenant has no further benefit in the use of the premises, whereas the borrower still has use of the loan proceeds. So clauses accelerating loan repayments are reasonable, whereas rent acceleration clauses are not. Moreover, in a landlord-mitigation jurisdiction, the landlord must relet and by doing so has the benefit of a new lease; to give her the benefit of a rent acceleration clause on top of that is to make her more than whole. Thus, enforcing a rent acceleration clause is in the nature of a penalty and unreasonable liquidated damages. Equity should refuse to enforce the acceleration clause when the clause gives the landlord such a windfall or when the landlord's mitigation efforts will actually determine the extent of the landlord's damages. See, e.g., Spialter v. Testa, 392 A.2d 1265 (N.J. Super. Ct. 1978) (holding that a lease covenant providing for payment of 25 percent of the rent for the unexpired term upon early termination of a lease by the tenant is a penalty and void in a jurisdiction imposing the rule of *Sommer* on the landlord).

Waiting for a Better Tenant

4. No. The duty to mitigate requires that the landlord not discourage offers to rent; while the landlord is free to make the decision to refuse to entertain a prospective offer to rent, the landlord cannot then charge the tenant with the risk and costs of that decision and recover rent for the extended waiting period it chose. See O'Brien v. Black, 648 A.2d 1374, 1378 (Vt. 1994) (holding just that).

The Abandoning Assignee

5. The easy answer is, not the landlord, who would have the same series of options as when the original abandonment occurred. See Novak v. Fontaine Furniture Co., 146 A. 525 (N.H. 1929). However, once a jurisdiction accepts a duty to mitigate in some form and it is imposed once, then in order to simplify matters and the law, the landlord should have a

duty to mitigate damages by making reasonable efforts to relet each time. The landlord has the prior experience in reletting, is in control of the premises, and is in a position to show it to prospective tenants. Certainly after the originally abandoning tenant is given notice of the default, the original liability of that tenant reemerges, and thereafter that tenant also has a strong incentive to make some efforts to find a new tenant, if only to check up on the landlord's renewed activity.

CHAPTER 19

Achieving Habitable Premises

EVICTIONS — ACTUAL AND OTHERWISE

When a landlord and a tenant enter into a lease, the landlord promises that neither she nor anyone else will interfere with the tenant's lawful possession. This promise, implied in all leases, is called the **covenant of quiet enjoyment**. The promise arises either from the written words of leasing — demise, let, lease, used as verbs — or in oral leases, from the relationship of landlord and tenant. See Cohen v. Hayden, 163 N.W. 238 (Iowa 1917). A landlord can breach the covenant of quiet enjoyment at common law by someone other than the landlord's exerting a superior legal title, or by the landlord's actually or constructively evicting the tenant from the premises.

(a) Actual Eviction

The landlord's **total actual eviction** of the tenant from the leased premises occurs when the landlord excludes or locks the tenant out of the premises. A padlock on the door to an apartment is sufficient for this purpose. The tenant's obligation to pay rent ends upon eviction and the tenant may sue for damages. An actual eviction may be a **partial actual eviction** as well, where the landlord renovates the property and makes some of the leased premises part of a common area of a multiunit property, such as a hallway or lobby. Even occupying a *de minimis* amount of the leased premises in this way may give rise to a partial actual eviction.

(b) Constructive Eviction

When the tenant's possession of the premises is disturbed by a landlord and, as a result, the premises are rendered unfit for habitation, in whole or in substantial part, the tenant may elect to vacate after giving the landlord notice of the disturbance and a reasonable opportunity to cure. In early cases, the landlord's action may have been a failure to control the common passageways of a building, with the result that bawdy or nuisance-like behavior of persons there affected the suitability of the tenant's premises. See Phyfe v. Dale, 130 N.Y.S. 231 (S. Ct., App. Term, N.Y. 1911) (noise and lewd conduct in halls). Or, it may be that the landlord's failure to control a noisy tenant disturbs other tenants in their premises. See Milheim v. Baxter, 103 P. 376 (Colo. 1909) (tenants on landlord's adjoining property).

Although there is some contrary authority, it should not make any difference that the interference by the landlord emanates from different property. Neither does it matter that the property was either owned by the landlord when the lease was executed or acquired later. The landlord's liability is imposed because of his failure to control interference with the tenant's possession, not because of the particular source of the interference.

In either event, the vacating tenant is said to have been constructively evicted by the landlord's conduct. **Constructive eviction** is a failure or interference on the landlord's part with the tenant's intended enjoyment of the premises, in such a way that the tenant is deprived of the enjoyment of those premises. Thus, the necessary elements of a constructive eviction are (1) intentional (actual or inferred) acts of the landlord that breach a duty owed to the tenant and (2) are the cause of substantial interference with the tenant's enjoyment of the premises, or render it unfit for the purpose for which it was leased, and (3) the tenant's vacating the premises (4) within a reasonable time after the landlord's actions. The tenant satisfying the elements of the doctrine, who is thus constructively evicted, is thereafter relieved from the obligation to pay rent. Constructive eviction is an affirmative defense, and a type of tenant self-help, best used when the tenant has somewhere else to go and rent. It is a clone of actual eviction, thus the tenant is required to vacate so that the constructive eviction looks as much like actual eviction as possible.

A landlord's failing to maintain basic services to premises also might form the basis of a constructive eviction. Thus, a constructive eviction occurs when the landlord fails to supply heat, utilities, or water when needed if the landlord has agreed to supply heat, utilities, or water. The actions of the landlord have compelled the tenant to leave, just as when the landlord actually evicts the tenant — retention of the premises and eviction are seen as logically inconsistent. However, a landlord's serving tenant with a compliant in ejectment is not a constructive eviction unless the landlord is abusing the legal process in doing so — service of process is not just like an actual eviction.

(c) The Covenant of Quiet Enjoyment

The doctrine of constructive eviction is based on the landlord's breach of the covenant of quiet enjoyment. Pursuant to the **covenant of quiet enjoyment**, the landlord promises the tenant shall have quiet and peaceful possession of the premises for the term, as against the landlord, any person holding through the landlord, or any person with a title superior or paramount to the landlord. As previously discussed, this covenant is implied in all leases — residential and commercial, written and oral. The parties can contract for quiet enjoyment and any express covenant of quiet enjoyment takes precedence over the implied covenant provided by operation of law.

Through this covenant, the landlord assures the tenant that no action or interest of his own, or of a third party, will deprive the tenant's quiet enjoyment of the premises during the term of the lease. Because of the common law doctrine of independent covenants, however, a landlord's breach of the covenant of quiet enjoyment traditionally gave rise only to a cause of action for damages, while the tenant remained liable for the rent. The covenant's breach as the basis for a constructive eviction, however, today lays the groundwork for the tenant's right to vacate the premises.

Absent a lease provision contrary, the covenant of quiet enjoyment is still an independent covenant — the tenant need not be in compliance with the leasehold covenants (including the covenant to pay rent) to enforce it. The tenant may vacate and then sue for damages. In this cause of action, the tenant's measure of damages under the covenant is for the difference between the rent reserved in the lease (often called "contract rent") and the fair rental value of the use that was in fact received, measured to include the unexpired period of the lease. This is a "difference money" measure of damages, using the values of what the tenant should receive and what the tenant in fact received.

Thus today a tenant has two options when the landlord breaches the covenant of quiet enjoyment. The tenant may stay in the leased unit and sue for damages or the tenant may vacate the premises and treat the breach as a constructive eviction. A constructive eviction requires the tenant to surrender the premises. There are dicta in some cases, particularly in New York, to the effect that upon a breach of the covenant the tenant must vacate; this is not generally so. The tenant must vacate to fulfill the last two elements of a constructive eviction, but not to sue for damages on the basis of the covenant itself.

(d) The Tenant's Dilemma

When asserting a constructive eviction due to a breach of the covenant of quiet enjoyment, the tenant runs the risk that after he or she moves out, a court will later find that no constructive eviction occurred. In such an instance, the tenant will owe the landlord rent. So the tenant bears the risk of a wrong guess about the law. To avoid this predicament, in a few jurisdictions a tenant may seek a declaratory judgment that a constructive eviction has occurred before vacating. In at least one case, a court in a declaratory judgment action found a constructive eviction to have taken place before the commercial tenants vacated the premises. See Charles E. Burt, Inc. v. Seven Grand Corp., 163 N.E.2d 4 (Mass. 1959).

As stated previously, the tenant who remains in possession does not give up a suit for damages for breach of a covenant of quiet enjoyment, of fitness, or of use for a particular purpose. See Stewart v. Childs Co., 92 A. 392 (N.J. 1914) (holding that the covenant to pay rent and the covenant of fitness were independent covenants). The measure of damages is again difference money.

(e) Scope of the Covenant of Quiet Enjoyment

The covenant of quiet enjoyment requires that the landlord act in such a way as to interfere with the tenant's peaceful possession. Usually the covenant is breached when the landlord has a duty to do or not do something. Hence, the failure to supply hot water or heat when the landlord is contracted to provide hot water or heat can be a violation of the covenant of quiet enjoyment. The failure of the landlord to make major repairs; to provide essential services or habitable premises; to properly maintain the heating or air conditioning facilities; to obtain a needed governmental permit; to control vermin, insects, or rodents; or to police the activities in the hallways or in other apartments can be a breach of the covenant of quiet enjoyment.

(f) Partial Constructive Eviction

It is also possible for a landlord to constructively evict a tenant from a portion of the premises. A partial constructive eviction must be clearly documented by the tenant who, after all, remains in possession of the rest of the premises. Because the tenant has not vacated, theories of partial constructive eviction are rarely used. The tenant's dispossession is less clear.

(g) Partial Actual Eviction

A *partial actual eviction* occurs when a landlord or her agent takes over part of the premises and denies the tenant use of a portion of the premises crucial to use of the whole. The underlying rationale for an actual partial eviction is that, absent some agreement to the contrary, the landlord conveyed the exclusive use of the demised premises to the tenant for the term and may not evict the tenant from any portion of the premises during the term.

Because the landlord is not permitted to apportion his wrong, courts have said that in this situation, there has been a total failure of consideration for the lease and, after providing the landlord with notice and a reasonable time to restore the premises to the tenant, the tenant is entitled to vacate the premises and is, in some jurisdictions, relieved entirely of the obligation to pay the rent. See Fifth Ave. Bldg. Corp. v. Kernochan, 117 N.E. 579 (N.Y. 1917) (Cardozo, J.) (denial of safekeeping area for jewelry store when safe was found to be under public sidewalk in the store's basement); Smith v. McEnany, 48 N.E. 781 (Mass. 1897) (Holmes, J.) (holding that an encroaching wall, making it impossible for dray wagons to deliver goods to retail premises, was such an eviction); Barash v. Pennsylvania Terminal Real Estate Group, 256 N.E.2d 707, 709 (N.Y. 1970) (attorney denied right to work weekends because landlord would not then heat or air condition a sealed office building). Other jurisdictions permit the tenant to vacate, but apportion the rent obligation so that the vacating tenant is only partially relieved of the rent obligation. While useful to commercial tenants, partial actual eviction has not been of much help to residential tenants denied habitable premises.

THE IMPLIED WARRANTY OF HABITABILITY

At common law, the covenant to pay rent and the landlord's covenant of quiet enjoyment were independent covenants — i.e., rent was due, no matter the condition of the premises for which rent was paid. An exception to this rule was developed early for a furnished house — particularly when, in a vacation location, such a dwelling was required to be habitable on the first day and every subsequent day of the lease, and if it was not, then no rent was due. The court's view of such a rental was that it was made for a specific purpose and the landlord was as much providing a service as an estate in the premises. See Pines v. Perssion, 111 N.W.2d 409 (Wis. 1961) (holding that, in a lease for student housing containing no express covenant of habitability and executed without opportunity to inspect the premises, but where landlord made oral promise to repair, the creation of an exception to the rule of caveat lessee is warranted). The unequal bargaining power of landlord and tenant and the greater ability of the landlord to repair are often additional grounds, along with the lack of inspection, for such holdings.

Traditionally, the landlord who delivers to a tenant quiet enjoyment, exclusive control, and reasonable use of the premises has performed her obligations. The delivery is a one-time obligation, satisfied on the first day of the lease. This is also a shorthand way of saying that the lease contained no implied covenants that the premises were fit for the purpose for which the tenant leased them.

As we have seen, the difficulty, from the tenant's perspective, with the remedy of constructive eviction is that the tenant must vacate to assert it. This is particularly difficult when the tenant is poor and has no place to go. Staying put but abating the rent, is what many poor tenants want instead. Their desire coincides with a judicial recognition that the fastest method to get a landlord's attention fixed on the condition of the premises is to reduce the landlord's cash flow or rental income stream from the property.

In addition, most residential tenants (poor or not) are inexperienced at repairing their premises, but bargain for and expect the structures thereon to be suitable for habitation. Most treat their rented premises as a bundle of services and many low-income tenants have little choice of premises and little bargaining power, and so face standardized leases and sometimes even racial and ethnic discrimination. In short, many need the law's protection when leasing a residence.

Faced with such conditions, many courts have adopted an **implied warranty of habitability**, requiring that rental premises be offered and maintained in a physical condition that provides safe, decent, and habitable housing for tenants. It is also consistent with the idea that landlords should comply with the standards found in building and housing codes enacted by many local governments around the country.

This implied warranty of habitability applies in most jurisdictions only to residential premises — and, on the facts of the cases that establish it, it is arguable that the warranty applies only to low-income housing, although there are no cases refusing to extend it to rental premises offered at high rents. It is both a warranty and a covenant. It is a warranty that residential premises are safe, clean, and fit for habitation at the time of the execution of the lease. It is also a covenant that the landlord will maintain and repair the premises so that they remain in that same condition throughout the term of the lease. It is both a representation of fact (a warranty) at the start of the lease, and a covenant (a contractual promise) of fitness during its term.

The warranty of habitability is implied and applies whether or not it is expressed in the lease. Any lease provision that purports to negate the warranty of habitability is void as a matter of public policy. The warranty of habitability applies to both written and oral leases. In most jurisdictions the tenant may not waive its benefits nor assume the risks inherent in uninhabitable premises, either in the lease or thereafter.

This warranty applies only to conditions that make the premises physically habitable. It requires that a landlord maintain the premises so that the essentials of habitable living are afforded. Luxury items are not included. Heat, hot water, plumbing, safe kitchen appliances, and safe and sound structural conditions are included. However, the warranty is not breached when the window blinds are broken, there are cracks in the plaster, or the premises need fresh paint. Thus, a landlord need not repaint the walls to satisfy the warranty, but the warranty will require a landlord to remove any lead paint that constitutes a safety hazard to a tenant's child. Moreover, things like the presence of radon, a virus, or loud noise on an adjacent property may affect the health and happiness of the tenant but, unless the landlord is somehow responsible for their presence or they are the subject of a special purpose statute or ordinance, they do not affect the physical conditions on the premises and so do not breach this warranty.

The impact on this warranty on prior law is substantial, but precise. It partially abrogates the doctrine of independent covenants to the extent that it makes the tenant's covenant to pay rent and the landlord's duty to repair uninhabitable conditions into dependent covenants. It applies this duty to repair to both patent and latent conditions. And it greatly expands a tenant's remedies for such conditions.

(a) Basis for the Warranty of Habitability

The basis for the implied warranty of habitability is most often found in the housing codes in the jurisdiction. Thus a substantial violation of the local housing code will breach the warranty. In some jurisdictions, the warranty of habitability derives from a common law concept of habitability. See Glasoe v. Trinkle, 479 N.E.2d 915 (Ill. 1985) (applying the warranty even where there was no housing code); Green v. Superior Court, 517 P.2d 1168 (Cal. 1974). Even when the housing code is not violated, the landlord may still be in breach of the warranty if the defect in the premises complained of makes the premises uninhabitable or unfit in the view of a reasonable person. Thus, an objectively reasonable standard of habitability is required by the warranty. No matter the source, the uninhabitable conditions complained of must be substantial to breach the warranty; de minimus defects will not do.

More than 40 states have adopted some form of the implied warranty of habitability, either by statute or judicial opinion. Some commentators argue that the imposition of this warranty is helpful to those tenants protected by it. Others respond that it just drives up rents to cover a landlord's legal liabilities for it. See Charles Meyers, *The Covenant of Habitability and the American*

Law Institute, 27 Stan. L. Rev. 879 (1975) (arguing that it drives up rents); D. Kennedy, *The Effect of the Warranty of Habitability on Low Income Housing: "Milking" and Class Violence*, 15 Fla. St. U. L. Rev. 485 (1987) (arguing it is a benefit to tenants).

(b) A Breach of the Warranty

There are three elements to a successful warranty of habitability claim. First, the landlord must have notice of the defective condition. Second, the defect must be substantial, considering its violation of the applicable housing code, its effect on the tenant's health or safety, the length of time it has existed, and its seriousness. Third, the landlord must have been given a reasonable time to repair the defect and not done so.

(c) Commercial Tenants and the Warranty of Suitability

In a few jurisdictions, the implied warranty of habitability has been extended, in a somewhat different form, to commercial as well as residential leases. See Davidow v. Inwood North Professional Group, 747 S.W.2d 373 (Tex. 1988) (finding an **implied warranty of suitability** for intended use), noted in 94 Colum. L. Rev. 658 (1994); cf. Reste Realty Company v. Cooper, 251 A.2d 268, 273 (N.J. 1969). Most courts that have considered this extension have not extended the warranty to commercial leases. See, e.g., Seoane v. Drug Emporium, Inc., 457 S.E.2d 93 (Va. 1995).

(d) Enforcement Remedies

If a landlord breaches the warranty of habitability, the tenant may (1) withhold rent until necessary repairs are made; (2) sue the landlord to collect damages, as will be discussed below; or (3) in some jurisdictions, repair the condition himself and deduct the reasonable cost of this repair from his next rent payment(s). A landlord cannot evict a tenant who pursues damages or withholds rent based on a breach of the warranty of habitability.

(e) Damages

A tenant may seek "difference money" contract damages: either (1) the difference between the fair rental value of the premises as warranted less the fair value in an unrepaired condition, or (2) the difference between the reserved or contract rent, as stipulated in the lease, less the fair value in an unrepaired condition. Some courts for practical reasons prefer a third measure of damages: the percentage of the contract rent by which a tenant's use and enjoyment of the premises has been reduced by the presence of the uninhabitable conditions. In addition to damages, a tenant may seek to abate his rent or to withhold rent altogether.

Emotional distress and punitive damages are possible as well, indicating that "slumlordism" has tort aspects, touching the personhood of the tenant. Punitive damages are likely when the landlord flouts tenant requests to repair up to code or puts exculpatory covenants into a lease, particularly after the jurisdiction has adopted the implied covenant of habitability.

Difference money measures of damages have come in for a good deal of criticism. They often require litigation to establish and collect. This litigation is likely to require the use of expert appraisers to establish the fair rental value of the property with and without the conditions alleged to breach the warranty. This may be expensive and time consuming, and in the end some courts have concluded that the result may not be worth the effort, being imprecise at best. As a result, some courts prefer the so-called "percentage diminution" measure of damage—the third measure of damages mentioned previously. Under it, a good deal of discretion is given the trial court, for it must figure out what, in percentage terms, a broken toilet or the lack of hot water is worth. In practice, this requires the buildup of case law and precedent on the subject, so that a judge can quickly determine that a broken toilet will permit the tenant to reduce the rent by (say) 20 percent, that the lack of hot water requires a 15 percent reduction, and so on. The advantage of this measure is a practical one: It simplifies fact finding and is cheap, expert-free, and sound in result, if not elegant in theory. See Wade v. Jobe, 818 P.2d 1006 (Utah 1991).

(f) Withholding Rent

Perhaps the most important remedy given tenants using this warranty is rent withholding by the tenant. Often this remedy is authorized by state statute. When it is not, the tenant should deposit the rent into escrow or a special account. When rent withholding is authorized by statute, the statute should be followed to the letter. The rationale for regulating this withholding remedy is that because the purpose of the warranty is the improvement in quality of the housing supply, tenants should not be permitted to put their rents beyond the reach of the court or the landlord. Withholding the rent disciplines landlords, but at the same time they should not be denied the rent money once they do remedy the uninhabitable conditions, else they will have no cash flow with which to maintain the premises in the future.

When withholding rent the tenant should (1) give the landlord a notice of breach and an opportunity to repair, followed by (2) a reasonable time for the landlord to make the repair, followed in turn by (3) a notice of rent withholding, establishment of an escrow account, and later (4) deposit the withheld rent in an escrow account. This remedy amounts to tenant self-help and a substitute for a suit for damages: Thus, a tenant unilaterally withholds the rent and waits for the landlord to sue him for the amount withheld. It thus shifts the burden of bringing suit to the landlord.

RETALIATORY EVICTION AS A TENANT'S DEFENSE TO EVICTION

Because in many jurisdictions the implied warranty of habitability or the standards by which habitability is defined are based on a housing or building code, tenants should report code violations so they can be brought to the landlord's attention and repaired. A tenant who reports a code violation to government officials and is evicted as a consequence of exercising her right to obtain a governmental benefit (premises up to code standards) has successfully defended a summary eviction procedure action by pleading that the landlord sought the eviction action with a retaliatory motive. See Edwards v. Habib, 397 F.2d 687 (D.C. Cir. 1968), cert. denied, 393 U.S. 1016 (1969). In Edwards, the tenant, Mrs. Edwards, defended herself in a summary procedure action. The opinion held that summary procedure may not be used when the landlord acts with a retaliatory intent and that, until that intent is dissipated, there can be no eviction. In a later opinion, the same court held that when the eviction procedure is begun shortly after the tenant reported the violation, there is a presumption that the intent is retaliatory and the landlord has the burden of showing that it is not.

Edwards concerned a month-to-month periodic tenancy and so the effect of the holding was to say that the landlord could not refuse to renew the tenancy as long as he or she had a retaliatory intent. The court was clear that retaliatory intent provides the basis for an exception to the common law rule that the landlord "may evict for any legal reason or for no reason at all." The elements of a retaliatory eviction doctrine are (1) the enactment of an applicable housing code statute or ordinance, embodying the objective of insuring safe and decent housing conditions; (2) the landlord's business being leasing residential housing; (3) the tenant at the time of the reporting of the code violation not being otherwise in material default on the lease; (4) the landlord's primary (or substantial or partial) motive for eviction being the tenant's reporting the code violation; and (5) the tenant's report being made in good faith and with cause.

This doctrine works in tandem with the implied warranty of habitability, particularly in jurisdictions in which it, too, is housing code-based.

As a practical matter, what violates the code will often also violate the implied warranty.

It is not necessary that the tenant give a notice of the code violation to the landlord in order to later invoke the retaliatory eviction defense. The defense's focus is on the report to public officials, rather than any preceding action by the tenant. In this regard, the defense may have a quasi-constitutional basis in the right to petition one's government, rather than just being based on the rationale that it promotes the objectives of and fosters the effective enforcement of the housing code. This basis was clear in *Edwards*, which arose in the District of Columbia, where, under the First Amendment, "Congress shall make no law . . . abridging . . . the right to the people . . . to petition the government." The retaliatory eviction theory has also been the basis for a tenant recovering damages in a separate suit against the landlord, or as the result of a counterclaim when the landlord sues the tenant in an action other than summary possession. There is, however, a split in the cases on this issue.

The burden of proof for establishing the elements of the doctrine is on the tenant, except when a statute provides to the contrary. Putting this burden on the landlord would be requiring proof of a negative. Putting it on the tenant seems to require what is seldom available — proof of the landlord's subjective state of mind. Thus, allocating this burden involves tough choices, and deciding whether it is satisfied often involves proof of objective actions that may indicate a subjective intent on the landlord's part to evict the tenant for reporting code violations to local authorities. Statutes are particularly helpful here in creating legal presumptions, usually rebuttable ones.

(a) Modifications to the Retaliatory Eviction Defense

Statutes have attempted to answer some of the questions raised by opinions such as *Edwards*. Some require that the retaliatory motive be dominant — not just one among many, but not the sole motive either. See Minn. Stat. Ann. § 566.03 (1971) (intent "in whole or part" may be deemed retaliatory), noted in 61 Minn. L. Rev. 523 (1977). Others have provided that a rent increase, or a decrease in services to a tenant, may be retaliatory as well. Still others have provided that the presumption of a retaliatory motive is dissipated after a certain time period — say, one year after the tenant reports the code violation. Without such a provision, the presumption might operate for a far longer period. See, e.g., Conn. Gen. Stat. Ann. § 47a-20 (1986) (six-month period), interpreted in Murphy v. Baez, 515 A.2d 383 (Conn. Super. Ct. 1986).

Statutes have also expanded the retaliatory eviction doctrine to include the tenant's assertion of statutory, contract, or other legal rights, such as those given by the implied warranty of habitability, and they have also established an objective, events-speak-for-themselves test for retaliatory intent. See Gokey v. Bessette, 580 A.2d 489 (Vt. 1990) (finding a landlord's lockout evidence of retaliation proscribed by statute as "change in the terms of the rental agreement" when coming after tenant's assertion of an implied warranty of habitability).

This doctrine has great potential for tenants. Consider the possibilities: retaliatory rent increases, retaliatory use of self-help (when peaceful self-help is permitted a landlord), retaliatory repairs, even a retaliatory going out of business.

In addition, when the doctrine is used in tandem with the illegal lease doctrine, discussed in the next section, the tenant has a potent arsenal of rights to use against the landlord.

ILLEGAL AND FRUSTRATED LEASES

(a) The Illegal Lease

Some leases are illegal from the moment of their execution because they offend some strongly held public policy — e.g., a lease made for running a gambling establishment in a jurisdiction where gambling is illegal, a lease for running a house of prostitution, or a lease for an anticompetitive purpose violating the antitrust laws. Such leases are said to be void *ab initio*. Other leases may be made illegal during their term, as when a use stipulated as the only use that is to be made of the leasehold premises is prohibited by an amendment to the applicable zoning code.

In one case, a landlord sued a tenant in arrears on her rent in a summary eviction process. The tenant moved out, contending all the while that no rent was due because numerous and substantial housing code violations in existence at the start of the lease rendered the lease illegal when executed. The court agreed the lease was illegal because of the housing code violations. See Brown v. Southall Realty Co., 237 A.2d 834 (D.C. 1968).

When a lease is made for an illegal purpose (say, for a use illegal under the zoning ordinance applicable to the premises), the law "leaves the parties to it, as it finds them." There is a presumption that both parties to the lease knew the law and so violated it in executing the lease. It is the execution of the lease that is illegal — so when the housing code is used as a basis for illegality, the violations of the code must exist at the time of execution.

The same District of Columbia court in a later case refused to extend *Brown*'s illegality doctrine to violations not proven to exist at the lease's execution. The problem is that the postexecution violation could not have been within the contemplation of the parties when the lease was made—so violating the housing code was not the purpose of the lease. A court may still find the lease to be illegal based on public policy. A court, more typically, will base the doctrine on the presumed knowledge of the parties and refuse to find an illegal lease for postexecution violations of the housing code. However, the supervening violations might render the lease impossible of performance, and this impossibility is another traditional ground for avoiding a lease. The illegal lease theory was more important before courts and legislatures recognized the warranty of habitability, which is the theory most residential tenants use.

The value of the illegal lease doctrine is that it works best in low-income housing contexts to remedy code or statutory violations in existence on the lease's first day; thereafter, the implied warranty of habitability extends a landlord's duty to keep the premises up to code. Rendering the lease illegal gives the tenant a ground to recover rent already paid; the implied warranty gives him a basis for avoiding liability for future rent at the level reserved in the lease. Depending on local law, Brown and any applicable implied warranty cases and statutes would seem to provide the tenant with an election to use one or the other theory on which to build a remedy for substandard housing.

(b) Frustration of Purpose

The doctrine of **commercial frustration** has been applied to commercial leases in many cases when the purpose for which the lease is made is nearly totally destroyed during its term. Thus, for example, a lease with a use restriction in its covenants is frustrated when that use is made illegal by a zoning change. Preexisting events do not give rise to frustration of purpose since, unless provided otherwise in the lease, tenants take the premises with all defects. See Chapter 17, supra. Only supervening and unforeseen events can legally frustrate the purpose of the lease. Supervening events that make the business less profitable or even unprofitable or more burdensome to conduct, however, are insufficient to constitute a frustrated purpose.

> ***Example:*** Tenant executes a five-year lease, intending to operate a bar. Six months after the execution of the lease, the county citizens vote to prohibit liquor sales in the county. Tenant can no longer sell alcohol. The change to Tenant's ability to sell alcohol does not qualify as a frustration of purpose since Tenant can still use the premises as a bar or restaurant that does not sell alcohol. The lease continues. If, on the other hand, the lease stipulated that the purpose was to sell alcoholic beverages, a court may find a frustration of purpose.

It is irrelevant that the lease has proven less profitable during its term than was anticipated at the start. The doctrine is not a means for investigating the level of profitability of leases and drawing lines between more and less

323

profitable ones. Not surprisingly, then, its greatest use comes when the premises that were the initial subject of the lease are destroyed, or nearly so, such that the operation or use contemplated in the lease is no longer possible.

When (1) a frustrating event is not reasonably foreseeable, and (2) the value of the consideration or the counter-performance of the lease is totally or nearly totally destroyed by the frustrating event, a tenant's defense based on the doctrine of commercial frustration will be successful in a landlord's action for rent. The courts stress that these two elements constitute rigorous tests, that the doctrine is not to be applied liberally, or that the doctrine is applied only in cases of extreme hardship. Whether stated as a procedural canon or more substantively, these statements mean that courts, in cases of doubtful applicability for the doctrine, will not use it to rewrite the contractual aspects of the lease in dispute.

If an event is foreseeable, then the tenant is generally said to have assumed the risk that it will occur. Thus, when the tenant could have foreseen an event, the tenant must provide for it in the lease or otherwise (with, say, insurance) or else be deemed later to have assumed the risk.

Examples

Not So Easy Access

1. Branch Bank leased premises on the lowest floor of a three-story office building to Echo on a five-year lease. The lease provided that Echo could use a "common right of access" to enter and leave its offices. A year into the lease Branch Bank renovated the building. The renovation created noise, dirt, and an occasional disruption of electric service. The construction also made the rear parking lot inaccessible. During most of a 12-month period, many of Echo's employees used street-level parking in front of the building, and entered the building, through the main street-level door to the building, walking downstairs to Echo's offices. Late in the year Branch Bank changed the locks to the main street-level door for security reasons. After that, Echo's employees could not use the main entrance before or after regular business hours and were forced to use a rear door, which often was obstructed and difficult to use. Echo sued Branch Bank, claiming that Branch Bank's not letting Echo employees enter and exit through the main street-level door before and after regular business hours harmed Echo's business. What result under the following claims?
   (a) Total or partial actual eviction
   (b) Constructive eviction
   (c) Breach of quiet enjoyment
   (d) Breach of covenant of habitability

Wade in the Water

2. Lister and Wade enter into a five-year lease for commercial space in the basement of a building. A driveway abutting the building is improperly graded, so that after a rainfall water covered much of the basement's floor. Lister, through an agent, promises to repair the condition. A new lease is signed for the unexpired term. In this new lease Lister promises in writing to repair the driveway. Lister does repair the drive, remedying the condition for a time, but not permanently. The water condition worsens until a rainstorm leaves five inches of water in the basement. Wade notifies the landlord of the water, and vacates a short time thereafter. Lister sues for rent for the remainder of the term. In this suit, what result?

Worst House in Town

3. Lee shows Toni the worst residential premises in town and then leases them to Toni at $100 per month. Toni finds living there disgusting and wishes to sue Lee for damages. The jurisdiction recognizes a right to difference money damages, but not a percentage reduction formula. What would you advise?

Habitable Habitats

4. (a) Does the implied warranty of habitability apply to housing other than low-income residential units, particularly units in a multiunit apartment building?
   (b) Does the implied warranty of habitability apply to premises without air conditioning in the summer months in an area in which the temperature rises into the nineties?
   (c) Does the implied warranty of habitability apply to premises inhabited by the deadly Ebola virus, even though it does not affect the physical condition of the premises?
   (d) What if a strike of local government garbage collection employees means that rotting garbage piles up in the basement, creating a health problem and odors and attracting rats — does the implied warranty require the landlord to arrange for alternative pickup?
   (e) Does the landlord warrant that the premises are secure so that the tenant will be free of a criminal assault on the premises?
   (f) A shower pipe in an apartment covered by the implied warranty of habitability breaks and water sprays over the tub and bathroom floor. The tenant does nothing, but does promptly report the break to the building manager. Before the manager responds, water covers the bathroom floor and seeps into the ceiling of the apartment below. (The tenant's throwing a bathroom towel over the broken pipe would have kept the water in the tub.) The landlord quickly repairs

the pipe and charges the tenant for the ceiling damage. The tenant refuses to pay. The landlord sues for the payment. What result in this suit, and why?

(g) Should the implied warranty of habitability apply to tenants in federally subsidized public housing?

(h) Does the implied warranty of habitability apply when the owner of a condominium unit sues the property owners' association for a defective ceiling in a hallway leading to the unit?

Retaliatory Conduct

5. (a) Larry leases a shop to Ted for five years, with an option to renew the lease for another five-year term. After Ted notifies Larry of his intent to exercise the option, Ted continues to negotiate with Larry for new lease terms past the end of the lease term. Ted reports electrical wiring failures in the shop to code officials and Larry promptly brings a summary possession action against Ted. Is the common law doctrine of retaliatory eviction available to Ted?

(b) What if in (a), Larry, having a clearly retaliatory motive, brings an ejectment action against Ted?

Explanations

Not So Easy Access

1. (a) No claim whatsoever for total actual eviction since Echo remained on the premises. The partial actual eviction claim is based on Echo's losing its rights to a "common right of access," particularly before and after regular business hours. As to partial actual eviction, the issue turns on whether Echo's employees should have a right to use the main access 24 hours a day or whether use of the rear door suffices (in which case no partial actual eviction). The court in Echo Investing Services, Inc. v. North Conway Bank, 669 A.2d 227 (N.H. 1995), concluded the lease provision giving Echo a "common right of access" required only that Echo's employees have access to the offices, not necessarily access through the main street-level door. No partial actual eviction.

(b) The court in *Echo* also concluded no constructive eviction occurred. Branch Bank has a duty under the lease to provide access and not to interfere with Echo's quiet enjoyment of its premises. Here there was some interference with access and interference from dirt and noise. The issue turns on whether the noise and dust and use of the rear door after hours substantially interfered with Echo's use of the premises. That is a factual issue. The trial court in *Echo* had concluded

Echo's use of its premises was not substantially affected and hence Echo was not constructively evicted — the premises were fit for Echo's business. The *Echo* court did not address but could have held that no constructive eviction occurred as a matter of law because Echo did not vacate the premises.

(c) Most courts conclude the covenant of quiet enjoyment insures the tenant maintains possession of the premises, and that its use is not substantially impaired by action or nonaction by the landlord. Unless the tenant is actually or constructively evicted, there is no breach of the covenant of quiet enjoyment. In these jurisdictions, Echo's loss on the constructive eviction claim disposes of this claim as well. The New Hampshire Supreme Court used the *Echo* case to expand the covenant of quiet enjoyment to include the denial of beneficial uses of the leased premises based on the tenant's reasonable expectations. Under this claim, the tenant need not vacate to prevail in its claim for damages. The practical difference in this covenant of quiet enjoyment and constructive eviction is that some landlord interferences with a tenant's quiet enjoyment justify a tenant's terminating the lease and collecting any damages that resulted from the landlord's action or nonaction. Other interferences do not justify the tenant's terminating the lease but do warrant damages for harm caused.

(d) The warranty of habitability applies to residential leases only, not to commercial leases. Echo has no warranty of habitability claim against Branch Bank. A few jurisdictions recognize a parallel warranty of suitability. Based on the trial court's finding the premises were fit for Echo's use, our guess is a court in New Hampshire would rule against Echo on a warranty of suitability claim.

Wade in the Water

2. Judgment for Wade the tenant. Rainfall covering the floors of the premises, particularly in a basement where, by force of gravity, it has nowhere to go, renders the premises unfit for use in heavy rains. The recurrences of the problem render it a substantial interference with the tenant's use of the premises: In this context, "substantial" need not mean continuing or permanent, it need only mean that the tenant cannot normally count on using the premises. All of the elements of a constructive eviction are present. The fact that commercial premises are involved is unimportant: The doctrine of constructive eviction applies to both residential and commercial leases. Its availability for commercial lessees remains an important feature of the doctrine in the many states adopting an implied warranty of habitability only for residential lessees. See Reste Realty Co. v. Cooper, 251 A.2d 268 (N.J. 1969).

Worst House in Town

3. Difference money damages can be either the difference between the fair
rental value of the premises in a habitable condition and in its unrepaired
condition, or the difference between the rent stipulated in the lease and
the fair rental value in an unrepaired condition. If this is the worst
housing, the two formulas are likely to produce the same result, and
almost nothing by way of recovery. For instance, the contract rent has
to be assumed to be higher than the fair rental value for the premises in its
unrepaired condition for there to be a difference greater than zero under
the second measure of damages. Quite often, the efficient method of
using both difference money formulas is to assume that the reserved
or contract rent in the lease is the same as the fair rental value, and the
amount recovered will then be the same as when the second measure is
used. In effect, the landlord charged and the tenant is already paying the
rental value of the premises in its uninhabitable condition. Thus, for slum
housing, these measures of damages produce the least when they are
needed the most. Moving out and then asserting the doctrine of constructive eviction may remain the best course of action for Toni (assuming she can afford to live somewhere else).

Toni might argue the lease was illegal and avoid rent altogether or
withhold rent until Lee makes the premises habitable. A risk then is that
Lee might board up the house or apartment and take it off the market,
especially if the cost to repair exceeds any rental he might get from it.

Habitable Habitats

4. (a) Yes. In some jurisdictions, the earliest uses of the implied warranty of
habitability were made by high-income tenants. Limiting some of the
implied warranty cases to their facts, involving low-income and periodic tenancies, is unfair to other tenants. Creating one set of legal rules
for low-income markets and another set for high-income markets
requires less than crisp line drawing, and is unwise policy. There is
no reason for public policy to deny a high-income tenant the benefits
and the remedies of the warranty. See Timber Ridge Town House v.
Dietz, 338 A.2d 21 (N.J. Super. Ct., L. Div., 1975) (permitting tenant a
rent abatement for patio attached to an adjacent, expensive townhouse, but denying abatement for pool and playground).

(b) Yes in Houston, Texas, but perhaps not in Vermont. The standards
for habitability inevitably will vary by region and court. Another
method of analysis would be to determine the source of the warranty, and then to answer yes in states that premise the warranty on
the common law, but no in states that premise the warranty on the
housing code. See Park Hill Terrace Associates v. Glennon, 369 A.2d
938 (N.J. Super. Ct., App. Div., 1977) (per curiam) (holding yes).

(c) No, Ebola is a deadly virus, but not a breach of the implied warranty — which is not a cure for all of a tenant's health and safety concerns. The implied warranty concerns only the physical condition of basic services and features of the premises, and that is not the concern here. So the presumptive answer is no, unless the physical condition of the premises is implicated somehow: The landlord might be a jack-of-all-trades in repairing the premises, but he is no doctor.

(d) The garbage strike is an event beyond any one landlord's control, and this Example raises the issue of whether the landlord must be at fault in causing the condition for there to be a breach of the implied warranty. The warranty is implied from the relationship of a landlord to a tenant. The fault of one party seemingly has nothing to do with it, and the status of the landlord everything to do with it. See Park West Management Corp. v. Mitchell, 391 N.E.2d 1288, 1294 (N.Y. 1979) (finding warranty breached regardless of whether the landlord is at fault, but with statements to the effect that the landlord is not supposed to provide every amenity under the warranty).

Another issue is whether the garbage is like the virus issue — i.e., not based on a physical condition on the premises. When the strike has gone on long enough and the garbage is piled up, it might be argued forcefully that the area where it is usually contained awaiting pickup is not being maintained in a habitable manner, and so the warranty is breached. Likewise, extermination of pests such as rats is basic to a landlord's job of maintaining habitable premises, and the presence of the rats is good evidence of a breach.

(e) This Example presents a matter of considerable controversy. Unless the security system fails and the assault results because of the failure, the landlord does not warrant that the premises are free of crime. In this respect, a landlord is not the guarantor or insurer of a tenant's safety. Shifting the risk of crime to the landlord is different in kind from shifting the duty to repair uninhabitable conditions, and is an ineffective way to fight crime, whereas the implied warranty of habitability may well be an effective way to improve the quality of rental housing. At the same time, the presence of security devices like locks and alarms in high crime areas is a physical condition required to keep the premises free of breach. A good security system for such premises makes them habitable, and the system's failure renders them uninhabitable and may breach the warranty.

Courts in California, the District of Columbia, New Jersey, and New York think security from crime is covered by the warranty. See, e.g., Note, *"Warranty of Security" in New York: A Landlord's Duty to Provide Security Precautions in Residential Buildings Under the Implied Warranty of Habitability*, 26 Ford. Urb. L. J. 487, 488, n.11 (1988) (collecting the cases). If the courts are willing to have the landlord warrant against third-party acts such as garbage workers' strikes, a warranty against criminal actions caused by the premises' insecure nature isn't likely to be far behind.

(f) Probably the landlord should obtain judgment if the implied warranty of habitability were viewed as a contractual covenant. The landlord then has a plausible argument that the tenant should have contained the leak with the towel. If the implied warranty is enforced by contract remedies, then the tenant generally has a contractual duty to mitigate the damages that the uninhabitable conditions cause. So the issue is whether the tenant has a duty to mitigate damages caused by a breach of the implied warranty of habitability. Many of the cases adopting the warranty also discuss contract remedies for its breach; a duty to mitigate damages normally attaches to the remedy of damages for breach of contract. Moreover, in the context of vendors and purchasers of new housing, the implied warranty of habitability imposed on the developers of new housing incorporates a purchaser's duty to mitigate damages. See, e.g., Wawak v. Stewart, 449 S.W.2d 922 (Ark. 1970). Whether tenants have a similar — and similarly strong — interest in the property is a question not addressed by courts: The length of the lease as well as the need for quick action on the tenant's part will bear on the answer. There is no definite answer to this issue in the case law, but the probable answer is that the tenant, too, has a duty to mitigate damages.

Viewing the matter as one to be litigated in tort might produce a different result, one not holding the tenant liable. First, the duty to mitigate acts is to reduce damages, not to require the injured party (the tenant) to pay the person who is primarily responsible (the landlord). Second, the tenant is not demanding the landlord fix the ceiling — such a demand might be made by the tenant in the unit below — so the tenant is not mitigating her own damages. Third, any duty to mitigate here more closely resembles the duty in a negligence action, which itself has two components. For the tenant to be deemed negligent, a reasonable person must know or should know that throwing a towel on the pipe would have kept the water in the tub, and would have recalled that when the crisis arose. In addition, to be liable in negligence, the tenant must owe a duty to the landlord to act. Placing that duty on the tenant here would require the tenant who saw a fire, for example, to have a duty to extinguish it or pay for the resulting damages. The general rule of tort is that no one must act absent a special relationship. Arguably landlord-tenant relationship is not such a relationship. Finally, broken pipes and resulting repairs are normal operating expenses in a multiunit dwelling, and are more properly the obligation of the landlord, who can spread the expected costs to all tenants as part of the monthly rental.

Lesson to be learned: how a case is pled, and the theory of a case, matters. So take your choice. The authors of this book have different views of the answer. No matter which one of us is correct, the authors enjoyed arguing over this Example. Law is fun.

(g) The answer is a qualified yes; the warranty imposed on public housing authorities as landlords is usually somewhat narrower in scope than is the warranty imposed by state law. Because the rent roll is crucial not just to the apartment house but to the program as a whole (and to payment of the government bonds guaranteed by the roll), the remedy of rent abatement is likely to be more closely supervised, and the opportunity for administrative action to remedy the defect given more time to work. See, e.g., Connille v. Secretary of Housing and Urban Development, 840 F.2d 105 (1st Cir. 1988) (imposing an implied warranty as a matter of federal common law). As a matter of policy, public housing tenants should have the same rights as tenants in private housing. Federal statutes generally require public landlords to extend roughly similar rights, but with different and more cumbersome enforcement mechanisms, as a condition of receiving federal grants and other assistance.

(h) In a condominium, each and every unit holder might generally think of the unit as his or her apartment, but in fact each holds a fee simple absolute to it, not a lease, so the conventional landlord-tenant relationship is absent. When the implied warranty of habitability is based on a state statute, its terms control the matter. Condominium regimes or developments are subject to detailed state statutes, and they are generally silent on this matter. See Agassiz W. Condominium Assn. v. Solum, 527 N.W.2d 244, 247 (N.D. 1995).

Where the warranty is based on the common law, however, the answer is less certain. Many condominium regimes were converted from rental apartments, and arguably landlords should not be able to escape the implied warranty just by converting. Moreover, insofar as common passageways and areas are concerned, the successor of the landlord is the unit owners' association, and applying the warranty to these areas is much less of a reach than making an association liable for conditions within the units. The association, however, is a common agent of all the unit owners, so permitting the suit is like permitting owners to sue themselves. Nonetheless, the policy behind the implied warranty is to make "landlords" pay attention to the uninhabitable premises, and associations should be given the same incentives. See Pershad v. Parkchester S. Condominium, 662 N.Y.S.2d 993, 995 (N.Y. Civ. Ct. 1997) (taking jurisdiction over condo owner's complaint for defects on common areas). Like tenants, unit holders expect a package of services, may not have the necessary repair skills, and cannot repair common areas without association permission.

Moreover, an association typically has remedies much like eviction when the unit owner does not pay assessments for maintaining the common areas, indicating that the association should be treated like a landlord as to those areas.

Imposing an implied warranty on an association may require that the remedies be limited. For example, assessment withholding probably is not a sound policy choice: If such withholding were permitted, all owners would be injured and the association would not be able to cover repair costs as expected. See Rivers Edge Condominium Assn. v. Rere, Inc., 568 A.2d 261, 263 (Pa. Super. Ct. 1990) (so holding). Thus, a unit owner might have a contract action against the association, but not be able to withhold assessments from it.

Retaliatory Conduct

5. (a) The first issue is whether the doctrine is applicable to commercial as well as residential tenancies. There is no sound public policy reason why it should not be, except that issues arising between commercial landlords and tenants often expressly involve a landlord's right to possession. Absent an express right of reentry, there is no reason not to apply the doctrine to a commercial lease, although statutes codifying the doctrine have typically limited it to residential leases.

The second issue is whether the doctrine applies to a term for years that under the traditional common law rule expires automatically at the end of the term. Here, Ted intends to exercise his lease's option to renew, but has not done so. Thus, if Larry and Ted were negotiating a new lease as a result of the option, then their failure to reach a new agreement bears on whether Ted is a holdover; if he is, then the doctrine may have no application because the rules on holdovers have strong policy reasons behind them as well — they dictate that the landlord is entitled to regain possession in order to release the premises. To avoid this conflict in the rules, a court might reasonably confine the doctrine to periodic tenancies because those are held by the type of tenants most likely to need the aid of code officials in maintaining the condition of their premises. Ted had the bargaining power to obtain the option to renew, did not exercise it, and so seems the type of tenant who does not require the protection of the doctrine.

(b) Ejectment is a common law cause of action. The doctrine of retaliatory eviction is the result of interpreting and attempting to reconcile two specific statutes: the housing code and the civil procedure code for summary possession. With ejectment, the statutory basis for the doctrine disappears, as does the doctrine itself. Unless the doctrine is seen more generally as a safeguard against abuse of the legal process, it is inapplicable to an ejectment action.

20

Premises Liability
of Landlords

PREMISES LIABILITY

Premises liability — the liability of landlords for injuries to tenants and nontenants — has undergone a major transition in the past century. Currently, the states' approaches to premises liability fall into three distinct camps.

(a) Landlord Liable for Injuries in Specific Situations

The majority of states fall into the first camp, which began with the old common law concept that the landlord's liability ended once the landlord delivered the premises to the tenant. It became the tenant's duty to keep the premises in repair. See Borders v. Rosenberry, 532 P.2d 1366 (Kan. 1975). The following exceptions to the general rule, however, have often become more important than the general rule.

(1) Latent Defects

The landlord must disclose latent defects where there is an unreasonable risk of physical harm present on the premises if the risk is known to the landlord but unknown to the tenant on the first day of the lease. (Some courts use the execution of the lease as the relevant date, and in most cases the different time frame is a matter of dicta.) Once the landlord discloses the defect to the tenant—either before, at, or after delivery to the tenant—the landlord's responsibility to the tenant and invitees ends.

(2) Prior Conditions Dangerous to Persons Off Premises

The second exception is for a landlord who transfers possession with the knowledge that there is a condition on the premises dangerous to persons off premises. This is a duty imposed on landlords on the first day of the lease. Typically, the landlord is liable for nuisances on the premises at the start of the lease. If the landlord was liable before the transfer, liability should remain and not be avoided just because of the transfer, even if the tenant is also aware of the dangerous condition.

(3) Leases for Public Use

Third, when the premises are transferred for a public use known to the landlord, the landlord has a duty to inspect and repair the premises in light of that contemplated use. A single-family residence would not be subject to this exception, but commercial premises, such as restaurants, theaters, and retail stores, typically are. If the landlord knows that the public will be admitted to the leased premises, the landlord is responsible for conditions that might foreseeably cause injury even if the tenant is aware of the condition and may be jointly liable.

(4) Negligence in Maintaining Common Areas

Fourth, the landlord remains responsible for negligence in maintaining common areas of multiunit premises and non-common areas if the areas are under the landlord's control. Hallway carpets that trip people, as well as lead paint used in hallways, are examples. The landlord is responsible for injuries caused by defects in a common area. This is a limited affirmative duty to inspect and repair.

(5) Landlord Contracts to Repair Leased Premises

Fifth, when the landlord contracts to repair, he assumes a duty to do so, no matter that the defect was in existence at the start of the lease or arose thereafter. Generally a landlord who contracts to repair but fails to do so is liable to persons injured because the landlord failed to act. The burden of proof is on the tenant to show the contract or agreement to repair.

(6) Negligent Repairs

Sixth, and finally, the landlord is liable for negligence in any repairs that he makes. This exception typically applies when the tenant neither knows nor should know of the negligence in performing the repair work. Thus, when the landlord makes the premises more dangerous with that work, or when the work has the deceptive appearance of being safe, the landlord is subject to liability for the physical harm caused thereby.

(b) Landlord Liable Under Negligence Standard

A few states have abandoned the classification scheme discussed above and will hold a landlord liable under the negligence standard based on how a reasonable landlord would prevent foreseeable harm. The landlord's duty under a negligence standard should extend to all persons likely to frequent the premises. The landlord's standard of care should be adapted to the right of access and the amount of control of the premises the landlord has. The negligence standard still leaves an injured tenant, as a plaintiff, the burden of litigation and proof as to the landlord's standard of care, its breach, actual and proximate cause, and duty; and subject to the defenses traditional in negligence cases such as assumption of the risk, contributory negligence, and comparative negligence.

(c) Landlord Strictly Liable

The California Supreme Court, for a few years, held a landlord strictly liable for all injuries to persons on leased residential premises, but has since reversed itself. Louisiana by statute holds landlords strictly liable for injuries to tenants resulting from the defective condition of the premises. As far as we know, no other state holds the landlord strictly liable for injuries resulting from defective conditions on the leased premises. See Raymaker v. Am. Family Mut. Ins. Co., 718 N.W.2d 154 (Wis. App. 2006) (rejecting strict liability).

LANDLORD LIABILITY FOR CRIMINAL ACTS

In most jurisdictions, absent some agreement to the contrary or the presence of a public or criminal nuisance on the premises, a landlord is not liable for the intentional criminal actions — murder, assaults, muggings, etc. — by third parties committed against tenants on the premises.

In other jurisdictions, however, a landlord has a duty to protect the common areas of a multiunit property against a known risk of foreseeable crimes. The same rationale used to impose premises liability for physical defects has been used to impose a duty on the landlord to protect tenants from criminals. When the implied warranty of habitability is based on a general duty to repair such defects (as opposed to a housing code), this warranty has been used as well. See Kline v. 1500 Massachusetts Ave. Apartment Corp., 439 F.2d 477 (D.C. Cir. 1970). *Kline* arose in a large multiunit apartment house, and the court noted "the duty of protection is the landlord's because by his control of the areas of common use and common danger he is the only party who has the *power* to make the necessary repairs or to provide the necessary protection." Id. at 477. Once the landlord knows of the insufficiency of the existing protection devices (doors, locks, etc.), a duty to take the necessary precautions arises. The landlord must "take those steps which are within his power to minimize the predictable risk to his tenants." Id. at 481.

For the tenant, the duty in *Kline* translates into a burden of proving that (1) the landlord knew of the defect and had control over it, and (2) it foreseeably increased the risk of criminal acts. Plaintiffs have been most successful in meeting this burden when the defect relates to a criminal's means of gaining access to common areas. Broken locks, missing passkeys, and accessible outside fire escapes are more easily made the basis of a landlord's liability than, say, defective lighting or alarms. The landlord is not an insurer of the tenant's safety; she must only act reasonably. Moreover, the landlord's duty is measured — and limited — by the measure of protection afforded the tenant at the start of the lease, for it is that standard on which the tenant relies in executing the lease. The same security must be maintained by the landlord throughout the lease.

The foreseeability of the increased risk of crime is best shown by other crimes occurring on the premises when the criminal's access was by a similar means. Foreseeability is an important element because the duty being discussed is a duty to undertake to prevent crimes, not to control the conduct of criminals. It is a duty to reduce a criminal's capacity to commit crimes in the common areas of the property.

Thus, a defect, in the common areas, subject to the landlord's control, and subjecting the tenant to a foreseeably increased risk are the four elements of a landlord's liability in jurisdictions where it is imposed.

The cases involving criminal activity involve both residential and commercial leases, and there is no reason why the same liability cannot be imposed in both settings. Shopping center landlords have been involved in litigation over crimes committed in parking areas around the center.

Finally, there has been some legislative activity affecting this area of the law. First, a landlord knowingly permitting his premises to be used for the conduct of a public nuisance is liable to have it closed down. Second, drug forfeiture statutes can result in the forfeiture of the landlord's interest in a property used routinely for drug trade. Finally, city ordinances have been upheld that require landlords in high crime areas to provide armed security guards in apartment houses with more than 100 rental units. See 515

Associates v. City of Newark, 623 A.2d 1366 (N.J. 1993) (upholding Newark, N.J., Ordinance § 15:13-1 (1991)).

EXCULPATORY CLAUSES

A landlord may insert an *exculpatory clause* into a lease whereby the landlord is absolved from liability for injuries on the premises or is indemnified by the tenant if the landlord is found liable to any person. Exculpatory clauses are often enforceable in commercial leases, but the trend is for courts to declare them void as a matter of public policy in residential leases. Early exceptions included actively concealed hazards and unfit conditions, or when the landlord's active negligence led to the injury. Later courts struck the clause when bargaining power between the landlord and tenant was unequal. Statutes, such as the Model Residential Landlord-Tenant Act, prohibit or severely restrict the use of exculpatory clauses.

Examples

Premises for Liability

1. A statute provides that "the presence on premises, rented for human habitation, of a paint containing more than five-tenths of 1 percent of lead by weight shall be construed as rendering said premises unfit and uninhabitable." Does this statute make a landlord on whose property such paint is present strictly liable, liable for negligence per se, or liable generally in negligence for the harm to a tenant's child caused by exposure to this paint?

Liable for Premises

2. (a) A tenant was assaulted in his apartment after the person committing the assault gained access to the common area of the apartment house through a defective lock on an outer door. Does it matter that the criminal activity occurred in the apartment and not in the hallway?

    (b) Same facts, except that the criminal gained access to an outside fire escape, and thence up the fire escape to and through an unlocked window in the tenant's apartment. The landlord had provided the lock for the window, and it was in working order at the time of the assault. What result?

    (c) Same facts, except that the person committing the assault was another tenant. What result? A very few courts have imposed liability when the landlord knew or should have known of the other tenant's criminal history involving assaults. The issue is, however, still the foreseeability of the assault, so that, even when the landlord knew of the other tenant's criminal history, foreseeability will be a fact question and difficult to show. An easier case might arise when the assault was committed by the landlord's employee.

Take a Hike

3. Lawrence leases land to a church that plans to use the property as a summer camp. A 12-year-old camper slips on a narrow pathway and is severely injured when he tumbles into a gulch by the pathway. Is Lawrence liable?

Shack Attack

4. Linda leases a farm to Fred. Linda shows Fred a storage shack and points out that the supporting posts for the shack have rotted. Six months later Edgar, a farm hand, climbs to the top of the shack. The shack collapses, injuring Edgar. Is Linda liable?

Explanations

Premises for Liability

1. Absent a clear legislative history on this issue, the language of the statute controls. A child who might ingest the paint is certainly subject to the health hazard such paint presents. The statute expands the implied warranty of habitability to conditions created by lead-based paint. The landlord, therefore, has a duty to repaint premises affected by lead paint, but only after it knows or has reason to know of its presence. Lack of notice of the condition, and denial of an opportunity to repaint, would be defenses to an action based on the statute. See Gore v. People's Savings Bank, 665 A.2d 1341 (Conn. 1995) (holding that the statute makes the landlord liable for negligence per se; that a jury need not decide the landlord acted (un)reasonably and (im)prudently — the statute establishes that the landlord acts imprudently when the lead paint is present — but that a landlord may defend that it had neither actual nor constructive knowledge of the paint on the premises).

Liable for Premises

2. (a) No, so long as the elements of liability are present. Aaron v. Havens, 758 S.W. 2d 446 (Mo. 1988). The landlord is not strictly liable and must know or should know of the defective lock before liability attaches.

(b) There are two issues. First, is the window, set in an outside wall, part of a common area? Pennsylvania courts have held not, but the authorities are split on this matter. If the window is under the tenant's control, there is no liability on the landlord. Second, if it is a common area, is the landlord liable for its unlocked state? No court has held that the landlord must provide a locked fence around an apartment house, so a holding that it is a landlord's duty to insure that all windows remain locked is similarly unlikely. Finally, in states that hold that contributory negligence is a complete defense, the landlord may escape liability even if a factfinder could find the tenant was contributorily negligent.

Take a Hike

3. Lawrence very well could be liable. If the factfinder concludes the narrow pathway on the edge of a gulch was a defective condition, or if the factfinder concludes the summer camp was for public use, or in other jurisdictions if a factfinder concludes a reasonable person should have foreseen someone falling into the gully at that point, Lawrence may be found liable since the dangerous condition was there when Lawrence delivered possession to the church. Lawrence may defend successfully if the church had an opportunity to learn about the hazard — again, a factual determination will decide the outcome of this case.

Shack Attack

4. Linda is not liable. Linda would be liable for latent defects in the shack if the tenant had no knowledge of the effect. As soon as Linda informed Fred, her tenant, of the rotted posts, her liability ended. Linda was not obligated to notify Edgar of the dangerous condition. Notice to the tenant was enough.

CHAPTER 21

The Holdover Tenant and Concluding Comments

HOLDOVER TENANT

A tenant continuing in possession of premises after the expiration of a lease is called a **holdover tenant** and is regarded as a **tenant at sufferance**. Any type of tenant — one for years, a periodic tenant, or a tenant at will — may become a holdover. So might any assignee, or a sublessee with regard to either her own or the primary landlord.

The general rule is that the landlord may elect one of two options when a tenant holds over: He may either treat the holdover as a trespasser or hold her for a further term. If the landlord elects to treat the holdover as a trespasser, the landlord can bring an ejectment action to evict or a summary procedure action for possession.

If the landlord elects to treat the holdover as a tenant for a new term, the duration of the new term will be measured by one of two rules: When the original lease was for a term of more than one year, the holdover is held to another year; when the original lease was for a term of less than a year, the holdover is held to the same term as the original lease. As to the rest of the lease covenants, the original lease covenants (absent the covenant on renewal, if any) are rolled over as well, binding the parties for that further term.

Most jurisdictions base the imposition of the extended lease on the holdover on the landlord's election. The law imposes the extended term on the tenant whether or not the tenant intends it or consents to it.

This election seems draconian. Three rationales are typically given for holding the tenant to a new lease term. First, it is a penalty for holding over, ultimately operating for the benefit of all tenants as a class, particularly incoming tenants bargaining for possession of premises at the expiration of the term of the tenant holding over. It gives outgoing tenants a strong incentive to vacate and gives security to incoming tenants that the premises for which they bargained will be available. This "penalty theory" is particularly apt in rental markets where there is a so-called natural term. In agricultural leases, for example, the turnover at the start of the growing season is necessary, and the landlord who misses this date likely also misses the opportunity to rent the land for that year. In fact, the market for agricultural leases provides the historic origin of the election rule. Sometimes rental markets in the neighborhood of a college or university work on the same turnover principle, premises turning over between academic years. Another policy for the election sometimes used by courts is that holding the tenant to a new term supplants the landlord's use of ejectment and summary proceedings. Thus, a residential tenant's inability to locate alternative housing does not justify holding over. (Were it otherwise, a housing shortage would result in tenancies lasting so long as the shortage does — a new type of tenancy indeed.)

Second, the landlord's election is sometimes thought of as the product of an implied (in fact) contract. From the landlord's perspective, this is not difficult to imagine. Here the implication is that, from the very fact of holding over, it may be implied that the tenant intends to prolong his tenancy by a further term. This implication arises regardless of the tenant's actual intent. Sometimes this implication is put in terms of its being an irrebuttable presumption. This rationale is an awkward one, not fitting too well with the idea of the further term's arising at the election of the landlord: It makes the tenant's "acceptance" of the extended term beside the point.

A minority of jurisdictions permit the landlord to elect to hold the tenant for a whole new term only when the parties intend the result, meaning that if landlord and tenant negotiate before the expiration of the original term, the negotiations are evidence that the parties may not intend a new term. This minority rule is consistent with the creation of a periodic tenancy for the holdover period — a result considered fairer under many circumstances. Moreover, if the parties also negotiated over the covenant to pay rent and the landlord insisted on a higher rent, then the tenant's holding over might be taken as an implied acceptance of the landlord's offer of a lease at a higher rent.

Third, it is sometimes said that the landlord's election rests on the idea of a quasi-contract, rather than an implied one. A quasi-contract is one that is implied in law, rather than in fact. It arises to prevent a person's retention of a benefit that another should in equity have. Here, this means that the trespassing holdover has the possession of premises that, had he exercised good faith, should be in the hands of the landlord; the holdover then owes the value of that possession to the landlord, who acquires a cause of action, quasi *ex contractu*. The landlord, waiving the option of suing the trespasser in tort, sues in contract instead: in tort, his suit is known as a waiver of the tort and suit in assumpsit.

The harshness of the landlord's election is sometimes additionally justified as reinforcing the landlord's duty to present any succeeding tenant with either possession free of paramount interests, or with actual physical possession of the premises. See Chapter 15, supra. Thus, the need for special rules governing the first day of a tenancy dovetails with the need for special, and especially harsh, rules governing its last day as well.

A landlord must exercise the election: Doing nothing leaves it intact. Only an acceptance of the next regular rent check establishes the tenancy for the new term, although a demand for the rent or a suit for it has the same result. The election, once made, is irrevocable. See Crechale & Polles, Inc. v. Smith, 295 So. 2d 275 (Miss. 1974).

Statutory Modification

Statutes in many states give the holdover tenant the status of a periodic tenant, usually a month-to-month tenant. This is the same result sought by courts looking to the implied intent of the parties, rather than the landlord's election. Under such statutes, the landlord may recover "actual damages" or recovery "for the use and occupation" of the premises by the holdover. Some permit the recovery for use and occupation to be apportioned for the actual holdover period; others require the payment of the full periodic rent — no matter that the holding over was only a matter of days. Check state law on this!

Exceptions

The harshness of the landlord's election is recognized in the exceptions to its general rule. For example, the holding over must be a voluntary and intentional act on the tenant's part, and so where it is involuntary, the tenant may quit after a reasonable time. An illness in the tenant's family — meaning that a member of the family should not, for medical reasons, be moved off the premises — justifies a tenant's holding over. See Herter v. Mullen, 53 N.E. 700 (N.Y. 1899) (tenant stays on in one room of an apartment for 15 days after his term because his mother is so sick that it is dangerous to move her); contra, Mason v. Wierengo's Estate, 71 N.W. 489 (Mich. 1897) (where the tenant dies five days after the end of the term, but was not sick on the premises). Similarly, a strike by building janitorial staff justifies a delay in moving out past the expiration date. Commonwealth Building Corporation v. Hirschfield, 30 N.E.2d 790 (Ill. App. 1940) (involving a high-rise apartment not completely vacant at term's end because of elevator difficulty). When the delay was not the tenant's fault or is beyond his or her control, the landlord is denied the usual election.

An additional exception is for holding over a short time. It is said that the law does not regard a fraction of a day as important to holding over. The tenant may normally stay this *de minimis* time without liability for a new term. A further example might involve a tenant's leaving some items of personal property on the premises; they are not taken as showing a tenant's intention to hold over.

A third exception involves negotiations with the landlord that spill over past the expiration of a term. See A. H. Fetting Manufacturing Jewelry Company v. Waltz, 152 A. 434 (Md. 1930). When the landlord and the tenant are negotiating in good faith, the tenant may stay until the conclusion of those negotiations. Were it otherwise, the landlord would be tempted to drag out the negotiations. This exception rests on a theory of estoppel; but see *Fetting*, op. cit. (suggesting that negotiations alone, without some assurance from the landlord, will not be enough to work an estoppel and deny the landlord his common law election). Were this exception not available, the tenant would be negotiating at a considerable disadvantage and the exception is intended to even the bargaining power of the tenant, making it comparable to the landlord's. Because this exception is based on a theory of estoppel, when the landlord insists throughout the negotiations that the tenant vacate as scheduled, it is unlikely that the court would not honor this insistence. Because of this exception, leases often prohibit an oral waiver by a landlord of the covenants in the lease, including covenants setting out the exercise of any option to renew. This exception encourages the parties to bargain clearly about when the lease ends.

Concluding Comments on Leases as a Contract or Conveyance

In the area of holdovers as well as many other areas of landlord tenant law, much ink has been spilled on the question of whether the lease is a conveyance or a contract. The answer is that a lease is neither and both at the same time. A lease certainly continues to be the conveyance of an interest or estate in real property. Were it not so, the landlord could, any day of the week, walk onto the premises, jerk his thumb at the door, and say "Get out. I'll pay your damages." So take language to the effect that it is one or the other with a grain of salt and as an analogy, not a metaphor: Ask yourself, for what purpose is it being called a contract or a conveyance? Sometimes the purpose of the label will be to change the substantive law, sometimes the remedies.

Examples

Co-Holders Over

1. Len is a co-tenant in a term for years. Len vacates the premises at the end of the term, but Lannie, his co-tenant, does not vacate. Is Len responsible in damages for Lannie's holding over?

Curtailed Negotiations

2. (a) Taft has a year to run on its remaining term for years, leased from Lonnie. Taft receives an offer from Timmy to take over Taft's premises. Taft asks Lonnie whether Taft's lease will be renewed at its expiration in a year and encloses a letter with the offer from Timmy. Lonnie's representative orally confirms that Taft's lease will be renewed and that Lonnie wrote a letter to Taft indicating that Lonnie "was glad that Taft would remain on the premises for many years to come." Taft discontinues talks with Timmy about taking over Taft's premises. Later Lonnie informs Taft that Lonnie will not renew the lease, but will offer Taft other premises at double the rent. Would you advise Taft to sue Lonnie to enforce Lonnie's offer of a renewed term?

   (b) Ted leases Redbrick from Larry for a term of five years, and after the fourth anniversary of the lease negotiates for a renewal of the lease. Larry confirms what progress has been made for the new lease by letter, but indicates in the letter that "we've got a way to go yet before a complete agreement is reached." Larry attaches a form lease, unsigned but approved by Larry's agent. Negotiations continue past the expiration of the term, when Larry breaks them off unexpectedly and declares Ted to be holding over, threatening suit to evict him or hold him to a new term. May Ted vacate Redbrick without further liability?

Taking His Home to Work

3. (a) Eddy is the caretaker of a swank residential club (C). Eddy's sole compensation is the right of occupancy of an apartment there. Eddy's "employment agreement" contains the occupancy right, but also gives C the right to terminate Eddy's employment without cause and at any time. C terminated Eddy's employment, padlocked Eddy's apartment, and removed Eddy's personal property from the apartment. In the applicable jurisdiction, padlocking has been found to violate the

state's prohibition against a landlord's using self-help, and by statute, moving costs and triple damages are available against the landlord using self-help. What is Eddy's best argument for being treated as a tenant, with regard to self-help as well as, say, C's notice obligations and remedies?

(b) Owen agrees to occupy Lawrence's land in exchange for driving off trespassers. Owen enters the land, improves it, and grows crops there. Is Owen a tenant?

Explanations

Co-Holders Over

1. No. The landlord's election is to treat the holdover as an intentional trespasser, and a vacating co-tenant like Len is not that. In addition, the holdover's extended lease is treated as a new lease and not a continuation of the old one — so Len is not a party to the extended lease. Further, the relationship of co-tenancy exists only so long as the parties hold a concurrent estate in the premises — and after Len vacates, they do not have any concurrent estate. In the same vein, if the lease had an option to renew, could one co-tenant exercise of it, bind the others? Again, no. The co-tenants would have to exercise it together. See *Bockelman v. Marynick*, 788 S.W.2d 569 (Tex. 1990) (so holding when Len and Lannie were husband and wife).

Curtailed Negotiations

2. (a) No. Although the reliance of the tenant on the landlord's letter is clear, it is not enough to enforce under an estoppel argument. Estoppel requires (1) a promise, upon which there is a (2) reasonable reliance, causing (3) subsequent injury or damage to the relying person. The letter indicated Lonnie was glad Taft would remain on the premises. It never mentioned a lease renewal. The landlord's wish for a continuing relationship with the tenant does not amount to a promise that most courts enforce by estoppel. Since lease renewals must be in writing to satisfy the statute of frauds, Taft's reliance on an oral communication was not reasonable. See Peter E. Blum & Co. v. First Bank Bldg. Corp., 275 S.E.2d 751, 753 (Ga. App. Ct. 1980).

(b) Yes. The unsigned form gives the court something on which to base Larry's promise, which Ted relied on by holding over. Rendering Ted liable as a holdover would represent subsequent injury or damage that Ted can avoid by vacating the premises. Ted thus has an estoppel defense to any suit of Larry's, either to hold Ted over for a further term or to hold Ted liable as a trespasser. See Daehler v. Oggoian, 390 N.E.2d 417 (Ill. App. Ct. 1979).

Taking His Home to Work

3. (a) Eddy's best argument is that the title of the "employment agreement" does not control its substance, and that this agreement establishes both an employer-employee and a landlord-tenant relationship; that the latter is not an incident of the former, but independent of it; that the landlord-employer's dual status does not excuse noncompliance with both landlord-tenant and employment law; and that the performance of the employment contract is consideration for the lease. Rent may be paid in services, as well as money, and a contractually enforceable lease results no matter how the rent is paid. See Grant v. Detroit Assn. of Women's Clubs, 505 N.W.2d 254 (Mich. 1993).

   The argument to the contrary is that the overriding intent of the parties in the agreement is to create an occupancy right linked to and incidental to an employment relationship — occupying the apartment enables Eddy to better perform the caretaker function of the job; the agreement taken as a whole reserves no rent, and but for the employment Eddy would not be occupying the apartment in any event. This creates at least a presumption that the employment relationship is the principal one between the parties, that Eddy's interest in the apartment is no more than a license. Thus labor and employment law provides the controlling set of legal rules — so, for example, if Eddy went on strike, those rules, rather than those of landlord and tenant law, would control. As is apparent in this and the preceding paragraph, labeling the agreement as a contract does not advance either argument greatly.

   (b) Probably. This is, if anything, an easier case than the Eddy and C one above. Driving off trespassers provides continuing consideration for Owen's right of occupancy, so that Owen is Lawrence's tenant at will. Owen's driving off trespassers is the service, payment that allows Owen to use the land for purposes benefiting himself — i.e., his farming. In addition, if Owen's improvements were for use during the agricultural growing season, Owen may be, in the alternative, a periodic tenant, entitled to appropriate notices to quit and limiting Lawrence to a landlord's remedies.

Transfers of Land

22

The Sales Contract

INTRODUCTION

This chapter introduces issues relating to the purchase and sale of real property. Two key dates in the process are the date the parties enter into a sales contract and the closing date. Legal issues may arise before execution of a sales contract, between the execution of the sales contract and the closing, or after closing. How courts resolve issues depends on the issue presented and at which point on the time continuum the issue arises.

```
-----------------------------|-------------------|-------------------- → ∞
                        Sales Contract        Closing
```

With some obvious exceptions, a selling landowner typically places real estate on the market, often listing the property with a real estate broker. The broker is the selling landowner's agent. Purchasers often contact a real estate agent to locate suitable property. Ideally, the landowner's attorney will draft or at least review the listing agreement. In practice most sellers enter into listing agreements without involving an attorney.

Sellers and potential purchasers negotiate the details of the sale, often through real estate brokers. The purchasers may conduct studies related to the suitability of the land for their needs. Assuming the parties agree on such matters as the sales price, the parties enter into a **sales contract**, also known as a sales agreement, contract of sale and purchase, contract of sale, contract of purchase, earnest money contract, or other such name. Both seller and purchaser incur enforceable obligations on the execution of the contract.

Because of the importance of the sales contract, each party should be represented by an attorney before signing it. In many cases, and in most residential sales, however, the parties do not seek legal counsel, relying instead on a preprinted form contract supplied by the seller's broker. In nearly all states, a real estate broker's filling in the blanks on a preprinted form contract does not constitute the unauthorized practice of law.

The sales contract identifies the parties, sets the sales price or at least a method to determine the sales price, describes the property to be conveyed, includes language that the seller will convey and the purchaser will acquire the property, sets the closing date, delineates the manner of payment including cash and seller-financing, records the deposit or earnest money paid at the time the parties sign the sales contract, and explains what happens to the deposit at closing or if the buyer defaults or repudiates the contract. If the property is mortgaged, the contract should provide either that the purchaser will assume the debt or take the property subject to the debt, or that the seller will pay off the debt at or before closing.

Real estate brokers often supply a form sales contract that contains a provision detailing the amount of the sales commission payable to the broker from the deposit. The parties may insert other conditions, such as making the sale contingent on the purchaser's obtaining financing, having the land rezoned, or selling an existing residence.

CLOSING

After entering into the sales contract, the parties work toward a successful closing. The purchaser or his broker may inspect the property, review title documents, survey the property, and secure loan commitments. The seller may need to correct any title imperfections or repair the property. Based on some findings or failures, one of the parties may decide not to proceed to closing.

At closing, the parties consummate the deal. The seller transfers the property to the purchaser by deed (general warranty deed, special warranty deed, or quitclaim deed). The general and special warranty deeds warrant the seller owns the property and has the right to convey the property, the property is not burdened with undisclosed encumbrances, the purchaser can enjoy the property in "quiet enjoyment," and other matters to be discussed infra in Chapter 25. The seller might assign all contracts, leases, and personal property on the property to the purchaser. The purchaser will pay the seller cash or execute a note to the seller (or a combination of the two). The closing agent will prorate (allocate) the current year's taxes, insurance, and other items between the seller and the purchaser. If, as is common, the purchaser borrows money to purchase the property, the buyer and the seller must execute documents to satisfy the lender's demands relating to the loan.

REMEDIES FOR BREACH

Various remedies are available if one of the parties breaches or repudiates the sales contract or fails to close. Each parcel of real property is considered unique. Courts often cite this uniqueness and order **specific performance** of the sale and purchase. If specific performance is not sought or not awarded, the non-defaulting party may receive **nominal damages**, meaning out of pocket expenses, and possibly **actual damages**. Actual damages equal the excess of the property's fair market value at the time of the breach over the contract sales price (if the purchaser is the non-defaulting party) or the excess of the contract sales price over the property's fair market value (if the seller is the non-defaulting party). A non-defaulting party may also receive some **foreseeable consequential damages**. See also Chapter 23, infra (Remedies for Breach of Sales Contract).

If a sales contract provides for **liquidated damages**, the prevailing party may receive the liquidated damages amount in lieu of actual damages as long as the prospective damages were difficult to determine at the time the sales contract was executed, and the amount of the liquidated damages is reasonable (and is not a penalty). Many contracts provide that the liquidated damages will equal the earnest money deposit, and the seller is limited to retaining the deposit in lieu of actual damages. If the sales contract does not specify what happens to the earnest money in case of breach, the seller must return the deposit to the purchaser and seek actual damages. If the contract provides, a prevailing party may recover attorney's fees. Otherwise, each party is responsible for his or her own attorney's fees.

REAL ESTATE BROKERS AND AGENTS

Sellers often engage real estate brokers or real estate agents (a/k/a salespersons) to market the property to be sold. Real estate agents possess a more limited license and work under the supervision of real estate brokers. Both a broker and an agent under the law of agency owe fiduciary duties to the seller. Although the broker is the seller's agent, unless the seller specifically grants the broker a power of attorney to sign or negotiate on behalf of the seller, the broker cannot obligate the seller to sell the property and cannot sign any documents on behalf of the seller.

The broker's or agent's right to represent the seller and to collect a commission must be set out in a written contract or listing agreement to satisfy the Statute of Frauds (discussed below). If the seller uses more than one broker or agent, the contract is said to be **open or nonexclusive**. If the seller is limited to only one broker, the contract is said to be **exclusive**.

Exclusive contracts fall into two categories. In one, known as the **exclusive agency contract**, the broker is the only broker representing the seller. The seller, however, is free to find her own purchaser; and if the seller finds a purchaser without the broker's assistance, the seller owes no fee to the broker.

Under the second type of exclusive contract, known as the **exclusive right to sell**, the broker receives a fee no matter who locates a purchaser, even if the owner sells the property without any assistance from the broker. Traditionally, unless the seller's listing agreement provides otherwise, the seller's or listing broker earns a commission or fee when he procures a **ready, willing, and able** purchaser and the seller and purchaser execute the sales contract. Payment of the broker's fee likely will be deferred until closing, but the broker earns his fee when the parties enter into the sales contract. Under the traditional rule, it does not matter if the sale ever closes. The broker's fee has already been earned and the putative seller still owes the fee to the broker.

Strictly speaking, under the traditional rule, a broker earns her fee when she introduces the seller to a prospective purchaser who is "ready, willing, and able" to meet the terms set out in the listing agreement. Only a few states have cases so holding. The broker's fee is earned in these jurisdictions whether or not the seller actually enters into a sales contract with the purchaser, and whether or not the sale closes.

Example: Owen lists Blackacre with a broker in a state where the "procuring a ready, willing, and able purchaser" rule determines when brokers are entitled to commissions. The broker locates a prospective purchaser who signs a valid contract of sale with Owen for Blackacre. The contract provides that the broker's commission is "due at closing." The purchaser breaches the contract and refuses to close. The broker is still entitled to a commission according to most cases considering the issue. There is a difference between being entitled to the commission and its being payable at closing. It might be convenient for Owen in the example to pay the commission out of the sale proceeds, but the quoted contract language is not sufficiently clear that it changes the state's default rule on brokers' commissions to give it that effect. The phrase "due at closing" does not make closing a condition precedent to the broker's receiving a commission.

A number of states, and probably you, feel the broker's fee should not be payable unless the sale is completed: No closing, no commission. The majority rule awarding brokers fees as soon as the sales contract is executed, even if payment is deferred until closing, assumes the seller is satisfied the prospective purchaser is a "ready, willing, and able" purchaser. The minority view that the broker's commission is not owed unless the sale closes sees the seller as hoping the purchaser will perform, but not being responsible for investigating the purchaser's personal and financial capacities before signing the sales contract.

The above rules are not as different as they seem. In many states retaining the traditional rule, courts often find no commission is due because, among other reasons, the broker did not procure a "ready, willing, and able" buyer, or the broker breached some fiduciary duty. In states where the sale must close before a commission is owed to the broker, a court nonetheless might find it due if the seller's default was the reason the sale did not close. Thus, if the seller refuses to close for personal reasons, the seller tries to add a condition to the original sales contract, or the seller materially misleads the purchaser (and the broker) concerning a material fact related to the property, a court would force the seller to pay the broker his fee even if the sale never closes. Whatever the state's common law rule, the parties can specify in the sales contract precisely when the broker's fee is earned and what contingencies if any affect the broker's right to the commission.

Courts differ on results when the parties do not close because of a failure to satisfy a condition precedent in the contract, such as a rezoning or financing clause, or for some other reason not the fault of either party, such as a building being destroyed by storm or fire. Usually no commission is due to the broker for these no-fault failures to close (although exceptions occur). Sensibly, if a deal does not close because the purchaser breaches, and the seller therefore does not owe the broker a commission, some courts force the breaching purchaser, who was not even a party to the listing agreement, to pay the commission to the broker as a third party beneficiary of the sales contract. Though a sensible solution, this last remedy is a minority rule.

Although real estate brokers and agents are involved in the majority of home sales, a growing number of homeowners have taken to using websites and yard signs to offer homes "for sale by owner" (FSBO). The FSBO option eliminates or reduces the broker's commissions, but places a higher priority on the homeowner's consulting with appraisers and attorneys.

BROKER AS SELLER'S AGENT

A series of issues surround the duty of brokers to sellers and to buyers. The listing broker is the seller's agent and owes a duty of loyalty, fair dealing, and good faith to the seller. The listing broker can buy property from his principal (the seller) but must disclose to the seller that the broker is buying the property and must disclose, if true, that the seller has set a below-market asking price. Similarly, a broker cannot intentionally delay efforts to sell the property for months until his principal lowers the asking price just so the broker, or a friend or relative of the broker, can buy the property at a lower price. The broker must diligently seek a purchaser (though the broker does not guarantee success). The broker cannot perform any act showing disloyalty. In some states, this duty prohibits the broker from indicating to potential purchasers that the seller is desperate to sell or would accept a lower price.

Selling brokers, those brokers that show properties to prospective buyers, pose an interesting dilemma: Are they the seller's agent or the buyer's agent? Their main contact is with prospective purchasers. In fact, they may show a single prospect many properties, all owned by different sellers, yet they are paid their commission pursuant to a sharing arrangement with the listing broker through a listing agreement with the seller. In the majority of states, absent a buyer's broker agreement, the selling broker is the seller's subagent. As such, he owes a duty to the seller despite having considerably greater contacts and discussions with the purchaser. Recognizing this reality, and in line with what most buyers consider the true relationship, a minority of courts hold the selling broker to be the buyer's agent. In any state, a broker may become a dual agent, representing both the buyer and the seller, a situation rife with conflicts of interest. A small but growing number of prospective purchasers engage the services of a buyer's agent, whose loyalty is to the prospective purchaser.

BROKER'S DUTY TO DISCLOSE LATENT DEFECTS TO PURCHASERS

A broker may have a duty to disclose latent defects; or more specifically, she may have a duty to disclose facts materially affecting the property's value or desirability when the broker, using reasonable diligence and making a reasonable inspection, discovered or could have discovered them, even though the purchaser did neither of those things. In Chapter 23, we discuss the seller's obligation to disclose material latent defects. The broker usually has an independent duty to make the same disclosures. The broker may be directly liable for her breach of the duty to disclose. The seller may be liable both for his failure to disclose and for the broker's breach of her duty to disclose.

Traditionally, the broker (and the selling landowner) owed no duty to purchasers to disclose defects under a theory known as *caveat emptor: let the buyer beware*. Caveat emptor is still the default rule in many states. Even when caveat emptor prevails, however, a broker can be liable for **intentional misrepresentations** or affirmative acts to conceal facts or to mislead purchasers about material facts. Most states also hold the broker liable for **negligent misrepresentation**, i.e., where a broker knows or should know of matters underlying a false statement. Generally, negligent misrepresentation occurs when a broker gives erroneous information about a matter of general knowledge affecting all property in the community: zoning laws, location within a flood plain, or building codes, for example. Eight states even hold the broker liable for **innocent misrepresentation**, in effect making the broker liable for good faith statements that turn out to be incorrect.

In states where caveat emptor is not the rule, a broker must avoid misrepresentations of material facts, and must disclose latent and material defects that the broker either knew about or could have discovered upon reasonable inspection. **Latent defects** are those not discoverable by a buyer or his representative upon a reasonable inspection. In order to hold a broker liable, not only must the defect be latent, rather than open and discoverable on reasonable inspection, the condition or defect must be a **material defect**, one significantly affecting the value or use of the property.

Finally, the broker's duties outlined above apply predominantly to the sales of residential property. Brokers (and sellers) have fewer duties in the sale of commercial properties.

THE STATUTE OF FRAUDS

Every American jurisdiction has enacted a Statute of Frauds. The **Statute of Frauds** requires that deeds and real estate contracts be in writing and signed by the person to be bound. The Statute of Frauds applies to transfers of any interest in real estate, including easements, real covenants, mineral rights, water rights, long-term leases, life estates, remainders, and liens. Some states require options to purchase to be in writing. In most states, modifications of provisions included in a writing also must be in writing. In contrast, a slight majority of states allow a person entitled to rescind a contract to orally rescind the contract. In most states, a special Statute of Frauds applies to commissions payable to real estate brokers, which explains why agents and brokers are adamant about getting signed written listing agreements.

Not all provisions of the real estate contract or deed must be in writing to satisfy the Statute of Frauds. Oral provisions will be enforced as long as a sufficient writing exists concerning the transaction. Even a memorandum of an oral contract satisfies the writing requirement. Although the Statute of Frauds does not set out minimum requirements of a "writing" (except the writing must be signed by the person to be bound), courts have established essential requirements.

Although some courts demand more, the essential requirements of a writing that satisfies the Statute of Frauds include identification of the parties, a sufficient description of the property, the price or at least a method to determine price, and an intention to convey the property (and the writing must be signed by the party to be bound). The basic essentials do not have to be contained in the same document or even in formal documents. Courts have concluded that a series of letters can constitute a writing, for example, or that a check can be the writing or part of the series constituting the writing if it contains all the required information. Courts require at least one of the writings to reference the other writings before they consider the separate documents to be one writing.

The advent of the internet and email has added a wrinkle to what constitutes a writing under the Statute of Frauds: Whether the exchange of emails that contain all the requirements of the Statute of Frauds constitute a writing. Some lower state courts have found emails with electronic signatures do constitute a writing if the elements otherwise are met. Other lower courts refuse to accept emails as writing since emails lack the cautionary and memorializing safeguards inherent in a traditional paper writing. State legislatures are enacting laws permitting emails and electronic signatures to have legal effect; though at least one state refused to extend the new law to real estate contracts, requiring the more traditional paper writing.

In interpreting a contract with both oral and written provisions, courts do not allow testimony to contradict any written provision but will allow testimony to clarify written provisions and to clarify or contradict oral provisions. Testimony also will be allowed to contradict the terms of a memorandum of an oral contract.

With some exceptions as discussed below, a court will not mandate specific performance of an oral contract even if all parties agree an oral contract exists. Oral contracts for real estate are said to be voidable. They therefore are not absolutely void. The parties may perform the contract and, if carried to fruition, the sale will not be undone.

PART PERFORMANCE AND OTHER EXCEPTIONS

Despite the seeming absoluteness of the writing requirement of the Statute of Frauds, courts have crafted exceptions to the writing requirement. The exceptions to the Statute of Frauds are based on equitable principles. In all cases, the moving party (1) must prove an oral contract exists, and (2) must persuade a court to excuse the party's failure to produce a writing containing the essential elements of the contract.

(a) Part Performance

At least one commentator lumps all possible equitable exceptions under the rubric "**Part Performance**." Other commentators, and many courts, limit the Part Performance theory to cases where the purchaser does some combination of the following:

(1) Pays the contract price
(2) Takes possession of the property
(3) Improves the property

Paying the purchase price alone is insufficient to warrant enforcement of the contract since the complaining party can be put back into the position he would have been in if there had been no contract simply by having the money returned to him (i.e., by restitution). Some courts accept partial payment, some require substantial payment, and some require full payment of the purchase price. Even with payment of the full purchase price, courts usually require at least one of the other two requirements before excusing noncompliance with the Statute of Frauds.

Taking possession entails more than delivery and acceptance of title. The buyer must physically move onto the property and perhaps even incur substantial moving expenses from another location. A party who substantially improves the property — i.e., the improvement must result in the property's value being increased more than the fair rental value accruing to the moving party during the time he possessed the property — may be excused from complying with the Statute of Frauds. Usually, the improvements must entail more than clearing, digging wells, fencing, cultivating, or planting trees.

(b) Equitable Estoppel or Equitable Fraud

Sometimes grouped with Part Performance, but having a slightly different emphasis, is **equitable estoppel or equitable fraud**. Under this theory, courts in a few states will excuse an oral contract's noncompliance with the Statute of Frauds if a party seeking performance, in justifiable reliance on an oral contract and the continuing assurances of the other party, so substantially changes his position that injustice would result unless the contract is enforced. The equitable estoppel or equitable fraud theory usually is invoked in cases involving persons, often family members, who move to the property to care for the property's owner, who also lives there, on the oral promise that the owner at her death will devise the property to the moving party. The consideration for the contract is the services performed.

The following are the requirements for the equitable estoppel or equitable fraud theory:

(1) A certain and definite oral contract;

(2) Acts that refer to, result from, or are made in pursuance of the agreement; and

(3) A refusal to fully execute the oral contract would operate as a fraud on, and place the moving party in, a situation not remediable by damages.

(c) Unequivocal Reference to Oral Contract

Related in theory, but with a slightly different emphasis, some courts say the Statute of Frauds furnishes evidence a contract exists. In these jurisdictions part performance serves as an alternative form of evidence of the contract. These courts recognize that substantial or full performance of the contract by one party is strong evidence of the oral contract. For these courts to accept the part performance in lieu of a written contract, the acts constituting the performance must be **unequivocally referable** to the oral contract; that is, the acts must make sense only if they are in furtherance of an oral contract. Generally, the owner of the property has received the bargained for benefit. Thus the avoidance of unjust enrichment by the granting party may underlie this approach, especially if, as is often the situation in these cases, the performance relates to the care of the property owner until her death.

Examples

The Richer or Broker Broker

1. Maxine is a real estate broker. Maxine entered into a listing agreement with Jacob to sell Jacob's home. The listing agreement provided in part:

> The commission due to Broker herein shall be 6% of the sales price stipulated in the Sales Contract signed by Seller and a prospective buyer, payable as, if, and when the deed is delivered to the buyer. Should the deed not be delivered for any reason whatsoever, except for the willful default of the Seller, no commission shall be due.

Maxine showed the home to prospective purchasers Harry and Hazel Harley, who with two friends rode to the home on motorcycles. The Harleys liked the home and submitted an offer meeting all of Jacob's stipulations. Between the time the Harleys viewed the home and the time they submitted an offer to Jacob, a neighbor called Jacob angry and upset that Jacob might sell to a "motorcycle gang." Jacob refused to sign the sales contract because his neighbor would be angry with him if he sold to the Harleys. Maxine sued Jacob for her lost commission. What result?

Where There's a Will

2. Alta Mae owned an eight-unit apartment complex at 6002 Fullerton Avenue worth $250,000. Due to her declining health, Alta Mae felt she no longer could manage or maintain the units. Desiring to receive a steady stream of income for the rest of her life, she considered selling the units for cash. Instead, believing a cash sale would result in detrimental tax consequences, she sold the apartment complex to her longtime friends, Donnie and Marie, who had lived in one of the apartment units for 15 years.

Donnie and Marie paid $25,000 cash and gave Alta Mae a note for the remaining $225,000. The note provided for interest at the prevailing market rate. The note provided for monthly payments of interest only. The $225,000 principal of the note was due in a lump sum in 15 years.

As part of the sale, Alta Mae agreed that if she received timely monthly payments, the unpaid balance of the note would be forgiven at her death. Alta Mae declined to put this agreement in writing at closing, but acknowledged the agreement in the presence of others, and agreed to put it in a writing after closing. Three weeks after closing, Alta Mae executed her will. Her will contained the following provision:

> Any note still owing to me or my estate by Donnie and Marie should be given to Donnie and Marie. This gift is in accord with a contractual agreement made when I sold my apartment units at 6002 Fullerton Avenue in the City of Buena Park to Donnie and Marie but never put in writing. I intend that the contractual obligation shall be honored.

Eight years later Alta Mae executed a new will revoking all previous wills. The new will made no reference to Donnie and Marie, the note, or the apartment complex. Donnie and Marie regularly paid monthly interest payments to Alta Mae until they learned of her death, at which time they stopped making payments, relying on their understanding the remaining debt was canceled on Alta Mae's death.

Alta Mae's legatees claim Donnie and Marie must pay the $225,000 note. Does the Statute of Frauds prevent Donnie and Marie from enforcing Alta Mae's agreement to forgive the note at her death?

Marital Bliss

3. Sal and Sally, husband and wife, own a house as tenants in common. Ben and By, husband and wife, negotiate to purchase the house.
   (a) Sal and Sally (the sellers) sign the sales contract, and Ben signs on behalf of himself and By (the purchasers). Ben and By refuse to close.

Does the Statute of Frauds prevent Sal and Sally from enforcing the sales contract?

(b) Assume Sal signs the sales contract on behalf of himself and Sally (the sellers), but Sally does not sign. Both Ben and By sign the sales contract. Sal and Sally (the sellers) refuse to close. Does the Statute of Frauds prevent Ben and By from enforcing the sales contract?

(c) Under the facts of (b) where Sal signs but Sally does not sign the sales contract, can Ben and By invoke the Statute of Frauds to rescind the sale if Sal and Sally seek specific performance?

(d) Assume Sal signs; Sally does not sign; both Ben and By sign; and, in addition, the contract contains a provision that "This sales contract to be effective upon the execution thereof by both sellers and both purchasers." Ben and By refuse to close. Can Sal and Sally enforce the sales contract?

Handshake Deal

4. Cain orally agreed to purchase 806 acres from Solomon for $1000 per acre. Pursuant to the agreement, Cain gave Solomon a $10,000 check as a down payment. Cain agreed to pay $400,000 on delivery of possession, and to pay the balance with interest later. Cain applied for and acquired a written loan commitment from Bank for the $400,000 to be paid at closing. Solomon refused to deed the property to Cain, and conveyed the property to a third party instead. Cain brings suit seeking money damages in excess of $50,000.

(a) Did the delivery of the check and securing the written loan commitment satisfy the Statute of Frauds?

(b) Assuming the check and loan commitment fail to constitute a "writing," does the transaction fall within the Part Performance or other exception to the Statute of Frauds?

The Knoll in the Hog Field

5. Red Fox owned a farm when he died intestate. His heirs were his eight children. Wishing to unify ownership in himself, one of the children, Sly Fox, made agreements with six of his siblings to purchase their undivided interests in the farm. One sister, Leona Fox Lamb, did not want to sell. She desired a particular lot on the farm, the lot known as the knoll in the hog field, on which she someday wanted to build a home. Sly and Leona orally agreed Leona would convey her undivided interest in the farm to Sly; and in exchange Sly at some future time would convey the knoll in the hog field to Leona (or, if they agreed, some other parcel). The seven siblings (including Leona) executed a deed transferring their interests in the farm to Sly. Sly paid six siblings (excluding Leona) $1,000 each for

their respective one-eighth interest in the farm. Leona was the only grantor who did not receive any money.

Over the next ten years Leona often discussed "her lot" on the farm with Sly and his wife. Sly often complained about the costs and hassles of subdividing, but never disavowed the original oral agreement. Sly never developed the property but he did sell some land from the farm (but not the knoll in the hog field).

Following some family discord between Sly and Leona, Leona by letter demanded Sly fulfill his agreement to transfer the knoll in the hog field to Leona. Sly balked at transferring the land, offering instead to pay Leona the same $1,000 he had paid the others. Leona sues. Sly defends, citing the Statute of Frauds. Does the contract fall within the Part Performance doctrine or other exception to the Statute of Frauds?

Explanations

The Richer or Broker Broker

1. Some states hold that Maxine, the broker, earns her commission when she produces a ready, willing, and able buyer. Others require the seller and purchaser execute a sales contract. Yet others require a closing. Those states requiring a closing make an exception, and still order the seller to pay the broker, if the closing did not happen because the seller breached the contract.

Whatever the state's common law rule, the seller and broker can modify, change, or reverse the default rule or common law by contract. The listing agreement between Maxine and Jacob stipulated that Jacob owed Maxine a commission only if the closing occurred and Jacob deeded the home to the Harleys, events that did not happen. The listing agreement, however, contained an exception, providing that Maxine earned her commission on the "willful default of Seller."

The case thus turns on whether Jacob's not signing the sales contract in the first place amounted to a default. If Jacob had signed the sales contract and later refused to close because he did not want to upset his neighbors, Jacob would owe Maxine her commission under the listing agreement. Unfortunately for Maxine, the default referenced in the listing agreement was a default of the sales contract and not a default of the listing agreement. Jacob never entered into a sales contract, and was not obligated to execute a sales contract. Since there was no sales contract for Jacob to breach, Jacob does not owe Maxine a commission.

Where There's a Will

2. No. A writing satisfies the Statute of Frauds if it identifies the parties, sufficiently describes the property, states the purchase price, and states an

intent that the property will be conveyed. If the seller finances the sale, the writing must document the essentials of the financing, including the interest rate, if any. A provision that the balance (the principal) of a note is to be forgiven upon some condition other than full payment is an essential element related to the financing of the purchase and must be included in a writing signed by the party to be bound.

Multiple documents may constitute the "writing" if a signed writing indicates the documents are related to the transaction. Prior to Alta Mae's executing the first will, the agreement that the balance of the note was to be forgiven at Alta Mae's death was merely an oral or parol contract and thus unenforceable under the Statute of Frauds. Alta Mae's first will referencing the sale of the apartments, including the note, and the contractual forgiveness of the note, memorializes the agreement and refers unequivocally to it. Alta Mae signed the will and thus she is bound. Donnie and Marie did not sign Alta Mae's will, but since they are not being bound, they are not required to sign.

Alta Mae's revoking the first will is irrelevant since the debt forgiveness was a part of the original contract and was not a testamentary transfer. A will may serve as a writing for purposes of the Statute of Frauds even if it is not a valid will or the will is later revoked.

Donnie and Marie must rely on the Statute of Frauds writing to prevail. The part performance exception is not applicable since Donnie and Marie have not paid the purchase price. The equitable estoppel exception does not apply since Donnie and Marie did nothing so substantially extra in reliance on the agreement that would shock the judicial conscience enough to excuse a failure to get a writing.

Marital Bliss

3. (a) A husband is not his wife's agent merely because of the marriage. No husband-wife exception to the Statute of Frauds exists. Since By did not sign, the Statute of Frauds prevents enforcement of the sales contract against her. Ben, on the other hand, did sign, and the contract can be enforced against him.

   (b) The Statute of Frauds insulates Sally but not Sal. Sal is not Sally's agent absent a writing signed by her designating Sal as her agent. Sally therefore has no legal obligation to sell her interest. Sal did sign and thus is liable under the contract. If, as is likely, Sal contracted to transfer the entire interest in the house and not just "his" one-half interest, Ben and By may seek damages for breach of contract. A court in theory might allow Ben and By to elect to acquire Paul's interest, but most courts prohibit the sale and limit purchasers' remedy to damages under these facts.

   (c) No. Ben and By are still bound. Sal and Sally can seek specific performance of the sales contract. Alternatively, Sally can ratify Sal's actions as her agent; or sign the sales contract if the offer has not been revoked; or sell her interest to Sal so he could seek specific performance.

(d) None of the parties is bound. The sales contract in (d) specifically conditions the contract on all four parties' signing. Even though the parties to be bound signed, there is no effective contract until all four parties sign. Either side may rescind prior to all four parties' signing. Under these facts, a court will hold the sale was contingent on all parties' signing since the evidence suggests the sale was an "all or nothing" proposition. See, e.g., Wachter Development, L.L.C. v. Gomke, 579 N.W.2d 209 (N.D. 1998).

Handshake Deal

4. (a) The $10,000 check may satisfy the Statute of Frauds if it contains enough information. While the check may come close to satisfying the Statute of Frauds, it probably will not contain all the essential information. The check may have contained a notation describing the property, named both parties (Solomon as payee and Cain printed on top of the check or on his signature), and probably Solomon's endorsement on the back and Cain's signature on the front of the check. Lacking in all probability would be the full purchase price and, since Solomon was to finance approximately half the purchase price, the terms of the financing. The loan commitment would not add any essential information. The check and loan commitment would not satisfy the Statute of Frauds. Cain has no action.

(b) No. Oral contracts saved by the Part Performance doctrine require more than the mere payment of earnest money. Even full payment of the contract price will not save the putative purchaser when the putative purchaser, like Cain, could be put back into his original position by the return of the earnest money deposit or the full purchase price. Since Cain never took actual possession, much less made substantial improvements to the property, equitable principles do not call for the transaction to be recognized.

The facts are not so sympathetic to Cain that a court should excuse Cain's noncompliance with the Statute of Frauds. Similarly, since Cain performed no acts other than payment of the earnest money, the evidentiary exception's requirements that the putative seller be unduly enriched and the putative purchaser's acts be "unequivocally referable" to the oral contract are not met.

The Knoll in the Hog Field

5. Leona will prevail, and a court will find an exception to the Statute of Frauds. Even though Leona has fully performed by deeding her interest to

Sly, she is not in a position to meet the other Part Performance requirements as to the knoll in the hog field: She has not taken physical possession and she has not substantially improved the property. So far as we can tell from the facts, Sly has not improved or harmed the knoll in the hog field in any significant respect.

Under an equitable estoppel or equitable fraud theory, however, Leona, in reasonable reliance on the oral contract and Sly's continuing assent had so changed her position that injustice could be avoided only by ordering specific performance of the oral contract. Leona's change of position was deeding her interest to Sly ten years earlier. Generally, deeding her interest in the property would be insufficient in itself since returning a one-eighth interest to Leona would undo any harm. Sly's use of the property as a farm over the previous ten years would have been consistent with his being Leona's tenant-in-common. The court noted that in this particular case Sly conveyed away part of the land, keeping Leona's inheritance from being fully restored. Not enforcing the oral contract under these facts would amount to an equitable fraud on Leona.

Moreover, Leona's joining her siblings on the deed to Sly was unequivocally or exclusively referable to their oral contract. This coupled with Leona's having no adequate remedy other than specific performance is enough to estop Sly from successfully pleading the Statute of Frauds.

Executory Period Issues

INTRODUCTION

Once a seller and purchaser enter into a sales contract, each takes steps in preparation for closing. The interim period between the signing of the sales contract and the closing is called the **executory period**. Not all sales contracts are consummated.

The sales contract itself may condition the parties' obligation to close. A party's failure to satisfy a sales contract **condition** allows the other party to rescind the contract without liability, and in some cases allows the party not meeting the condition to rescind.

A clause, for example, may allow the purchaser to rescind the contract after consulting with an attorney. A common condition, known as the **subject to financing** clause, conditions the purchaser's obligation to close on securing a loan commitment under suitable terms, including the amount, repayment schedule, and maximum interest rate. Often what is considered suitable is included in the sales contract. Implied in the subject to financing clause is the purchaser's reasonable effort to obtain the loan commitment. Other clauses may condition the closing on the purchasers' selling their current residence, on a rezoning of the property, or on the seller's removing a mortgage or other lien on the property.

State or federal law may impose conditions such as a termite inspection or CERCLA (Comprehensive Environmental Response, Compensation, and Liability Act) disclosures. Predictably, some matters escape statutory requirements and explicit contractual provisions. Courts have crafted common law default provisions for some of these matters. The common law rules are default provisions only, however, and the parties can contract around and contrary to the common law rules.

Under contract law, a purchaser can rescind a contract for fraud or misrepresentation. Similarly, either party can cancel a contract in the case of **material mistake** when both parties are mistaken about a material fact underlying the contract.

MARKETABLE TITLE

(a) Definition of Marketable Title

Title implies the elements or attributes constituting ownership. "Title" is often preceded by an adjective clarifying the intended meaning in context. Legal title, equitable title, perfect title, record title, insurable title, and marketable title are all variations. Unless the sales contract specifically stipulates a different standard, every land sales contract contains an implied condition that the seller will convey "marketable title" to the purchaser. Often a seller will contract to convey a lesser title such as **insurable title** (that title a title insurance company will insure; sometimes a title insurance company will issue a title policy even though the seller cannot convey marketable title).

Marketable title (or merchantable title) allows for some possibility the purchaser's title will be successfully challenged, but the title is solid enough that a reasonable person knowing all the facts would accept and pay for the title. Marketable title means a title free from reasonable doubt as to the promised title's validity. A reasonable person having knowledge of all the relevant facts, and the legal consequences flowing from those facts, would be willing to accept the title. Generally, a title is unmarketable if there is a reasonable probability the seller does not own the full title alleged, the property is subject to an undisclosed encumbrance, or the purchaser bears an unreasonable risk he or she would be subject to litigation related to the property in its current condition. A good rule of thumb is that a title is unmarketable if acquiring the property would subject the purchaser to a real risk of litigation (to remove a condition, to challenge a creditor's or nonparticipating co-owner's rights, or to bring or defend an adverse possession suit, as examples). A purchaser, in other words, is not required to "buy a lawsuit."

Unless the seller cures all defects before the scheduled closing date, a purchaser can refuse to close and can rescind the sales contract if the title is unmarketable. If a purchaser intends to rescind a sales contract based on unmarketable title, he or she must rescind before closing. If closing occurs, courts historically held the sales contract **merged** with the deed, and the purchaser generally was limited to rights flowing from the warranties of title included in the deed. As a modern trend, however, courts find ways to allow some sales contract provisions to survive closing. See Warranties of Title in Chapter 25, infra.

(b) Examples of Unmarketable Title

Minor encumbrances or unlikely occurrences do not make a title unmarketable. Thus, a mere possibility or suspicion the title is flawed is not enough to make the title unmarketable.

Example: A, a single person with no siblings, died intestate 20 years ago. A chance exists some heretofore unknown or long lost heir may appear claiming an interest in the property. That possibility without evidence an unknown or missing heir survived the decedent and still has a claim to the property would not make a title unmarketable today. Likewise, a lien or mortgage many decades old involving persons long since dead probably would not make the title unmarketable.

Marketable title is not the same as a title without encumbrances. In practice, most property is transferred subject to encumbrances. It is not the existence of an encumbrance or possible defect that causes a title to be unmarketable. Rather, it is the existence of an **undisclosed encumbrance** and thus not made part of the bargain that makes the title unmarketable.

Example 1: A purchaser contracts to buy Blackacre subject to a restrictive covenant restricting the property to use for residential purposes only. Assuming no other restriction, encumbrance, or defect surfaces, the title is **marketable** and the purchaser is legally bound by the sales contract.

Example 2: After signing the sales contract and before closing, the purchaser discovers a covenant binding on the property's current and future owners that prohibits multistory homes on the property. As to this purchaser, the title is **unmarketable** because the sales contract did not disclose the prohibition against multistory buildings. The purchaser can rescind the sales contract. It does not matter whether the purchaser intends to build a one-story or two-story home, or whether the seller knew of the multistory covenant. The title is unmarketable and the purchaser is not obligated to buy the property (unless the seller removes the restriction, encumbrance, or defect by the closing date).

Example 3: Assume the same facts of Example 2 and a second purchaser contracts to purchase the property. The sales contract makes the transfer subject to both the residential-use-only restriction and the one-story-only restriction. The title as to the new purchaser is **marketable** because the purchaser executed the sales contract aware of both encumbrances.

The difference between the two purchasers is critical. The purchaser in Example 2 did not contract to purchase the property with a restriction that limits houses to one story. As a common sense result — and under the legal theory of unmarketable title — the purchaser is not required to complete a contract for something less than he or she bargained to buy. The purchaser in Example 3, on the other hand, is purchasing exactly what the sales contract described. The Example 3 purchaser should be, and will be, liable on the sales contract.

Typical **encumbrances** or **defects** in title are undisclosed co-owners (concurrent or future estates), mortgages or liens, easements, real covenants or equitable servitudes, leases, mineral rights, options, flaws in the deed records, erroneous acreage designations, or ownership based on adverse possession. Violation of a federal or state statute or a zoning ordinance may be a defect in title only if a violation is likely to be prosecuted.

For purposes of the marketable title discussion, **real covenants** and **equitable servitudes** are contractual restrictions and duties included in prior deeds or other documents that affect the use of the property. Some common covenants and servitudes (the difference between the two are unimportant to the present discussion) are restrictions of land to residential uses only (used in the previous example); restrictions on certain types of businesses; prohibitions of animals, mobile homes, or alcohol sales; minimum lot sizes; or other building or use restrictions. For more, see Chapter 30, infra. **Easements** are rights of nonowners to use the land for particular purposes. The most common easements are private roadways, utility easements for poles or wires, sewer easements, and easements for railroad tracks. While both lists are incomplete, they should give you an idea why a purchaser not knowing about them should be permitted to rescind the contract if he or she does not choose to accept the restrictions or easements. For more see Chapter 28, infra.

Monetary obligations secured by the property, such as undisclosed mortgages, liens, or unpaid property taxes, in amounts less than the sales price likely do not justify rescission of the sales contract since the mortgage, lien, or back taxes can be retired at closing. Nonetheless, the prudent seller in the sales contract will disclose the existence of all liens, mortgages, and taxes owed.

Because the marketable title inquiry entails ascertaining a reasonable person's response to the likelihood a lawsuit may ensue, sellers often try to promise to furnish **insurable title**, which more objectively is satisfied if a title insurance company will insure the title. Insurable title also aids sellers because title insurance companies are more willing to undertake the risk no litigation will arise on minor or technical defects in title.

(c) Defective Deed Records

Any flaw in the deed records that could lead to litigation makes the title unmarketable. Deeds and other documents (liens, mortgages, etc.) affecting real property are filed ("recorded") in local government offices in counties where the land is situated. Usually the deed records are found in the county courthouse. A person can trace all filed documents related to a particular piece of land back to the original grant from the state or federal government (*chain of title*). The deed records thus serve an important function in assuring purchasers their sellers in fact own the property being bought and sold. Because of the importance of the deed records to our society, the person who is the *record owner* — i.e., the person who is deemed the landowner by looking solely at the deed records — often will prevail over the *legal owner* — i.e., the person who would be owner if there was no official recording system and the history of all actual transactions is known.

The deed records can be defective in many ways. The property can be misdescribed in a prior deed, or some names are different from one "link" to the next in the record "chain." A deed may not be properly notarized or otherwise not legally authorized to be recorded, or recorded out of order; in either case the document will be deemed unrecorded and of no legal effect. A party to a deed may have lacked capacity to transfer the interest in the property (either being a minor, lacking mental capacity, or lacking authorization for a corporate officer, as examples). Any serious flaw or missing link in the deed records makes the title unmarketable.

Searching the deed records is the most common manner of finding evidence the title is either marketable or not due to a defect in the chain of title. An exception to the rule that an encumbrance found in the deed records that was not disclosed in the sales contract makes the title unmarketable relates to visible easements. Visible easements are easements so apparent upon inspection that the purchaser saw or should have seen the easement and is, therefore, to have contemplated purchasing the property subject to the easement. Many states reject the exception for visible easements, however, and look solely to whether the sales contract disclosed the easement. Some courts also find the title to be unmarketable if a structure on the property encroaches on neighboring land or if property on neighboring land encroaches on the property being transferred since, in either case, resolution of the matter could lead to litigation.

(d) Violations of Covenants, Ordinances, Regulations, or Other Laws

Special considerations surround zoning laws, building codes, and other government laws and regulations. In general, a seller is not required to disclose the applicability of any law or government regulation, including zoning laws and building codes. The failure to disclose these regulatory matters will not make the title unmarketable.

Example: In Example 2, above, an undisclosed restrictive covenant limiting homes to one story made the title unmarketable (when the restriction was found in an earlier deed in the chain of title). Assume now the one-story restriction is part of the local zoning ordinance rather than a restriction in a prior deed. The restriction imposed by a local zoning ordinance would not make the title unmarketable.

The logic behind this seeming anomaly is fairly simple: all people are expected to know zoning laws apply to all property within a political subdivision, including a city or county. A reasonable person would research the zoning laws before entering into the sales contract. A person entering into a sales contract without reviewing the zoning laws risks being bound by an unanticipated zoning ordinance. The same logic applies to all federal and state statutes and local ordinances, including building codes. Only private restrictions must be disclosed in the sales contract.

Another ticklish situation arises when the property in its current state violates a disclosed covenant or servitude, a zoning ordinance, a building code, or other federal or state statute. A violation of a **restrictive covenant** makes the title **unmarketable.** Most courts hold that an undisclosed **zoning code** violation does not make a title unmarketable unless an enforcement action has been docketed, or is being pursued in litigation, against the seller. Courts seemingly agree that **building code violations** relate to the property's **condition** and not to **title**. Thus an undisclosed building code violation does not make a title unmarketable.[1]

(e) Adverse Possession

Adverse possession complicates the determination of marketable title for both the record title owner and the self-styled adverse possessor. Title acquired by adverse possession constitutes marketable title in most states. See Chapter 8, supra. Title by adverse possession is marketable even if the claimant has not filed a quiet title action. Yet the mere allegation by a seller he owns property by adverse possession is insufficient to establish marketable title. Adverse possession must be established by clear and convincing evidence. Serious controversy as to any element of adverse possession prevents the seller from having marketable title. A seller claiming title by adverse possession bears the burden of proof that he would prevail against record holders and other outstanding claimants. Similarly, a record

---

1. A purchaser may be able to rescind a sales contract if the building code violation is serious and if the seller failed to disclose the material defect. See Caveat Emptor and the Duty to Disclose Defects, infra (a purchaser may rescind a contract if the seller fails to disclose material defects). Serious zoning violations also may constitute material defects required to be disclosed.

title owner cannot convey marketable title if a third party, especially a present possessor, claims to own an interest in the property by adverse possession unless the claim is clearly frivolous. The record title owner might be required to bring a judicial action to defeat the adverse possessor claims and eject them from the property, if need be, as trespassers.

(f) Landlocked Property

Courts favor access to property. Thus, even though technically not a title defect, a court may find title to be unmarketable if there is no *access* to the property — i.e., if the property is **landlocked** (unless the sales contract discloses the lack of access or, in some jurisdictions, if the purchaser was aware of the access problem when he or she signed the sales contract). See, e.g., Howell v. Brozetti, 246 A.D. 929 (N.Y. 1998). Courts in at least two states have held property without access is still marketable. See, e.g., Sinks v. Karleskint, 474 N.E.3d 767 (Ill. App. 1985). In both those cases the courts alternatively held the purchaser was aware the property lacked access.

CAVEAT EMPTOR AND THE DUTY TO DISCLOSE DEFECTS

Marketable title issues generally stress **title** — i.e., ownership of the property. Violations of zoning laws or restrictive covenants concern the **condition or use** of the property and do not directly bear on title. Nonetheless, many courts use a marketable title analysis when there is a violation and enforcement is imminent since the violation could involve the seller in a lawsuit.

A more recent (and sensible) approach evaluates violations of covenants, ordinances, and other material latent defects under a **duty to disclose**. The failure to disclose material latent defects is a rapidly gaining independent theory for rescinding sales contracts. Courts imposing a duty to disclose material defects abrogate the long recognized theory of **caveat emptor** — **let the buyer beware**. Where courts impose the duty to disclose, purchasers can rescind the sales contract or seek damages if the seller does not disclose known material latent defects in the condition of the land or improvements.

(a) Caveat Emptor

In some states, probably now a minority, **caveat emptor** reigns, and a seller owes no duty to disclose patent or latent defects to a purchaser. The purchaser should inspect the property before executing the sales contract. Unless a seller is in a fiduciary relationship in a caveat emptor state, the seller is under no obligation to disclose defects. A seller who remains silent escapes liability. Even where caveat emptor is the rule, however, sellers cannot actively mislead purchasers by affirmatively misrepresenting facts, and cannot actively conceal facts, such as putting up fake ventilation coverings.

The purchaser of defective premises in caveat emptor jurisdictions may bring a claim based on fraudulent misrepresentation. The elements of **fraudulent misrepresentation** are (1) a representation of a fact, (2) which is material to the sale, (3) made falsely, with knowledge of its falsity, or with such utter disregard and recklessness as to whether it is true, (4) with the intent of misleading the purchaser into relying on the representation; (5) the purchaser justifiably relies on the representation; and (6) the purchaser suffers some injury proximately caused by his reliance on the misrepresentation (or injury would be suffered if the purchaser goes through with the purchase).

(b) The Duty to Disclose Material Latent Defects

States are moving, sometimes judicially and often by statute, to a rule requiring sellers to disclose material latent defects to purchasers. **Material defects** are those that materially affect the property's value, or that could significantly impair the occupant's health and safety, or that the seller knows affects the desirability of the property to the buyer. **Latent defects** are those defects known to the seller and not discoverable by the purchaser or her representative upon reasonable inspection.

Courts and states differ on what latent defects must be disclosed. A few courts limit a seller's duty to disclose material latent facts relating to conditions that affect the **health or safety** of the buyer. Some limit the duty to disclose to professional sellers — **builders and developers** — of **new** homes. Others extend the duty to all sellers and to real estate brokers and agents.

Those courts requiring disclosure demand the seller disclose material latent **physical defects** on the property, including leaky roofs, termites, cockroach infestation, or that the house is built on a filled-in swamp. Some courts also require a seller to disclose **off-site conditions** that may affect the property's value or the occupant's safety or health. The greatest number of off-site condition cases involve nearby hazardous waste disposal sites. Other off-site matters that should be disclosed are nearby landfills, noisy neighbors, underground gas pipelines, or proposed developments.

A small minority of courts require sellers to disclose some **nonphysical defects** or conditions, both associated with the property itself and on nearby properties. In one famous case, sellers were required to disclose a home had a reputation of being haunted by ghosts. Another court required disclosure that a mass murder occurred in the home. Some states' laws, known as "stigma statutes," to the contrary specifically absolve sellers from disclosing the home was occupied by a person with HIV or other disease unlikely to be transmitted through occupancy of the home; or that the home was the site of a homicide, suicide, felony, or death by accidental or natural causes.

Even when a seller must disclose latent defects, a seller does not have to disclose **patent** (visible) defects or defects that are not material. Likewise, a seller must know of the defects before the obligation to disclose arises.

The duty to disclose latent defects, where it exists, relates only to **residential** properties. Courts to date have not extended the duty to disclose to **commercial** property sales. They reason commercial purchasers are more sophisticated and can have their own agents inspect the property. Off-site conditions and nonphysical defects, moreover, are not as crucial to commercial owners. Sellers of commercial property still can be liable for affirmative misrepresentation; but for the most part, caveat emptor remains the rule for commercial properties.

TIME FOR PERFORMANCE

A purchaser cannot rescind a contract as soon as a title defect or physical defect is discovered. The seller has time to rectify or remove the defect. Similarly, the purchaser has time to obtain financing, inspect the property, secure government permits, etc. Yet there must be an outside time limit to close the transaction. If the sales contract does not specify a time, the parties have a "reasonable time" to perform. What is reasonable varies with the surrounding facts. A seller may even have time to bring an adverse possession suit without breaching the contract for unreasonably delaying closing. Even if the parties set a date for closing, courts in equity, recognizing all the unavoidable delays that may occur, tolerate delays in closing unless the sales contract stipulates that "**time is of the essence**." Even when time is of the essence in the performance of the contract, some minor delays will usually be tolerated if no harm occurs.

REMEDIES FOR BREACH OF SALES CONTRACT

If the seller cannot deliver marketable title at closing, the purchaser generally may elect to rescind the sales contract. Alternatively, the purchaser may choose to go forward with the closing and seek **specific performance** of the contract — i.e., compel the sale and purchase be carried out. Additionally, if the seller partially breaches the contract — does not disclose a title defect, encumbrance, or acreage, for example — the purchaser can seek an abatement of the purchase price. If a purchaser breaches — generally refuses to close — the seller like the purchaser can seek specific performance; but while courts do order specific performance at the seller's request, they often limit the seller to monetary damages.

A purchaser may decide not to seek specific performance, or a court may decide against ordering specific performance. In such cases, a court could award monetary damages (**loss of bargain damages**) equal to the difference between the fair market value at the time of the breach and the agreed upon contract price. In many cases this is a nominal amount. In some cases, of course, the amount could be substantial.

Example: Linda contracts to sell property to Marcus for $400,000. During the executory period, Marcus discovers an undisclosed easement making the title unmarketable. The property's value has increased to $450,000 since Linda and Marcus executed the Contract of Sale. In jurisdictions allowing loss of bargain damages, Marcus can rescind the contract and collect $50,000 loss of bargain of damages from Linda. If the property's value had decreased to $375,000 during the executory period, Marcus would not have suffered (and thus could not collect) any loss of bargain damages.

The courts split on whether a purchaser can get loss of bargain damages when a seller acts in good faith yet fails to deliver marketable title. The majority of courts allow loss of bargain damages, but many courts allow only restitution of the earnest money deposit and incidental out of pocket expenses.

The nonbreaching party also may seek "**incidental**," "**nominal**," or "**reliance**" **damages** and expenses incurred up until the time of breach. Funds spent on appraisers, surveyors, lawyers, fix-up costs, utilities, taxes, interest on loans, title examination fees, moving expenses, temporary housing expenses, and increased construction costs qualify as incidental, nominal, or reliance expenses. Awarding incidental expenses to the nonbreaching party puts the nonbreaching party back in the financial position he or she would have been had the parties not entered into the sales contract in the first place. Noting the inconsistency of allowing both loss of bargain damages and incidental damages, most courts do not allow the nonbreaching party to collect all incidental damages if the party receives loss of bargain damages, the theory being that the nonbreaching party would have incurred the incidental expenses had the sale closed, and thus the nonbreaching party is fully compensated by the loss of bargain damages. Incidental expenses not related to the sale or acquisition of the property still can be awarded in addition to loss of bargain damages.

In some circumstances a nonbreaching party can collect **consequential** damages for damages foreseeable by the breaching party. Generally, lost profits on anticipated resale of the property or lost rents would fall into this category. Since the profits need to be proved and not be merely speculative, courts are reluctant to award consequential damages in many cases. Courts not awarding loss of bargain damages for good faith defaults will not award consequential damages on good faith defaults, either.

The difficulty of proving damages at times leads parties, especially sellers, to insert liquidated damages clauses, either as an option or as the exclusive remedy, into the sales contract. The **liquidated damages** clause fixes the amount of damages on default and often provides that upon the purchaser's default the purchaser forfeits the downpayment or earnest money to the seller. As long as the liquidated damages clause is reasonable and not punitive and does not serve as a penalty, a court will enforce the liquidated damages clause. Technically, a court must find the liquidated damages clause to be a reasonable estimate of potential damages, and the seller's actual damages must be difficult or impossible to measure. If a court finds the liquidated damages clause is unreasonable, the seller must prove actual damages and refund any excess earnest money to the purchaser.

EQUITABLE CONVERSION AND RISK OF LOSS

Although the seller holds legal title to, and probably possession of, the property until closing, many ownership risks and benefits pass to the purchaser immediately upon execution of the sales contract. The purchaser, for example, suffers or benefits from any changes in the property's fair market value between the date the sales contract is signed and the closing. This "shift" of many of the incidents of ownership to the purchaser once the sales contract is executed is called **equitable conversion**. The purchaser's interest is deemed an interest in **real property**. Meanwhile, although the seller is still the legal and record owner, the seller no longer is deemed to own an interest in real property. His ownership interest is in the sales contract, which is deemed to be **personal property**. Thus, for example, if a seller or purchaser dies intestate during the executory period, the seller's interest passes according to the personal property provision of the intestate succession statute and the purchaser's interest passes according to the real property provisions. Similar results follow if the testator's will transfers real property to one beneficiary and personal property to another beneficiary: the seller's interest passes as personalty and the purchaser's interest passes as realty.

One troubling issue (unless the sales contract specifically addresses it) is which party bears the **risk of loss** during the executory period if the property is completely or partially destroyed by fire or by natural causes such as by flood, storm, or earthquake, or is affected by government actions such as rezoning, annexation, or condemnation. The answer varies depending on the jurisdiction, and sometimes on who has possession and on whether the property is insured. Consistent with the idea of equitable conversion that the purchaser is the equitable owner of the property, the traditional rule places the risk of loss from events in the executory period on the purchaser. In contrast, a growing number of states demand the seller deliver the subject of the contract—i.e., the building—and if the seller cannot deliver the building, there is a **substantial failure of consideration**. In these states, therefore, the seller bears the risk of loss. Yet other states place the risk of loss on the seller unless the purchaser goes into possession, at which point the purchaser bears the risk of loss.

Seeking equity, courts may order specific performance, but **abate** (reduce) the purchase price for the loss of value attributable to the damaged or destroyed building. In these states, either the buyer or seller can seek specific performance, and a court in equity may abate the purchase price.

Property insurance complicates the analysis. In most but not all states both seller and purchaser have insurable interests in the property during the executory period. As long as the party saddled with the risk of loss carries insurance, no problem arises. Only when one party, usually the purchaser, bears the risk of loss and the other party, usually the seller, carries the insurance do courts adjust rights. While a few courts allow a seller both to receive insurance proceeds and collect the full sales price, the majority generally require the seller to apply the insurance proceeds against the sales price on the theory the seller holds the insurance in **constructive trust** for the purchaser.

If the risk of loss is on the seller and the purchaser carries insurance, some courts allow the purchaser both to keep the insurance proceeds and to rescind the sales contract. Other courts impose a constructive trust on the purchaser, requiring the purchaser to turn the insurance proceeds over to the seller, but allowing an abatement in the purchase price if the purchaser closes the sale, or allowing the purchaser to keep the proceeds but allowing no abatement in the purchase price. Yet others prohibit the purchaser from receiving the insurance proceeds, and deem the seller, as legal owner, to receive the proceeds as the third party beneficiary of the insurance contract.

Examples

Restrictions of Record

1. The Balboas contract to sell their home to the Ricardos. The sales contract does not mention the quality of title to be transferred. The sales contract merely says the Balboas will transfer the property "subject to all covenants, easements, restrictions, and encumbrances of record applicable to this property." While researching the deed records in the county courthouse, the Ricardos' attorney finds, among other documents, an easement held by Exxon Corporation to run a gas pipeline through the northeast corner of the property's backyard. Can the Ricardos refuse to close?

Violation? What Violation?

2. The Nelsons contracted to sell their home to the Andersons. The Andersons paid the Nelsons $2,000 earnest money on executing the sales contract, with the balance of the purchase price to be paid on delivery of a warranty deed conveying marketable title, the title to be free and clear of all encumbrances except those encumbrances enumerated in the sales contract. One of the referenced encumbrances was the recorded subdivision plat and its restrictions. The recorded subdivision plat contained a ten-foot setback that prohibited any building or part thereof from being located within ten feet of the adjoining property line. The Nelsons' house was four feet from the north boundary line in violation of the subdivision plat covenant. The Nelsons obtained written assurances from a title insurance company that, for an additional fee, which the Nelsons were willing to pay, the title company would insure the "over the building line" exception at issue.

   The Andersons refused to close, buying another home instead. The Nelson sold their home to other people for $5,000 less than the price in the sales contract with the Andersons. The Nelsons sued the Andersons for damages. The Andersons countersued to recover the $2,000 earnest money. What result?

What Violation? Part II

3. Willie Sellit bought his home in 1955. In 2002 he contracted to sell the home to the Knoweighs. The sales contract provided Sellit would transfer to the Knoweighs "good and marketable title, free of liens and encumbrances except for use and occupancy restrictions of public record that are generally applicable to properties in the immediate neighborhood or subdivision." A covenant in every deed to every house in the subdivision, including Sellit's deed in 1955, contained the following restriction: "No residence or dwelling shall be erected within 75 feet of the streets and avenues designated in the subdivision plat." The front of Sellit's home was 44 feet from Woodlawn Avenue. The four homes closest to Sellit's home were 40, 44, 45, and 45 feet, respectively, from Woodlawn Avenue. There never has been any litigation with regard to any of the violations. Two title insurance companies were willing to insure the property as marketable. A third title insurance company would guarantee the dwelling could remain as located, but would not guarantee or insure the property's marketability. The Knoweighs refused to close. Sellit seeks specific performance. The Knoweighs counterclaim for a return of their earnest money. Who prevails?

Stop, Look, and Pay Attention

4. Lionel contracted to buy 200 acres of land he intended to use for cattle grazing. Before committing to the purchase, he walked the

fence forming the boundary of the farm. At one point Lionel stood on some railroad tracks while the real estate agent explained how the current owner used gates to rotate cattle from one grazing field to another. The sales contract provided that Lionel would receive marketable title and that the property would be free from all restrictions, covenants, easements, and encumbrances except for two utility easements, an easement for an underground gas line, and an easement across the easternmost part of the farm in favor of a neighbor to reach the county road adjoining the property. The sales contract did not mention a railroad easement on record nor an outstanding $50,000 mortgage. Can Lionel rescind the sales contract, claiming unmarketable title?

Buyer Beware: Caveat Emptor

5. The Dixons plan to sell their home. Which of the following must they disclose to prospective purchasers?
   (a) Basement floods after heavy rains.
   (b) Leaky water pipe in basement.
   (c) Home being connected to a new sewer system for which a special property tax assessment was likely.
   (d) Empty, out-of-service underground petroleum storage tanks in backyard.
   (e) Seven people murdered in the house ten years ago.
   (f) Reputation in the community that the ghosts of the seven murder victims haunt the house (an article has appeared in the local paper).
   (g) A landfill is located one-half mile from the home.
   (h) A convicted child molester lives on the block.

Fire Sale

6. (a) Ernest and Julia Gallow on March 15 contracted to sell a cabin on five acres to Christian and Christie Crier. The Criers deposited $1000 earnest money toward the $100,000 purchase price. Closing was scheduled for May 1. On March 25 the cabin was destroyed by fire. The fire was not the fault of either the Gallows or the Criers. The Criers refuse to close and demand a refund of their earnest money. The Gallows seek specific performance. Who prevails?
   (b) Under the sales contract, the Criers were allowed immediate possession of the cabin and five acres. The Criers moved their personal belongings into the cabin on March 20. Does this affect your answer?
   (c) Assume the sales contract provided that "should the premises be materially damaged by fire or other casualty prior to closing, this contract shall be voidable at the option of Buyer." Would this clause change the result in (a)?

(d) Assume the Criers purchased insurance on the cabin, $50,000 coverage on the cabin and $50,000 coverage on the contents of the cabin. The Criers were the insureds. Ernest and Julia Gallow were listed as other persons having an interest in the property. Would the existence of the property insurance affect your answer? Who receives the insurance proceeds?

Death and Other Incidental Matters

7. On May 1 Michelle contracted to sell and Barry contracted to buy for $100,000 a vacant lot subject to all covenants, easements, restrictions, and encumbrances of record. The contract set August 1 as the closing date.

   (a) Michelle died June 1. Her will directed that all her real property pass to her husband and that all her personal property go to a trust for the benefit of her two children. Who receives the $100,000 at closing? What result if Barry is able to rescind the contract?

   (b) Michelle survived, but the city on June 1 rezoned the lot from commercial to residential use only. Barry intended to use the lot to carry on his clothing business. The value of the lot dropped to $75,000 immediately upon the rezoning. Barry wants to rescind the contract. What result?

   (c) Michelle lived. The property is zoned residential. Because of the large number of loans and real estate purchases being made, and delays by surveyors, appraisers, and title researchers, the lending institution did not approve Barry's loan application until August 10. By the time all documents were drafted, the earliest the parties could close would be August 15, which was two weeks after the August 1 closing date stipulated in the sales contract. A second purchaser approached Michelle in July, offering her $125,000 for the lot. Barry wants to close. Michelle wants to rescind the contract and sell to the second purchaser. What outcome?

Explanations

Restrictions of Record

1. No. Even though the sales contract did not mention the quality of title to be transferred, unless otherwise stated, a sales contract contains an implied condition that the seller will convey marketable title. The sales contract did not mention Exxon's easement. If the Balboas in the sales contract had listed specific covenants, restrictions, easements, and other encumbrances on the property, accidentally omitting Exxon's gas line easement, the omission would have made the title unmarketable. In the Example, however, instead of listing covenants, restrictions, easements,

and other encumbrances, the Balboas transferred the property subject to all restrictions of record. A transfer of this type means the purchaser is willing to accept the property subject to all documents filed in the deed records. The sellers are protected against inadvertent omissions by inserting the general reference to all documents in the deed records. The purchasers, on the other hand, are best served by specific enumerations of the encumbrances.

Violation? What Violation?

2. The putative purchasers, the Andersons, win and are entitled to a return of their earnest money. The sellers, the Nelsons, must convey marketable title. Marketable title is not perfect title. It is a title that a reasonable person would accept because the indicated defect would not affect market value or subject the owner to an unreasonable risk of litigation.

   The title defect in the Example is not the existence of the ten-foot setback restriction. The purchasers (the Andersons) accepted the restriction in the recorded subdivision plat, including the ten-foot setback restriction. The violation of the setback requirement is a defect, however. Since this is a restriction in a subdivision plat, every landowner in the subdivision has standing to enforce it. A reasonable purchaser understandably might be reluctant to buy the property for fear of future litigation. A reasonable fear of potential litigation is a polestar of unmarketable title.

   The title insurance company's willingness to insure the "over the building line" exception does not change the result. Buying insurance would not "cure" the defect. It may reduce the financial concern of litigation and possibly the cost of reconstructing the home, but it does nothing to remove the specter of litigation. The Andersons contracted for marketable title, not the lower insurable title standard. Finally, although the reason is unknown why the Nelsons sold the home to the second purchasers for a lesser price, unless market conditions changed, the purchase price reduction may be directly related to the new purchasers knowing about the violation: another indication the title was unmarketable.

What Violation? Part II

3. Sellit wins. Specific performance ordered. Willie Sellit agreed to transfer marketable title. Marketable title is not perfect title, but is that title that a reasonable purchaser, who is well informed as to the facts and legal consequences, would accept in the exercise of prudence of a reasonable business person. Here, as in Example 2, the defect is the violation of a restriction: the house being 44 feet from Woodlawn Avenue when a covenant mandates any residence to be 75 feet from the avenue.

Not every defect or threat of suit makes a title unmarketable. Minor encumbrances or unlikely occurrences, for example, do not make a title unmarketable. The issue in this Example turns on whether a reasonable purchaser would fear a lawsuit because of the violation. A reasonable purchaser would purchase the house — the houses have been so situated for nearly half a century with no hint of litigation, other owners would be barred by acquiescence or some prescriptive period, and at least the four closest neighbors are estopped from enforcing the covenant since their homes too are in violation of the restriction, so no reasonable purchaser would anticipate a lawsuit. The title being marketable, the Knoweighs must honor the sales contract.

Can we reconcile Examples 2 and 3? Certainly, in the sense we can (or at least should) agree no lawsuit would occur in Example 3, and a real chance exists a lawsuit could occur in Example 2 since the house may have been the only one in the neighborhood that so substantially violated the ten-foot setback. That distinction accents the importance of the necessary factual inquiry into how a "reasonable purchaser" would react, a reminder that facts drive the law.

Example 2 is the more difficult factual inquiry. While the facts do not indicate how long the house has been in violation of the subdivision restriction, it seems unlikely that anyone would sue to have the house removed at this stage. If that is so, Example 2 should be resolved the same as Example 3. Some jurisdictions, when dealing with Example 2, do not look at the degree of risk of litigation for violations of restrictive covenants or of zoning ordinances. These jurisdictions find the title unmarketable because the possibility of a lawsuit exists, and the purchaser should not have to enter into a lawsuit to determine if a court would find a reasonable purchaser would purchase the property. In those jurisdictions a court might rule in favor of the Knoweighs in Example 3.

Stop, Look, and Pay Attention

4. The outstanding $50,000 mortgage does not make the title unmarketable. Lionel must notify the seller of the defect and the seller has until (and including) closing to remove the mortgage. In most cases, the seller uses the sales proceeds to satisfy the $50,000 debt and the mortgage is released. Courts seldom if ever find a title unmarketable as long as the sales price exceeds the cumulative amount of outstanding debt against the property since it is so customary to use the sales proceeds to retire outstanding mortgages at closing.

    The railroad easement poses a more interesting question. Lionel saw the railroad tracks. He even stood on them. Many states, probably the majority of states, hold visible easements do not make a title unmarketable. Courts following this approach conclude the purchaser was willing to purchase the property subject to the easement, and probably adjusted the sales price for the easement. At the other extreme, some courts, probably a minority of courts, would find the title unmarketable even though Lionel admittedly saw the tracks. All encumbrances must be mentioned or referenced in the sales contract for title to be marketable in these states. A third grouping of cases seems to indicate visible easements on the edge of the property or that benefit the property such as roads and utility easements do not make the title unmarketable, but that other visible easements do make the title unmarketable. Since the railroad easement would not benefit Lionel, under this third approach the title is unmarketable.

Buyer Beware: Caveat Emptor

5. In many states, as long as the Dixons do not affirmatively deceive any purchasers or engage in any active concealment, they would not be required to disclose any of the listed items. CAVEAT EMPTOR! Because the Dixons are selling a used home and are not builders or developers, they may not have a duty to disclose even in some states imposing a duty to disclose. In states judicially requiring disclosures, the Dixons could avoid the duty to disclose several of the listed conditions because the purchaser or his agent by reasonable inspection could spot the defects.

If a state has a statutory disclosure law or forms, the statutory provisions control. Under California law, to illustrate, a disclosure form (see West's Ann. Cal. Civ. Code § 1102.6) would require disclosure of the following from the Example: Plumbing problems, which may reach the leaky pipes; sewer problems, which probably does not reach the prospective future sewer; fuel or chemical storage tanks, which probably reaches the empty, out-of-service tanks; flooding problems, which should reach the basement flooding; and neighborhood noise problems or other nuisances, which may or may not reach the landfill. Apparently mass murders and poltergeists are not material defects in California. Compare these results to the discussion of the specific Examples below when there is no statute on point:

(a) Basement flooding epitomizes defects that can be discovered upon inspection, even when no rain has fallen and the basement is dry. Courts find most basement flooding to be visible and not latent. No duty to disclose.

(b) Leaky pipes in the basement are open and visible if the pipes are visible (which most pipes in basements are) or if the evidence of previous damage is observable. There is likely no duty to disclose.

(c) The New York court resolving this issue said normally there is no duty to disclose future tax assessments. See Bethka v. Jensen, 672 N.Y.S.2d 494 (App. Div. 1998). New York is a caveat emptor, no duty to disclose, state. Thus normally the holding would not be helpful in answering Example 5(c) in a state mandating disclosure of material latent defects. In *Bethka*, the plaintiff purchaser alleged the seller affirmatively engaged in conduct that deceived the purchaser. The appellate court remanded on this issue.

The court held that if the purchaser could have found out about the sewer and the tax assessment by inquiring of government officials, the seller would not be liable even though the seller had acted deceptively. The implication is that the Dixons would not have to disclose the facts, even if the state requires disclosure of material latent defects, as long as the purchasers could learn of the situation by inquiring of proper authorities.

(d) As long as the tanks are not being used and pose no health or environmental risks, no disclosure is required under state law. But — and this is a big but — disclosure probably is mandatory because of state environmental statutes.

(e) If the state has abolished caveat emptor for material latent defects, the seller may be required to disclose the facts of the seven murders. Clearly the fact of the murders is not observable by inspection (we hope the bodies are no longer there!). The remaining issue is whether the fact of the murders is material. Materiality is determined by whether the occurrence of the seven murders significantly affects the value of the house. The defect involved here is known as a psychological defect. Since some people would not want to live in a house where a mass murder occurred, and others would not want to have people constantly reminding them they live in the house where the mass murders occurred, it seems a good case could be made that disclosure be made. CAVEAT: In some states, by statute, sellers are not required to disclose psychological or stigma conditions. Such a statute would result in no duty to disclose in this Example.

(f) Seven ghosts for seven murders! If required to disclose under (e), the Dixons would be required to disclose here also. Your casebook likely reproduces the only case to address this haunting issue, Stambovsky v. Ackley, 572 N.Y.S.2d 672 (App. Div. 1991). In that case the court held a seller who had disseminated information to publicize her haunted house was obligated to disclose that reputation to purchasers. The court mentioned, but did not develop, that the seller may have to disclose a reputation resulting from actual possession of poltergeists, presumably whether or not the seller actively sought the publicity. The court had no reason to discuss actual possession, or what happens if the seller did not publicize the haunting.

We could get into a spirited debate whether sellers who did not publicize the haunting must disclose the presence of ghosts or the reputation that ghosts haunt the house. The cautious seller would be advised to disclose since in all likelihood seven apparitions sharing the house embody the essence of a material psychological defect. Presumably the ghosts are not easily observable on inspection. In states where caveat emptor survives, no disclosure is required except in the *Stambovsky* situation.

(g) Generally, a seller is required to disclose only conditions on the property, not off-site conditions. The case discussing this exact problem limited the duty to disclose the existence of the landfill one-half mile from the home to professional sellers — generally the developer or builder. See Strawn v. Canuso, 140 N.J. 3, 657 A.2d 420 (1995). Sellers of used houses, such as the Dixons, would have no duty to disclose. Note that if the test truly is whether the condition is a material latent defect known to seller and important to a reasonable purchaser, the status of the seller as a private citizen or professional seller should not matter. Strawn's holding sensibly recognizes that a nonprofessional seller will not know what should be disclosed. The Example also shows why legislated disclosure forms are gaining favor with both sellers and purchasers.

(h) A convicted child molester is not only an off-site matter, but arguably is a person and not a condition. Some disclosure-prone states might require disclosure of noisy neighbors, or noise from a nearby bar, on the theory that they are nuisances. Generally, however, sellers of used property have limited duties to disclose off-site conditions. There is some question whether a person constitutes a condition. A few commentators, citing the proliferation of Megan's Laws designed to inform citizens of sex offenders residing in the community, push for sellers' disclosing sex offenders and child molesters in the neighborhood.

Fire Sale

6. (a) Under the doctrine of equitable conversion, purchasers are deemed equitable owners of the property as soon as the parties enter into the sales contract, and must bear or benefit from changes in value and bear the risk of loss should the property be destroyed or damaged between the execution of the sales contract and the closing. Under the traditional rule, a court would order specific performance. Gallows win. Criers weep.

The doctrine of equitable conversion developed at a time when land tended to be more important to and a more valuable part of the transaction than the structures on the land. Arguably, that situation is reversed today and structures are often the most significant part of the purchased property. A growing number of jurisdictions in fact place the risk of loss on sellers under the theory the improvements are a substantial part of the bargain and the contract is voidable for failure of consideration or impossibility of performance of the contract. In the majority of jurisdictions, however, equitable conversion prevails and purchasers bear the risk of loss.

(b) Possession is important in some states. In those states, a seller bears the risk of loss if the seller retains possession or no one takes physical possession. The risk of loss passes to the purchaser once the purchaser takes possession or at closing, whichever occurs first. In these states the Criers bear the risk of loss.

In some states, on the other hand, the risk of loss remains with the seller notwithstanding the purchaser's possession. In these states the Gallows must bear the risk of loss, and the Criers would receive their earnest money back.

In the majority of states, where the risk of loss passes to the purchasers on execution of the sales contract, the Criers as purchasers would be liable with or without right of possession, and even if the Gallows remained in possession.

(c) The clause could reverse the result completely. Equitable conversion is a default provision. The parties can override the doctrine of equitable conversion by drafting a provision in the sales contract. The provision places the risk of loss squarely on the sellers. The Criers can void the contract and have their $1,000 earnest money returned. The sales contract says the Criers have the option of voiding the contract. If, in contrast to the facts of the Example, the Criers choose to go forward with the transaction, an issue arises whether the Criers should receive an abatement in the purchase price, reducing the price by the decrease in value resulting from the destruction of the cabin. While the ultimate answer is still to be determined, at least two courts have indicated the purchaser can receive an abatement in price.

(d) Issues and alternatives galore arise in this Example. The only easy part is that the Criers can collect for the contents of the cabin. If the Criers elect to continue the contract, the Criers receive the insurance proceeds. Since abatement of the purchase price is an equitable remedy, most if not all courts would refuse to abate the purchase price; or at least the courts would reduce the amount of abatement by the insurance paid to the purchasers. Otherwise the purchasers (the Criers) would receive a windfall ($50,000 insurance and $50,000 price abatement) and the sellers (Gallows) suffer a $50,000 economic loss. Courts, therefore, likely would require the purchasers electing to continue the purchase to pay the full purchase price.

If the Criers refuse to close: One line of analysis would treat the insurance contract and the sales contract as unrelated contracts, allowing the Criers both to void the sales contract and to collect the $50,000 on the insurance policy. Many courts, probably the majority, follow this logic.

A few courts consider this line of analysis a case of judicial tunnel vision. When purchasers refuse to close, these courts require the purchasers (the Criers) or the insurance company to pay the insurance proceeds to the sellers (the Gallows) under the theory the Criers hold the proceeds in constructive trust to be received by the party that ends up with the property. Some courts invoke this theory only if the sales contract requires the purchasers to carry the insurance. As noted in the previous paragraph, the majority of courts would not require the purchasers to pay proceeds to the seller.

A more common problem occurs when the insurance company refuses to pay the purchaser because the purchaser does not have an insurable interest or, more likely if the purchaser voids the sales contract, the insured purchaser suffered no loss on the fire and therefore is not entitled to any insurance proceeds. A minority of courts agree with the insurer's argument. Most courts reject this theory, holding instead that the insurer accepted the premiums and must pay the insured. Most courts receptive to the insurer's argument in this situation nonetheless find the seller to be a third party beneficiary of the contract, especially if, as in the Example, the seller is listed as a party having an interest in the property. Since the seller did suffer a loss, the insurer must pay the insurance proceeds to the seller, the Gallows, in our Example.

Death and Other Incidental Matters

7. (a) Unless a state statute to the contrary controls, under equitable conversion principles, the contract right to the proceeds passes as personal property. The $100,000 sales proceeds go to the trust for the benefit of Michelle's two children.

If Barry rescinds the contract because the title was unmarketable, most courts treat the property as real property. Under that approach, the property would pass to Michelle's husband. A similar result follows if the purchaser refuses to close based on a condition in the contract.

On the other hand, if the purchaser defaults, and a seller would have the option of accepting liquidated damages or of seeking specific performance, the property passes to the legatee of personal property: in the Example, for the benefit of the two children. Under this theory, the purchaser becomes the equitable debtor on the execution of the sales contract. When the debtor/purchaser defaults, the property is returned to the equitable creditor, the trust for the two children in our Example, to satisfy the outstanding debt and not as a rescission of the sales contract.

(b) If nothing in the sales contract specifically addresses the problem, the risk that the city would rezone the property is borne by the purchaser. Barry cannot rescind even though the property's value declined and even though the property no longer can serve Barry's intended purposes. If Michelle knew both that the zoning change was imminent and that Barry intended to use the property for commercial purposes, a few courts under equitable principles may refuse to order specific performance.

(c) The issue turns on whether Barry materially breached the sales contract by failing to close on August 1. Courts tolerate tardy performances of real estate contracts because of the many unavoidable delays commonly encountered in real estate sales. Time ordinarily is not regarded to be of the essence absent an express stipulation in the sales contract, or unless the surrounding circumstances indicate timing is critical. Barry would have a reasonable time to close. While what is a reasonable delay under the circumstances is a matter for a jury or judge as fact finder, the two weeks' delay in the Example appears reasonable. A court should order specific performance.

Real Estate Closings

THE CLOSING OR SETTLEMENT PROCESS

A seller or grantor usually transfers title to property to the buyer at a **closing** or a *settlement*. Typically at closing, a bank, savings or loan association, or other financial institution loans the buyer money to complete the purchase, the buyer pays the seller, and the parties sign a series of documents required by the sales contract, the lender, or federal or state law. Closing does not need to be this complex, however. A grantor can write a deed on any paper and receive money from the purchaser without any of the other incidents associated with a formal closing.

Sellers transfer interests in property by a **deed**. Property passes by other means, of course — by will, intestate succession, court order, adverse possession, and prescription, for example — but the normal manner, whether the transfer is a sale or a gift, is a transfer by deed. The "modern deed" must be in writing to satisfy the Statute of Frauds, and must contain (a) the grantor's name, (b) the grantee's name, (c) words that indicate an intent to convey the property or an interest in the property (the "words of grant"), (d) a description or identification of the property, (e) the interest being transferred (though a fee simple will be assumed unless the deed stipulates a lesser interest), and (f) the grantor's signature.

The deed should recite any covenants, conditions, easements, equitable servitudes, leases, mineral rights, or other encumbrances burdening the property (but not government regulations). If the grantee is to assume a mortgage or take the property subject to a debt, that too should be listed. A general reference, such as **subject to all restrictions of record**, is adequate to subject the grantee to all restrictions found in the official deed records.

Most deeds are recorded at a local government office, often the county courthouse. State statutes require that all documents to be accepted for recording be **acknowledged** before a notary public or other authorized person, or, alternatively in some states, to have witnesses sign or **attest** as to the grantor's signature on the deed. Recording a deed pursuant to a state's recording statute is critical to protecting title and to finding a willing purchaser or lender at a later date. As a practical matter, therefore, even though an unacknowledged and unattested deed transfers title, most purchasers insist on acknowledged deeds (or at least attested deeds). Strict compliance with the state's acknowledgment or attestation law is essential for an effective acknowledgment or attestation.

Although deeds are not limited to any one format, some forms have evolved. The two most common are referred to as the "long form" deed and the "statutory short form" deed. Both contain the essential items set out above. The main difference between the two is the statutory short form deed excludes (and the long form incorporates) the "habendum clause," a clause following the property description and beginning with the words, "To Have and to Hold. . . ." The habendum clause usually contains the warranties of title.

Only the grantor as the party to be bound must sign the deed. Grantees are NOT required to sign the deed. Grantees are not required to sign the deed even if, as is likely, the deed binds the grantee to honor covenants, conditions, easements, or other encumbrances included in the deed and even if the grantee through the deed agrees to assume or take the property subject to a mortgage. The oft-repeated rationale is that the grantee by accepting the benefits flowing from the deed accepts all the obligations and encumbrances stipulated in the deed.

If the grantor is married, the deed should indicate the grantor owns the property as his or her separate estate (assuming that is the case). If the seller's spouse has an interest under community property laws, as a tenant by the entirety, joint tenant, or tenant in common, or has a curtesy, dower, or homestead interest, the spouse also must execute the deed.

Nothing requires the deed to recite the consideration paid for the property. But partly from habit and partly for other reasons, including serving to show the purchaser is a **bona fide purchaser for value**, most scriveners include the consideration, or at least a symbolic consideration such as "ten dollars and other consideration." Centuries ago in England, when a large portion of the populace was illiterate, grantors embossed their **seal** onto the deed in lieu of or in addition to their signature. The seal became a requirement for an effective deed. A few states retain the seal requirement, but the majority of states have dispensed with the seal requirement.

DELIVERY

In general, a deed transfers title only when (1) the grantor intends to presently convey an interest in property, (2) the grantor delivers a deed to the grantee, and (3) the grantee accepts the deed. The easiest element to satisfy is the grantee's **acceptance** since the grantee's acceptance is presumed if owning the property would be beneficial to the grantee.

Of the three elements, **intent to presently convey** an interest is the most critical element. The grantor's delivery of the deed is a physical demonstration of the grantor's intent to convey title. Even though black letter law holds that a deed transfers title only when the deed is delivered and accepted, exceptions and variations abound. A deed, for example, can be delivered without title passing because the grantor did not intend to transfer title. Conversely, title can pass without delivery of a deed to the grantee in the right circumstances such as when the grantor records the deed in the deed records. Most cases turn on their particular facts.

Courts often resort to **rebuttable presumptions** to resolve delivery issues. For example, a court will presume a deed in the grantee's possession has been delivered to the grantee. Conversely, courts presume the grantor did not deliver the deed if the grantor retains possession of the deed. Likewise, courts presume acknowledged and recorded deeds have been delivered. In some states, in fact, a recorded deed forms an **irrebuttable presumption** the deed was delivered when one of the parties to a later dispute is a subsequent bona fide purchaser for value. In practice, the burden to rebut the presumptions is not high. Courts readily find a presumption of delivery or nondelivery rebutted if the facts so indicate. The presumptions merely establish who bears the burden of proof and persuasion in the controversy.

(a) Sales and Commercial Transfers

Delivery usually causes no problems in sales transactions since the grantor delivers the deed at closing or gives the deed to an independent third party, known as the escrow agent, who will deliver the deed on the happening of conditions precedent to the transfer. An occasional case involves someone who through some nefarious act picks up a deed or tricks the grantor into giving him the deed; or some confusion arises when the grantor and grantee enter into a **contract for deed** (also known as an **installment sales contract**). A court in these cases will conclude there was no delivery unless the grantor intended to convey title when the ostensible grantee took possession of the deed.

Delivery in many situations turns on whether the grantor can retrieve the deed and stop or revoke the transfer before the grantee takes possession of the deed. A grantor's giving the deed to the grantor's agent, for example, is not a delivery until the agent gives the deed to the grantee. Conversely, a grantor's handing the deed to a grantee's agent does constitute a delivery.

In some commercial transactions the parties use a third party — an escrow agent or escrowee — to hold the deed and pass the deed to the grantee after the grantee satisfies conditions set out in a valid sales contract. Under the escrow agreement the grantor cannot retrieve or revoke the deed unless the grantee materially breaches the sales contract or fails to satisfy a condition within a reasonable time. This is true even if the grantor dies before the conditions are met. As soon as the grantee meets the conditions, the escrow agent delivers the deed to the grantee. For theoretical tidiness, once the grantee satisfies the stipulated conditions, courts find the title **relates back** to the date the grantor initially delivered the deed to the escrow agent.

(b) Donative and Testamentary Transfers

Problems occur more frequently in informal transfers epitomized by donative or gift transfers related to the grantor's death. As background, you should know that a deed does not qualify as the vehicle for **testamentary transfers**; only documents meeting all statutory formalities under a **Statute of Wills** serve to transfer property at a grantor's death. A deed to be effective must deliver title during the grantor's lifetime. The deed does not have to guarantee **present possession**, and in fact may delay the grantee's possession until the grantor's death, but the deed must grant an immediate **interest** in the property to the grantee. To use the terminology learned when you studied estates in land, a deed is delivered if it passes a **present interest** or a **future interest**, but the interest must pass immediately, not at some future time. If the facts surrounding the handing over of the deed indicate the deed is to take effect at a later date, there is no delivery until that later date. Delivery occurring after the grantor's death in donative transfer situations cannot transfer title. Consider the following examples.

Example 1:   A grantor executes a deed but does not deliver the deed to the intended grantee. The grantee knows nothing about the deed until the deed is found after the grantor's death. A court in this situation usually will find the deed was not delivered. In most cases an executed deed still in the grantor's possession fails the delivery element.

Example 2:   A grantor places a deed someplace under the grantee's control but does not tell the grantee about the deed, knowing the grantee will find the deed later (perhaps after the grantor's death). The grantee finds the deed after grantor dies. A court might find the requisite intent and delivery under these facts.

Example 3: A grantor places a deed in a safe deposit box used by both the grantor and the grantee. Grantee finds the deed after grantor dies. Because the grantee has access and control over the safe deposit box, many courts find the grantor's placing the deed in the safe deposit box indicates grantor intended to deliver the deed and in fact did deliver the deed to grantee. Other courts find no delivery since the grantor also has control over the safe deposit box and can revoke the transfer simply by retrieving the deed before grantee takes physical possession.

Example 4: A grantor hands a deed to an intended grantee with instructions that the grantee is to record the deed if the grantee outlives the grantor. The grantor dies. Since the grantor attempted to pass an interest at some future date after his death rather than to pass a future interest immediately, the grantor had no intent currently to transfer title. Consequently, a court would conclude the deed has not been "delivered" until the grantor died. The grantor in this scenario tried to use the deed as a will. Since the deed does not meet the statutory prerequisites of a will, the deed cannot operate to effect a testamentary transfer.

Example 5: A grantor hands the deed to an intended grantee with instructions that the grantee is to record the deed *after* the grantor's death. The grantor dies. Courts differ on the result. A court rationally could hold the result should be the same as that in the previous Example for the same reason given there: no delivery because the grantor attempted a testamentary transfer. Other courts would uphold the deed as a present delivery of a future interest. Many courts holding the deed was delivered will conclude the oral condition is void as inconsistent with the delivery of a deed. Thus the grantee could record the deed at any time before or after the grantor's death.

Similar issues follow if the grantor hands the deed to an escrow agent with instructions to deliver the deed to a grantee after the grantor's death. Some courts hold no delivery occurred on the familiar theory that the arrangement is a failed testamentary transfer. A few courts hold the grantor's death terminates the agent's power to deliver the deed, so delivery is impossible. Other courts, possibly the majority of courts, liken the arrangement to a trust such that delivery occurs when the grantor hands the deed to the escrow agent, or hold that the delivery **relates back** to the time the grantor handed the deed to the agent as long as the grantor cannot revoke the deed and the grantor did not condition the agent's delivering the deed on the grantee's surviving the grantor.

Example 6: A grantor hands a deed to the grantee, the grantor reserving a life estate. The deed here is delivered since some interest in the property inures to the grantee immediately.

Example 7: A grantor gives a deed to a grantee, the grantor both reserving a life estate and retaining the power to revoke the deed. The reservation alone will not obviate an otherwise true delivery. Many courts look at the realities of the situation, however, and hold that the grantee holds no legal interest. To them, the grantor retains the life estate and current possession, and has the power until the grantor's death to revoke the deed. In effect, the deed is little more than an expectation that does not ripen into an interest until the grantor dies or releases the power to revoke the deed. Until that time, no delivery occurs. This is especially true if the grantor continues using the property, paying property taxes, and collecting income from the property. In contrast, other courts find the delivery good as long as the grantor intends to pass the interest immediately to the grantee. These courts regard the power to revoke as a condition subsequent, and the grantee owns an interest in the land until the grantor exercises the power to revoke. Since some interest is currently transferred to the grantee, the deed is delivered.

Either result can be justified depending on your view of the world. It appears the arrangement is a will substitute. If you believe the Statute of Wills is an important device to protect decedents and *heirs and devisees* from overreaching or fraud, and the grantor has a will, or his heirs are deserving, holding the deed is not delivered is consistent with those goals. If, on the other hand, you view the deed as a poor person's version of a trust, a trust being effective even if the grantor reserves a life estate and a power to revoke, and the deed carries out the grantor's intent, then a finding that delivery has occurred is the proper conclusion.

MORTGAGES

(a) Mechanics of Mortgages

Purchasers often borrow money to buy real estate, especially real estate improved with homes or other buildings. While a buyer may borrow from various sources, including her employer and family members, the most common sources of financing are the seller and financial institutions such as banks, savings and loan associations, and credit unions.

When a person borrows money to buy real property, say a home, he or she usually signs two documents. One document is the **promissory note**, a formal IOU by which the borrower (the debtor) obligates himself or herself to pay the money back to the lender according to certain terms, including the interest to be paid for the use of the money and the timetable for making payments. The other document is the **mortgage**, which provides collateral for or "secures" the debt. Should the **mortgagor** (the borrower) default on the loan (or otherwise breach the terms of the mortgage agreement) the **mortgagee** (the lender) can bring an action (foreclosure) to sell the home and apply the sales proceeds to retire the note.

All other terms and concepts build on this fundamental relationship. For example, if the seller lends the money and becomes the mortgagee, the mortgage is usually called a **seller-financed mortgage or purchase-money mortgage**. The adjectives, however, do not change the essential working of the mortgage as a security mechanism.

Ordinarily the property pledged as security in the mortgage is the purchased real estate, but that is not essential. Other property may serve as the collateral. To illustrate, a person buying a vacation home may pledge the purchased home to secure the mortgage. Alternatively, for various reasons, the vacation home purchaser may pledge his or her primary residence as the collateral underlying the mortgage. If in this last example the buyer defaults on the note, the mortgagee (lender) under the mortgage has priority rights as to the borrower's primary residence, but not to the vacation home.

Sometimes the purchaser gives promissory notes both to a financial institution and to the seller in order to purchase a home. The financial institution will demand it receive the "first" mortgage and the seller will take a "second" mortgage. The ranking of mortgages — "first," "second," "third," etc. — establishes which mortgagees (creditors) have the first right (**priority**) to any sale proceeds should the property be sold. Mortgages and liens of a lower priority are known as **junior liens** or **junior mortgages** while those of a higher priority are **senior liens** or **senior mortgages**. Thus if a person has given three mortgages, the second mortgage is senior to the third mortgage and junior to the first mortgage. As explained in more detail in Chapter 26, infra, a lender should record the mortgage in the local deed records office to protect its status as having first priority to the property.

The party having first priority may use all proceeds from any sale of the home (foreclosure sale) if necessary to satisfy any amounts still owing to the lender. If any sales proceeds remain after satisfying the first mortgage, the money goes to the second mortgage holder, and so on. Any proceeds remaining after satisfying all notes secured by the mortgages belong to the property owner (the mortgagor).

(b) Title Theory and Lien Theory

States fall into two camps concerning the legal ownership of the mortgaged property. A small minority of states subscribe to the **title theory of mortgages**, meaning the lender (mortgagee) has legal title to the mortgaged property until the debt is repaid. This theory developed at a time when the mortgagee (lender) actually took possession of the property or held its legal title until the underlying note was satisfied. Not so today. Today, the borrower retains possession of the property. Accordingly, the vast majority of states favor the **lien theory**, recognizing the mortgage as a security device giving the mortgagee rights to the property when the mortgagor breaches some term of the mortgage. In lien theory states, the mortgagee (lender) has legal title and the mortgagor (borrower) has equitable title in the property.

While some differences in law can be traced to which theory of mortgages a state adopts, generally, due to contracts, statutes, and judicial construction, the differences in practice are not that great. Under neither theory, for example, can the mortgagee's (lender's) creditors force a sale of the collateral to satisfy the mortgagee's debts, and under both theories the mortgagor's creditors can reach the proceeds from the sale of the mortgaged property after the mortgagee's claims have been satisfied.

The major difference between the two theories in actual practice is that under the title theory a mortgagee in some states can go into possession of the property as soon as there is a default and remain in possession during the foreclosure proceedings. In a lien theory state, on the other hand, the mortgagor retains possession until foreclosure proceedings are completed.

(c) Deed of Trust

Two popular alternatives to the mortgage are the deed of trust and the installment land sale contract (also known as the contract for deed). The deed of trust resembles the mortgage. Under the deed of trust the borrower delivers the **deed of trust** to a third party (the trustee), often the lender's attorney, instead of directly to the lender. If the borrower defaults, the trustee can foreclose on the mortgaged property. As discussed below, the deed of trust allows mortgagees to sell the collateral more quickly and cheaply than under the traditional foreclosure process (though traditional mortgages may achieve the same result by incorporating a **power of sale** right in the mortgage).

(d) Installment Land Sale Contract (Contract for Deed)

Under the **installment land sale contract (or contract for deed)**, the seller retains legal title and does not deed the property to the purchaser until the purchaser pays the full purchase price. In the interim executory period, the purchaser takes possession and the parties act pursuant to the sales contract. The payment period under an installment contract (or contract for deed) may be as long as the normal deed and mortgage period — i.e., ten, fifteen, or more years. The purchaser has an equitable interest in the property, but unless the purchaser records the installment sales contract or a memorandum of contract in the local deed records, the purchaser risks losing the property to the seller's creditors or to a bona fide purchaser for value. At one time if a purchaser missed a payment, the purchaser forfeited his interest in the property and the seller kept the property no matter how wide the disparity between the property's fair market value and the amount of the remaining outstanding indebtedness. Today courts treat installment land sale contracts like a deed and mortgage transaction, restricting the seller to proceeds of sale equal to the amount of the remaining debt obligation.

(e) Debt Satisfaction and Assumptions

Once a mortgagor (borrower) satisfies (pays) the underlying debt, the mortgagee releases the mortgage. This *release* should be recorded in the local deed records.

Many mortgages and notes contain a **due-on-sale** clause requiring the entire note balance be paid before the seller can deed the property to a new purchaser. Alternatively, some mortgagees allow subsequent purchasers of the property to continue making payments on the note under the original note terms. The subsequent purchaser can **assume** the note, meaning the purchaser becomes primarily liable on the note. If the underlying property cannot be sold for an amount great enough to retire the secured indebtedness, the mortgagee (lender) usually has **recourse** to the subsequent purchaser's other assets for the deficiency. Instead of assuming the note, a subsequent purchaser may take the property **subject to** a note and mortgage. In this situation the mortgagee (lender) is limited to taking the proceeds from the sale of the property and cannot go after the subsequent purchaser's nonpledged assets. Generally, in either situation, the initial purchaser remains secondarily liable to the mortgagee for any unpaid amounts.

(f) Foreclosure

If the mortgagor (debtor) defaults (generally by not making scheduled payments), a mortgagee (lender) has various options based on the mortgage terms and on state law. In earlier times, and in two states today under some circumstances, a mortgagee through a process known as **strict foreclosure** could petition a court to **foreclose** a mortgagor from **redeeming** his property after the foreclosure date. Once that date arrived, the mortgagee (lender) kept the mortgaged property and the mortgagor was barred (foreclosed) from asserting any rights to the property.

The most common alternative today is the **judicial foreclosure**. The judicial foreclosure affords the mortgagor (debtor) all the procedural safeguards inherent in a judicial proceeding. The mortgagee (lender) files a complaint, the mortgagor answers, and a trial is conducted should the mortgagor allege a foreclosure sale is inappropriate. An officer of the court determines what debts are to be paid from the sales proceeds. If the court orders the property be sold, pertinent auction information must be posted and advertised as prescribed by statute. The foreclosure sale usually is by auction (though an auction is not always mandated, and more traditional sales methods may bring a better price).

In contrast to the strict foreclosure where the mortgagee (lender) succeeds to the title, in the judicial foreclosure mortgagees are entitled only to the sales proceeds up to the amount owed them. Sales proceeds remaining after all creditors receive their share belong to the mortgagor. If the sales proceeds are inadequate to satisfy all debts and liens, the creditors get a "deficiency judgment" against the debtor personally. The creditors can go against the debtor's (mortgagor's) other assets to satisfy the deficiency judgment (if the underlying debt constitutes a **recourse** liability).[1]

Mortgagees wanting to avoid the delay and cost of a judicial foreclosure action may try a **private foreclosure sale** if (a) the state allows it and (b) the parties incorporate a **power of sale** provision in the mortgage or deed of trust. The mortgagee (lender) or the trustee in a deed of trust sells the property in a private sale, often by auction, bypassing the full judicial process. Statutes dictate the process, usually providing for notice and advertising. Some states require a court to approve or confirm the private sale.

Mortgagors can have the private sale voided if the mortgagee or trustee does not adhere to the statutory requirements. As a general rule, the mortgagor (borrower) cannot protest solely because the sales price was below the property's fair market value unless the purchaser at auction or the mortgagee (lender) acted fraudulently or did not comply with the statute. An exception to this rule occurs in some jurisdictions if the sales price is so inadequate it "shocks the conscience." In a small number of states, courts have interpreted statutory language of "good faith" and "due diligence" to impose a fiduciary

---

1. A debtor on a **recourse liability** is personally liable for a debt. A creditor can reach all of the debtor's assets to satisfy the debt. A debtor on a **nonrecourse debt** is liable on the debt; but if the debtor defaults, the creditor can reach only those assets pledged to secure the debt. The creditor cannot reach assets the debtor did not pledge.

To illustrate, assume a debtor borrows $100,000 from Bank A on a **recourse note** and $100,000 from Bank B on a **nonrecourse note**. Assume also the debtor pledged $100,000 of common stock to each bank to secure the respective loans. Assume further the debtor has $500,000 cash in the bank. Finally, assume the debtor defaults on both notes after the common stock serving as collateral for the two loans falls in value such that the common stock securing the note to Bank A is worth $70,000 and the common stock securing the note to Bank B is worth $80,000. Since the note to Bank A is a **recourse liability**, Bank A can sell the $70,000 stock, and can force the debtor to use $30,000 of her cash to pay off the rest of the note. On the other hand, since the note to Bank B is a **nonrecourse liability**, Bank B can sell the pledged stock for $80,000. That is all Bank B can get from the debtor. Bank B cannot reach any of the debtor's cash to satisfy the remaining $20,000 owed on the note.

duty on mortgagees and trustees to seek a fair and reasonable price or to refuse to sell below a reasonable price. See, e.g., Murphy v. Financial Development Corp., 495 A.2d 1245 (N.H. 1985). Most courts, however, uphold even exceedingly low foreclosure sale prices.

The mortgagor enjoys a right or **equity of redemption** until the property is sold. Thus, a defaulting mortgagor can keep the property by paying off the loan before the property is sold. About one-half of the states by statute give the mortgagor an extra right *after* the foreclosure sale, called the **statutory redemption right**, either to reimburse the purchaser at auction the amount she paid, with interest, and undo the sale, or to pay the court and to return the parties back to the legal relationships in place immediately before the foreclosure sale. The time in which the mortgagor must exercise his statutory redemption right, depending on the state, ranges from three months to two years.

Examples

Clarence Deed It

1. Clarence agreed to sell 1,000 acres of ranch land to Isby. Clarence and Isby executed a contract for a deed. Clarence signed not only the contract for a deed but also a warranty deed. The two documents were two of the many documents on the conference table when Isby picked up the deed, examined it, and put it with his papers. Isby left the meeting with the deed. A year later Isby recorded the deed. Was the deed delivered?

Home Delivery

2. Beulah, long divorced, owned her home. For years Elizabeth and Walter Raleigh helped Beulah around the house with repairs and yard work. They also drove her to the doctor's office and to social, cultural, and church functions. When Walter died, Elizabeth moved in with Beulah. Five years later Beulah decided she wanted Elizabeth to have her home if Beulah died before Elizabeth.

   Who owns Beulah's home after Beulah's death in the following situations? You may assume under the state's intestate succession statute the home would pass to Beulah's two sons, Ethan and Allen, if Beulah owned the home at her death.
   (a) Beulah handwrites a deed giving her home to Elizabeth. She puts the deed with her important papers and tells Elizabeth to read the important papers if Beulah dies. Beulah dies. Elizabeth sorts through the papers and finds the deed.
   (b) Beulah drafts and executes a deed. Beulah entrusts the deed to her minister with instructions to give the deed to Elizabeth if Elizabeth

survives Beulah. Before Beulah dies, she executes and delivers a deed to her son, Ethan. When Beulah dies, the minister gives Elizabeth the deed in his possession.

(c) Beulah hands Elizabeth a deed conveying the home to Elizabeth. Beulah orally instructs Elizabeth to hold the deed and to record it only if Elizabeth survives Beulah. Beulah dies.

(d) Beulah drafts a deed granting the home to Elizabeth if she survives Beulah, otherwise the home is to pass to Beulah's son, Ethan. Beulah reserved a life estate. Beulah hands the deed to Elizabeth. Beulah dies.

(e) Same facts as (d) except Elizabeth, one year after she received the deed, gave the deed back to Beulah (who was still alive). Beulah later dies.

(f) Same facts as (d) except one year after Beulah's death, Elizabeth hands the deed to Beulah's son, Allen.

(g) Beulah deeded the home to her minister in trust. Beulah was the life beneficiary and retained the right to revoke the trust (and thus to have the home returned to her). Upon Beulah's death the minister (the trustee) was to deed the home to whomever Beulah designated in her will, or, absent such designation, to Elizabeth if she survives Beulah, otherwise to Ethan. Beulah dies intestate. The minister, Elizabeth, Ethan, and Allen survive Beulah.

Foreclosing Options

3. Donatello bought a rental house for $100,000 from Trevor as an investment. Donatello paid Trevor the sales prices by transferring $5,000 cash from his savings, borrowing $80,000 from Hometown Bank and paying that money to Trevor, and giving Trevor an unsecured note for the remaining $15,000. At closing, Trevor deeded the house to Donatello, and Donatello signed and delivered a note and mortgage secured by the house to Hometown Bank. (You may assume that all deeds and mortgages are properly recorded.) Five years later when the house's fair market value (FMV) was $150,000, Donatello borrowed $50,000 from Local Bank to remodel his personal residence. Donatello gave Local Bank a note for $50,000 and a mortgage to his rental house (and not to his personal residence).

   Two years later Donatello sold the rent house to Zola for $170,000. Zola paid the sales price with $10,000 from her checking account, borrowing $50,000 from Friendly Savings & Loan and paying that money to Donatello, and agreeing to take the property subject to the notes to Hometown Bank ($65,000) and Local Bank ($45,000). Donatello deeded the house to Zola. Zola signed and delivered a note and a mortgage secured by the house to Friendly Savings & Loan.

One year later the state suffered an economic recession. Real estate values dropped. Donatello and Zola each suffered financial setbacks. Assume the following facts for all the questions:

Balance on Trevor note	$ 5,000
Balance on Hometown Bank note	$ 60,000
Balance on Local Bank note	$ 40,000
Balance on Friendly S&L note	$ 50,000
FMV of Donatello's home	$200,000
Cash in Donatello's bank account	$100,000
FMV of Zola's home	$ 90,000
Cash in Zola's bank account	$ 10,000

Please explain who has what rights and what is likely to occur in the following situations:

(a) Donatello stops making monthly note payments to Trevor.

(b) Zola continues monthly payments to Friendly S&L but stops making payments to Local Bank and to Hometown Bank.

(c) Zola continues making payments to Hometown Bank but not to Local Bank or to Friendly S&L.

Explanations

Clarence Deed It

1. No. Isby's possession of the deed raises a rebuttable presumption that Clarence delivered the deed to Isby. The recited facts, however, easily rebut the presumption. Clarence did not intend the delivery until Isby paid the full price. No intent to deliver; therefore, no delivery.

   Isby's recording the deed does not alter the result. If Isby had transferred the property to a bona fide purchaser for value, the recorded deed might form an irrebuttable presumption of delivery, at least as to the bona fide purchaser for value. Since Isby is the original party to the transaction and is not a subsequent bona fide purchaser for value, however, Isby cannot avail himself of the irrebuttable presumption. Clarence wins.

Home Delivery

2. (a) Ethan and Allen own the home. Beulah attempted a testamentary transfer, using the deed as a will substitute. Elizabeth does not gain access to Beulah's important papers until and unless she survives Beulah. There being no delivery until after Beulah dies, the transfer is void. Beulah's home passes by intestate succession to Ethan and Allen.

(b) Ethan wins. The result in this Example depends on whether Beulah delivered the deed during her lifetime. Clearly Beulah delivered a deed to her son, Ethan, during her life. Whether Ethan prevails depends on the transfers for Elizabeth's benefit. If the deed transferring the home to Elizabeth is deemed delivered before the deed to Ethan is delivered, Elizabeth prevails over Ethan. Beulah cannot revoke a completed gift, and she would have nothing to transfer to Ethan. (NOTE: The recording acts do Ethan no good since the acts protect bona fide purchasers for value, and Ethan is not a purchaser for value. The recording statutes, therefore, would not protect him. See Chapter 26, infra).

If Beulah's entrusting the deed to her minister constitutes the present delivery of a future interest — i.e., a springing executory interest — the delivery is good and Elizabeth prevails over Ethan, even though the minister delivered the deed to Elizabeth after Ethan received his deed.

The difficult issue in this Example is whether Beulah intended a present inter vivos transfer of a future interest or whether she intended a testamentary transfer. If Beulah intended a testamentary disposition, the delivery to the minister on Elizabeth's behalf is ineffective. The only good delivery under this interpretation is the one to Ethan, who would own the home. A court finding the minister to be Beulah's agent also would find there was no effective delivery since the agency ends at Beulah's death or, alternatively, since Beulah attempted a testamentary transfer without complying with the Statute of Wills.

Many courts, however, focusing on the donative aspect of the transfer would conclude the minister is a dual agent, that is, an escrow agent acting for both parties. In this situation, the delivery is good unless Beulah imposed a condition on the transfer other than her death. If Beulah had instructed her minister to deliver the deed to Elizabeth when or after Beulah died, for example, these courts would deem the delivery good. In this case, Elizabeth would prevail over Ethan.

Beulah, however, did not instruct her minister to deliver the deed to Elizabeth after Beulah's death. Elizabeth imposed a condition: Elizabeth must survive Beulah before the minister was authorized to deliver the deed to Elizabeth or Elizabeth's heirs or devisees. Moreover, as a practical matter, Beulah likely had the power to revoke the gift to Elizabeth by asking the minister to return the deed to her. Thus the attempted delivery to Elizabeth was ineffective. Ethan prevails since his is the only effective delivery.

(c) Beulah has attempted to condition the delivery. The question is: Does the orally imposed condition delay or prevent effective delivery until and if Beulah dies while Elizabeth is still alive? If so, the deed is a will substitute and, thus, ineffective as an attempted testamentary transfer not complying with the Statute of Wills. Many courts so hold, and many commentators agree with this rationale.

Under this analysis Ethan and Allen own the home as Beulah's heirs.

Other courts and commentators conclude a written deed that on its face conveys present title is good delivery. The oral condition, since the condition is not in writing and is inconsistent with the writing, is void and unenforceable, such that the grantee owns the property even if she dies before the grantor. This rule also prevents fraud after a party's death (especially the grantee's death). Moreover, many grantees will record the deed so the latter rule is necessary to protect the integrity of the recording system. Under this theory, Elizabeth owns the home.

On the final exam, which should you choose? It depends. If your class discussion indicates one rule is the majority or the "better" rule, choose that answer. A second option is to see if you have time to answer the rest of the question assuming different responses. This may occur, for example, if the problem is all but over if you choose one option, and lengthier if you choose the second option. If so, write an answer for each alternative, but *indicate which one you favor and the reason you like your chosen alternative.* If you must choose and nothing in the question helps you decide, identify the issue, pick the alternative that makes the most sense to you, explain why you picked that alternative, and go with it.

(d) Beulah has transferred alternative contingent reminders or executory interests to Elizabeth and to Ethan. Even though the interest to Elizabeth is a contingent interest, Beulah's handing the deed to Elizabeth is still a present delivery of an interest (to Elizabeth *and* to Ethan, even though Ethan may not have seen the deed), no matter that the interests are contingent and future interests. Delivery is good. Elizabeth survives Beulah, so Elizabeth owns the home after Beulah's death. If Beulah had survived Elizabeth, Ethan, his heirs, devisee or assign would take possession of the home. Ethan's brother, Allen, has no interest.

The deed contained the same condition Beulah put on Elizabeth's interest in (b) above: that Elizabeth survive Beulah before she takes a vested interest in the home. Yet the legal result is dramatically different. Courts do not deem Elizabeth an agent, as the minister was in (b). Courts utilize the analysis in (b) only in situations involving a third party escrow agent.

(e) Elizabeth owns Beulah's home. Elizabeth apparently intended to reconvey Beulah's home back to Beulah. Returning the deed does not "undo" the transfer, however. To transfer her interest back to

Beulah (note Elizabeth could not transfer Ethan's contingent interest), Elizabeth must satisfy all the requirements for a valid deed, including a writing signed by the grantor as required by the Statute of Frauds.

(f) Elizabeth owns Beulah's home. As soon as Beulah died, Elizabeth's interest became vested and Ethan's interest disappeared. Elizabeth handed a deed to Allen (Beulah's other son), but unless Elizabeth gave Allen some writing (or wrote on the front or back of the original deed) signed by her indicating she was conveying the property to Allen, the delivery of the original deed to Allen transfers nothing to Allen.

(g) Elizabeth owns the home. The trust is a popular vehicle for individuals to avoid the cost, publicity, and delay of probate administration. Generally, persons utilizing the trust are sophisticated or consult legal and financial advisors before entering into the trust arrangement. Courts honor the trust and will hold Beulah delivered the deed to the trustee, even though she retained the right to revoke the trust and all remainder interests, and even though she retained the power to control who would take after her death. She even had the power to sell to a third party during her life simply by revoking the trust and then transferring the property to the third party. Nonetheless, the delivery is good. When Beulah died intestate, her home passed to Elizabeth under the terms of the trust arrangement. Compare the result and analysis here with those in (b) and (d) above.

Foreclosing Options

3. (a) Donatello is the primary obligor only on the unsecured $5,000 Trevor note. Trevor did not receive a mortgage on the rental house so he has no security interest in Zola's house. Trevor is an unsecured creditor, however, and may get a judgment lien against Donatello's other assets (but not against Zola's assets). In all likelihood, Trevor will get his $5,000 from Donatello's cash in his bank account, depending on how many other unsecured creditors also are looking to the cash for payment.

Donatello also is secondarily liable on the $60,000 Hometown Bank note and the $40,000 Local Bank note. As long as Zola continues scheduled payments, the two banks have no action against Donatello.

(b) Zola has stopped making payments on the notes secured by the two senior mortgages (Hometown Bank and Local Bank), and continued paying only on the Friendly S&L note secured by the junior mortgage. Most mortgage agreements contain an **acceleration clause**, which allows mortgagees (lenders) to call the entire note balance on the happening of a material default. Thus any mortgagee seeking relief will seek full payment of the outstanding note balance.

Zola took title to the house subject to the Hometown Bank note and the Local Bank note. She did not assume any personal liability for the notes, however. The good news for Zola is that she is not legally obligated to pay the two banks. The bad news for Zola is that if no one pays the notes, the two banks can have her house sold to satisfy the debts since they have recorded mortgages secured by the house. Zola quit paying and, unless the banks can cajole Donatello into paying, the two banks will bring a judicial foreclosure action to compel a judicial sale of Zola's home. (This assumes the private sale is not an option either (a) because private sales are not allowed in the state or (b) because the mortgages did not incorporate "due-on-sale" clauses.) Assuming the house will bring its $90,000 fair market value at auction (probably not the case) and assuming the transaction costs associated with the foreclosure and sale are zero (definitely not the case), Hometown Bank, which holds the first mortgage and enjoys the highest priority to the sales proceeds, will receive $60,000 to retire its note.

Local Bank will receive the remaining $30,000 from the sales proceeds. Local Bank is still due $10,000 under the note. Local Bank has no action against Zola for the $10,000, however, since Zola has no personal liability on the note. Donatello is still personally liable, however. Local Bank will turn to Donatello as an unsecured creditor. If Local Bank is the only unsecured creditor, it likely will get $10,000 from Donatello's bank account. Otherwise, Local Bank must share pro rata with any other unsecured creditors.

Friendly S&L is in an uncomfortable position. Friendly S&L normally would be named a party to the foreclosure action. As such (and in most states even if not made a party), Friendly S&L as a junior creditor can receive proceeds from any foreclosure sale only after the note to Hometown Bank and Local Bank are retired. Since no proceeds remain after paying off the notes, Friendly S&L gets no money from the sale, and also loses all rights to Zola's house through the foreclosure sale. Nonetheless, Friendly S&L still has recourse against Zola personally for the $50,000 since Zola signed the original note. Friendly S&L is no longer a secured creditor, however, and must exercise any rights it might have as an unsecured creditor. Zola has only $10,000 in her bank account, so the S&L will not get full payment immediately from Zola. Friendly S&L does have the option of paying off the notes to Hometown Bank and to Local Bank (and thus "stepping into their shoes"), but since Zola's house's FMV is less than the two notes' balances, that is not a rational solution under the facts. Friendly S&L's only realistic option is to hope Zola continues making the note payments.

Zola is out a home and still owes Friendly S&L $50,000. Can Zola demand Donatello reimburse Zola for the $90,000 value of the home lost in the foreclosure, or for the money Zola paid Donatello to buy the home? Answer: No. Zola's taking the house subject to the two bank notes was part of the consideration for the house. That is why Zola was able to buy a $170,000 home for $60,000 cash in the first place!

If Zola's taking the house subject to the two bank notes was consideration for the sale of the house, can Donatello demand Zola indemnify Donatello for the $10,000 he must pay Local Bank from his personal funds? Answer: No, again. Zola did not obligate herself to pay the banks, Donatello, or anyone else for the two bank loans. Zola only risks losing the house, which is exactly what happens.

(c) Zola is no better off under this course of action and may fare worse than in (b). The chain of events here would parallel those in (b). Local Bank and Friendly S&L would accelerate the balance due. Hometown Bank, however, maintains its senior mortgage status. If the parties notify Hometown Bank as a party-in-interest of the lawsuit, Hometown Bank will insist on and receive the first $60,000 of any sales proceeds. Thus, only $30,000 of the sales proceeds remain, which as in (b) would go to Local Bank. Local Bank has recourse against Donatello for the balance still owed it, and Friendly S&L has recourse against Zola for its note. Both financial institutions are reduced to unsecured creditors.

If no one notifies Hometown Bank of the foreclosure action, any purchaser will take the property subject to Hometown Bank's recorded mortgage, and must continue making payments to Hometown Bank or risk a foreclosure action later. Prospective purchasers, aware of the bank's rights, would reduce the amount of cash paid for the house, in our Example, to $30,000.

As an observation, Zola is worse off paying Hometown Bank instead of Friendly S&L. Zola will lose the home either way, but she is personally liable for the Friendly S&L loan. Every dollar diverted from reducing the Friendly S&L loan balance prior to foreclosure to reducing the amount owed to Hometown Bank reduces the amount Donatello ultimately must bear, but does not reduce how much Zola must pay. (Do you see why? Answer: All Zola can lose to Hometown Bank and Local Bank is her house. Paying down the principal on the Hometown Bank loan reduces the amount owed to Hometown Bank; but unless Zola reduces the amount owed to Hometown Bank and to Local Bank to less than her home's fair market value, she receives no benefit from her payments. She reduces the loan principal, but on foreclosure she still loses her home and gets no money from any sale since all proceeds will go to reducing the Hometown Bank and Local Bank loan balances. Meanwhile, Zola remains personally liable on the loan to Friendly S&L. She must pay the loan from her personal funds. Thus, under the facts of the Example, by reducing the

Hometown Bank loan rather than the Friendly S&L loan balance, Zola does not reduce the amount of her personal liability. If, on the other hand, Zola pays down the loan owed to Friendly S&L, on foreclosure she still loses her home, but she is not liable for any excess balance owed to Hometown Bank and to Local Bank. She remains personally liable to Friendly S&L, but the amount owed to Friendly S&L is lower than if Zola had not reduced the principal.)

Post-Closing Title Assurances

MERGER DOCTRINE

The sales contract controls the relationship between the buyer and seller during the executory period. See Chapter 23, supra. A purchaser, for example, pursuant to the sales contract, may refuse to close if the seller cannot deliver marketable title. Traditionally, the sales contract's provisions were no longer enforceable after closing; the sales contract **merged** into the deed and the purchaser's rights were limited to those warranties and covenants contained in the deed or other document (note, mortgage, etc.). Warranties and covenants are the grantor's promises either that certain facts are true as of closing, or that the grantor will remedy the problem or pay damages if a third party successfully asserts an undisclosed interest in the property.

Exceptions are chipping away at the merger doctrine. The purchaser can resort to the sales contract to combat a seller's fraud, for example. Alternatively, the sales contract itself may provide expressly that a sales contract provision will survive closing. Moreover, courts are more willing to identify some sales contract matters not normally incorporated into the deed and to enforce these sales contract provisions as **collateral** or **independent covenants**.

TYPES OF DEEDS

Fortunately, the deed covenants and warranties in many cases parallel those promised in the sales contract. Three types of deeds are used in the United

States: the "general" warranty deed, the "special" warranty deed, and the quitclaim deed. Under the **general warranty deed**, the seller warrants against all defects and encumbrances in title except those specifically excepted in the deed itself, no matter whether the seller or some predecessor created the defect or whether the seller even knew of the defect. The grantor in a **special warranty deed** also warrants against defects in title, but the grantor limits his or her warranty to those defects or encumbrances that are attributable to some act by the grantor. The grantor makes no warranties about defects or encumbrances created before the grantor took title. The grantor may include each preexisting exception and encumbrance in the deed, but these representations will not open the grantor to liability for unknown, unspecified preexisting defects or encumbrances.

Example: A in 1990 granted Corporation, Inc. a pipeline easement over Blackacre. A conveys Blackacre to B, the deed mentioning the easement. B conveys Blackacre to C without mentioning the easement. C then conveys to D, who conveys to E, all without mentioning the easement. Finally, E conveys Blackacre to F by warranty deed. One year later Corporation, Inc. notifies F of its plans to dig up the land to place pipes in the easement. If the warranty deed from E to F was a general warranty deed, E would be liable to F for damages because E would have warranted no such easement encumbered Blackacre. On the other hand, E would not be liable to F if the deed was a special warranty deed since E did not create or grant the easement.

The **quitclaim** deed contains no warranties. The grantor conveys whatever interest he or she owns, but the grantor does not even warrant he or she has title. In the above example, E would not be liable to F for any defect in title if the transfer was by quitclaim deed. You can recognize a quitclaim deed easily enough because the deed uses the word "quitclaim" or another verb conveying the property that indicates the transfer is without warranties. Quitclaim deeds serve useful purposes, especially in transfers between family members, short-term ownership situations, and boundary dispute resolutions.

DEED COVENANTS

Deed covenants, also known as deed warranties, are promises or representations that title is as presented at closing and no one will step forward later claiming an undisclosed interest in the property. There are six common deed covenants: seisin, right to convey, against encumbrances, warranty, quiet enjoyment, and further assurances. In some states, the grantor must list the covenants in the deed. The grantor is not obligated to make all covenants, and will be held only to those covenants specifically included in the deed. Other states work from the other direction, concluding deeds containing words such as "grant" or "convey" carry the six covenants with them unless the deed expressly excludes them. In these states, if the grantor does not expressly limit or exclude covenants, the covenants are implied.

The first three covenants — seisin, right to convey, and covenant against encumbrances — are called **present covenants**. The present covenant or warranty is breached or violated, if ever, the moment the deed is delivered. A grantor either has seisin and a right to convey the interest, or she doesn't, when she delivers the deed. Similarly, any undisclosed defect or encumbrance already exists when the deed is delivered. Two consequences flow from the present covenant designation. First, in favor of the grantee, the grantee can bring suit for breach of the covenants immediately even though no person has stepped forward to assert a superior right to the property. Second, and detrimental to the grantee's right, the statute of limitations begins running on the delivery date. Consequently, the statute of limitations may expire before the grantee discovers the breach — e.g., before a person having a higher priority exercises those rights.

In contrast, the **future covenants** — warranty, quiet enjoyment, and further assurances — obligate the grantor to perform some act, such as defending against a third party asserting a higher claim to the property, upon some future event. Future covenants cannot be violated until the grantor refuses to act or the grantee has been ousted or evicted by someone having a paramount title. Two consequences of future covenants are mirror opposites of the present covenant consequences. First, the grantee cannot bring suit against the grantor unless and until the future covenant is actually breached. Second, the statute of limitations does not begin to run until a third party asserts a superior title (in the case of the covenants of warranty and quiet enjoyment) or the grantor refuses to execute a needed document (in the case of the covenant of further assurances).

In many cases, the grantee is protected against defects or encumbrances under both the present covenants and the future covenants. The grantee may assert a breach of the **present covenant of power to convey** or of the **covenant against encumbrances**, for example, if the grantee discovers the encumbrance before the third party asserts a paramount title to the property, or can assert either the breach of a present covenant or breach of the future **covenant of warranty** or **quiet enjoyment** if the grantee has been evicted (as long as the statute of limitations on the present covenant has not expired). If the statute of limitations on the present covenant has expired, the grantee can resort to an action for the breach a future covenant once the third party asserts his or her paramount title.

Unfortunately, sometimes a grantee gets caught without a cause of action. Consider the following example based on the classic case, Brown v. Lober, 389 N.E.2d 1188 (Ill. 1979):

Example: Landowners could not sell coal rights to a coal company because, unbeknownst to the landowners, a predecessor-in-interest owned two-thirds of the mineral rights. The landowners sued their grantor for breach of both present and future covenants. The court concluded the landowners could not bring an action on the **present covenants** because the statute of limitations had run. The court also denied the landowners a claim based on breach of a **future covenant** because the third party had not attempted to mine the coal or to prevent the landowners from mining the coal. Thus the landowners' breach of the future covenant of warranty claim action was premature. The mere existence of the superior title and the inability to sell the interest because of the cloud on the title were not breaches of the **future covenants** (though they would have been breaches of a present covenant if the statute of limitations had not run).

PRESENT COVENANTS

(a) Seisin

A grantor by the **covenant of seisin** warrants she owns the interest she is conveying. In most states, this means the grantor has legal rights to the estate conveyed. The grantor in this covenant does not warrant that no encumbrances affect the interest conveyed. The relevant issues arise under the warranty of seisin when the grantor does not have any interest, or the grantor's claim is through adverse possession before all the elements of adverse possession (including time of possession) have been fulfilled.

(b) Right to Convey

The **covenant of right to convey** closely parallels the covenant of seisin. The grantor may not have a right to convey someone else's interest when, for example, the purported grantor is not an authorized corporate officer, or trust terms limit a trustee's right to convey, or a restraint on alienation included in the deed or some other document restricts or forbids the transfer. In some states, the warranty of seisin merely indicates the grantor is in possession of the land, whether or not he holds legal title. Under this, an adverse possessor would have seisin, but would not have the right to convey since he does not have legal title. The present covenants of seisin and right to convey are often breached on the same set of facts.

(c) Warranty Against Encumbrances

Under the **warranty against encumbrances**, the grantor warrants no encumbrances burden the title except for those mentioned or referenced in the deed. **Encumbrances** include mortgages, liens, easements, restrictive covenants, and leases. Improvements encroaching onto neighboring land also are encumbrances.

An encumbrance mentioned in the deed cannot be the foundation of a breach of warranty against encumbrances claim. Neither can a government action pursuant to an ordinance or other law. "Encumbrances" as used here parallels "encumbrances" justifying a grantee's rescission of the sales contract for lack of **marketable title**. Encumbrances are developed more fully in Chapter 23, supra.

One interesting difference between the definition of "encumbrance" during the **executory period** and during the **post-closing period** has developed. Whereas many courts will allow a purchaser during the executory period to rescind a sales contract because of a violation of a zoning ordinance or environmental law, courts tend not to find an encumbrance under the deed covenants in this situation. The apparent reason for this distinction is that a prospective purchaser during the executory period should have the right to refuse to purchase the property if a prospective lawsuit looms even though the violation does not affect title. The grantee can rescind the sales contract, and the parties are returned to their original positions. Once closing occurs, however, judges apparently do not believe grantors should be liable for all potential violations of government regulations. The defect does not affect title, and may not be enforced by government authorities.

FUTURE COVENANTS

(a) Warranty

Pursuant to the **covenant of warranty**, the grantor covenants to defend against and compensate the grantee for any **lawful** claims made against the title. Thus the grantor must pay attorney fees and damages resulting from claims of persons actually owning the property, having any superior interest in the property, or having any interest by way of an easement, restrictive covenant, equitable servitude, or lease. Similarly, the grantor warrants improvements on the property do not encroach onto a neighboring property. Just as with the present covenant of warranty against encumbrances, government regulations and ordinances cannot form the basis of a covenant of warranty action.

A grantee's cause of action under the covenant of warranty does not arise until the grantee has been evicted by a party having a superior interest. The mere existence of the paramount interest is not enough. The grantee must be evicted or at least have an interest enforced against him.

(b) Quiet Enjoyment

The **covenant of quiet enjoyment** is treated in nearly all cases the same as the **covenant of warranty**. The covenant of quiet enjoyment probably should not be listed as a separate covenant any longer. Note, however, that "quiet enjoyment" means no one with superior title will interfere with the grantee's possession. Contrary to its name, the covenant of quiet enjoyment has nothing to do with noise or freedom from noise.

(c) Further Assurances

The **covenant of further assurances** requires the grantor to execute any document needed to cure a defect or possible defect in the conveyancing document. The covenant prevents the grantor from extorting extra money to sign documents later. One example is where a technical defect exists in a previously signed document and the parties need to execute a corrected document. A grantor under the covenant of further assurances must execute the new deed and cannot demand additional compensation from the grantor. As another example, the grantor may deliver a deed to the land before the grantor acquires the land. A grantee in this situation may insist on receiving a second deed conveying the land from his grantor to him after his grantor purchases the land. A special characteristic of the covenant of further assurances is that it alone of the deed covenants can be enforced by **specific performance**. Despite the covenant's theoretical importance, grantees do not resort to the covenant of further assurances much in practice.

DAMAGES

A grantee can receive monetary damages from the grantor for the breach of a deed covenant. The amount of damages depends on which covenant has been breached. A court may allow nominal or actual damages for a violation of the covenant of seisin or covenant of right to convey; or may award the property's full value if the grantee transfers the property back to the grantor. The damages for a violation of the covenant against encumbrances will either be the cost of removing the encumbrance, or, if that is impractical, the decrease in the property's fair market value (but see below).

Two rules apply in calculating damages. First, the maximum the grantee can receive on the breach of a covenant is the original amount the **grantee paid** his grantor for the property. Second, the maximum the grantee can receive from a remote grantor will be the amount the **remote grantor received** from a bona fide purchaser.

Example 1: Grantee pays $10,000 for a lot and later builds a $100,000 home on the lot. On the breach of a deed covenant, the maximum damages a grantor must pay Grantee will be $10,000.

Example 2: Grantee paid $100,000 for a lot and land, and the value increased to $150,000 before Grantee discovers the breach. The maximum Grantee can receive from a grantor is the $100,000 Grantee paid originally.

This limitation on damages fosters several problems.

Example 3: Abel sells land to Baker for $100,000. When the land is worth $160,000, Baker learns that Clements owns a one-quarter interest in the property. How much in damages can Baker get from Abel? Since Baker's interest is one-quarter less than she expected, her damages presumably are one-quarter of the property's fair market value. The key question — and one on which courts differ — is which number is the fair market value, the price Baker paid for the property or the fair market value when the breach occurred or was discovered. In some states Baker's recovery is limited to $25,000 and in others to $40,000.

Example 4: Assume the same facts as in Example 3, except Clements actually owns a three-fourths interest in the land. What damages can Baker get from Abel? In states using the $100,000 original sales price as the relevant fair market value, Baker's damages would be $75,000. In states using the $160,000 fair market value on the date the breach occurs or is discovered as the relevant fair market value, Baker suffered $120,000 loss of value, but would be limited to $100,000 damages (the amount Baker paid for the property).

ATTORNEY FEES

In addition to the **loss of bargain** damages, a grantee bringing an action against the grantor under the **future covenants of warranty, quiet enjoyment**, and **further** *assurances* can collect attorney fees for the cost of defending against a third party's **lawful** claim. Three important observations are needed here:

1. The grantor is obligated to reimburse the grantee for attorney fees the grantee incurred in defending the lawful claim since the grantor warranted no person had a superior interest in the property.
2. The grantor is liable for attorney fees **only if the third party prevails** against the grantee. The grantor did not covenant to defend against unfounded claims.
3. The grantee can receive only those reasonable attorney fees incurred to mount the unsuccessful defense against the third party.

Those are the only attorney fees the grantee can collect from grantor. The grantee cannot receive attorney fees incurred in a second suit to collect the attorney fees incurred in the first action, for example; nor can the grantee collect attorney fees for suing the grantor for losses suffered because of the paramount claim in the third party.

Example 1: Assume in Examples above that Baker spent $20,000 in an unsuccessful defense against Clement's claim to a one-quarter interest in the conveyed property. Baker's actual loss of value damages were $40,000. In addition, Baker incurred $5,000 attorney fees in a suit against Abel to collect the $40,000 actual damages and any attorney fees owed her. Baker should collect from Abel the $40,000 actual loss of bargain damages and the $20,000 attorney fees for the unsuccessful defense. Baker would not receive the $5,000 in attorney fees incurred in the suit against Abel.

Example 2: Baker incurred $20,000 in attorney fees in a successful defense against Clement's claim to the one-quarter interest in the property. In addition, Baker incurred $5,000 attorney fees in a second suit for attorney fees against Abel. Baker would not collect any attorney fees. Baker would not collect the $20,000 since she was successful in her defense. Abel warranted no one had a superior interest in the property. Abel did not warrant no one would make an unfounded claim. Baker's successful defense is proof Clements did not have a superior interest. Thus Baker cannot collect the $20,000 for the successful defense. Baker could not collect the $5,000 incurred in the case whether she won or lost the case against Clements. Baker will not collect any attorney fees from Abel.

REMOTE GRANTEES

A grantee may transfer the property to other persons, known as **remote** or **subsequent grantees**, who will own the property when the breach of a covenant made by a prior or remote grantor occurs or is discovered. To illustrate, assume A transfers land to B, who later transfers the land to C. As to A, B is the grantee and C is a remote grantee. As to C, B is the grantor and A is the remote grantor. The presence of remote or subsequent grantees raises additional issues.

The first issue is whether a remote grantee can seek relief against any prior covenanting grantors in the chain of title. Stated another way, do deed covenants run with the land to remote or subsequent grantees? In all states **future covenants** run with the land, and a remote grantee can seek relief against any **remote grantor** in the chain of title who breached his or her deed covenants. As a corollary, a grantor who pays a grantee because of a warranty has recourse against the prior warranting grantors (subject to the statute of limitations).

States differ as to the remote grantees' rights to enforce **present covenants** against remote grantors. Since present covenants are breached immediately on delivery of the deed, the cause of action vests in the first grantee (the non-remote grantee) immediately. At common law, causes of action were not assignable. Consequently, since the original grantee could not assign his cause of action to subsequent owners, states held remote grantees could not bring actions against remote grantors for breaches of the present covenants. Only the grantee named in the original deed could enforce a present covenant. Many states adhere to this prohibition. Other states, by statute or judicial opinion, allow remote grantees to sue remote grantors for breach of present covenants since today causes of action and contract rights are freely assignable. The statute of limitations for a breach of a present covenant as to remote grantors begins running on the initial transfer out from the defendant grantor, not when the remote grantee receives the deed.

A second issue involving remote grantees concerns the **maximum** amount of **damages** a remote grantee can receive from a remote grantor if, as is likely, the amount the remote grantee paid differs from the amount received by the remote grantor. The general rule is that the remote grantee is limited to the lesser of the remote grantee's actual damages, the remote grantor's sales price, or the remote grantee's purchase price.

Example 1:   Wesley by general warranty deed sold Greenacre to Yodi for $50,000. Subsequently Yodi by general warranty deed sold Greenacre to Zane for $40,000. The most Zane could collect from Wesley, the remote grantor, for breach of a warranty would be $40,000, Zane's purchase price.

Example 2:   Wesley by general warranty deed sold Greenacre to Yodi for $50,000. Yodi by general warranty deed sold Greenacre to Zane for $60,000. The most Zane could collect from Wesley, the remote grantor, for a breach of a warranty would be $50,000, Wesley's sales price. In this last situation, Zane would be better off going against Yodi, from whom Zane could collect $60,000. If Yodi paid Zane the $60,000. Yodi could seek relief against Wesley, but only up to $50,000, the amount Yodi paid Wesley for the property (and not the $60,000 he paid Zane).

IMPLIED WARRANTY OF QUALITY

In many states there is an implied warranty of habitability for leased residential property. See Chapter 19, supra. Likewise, during the executory period, a purchaser can rescind his sales contract if the seller does not disclose the property's material latent defects. See Chapter 23, supra. A similar implied **warranty of quality** (sometimes called the **warranty of habitability** or **warranty of suitability**) exists in the sale of new and remodeled homes by developers and other commercial vendors. The **implied warranty of quality** permits a purchaser to recover from the contractor, developer, or other commercial vendor for defective construction or construction not done in a workmanlike quality. This implied warranty of quality is yet another exception to doctrine of **caveat emptor**. See Chapter 23, supra.

The warranty of quality extends to **latent defects** resulting from **poor workmanship** that are discovered within a reasonable period of time. The defect must be due the builder's poor workmanship, and cannot result in whole or part from subsequent substantial changes to the structure, from misuse of the structure, from substandard materials (unless the builder should not have used the materials), or from normal deterioration. Currently, the implied warranty of habitability extends only to residences. It does not apply to commercial buildings (despite commentators' arguments it should extend to commercial buildings).

Only developers and other commercial vendors have been held liable under the warranty of quality. Thus, most courts find a warranty on the sale of new residences (including houses, townhouses, and condominiums). The warranty of quality likely also applies to the sale of commercially renovated or remodeled used homes. So far courts have refused to extend the warranty to the sale of used residences (other than those remodeled by commercial developers or builders).

Courts implying a warranty of quality on the sale of new homes treat the covenant of quality as a unique legal theory, based partly on tort law and partly on contract law. Most courts, for example, borrow from contract law and allow replacement or repair costs or the decrease in value of the building (known as economic losses) as damages for breach of the implied warranty. If the defect renders the house uninhabitable, some courts allow the purchaser to rescind the sale and grant the purchaser complete restitution of the purchase price.

A small number of courts, relying on tort principles, do not allow any recovery of economic losses unless a person has been injured or is likely to be injured. A latent defect that causes only economic damages does not give the buyer a claim for relief under the tort theory. Commentators and most courts question the wisdom of the tort approach, preferring the contract approach allowing economic damages even without physical injury.

One intriguing issue concerns the **grantor's power to disclaim** responsibility and the **grantee's power to waive** any rights under the implied warranty of quality. Although some states hold attempts to disclaim to be void as against public policy, most states honor disclaimers that are clear, unambiguous, and conspicuous (bold print, larger print, different colored print, for example) or are otherwise brought to the purchaser's attention, particularly if the buyer knows of the specific defect in advance. General disclaimers, such as a property is transferred "AS IS," probably do not suffice in most jurisdictions (although this general disclaimer is effective in some states). Courts usually limit the "AS IS" general disclaimer to patent defects, not to the latent defects covered by the implied warranty of quality.

In jurisdictions where the implied warranty of quality is based on public policy rather than implied contract, any express warranty of quality given by the builder generally supplements but does not negate or override the implied warranty. The implied warranty remains the minimum that the builder offers. In some jurisdictions, however, freedom of contract principles allows an express warranty to trump the implied one if both have the same subject matter, such as the roofing or the heating and air conditioning system.

The **statute of limitations** for the implied warranty of quality generally runs from the date construction is completed, or from the date the property is sold to the first purchaser, if later. Alternatively, some states begin the running only when the homeowner discovers, or should have discovered, the defect. The statute of limitations in theses states is usually shorter than in those states that begin the running the day construction is completed. Many states toll the running of the statute of limitations from the time the homeowner gives the builder notice of the defect as long as the builder promises to fix the defect.

In most states that have addressed the issue, the implied warranty of quality runs with the house to subsequent purchasers. In a higher than expected number of states, however, courts have ruled subsequent or remote purchasers are not in **privity of contract** with the builder and thus the warranty does not run to them. Some of these states nonetheless allow subsequent purchasers to proceed with a negligence claim against the builder.

Commentators prefer the view that the implied warranty should run to subsequent purchasers. The logic is the warranty protects homeowners, not just the immediate purchaser, from defects; defects often take time to become apparent; subsequent buyers are not likely to discover latent defects before purchasing; the builder/vendor should anticipate homes will be sold to subsequent purchasers; and the builder/vendor is in a better position to prevent the defect and to repair any discovered defects.

The subsequent purchaser must prove the vendor/builder caused the defect. Perhaps more critically, since the statute of limitations runs from the date of the original sale from the builder to the first purchaser, the subsequent purchaser much show the suit was brought within the relevant statutory period. The builder can defend by showing he did not cause the defect, that previous owners made substantial changes to the structure, or that the damages were the result of normal wear and tear or due to other natural causes.

AFTER ACQUIRED TITLE (ESTOPPEL BY DEED)

Sometimes — and this is not recommended as a general practice — a person conveys property or an interest in property without having legal title, in anticipation of gaining that title later. Under the doctrine of *after acquired title* (also known as *estoppel by deed*), the legal title to the property passes to the grantee as soon as the grantor gets her title. The doctrine applies only where the grantor warranted she had title. If the grantor quitclaimed the property to the grantee, the grantee acquires no interest if the grantor later acquires the property.

Examples

Remote Control Problems

1. Jennifer conveyed a retail building to Turner by general warranty deed subject to utility easements and a covenant restricting the building to two stories. One year later Turner sold the building to Walter by general warranty deed containing the same restrictions included in his deed. Walter subsequently learns of a $60,000 note Jennifer owed Bay Bank. The note was secured by a mortgage on the building now owned by Walter. Bay Bank's mortgage was recorded in the County Deed Records, but Jennifer's warranty deed to Turner did not mention the mortgage. Jennifer has made all payments and the note is current. Bay Bank has not given any indication it plans to foreclose on the mortgage. Walter does not want his building to secure the Bay Bank note. What should Walter do?

The Defective Subdivision

2. Seymour owned 100 acres of land. He sold three acres to Coleman. Six months later, Seymour sold two acres to Daughetee and three acres to Evans. All three deeds were general warranty deeds. Seymour conveyed

easements across his remaining property for egress and ingress to all three grantees' properties. Coleman, Daughetee, and Evans intended to build residences on their newly acquired lands.

Two years later Evans applied to the County Planning Department for a permit to build his home. The county refused the permit and said it would continue to refuse to issue a permit until Seymour and Evans subdivided Seymour's original property, secured a plat approval, and paved a road as required by the local subdivision ordinance. Evans called Seymour, who said there was nothing Seymour could do or would do about the matter.

Evans, Coleman, and Daughetee brought a suit against Seymour to rescind their deeds and have their money returned since the conveyances violated the county subdivision ordinance. Do the plaintiffs have any rights under their general warranty deeds?

A2B2C2D

3. Algernon by general warranty deed conveyed Blackacre to Bartley for $100,000. Bartley in Year 2 quitclaimed his interest in Blackacre to Carlotta for $110,000. Carlotta in Year 3 conveyed Blackacre by special warranty deed to Dudley for $80,000. In Year 6, when Blackacre was worth $90,000, Trudy Owner, the legal owner, appeared and evicted Dudley. Under state law, present covenants do not run to remote purchasers.

   (a) Explain how all resulting issues among Algernon, Bartley, Carlotta, and Dudley should be resolved.

   (b) How would your answer change if Algernon sold for $100,000, Bartley sold for $80,000, Carlotta sold for $110,000, and Blackacre was worth $125,000 when Trudy Owner evicted Dudley?

   (c) How would your answer change if the actual amounts paid were those set out in the facts but each deed recited consideration received as $10?

A Quality Question

4. Flawless Construction built a residential townhouse, which it sold to Amos. After living there a few months, Amos noticed excessive humidity and dampness in his basement, accompanied by mold, mildew, and an offensive odor. Some personal property stored in the basement was damaged also. The moisture originated from the groundwater table underlying the basement. A $2,000 "capillary break" would eliminate the problem. Amos wants Flawless Construction to pay to fix the problem. Flawless Construction contends it bears no liability for this act of nature, especially since Amos can and does still live the home. What result?

Implied Inference

5. Development Inc. contracted with Building Company to build several townhouses. Development Inc. sold one of the new houses to the Sotos. The form sales contract between Development Inc. and the Sotos, among other provisions, contained the following two provisions:

> 17. ONE-YEAR WARRANTY: Development Inc. warrants that it will repair all defects due to faulty materials or workmanship if Development Inc. receives written notice of such defects within one year of the sale to Purchaser.

> 18. ENTIRE AGREEMENT: This contract and the matters referred to herein constitute the entire agreement between the parties. No representations, warranties, undertakings, or promises, whether oral, implied, or otherwise, have been made by Development Inc. or Purchaser to the other unless expressly stated herein, or unless mutually agreed to in writing between Development Inc. and Purchaser.

These provisions were on a standard printed form in like-sized small print. The form contained blanks for the purchaser's name, the house description, the sales price, and the financing terms, if appropriate.

A year and a half after buying the home, the Sotos sold the house to Sabrina. A month after moving into the house, Sabrina discovered the exterior walls did not prevent water from coming into the house after a big rain and that the central heating system did not heat one of the bedrooms adequately. There was nothing to indicate previous water damage or heating problems. Sabrina called and wrote Development Inc., demanding Development Inc. repair the house. Development Inc. refused.

(a) Sabrina sued Development Inc., but not the Sotos or Building Company. Is Development Inc. the proper defendant under the implied warranty of quality?

(b) Did Sabrina buy a "new" house for purposes of the implied warranty of quality? Does Sabrina as purchaser from the Sotos have any rights against Development Inc.?

(c) How does Provision 17's express warranty affect of the analysis? Specifically, does an express warranty covering the same subject matter as the implied warranty of quality displace the implied warranty?

(d) Was Provision 18 an effective disclaimer of the implied warranty of quality?

After Acquired Thought

6. Adam was the original owner of 700 acres. Adam contracted to sell the 700 acres to Lanis. One month later, and two months *before* closing, Lanis by general warranty deed conveyed ten acres of the 700 acres to Marty. Marty recorded. Two months later, Adam and Lanis closed, Adam

delivering a warranty deed to Lanis for the 700 acres. A year later Lanis contracted to sell the 700 acres to Nick. When Marty heard Lanis planned to include the ten acres Marty had bought earlier in the sale, Marty protested. Who owns the ten acres, Lanis or Marty?

Explanations

Remote Control Problems

1. Walter wants Jennifer either to pay off the loan or to substitute other collateral to secure the Bay Bank note. Whether Walter can demand Jennifer do so under the deed covenants depends on whether the present covenants "run with the land." A mortgage is an encumbrance for purposes of the covenant against encumbrances. A few jurisdictions allow remote grantees like Walter to enforce present covenants. If the building is in one of those states, Walter can enforce the covenant against encumbrances against Jennifer. The proper remedy in these jurisdictions would be for Jennifer to pay the mortgage, though Walter would be happy as long as Jennifer got Bay Bank to release the mortgage either by Jennifer's retiring the debt or substituting collateral.

   If the building is in a jurisdiction in which remote grantees cannot enforce present covenants, the case gets messier. For one thing, Walter has no standing to bring an action for breach of the present covenant against Jennifer. In addition, Walter cannot bring an action for breach of the future covenant, which remote grantees can enforce in all jurisdictions, because Bay Bank has not evicted him.

   Having no direct case against Jennifer, Walter must enforce the covenant against encumbrances against Turner. Turner is liable since he gave Walter a general warranty deed that did not mention the mortgage securing Jennifer's note. A court may require that Turner pay the mortgage, leaving him with an action against Jennifer; or require that Turner place funds in trust in case Bay Bank forecloses on the building. Turner might make Jennifer a third party defendant to resolve all matters in one proceeding, but that is beyond Walter's control.

   If, in a worst-case scenario where Walter cannot locate Turner (say he moved to another state) or Turner is bankrupt, Walter may be left without a remedy unless and until Bay Bank forecloses on the building. At that point he has an action against Jennifer on the future covenants of warranty and quiet enjoyment.

The Defective Subdivision

2. As a preliminary matter, courts generally award damages only for a breach of a deed covenant. Courts will order complete rescission of

the deed, however, if the breach is so material it amounts to a constructive eviction.

Seymour did not violate the present covenant of seisin. Seymour owned the fee simple. The big issue is whether the county's subdivision ordinance served as a restraint on Seymour's power to convey. The court from which the Example is based, Seymour v. Evans, 608 So. 2d 1141 (Miss. 1992), refused to treat the violation of the subdivision ordinance as a breach of the covenant of right to convey. As an aside, the court also noted that the ordinance did not render the attempted deed illegal, or cause any party to engage in illegal conduct, so the sales contract and deed were not void for illegality.

Seymour's transferring the land also did not breach the present covenant against encumbrances. The existence of a zoning ordinance does not breach the covenant. That's easy enough. In the Example, however, there existed a violation of the subdivision ordinance; or more precisely, the transfers themselves were in violation of the subdivision ordinance. The majority of courts would agree with the Mississippi Supreme Court that the violation of an ordinance or land-use regulation does not breach the covenant against encumbrances.

Note that this answer differs from the same situation in the executory period, where a violation is grounds for rescinding the sales contract. The rationale for the different conclusions may be that during the executory period, the parties can be placed back into their original positions without much cost; and the grantor can decide how or if to resolve the problem. After closing, the grantor's flexibility disappears and the cost may be too high for the grantor to bear based on the sales price. This is especially true where, as in the Example, both buyer and seller understood the transaction and both had equal access to the land-use regulation. In the majority of states, therefore, Seymour would prevail on the covenant against encumbrances argument.

A minority of states, on the other hand, would hold a violation of land-use regulations violates the covenant against encumbrances, especially where the state took action to enforce the provision and no variance or other permit was forthcoming. In these states, the plaintiffs would have prevailed.

The future covenants of warranty and quiet enjoyment are not violated since the future covenants assure grantees that their enjoyment will not be disrupted by the grantor, by a person acting through the grantor, or by someone having paramount title. The county is acting without any claim of title. The future covenants are inapplicable in this situation.

The covenant of further assurances also does not apply since it does not require grantors to expend money, only to sign documents necessary to perfect title. Seymour's deed granted good title.

A2B2C2D

3. (a) Working in reverse chronological order, Dudley has no claim against Carlotta since Carlotta, by using a special warranty deed, warranted only against title defects that arose while Carlotta owned Blackacre, not any defects already in effect when she acquired her interest. Trudy Owner has owned the land since before the relevant transactions began so her interest in the land preceded Carlotta's purchase.

Dudley also has no cause of action on the deed covenants against Bartley since Bartley quitclaimed his interest, meaning he made no warranties whatsoever as to title. The state's laws against fraud may apply if Bartley knew he owned no interest; but nothing in the facts indicate Bartley (or anyone else) knew of Trudy Owner's interest until Year 6.

Dudley can bring an action against Algernon since Algernon conveyed by general warranty deed. Dudley cannot bring a claim based on the present covenants of seisin, the right to convey, or against encumbrances, however, since, according to the Example, present covenants do not "run to" subsequent or remote purchasers in this jurisdiction. Fortunately for Dudley, future covenants do run; so Dudley can seek relief under the covenant of warranty or covenant of quiet enjoyment. Dudley had rights under the covenants of warranty and quiet enjoyment as soon as Trudy Owner evicted him. Algernon owes Dudley $80,000 in damages (the amount Dudley paid for Blackacre) even though Algernon received $100,000 when he sold Blackacre and Blackacre was worth $90,000 (when Trudy evicted Dudley) since Dudley's damages are limited to the amount he paid for Blackacre.

If Dudley had litigated to defend his interest against Trudy Owner, and lost, Dudley could under the covenants of warranty or quiet enjoyment recover reasonable attorney fees and court costs from Algernon. Dudley cannot receive attorney fees incurred in suing Algernon. (NOTE: Dudley would not be able to collect attorney fees for the defense if he had prevailed against Trudy Owner since the covenant of warranty only warrants against successful third-party challenges.) In addition, the court may award Dudley interest on the $80,000. Courts differ as to when the interest should begin running, the options being either from when Dudley bought Blackacre, or when Trudy Owner evicted Dudley. The better rule seems to accrue the interest from the date Trudy evicted Dudley since before that day he possessed and used Blackacre. The rule is even more sensible in cases, like the one in the Example, where the true owner does not seek back rent or profits from the innocent trespasser (Dudley in the Example).

Carlotta has no claim against Bartley since Bartley quitclaimed Blackacre. Carlotta has no claim against Algernon unless and until Carlotta becomes liable to either Dudley (and Carlotta is not liable to Dudley because she gave a special warranty deed) or to Trudy Owner. Nothing in the Example indicates Trudy Owner sought any damages from Carlotta so Carlotta has no action against Algernon.

Carlotta lost money on Blackacre, selling Blackacre for $30,000 less than she paid for it. Carlotta cannot demand Algernon reimburse her for this loss, however. Presumably, the loss resulted from a general decrease in Blackacre's market value and not from the title defect. Deed covenants do not warrant against general market changes.

For the same reasons, Bartley has no action against Algernon based on a breach of the future covenants. Bartley, however, may have a claim for breach of a present covenant since he is the only person who could enforce the present covenants against Algernon. Bartley, however, sold Blackacre for a profit before any title defect surfaced and thus he suffered no cognizable loss. Even if Bartley sold Blackacre for a loss, since he and his purchaser, Carlotta, did not know of any title defect, the decreased value would have been attributable to general market conditions, and not reimbursable as damages from Algernon.

(b) The Explanation for this Example parallels the Explanation to (a) in all respects except that Dudley can receive only $100,000 damages in the large majority of states. Dudley cannot recover the full $110,000 he paid for the property or the property's current $125,000 value. His maximum loss of bargain damages is limited to the amount the defendant, Algernon, received for the property.

In a minority of states Dudley would be able to collect the $110,000 he paid for the property. In addition to the loss of bargain damages, Dudley may recover reasonable attorney fees incurred in his unsuccessful defense against Trudy Owner, and interest (see (a) above).

(c) This Explanation parallels Explanations (a) and (b). Dudley should collect $100,000 in loss of bargain damages and perhaps interest and reasonable attorney fees. The parol evidence rule, which makes oral testimony or other extrinsic evidence inadmissible to construe the plain terms of a contract or deed, causes problems in some states as to remote grantees. A few courts adhere to a strict parol evidence rule, looking only to the consideration stated in the deed. Some courts allow the original parties to offer parol evidence to contradict the deed, but will not allow remote grantees that same privilege. See, e.g., Rockafellor v. Gray, 191 N.W. 107 (Iowa 1922). Most states, however, allow parol evidence even as to remote grantees, apparently acknowledging the general practice of parties' inserting token consideration amounts into deeds. Other states seemingly feel obliged to honor the parol evidence rule, yet admit parol evidence as to the actual consideration by treating the amount stipulated in the deed as a statement admitting receipt of the consideration rather than as a statement of the actual consideration paid. Parol evidence then is allowed to flesh out an unclear fact. This approach is especially easy for a court if the deed recites "$10 and other consideration received" or some like language.

In the Example, the $10 stated price was less than the actual consideration. In some situations, the deed consideration may in fact be greater than the actual consideration. It would seem in that case that the grantor would be estopped from limiting his liability to a lower amount. This may explain the *Rockafellor* holding.

A Quality Question

4. A damp basement is not a title defect, and the Example does not reproduce any express contract or deed provisions. Therefore, Amos' case hinges on the implied warranty of quality. To prevail, Amos' prima facie case must prove (a) Amos bought a "new" home from Flawless Construction; (b) Flawless Construction was the builder/vendor of the townhouse; (c) the townhouse at the time of sale was not delivered in a workmanlike condition; and (d) Amos suffered damages as a result of the defective condition. The first two elements are not in dispute. Flawless Construction is a builder/vendor and the townhouse is Amos' home. The townhouse is a new home. The $2,000 cost to fix the defect indicates Amos suffered some damages from the moisture. The damage issue in (d) depends on whether Flawless Construction is responsible for damages caused by moisture from the surrounding groundwater table seeping into the basement. That issue follows from the resolution of the issue in (c), whether the townhouse was delivered to Amos in a workmanlike condition.

Courts do not demand homeowners prove exactly how the builder failed to build the house in a workmanlike manner. The homeowner can show either that the home was not built in a workmanlike manner or, in the alternative, that the home was not suitable for habitation. In the Example, Amos proved Flawless Construction did nothing to prevent groundwater from seeping into the basement. He also showed the mold, mildew, and odors made part of his home unuseableunusable for its intended purposes.

The issue in the workmanlike manner alternative is whether builders in the community must anticipate and prevent water seepage into the basement, or whether seepage protection is a nicety some homeowners will pay extra to have. That is, does a leaky basement fall into the same category as a leaky roof or cracked foundation? Or is it more like central air-conditioning, a dishwasher, or storm windows? The issue is one for the fact finder. In the few cases to date on this issue, the fact finder has found a builder should prevent water seepage into basements.

Similarly, the alternative question whether the home was suitable for habitation is a fact question. The defect does not have to make the home completely uninhabitable. The test is one of merchantability: whether the home's condition meets the reasonable homeowner's expectations for its intended use. A fact finder here likely would find the leaky basement was ill-suited for use as a bedroom or storage area. Thus the conclusion must be that Flawless Construction did not deliver the home in a workmanlike condition.

Flawless Construction could defend by arguing the leakage was a patent defect. The implied warranty of quality does not cover patent defects. In the earlier discussion of marketable title, Chapter 23, supra, leaky basements often were deemed patent defects since an inspector would find water stains, molds, mildew, or odors of some sort. In a new house, however, the defect may not have occurred, or not been significant enough to leave telltale evidence of the defect. Nothing in the Example indicated Amos should have discovered the defects prior to closing.

Flawless Construction must fix or pay to have the basement fixed.

Implied Inference

5. (a) Yes, Development Inc. is a proper defendant. In most cases the defendant is the builder/vendor. Development Inc. is not the builder, but Development Inc. is a commercial vendor. Commercial vendors can be liable under the implied warranty of quality. Building Company, moreover, was Development Inc.'s agent. Development Inc. cannot escape liability by contracting out the work. As a public policy matter, moreover, Development Inc. is in a better position to monitor and discover the defects than are consumers.

   (b) Sabrina bought a "new" house for purposes of the implied warranty if she is seeking relief from Development Inc. The issue is whether the latent defect existed at the time Development Inc. sold the house to the Sotos. The sale from the Sotos to Sabrina would be deemed the sale of a "used" house if Sabrina tried to sue the Sotos, thus defeating the implied warranty of quality claim against the Sotos.

   The second question is more than a restatement of the first question. In fact, courts disagree as to whether a subsequent purchaser can enforce the implied warranty of quality against a commercial vendor if the second purchaser is not in privity of contract with the commercial vendor. Most courts, and virtually all commentators, support the legal conclusion that Sabrina, as a remote grantee in the Example, could enforce the covenant against Development Inc.

Only a minority of courts would hold Sabrina, as a remote grantee, did not have standing to sue Development Inc.

(c) Provision 17, "One Year Warranty" is an express warranty covering the repairs of all defects due to faulty materials or workmanship if the purchaser notifies Development Inc. in writing within one year of the sale. If the provision controls, Sabrina has no rights since she did not even buy the house until a year and a half after Development Inc. sold the house to the Sotos (even if we assume she qualifies as the "Purchaser" under the sales contract). The one year period begins when Development Inc. sold the house to the Sotos. It does not start anew when the Sotos sold the house to Sabrina.

Fortunately for Sabrina, courts will not hold Sabrina to the one-year period. A court likely would interpret the sales contract provision as applying only to *patent* defects, not to the *latent* defects at issue here. Although their analysis appears disingenuous, courts fear a contrary ruling would lead to commercial vendors' effectively negating all warranties by conditioning the express warranty of quality to one year, even one month. Sabrina has the time set out in the statute of limitations under state law.

The next provision, Provision 18, seemingly disclaims all implied warranties, strengthening Development Inc.'s claim the express warranty of Provision 17 constitutes Sabrina's sole remedy. A court likely will reject that claim also since a reasonable consumer would not associate the two provisions nor appreciate the legal consequences of the two provisions. Sometimes, especially in consumer protection law, a consumer's ignorance about a contract provision works to the consumer's benefit!

(d) Development Inc. in Provision 18 attempts to disclaim all implied warranties. While most courts will allow disclaimers or waivers in appropriate circumstances, the courts would not approve this disclaimer. The disclaimer is part of a boilerplate, preprinted form contract, sometimes called a contract of adhesion. The print is small and appears no different from the rest of the document. To be effective, the disclaimer must be clear and conspicuous, maybe even containing some indication the purchaser read and understood the legal consequences of the provision. Provision 18 did not even mention habitability or quality. Provision 18 was legally insufficient to disclaim the implied warranty of quality.

After Acquired Thought

6. Marty owns the ten acres. Under the doctrine of **after-acquired title** or **estoppel by deed**, title to the ten acres automatically inured to the earlier grantee, Marty in our Example, as soon as Lanis acquired legal title.

Thus, as soon as Adam deeded the 700 acres to Lanis, title to the ten acres passed to Marty. Lanis had no interest in the ten acres he contracted to sell to Nick.

PREVIEW NOTE: If Adam already had deeded the 700 acres (including Marty's ten acres) to Nick, the recording acts, discussed infra, might reverse the result. In some jurisdictions, Marty's deed, recorded before Lanis purchased the property, will be found to be out of the chain of title. Thus the deed legally is not properly recorded and will not be treated as a recorded deed. In those states, Nick, as a bona fide purchaser without notice, prevails against Marty. This will become clearer to you later when you study the recording acts in the next chapter.

CHAPTER 26

The Recording Systems

INTRODUCTION

Land purchasers do not like discovering unpleasant surprises after closing, especially surprises affecting title. Similarly, landowners, creditors, and others having an interest in land do not want future claimants to challenge their interests. Currently, a public recording system serves the needs of society in facilitating land ownership and land transfers. The system is not the most efficient. In fact, it is often inefficient, time-consuming, and costly.

The recording systems supplant, not supplement, common-law systems. As a rule of thumb, **record title holders** prevail over **legal title holders**. Quite often, recording systems reverse outcomes that would have been reached under common law. A legal title owner under common law rules may lose all rights under the recording system, and a person with no interest under the common law may prevail under a recording system. If a recording system protects a person, that person prevails over other claimants having an inferior or competing interest. If the recording acts do not protect any person involved in a dispute, common law principles control.

Recording systems serve two practical functions. First, the recording systems **assure** title or, more accurately, determine a **priority of rights** to a parcel of land. Generally, a person recording a document in the local deed records takes priority over persons later recording an interest in the same property. In line with this function, much of the study of recording statutes emphasizes the concept of proper recording and discerning which persons are protected by the recording acts.

The recording system's second purpose is **informational**. A prospective purchaser or lender can search the deed records to determine whether the prospective seller or borrower has record title, and to locate other recorded interests affecting the property. Gaining knowledge of other record owners, easements, restrictive covenants, cotenants, leases, mortgages, liens, and other recordable encumbrances to title, the prospective purchaser during the executory period may rescind the sales contract if the seller cannot deliver marketable title. Even before entering into the sales contract, the prospective purchaser can decide if he would be willing to purchase the property subject to the restrictions and encumbrances of record.

The assurance and informational purposes are interrelated. First, a person recording an interest usually can rest assured a subsequent purchaser must honor the previously recorded interest. Second, with knowledge or "notice" of the previously recorded documents, a prospective purchaser will be bound by all recorded encumbrances and interests in the property, and cannot later protest he did not think he would be bound by any of the encumbrances. To encourage prospective purchasers to review the deed records, the prospective purchaser is deemed to have **constructive notice** of all properly recorded documents regarding the property. In other words, the wise prospective purchaser checks the deed records and does not rely solely on a seller's representations.

Conversely, a person who fails to record takes the risk a court will find a subsequent **bona fide purchaser for value** will not have to honor the first person's interest either because the first person did not qualify for protection under the state's recording act or because, of the two innocent parties, the first person could have avoided the problems by recording.

Local governments maintain the official deed records. Usually, one office in each county — titled variously as clerk, register, registrar, recorder, probate judge, circuit court, or bureau of conveyances — maintains the deed records for all land in the county or parish. Each state's recording act specifies the mechanics of the recording process, including the formal requirements needed before the recording office can accept a document for recordation. Once accepted, the recording office dates the document, assigns the document a number, and notes the document in a log. The clerk makes a copy of the document and records pertinent data in appropriate indices: the grantor and grantee index being the most common.

Some recording acts give long lists of documents that may be recorded — e.g., "deeds, mortgages, agreements that convey, transfer, assign, encumber, or affect the title to real property." Other acts permit the recording of "every grant of an estate in real property." Some interests are not recordable. Short-term leases are often expressly excluded. Interests that arise from possession (e.g., adverse possession and prescriptive easements) or involve marital property are excluded as well: They don't arise by written instrument, so there is nothing to record.

Before delving into the recording acts, you must be comfortable with the fundamentals of using a *grantor-grantee* index to create a **chain of title**. Governments are quickly placing documents and indices on computers, which should simplify the search for documents. Until all documents are accessible on computers, however, you must be able to construct a chain of title using the traditional grantor-grantee indices.

Chain of title means the series of documents affecting ownership of, rights to, and encumbrances on a parcel of land "linked" together in some manner. Generally, the links are organized by the grantors' and grantees' **names**. In "searching" title using a grantor-grantee index, the title searcher first checks the grantee indices (moving back in time). This gives him a list of past owners dating back however many years he needs to search. He then searches the grantor index for conveyances made by each past owner in the chain of title, tracing from the earliest grantor to the most recent. This second step tells him whether any owner rendered the title unmarketable in some way. The second step is the more difficult and more critical. For more on the mechanics of the search, see the next section.

SEARCHING A CHAIN OF TITLE USING THE GRANTEE INDEX

The **grantee index**, as the name implies, indexes by grantees' names. The index includes the name of each grantee for all land in the county for a given period of time — one year, ten years, etc., depending on the volume of transactions in the county. Along with the grantee's name, the grantee index will contain a date, the grantor's name, a description of the document being indexed (deed, lease, easement, mortgage, release, lien, etc.), a brief description of the affected property, and a reference to an instrument number or the page and book in the deed records where a copy of the document is filed.

A title searcher begins the search by locating the current owner in the grantee index. The grantee index attempts to list **grantees'** names alphabetically (computers help) so if the current owner is Richard Grayson, the searcher would look in the most recent grantee index under "G" or "Gr" for Grayson, Richard. Richard Grayson may have received several parcels so a check of the brief property description is important.

A prudent title searcher, looking through the grantor or grantee indices, will be on the lookout for similar names — for example, past owner Johnson Smith may have used the name Johnson A. Smith in a mortgage transaction in the chain of title. In some states, when one name is inconsistent with another, checking the documents involving both may be required.

Some other states require that names that sound alike be treated alike: Thus a phonetic search may be required because Johnny Smith should also be searched under the name of John E. Smith.

Once the grantee's name is found, the searcher finds, copies, and reads the complete document indexed at that entry (the deed, lease, mortgage, etc). The searcher also should locate all documents referenced in the indexed document. Next, if the found document was a deed, the searcher notes the name of the grantor and searches the grantee index again, this time using the grantor's name as the grantee. The searcher repeats the process back in time to the **root of title**, which usually is the document by which the federal or state government granted the land to a private person, but which may be an adverse possession judicial proceeding or some other document established by state law as a "root of title."

If the searcher cannot locate the prospective seller in the grantee index, or cannot complete some link back to the root of title, the searcher must inquire as to why the deed records are incomplete. A prospective purchaser should refuse to close the sale until the grantor has corrected or completed the chain of title. As you will discover, for the recording system to work, courts often favor maintaining the integrity of the system over seeking equity or justice in any individual case. This judicial attitude puts the onus on the latest person in the chain of title to verify that the chain of title is complete and documents are filed properly in the chain of title. In practice, chains of title are maintained because purchasers (or, more precisely, their attorneys or the lender's attorneys) refuse to close until sellers rectify problems in the chain of title.

SEARCHING A CHAIN OF TITLE USING THE GRANTOR INDEX

The mechanics of searching the **grantor index** are similar to those to search the grantee index, except the search order is reversed. The title searcher begins with the root of title found by searching the grantee index and then searches chronologically for grantors up to the present day. A search of the grantor index may turn up more documents since easements, mortgages, leases, etc. are more easily found in the grantor index than in the grantee index. As with the grantee index, the searcher should find, photocopy, and read each located document. The chain of title resulting from the search should lead back to the seller. The title searcher must continue the search up to the day of closing to be sure the seller has not granted the property or an interest in the property to someone else.

Example: A searcher finds deeds showing *A* conveying Blackacre to *B*, and *C* conveying Blackacre to *D*, but cannot find a deed from *B* to *C* in the deed records. The searcher may find the documents to fill the gap in the probate records, the divorce records, or the bankruptcy records, but not always. A purchaser should not purchase property if there is a gap between record owners. The prospective purchaser should notify the seller immediately. The burden falls on the seller to search for and to record proper documents to clean up the chain of title.

SEARCHING A TRACT INDEX

Some states use a **tract index** instead of the grantor-grantee index. In a tract index, all documents affecting a parcel of land are indexed on a page for that parcel of land. A searcher in a tract index finds the page for the property in question and copies the page that summarizes all documents affecting the parcel. The searcher then can pull all referenced documents.

The more you study all the problems associated with grantor-grantee indices, the more you will begin to favor the tract index. The large majority of states, however, retain the more cumbersome grantor-grantee index system. One reason is that most states began with the grantor-grantee index system and are reluctant to change. Second, the government employees in a grantor-grantee index system merely index the documents. They do not decide what properties are affected, and thus avoid claims, possible in a tract index system, that the government employees' negligence caused a title problem.

Third, and maybe more important, private companies, known as **abstract companies** or **title insurance companies**, usually maintain a **plant** by which they reconstruct all deed records, creating the equivalent of a tract index. The abstract company or title insurance company updates the plant daily for all documents filed that day in the county's deed records. With the equivalent of a tract index available in the private sector, governments perceive no need to change the current recording system. Moreover, the private abstractors and title insurance companies lobby zealously against changes.

THE RECORDING ACTS

Recording acts establish the priority persons have to a parcel of land. Purchasers and creditors must strictly comply with a state's administrative, statutory, and judicial laws regarding recording to be protected by the recording acts. With all the transactions, documents, people, and parcels of land involved, errors and other problems are sure to develop. The first step in resolving many problems is determining the type of recording act adopted in the state.

State recording acts fall into three categories: race, notice, and race-notice. It is critical you know which recording act applies to the jurisdiction before you analyze the issues. Which recording act applies may alter dramatically the outcome of any question. Determining a recording act's category is not always easy to do.

RACE OR PURE RACE STATUTE

Under a **race** or **pure race** statute, when two persons hold competing claims to real property, the first person to officially record (not the first to receive the deed, mortgage, etc.) prevails. Only a couple of states have pure race statutes. Louisiana has a pure race statute. So do Delaware and North Carolina, although some commentators interpret court cases as moving North Carolina from race to race-notice. The North Carolina recording statute, N.C. Gen. Stat. § 47-18 (LEXIS 2000), in part reads as follows:

§ 47-18 (a) No (i) conveyance of land, or (ii) contract to convey, or (iii) option to convey, or (iv) lease of land for more than three years shall be valid to pass any property interest as against lien creditors or purchasers for a valuable consideration from the donor, bargainor or lessor but from the time of registration thereof in the county where the land lies. . . .

Do you see why this is a pure race statute?

Under a **pure race statute,** the first person to record wins even if he knows about a previously unrecorded conveyance. Under the North Carolina statute, the key phrase is "but from the time of registration." In addition, there is no mention of the good faith of the parties protected by the statute — the "lien creditors or purchasers." As you will notice in the next two sections, that omission is a good indication that the statute is not a notice (and so not a race-notice) statute.

The most attractive part of a pure race statute is its certainty. The prevailing party is easily determined by seeing who recorded first. A person who delays recording risks having other persons' claims to the property take higher priority than her interest. In its most dramatic scenario, a nonrecording owner risks losing her entire interest. That potential for losing the interest to a subsequent purchaser serves as a strong incentive to record a document the day of any transaction. Unfortunately, race jurisdictions chance too many unsatisfactory results.

Example: O conveys Redacre to A, who does not record. B learns A has failed to record, and convinces O to convey Redacre to B. B records. Under a pure race statute, B will own the property because she recorded before A recorded (A may have an action against O on the deed covenants, of course).

Many states reject the pure race statute because B in the above Example was in a better position to avoid the problem since B knew A already had an interest. B's acquiring the property seems unfair at best, and fraud at worst. Most state legislatures have decided a person with notice of a prior transfer cannot defeat that prior interest.

Similarly, a person purchasing without notice of a prior transaction because no notice is available also is at risk in a pure race jurisdiction.

Example: O conveys Blueacre to A. Before A records, O conveys Blueacre to B, B having no actual knowledge of A's interest. A records before B. Under a pure race statute, B, the innocent subsequent purchaser, has no interest in the property since A was the first to record.

Many states reject the pure race statute in this situation because A was in the better position to avoid the confusion simply by recording quickly. B, being the more innocent of the two, conclude these state legislatures, should prevail. The states that reject the pure race statute adopt one of the two recording acts with a notice component: pure notice or race-notice.

Only Delaware, Louisiana, and North Carolina have generally applicable race statutes, and a few states (e.g., Pennsylvania) have race statutes for mortgages and for transactions involving mortgage remedies (e.g., foreclosure by the holder of a deed of trust, as in California). The rest of the states have either race-notice or notice statutes — and these two categories of statutes have each been adopted in roughly the same number of jurisdictions.

RACE-NOTICE STATUTE

Under a **race-notice statute**, a subsequent bona fide purchaser or creditor who **first records** prevails against a person claiming a prior, unrecorded interest as long as the subsequent purchaser did not have notice of the preceding interest when she acquired her interest (she can know about the interest when she records the document as long as she did not have notice when she purchased). The race-notice statute is a variation of the pure race statute. As with the pure race statute, if the **first purchaser** in a race-notice state records first, she prevails. The **second or "subsequent" purchaser** in a race-notice jurisdiction, to prevail, must acquire her interest **without notice** of the preceding interest **and** must **record first**. The race-notice statute therefore resolves the issue of the unscrupulous subsequent purchaser in the pure race jurisdiction who knew about an unrecorded document and took unfair advantage of the situation. The following California race-notice recording statute, Cal. Civ. Code § 1107 (West 1999), is a representative race-notice act:

§ 1107. Every grant of an estate in real property is conclusive against the grantor, also against everyone subsequently claiming under him, except a purchaser or incumbrancer who in good faith and for a valuable consideration acquires a title or lien by an instrument that is first duly recorded.

Do you see why this is a race-notice statute? The significant phrases in this statute are "good faith" and "first duly recorded." They establish that the class of persons protected by the act must be without notice (as explained below) and record first. These phrases are fairly typical.

Since (hopefully) the vast majority of persons do not engage in fraud and unscrupulous behavior, the result in a race-notice jurisdiction should parallel that in a pure race jurisdiction, except for one thing: **Notice** is defined broadly and includes, in addition to the **actual notice** or knowledge the race-notice statute anticipates, notice or knowledge not actually known, but which the purchaser should know or should ask about. The courts label these latter types of notice as **constructive notice** and **inquiry notice**.

(a) Actual Notice

Actual notice or knowledge means the subsequent purchaser or her agent had actual notice of a prior claim. The subsequent purchaser can gain this knowledge from personal observations, a document in the deed records, or hearing about it either during negotiations or from conversations outside the transaction itself.

(b) Constructive Notice

Constructive notice, also called *record notice*, refers to knowledge or notice a purchaser could gain by searching the deed records. The purchaser is deemed to know all matters contained in documents legally recorded in the deed records, even though the purchaser did not search the deed records. In fact, constructive notice or record notice usually is asserted when a purchaser did not search the records (a purchaser who searched the records likely has **actual** notice of prior recorded claims). Constructive notice is less important in race-notice jurisdictions since documents giving constructive notice also are the first recorded documents; and the recording party prevails on the "race" portion of the race-notice requirements. Constructive or record notice plays a much more important role in pure notice jurisdictions.

(c) Inquiry Notice

A prospective purchaser or creditor has **inquiry notice** when the purchaser hears or observes something that would cause an ordinarily prudent person to inquire further. If a prudent person would have investigated further, and that investigation would have revealed some unrecorded interest in the property, the purchaser is deemed to have notice of the unrecorded claim.

The most important source of inquiry notice comes from visiting the property. A purchaser has inquiry notice of all rights belonging to possessors and users of the property. The user may be the owner, a tenant with a long-term lease or with an option to purchase, or the tenant's landlord may own the property (and not be the person trying to sell). If, as in the case of an apartment building, the property contains multiple units, the purchaser must inquire of each user.

Structures, railroad tracks, roads, and power lines may prompt an inquiry. A prospective purchaser also may have inquiry notice based on a **common scheme of development**, or may be required to check deeds to neighboring property if the properties were conveyed by a **common grantor**. In summary, the prospective purchaser has a duty to view the property, and it is no defense that the property is far away.

A second category of inquiry notice (though it easily could be considered a subset of constructive notice) involves documents mentioned in properly recorded documents. A subsequent purchaser has inquiry notice of all matters specifically identified in properly recorded documents, whether or not the subsequent purchaser read the recorded documents.

Inquiry notice plays an important role in race-notice jurisdictions. A subsequent purchaser who searches the deed records (not finding the claims at issue) and who first records can lose to a person claiming an interest that would have come to light had the purchaser inquired.

As a caveat, some states do not recognize inquiry notice or even constructive notice. These jurisdictions limit notice to actual notice or knowledge. In these states, the subsequent purchaser has no duty to inquire. Unless the subsequent purchaser has actual notice, the subsequent purchaser will prevail.

NOTICE OR PURE NOTICE STATUTE

Under a **notice or pure notice statute**, a subsequent bona fide purchaser or creditor for value prevails over prior claimants as long as the subsequent purchaser acquires the interest **without notice** of the prior claim. A subsequent bona fide purchaser without notice prevails immediately **upon closing**. The subsequent purchaser does not have to be the first to record. In fact, the subsequent purchaser is not required to record at all to prevail against **prior unrecorded** claimants (although the subsequent purchaser must record to protect his or her interest against yet later subsequent purchasers).

Notice contemplated in the statute could be actual, constructive, or inquiry notice (see above discussion). States adopting a pure notice statute reward bona fide purchasers without notice, and refuse to condition that protection on the subsequent purchaser's winning the race to the courthouse. In a pure notice state, a purchaser can rely on the deed records as they exist at closing.

The following Example illustrates the difference between race-notice and pure notice statutes:

Example: O conveys Blackacre to A, who does not record. O then conveys to B, who purchases without actual, constructive, or inquiry notice of A's interest. A records. Then B records. In a race-notice jurisdiction, A has record title and owns Blackacre since B to be protected must purchase without notice (which she did) and be the first to record (which she was not). In a pure notice jurisdiction, in contrast, B, the subsequent bona fide purchaser, prevails since she purchased without actual, constructive, or inquiry notice of A's interest.

A matter that troubles many students is what incentive a subsequent purchaser has to record in a pure notice jurisdiction if the subsequent purchaser prevails against prior unrecorded claims even if she does not record. The answer is simple, obvious, and easily overlooked: The subsequent bona fide purchaser without notice prevails over prior unrecorded claims; but unless she records her document, she risks losing to yet a later purchaser for value without notice of her deed. The surest protection a purchaser has that all subsequent purchasers or creditors will have notice of her claim under a pure notice statute is to record the document. The whole world, including prospective purchasers and creditors, then has constructive or record notice of her interest.

Example: O conveys Blackacre to A, who does not record. O later conveys Blackacre to B, who purchases without notice of A's claim. In a pure notice jurisdiction B's claim to the property is superior to A's. Assume now that O or A conveys to C (a mortgagee), who does not have actual or inquiry notice of B's interest. Who has the greater rights, B or C? If B did not record before C acquired his interest, C prevails since he is a subsequent bona fide purchaser for value without notice of B's claim. On the other hand, if B had recorded before C purchased, B would prevail since C, the subsequent purchaser, is charged with constructive notice of B's recorded document (deed, mortgage, lease, etc.).

The following Texas statute, Tex. Prop. Code Ann. § 13.001 (West 1999), is a pure notice statute:

> § 13.001 (a) A conveyance of real property or an interest in real property or a mortgage or deed of trust is void as to a creditor or to a subsequent purchaser for a valuable consideration without notice unless the instrument has been acknowledged, sworn to, or proved and filed for record as required by law.
>
> (b) The unrecorded instrument is binding on a party to the instrument, on the party's heirs, and on a subsequent purchaser who does not pay a valuable consideration or who has notice of the instrument.

Do you see why this is a pure notice statute? Subsection (a) says a deed or mortgage is void against subsequent creditors or purchasers for valuable consideration "without notice." The notice element is straightforward. The provision is not a race-notice statute, however, even though subsection (a) also mentions recording, because the section does not say anyone must be the first to record. The recording language merely indicates the date the document gives constructive notice to potential purchasers and creditors — the day the document is recorded.

Subsection (b) of the Texas statute makes an important point, one that courts recognize even if it were not expressly stated: The recording act does not affect the validity of a conveyance between the parties to it. This is important not just for this category of statute but for every recording act because the party not obtaining recording act priority will want to sue his grantor either for fraud or on account of the representations made by deed covenants. The continuing validity of the "instrument" makes that possible.

One rule of thumb holds true for race, race-notice, and notice jurisdictions: Purchasers, mortgagees, lessees, and other parties acquiring an interest in property should insist that the chain of title be complete up to the date of closing, and should record their new document the day of closing.

PURCHASERS FOR VALUE

The notice and race-notice recording statutes protect **subsequent bona fide purchasers without notice**. "Purchasers" are not just purchasers of the fee simple. They include mortgagees, lessees, and anyone else who gives **value** for any interest in the property. Persons who receive an interest as a gift, devise, or inheritance are not purchasers for value, however, and thus the recording acts do not protect them or their interest against unrecorded prior transfers. Donees, devisees, and other persons not qualifying as a purchaser for value can prevail over later subsequent purchasers, however, by promptly recording since a subsequent purchaser will have constructive notice of the donee's interest and thus cannot be a protected purchaser without notice.

Most statutes provide the subsequent purchaser be a purchaser for value or for valuable consideration. Even if the statute omits the value or valuable consideration language, almost all courts would imply it. Only in Colorado do courts not imply the valuable consideration element.

To be a protected subsequent purchaser **for value**, the purchaser or creditor must furnish some value. Money or other consideration less than the full value of a mortgage will suffice. Unfortunately, what constitutes adequate value is a fact-and-circumstances test.

A promise to pay consideration later is not value. Thus a purchaser who gives the seller a note for a substantial part of the purchase price has not given value yet. If the purchaser receives *actual* notice of a prior claimant before retiring the note, she loses to the prior claimant. However, under a concept termed **bona fide purchaser pro tanto**, the prior claimant must reimburse the subsequent purchaser for all consideration paid prior to the subsequent purchaser's learning of the prior claim.

One frustrating twist concerning mortgages complicates matters a bit. As stated above, in the common situation a financial institution or individual that takes a mortgage for a loan, or a home seller who takes back a note and mortgage as part of the purchase price, qualifies as a **purchaser for value** (the loan of money or deeding the property is the value). That seemingly straightforward rule does not apply to the creditor who is owed a **preexisting debt** and, seeking security for the debt, persuades the debtor to give the creditor a mortgage on land as collateral. The courts demand some **new value** be given for the mortgage before the mortgagee can qualify as a purchaser for value. The mortgagee (creditor) is not a purchaser for value, conclude the courts, on the theory that the creditor gave no new value for the mortgage and the mortgage was not part of the original loan. Most mortgagees in this situation get around this problem by giving the debtor extra time to pay. The time extension constitutes the requisite "value." "Value" does not have to be more money. Thus, an unsecured creditor with a demand note or a note due and payable who gives the debtor an additional year to pay in return for the mortgage suddenly becomes a purchaser for value. As an editorial comment, the rule that a preexisting debt cannot be the value for the recording acts seems silly and a trap for the unwary, which may explain why commentators criticize it so much.

PROBLEMS IN GRANTOR-GRANTEE INDICES

The potential for problems in grantor-grantee recording systems is great indeed. One category of problems involves errors in the recorded documents, such as mistaken property descriptions or misspelled names of the parties. Sometimes documents are improperly filed or erroneously indexed. Another class of problems falls under the category of chain of title problems.

One problem occurs when a property owner of two adjoining lots transfers one of the lots and incorporates an easement or covenant (discussed in Chapters 28 and 30, infra) into the deed of the transferred lot that benefits or burdens the current and future owners of the retained lot.

Example 1:   O, the owner of Lot A and Lot B, transfers Lot B, the deed to Lot B incorporating a provision that both Lot A and Lot B will be restricted to single-family residences (a covenant) and another provision giving the owners of Lot B the right to travel over Lot A to get to a specific road (an easement). Later O sells Lot A to Z without telling Z about the easement or the residence-only covenant. The owner of Lot B wants to enforce the covenant and easement against Z even though Z did not know about the covenant or the easement.

The grantor-grantee index flaw is that Z dutifully can check the grantor-grantee index and not find anything in the chain of title for Lot A that mentions the easement or the covenant. Is Z obligated to check out deeds to Lot B and other surrounding lots? If not, how is the owner of Lot B able to protect her bargain? About half the states conclude Z prevails because he should not be obligated to check on all deeds to surrounding property or on deeds to lots transferred by O, the **common grantor**, or by other owners of Lot A in the chain of title. In the other half of states, the owner of Lot B prevails (and Z loses) because purchasers and their representatives should know many covenants and easements are included in only one deed from a common grantor. Either way, somebody will be understandably upset.

A familiar problem with grantor-grantee indexes is the so-called **wild deed**, a recorded deed or other document that cannot be found easily by a search of the grantor-grantee indexes because a link in the chain of title is not recorded or is recorded out of order.

Example 2:   O deeds Blackacre to A, who does not record. A later deeds to B, a purchaser for value, who records. Still later O deeds Blackacre to X, a purchaser for value with no actual knowledge of the grants to A and to B. X records.

Note the quandary. B purchased from A, the legal owner, and recorded his deed, so B is the first of B and X to purchase and to record. X, on the other hand, recorded after B, but if he searched the grantee index back from O to the root of title, and searched the grantor index forward from the root of title to the present day, X would not find the deed from O to A since it was unrecorded, and would have no reason to know to look for a deed from A to B. Who owns Blackacre: B or X?

X prevails. A court would brush aside the fact that B recorded before X by concluding either that X does not have constructive notice of a deed following a missing link in its chain of title, or that B's deed was not legally recorded. The courts favor X not because X is a more innocent party but because it is critical that the integrity of the recording system be maintained. The result puts a premium on a purchaser demanding the seller take all steps to insure a complete chain of title exists. If B had required A to record the 0-to-A deed before B closed, X would have had constructive notice of B's interest and B would have prevailed.

Documents recorded out of chronological order create more grantor–grantee index problems.

Example 3:   A, anticipating his acquisition of Whiteacre, deeds Whiteacre to B, who promptly records the deed. A subsequently purchases Whiteacre from 0, and 0 deeds Whiteacre to A. A records. Later A deeds[1] Whiteacre to X, a purchaser for value who does not know about B's deed. X records.

Note the quandary. Absent the recording acts, B holds legal title. Even though A did not own Whiteacre when he transferred it to B, B takes legal title by the doctrine of estoppel by deed or after-acquired title. See Example 6 in Chapter 25, supra. B also was the first actually to record. X, however, bought in good faith. Moreover, if X had searched the deed records she would have found the 0-to-A deed, but very likely would not have located the A-to-B deed.

Courts differ on whether the A-to-B deed is legally recorded, or if X has constructive notice of the A-to-B deed. Some older cases, presumably on the thought a searcher could find the A-to-B deed because the A-to-B deed would be located in a recent grantor index, ruled in favor of B. The majority of cases, including the more recent ones, hold for X. The integrity of the recording system requires a purchaser, including B in this example, insure all links in the chain of title are properly recorded in order before purchasing; or at least the purchaser (B in this example) should have re-recorded the A-to-B deed after the 0-to-A deed was recorded.

Another problem inherent in the system of deed records is that the deed records do not disclose whether a subsequent purchaser had actual notice or inquiry notice of an unrecorded document or a wild deed, or whether a person in the chain of title bought knowing of an earlier claimant.

Example 4:   0 deeds Greenacre to A. Greenacre is the place to be and, before A can record, 0 deeds Greenacre to B, who has actual knowledge of the 0-to-A deed. B promptly records. Then A records. B later deeds Greenacre

---

1. The transfer from A to C may have been a mortgage. The results are the same whether the transfer was a deed or a mortgage.

to X, a purchaser for value without actual notice of the deed from O to A. X records.

Note the dilemma. B wins between A and B in a race state. B loses between A and B in a notice and a race-notice state because B had actual notice of the O-to-A deed. X, on the other hand, did not have actual notice of the O-to-A deed. Moreover, if X searched the deed records she would find the deed from O to B, and would conclude that B was the legal and record owner of Greenacre.

Who should prevail between A and X? States disagree. Some conclude X prevails because she likely would not find the O-to-A deed because it was recorded after the O-to-B deed. X's chain of title appears complete. Other notice and race-notice states, on the other hand, favor A because the O- to-A deed was the first deed legally recorded. The O-to-B deed is not deemed legally recorded since B had notice of the O-to-A deed. Since the O-to-B deed was not legally recorded, the O-to-A deed was the first legally recorded deed in the chain of title. A prevails. In these jurisdictions, a purchaser to be secure must search all previous owners' names up to the date of closing, a formidable task, and still not be certain she will get record title.

A variation of the above facts introduces the **shelter rule**, an important concept in recording acts whereby a grantee can rely on his predecessor in interest taking without notice even if the grantee has notice of an earlier conveyance.

Example 5: O deeds Brownacre to A, who does not record. O then deeds Brownacre to B, a purchaser for value who has no actual knowledge of the O-to-A deed. B records. Then A records. B later sells and deeds Brownacre to X, a purchaser for value who knows about the O-to-A deed. X records.

As between A and X, who owns Brownacre? X prevails over A even though she has actual knowledge of the O-to-A deed and the O-to-A deed was recorded before the B-to-X deed because B, a prior owner in X's chain of title, prevailed over A. As between A and B, B prevails in a notice state because he purchased without notice of the O-to-A deed, and in a race-notice state because he purchased without notice and he recorded first. B therefore owned Brownacre. To protect B in his enjoyment of Brownacre, the shelter rule allows B to transfer Brownacre to whomever he desires, even to those persons knowing of the O-to-A deed. B, therefore, was free to transfer record title to Brownacre to X even though X knew of the O-to-A deed.

MARKETABLE TITLE ACTS

Several states have enacted marketable title acts to facilitate more efficient searches of the records and to void some long-outstanding interests in the

447

land. Marketable title acts facilitate title searches by stipulating a document conveying title will be the root of title even though the true root of title may have been decades, or even centuries, earlier. Generally, the state marketable title act will specify a period of number of years, ranging from 20 years in some states to 50 years in others, as the marketable title search period. A searcher must trace back in a grantee index to the first document transferring title (the title transaction) that was recorded earlier in time than the earliest date in the marketable title search period. This title transaction becomes the root of title.

Example: State has a marketable title act similar to the Model Marketable Title Act: Any person having the legal capacity to own land in this state, who has an unbroken chain of title of record to any interest in land for forty (40) years or more, shall be deemed to have a marketable title to such interest [subject to some exceptions].

The following transactions apply to Whiteacre:

State gave a patent for Whiteacre to A in 1801.
A sold to B in 1825.
B sold to C in 1870.
C granted D an easement in 1900. C died in 1910, devising the property to E. E sold to F in 1940.
F mortgaged Whiteacre in favor of G in 1950.
F sold Whiteacre to H subject to the mortgage to G in 1955. H sold Whiteacre to I in 1960, the deed not mentioning the 1950 mortgage or the 1900 easement.
I sold to J in 1977. J sold to K in 1998.
Now L in 2010 wants to purchase Whiteacre from K.

Without a marketable title act, the **root of title** is the patent from the state to A in 1801. Under the **marketable title act**, however, the searcher need not search back two centuries for all documents relating to Whiteacre. Instead, the searcher must search only to the title transaction recorded at least 40 years earlier. Since the search begins in 2010, the searcher must find a title transaction recorded prior to 1970. That document is the deed from H to I recorded in 1960. L can search the grantor index back to 1960 and the grantee index forward to 2010. L would have constructive notice of documents recorded or mentioned in documents recorded since 1960, but will not be deemed to have constructive notice of documents recorded before 1960 (unless, as discussed below, an exception applies).

The corollary to the limited search required, and a second objective of marketable title acts, is that interests deriving from documents recorded before the statutory root title cannot be enforced against the new purchaser unless the documents have been re-recorded after the new root of title or unless the old interest meets one of the exceptions to re-recording.

In the above example, since the 1950 mortgage and the 1900 easement were recorded before the statutory root of title, L does not have constructive notice of them. If the 1960 deed from H to I had mentioned the mortgage or easement, L would have been on inquiry notice of them. Similarly, L would have been on inquiry notice of the easement if he would have noticed them had he visited the land.

Statutory exceptions to the marketable title act greatly reduce the effectiveness of the act. While the exceptions vary among the states, the exceptions often include interests held by federal, state, and local governments; utility easements; railroad easements; water rights; and mineral interests. A few states except reversions, remainders, rights of entry, and possibilities of reverter. A few states even except restrictive covenants. Rights acquired by adverse possession or prescription also escape the reach of the marketable title acts. Since exceptions recorded long before the statutory root of title remain enforceable, a conscientious searcher will continue searching back into the deed records for these exceptions.

TITLE INSURANCE

Title insurance is another means to assure title. Although title insurance offers insurance protection, title insurance's **information function** is as important as its **insurance function**. Generally, title insurance companies maintain "title plants" where the companies keep real estate records that are the equivalent of a tract index. Each day the company makes copies of all documents filed in the local government recording office and incorporates the data into its own records.

(a) Informational Use

When some party to a real estate transaction requests title insurance, the title insurance company issues a **preliminary title report** or **binder** setting out the status of the property's **record title**, not its legal title. Because the title company can quickly issue a preliminary title report, purchasers and creditors can quickly review the record defects and encumbrances and decide during the executory period whether the property is marketable under the sales contract. Often, in practice, the preliminary title report is more useful than the title insurance itself.

The information furnished in the preliminary title report usually is limited to information found in the local deed records. The preliminary title report and title insurance policy do not purport to furnish information about or insure against matters created by or that are known by the insured;

defects that result in no loss or damage; defects or encumbrances created after the policy date; rights of persons in possession of the property; encroachments, boundary line disputes, and other matters that would be disclosed by an accurate survey; easements not shown by public record; mechanic's liens; and taxes and special assessments not in the public records. Not all policies except all the above, but many policies come close to limiting the title insurance company's liability solely to damages flowing from the company's not finding documents filed in the deed records.

(b) Lender's Policy and Owner's Policy

Another problem with the insurance aspect of title insurance policies is that property purchasers often are not beneficiaries under the policy, even though many mistakenly believe they are beneficiaries. There are two types of policies based on who is insured. Most title insurance policies insure lenders and mortgagees (**lender's policy**), not the property owners (**owner's policy**). The reason for this is that there is a huge **secondary market** for mortgages.[2] To facilitate assignment of mortgages in the secondary market, financial institutions condition loans on the purchaser/borrower purchasing a lender's policy. A purchaser also may purchase (or the seller may purchase on behalf of the purchaser) an owner's policy for an additional fee. Unless the seller is paying for the policy, most purchasers do not choose to purchase an owner's policy.

(c) No Assignment or Running of Benefits

Another problem with title insurance is that the named beneficiary is the only insured. Title insurance policies are not assignable and do not run with the land. Each new property owner must buy a new policy. This can be costly in a series of quick sales.

(d) Insurer's Duty to Disclose Excepted Defects

A common issue is whether a title insurance company must disclose defects or encumbrances filed in the deed records but excepted from coverage under the policy. Title insurance companies argue, often successfully, that deed records searches are done for the benefit of the title company

---

2. The secondary market for mortgages lets the original mortgagee, generally a financial institution such as a bank, or savings & loan association, sell its mortgages to other lenders or groups of investors.

to determine whether it will issue a policy. Under this view, the insured's only rights are those provided in a title insurance contract. The majority of courts, rejecting the title insurance companies' contract theory, now hold a title insurance company searches the deed records both for its own benefit and for the insured's benefit. The company's failure to disclose defects in these jurisdictions makes a title insurance company liable for not finding the record defect (a negligence standard) or for not reporting the defect to the insured (a breach of a good faith and fair dealing standard).

(e) Damages

When a title insurance company pays a claim under its policy, the amount of the claim is measured by the extent the insured property is damaged by the insurer's failure to discover or disclose a title defect. Damages are limited to the amount stipulated in the policy. Subject to the contract maximum, damages are based on the decrease in fair market value resulting from the defect. Most courts use the values as of the date the defect is discovered to calculate the damages. Other courts prefer the purchase date or even the trial date. Notwithstanding their duty to pay damages, title insurance companies usually reserve the right to cure any defect instead of paying for any loss of value.

(f) Other Benefits of Title Insurance

Title insurance policies do offer some benefits that make a title insurance policy superior to relying solely on the grantor's warranties of title in the deed covenants. One such benefit is that the insurance company will pay attorney fees to defend the title against third-party claimants, whether or not the adverse claimant has a legitimate claim. Another benefit is a title insurance company likely can be found and will have money to pay damages. In contrast, a big hurdle in enforcing deed covenants is finding the grantor. A related hurdle is finding a grantor solvent enough to pay a claim. Those problems usually are minor when dealing with a title insurance company.

Title insurance is not, however, a solution for every problem, as the Example below shows.

Example: In the following situations, O is the owner of Blackacre, whose fee simple absolute title is insured in a standard owner's title policy. Thereafter, the following events occur in the alternative:

1. O is evicted by Blackacre's true owner, who proves that a deed in O's chain of title was not delivered to its grantee. Does O have a claim against

the insurer? Yes, because the policy is intended to provide more than information; one of its functions is to insure against the risk that what looks like a good record title, leading in a chain of title to the insured, has an inherent defect not appearing on the face of the documents. Nondelivery is such a risk. So is the incompetence of a grantor, or the fact that a grantor in the chain conveyed under duress or in some other situation that gave him the power to recall the deed. (These are known collectively in the title insurance industry as "off-record" risks.) Moreover, here O is actually evicted and so can show the insurer an "actual loss" as required by the policy. This is an indemnity agreement after all, not a guarantee of good title, so a loss must be more than theoretical or potential — it must be actual before the insurer will pay a claim.

2. O knew of an easement over Blackacre; it is recorded but does not appear as an exception to coverage in O's policy. Does O have a claim against the insurer? Yes again. Under the policy, the insured has a duty to disclose what she knows about the easement to the insurer (until the closing or the date of the policy), but the insurer also has a duty to discover and disclose what the records would reveal about the title, and it failed in that duty. So an exclusion for defects "known to the insured and not in the public records" only half applies. Any exclusion or exception in the policy will be narrowly construed and also construed against the insurer, and if not excluded, the coverage for record title controls and validates the insured's claim.

3. The county rezones Blackacre, substantially reducing its fair market value. Does O have a claim against the insurer? No, on two grounds. First, the policy provides title insurance, not fair market value insurance. It does not insure against the possibility of public regulation that might affect the use of the property (as zoning does) but not affect its title. In short, the policy insures only against defects in the title, not the property itself. The value of the property after the date of the policy could drop like a rock, falling to zero, and that would not affect the insurer's liability. Second, the rezoning occurred after the policy was issued, and title insurance is retrospective in nature: It indemnifies the insured for defects in title that arose before the policy was issued, not thereafter.

4. O finds that the barn on Blackacre sits partially on a neighbor's land. Does O have a claim against the insurer? No. In its schedule describing the coverage, the policy will use whatever legal description of the property appears on the insured owner's deed, and if the barn is beyond the boundaries of that description, it is not insured.

5. O is forced to buy a quitclaim deed to the marital rights of a spouse of a grantor in O's chain of title. Does O have a claim against the insurer? Maybe. The existence of a marital interest should have been discovered

and disclosed if, for example, property in the insured chain of title was purchased by spouses, only one of whom conveyed to the next grantee, or if a grantee who took title and conveyed it later was really married and nothing about the marriage was reflected in the chain. If, however, O bought the right without first giving the insurer notice of the claim, O probably violated the conditions and stipulations in the policy. The insurer, for instance, might have wanted to participate in the buyout, thinking that its attorney was a better negotiator. At this point, the insured O will have to show that the insurer is not prejudiced by anything that O did in the buyout; even then, a few courts might deny the claim as not in compliance with the claims procedure set out in the policy.

Examples

Name That Recording Act

1. Classify each of the following recording acts as either race, notice, or race-notice:

   (a) No sale, contract, counter letter, lien, mortgage, judgment, surface lease, oil, gas, or mineral lease, or other instrument of writing relating to or affecting immovable property shall be binding on or affect third persons or third parties unless and until filed for registry in the office of the parish recorder of the parish where the land or immovable is situated. Neither secret claims or equities nor other matters outside the public records shall be binding on or affect such third parties.

   (b) A conveyance of real property, within the state, on being duly acknowledged by the person executing the same, or proved as required by this chapter, and such acknowledgment or proof duly certified when required by this chapter, may be recorded in the office of the clerk of the county where such real property is situated, and such county clerk shall, upon the request of any party, on tender of the lawful fees therefor, record the same in his said office.

   Every such conveyance not so recorded is void as against any person who subsequently purchases or acquires by exchange or contracts to purchase or acquire by exchange, the same real property or any portion thereof, . . . in good faith and for a valuable consideration, from the same vendor or assignor, his distributees or devisees, and whose conveyance, contract or assignment is first duly recorded.

   (c) Every such instrument in writing, certified and recorded in the manner herein prescribed, shall, from time of filing the same with the recorder for record, impart notice to all persons of the contents thereof and all subsequent purchasers and mortgagees shall be deemed, in law and equity, to purchase with notice. No such instrument in writing shall be valid, except between the parties thereto, and such as have actual notice thereof, until the same shall be deposited with the recorder for record.

(d) All deeds, powers of attorney, agreements, or other instruments in writing conveying, encumbering, or affecting the title to real property, certificates, and certified copies of orders, judgments, and decrees of courts of record may be recorded in the office of the county clerk and recorder of the county where such real property is situated; except that all instruments conveying the title of real property to the state or a political subdivision shall be recorded pursuant to section 38-35-109.5. No such unrecorded instrument or document shall be valid against any person with any kind of rights in or to such real property who first records and those holding rights under such person, except between the parties thereto and against those having notice thereof prior to acquisition of such rights. This is a race-notice recording statute. In all cases where by law an instrument may be filed in the office of a county clerk and recorder, the filing thereof in such office shall be equivalent to the recording thereof, and the recording thereof in the office of such county clerk and recorder shall be equivalent to the filing thereof.

(e) Every deed conveying lands shall be recorded in the office of the clerk of the superior court of the county where the land is located. A deed may be recorded at any time; but a prior unrecorded deed loses its priority over a subsequent recorded deed from the same vendor when the purchaser takes such deed without notice of the existence of the prior deed.

(f) A conveyance of an estate in fee simple, fee tail or for life, or a lease for more than seven years from the making thereof, or an assignment of rents or profits from an estate or lease, shall not be valid as against any person, except the grantor or lessor, his heirs and devisees and persons having actual notice of it, unless it, or an office copy as provided in section thirteen of chapter thirty-six, or, with respect to such a lease or an assignment of rents or profits, a notice of lease or a notice of assignment of rents or profits, as hereinafter defined, is recorded in the registry of deeds for the county or district in which the land to which it relates lies.

A Common Problem

2. O conveys Blackacre, which he owns in fee simple absolute, to A. A does not record. O conveys Blackacre to B, who does not record. Who owns Blackacre?

A Noted Inquiry

3. M sold her home to A in Year 1. As part of the purchase price, A gave M a $100,000 note and a mortgage on the home as collateral for the note. A recorded her deed, but M did not record the mortgage. On April 21, Year 2, A sold the home to B for $120,000. During the negotiations A told B she still owed $100,000 on the home, but neither the sales contract nor the deed mentioned the note. B borrowed $105,000 from Valley Bank. At closing A received $120,000; B received a warranty deed to the home; and Valley Bank received a note and a mortgage on the home. The closing attorney recorded B's deed and Valley Bank's mortgage the day of closing. M finally recorded her mortgage on July 14, Year 2.

   The state recording act reads, in part, as follows:

   > Every deed conveying land shall be recorded in the office of the clerk of the superior court of the county where the land lies. The record may be made at any time, but such deed loses its priority over a subsequent deed from the same vendor, taken without notice of the existence of the first. Deeds, mortgages, and liens of all kinds, which are required by law to be recorded in the office of the clerk of the superior court, shall, as against the interests of third parties acting in good faith and without notice, who may have acquired a transfer or lien binding the same property, take effect only from the time they are filed for record in the clerk's office.

   B and Valley Bank learn of M's recorded mortgage and bring suit to remove the cloud from his title. What result?

Chain! Chain! Chain!

4. Albert contracted to purchase Velda's home for $100,000. Albert borrowed $90,000 from Nice Bank. At closing Nice Bank's $90,000 check was given to Velda, a warranty deed executed by Velda was given to Albert, and a mortgage on the home executed by Albert in favor of Nice Bank was given to Nice Bank. Nice Bank recorded. Albert recorded his deed one year later. Two years later Albert sold the home to Jules for $125,000, giving Jules a warranty deed. To buy the home, Jules borrowed $100,000 from Residential Savings & Loan, for which Jules gave Residential Savings & Loan a note and a mortgage on the home. Jules promptly recorded his deed. Residential Savings & Loan recorded the mortgage the next day. Neither Jules nor Residential Savings & Loan knew about Nice Bank's mortgage. Who has what rights to the home?

Doing the Wild Deed

5. O sold Blackacre to A, a bona fide purchaser. A did not record. A year later A conveyed Blackacre to B, a purchaser for value who lives out of state.

B promptly recorded. A year later, O conveyed Blackacre to C, a purchaser for value with no actual knowledge of O's deed to A or A's deed to B. C recorded. A year later B inspected the property and saw C building a house on the land. B brought a lawsuit to evict C. Who prevails?

The Fashionably Late Recording

6. Oscar sold his home at its fair market value to Avery in Year 1. Avery did not record in Year 1. In Year 5, Oscar sold the home for its fair market value to Mary, who knew about Avery's deed. Mary recorded promptly. Avery finally recorded his deed in Year 7. In Year 8, Mary sold to Nancy, a purchaser for value without actual knowledge of Avery's deed. Nancy recorded.
   (a) As between Avery and Nancy, who owns the home?
   (b) What result if Mary did not know about Avery's deed, but Nancy did?
   (c) What result on the original facts if Avery finally recorded in Year 10 instead of Year 7?

The Purchaser Who Recorded Too Soon

7. Big Poppa contracted to buy Whiteacre from Owner. Before closing on Whiteacre, Big Poppa conveyed Whiteacre by general warranty deed to First Purchaser. First Purchaser recorded. Six weeks later, Big Poppa acquired title to Whiteacre from Owner. Big Poppa recorded. Three months later Big Poppa conveyed Whiteacre to Second Purchaser, a purchaser for value who had no actual knowledge of the deed to First Purchaser. Second Purchaser recorded.
   (a) As between First Purchaser and Second Purchaser, who owns Whiteacre?
   (b) What result if First Purchaser moved onto Whiteacre immediately after receiving his deed from Big Poppa?

Search Me, Neighbor

8. Mike owned two lots (Lot 1 and Lot 2). Mike sold Lot 1 to Phil by a warranty deed containing the following covenant: "Grantor and Grantee covenant for themselves, their heirs and assigns, that Lot 1 and Lot 2 will be used for single-family residence purposes only." Phil recorded the deed. Five years later Mike sold Lot 2 to Sara by a warranty deed that did not mention the single-family residences only covenant. Sara wanted to build a shop on Lot 2. Phil protested, citing the covenant in his deed. Who prevails?

Schooling Daughter

9. (a) Dad conveyed five acres to Daughter as a gift. Daughter did not record. Daughter immediately moved out of town. Dad, feeling Daughter deserted him, *sold* the five acres to Local School District at its fair market value. Local School District did not know about the prior transfer to Daughter. Local School District recorded. Who prevails as between Daughter and Local School District?

   (b) Dad sold five acres to Daughter at its fair market value. Daughter did not record. Daughter immediately moved out of town. Dad, feeling Daughter deserted him, *donated* the five acres to Local School District. Local School District recorded the deed. Who prevails as between Daughter and Local School District?

   (c) What result in (a) if Daughter recorded before Dad sold the five acres to Local School District?

   (d) What result in (b) if Local School District sold the five acres to Farmer John for its fair market value and Farmer John promptly recorded?

Explanations

Name That Recording Act

1. (a) Race. This is the Louisiana recording act. La. Rev. Stat. Ann. § 2721 (West 1999). It is a pure race statute. Notice is never mentioned.

   (b) Race-notice. This is the New York recording statute. N.Y. Real Prop. Law § 291 (West 1999). The first sentence sets out the essentials for a document to be recorded. Every state has the same or similar prerequisites. New York is one of the few states that combines the prerequisites of recording with the priority granting provision. The second sentence of the excerpt is the critical one for this Example. First, the subsequent purchaser must pay valuable consideration for the interest. Second, the sentence never mentions notice, but it does mandate that the purchaser must have purchased "in good faith." Courts equate the term "good faith" with "without notice." Finally, the subsequent purchaser's document must be "first duly recorded."

   (c) Notice. This is the Missouri notice recording act. Mo. Ann. Stat. §§ 442.390 & .400 (West 1999). The first sentence expressly states that recorded documents impart constructive notice to subsequent purchasers and mortgagees, who in law and equity will have notice of the recorded document. According to the second sentence, a document is not binding on subsequent purchasers and mortgagees who do not have notice of the document. The last clause "until the same shall be deposited with the recorder for record" mentions "record" but not in the context of mandating a race to record. The clause is a subtle but definite reference to the first sentence that a recorded deed imparts "constructive notice." Earlier in the last sentence, the statute denies protection to subsequent purchasers who have actual notice, leaving the last clause to incorporate the constructive notice element.

(d) Race-notice. The Colorado statute, Colo. Rev. Stat. Ann. § 38-35-109(a) (West 1999), is interesting for several reasons. The first reason is historical. The second sentence mandates the subsequent purchaser be the first to record to be protected and then excepts from the act's protections those subsequent purchasers who acquired their interest with notice of the prior interest: the classic race-notice statute. To clear up the confusion in its case law, the Colorado legislature added the third sentence, "This is a race-notice recording statute."

The second reason the Colorado statute is interesting is that same third sentence, "This is a race-notice recording statute." After toiling through the second sentence, the third sentence is startling in its directness. Why don't all statutes convey important information this way?

(e) Race-notice. This is the Georgia statute. Ga. Code Ann. § 44-2-1 (West 1998). For a subsequent purchaser to prevail, the purchaser must acquire the deed without notice of the prior unrecorded deed and must be the first to record.

(f) Notice. This is the Massachusetts recording act. Mass. Gen. Laws Ann. ch. 183, § 4 (West 1999). Under this act, unrecorded deeds are void against all persons except the grantor, his heirs and devisees, and subsequent purchasers having actual notice of the deed, unless the deed is recorded, in which case the recorder of deed prevails against all subsequent purchasers, whether they have actual knowledge or not. Until the deed is recorded, however, any subsequent purchasers without actual knowledge of the deed prevail over the holder of the unrecorded deed. Nothing in the statute requires the subsequent purchasers to be the first to record; hence, no race element.

A Common Problem

2. Under a race statute, the fact that neither A nor B has recorded means that neither has the benefit of the statute, so the common law rule of first in time, first in right controls: A has priority of title.[3] In effect, under the

---

3. The common law rule serves as the default rule when the matter cannot be resolved under the recording act. Consider the situation of an owner who signs a contract of sale with A and later another contract with an unsuspecting B. Contracts are not recordable in some states, and in others won't be recorded because the owner does not put an acknowledgment on it. Acknowledgment is a precondition to recording in almost all states. The common law rule of first in time, first in right applies to two legal interests like deeds and to two equitable

common law, O's second conveyance was a nullity, except that as between O and B, B can use it as evidence of O's defrauding him. No vendor can convey more than he has, and O then had nothing to convey to B, having previously conveyed the fee away. Under a notice statute, however, B could become a subsequent purchaser protected by the statute if he is without notice of A's deed, and so achieves priority over A. (And a moment's thought should tell you that because it will be A who will have to allege and prove that B had notice, A is unlikely to prevail under such a statute.) Now it is A who is left to sue O for fraud or on his deed's covenants of title. Under a race-notice statute, neither A nor B again can satisfy the statute, and the common law controls as before.

A Noted Inquiry

3. Judgment for Valley Bank. B's rights depend on a factual determination. The statute is a pure notice statute. B recorded before M recorded, so B did not have constructive notice of M's mortgage. But A told B about her note to M. The factual issue is whether this information about the note constitutes actual notice of the mortgage, or whether knowing about the debt in these circumstances would induce a reasonably prudent person to inquire about a mortgage to secure the $100,000 debt. If either, B would have notice of the mortgage when B acquired title, and thus not be protected by the recording act. B's home would continue to secure the $100,000 note and mortgage. If neither, B prevails against M's claims.

As a review of deed warranties, see Chapter 25, supra, if M the mortgagee prevails, B still has an action against A based on the present covenant against encumbrances that B may enforce (assuming B can locate A).

If, instead, B prevails, M still has a right to collect the note from A. M cannot foreclose on B's home if A defaults, however. M becomes an unsecured creditor, sharing rights with A's other unsecured creditors.

Valley Bank prevails over M in either situation. Valley Bank took the mortgage without actual notice of M's mortgage since no one, according to the facts, told the bank about M. Also, since Valley Bank received its mortgage before M recorded, Valley Bank did not have constructive notice of M's mortgage, either.

The result is that, while M may have a higher priority than B, M has a lower priority than Valley Bank. In a foreclosure action, M does not have any rights to the sales proceeds until Valley Bank's note is satisfied. In effect, although the problem seemed to pit M the mortgagee against B

---

interests like executory contracts. If A held a contract, and B a deed, B's interest would trump A's at common law because B's was the first *legal* interest: B reached the closing table first and took legal title in his grantor's deed, trumping even the earlier interest in A's equitable title in the contract.

the subsequent purchaser, O and B share a common goal of having A immediately satisfy the debt to O.

Chain! Chain! Chain!

4. Because the subsequent purchasers and creditors for value, Jules and Residential Savings & Loan, did not have actual notice, they should prevail against Nice Bank in a pure notice jurisdiction unless either had constructive notice or inquiry notice. Both Albert's deed and Nice Bank's mortgage were recorded before Jules bought the property and Residential Savings & Loan received the mortgage.

The issue turns on whether the Nice Bank mortgage is in the chain of title or, more precisely, on whether subsequent purchasers and creditors must search the deed records for documents filed before the prior fee owner recorded his interest. Black letter law holds a searcher must examine documents filed from the date the record title owner acquired his interest and not just from the date the deed was recorded. In our Example, both Jules and Residential Savings & Loan should have searched from the date Albert acquired the property. That search would have uncovered the Nice Bank mortgage. Thus Jules and Nice Bank had constructive notice of the Nice Bank mortgage. In a notice jurisdiction, Nice Bank's mortgage takes priority over Jules' deed and Residential Savings & Loan's mortgage. (Jules, of course, owns his home and will continue living there. Nice Bank may have priority, but Nice Bank cannot exercise its rights to the home unless and until Albert defaults on his note to Nice Bank. Jules currently has an action against Albert for breach of the present covenant against encumbrances, and maybe for a breach of the future covenants of warranty and quiet enjoyment. See Chapter 25, supra.) As an aside, some jurisdictions, led by New York, recognize that some purchasers execute mortgages before closing and place the duty to begin searching the deed to sometime before the date the seller acquired title. That approach definitely is the minority rule.

For the reasons given above, Nice Bank also prevails in a race-notice jurisdiction. Nice Bank also prevails in a pure race jurisdiction since Nice Bank recorded before Jules and Residential Savings & Loan recorded.

Doing the Wild Deed

5. C prevails under race, notice, and race-notice statutes. The seemingly paradoxical reason C prevails is that B's deed, though recorded, is a wild deed and a court will conclude that B's deed was not legally recorded. B's deed will be deemed recorded only when all links needed for the chain of title to be traced to B's deed are recorded. The deed from O to A is not recorded, so all conveyances out from A, including B's

recorded deed, also must be deemed unrecorded. Since B's deed is deemed unrecorded, B's deed cannot give constructive notice to subsequent purchasers. Moreover, because B's deed is still unrecorded, C also prevails in a race jurisdiction by being the first to record.

The only way B could prevail is if B could show that C, in searching the deed records, actually found B's deed from A. B then would prevail in a notice or race-notice state since C would have actual notice. The facts, however, say C did not have actual knowledge, and there is no reason to believe C would have found B's deed in a search of the grantor-grantee indices. In a jurisdiction using a tract index, on the other hand, C may have found the deed had he actually searched, and thus would have actual notice.

C's prevailing under these facts is not as unjust as it may appear to you. B was in the best position to prevent the problem by requiring A record A's deed before B would agree to close. The integrity and workability of the grantor-grantee indices depends on each person in every real estate transaction demanding a complete chain of title.

The Fashionably Late Recording

6. (a) Nancy prevails in a race jurisdiction. Avery wins in the majority of notice and race-notice jurisdictions. Nancy prevails in a race jurisdiction because Mary was the first to record, and thus Mary wins the "race" as between Mary and Avery. Because Mary prevails, her successors continue forming the links in the chain. The principle that subsequent purchasers can profit from a predecessor's being protected by the recording statute is known as the shelter rule or shelter principle. In effect, once a person, like Mary, has perfected her priority under the recording acts against a prior claimant, like Avery, all persons claiming through the perfected interest (Mary's interest) also prevail against the prior claimant (Avery). Nancy falls into that happy class, so she prevails in a race jurisdiction.

The situation is different in notice and race-notice jurisdictions. Mary cannot prevail against Avery in either jurisdiction because Mary had actual notice of Avery's deed. Unlike the situation under the shelter principle where Nancy's interest was secured as soon as Mary prevailed, Nancy does not lose because Mary is not a protected person under the recording statute: Nancy still may prevail strictly on her own merits.[4] Unfortunately, Nancy loses on her own in a

---

4. Some jurisdictions hold the reverse. In those states a subsequent purchaser without notice cannot prevail as record owner in a race-notice jurisdiction unless all deeds in his chain of title were properly recorded. See Messersmith v. Smith, 60 N.W.2d 276 (N.D. 1953). This may mean all previous parties in the chain must be protected parties under the recording statute. If so, Nancy cannot prevail since Mary failed to qualify as a protected person.

majority of states. In a race-notice state, Nancy loses and Avery prevails because Avery recorded prior to Nancy. Avery also prevails in the majority of notice (and race-notice) states because Nancy has constructive notice of Avery's deed since Avery's deed was recorded.

A minority of states would find in favor of Nancy, at least in pure notice jurisdictions because, had Nancy searched the deed records, she would have found a deed from Oscar to Mary and she would not have discovered the deed from Oscar to Avery unless Nancy extended her search of Oscar's transactions all the way to Nancy's closing. That being impractical (unless a tract index is used), Nancy should not have constructive notice and thus she should prevail in a pure notice jurisdiction. Again, only a minority of states would find in Nancy's favor. The majority would find in Avery's favor.

Some race-notice jurisdictions also would hold in Nancy's favor on the theory that Nancy is a purchaser without notice of Avery's deed, and Nancy's recording somehow removes the taint from Mary's recording. With her taint removed, Mary's deed is the first recorded. Mary and Nancy then prevail in a race-notice state. These states note that for all subsequent searches, Avery's deed will be outside the chain of title. In addition, Avery's late recording was the reason the problem occurred. Thus, as between Avery and Nancy, Nancy is the more innocent; so courts can favor her and guarantee the integrity of the recording system at the same time. Nonetheless, as developed above, the majority of courts in race-notice jurisdictions would find in Avery's favor.

If Avery had contested ownership before Mary conveyed to Nancy, Avery would have prevailed in all race, notice and race-notice jurisdictions. Only when a subsequent purchaser without notice is introduced does the matter become more complicated.

(b) Nancy prevails in race, notice, and race-notice jurisdictions since, under the shelter rule, Nancy prevails if Mary prevails. Mary prevails in a race state because she recorded before Avery recorded. Mary prevails in a race-notice jurisdiction because she was the first to record and she acquired her interest without notice of Avery's deed. Mary prevails in a notice jurisdiction as soon as she receives the deed because she bought without notice of Avery's deed (which was still unrecorded when Mary bought the property from Oscar). Under the shelter rule Mary can pass her interest to others, who succeed to her rights even if they, like Nancy, knew of the prior adverse claim.

(c) Nancy wins. Under race statutes, both Nancy and Mary recorded before Avery. Under a notice statute, Nancy prevails because she acquired the property without notice of Avery's deed. The fact that Mary knew of Avery's adverse claim does not prevent Nancy from prevailing in her own right. Under race-notice, Nancy wins because she recorded before Avery and she had no notice of Avery's deed.

The Purchaser Who Recorded Too Soon

7. (a) A majority of courts would hold for Second Purchaser, the subsequent purchaser. The facts highlight a conflict of legal preferences. On the one hand, First Purchaser, the first purchaser, properly recorded, and is deemed the legal owner under the doctrine of estoppel by deed (or after-acquired title). See Chapter 25, supra. On the other hand, First Purchaser's deed is not in the chain of title, and Second Purchaser likely would not find the deed in a typical search.

Most courts would find in Second Purchaser's favor, thereby ensuring the integrity of the recording system (and the demise of the significance of after-acquired title (estoppel by deed) in many cases). As between First Purchaser and Second Purchaser, First Purchaser was in the better position to avoid the problem by rerecording his deed after Big Poppa acquired Whiteacre from Owner.

Courts in race and race-notice jurisdictions would hold Second Purchaser recorded first in the chain of title. Second Purchaser prevails in a notice jurisdiction because she purchased without actual notice and with no constructive notice of First Purchaser's deed since First Purchaser's deed was filed outside the chain of title. A few jurisdictions, on the other hand, led by New York and Mississippi, would find in favor of First Purchaser, concluding, on a literal reading, the recording acts protect persons who record, not just those who record in the chain of title, and it is the duty of the subsequent purchasers to expand their search of the deed records if they wish to be protected.

(b) Second Purchaser would have inquiry notice of whatever interest First Purchaser possessed. With notice, Second Purchaser loses in both race-notice and pure notice jurisdictions. Second Purchaser prevails in a pure race jurisdiction since she was the first to record in the chain of title.

Search Me, Neighbor

8. The states seem to be evenly divided. Mike is a common grantor (he owned both lots at one time). When searching the grantor index, a searcher would find Mike's name associated with his conveying Lot 1 to Phil. The property description in the grantor index by accident may mention the restrictive covenant as affecting Lot 2, but most likely the grantor index brief description will describe Lot 1 and not mention Lot 2.

Assuming the grantor index for Lot 1 does not mention Lot 2, the issue becomes, does the subsequent purchaser of Lot 2 have the duty to search deed records for all transfers from a common grantor of neighboring properties? Stated another way, is the fact of a common grantor, coupled with the knowledge that many restrictive covenants and easements are contained in only one deed out from the common owner, enough to put all subsequent purchasers on inquiry notice of all restrictions in deeds of neighboring lands?

The required search extension is not as broad as searching all deeds in the record, and searching the common grantor's name from the time the common grantor originally acquired the property to the closing of the subject property narrows a search (unless, of course, the common grantor began selling off property in 1901 or some other long-ago date). If a state places the burden on the subsequent purchaser to read deeds of neighboring lands from a common grantor, Sara would have constructive notice of the deed restrictions, and thus be bound by the covenants under notice and race-notice statute. Since Phil was the first to record, Sara also would be bound under a race statute. About half the states would rule in favor of Phil and hold the subsequent purchaser, Sara, bound.

The other half of the states find the deed to Lot 1 outside the chain of title of Lot 2. To these states, it is more efficient to require the person receiving the benefit in the first deed (Phil in our Example) to be sure the deed was properly indexed as affecting both Lot 1 and Lot 2 than to require subsequent purchasers to search old deeds from the common grantor. In these states Sara as the purchaser of Lot 2 would not be bound by the restrictive covenant contained in the deeds to Lot 1.

Of the Examples in this section, this is the first one that could not be avoided by a tract index. The problem of indexing Lot 1's deed to Lot 2 remains.

This question will be addressed again in Chapter 31, infra. That chapter explains that for the residential restriction to "run with the land" so as to bound the subsequent purchaser (Sara in our Example), the subsequent purchaser must have notice of the residential-use-only restriction on her lot, either by it being recorded in the deed records (constructive notice) or by a common development scheme (inquiry notice).

Schooling Daughter

9. (a) Local School District prevails. Daughter did not record, so Local School District prevails in a race jurisdiction because it recorded first. Local School District has no actual or constructive or inquiry notice of the deed from Dad to Daughter, so Local School District also prevails in notice and race-notice jurisdictions.

(b) Daughter prevails. Local School District as a donee is not a "purchaser for value." Thus Local School District cannot seek protection under the recording statute. Resort to common law principles favors Daughter since she acquired her title first.

(c) Daughter prevails. Daughter would have been the first to record and Local School District would have had constructive notice of Daughter's interest.

Daughter's receiving the property as a gift is immaterial. Daughter as donee (protected) differs from the Local School District as donee in (b) above (not protected) because Daughter was the first to receive the property and sought protection against subsequent grantees. A prior grantee who records in the chain of title prevails against subsequent grantees. It is subsequent grantees who seek protection that must be purchasers or creditors for value. Daughter having received and recorded her interest prevails against Local School District.

(d) Since Farmer John is a subsequent purchaser for value without actual notice of Daughter's unreported deed and he was the first to record, Farmer John will prevail against Daughter under race, notice, and race-notice statutes. Farmer John's rights are not tainted by Local School District's failure to qualify as a purchaser for value. Farmer John would have benefited from the shelter rule if Local School District was protected under the recording act, of course, but he still can triumph even if the recording act does not protect Local School District. Farmer John can qualify based on his own merits. Farmer John on the facts prevails.

Private Land
Use Controls

PART V

27

Private Nuisance

INTRODUCTION

Private nuisance law is one of the oldest bodies of law, and one that continues to evolve.

A **private nuisance** is an act or condition on the defendant's land that **substantially and unreasonably interferes** with the plaintiff's use and enjoyment of plaintiff's land. The **interference** is usually an **intangible invasion** such as smells, light, sounds, vibrations, dust, and pollution of air and water rather than a **physical invasion**, which is the subject of the **trespass** claim. A person who walks his dogs on his neighbor's land trespasses, and will be liable for nominal damages, at minimum. If that same person allows his (many) dogs to bark all night, the barking dogs may be a nuisance if a court determines the barking — noise or sounds — substantially and unreasonably interferes with his neighbors' use and enjoyment of their property. A plaintiff more easily can prove trespass than nuisance since only the invasion need be shown in a trespass action, and not the substantiality and unreasonableness of that invasion. In close calls — dust (nuisance) or rocks (trespass) coming from one property to another, for example — plaintiffs will try for a trespass action, and defendants will argue private nuisance law applies.

Historically, courts in private nuisance cases brought early in our legal history looked solely at the interference with plaintiff's use and enjoyment of his land, much the way courts evaluate trespass actions today. A defendant was not allowed to interfere with a plaintiff's use and enjoyment at all. If a defendant's activities interfered with a plaintiff's use and enjoyment of

469

plaintiff's own land, the defendant's activities constituted a private nuisance and a court enjoined the defendant's activities.

With the advent of the Industrial Revolution at the beginning of the nineteenth century, courts accommodated progress by implementing a **balancing of the utilities** approach. Each landowner had to tolerate some inconveniences and annoyances for the benefit of technological advances, and only if the harm to the plaintiff outweighed the social utility of the defendant's activities would an injunction issue. Otherwise, the defendant could continue his activities. Neither was the plaintiff entitled to monetary damages in that case, because by law the defendant's activities were not a private nuisance.

A century later, courts recognized the new balancing rule favored a finding of no nuisance when plaintiff landowners were harmed by major economic entities. Courts then began allowing damages if the plaintiff seemed entitled to some relief but an injunction seemed inappropriate. Relatively recent judicial decisions can be found using each of the three approaches, though a definite trend toward the approach allowing damages is apparent.

In many cases, the plaintiff's and the defendant's uses both are socially beneficial, but the two uses are incompatible. Generally, which one is labeled a private nuisance would depend on which is less suited to the general locale. Sometimes, in close cases, the use in place first will prevail over the other use since the second party came to the nuisance, but that is not always the case.

INTENTIONAL AND UNINTENTIONAL INTERFERENCES

Interferences with a plaintiff's use and enjoyment of the plaintiff's land may be one of two types. The first type is an **unintentional interference**, usually resulting from negligent, reckless, or abnormally dangerous activities. These activities are either disfavored as falling below expected standards of conduct (negligence and recklessness) or as imposing such a high standard of care than a strict or near-strict liability standard applies as long as the interference is substantial (abnormally dangerous activities). Many commentators prefer to isolate unintentional interference from private nuisance analysis, consigning unintentional interferences to the more traditional negligence or strict liability actions.

The second type, and the more important one for the immediate discussion, is the **intentional invasion** or **intentional interference**. "Intentional" does not mean the defendant intends to interfere with the plaintiff's use and enjoyment of his land. "Intentional" mainly distinguishes the acts or conditions from negligent acts or conditions. When an "intentional invasion" occurs, the defendant in fact knows or should know its activities or property condition will affect the use or enjoyment of neighboring property, but feels society should tolerate or even encourage the defendant's activity or condition despite the inconveniences to neighboring landowners.

Example: A person mowing his lawn knows or should know the noise from the lawnmower and some dust will pass over the property line to neighboring property, and that the exhaust from the lawnmower pollutes the air flowing to neighboring lands. Despite this knowledge, the person probably considers the invasions normal, acceptable consequences of mowing the lawn (even though his innocent neighbor may have to turn up the sound on the television he's watching). He means his neighbor no harm. The invasions in this Example, nonetheless, are characterized as "intentional." They probably are not unreasonable (or even substantial) interferences with his neighbors' use and enjoyment of their lands, but they are intentional interferences.

SUBSTANTIAL INTERFERENCE

Only a *substantial interference* with the use or enjoyment of property will amount to a private nuisance. As members of the community, individuals must tolerate certain annoyances, such as children at play during daylight hours (unless someone operates a preschool next door), automobile noises, and other annoyances. **Substantial** as used here does not necessarily mean egregious. It only means that persons of normal sensitivities would consider the interference to be substantial. The element forecloses actions for invasions that are insubstantial and deters complaints by petty or overly sensitive plaintiffs. Two hundred years ago, this was the main inquiry. Once a defendant was found to have substantially interfered with his neighbor's use and enjoyment of the neighbor's land, a court would enjoin the activity. Today courts consider the next factor, unreasonable interference, more important.

UNREASONABLE INTERFERENCE

The main task of a court in a private nuisance case is to determine whether the defendant's actions or the condition on the defendant's property is a reasonable or an **unreasonable interference** with the neighbors' use and enjoyment of their property. While courts and commentators agree on the necessity of a substantial and unreasonable interference with the use and enjoyment of neighboring lands, they disagree on how exactly to determine unreasonable interference and what remedies are available once a private nuisance is found. The following, drawn from the Restatement (Second) of Torts, seems to be the current trend (but not the universal approach by any means): Defendant's acts or the condition on defendant's property will be a private nuisance if either:

> (a) the **gravity of the harm** to plaintiff's use and enjoyment outweighs the **social utility** of defendant's conduct or the condition on defendant's property; (b) the harm to plaintiff is sufficiently grave and greater than the plaintiff should be required to bear without compensation; (c) the harm to plaintiff is sufficiently grave and the financial burden of defendant's compensating for the harm and for similar harm to others would not make the continuation of the defendant's activities infeasible; (d) the harm to plaintiff is sufficiently grave and the defendant could avoid the interference in whole or in part without "undue hardship"; or (e) the harm to plaintiff is sufficiently grave, plaintiff's use is well-suited to the character of the locality, and the defendant's conduct or property condition is unsuited to the locality.

See Restatement (Second) of Torts §§ 825-831.

To reiterate, not all courts have adopted the Restatement's view. Some courts, for example, limit the definition to situation (a) and deny relief in the other four situations. A few states look solely at the severity of the interference with the plaintiff's use and enjoyment of his property without considering at all the social utility of the defendant's activities.

In evaluating the **gravity of the harm to plaintiff**, a court considers the extent and the character of the harm, the social value attached to the plaintiff's use or enjoyment, the suitability of the use in the character of the locality, and the burden on the plaintiff to avoid the harm. In regard to the character of the locality, courts look to whether the plaintiff **came to the nuisance** as one of the factors considered (though it is only a factor and is not determinative). A court can consider other relevant factors as well.

In evaluating the **social utility of the defendant's conduct**, courts consider the social value the law attaches to the defendant's conduct or the condition on the land, and the suitability of the defendant's activities or property condition to the character of the general locality. Zoning ordinances may help ascertain the suitability of the location for the defendant's and the plaintiff's uses, but zoning status is just a factor and is not determinative.

INJUNCTIONS AND DAMAGES

As to remedies for a private nuisance, some courts hold that once a private nuisance is found by **balancing the utilities**, the plaintiff is entitled to an **injunction**. Probably most courts today would engage in a second, more critical "balancing of the equities" during the remedy phase to determine the appropriate relief. An injunction seems appropriate if the harm to the plaintiff outweighs the social utility of defendant's conduct, where the defendant can avoid the harm without undue hardship, or where the plaintiff's conduct is suited to the locale and the defendant's activity is not. While some courts will grant **injunctive relief** only, the vast majority will grant **damages** under equitable principles, sometimes in addition to injunctive relief, and sometimes in lieu of injunctive relief. Monetary damages seem appropriate where the defendant provides significant social utility, and it cannot prevent the nuisance. In many jurisdictions, a defendant can escape an injunction only if the social utility of the defendant's primary activity benefits the public at large rather than merely benefiting the defendant personally (known as the **rule of necessity** or the **stern rule of necessity**).

LATERAL SUPPORT AND SUBJACENT SUPPORT

Related to private nuisance because it relates to rights and obligations between owners of neighboring property, but with its unique legal character, is the landowner's right to adjacent and subjacent support, and the concomitant obligation not to do any act that causes neighboring lands to subside or move. A landowner in hilly terrain, for example, cannot remove so much dirt on his land that the uphill land shifts, subsides, or gives way. A landowner can remove soil from his property but not so much or so near his property line that it changes his neighbor's land.

The rights and obligations relating to **lateral support** vary depending on whether the supported land is in its natural state or if structures or other improvements have been built on the supported land. The owner excavating or changing his land so as to cause a shift of the soil of the supported land is strictly liable for damage caused by removing the lateral support if the supported land is in its natural condition, and is liable for damages to improvements on the supported land if his excavation would have caused the supported land in its natural condition to shift or move.

If the supported land has been improved such that the land needs support greater than if the supported land was in its natural state, the supporting land owner's standard of care changes from a strict or absolute liability to one based on negligence. The standard of care to which an excavator is held anticipates the excavator considering the effect the excavation has on neighboring property. If the excavating landowner makes an unnecessary excavation and can or should foresee that the unnecessary excavation will cause the soil to shift or subside, his removing the soil will be negligent. If, however, the excavation benefits the supporting land, the landowner must use accepted methods of excavation as determined by engineers, he must give notice to the supported land owners, and he must allow the supported land owners sufficient time to take steps to prevent harm to their land and improvements. It is a defense to a negligence claim that the owner of the supporting land gave sufficient notice and time to the owner of the supported land, and the owner of the supported land did not shore up his land.

In contrast to lateral support rights and obligations, which relate to the removal or changing of soil on the supporting property, the rights and obligations related to **subjacent support** involve actions that may cause the land surface to subside. Two variations of subjacent support cases can be found. In the first, the owner of a minerals interest can be liable to the surface owner if the mineral owner in extracting the minerals removes the subsurface support resulting in the subsidence of the surface land.

The second variation of subjacent support cases occurs when pumping water from one parcel of land leads to the subsidence of neighboring land. As background, water flows underground similar to how it flows above ground. Water in underground lakes, called **percolating water,** flows to areas of low pressure. If water is pumped from one area of an underground lake, water moves toward that lot. If enough water flows from one area to another, the underground infrastructure may collapse and the surface will subside.

Under the English Rule, a landowner owns all the underground lake or percolating water he can pump from the ground (as contrasted with water from underground streams). The landowner can remove as much of the water for any purpose without regard to the effect on neighboring land. Most American jurisdictions reject the English Rule and substitute one of several approaches.

One approach, called the American Rule, limits the landowner to removing only so much water as can be used to reasonably benefit the property where the water is located. Another approach views the percolating water as jointly owned by all the surface owners. A landowner can take out only his "correlative" share. Under a third approach, landowners can withdraw water as long as the removal does not affect other landowners' beneficial use of the water. Under these approaches as long as the landowner does not exceed the amount of water he legally can remove from the land and he does not act maliciously, he is not liable for subsidence of neighboring land. A fourth approach is to apply a negligence standard that addresses the subsidence issue directly, holding that a landowner is negligent, and hence liable, if he withdraws water in a manner that negligently damages or destroys the lands of others. In some western states a landowner whose removal of water from under his land causes his neighbors land to subside is strictly liable for any damages his neighbor's property.

Examples

Bark All Night, Bark a Little Louder

1. Five plaintiffs and the defendant, Shepherd, live in a semirural area with homes in relative close proximity. The closest of any plaintiffs' home to Shepherd's is 50 yards. Plaintiffs already lived in the area when Shepherd moved to his place. Two years ago Shepherd built a dog kennel for his 16 Australian Shepherd show dogs. The dogs stayed penned outdoors during the daytime. Shepherd moved them indoors each evening, and the dogs remained inside the kennel all night. The 16 dogs barked all night and much of the day. Plaintiffs could not sleep, perform yard work, or enjoy their porches or yards because of the dogs' constant barking. The plaintiffs became annoyed, irritable, and physically upset. They lost sleep and became short-tempered. Shepherd says the dogs never woke him. The five plaintiffs brought a private nuisance action. What result?

Slam Dunk at the Buzzer

2. Shields, a lawyer, and Ruben, a lawyer, are neighbors, sharing a back property line. A six-foot-high solid adobe wall separates the two lots. Shields built a basketball court (one basket) in his backyard 60 feet from the back property line. Ruben's house is ten feet from the back property line. Mrs. Ruben was pregnant and became nervous when she heard Shields or Shields' son, Jonathan, playing basketball. In addition, weekend basketball games interrupted Ruben's naps. The basketball games lasted between five and thirty minutes. Since the basketball court was not lighted, the Shields only played during the daylight hours.

   Ruben complained to Shields about the noise. Shields poured additional concrete into the hollow pole supporting the backboard and added four inches of foam rubber with a plywood backing to deaden the sound of the backboard. The noise still annoyed Ruben. Twice, to abate the noise, Ruben sprayed the basketball court with water while Shields and Jonathan were playing. Ruben also hired an acoustic engineer, who concluded the noise was below the municipal code maximum noise level, but that the noise could exceed the maximum noise level if more people played. Mrs. Ruben could hear the noise in her bedroom if the window was open. Closing the window substantially reduced the noise.

   Ruben, extremely distressed and frustrated because Shields continued playing basketball despite Ruben's complaints and self-help, brought a private nuisance action to halt Shields' basketball playing. What result?

Feedlot Feud

3. Adrian and Ruth Carpenter and five of their neighbors brought a private nuisance action against Sunnyland Feedlot, a feedlot that services approximately 9000 head of cattle daily. Plaintiffs allege the manure, pollution of river and groundwater, odor, pest infestation, increased concentration of birds, dust, and noise caused by the feedlot constitute a private nuisance. The state's economy depends largely on agriculture. What result?

Fuel for Thought

4. John Wayne Airport leased property on the northwest quadrant of the airport to Snafuel, a venture by various airlines using the airport. Snafuel built three 300,000-gallon *above-ground* fuel storage tanks on the leased property. Studies indicated the three tanks presented a severe and unnecessary risk of a potential disaster. Federal regulations stipulated the tanks should have been placed underground.

   Bishop Office Park is located on the northwest border of John Wayne Airport, about 100 feet from the three fuel storage tanks. Bishop Office Park tenants fear that, in the case of an explosion, they and their property will be burned to a crisp instantaneously. They also worry their insurance premiums will become unaffordable. Bishop Office Park also contends its proximity to the fuel storage tanks has decreased the property's market value.

   Bishop Office Park, for itself and its tenants, brings an action alleging a private nuisance. What result?

Strip Mine, Will You?

5. Landowner conveyed all the coal, minerals, oil, gases, iron ore, and stone to Coal Company. Two years later Landowner conveyed the property to New Owner, excepting the rights transferred to Coal Company. Coal Company wrote New Owner that Coal Company planned to strip mine the coal (strip mining destroys the land surface). New Owner brought an action to prevent Coal Company from strip mining the coal. What result?

A Sinking Feeling

6. Quarry Company has operated a stone quarry for 40 years on a 100-acre parcel of land adjoining Farmer's land. The quarry covers the entire 100 acres and is about 80 feet deep. Water seeps into the quarry. To mine the quarry, Quarry Company must continually pump water from the quarry. Quarry Company has drained so much water from its pits that the water table beneath Farmer's land has dropped and the water support for the clay under Farmer's land has been destroyed, resulting in a series of sink

holes up to 10 feet deep and 30 feet wide on Farmer's land. Farmer brought an action against Quarry Company for damages to his land. What result?

Explanations

Bark All Night, Bark a Little Louder

1. Plaintiffs prevailed in the actual case. Tichenor v. Vore, 935 S.W.2d 171 (Mo. Ct. App. 1997). A private nuisance is a condition on defendant's land that substantially and unreasonably interferes with the plaintiff's use and enjoyment of the plaintiff's property. Generally, there must be some invasion. Here that invasion was noise — 16 dogs' barking. The interference was substantial: a normal person of the community would regard the noise as seriously annoying or intolerable.

   Shepherd's raising the show dogs was a hobby. The harms to the plaintiffs are serious disruption of sleep and social activities, some physical stress, mental stress, and anxiety. The balancing result is that the condition, the dogs' barking, constitutes an unreasonable interference with the use and enjoyment of the neighboring property. The kennels with 16 dogs is not suited to the area. The court so ruled, and issued an injunction limiting Shepherd to two dogs.

Slam Dunk at the Buzzer

2. Shields prevails. The most that can be said for Ruben is that noise invaded his property. Some doubt exists whether the noise substantially interfered with Ruben's use of his property. Mr. and Mrs. Ruben's statements they lost sleep and suffered emotional distress sounds like the noise was substantial to them, but it is doubtful persons of normal sensibilities would have been disturbed by Shields' basketball playing. As the actual court wrote,

   > A reasonable person must realize that complete emotional tranquility is seldom attainable, and some degree of transitory emotional distress is the natural consequence of living among other people in an urban or suburban environment. . . . Every annoyance or disturbance of a landowner from the use made of property by a neighbor does not constitute a nuisance.

   A reasonable person probably would not find the noise to be substantial.

   Even if the "substantiality" factor is conceded, Shields' conduct does not appear unreasonable. Basketball furthers exercise and family cohesion (Shields usually played alone or with his son). Shields made changes to soften the sound of the backboard. The noise was not greater than expected for reasonable use, and was below the municipal code noise level maximums. Play occurred during the daylight hours when such noise normally occurs. Ruben, moreover, could eliminate much of the noise simply by closing his windows. On balance, Shields' basketball playing was not an unreasonable interference with Ruben's use and enjoyment of his property.

Feedlot Feud

3. This case highlights a controversial aspect of private nuisance law: what to do when the social utility of defendant's conduct outweighs the harm to the individual plaintiffs. As a preliminary matter, the feedlot certainly **interfered substantially** with the plaintiffs' use and enjoyment of their property. The harder question is whether the feedlot **unreasonably** interfered with that enjoyment.

   To decide under the Restatement guidelines, a court would balance the social utility of the feedlot against the harm to the plaintiffs. In Carpenter v. Double R Cattle Co., 701 P.2d 222 (Idaho 1985), a judge and a jury decided the social utility of the feedlot, as an essential activity in the local economy, outweighed the private discomfort and health risks suffered by the individual landowners. At one time and in some jurisdictions (including Idaho in Double R Cattle Co. as it turns out) this determination ended the case, and the feedlot as a matter of law would not be a private nuisance. No injunction would issue and no damages would be awarded.

   The Restatement (Second) of Torts, however, envisions a situation where an injunction may not be appropriate, but where damages would be in order if the harm to plaintiffs' use and enjoyment was severe and greater than the plaintiffs should bear without compensation, or if the harm was serious and the defendant's paying damages would not make the defendant's activities infeasible. The limited facts suggest one of these two situations fits the Example, so that Sunnyland Feedlot should pay the plaintiffs' damages. Otherwise, the feedlot could "externalize" the cost onto its unfortunate neighbors.

   The Idaho Supreme Court in *Double R Cattle Co.* refused to adopt the Restatement (Second) provisions providing for damages for serious or severe interferences. These rules would place an unreasonable burden on agriculture, a critical component of the state's economy, wrote the majority. In effect, some citizens must suffer some inconveniences so that all the people in the long run live better lives. Thus, in the actual case, Sunnyland Feedlot owed plaintiffs nothing.

   Neither the facts in the Example nor those of the actual opinion develop the nature of the surrounding area. Residences may be moving toward the feedlot, for example; and at some later point in time the feedlot will become a private nuisance and thus be forced to relocate.

Notwithstanding the approach taken by the Idaho Supreme Court, and notwithstanding the Restatement's balancing-of-the-utilities formulation, a few states would have found for the plaintiffs by looking exclusively to the interference with the plaintiffs' use and enjoyment of their land. In those states, the courts would order Sunnyland Feedlot to cease the activities constituting the private nuisance — the feedlot in the Example — due to the interference with plaintiffs' use and enjoyment of their properties. The injunction issues, end of matter. Any other response would give the defendant a private right of eminent domain over neighboring property. The injunction returns the parties to a non-nuisance status. The parties are free to contract to resolve the issue amongst themselves. If they cannot agree, the feedlot must close. In most jurisdictions today, however, a court would balance the equities to determine if an injunction or damages or both is the most equitable remedy.

Fuel for Thought

4. The result depends on whether the jurisdiction recognizes an action for private nuisance when invasion of the property has not occurred. The court in Koll-Irvine Center Property Owners Assoc. v. County of Orange, 29 Cal. Rptr. 2d 664 (1994), held a private nuisance action cannot be maintained for an interference in the use and enjoyment of land caused solely by the fear of a future injury. The list of consequences and effects given by plaintiffs, wrote the court, cannot substitute for an invasion of property rights. Plaintiffs' only option, it appears, was to lobby the county, state, or federal regulatory agencies to act for the public good.

   Other states do not require an invasion as an essential element of a private nuisance. All that is required is a condition on the defendant's land that unreasonably interferes with the plaintiff's use and enjoyment of its land. Stored explosives or above-ground fuel storage tanks, therefore, could be the grounds for a private nuisance action. Other conditions that have constituted a private nuisance have been houses of prostitution, crack houses, funeral homes, and a tuberculosis hospital.

   Interestingly, even states that recognize noninvasive conditions as the basis for a private nuisance claim may not have found this interference to be "substantial" if the parties merely feared for their lives and property. It is only when that fear is reflected in the decline in the property's fair market value that many courts will conclude the interference would be the considered substantial to the normal person in the community.

   Assuming the tanks are a private nuisance, a court would issue an injunction only against the use of the above-ground fuel tanks. The airport itself could continue and underground tanks would be allowed as more suited to the locale.

Strip Mine, Will You?

5. New Owner as the surface owner has a right of continued subjacent support, and Coal Company as the owner of a mineral estate and miner of the minerals has an obligation not to remove or destroy that support. New Owner prevails since Coal Company by strip mining would destroy the surface and its subjacent support. The parties can contract to allow Coal Company to strip mine but it is not an inherent right of ownership of the coal or other minerals.

A Sinking Feeling

6. The result depends on the jurisdiction. Jurisdictions focusing on a landowner's right to withdraw water, such as those states employing the English Rule (not many states) or the American Rule, allowing a landowner to remove as much water as it needs to reasonably benefit the use of the land, would hold Quarry Company is not liable for the damages to Farmer's land. See, e.g., Finley v. Teeter Stone, Inc., 248 A.2d 106 (Md Ct. App. 1968). Jurisdictions that hold a landowner strictly liable for causing harm to neighboring land by removing the subjacent support would find Quarry Company liable for damages to Farmer's land. Those states adopting a nuisance standard likely would find Quarry Company liable to Farmer. See, e.g., Henderson v. Wade Sand & Gravel Co., 388 So. 2d 900 (Ala. 1980).

CHAPTER 28

Creation of Easements

INTRODUCTION

Easements, along with restrictive covenants and equitable servitudes, are interests one person has in another person's property. Easements, restrictive covenants, and equitable servitudes are similar concepts, yet their elements and the rights of the respective parties to them differ. We explore easements first. Chapters 30 and 31 develop restrictive covenants and equitable servitudes.

An **easement** is an irrevocable right to use another person's land for a specific purpose. The Restatement of Property § 450 (1944) offers the following definition:

> An easement is an interest in land in the possession of another which (a) entitles the owner of such interest to a limited use or enjoyment of the land in which the interest exists; (b) entitles him to protection as against third persons from interference in such use or enjoyment; (c) is not subject to the will of the possessor of the land; (d) is not a normal incident of the possession of any land possessed by the owner of the interest; and (e) is capable of creation by conveyance.

The most frequently encountered easements give the holder a right to travel over another's land, or a right to place utility lines, sewer lines, pipelines, or railroad tracks across another's property, but easements may be used for many purposes. The easement holder and the landowner both may use the same area of land, but the landowner's use may not

481

unreasonably interfere with the easement holder's use of the easement for its intended purposes.

One issue, often litigated in grants of a strip of land to a railroad for "railroad purposes" or "railroad right-of-way," is whether the interest granted is an easement, a fee simple absolute, or a fee simple determinable. The matter often comes to a head when a railroad abandons a line and plans to sell the strip (or many adjoining strips) to a third party. Courts try to ascertain the grantor's intent in conveying the interest to the railroad company. Generally, each case turns on state law and the particular language used in the original grant. In drafting deeds, the prudent attorney should clearly identify easements as such.

TERMINOLOGY

To appreciate the many facets of easements law, you must master its terminology. To begin, an easement may be an **easement in gross** (or personal easement) or an **easement appurtenant**. An **easement in gross** is one benefiting a person whether or not the person owns any specific property (or any property at all). An **easement appurtenant**, in contrast, benefits the owner or possessor of a particular parcel of land. The easement appurtenant passes with the property it benefits. An easement appurtenant has the potential to continue indefinitely. An easement in gross, on the other hand, unless assignable, ends at the holder's (grantee's) death.

Example: Jacob deeds to his next-door neighbor, Dolores, the right to park in his parking lot. Dolores has an easement. Dolores sells her home to Roger and moves to a house five miles away. The easement is an **easement in gross** if, under the terms of the original grant from Jacob to Dolores, Dolores can continue parking in Jacob's parking lot after she sells her home to Roger. On the other hand, the easement is an **easement appurtenant** (benefiting Roger as the current owner of the home) if the original deed provided that any new owner of the house succeeded to the right to park in Jacob's parking lot. The easement will not be interpreted to benefit both Dolores and Roger.

In deciding whether an easement is an easement in gross or an easement appurtenant, courts express a constructional preference for the easement appurtenant, which means an easement in gross must be clear from the express grant or from surrounding circumstances.

An **easement appurtenant** affects at least two parcels of land. The owner of one parcel has an easement over the other parcel of land. The property **burdened** by the easement is called the **servient estate** or the **servient**

tenement. (Use the term favored by your professor.) The land **benefited** by the easement is the **dominant estate** or **dominant tenement**. We speak of benefited and burdened property, but it is the owners of the parcels who are actually benefited or burdened in their use of the properties.

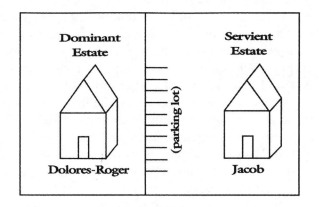

In our previous example, Jacob's land was the servient estate, and the Dolores-Roger property was the dominant estate. The term "servient estate" describes the burdened property for both easements appurtenant and easements in gross. The term "dominant estate" is used only when discussing easements appurtenant. Since an easement in gross benefits a specific person and not the owner of a particular parcel of land, there is no dominant estate.

Easements are only one form of nonpossessory interest a person may have in another's land. You must be able to distinguish easements from other nonpossessory interests in land. **Leasehold interests**, for instance, are contractual rights between a landlord and a tenant. In the parking lot example, Jacob and Dolores could have entered into a contractual lease rather than Jacob's granting Dolores an easement.

A **profit a prendre** or "profit" is the right to enter another's land, without liability for trespass, and remove minerals, timber, wild animals, fish, soil, water, or other things constituting a natural part of the land. A person usually has a profit in only one of the listed items. A person with a profits interest has an easement to venture onto the property as necessary to enjoy the profits interest. At one time, major differences existed between profits and easements. No notable differences exist in modern American law.

Sometimes a landowner permits another person to use property, the permission revocable at the landowner's will. This permission is a **license**. A person invited to swim in his neighbor's pool has a license, for instance. Jacob, in our earlier example, may have given Dolores a mere license instead of an easement to park in his parking lot. Tickets to see a movie, concert, or sporting event often are characterized as licenses, as are many short-term parking arrangements. The main attribute of a license is that it is revocable or terminable at will. Some commentators do not consider a license to be an interest in land. Others call a license a revocable nonpossessory interest in land. Either way, it is revocable at will. That said, licenses in some circumstances become irrevocable, and in practice become indistinguishable from easements. More on this later.

A final classification dichotomy distinguishes affirmative easements (also known as positive easements) from negative easements. **Affirmative easements** give the holder the right to go onto the servient estate for a specific purpose. Dolores, in our on-going example, has an affirmative easement to park on Jacob's property. Most easements today are affirmative easements.

A **negative easement** gives the holder the right to prevent the possessor of the servient estate from doing some act on the servient estate. English courts recognized four negative easements: right of airflow (duty not to interfere with airflow), right to light (duty not to block light or the easement holder's windows), right to channeled water flow (duty not to interfere with water flow in artificial streams to the dominant estate), and right to lateral support (duty not to remove support from a house on the dominant estate). English courts refused to extend negative easements beyond these four. American courts accepted these four, and though reluctant to recognize other forms, have added view easements (duty not to block view), solar easements (to protect access to solar energy), and conservation easements (usually given to a government or charity to protect or maintain historical or scenic areas). For the most part, courts do not recognize other negative easements, entrusting what could be called negative easements to the domain of restrictive covenants and equitable servitudes, to be discussed in Chapters 30 and 31, infra.

Negative easements, like affirmative easements, are not absolute rights of ownership, but because they are not evidenced by use of the servient estate, their nature and scope must be more precisely defined in the deed creating them. Thus, a landowner needing air flow for a windmill or to cool her house cannot object to a neighbor's new wall or building just because it blocks the flow. Only if the neighbor or one of the neighbor's predecessors deeded the landowner or one of the landowner's predecessors a negative easement will the landowner have an enforceable right.

EXPRESS EASEMENTS

Easements can be created several ways. Most easements result from an **express grant** or **express reservation** in a deed. Easements being interests in land, an express grant or reservation of an easement must be in writing to satisfy the Statute of Frauds. All Statute of Frauds requirements, developed in

Chapter 22, supra, apply to easements as well. Like other interests in land, for an express easement to bind bona fide purchasers, it must be recorded. See Chapter 26, supra.

Express grants of easements usually are created by deed. The grantor often sells only part of her property and grants the purchaser an easement over the seller's retained land. The grantee owns the dominant estate and the grantor retains the servient estate. Courts have no problem recognizing the grantee's easement over the grantor's land.

Conversely if the grantor was to have an easement over the grantee's land, the deed likely would incorporate a clause **reserving** an easement or **excepting** an easement. At one time, in some jurisdictions, which word chosen ("reserve" or "except") was key to whether the deed created an easement in favor of the grantor at all. A reservation created an easement; an exception did not. The theory was that a **reservation** was a grant of the property to a purchaser and a regrant of the easement back to the original grantor. An **exception**, in contrast, was merely a statement the property might be subject to an outstanding easement. The proof the outstanding easement existed had to be found in another, independent deed, however. Since most people, including lawyers and judges, were not aware of the distinction, and after a while used the terms concurrently and interchangeably, over time the two terms became synonymous. That's the good news.

A third example, incorporating the **reservation to a stranger to the deed**, presents the confusing aspect. Assume the grantor is selling part or all of her property and wishes to provide that a third party be given an easement over the transferred land. In Willard v. First Church of Christ, Scientist, 498 P.2d 987 (Cal. 1972), as an illustration, a landowner sold property on the condition a church located across the street would have an easement to park on the transferred property. The court interpreted the deed transferring the property as **reserving** a parking easement to the church. One of the issues in the case — and the relevant one for this discussion — was whether a grantor can reserve an interest (here an easement) to a "stranger to the deed" (here the church). "Sure, why not?" was the court's attitude: The grantor's intent clearly was that she wanted the church to have the easement. A primary rule of construction is to ascertain and carry out the grantor's intent. The grantor's intent controls. The church got its parking easement.

While enforcing an easement reserved to a third party seems eminently sensible, a large majority of states still follow the old common law that a reservation or exception in favor of a third party (the stranger to the deed) is invalid. While sometimes acknowledging that the rule forbidding a reservation to a stranger is an "obsolete vestige of feudalism," the majority of courts still retain the old rule because, as explained by one court, "Where it can reasonably be assumed that settled rules are necessary and necessarily relied upon, stability and adherence to precedent are generally more important than a better or even a 'correct' rule of law." Estate of Thomson v. Wade,

509 N.E.2d 309 (N.Y. 1987) (per curiam). A few states, such as California and Montana, will enforce a reservation to a stranger to the deed if the deed clearly identifies the third party, the deed specifically locates the easement on the servient estate, the grantors testify that they intended to create the easement, and the price paid was less than if the easement had not been reserved.

EASEMENTS BY ESTOPPEL AND IRREVOCABLE LICENSES

Express easements must be created in a writing to satisfy the **Statute of Frauds**. What would otherwise be an express easement may fail because a document may not qualify as a writing under the Statute of Frauds or, more likely, the parties may never have memorialized the transfer in writing in the first place. In the latter case, the owner of the servient estate may have given the owner of the dominant estate permission or authorization to use the burdened property for a specific purpose.

The failure to create an easement because the parties did not execute a writing generally results in the grantee's receiving a **license**. As discussed supra, the license is revocable at will. To be more specific, the license is revocable at will *at law*. Some courts, however, **in equity** will enforce the license under either an easement by estoppel or irrevocable license theory. These two theories center on similar elements: The owner of the servient estate consents to the dominant estate holder's use of the servient estate; the servient estate owner knows or should know the dominant estate owner will materially change his position believing the permissive use will not be revoked; and the dominant estate holder reasonably believing the permission will continue substantially changes his position by investing in improvements on the servient estate or on the dominant estate.

Most courts use an **easement by estoppel** theory, concluding that under the facts, the servient estate holder cannot deny the existence of the easement. Broadly applied, an easement by estoppel will result every time a person uses another's land and a court finds that person will be inconvenienced if he is stopped. Courts say they disfavor easements by estoppel, but they choose different ways to rein in the theory. (1) Some courts require the servient estate owner's representation specifically be that an easement exists. In these states, mere permission to use property will not ripen into an easement, even if the claimant materially changes his position on the expectation his right to use the property would continue. (2) Other courts extend the easement by estoppel theory to all representations of fact. In some of these courts, even silence in the right set of circumstances forms the basis for an easement by estoppel. (3) Another group of courts allows estoppel only when the speaker intended the claimant act in reliance on the statement. (4) Still other courts allow estoppel only if the representation occurred in a sales transaction.

The claimant, moreover, must act in justifiable reliance on the statement. Most courts will not find an easement by estoppel if the claimant should have verified the fact represented before relying on it.

The character of the transaction and the relationship between the parties are critical factors in determining whether an easement by estoppel exists. Purchasers from a developer, for example, who buy after seeing a plat or a brochure purporting to show streets in the subdivision, often succeed in easement by estoppel actions to use the depicted roads. When evaluating actions between neighbors, courts more willingly enforce informal agreements as easements by estoppel if the claimant made a long continued use of the claimed easement and spent money to improve, repair, or maintain the claimed easement. Overall, courts evaluate the facts, and will find an easement by estoppel where they feel the claimant acted in good faith on the servient estate owner's words or actions, and the servient estate owner's words or actions are such that he rather than the claimant should bear the consequences of any confusion.

A few courts, adhering to the rule that an express easement must be in writing to satisfy the Statute of Frauds, refuse to recognize the easement by estoppel at all. These courts recharacterize whatever writing they have as the grant of an **irrevocable license** (which, as a practical matter, is the same as an easement by estoppel, though in a way that preserves the integrity of the Statute of Frauds).

Some courts prefer yet a third theory, based on the **part performance** exception to the Statute of Frauds. See Chapter 22, supra. This theory excuses the dominant estate owner from complying with the Statute, but it still permits the court to craft the easement as if there had been a writing.

The three theories yield similar consequences. The easement or irrevocable license becomes irrevocable, although how long it becomes irrevocable is subject to dispute. Some courts hold that once the easement or irrevocable license is conceded, it continues as long as would any express easement—i.e., potentially forever. Other courts allow the easement to continue "to the extent necessary" for the dominant estate holder to amortize his expenditures, which implies a limited duration. Not clear is how future repairs and improvements affect the duration of the easement, nor even how to measure when a dominant tenement owner has amortized his expenditures.

A final and fundamental issue is whether courts should permit easements by estoppel at all. One or two jurisdictions acknowledge neither the easement by estoppel nor the irrevocable license. The large majority, however, recognize its essential function: one party has so substantially changed his position in reasonable reliance on his neighbor's consent that it borders on the unconscionable not to enforce the agreement.

The easement by estoppel theory, moreover, is consistent with the general estoppel theory commonly invoked to justify equitable relief in many areas of contract law.

IMPLIED EASEMENTS

Most easements are express easements, but under the right circumstances a court will imply an easement. Implied easements may be created even though they are not in a writing; the servient estate owner has not given permission for the dominant estate owner to use her property; in all likelihood the two landowners never even discussed one party's use of the other's land; and in some cases the two landowners never even met! Despite this, implied easements make sense.

EASEMENTS IMPLIED FROM PRIOR USE

Courts imply easements from **prior use** when the use was in place at a time a single parcel of land was divided into two parcels. In most cases, the seller and purchaser did not discuss or even think of the legal niceties involved at the time they bought and sold the land. The parties' oversight as a matter of human behavior is understandable and the **implied easement from a prior use** theory permits courts to reach results reasonable parties would have reached had they discussed the matter. The emphasis is on the parties' likely **intent at the time of severance** (not at time of trial).

In a typical scenario, a common owner conveys some part of her land to another person, and keeps some of her land, the two parcels becoming adjoining properties. When the common owner possessed the whole parcel, she made use of the part she ultimately sold to benefit the part she retained (or, vice-versa, she made some use on the land she later retained for the benefit of the land she later conveyed).

Example: George owned two adjoining lots. He sold one to Meg. A driveway and a sewer line ran from Meg's house to the street. After the sale, part of the driveway and part of the sewer line ran over (and under) George's lot. The deed conveying the lot to Meg, predictably, did not mention the driveway or the sewer line. The issue that ends up in court: Does Meg have a right to continue using the driveway or sewer line? Since the deed did not expressly give Meg an easement over George's land, Meg can continue the prior driveway and sewer uses only if the elements of an easement implied from prior use are shown.

All of the following elements are necessary for an **easement implied from prior use**:

(1) The unity of ownership is severed (i.e., a common owner);
(2) The use was in place before the parcel was severed (i.e., a pre-existing or prior use);
(3) The use must have been visible or apparent at the time of the severance; and
(4) The easement is necessary for the enjoyment of the dominant estate (i.e., necessity).

Since the implied easement from prior use is premised on one person owning the whole parcel of land when the pre-existing use was in place, the common ownership or **unity of ownership** element seems self-explanatory. The second element requires the use to be a **pre-existing use**. The common owner must have engaged in the use before the severance occurred. Some courts add that the pre-existing use be continuous or permanent. All the "continuous or permanent" requirement means is that the common owner used the property in such a way that a reasonable person would expect the use to continue no matter who owned the property. It does not require a use for years. The continuous or permanent use element's major practical function is to eliminate temporary or casual use from consideration as an easement.

At this point, we need to explain the term **quasi-easement**. While the concept of the prior or pre-existing use is simple enough, courts felt a need to create a new term for the pre-existing use because, under law, an easement is an interest in **another person's** property. A person cannot have an easement over her own land (As developed later, one way to terminate an easement is for one person to become owner of both the dominant estate and the servient estate.). Since the common owner, while she owned the whole property, could not have an easement over her own land, courts labeled the use on the unified parcel the **quasi-easement**. The change in label accommodates a legal purist's sensibilities. Courts even refer to various parts of the pre-divided property as the **quasi-dominant estate** and the **quasi-servient estate** to conceptualize the situation as it existed before the common owner sold part of her land.

Back to the elements. The third element requires the pre-existing use be **visible** or **apparent** at the time of severance. Driveways, roads, and other quasi-easements on the surface easily satisfy the requirement. Potentially more difficult are underground quasi-easements, exemplified by sewers or underground utility lines. Happily, at least for exam purposes, courts have interpreted **visible or apparent** to reach those uses or conditions discoverable by a reasonable inspection. In other words, sewers and underground utilities are visible or apparent.

The fourth element — *necessity* — is the most complex element. Courts may impose a different standard of necessity depending on whether there was an **implied grant** or an **implied reservation** of the easement. The degree of necessity will be less for an implied grant of the easement. The theory is that the grantee of the dominant estate can be excused for not knowing the location of a use or quasi-easement on the adjoining parcel. (Is that a reasonable assumption, especially for visible uses such as driveway and roads?) The common owner who tries to reserve an implied easement, on the other hand, is not so easily excused since she had greater knowledge, plus she executed the deed transferring the property without reserving any easement. (Is that a reasonable assumption? Is the common owner thinking she may have to disconnect her sewer line unless she expressly reserves an easement in the deed? Does she know she must reserve sewer lines in the deed, or does she simply rely on the drafting attorney to draft a valid deed? Does the attorney or other drafter have any idea where the sewer line runs?) Some states set a **reasonable necessity** standard for an **implied grant** and a **strict necessity** standard for an **implied reservation** of an easement implied from a prior use. The commonly given definition of **reasonable necessity** is "reasonably necessary for the fair enjoyment" of the dominant estate. In some states it means little more than convenient. A **strict necessity**, on the other hand, mandates a finding that the owner of the dominant estate could not fairly enjoy the property without the easement. Strict necessity resembles absolute necessity. A current trend is to subject both the grantor and the grantee to the **reasonable necessity** standard. Another current trend, influenced by the Restatement of Property, evaluates the totality of the facts to determine whether the parties would have intended the easement if they had thought of it at the time the property was subdivided.

The above discussion on easements implied from prior use assumes the parties did not negotiate the matter or otherwise indicate some intent. Some indication that the right to use the property was to be a revocable license or that one party attempted but failed to purchase the easement would preclude this implied easement, no matter how necessary the easement might be.

EASEMENTS IMPLIED BY NECESSITY

The second category of implied easement is the **easement implied by necessity**, also known as the easement implied by necessity for egress and ingress, or the easement implied for right-of-way. Although technically an easement will be implied by necessity for any purpose if the easement is strictly necessary for the enjoyment of a parcel of land, easements by necessity involve access to and from landlocked property. Landlocking a property destroys so much of its use that the law, as a matter of either public policy or an implied contract, presumes that the parties to the landlocking transaction could not have intended *not* to include a right-of-way onto the land. An easement by necessity is completely different from an easement implied by prior use.

The elements for any easement implied by necessity are as follows:

(1) A common owner severed the property (unity of ownership);
(2) The necessity for egress and ingress existed at the time of the severance (the severance caused the necessity); and
(3) The easement is strictly necessary for egress from and ingress to the landlocked parcel.

As with the easement implied from prior use, the easement implied by necessity requires there have been a common owner. The common owner must have conveyed part of the property to another person, and in severing property caused one of the parcels to become landlocked. A court will not imply an easement by necessity for egress and ingress unless the severance of the property caused the dominant estate to be landlocked.

No easement will be implied by necessity unless the easement is **strictly necessary** for egress and ingress. The party seeking the easement (which can be either the grantor or the grantee) must show the easement is strictly necessary. Strictly necessary can mean absolutely necessary, but most courts interpret the term to mean strictly necessary for the effective use of the property. A court, for example, may imply an easement by necessity even if an alternate route is technically available but the alternate way goes over unusually inhospitable terrain or involves water access, as with riparian land. Easements by necessity will not be implied for mere convenience, however, or even for reasonable necessity. This implied easement lasts only so long as the necessity lasts. Once a new road is built or a new way is available, the easement ends.

A problem peculiar to easements by necessity is physically locating the easement on the servient estate. Generally, the servient estate owner has the first opportunity to locate the easement, having due regard for the dominant estate holder's situation. If the servient estate owner's location is unreasonable or the servient estate owner delays locating the easement, the dominant estate holder has the right to locate the easement at some reasonable location, having due regard for the servient owner's use of the land. As with other easements, once an easement by necessity has been located, it can be moved only with the consent of both parties.

PRESCRIPTIVE EASEMENTS

A person can gain an **easement by prescription** by long-continued adverse use. The elements for an easement by prescription parallel in many respects those of adverse possession, substituting "use" for "possession":

(1) Actual use
(2) Open and notorious use
(3) Hostile use (adverse use) (claim of right)
(4) Continuous and uninterrupted use
(5) Exclusive use (in a minority of states)
(6) For the statutory prescriptive period.

In addition to these six elements, at least one state requires color of title as an element of easement by prescription. Since this is definitely the minority view, color of title will be discussed under Hostile Use rather than as its own subcategory.

(a) Actual Use

Actual use demands a physical presence on the servient estate. The actual use element's main function is to prohibit *negative* easements by prescription. That is, only *affirmative* easements can be implied by prescription. Thus a claimant cannot compel his neighbor to take down a fence, wall, or building because the claimant has an implied negative easement to light and air.

(b) Open and Notorious Use

Open and notorious use means the use must be so open and visible that the landowner will or should notice the use. The landowner's actual knowledge suffices even if the use is not noticeable by anyone else. Absent actual notice, something observable on the claimed estate (such as a roadway, utility lines, or paths) would give notice to the landowner. Even without physical evidence, some uses are so open and notorious that courts will find the use satisfies the open and notorious element.

(c) Hostile Use (Adverse Use) (Claim of Right)

Hostile use, also known as *adverse use* or use by *claim of right*, means the claimant uses another's property without permission. A person who receives permission from the landowner to be on the property cannot gain an easement by prescription, no matter how long the claimant uses the property. A person who enters pursuant to a defective deed enters by claim of right, for example, and not by permission. His use is hostile and adverse.

From the landowner's perspective, acquiescence is not permission. The landowner who tolerates another's use of the land has not given permission. The claimant's use remains hostile. For the hostility element to be destroyed once it begins, the claimant must renounce his claim of right and concede he uses the land by permission. Oral or written consent given after the use began may or may not constitute permission, depending on how the claimant reacts. A user who concedes he is a wrongdoer or trespasser and agrees, preferably in writing, that he will continue only as a licensee no longer is hostile. He cannot change his mind later. The claimant who either denies he needed permission or remains noncommittal in the face of the landowner's attempted consent remains hostile.

Possession that began as permissive use, moreover, can become adverse use if the claimant acts beyond the scope of the permitted use or otherwise has made an identifiable and definite assertion of greater rights than he originally received. The expanded claim must be so obvious, however, that it becomes tantamount to actual knowledge by the landowner. Gradual abuses will not qualify as the necessary "identifiable and definite" assertion of an independent right.

Courts engage in rebuttable presumptions to determine whether a claimant's entry was with permission. Some states presume continued use that satisfies the other elements also satisfies the hostility element unless the landowner can prove the entry was with permission. Other courts, noting that prescriptive easements are disfavored at law, refuse to presume hostility and place a heavy burden of proof on the claimant that the use was not permissive. This issue often arises in cases concerning a common driveway.

Example: Two neighbors jointly build a driveway along their mutual property line, part of the driveway on one lot and part on the other. The neighbors do not discuss whether any easement exists, much less put it in writing. Years later (after the statutory period has run), a dispute will arise and one neighbor will attempt to stop the joint use of the driveway. Courts that presume a hostility will find a prescriptive easement arose. Those courts that presume a permissive use will hold the use to be a revocable license. (Query whether an easement by estoppel or an irrevocable license, discussed above, might be in order.)

While states engage in a variety of rebuttable presumptions in determining hostile or permissive use, the following are some of the common ones. Many courts consider use by immediate family members (parents, children, brothers, and sisters) to be permissive unless evidence to the contrary is furnished. Cousins and good friends are not immediate family members!

In many states, courts will presume the use of unenclosed and unimproved property to be permissive unless the claimant affirmatively can prove the use to be hostile. The fitting corollary in these states is the use of enclosed, improved, or cultivated property will be presumed to be hostile absent evidence to the contrary.

At least one state requires the claimant have color of title — a defective deed or other writing, for example — to show hostility. (Color of title is not the same as claim of right or claim of title. See Chapter 8, supra.) This approach authorizes prescriptive easements only if the claimant asserts a right under color of title. In most states, however, color of title is not a necessary element. Nonetheless, having color of title benefits the claimant considerably. It shows hostility, for one thing. It also helps prove when the adverse use began. The document establishing color of title, moreover, proves the location and scope of the easement. Some states impose a shorter statute of limitations period for easements claimed under a color of title that accords up with any shorter statute of limitations period afforded adverse possession actions under color of title in the state. Recognizing an innate difference in character of use between prescriptive easement and adverse possession, however, most states that have addressed the issue do not shorten the statutory period in a prescriptive easement case for someone holding under color of title (it remains an open issue in most states).

(d) Continuous and Uninterrupted Use

Continuous and uninterrupted use does not mean the claimant uses the easement all the time; only that the claimant's use is consistent with that of a reasonable easement holder's use. Mainly the continuity element looks to whether the landowner effectively interrupted the claimant's activities on the claimed easement, or whether the claimant abandoned the use. The interruption envisioned is a real interruption, not just an attempted interruption. A successful ejectment or trespass action by the landowner destroys the continuity. A fence that interrupts the claimant's use of a road in fact also will defeat the continuous use element. On the other hand, a legal owner's erecting a fence to block a roadway is not an interruption if the claimant removes the fence or installs a gate in the fence within a reasonable time. Finally, a claimant's changing the location of a claimed right of way may be interpreted as the abandonment of the road in the first location and the start of a new easement at the new location. If the claimant discontinues her own use of the road, the statute of limitations must begin running anew on the new location.

(e) Exclusive Use

Exclusive use for a prescriptive easement claim is not as major a factor as exclusive use is for a finding of adverse possession. Concurrent use of property by the servient estate owner and the dominant estate owner is consistent with an easement. Most states, therefore, omit the exclusive use requirement as unnecessary, preferring the continuous, nonpermissive use for the statutory period as reason enough to imply the prescriptive easement.

A sizeable minority of states do impose an exclusive use element. These states tend to limit exclusive use to two narrow meanings. One meaning is that the claimant's use is distinguishable from the use made by the general public. The exclusive element requires the claimant show his claim for some reason is unique to him. Others may have independent claims to the same or similar easement, but this will not destroy the claimant's exclusive use. This interpretation makes it harder for a person to claim an easement in gross by prescription.

The second narrow meaning of exclusive use is that the landowner is not using the property in a way that would prevent the claimant from enjoying the easement. The owner's using the property in a way that prevents the claimant's effective use also defeats the continuous and uninterrupted use element.

A small number of states expand the role of the exclusive use element and will find no exclusive use if the claimant uses the claimed easement for the same purposes the land owner uses his property. In fact, a few courts conclude a similar use of the land by the claimant and the landowner, especially as to a road, constitutes *permissive* as well as *nonexclusive* use, thus defeating the prescriptive easement claim. Most courts, however, find similar use will not defeat the exclusive use element.

(f) Statutory Prescriptive Period

The **prescriptive period** is the time a claimant must use the property before a court will imply the easement by prescription. Generally the time is taken directly from the state's statute of limitations period for adverse possession.

Examples

Easement Genesis

1. Common Owner owned two adjoining parcels (Parcel A and Parcel B). Parcel A abutted Major Road. Parcel B bordered a river and a public timber road that meandered ten miles to a county road. Common Owner never used the timber road, preferring to cross Parcel A to Major Road. In 1965,

Common Owner sold Parcel B to Cornelius. The deed to Cornelius did not grant Cornelius an easement over Parcel A.

Two years later, in 1967, Common Owner sold Parcel A to Dan, the deed to Dan "excepting and reserving to Cornelius, his heirs and assigns, a right-of-way located at [a description locating the roadway over Parcel A]" from Parcel B to Major Road. In the ensuing years, members of the public generally and the various owners of Parcel B used the right of way to get to and from Major Road.

After several interim conveyances, Escovedo bought Parcel A. Last year Hilton bought Parcel B and built River Inn, a 50-room motel, on Parcel B. Escovedo, worried the expected increase in traffic would disturb her use of Parcel A, sought to bar Hilton from using the right-of-way over her land to reach Major Road. The case turns on whether Hilton has an easement over Escovedo's land. (You may assume all deeds were properly recorded. Exceeding the scope of the easement might be an issue in a case like this. The next chapter covers scope of easement issues. You may assume for this Example no issue arises as to the scope of the easement.)

(a) Is Hilton claiming an easement appurtenant or an easement in gross?

(b) If there is an easement, is Escovedo's land (Parcel A) the dominant estate or the servient estate?

(c) Is Hilton seeking an affirmative easement or a negative easement?

(d) Does Hilton have an express easement?

(e) How would your answer change in (d) if Common Owner conveyed Parcel B to Cornelius in 1965, deeded an easement to Cornelius in 1966, and deeded Parcel A to Dan in 1967?

(f) Does Hilton have an easement by estoppel (or an irrevocable license)?

(g) Does Hilton have an easement implied from prior use?

(h) Does Hilton have an easement implied by necessity?

(i) What result in (h) if the state does not require landowners to use navigable waters, and a bridge on the timber road that once crossed a chasm collapsed ten years ago? The timber road from the chasm back to Parcel B over the past ten years has become overgrown with shrubs, trees, and undergrowth.

(j) Does Hilton have an easement by prescription?

(k) What is Hilton to do if a court rules he has no easement over Parcel A?

Easement Exodus

2. Curly owned 100 acres of undeveloped land just east of town. Curly sold the land in nine separate parcels in the order shown below (Lot 1 first, Lot 2 second, etc., finally selling Lot 9 to Jack and Jill).

(a) Assuming Jack and Jill can get an easement implied by necessity, over which lot will it go?

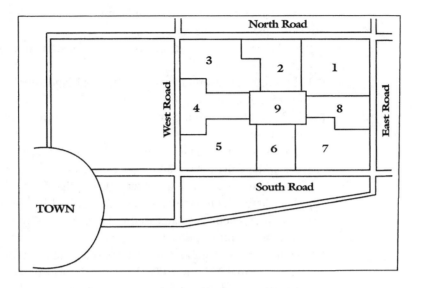

(b) Would your answer to (a) change if after Curly sold Lot 8 but before he sold Lot 9 to Jack and Jill, Margie bought a 200-yard strip of land on East Road running from the northernmost point of Lot 1 to the southernmost point of Lot 7?

(c) Assume, instead of the given facts, Curly sold Lot 9 to Jack and Jill before Curly sold Lots 5 and 8. After Curly sold Jack and Jill Lot 9, he sold Lot 5 to Owen. Over which lot will Jack and Jill's easement by necessity go?

Paul's Easement to Timothy

3. Paul owned two adjoining lots in 1975. He built a house and a detached garage on each lot. Paul built one driveway between the two houses leading to the two garages. Paul lived in a house and rented out the second home. In 1985, Paul sold the rent house to Timothy. The property line between the two lots was placed so that the driveway was located exclusively on Paul's land until it reached the back of the houses, where it widened giving access to both garages. The deed did not mention the driveway, but Paul orally assured Timothy he could continue using the driveway to get to his garage.

In 2010, Timothy sold his home to Magdalene by a deed transferring the lot "with all easements, rights and appurtenances." A week after moving into her new home, Magdalene went out of town for the weekend. She left her car in the driveway, thereby preventing Paul from driving his car out the driveway. As a consequence, Paul missed church services that Sunday morning. When Magdalene came home that Monday, Paul told her she could not use his driveway anymore. Magdalene brings suit for the right to continue using the driveway.

(a) Is Magdalene claiming an easement appurtenant or an easement in gross?

(b) If there is an easement appurtenant, is Magdalene's property the dominant estate or the servient estate?

(c) Is Magdalene seeking an affirmative easement or a negative easement?

(d) Does Magdalene have an express easement?

(e) Does Magdalene have an easement by estoppel?

(f) Does Magdalene have an easement implied from prior use?

(g) Does Magdalene have an easement implied by necessity?

(h) Does Magdalene have an easement by prescription (assume a ten-year prescription period)?

(i) Assume no garage and no driveway existed when Paul sold to Timothy in 1985. In 1986, Paul and Timothy agreed to build a driveway, and shared the cost for a contractor to build the driveway in the same location stipulated in the main facts. Paul and Timothy contracted with separate builders to build their detached garages at the back of their respective lots. Would these facts change your answer to any of the questions?

Explanations

Easement Genesis

1. (a) Easement appurtenant. The easement benefits owners of specific land, Parcel B. We can reach this result several ways. First, the deed reserving the easement reserves it to Cornelius, his heirs and assigns, which is traditional language indicating an easement will run with the land. Second, the surrounding facts indicate the main reason for the easement is to gain access to Parcel B from Major Road for all purposes and not for a use peculiar to Cornelius. Finally, an easement appurtenant is presumed unless there is some indication an easement in gross was intended. Nothing favors an easement in gross here. This is an easement appurtenant. Hilton asserts his rights as the current owner of Parcel B.

(b) Servient estate. The right-of-way would go over Escovedo's property. Her land would be burdened. The owner of the burdened property owns the servient estate. The owner of the benefited property has the dominant estate.

(c) Hilton seeks an affirmative easement: the right to travel over Escovedo's land to reach Major Road.

(d) In the majority of states, Hilton does not have an express easement. In a minority of states, he does. See Estate of Thomson v. Wade, 509

N.E.2d 309 (N.Y. 1987) (per curiam) (this case is mentioned in the overview supra).

According to the New York court, Hilton did not have an express easement. The deed from Common Owner to Cornelius did not grant Cornelius, Hilton's predecessor in interest, an easement. Common Owner did attempt to reserve an easement in favor of Parcel B for a right-of-way over Parcel A in his deed conveying Parcel A to Dan. Cornelius was a stranger to the deed, however. The controversy then turns on whether the jurisdiction would allow Common Owner to reserve an easement to a stranger to the deed. The New York Court of Appeals explained its reasoning as follows:

> It is axiomatic that [Common Owner] could not create an easement benefiting land which he did not own. Thus, having already conveyed [Parcel B], he could not "reserve" in the deed to [Dan] an easement appurtenant to [Parcel B] for the benefit of [Cornelius, his heirs and assigns]. The long-accepted rule in this State holds that a deed with a reservation or exception by the grantor in favor of a third party, a so-called "stranger to the deed," does not create a valid interest in favor of that third party. [Hilton] invites us to abandon this rule and adopt the minority view which would recognize an interest reserved or excepted in favor of a stranger to the deed, if such was the clearly discernible intent of the grantor (see, e.g., Willard v. First Church of Christ, 498 P.2d 987 [(Cal. 1972)]).
>
> Although application of the stranger-to-the-deed rule may, at times, frustrate a grantor's intent, any such frustration can readily be avoided by the direct conveyance of an easement of record from the grantor to the third party. The overriding considerations of the "public policy favoring certainty in title to real property, both to protect bona fide purchasers and to avoid conflicts of ownership, which may engender needless litigation" persuades us to decline to depart from our settled rule. We have previously noted that in this area of law, "where he can reasonably be assumed that settled rules are necessary and necessarily relied upon, stability and adherence to precedent are generally more important than a better or even a 'correct' rule of law[.]" Consequently, we hold here that any right-of-way reserved to [Cornelius, Hilton's] predecessor-in-interest in [Dan's] deed was ineffective to create an express easement in [Hilton's] favor.

The New York case represents the majority rule. The Supreme Court of California in a case reproduced in many casebooks, Willard v. First Church of Christ, Scientist, 498 P.2d 987 (Cal. 1972), adopted the minority rule allowing the reservation to a stranger to the deed, explaining its reasoning as follows:

> [O]ur courts no longer feel constricted by feudal forms of conveyancing. Rather, our primary objective in construing a conveyance is to

try to give effect to the intent of the grantor. . . . In general, therefore, grants are to be interpreted in the same way as other contracts and not according to rigid feudal standards. . . . The common law rule conflicts with the modern approach to construing fees because it can frustrate the grantor's intent. Moreover, it produces an inequitable result because the original grantee has presumably paid a reduced price for title to the encumbered property. . . . [We] abandon it entirely.

(e) Hilton has an express easement in all states, including New York and California. Bryan no longer relies on the reservation in the easement to Dan. Instead, his easement comes from a deed specifically granting Cornelius, Hilton's predecessor in interest, an easement appurtenant. Cornelius recorded the deed and the deed to Escovedo excepts the easement. The answer would be the same if Common Owner had deeded the easement to Cornelius one minute before delivering Parcel A to Dan. The ceremonial two documents instead of one makes a huge difference in outcome.

(f) Even assuming the jurisdiction recognizes an easement by estoppel or an irrevocable license, on the facts given, Hilton would not have an easement by estoppel or an irrevocable license. Nothing in the facts indicates Escovedo gave any reason to believe the easement would not be revoked. Current use of a license does not imply the license will be continued indefinitely. If Hilton used the right-of-way as a license, it would be a revocable license, despite its being a long-standing use.

(g) Hilton should prevail on an easement implied from prior use claim. The easement will be an implied grant. Common Owner owned both parcels. He crossed Parcel A to reach Parcel B. It is not clear whether Common Owner used the same road each time he traversed Parcel A but it seems likely, especially if he traveled by car. The quasi-easement was apparent, probably by some trail or road. Common Owner himself drove on it.

The matter may turn on the necessity element. If the state demands strict necessity, Hilton probably loses since Hilton can use a winding timber road that was in place when the property was severed.

Additionally, a dwindling number of states might require Hilton to use the river. Since this is an implied grant and not an implied reservation, however, most states utilize a reasonable necessity standard rather than the strict necessity standard. Since the roadway over Parcel A seems reasonably necessary for the fair enjoyment of Parcel B, Cornelius likely received an implied easement from prior use, which passed with the property to Hilton. This interpretation seems consistent with the actual use made of the easement over the decades.

For this Example, you were not to consider whether the road to a 50-room motel exceeded the easement's scope. If it does, Hilton cannot rely on the easement implied from a prior use to preserve his rights since, obviously, no motel existed when Common Owner owned both parcels. See Chapter 29 infra.

(h) Hilton does not have an easement implied by necessity. Two elements for implying the easement by necessity for right-of-way took place: Common Owner was the common owner and the severance of the property caused the necessity. Unfortunately, the resulting necessity was at most a reasonable necessity and not a strict necessity since the owner of Parcel B, Cornelius, could have left and entered Parcel B by way of the timber road, time consuming as that may have been.

This Example serves as a reminder that a court may imply an easement from prior use even where it would not imply an easement by necessity. The opposite is also true: a court may imply an easement by necessity where it would not imply an easement from prior use.

(i) Same result as in (h). Hilton still does not have an easement by necessity. While Parcel B certainly seems landlocked now, the action for an easement by necessity requires the necessity to have existed at the time of the severance. Property landlocked due to subsequent events does not qualify.

QUERY: Should this Explanation be correct? The Explanation states the black letter law, and it works well if a subsequent sale causes property to become landlocked. The rule in that context identifies which property will be the servient estate, that being the property belonging to the common owner at the last severance. The rule does not work in situations like our Example where the subsequent event causing the property to be landlocked is not a severance, but an act of nature, government, or other event destroying the only access to the land. It seems the landowner, Hilton, should be able to gain access over property that would have been the servient estate at the last severance if the strict necessity existed then. The rationale given for the black letter rule is that the implied easement by necessity follows from the parties' presumed intent at the time of severance, and the parties could not have presumed an easement for egress and ingress if there was already one in place. It seems presumed intent should include permitting the easement if the lack of access results from a later event outside the dominant estate owner's control. That's my spiel, and I'm sticking to it!

(j) Hilton may have an easement by prescription. Parcel B landowners have been traversing Parcel A since 1965, when Common Owner initially sold the property to Cornelius. (Common Owner himself traversed Parcel A, but Common Owner's time cannot be tacked to determine the time of actual use.) All Parcel B owners' use from

Cornelius to Hilton can be tacked to satisfy the statute of limitations period and other elements. Use since 1965 will satisfy even the longest statutory period. In a few states, Hilton could benefit from a shorter statutory period if the reservation to Cornelius in the deed to Dan constituted color of title. Many of the elements are noncontroversial: Actual use, open and notorious use, and continuous and uninterrupted use (or so it seems from the facts) all appeared met.

Most states do not require exclusive use, so the exclusive use element would be no problem in those states. The exclusive use element in the states that do demand exclusive use may be a problem, however, since the facts say the general public used the right-of-way. Cornelius and all successors, as far as we can tell, used the right-of-way as the owner of the adjoining tract rather than as a member of the general public. Hilton should persuade a court he and his predecessor satisfy the exclusive use element.

The hostile use element should be satisfied, also. Common Owner's attempted reservation of an easement to Cornelius indicates he recognized a claim by Cornelius to an easement over his land at least as of the day the reservation was included in the deed to Dan. (Alternatively, a court easily could conclude Cornelius claimed a right from the date he bought the property.) No evidence even suggests Cornelius or anyone else in the chain of title renounced the claim to the right-of-way.

In summary, Hilton should have an easement over Parcel A, either as an easement implied from prior use or an easement implied by prescription. In some states Hilton would have an express easement, though in a majority of states he does not qualify since his predecessor was a stranger to the deed reserving the easement.

You were not to consider in this Example whether the use of the right-of-way for guests to get to a 50-room motel exceeded the scope of the prescriptive easement. If, however, the use exceeded the scope of the easement implied by prescription, Hilton could not gain a prescriptive easement over parcel A for a roadway to his motel because the time he used the road for that purpose was virtually nil.

(k) Assuming Hilton accepts the court's decision or he has exhausted his appeals, Hilton has a few options, none of which is as good as having the easement over Parcel A. Hilton could negotiate with Escovedo to purchase an easement over Parcel A or to purchase Parcel A itself. Hilton may consider purchasing an easement over other adjoining lands for access to Major Road.

Some western states by statute authorize private condemnation actions under certain circumstances. Hilton may have such a right under the statute. If he does, he will have to pay Escovedo the fair market value of the roadway, but at least she could not refuse to complete the transaction.

Hilton might convince the local government a road along his property line would serve a public need, and have the local government purchase the land and build a road. This may take longer than Hilton wants to wait, however. If all else fails, Hilton apparently could rebuild the bridge, then grade and use the meandering ten-mile timber road.

Easement Exodus

2. (a) The easement goes over Lot 8. An easement implied by necessity arises only when property becomes landlocked. The easement must run over some portion of the severed property that was part of the commonly owned property right before the severance. Lot 9 was not landlocked until Curly sold Lot 8. Only when Curly sold Lot 8 did an easement implied by necessity materialize. Lot 8 is not the most convenient for Jack and Jill, but they cannot pick and choose the most convenient lot.

   (b) It does not affect the answer to (a). Once the servient estate has been identified, it remains the servient estate. The easement still runs over Lot 8.

   (c) Jack and Jill bought landlocked property. Curly, the common owner, still owned Lot 5 and Lot 8 when he sold landlocked Lot 9. The implied easement by necessity in this situation can run over either Lot 5 or Lot 8. Most courts would give Curly as the servient estate owner the first opportunity to locate the easement. Only if Curly does not locate the easement or his location is not reasonable will Jack and Jill be able to locate the easement. If they locate the easement, they probably should choose locating it over Lot 5 since it appears to be the most convenient for them to get to town.

Paul's Easement to Timothy

3. (a) Easement appurtenant. An argument could be made that, if Timothy had an easement at all, it was an easement in gross. Paul told Timothy that Timothy could use the driveway to reach his garage. Paul literally may have meant Timothy and not anyone else could use the driveway. This then would sound more like a revocable license. On the other hand, Paul may have meant Timothy could use the driveway as long as Timothy used the house, and whoever went into possession of the house after Timothy would have the right to use the driveway. That could be an easement appurtenant. This second scenario rings truer. Courts, moreover, have a construction preference for easements

appurtenant. In all likelihood, therefore, a court would find any easement here to be an easement appurtenant. More importantly for Magdalene, she will have a right to use an easement appurtenant, whereas an easement in gross may be used by Timothy but not by Magdalene.

(b) Dominant estate. Magdalene's property is the one benefited by any easement. The benefited property is the dominant estate. Paul's property, burdened by the easement, would be the servient estate.

(c) Magdalene seeks an affirmative easement. She wants to drive over Paul's land.

(d) Magdalene does not have an express easement. An express easement must be in writing to satisfy the Statute of Frauds. Paul did not deed Timothy the easement. He merely told Timothy that Timothy could use the driveway to reach his garage. The deed from Timothy to Magdalene could not create an easement over Paul's land.

(e) Although this may be Magdalene's strongest case, Magdalene probably does not have an easement by estoppel.

As a preliminary matter, Paul made no statement to Magdalene before she bought the house or otherwise gave her any indication she might be able to drive over his property. She therefore cannot gain an easement by estoppel based on anything Paul said to her.

On the other hand, Magdalene succeeds to any easement that Timothy had in the property. If Timothy had an easement by estoppel, Magdalene also owns the easement. Timothy's claim is based on Paul's oral statement that Timothy could use Paul's driveway. It appears Paul made the statement after Timothy decided to buy the home. If so, then Timothy could not have changed his position based on the statement and thus he does not qualify for the easement by estoppel.

If, however, Magdalene can show Timothy purchased the house only because of Paul's assurances that Timothy could use the driveway, she should get her easement by estoppel. Paul made a representation to persuade Timothy to commit to the house purchase. He should have known that Timothy would rely on the representation in buying the home, and that it was an important factor in Timothy's decision to buy the home. Finally, Timothy bought the home as a consequence of relying on the representation. While some courts might find an easement by estoppel here, the surrounding circumstances seem to indicate Timothy was going to buy the house, and Paul's assurances were just a neighborly act. The facts are sketchy, but it appears that if Timothy was relying on the assertion, and the assertion was as critical as Magdalene needs a court to believe, Timothy should have fleshed out the matter more at the time, and asked his attorney or closing agent (hopefully an attorney) how best to document his rights. Not doing so, Timothy should be denied the easement rather than having Paul lose his right to exclude others from his property. The matter is even less sympathetic to Timothy and Magdalene than it could be because the facts do not indicate that Timothy expended any money on the easement itself.

(f) Magdalene probably does not have an easement implied from prior use even though the elements do seem satisfied. Paul was the common owner. The use was in place at the time the commonly owned parcel was divided into two parcels. The use was visible at the time of severance. The easement seems reasonably necessary for the enjoyment of the dominant estate. So far so good. The fact that Paul told Timothy that Timothy could drive over Paul's driveway to reach his garage, however, is evidence that Timothy used the driveway pursuant to Paul's permission. The conversation indicates the parties did not overlook the issue. The opposite seems true. The two presumably believed the right to use the driveway was not part of the transfer to Timothy. If so, the presumed intent underlying the easement implied from prior use theory disappears. Timothy did not receive an easement implied from prior use, only a revocable license. Since Timothy did not get an easement from prior use, neither will Magdalene.

(g) Magdalene does not have an easement implied by necessity. Her property borders a street so she does not need a way of egress and ingress. Presumably she can build a driveway elsewhere on her lot or park on the street.

(h) Magdalene does not have an easement by prescription. She has been on the property less than a month. The only way she could prevail is by tacking Timothy's use. Timothy did use the driveway long enough to satisfy most state's statutory period. His use was open, continuous, and exclusive. His use was not hostile or under a claim of right, however, since the facts indicate Timothy used the driveway with Paul's permission. A person who begins using property pursuant to a landowner's permission cannot gain an easement by prescription, no matter how long the use. This easement by prescription Example and the earlier easement by estoppel Example both hinge on state of mind: Did Timothy begin using the easement because he thought he had a right, an easement in legal parlance, to continued use as the new owner of his house, or was he grateful for the kindly gesture of his saintly grantor/neighbor? A court's conclusion as to Timothy's state of mind affects dramatically the results under the two theories.

(i) Magdalene's chances increase tremendously under these facts. First, the facts increase the likelihood that a court will find an easement by prescription. Timothy spent money to build the driveway and built his garage, indicating that Timothy believed that he could use the driveway for a long time. Timothy's use, therefore, was hostile and under claim of right based on his reasonable belief that the agreement was that he would have a long continuing use. Timothy's claim is hostile even if the word "easement" was never spoken between Paul and Timothy. Once Timothy used the driveway for ten years, he had an easement by prescription. Since Timothy had an easement appurtenant, he could transfer it to Magdalene.

Timothy also may have had an easement by estoppel. Paul and Timothy discussed jointly building a driveway for their common use. Paul must have known (in fact Paul encouraged Timothy) that Timothy would expend money to pay for the driveway and to build a garage based on Timothy's right to continue using the driveway. Timothy in fact spent the money. Timothy's actions indicate that he reasonably believed that Paul would not attempt to revoke Timothy's right to use the driveway. Thus, it seems Magdalene has an easement by estoppel.

The new facts lessen the chance Magdalene will prevail in an easement implied from prior use action since the use was not in place when the property was severed. The change in facts will not affect the easement by necessity discussion in (g).

Assignability, Scope, and Termination of Easements

ASSIGNABILITY OF EASEMENTS

Most easements are assignable. Some, however, are not. **Assignable** means the easement can be sold, gifted, devised, inherited, or otherwise conveyed. Rules concerning assignability of easements depend on several factors, the major factor being whether the easement is an easement in gross or an easement appurtenant.

Easements appurtenant run with the land. Logically enough, whoever possesses the **dominant estate** (by purchase, gift, devise, or inheritance) has the right to continue the easement over the **servient estate**. A person selling the dominant estate loses her easement rights to the person buying the dominant estate. Likewise, the servient estate remains burdened with the easement no matter who owns the servient estate.

An **easement in gross** benefits a person whether or not he owns a particular parcel of land. In other words, there is no dominant estate. The law relating to the assignability of easements in gross is still evolving. Rules are developing separately for *commercial* easements in gross and for *noncommercial*, or personal, easements in gross. **Commercial easements in gross** are those easements that further a money-making activity (as opposed to **noncommercial** or **personal easements in gross**, which are those easements granted for the owner's personal enjoyment or pleasure). Railroad easements, utility easements, and pipeline easements are commercial easements in gross. The commercial easement in gross also might be the right to use a lake to operate a fishing, boating, or swimming operation, or the right to remove timber or minerals from the land (the latter two are known as **profits a prendre**, or **profits**).

Unless expressly made nonassignable or the circumstances surrounding the creation of the commercial easement in gross indicates otherwise, **commercial easements in gross** are assignable. A telephone company with easements throughout the region for its telephone poles and lines (commercial easements in gross) can assign its easements in gross to a successor telephone company, for example. (The same goes for easements for railroad companies assigning railroad easements for tracks or water companies assigning easements for water lines.) The significance of the right to assign in this case should be obvious: If the easements were nonassignable, the purchasing telephone company (or railroad or water company) would not be able to use any of the poles or lines (or tracks or pipes) on any servient estate. And without those wires (or tracks or pipes) the company could not operate.

Noncommercial easements in gross (or personal easements) are a different matter. Many courts prohibit the assignment of noncommercial easements in gross even if they allow assignability of commercial easements in gross. A few courts, however, permit holders to assign noncommercial easements in gross. The majority rule is that a noncommercial easement in gross is not assignable unless circumstances or the document creating the easement expressly stipulates the easement in gross is assignable.

DIVISIBILITY AND APPORTIONMENT

An issue separate but related to assignability concerns the **divisibility** or **apportionment** of easements. In the assignability discussion, the holder of the easement transferred all her interest in an easement to one other person. Under divisibility or apportionment, the easement holder attempts to share the easement with others or to assign, divide, or apportion the easement to multiple grantees. The issue is whether an easement holder can divide or apportion an easement among several grantees — i.e., whether a person owning an easement can transfer an otherwise assignable easement to more than one person.

(a) Easements Appurtenant

Once again, the distinction between easements appurtenant and easements in gross is important. The holder of an **easement appurtenant**, by subdividing and selling parcels of the dominant state, transfers the easement with each parcel. Each resulting parcel becomes a dominant estate and the owner enjoys the easement over the servient estate so long as the several dominant estate owners do not overburden the servient estate.

Example: Faye owns Blackacre, and as owner of Blackacre she has an easement for egress and ingress over Greenacre. Faye subdivides Blackacre, selling subdivided lots to 20 different people, and retaining a lot for herself. Who has a right to cross Greenacre: Faye as long as she owns any part of the original Blackacre? Only the new owner of the lot where the right of way enters the former Blackacre from Greenacre? All 21 property owners? Or no one since in subdividing Blackacre (the dominate estate) Faye destroyed the easement over Greenacre? The answer is that all 21 property owners have an easement of right of way over Greenacre. Easements appurtenant are divisible and apportionable.

(b) Easements in Gross

Easements in gross that are not assignable under state law obviously are not divisible or apportionable, either. Since most noncommercial easements in gross are nonassignable, the following discussion applies to *commercial easements in gross*.

In the states where commercial easements in gross are assignable, courts often distinguish between exclusive easements in gross and nonexclusive easements in gross. **Exclusive easements in gross** are those where the easement holder has the sole right to use an easement. Generally a person owning an exclusive easement in gross has the sole power to authorize others to use the easement. Even the servient estate owner cannot allow others to use the easement. In general, if a person (or a company) has an **exclusive easement in gross**, that person may permit many others to use the easement as long as the total burden on the servient estate does not amount to a surcharge or misuse of the easement.

Persons granted nonexclusive easements in gross, on the other hand, cannot subdivide or apportion any rights to the easement. A **nonexclusive easement in gross** is one in which the easement holder has right to use the easement, but the servient estate owner (or other exclusive easement holder) can authorize others to use the easement and the holder of the nonexclusive easement in gross cannot prevent the servient estate owner (or some other person having the exclusive easement) from granting the right to use an easement to other persons. The servient estate owner (or other exclusive easement holder) in effect retains the power to decide how many persons can use the easement

When two or more persons inherit or otherwise share the exclusive right to an easement, at least one court has concluded the multiple owners must act with one voice (known as the **one-stock rule**). See Miller v. Lutheran Conference & Camp Association, 200 A. 646 (Pa. 1938). Each of the multiple owners under a one-stock rule has a veto on any action taken with regard to the easement or profit. This resolution is thought to encourage reasonable exploitation without overutilizing the easement or profit. As developed more fully infra, should the exclusive holder, a "one-stock" group, or the many nonexclusive users of an easement or profit overburden the easement, the servient estate owner has a right to enjoin the uses that overburden or exceed the scope of the easement.

SCOPE OF EASEMENTS

The *scope* of the easement delineates the extent of use an easement holder may make of the servient estate. An easement holder's use cannot exceed the *scope* of the easement. Scope issues take several forms.

(a) Location

Easements must be located on an identifiable part of the servient estate. Once the location is established, the easement owner must remain within the located easement. The easement owner's use of the servient estate outside the boundaries of the easement, even for the same purposes privileged in the easement, is not authorized and is a trespass.

An express grant or reservation should state the precise location of the easement. In a few states, an express grant or reservation of an easement that does not locate the easement is invalid. In most states, however, the easement is valid even though no specific location is given. Easements implied from prior use and by prescription are usually apparent from the current use.

Easements implied by necessity (and express easements if not located in the grant or reservation deed) must be physically located after the easement is recognized. The general protocol is that, if the location cannot be ascertained from the deed or other document, the servient estate owner can situate the easement, but if the servient estate does not locate the easement or if the location is not reasonable, the dominant estate holder (or holder of an easement in gross) can locate the easement, having due regard for the convenience of the servient estate owner.

In most states, an easement's location cannot be changed or moved unless both parties agree. Several states and the Restatement (Third) of Property (Servitudes) permit the servient owner to move the easement at the servient owner's own expense as long as moving the easement does not inconvenience the easement holder's use of the easement. An easement holder's unilateral change in location of the easement constitutes a **misuse** of the easement. The forbidden move may be from one part of the servient estate to another, or from a surface location to underground placement (or from an underground placement to a surface location).

Example: A utility company owns an easement to place poles and wires over property. The easement to place poles over property does not give the utility company the right to move the wires underground.

(b) Intensity of Use

Even express grants or reservations do not address every potentiality (and usually address no potentiality beyond the basic purpose of the easement). The general rule, that a easement holder can use the easement as long as the use does not overburden the servient estate, has both flexibility and uncertainty. Courts stress the original parties' unexpressed but presumed "intent" in determining what qualifies as authorized uses of an easement. In ascertaining the original parties' intent, courts presume the parties intended the scope of the easement would evolve to accommodate reasonably foreseeable changes in the surrounding area and in society.

Example 1: Pauline in 1900 granted Sarah an easement appurtenant over Pauline's land so Sarah could reach a public road. In 1900, both properties were rural, and travel was by foot, horse, and buggy. One hundred years later Pauline's heirs and Sarah's successors and assigns own the respective properties. Are Sarah's successors limited to using foot, horse, and buggy to travel over a dirt path easement? Of course not! Cars, trucks, and even motorcycles, are natural developments and the scope of the easement will be adjusted to accommodate progress.

Example 2: Under the same facts as Example 1, Sarah's successors-in-interest, reacting to urban sprawl, subdivide Sarah's original property into 100 homesites. They sell the individual lots to individuals who build residences. Each new homeowner uses the easement to travel to the public road. The owners of each and every lot within the original benefited property will receive the right to use the easement appurtenant over Pauline's property. Most courts will allow the increased use as not overburdening the easement.

Example 3: Sarah's successors in some states (not in others) can widen what was once an eight-foot-wide easement to a twenty-foot-wide easement. To better accommodate (and market) their land, Sarah's successors can lay shell, asphalt, or concrete to make a modern road out of the easement. The improvements are privileged as being consistent with the original parties' presumed intent. (What do you think: Was this Pauline's original "intent" as to the scope of the easement? Should courts admit they evaluate the scope of an easement based on the reasonableness of the use taking into consideration what is currently occurring in the general vicinity of the servient estate?)

The easement holder's use is not unbounded, however. The easement holder is limited to using the easement only for the authorized purpose of the easement. A dominant estate owner having a right of egress and ingress through an alleyway over a neighboring lot, for example, cannot use the alleyway to park vehicles, even though those same vehicles may be driven through the alley.

Example 4: Assume in the above Pauline-Sarah example that Sarah's successors, instead of subdividing the property, build a shopping mall, with hundreds or thousands of cars daily streaming across the servient estate. A court likely would find either (a) that the intended use was for access to residential not commercial property or (b) that the intensity of use with the resulting noise, pollution, and traffic was beyond the original parties' reasonable expectations, even if the general vicinity, including the servient estate, was commercial.

(c) No Benefit Allowed to Nondominant Property

The easement appurtenant may benefit only the dominant estate. The easement cannot benefit adjoining property, even if the owner of the dominant estate also owns the adjoining property, and even if the adjoining property is used in an integrated activity with the dominant estate. Any extension of the benefit to another property is a misuse of the easement.

Example 1: Wilson owns land he wants to develop into a residential subdivision. He would like access to Main Street. Wilson discovers an adjoining lot owner that has an easement appurtenant over Jackson's land for egress and ingress to Main Street. Wilson buys the lot. Can Wilson use the easement over Jackson's land to get to Main Street? The precise answer is that Wilson can use the easement of egress and ingress to Main Street to benefit the newly acquired lot, but not to benefit his adjoining land. In other words, Wilson, his workers, and his prospective purchasers cannot get from the back property to Main Street by going over the newly acquired lot.

Example 2: Washington owns a restaurant with the easement for egress and ingress over Erin's property. Washington's restaurant is successful and he plans to enlarge the restaurant. If the enlarged restaurant remains on the dominant estate, Washington and his customers can continue using the easement over Erin's land. If, however, Washington buys a 50-foot-wide strip behind his lot to accommodate the larger building and to provide extra parking spaces, Washington and his customers will not be able to use the easement over Erin's property to reach the part of the building and parking area on the adjoining 50 feet. Washington somehow must take steps to prevent the misuse. If Washington cannot effectively prevent the misuse, he and his customers may not be able to continue using the easement at all!

(d) Improvements, Maintenance, and Repair

An easement holder has the right to make improvements to her easement as long as the improvements promote the use of the easement within the scope of the easement and does not unreasonably burden the easement or the servient estate owner's use or enjoyment of her property. A prior Example involved the asphalting of a right-of-way. Similarly, a company or individual having the right-of-way for utility lines or pipelines has a right as necessary to install the pipes, poles, and wires essential to the enjoyment of easement. In contrast, a utility company that has the surface rights to install utility poles and lines cannot remove the poles and place the wires underground. Placing the wires underground exceeds the scope of the easement and hence is a misuse of the easement. The utility company in this case must secure a grant of the underground easement.

Predictably, an easement holder is responsible for maintaining the easement and any improvements it places on the easements. The easement holder has a right to enter the property to maintain its easement. Although the easement holder has a right to enter the servient estate to maintain the improvements in the easement, the easement holder must repair any damage it does to the servient property.

Example: A utility company that installs poles and overhead wires has a right to enter the property to repair and maintain the poles and wires, to remove or replace the poles or wires, to clear out undergrowth, and to cut back trees endangering the wires. Likewise, a pipeline company with a pipeline easement or a person having an underground sewer or water line easement has a right to go onto the servient estate and dig up the ground as necessary to maintain the underground improvements.

TERMINATION OF EASEMENTS

An easement, whether an express or implied easement, potentially lasts forever. Nonetheless, easements can be extinguished or terminated. Let's count down the ways:

10. **By the Terms of the Grant.** The deed or will granting or reserving the easement may set an expiration date, a term of years, or a

condition. The grant may allow an easement of egress and ingress as long as the grantee continues mining operations or until a highway opens, for example; or a landowner may grant an oil company a pipeline easement for 50 years. The easement expires automatically according to the express terms of the grant or reservation.

9. **Purpose for Easement Ends.** An easement terminates when the purpose for the easement ends. For instance, an easement to enter an apartment complex to install and service cable lines ends if the apartment building is destroyed. Although the doctrine has been applied to all types of easements, it is most often applied to terminate *easements implied by necessity*. The easement implied by necessity ends as soon as another way to enter the property appears and the strict necessity for the easement for egress and ingress ends.

8. **Merger.** An easement is a right to use another person's property. Once a person gains concurrent ownership of both the dominant estate and the servient estate, the estate **mergers** and the easement disappears. If the common owner later severs the property, the old easement does not reappear automatically. A new express or implied easement may be created on a later severance, of course.

7. **Forfeiture for Misuse.** A court may declare an easement forfeited for **misuse**. This is an extraordinary remedy, and only imposed in the most egregious cases of misuse. The more common action is an **injunction** halting the misuse. Where the easement cannot be used without benefiting property adjoining the dominant estate, a court will enjoin all use of the easement until the easement holder can stop the misuse.

6. **Release.** An easement is an interest in property of another. As such, the easement holder by deed can transfer part or all of the easement to the servient estate owner. This transfer is called a **release**. The release must be in writing to satisfy the Statute of Frauds.

5. **Abandonment.** An easement holder may abandon an easement. Abandonment has two elements: intent to abandon and subsequent nonuse. **Mere nonuse, no matter how long the duration of the nonuse, does not constitute an abandonment.** Intent to abandon is hard to prove. Intent to abandon must be evidenced by some identifiable and unambiguous act inconsistent with the continued ownership of the easement. Nonuse, no matter how long continued, is not an identifiable event or an unambiguous fact, or an act inconsistent with the ownership of the easement. Nonuse for a long enough time, however, does give credence that some oral pronouncement or act taken long ago constituted the requisite unambiguous act denoting the intent to abandon. This is a thin reed, however, and not often a fruitful one. The best evidence of intent to abandon, of course, is a deed or other written document, which moves abandonment very close to release.

4. **Estoppel.** Just as an easement by estoppel may be created, see Chapter 28, supra, in some states the servient estate owner can extinguish an easement by estoppel. The same standards apply: the easement holder consents to the servient estate owner's use of the easement location in a manner inconsistent with the use of the easement; the easement holder knows or should know the servient estate owner believing the consent will not be revoked will materially change her position; and the servient estate holder, reasonably believing the consent will not be revoked, substantially changes her position, usually by constructing improvements over the easement.

3. **Prescription.** Just as a person can gain an easement by prescription (see Chapter 28, supra), a servient estate owner can terminate an easement by prescription. Easements terminated by prescription are not limited to easements initially acquired by prescription. Easements of all sorts, whether express or implied, can be extinguished by prescription.

   Terminating an easement by prescription is not as easy as it sounds, however. To terminate an easement by prescription, the servient estate owner must use the easement in a manner adverse to the easement holder's right. This is not easy to do. Recall the servient estate owner has the right to use the easement as long as her use does not unreasonably interfere with the easement holder's use. Thus, to terminate an easement by prescription, the servient estate owner must prove her use of the property was inconsistent with continuation of the easement. Improving the right-of-way before a pipeline company "installs" its pipes is not adverse enough. Farming over an easement during a period the easement holder is not using the easement is not adverse enough, either. A fence blocking a road usually is not adverse enough, especially if there is an unlocked gate over the road. If a fence blocks the easement holder's anticipated use, however, it may be adverse. A stone wall over the roadway might be the adverse use if the easement holder attempts to use the road after the wall has been constructed. Until then, however, the servient estate owner's wall is consistent with the easement holder's nonuse of the easement.

2. **Recording Acts.** The easement as an interest in property is subject to a state's recording acts. See The Recording Systems, Chapter 26, supra. A subsequent bona fide purchaser who takes without actual, constructive, or inquiry notice of the easement is not bound by the easement. Likewise, a creditor that records a mortgage before an express easement is recorded is protected by the recording acts and, if necessary, may sell the property in a foreclosure action. The purchaser at the foreclosure sale is not bound by the easement. If, on the other hand, the easement was recorded before the mortgage (or the easement holder is a otherwise protected under

the recording act, such as the mortgagee having actual or inquiry notice of the easement), the easement holder has **priority** and the purchaser at the foreclosure sale takes the property subject to the easement. In states having marketable title acts, an easement recorded prior to the "root of title" faces extinguishment unless one of many possible exceptions in the act applies.

1. **Eminent Domain.** Federal, state, and local governments through a process known as *eminent domain* or *condemnation* can force landowners to sell property to the government as long as the government pays for the property. See Chapter 35, infra. The government in an eminent domain action takes the whole property, including any easement. This has two consequences for the easement holder. First, the easement is extinguished. Second, because the government took the easement, a property interest, the government must compensate the easement holder.

Examples

Gone Fishing

1. Landowner's 200 acres includes a 50-acre lake. Landowner deeds Marty the right to fish and boat on the lake.
   (a) Marty wants to hold a ski show on the lake. Can he?
   (b) Marty wants to bring his friend, Catfish, along to go fishing with him. Landowner does not like Catfish and wants to prohibit him from using the lake. Can he?
   (c) Marty planned to take two working buddies fishing. Marty awoke, feeling ill. He gave his buddies a map to the lake and a note giving them permission to fish without him. Landowner does not want anyone using the lake unless Marty accompanies them. Can Landowner refuse to let the two buddies use the lake?
   (d) Marty died, devising his fishing rights to his fishing pal, Catfish. Does Catfish have an easement to fish on the lake?
   (e) Assume Landowner sold Marty ten acres of adjoining land, and the deed conveyed the easement to fish and boat on the lake on Landowner's property. Marty died, devising the ten acres to his fishing pal, Catfish. May Catfish fish and boat on Landowner's lake?

She Sells Easements to Seashore

2. Debbie granted Seashore Pipeline an express easement across her property for the construction, maintenance, and operation of pipelines. Debbie gave Seashore Pipeline the exclusive right to install additional pipelines as long as Debbie and the company negotiated an additional

compensation arrangement for each extra pipeline that was laid within the easement. Seashore Pipeline constructed a 12-inch pipeline through the easement. Two years later Seashore Pipeline constructed a 20-inch pipeline within the easement. Seashore compensated Debbie when it added the second pipeline.

Twenty years later Seashore Pipeline sold and assigned the 12-inch pipeline and the easement to Triton Company. Seashore Pipeline reserved an undivided one-half interest in the easement. Seashore Pipeline did not assign any interest in the 20-inch pipeline.

(a) Debbie brought a trespass action against Triton Company and sought to terminate Seashore's easement. What result?

(b) Instead of giving Seashore an exclusive easement, Debbie deeded separate easements to Seashore Pipe for each pipeline, one for the 12-inch pipeline and one for the 20-inch pipeline. Seashore later sold the 12-inch pipeline and the easement for the 12-inch pipeline to Triton Company, which attempted to dig up the pipeline and replace it with a 20-inch pipeline. Debbie protests. What result?

Cable Ready Easement

3. Optical Cable Network plans to offer television, telephone and internet cable services. It is critical to the company's success that it be able to lay cable either underground or over poles to businesses, schools and residences. Optical Cable Network contracted with Flat Hills Electric Company to attach cable lines to existing poles on easements the electric company assembled years ago. Optical Cable Network entered into a similar contract with Statewide Telephone Company. In addition, Optical Cable Network contracted with four railroad lines to place cable underground or on poles parallel to railroad tracks in easements acquired by the railroad decades ago. Landowners have challenged these arrangements, arguing the electric company, the telephone company and the railroads cannot authorize Optical Cable Network to string or lay its cable in the easements, and that Optical Cable Network therefore was trespassing.

(a) The original easement grant to Flat Hills Electric Company was worded as an easement "for the purpose of constructing and maintaining an electric transmission or distribution line or system." Can Optical Cable Network use the Flat Hills Electric Company easement without compensating the servient landowners?

(b) The original easement grant to Statewide Telephone Company was worded as "the right to construct and operate equipment for the distribution of electricity and messages upon or across the" property. Can Optical Cable Network use Statewide Telephone Company's easement without compensating the servient landowners?

(c) The original easement grant to Dixie-Northern Railroad was worded "to be used by the Railroad Company as a right of way for a railroad together with the right to construct, maintain and operate a railway or railways across the property." Can Optical Cable Network use the railroad easement without compensating the servient landowners?

The Use and Misuse Truce

4. Bagwell bought two five-acre parcels. Parcel I is east of and adjacent to Route 53. Parcel II is a landlocked tract just east of Parcel I. Shortly afterward Bagwell deeded Parcel I to Caminiti, reserving an easement for himself, his heirs and assigns, to use a right-of-way running from Route 53 across the southern boundary of Parcel I to Parcel II. Bagwell stored equipment and sewer pipes on Parcel II.

   Caminiti owned and operated a construction company on Parcel I. The construction company's office building was located 20 feet from the easement.

   Five years later, Bagwell sold Parcel II to Asphalt Road Graders (Asphalt), the deed including the easement over Parcel I. Over the next ten years Asphalt trucks made an average of 200 daily round-trips from Parcel II to Route 53.

   Asphalt bought Parcel III (not landlocked) ten years after it bought Parcel II. Parcel III is directly east of Parcel II. Asphalt built a new asphalt plant on Parcel III. Trucks going to the asphalt plant entered and exited from Route 53 over Parcel I and Parcel II. Because Asphalt's business increased after the new plant opened, the average number of trucks using the easement on Parcel I doubled. As traffic increased, the trucks began driving faster and raised dust. Dust entered Caminiti's showroom through the ventilation and air-conditioning system. Dust also fell on employees' and customers' cars. Although Asphalt paved the road in when it bought Parcel II, it had not repaired the road since then and the heavy truck use caused the pavement to deteriorate, adding to the dust problem. The parties agree the road had deteriorated so much it had to be rebuilt completely.

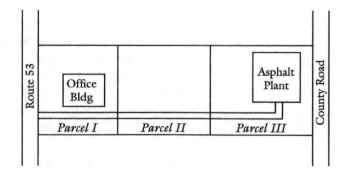

This year Caminiti installed four eight-inch high-speed barriers on the easement in an effort to slow the trucks. Asphalt built up the road on either side of the four speed barriers with asphalt in an effort to minimize the damages caused to its trucks when the trucks went over the speed barriers. Caminiti removed the asphalt gradings, leaving the barriers with eight-inch-high horizontal edges. When Asphalt attempted to replace the asphalt inclines, Caminiti parked his truck on one of the barriers, locked the gate on the easement for one hour, and told the Asphalt workers to remove the asphalt. The parties ended up in court.

(a) Caminiti claims Asphalt's almost constant running of trucks over the easement is a misuse. How would a court rule?

(b) Caminiti claims trucks cannot use the easement to get to the asphalt plant on Parcel III. How would a court rule?

(c) Caminiti claims the facts justify terminating Asphalt's easement over Parcel I. How would a court rule?

(d) Asphalt Road Graders wants the speed barriers removed. Caminiti wants the speed barriers to stay. How would a court rule?

(e) If the easement continues, who should pay to rebuild the road? Once the road is paved, who should pay for the repairs and maintenance of the road?

The End of Easements

5. Farmer sold Heather a landlocked lot. He deeded Heather a ten-foot-wide easement for ingress and egress over Lot 24 to reach Clampett Cove Road. Farmer continued selling lots. A year later he deeded Lot 24 to Edward Wilbur subject to Heather's easement. Edward Wilbur has wanted to get rid of the easement from the start.

(a) Heather purchased Lot 35, which adjoins her original lot and fronts on Drysdale Avenue. Does her easement over Wilbur's property end?

(b) The county constructed a road fronting on Heather's original property. Does her easement over Wilbur's property end?

(c) Assume both (a) and (b) occur, and Heather fences in her yard, without a gate in the fence at the point where her easement begins. Does the easement over Wilbur's property end?

(d) Assume all the above, plus Heather plants a hedge along the fence. Is her easement still in existence?

(e) Assume all the above, plus Wilbur built a storage shed on the easement and ten years pass (the statute of limitations period is ten years). Is Heather's easement still in existence?

(f) Assume all the above occurred. Edward Wilbur sells his property to Heather, who moves into Edward Wilbur's home. Six months later Heather sells her old home to Dante Wilbur (Edward's son, who wanted to move back to the old neighborhood). Is the easement still in existence?

(g) What result in (f) if Heather sold her home to Dante one day before she closed on Lot 24?

(h) Would any of the answers above change if Farmer's deed to Heather had granted her a right-of-way over Lot 24 as long as Heather's property remained landlocked?

Explanations

Gone Fishing

1. (a) Marty has an easement in gross. The easement is a noncommercial easement for Marty's personal pleasure and enjoyment rather than a commercial easement in gross. The scope of a personal easement for fishing and boating normally would not include such an intense use by the easement holder as holding a ski show. Marty cannot hold a ski show on the lake. The ski show may have other problems. Since the easement is personal and not commercial, Marty's use of the easement for commercial purposes probably exceeds the scope of the easement. In addition, the ski show would use much of the land surrounding the lake for both participants and spectators. The easement to use the lake for fishing and boating carries it with it the right to travel over the land and use it as reasonably necessary to enjoy the fishing and boating rights, but it does not carry with it the right to use the grounds for other reasons, such as accommodating large crowds.

(b) Bait that hook, Catfish. Marty has a noncommercial easement in gross. The easement in gross, even a personal or noncommercial easement in gross, includes reasonable ancillary use by the easement holder beneficial to the use of the easement. Unless the grant specifically limited access to Marty to use the lake alone, an easement to fish and boat includes the right to bring a reasonable number of others (for social, safety, or other practical reasons). Catfish can accompany Marty.

(c) Noncommercial, nonexclusive easements in gross are not apportionable. Marty, for example, could not give his buddies the right to fish on the lake anytime they wanted. The Example is narrower than that, however, with Marty allowing his buddies to go just this one time without him. They could argue Marty has not assigned them any rights, and that they came as Marty's guests even though Marty himself could not come. A court probably would hold the easement is personal to Marty, and buddies can fish on the lake only when they accompany Marty. Landowner can refuse to let Marty's two buddies fish on the lake.

(d) Noncommercial easements in gross generally are nonassignable unless the circumstances or the grant indicates the easement is assignable. Nothing in the facts even hints at Marty's easement being assignable. Marty cannot assign the easement in gross during his lifetime or by will at his death. Marty's easement terminates on his death. Unfortunately for Catfish, he loses this one hook, line, and sinker.

(e) Marty had an easement appurtenant. The easement appurtenant is assignable and passes with the dominant estate. When Marty devised the ten acres to Catfish, Catfish acquired the easement to fish and boat on Landowner's lake.

She Sells Easements to Seashore

2. (a) Seashore Pipeline has a commercial easement in gross. The easement is an exclusive easement. Seashore has the right to assign its commercial easement in gross to Triton Company. Seashore Pipeline assigned one of the pipelines to Triton, but only made a partial assignment of its easement; or, stated otherwise, Seashore attempted to subdivide or apportion its easement. The issue becomes whether Seashore Pipeline can subdivide or apportion its easement rights as long as it compensates Debbie for each additional pipeline. And the answer is: Yes it can. Seashore Pipeline has an exclusive easement. Unless the deed or contract specifies the easement is nonassignable or nonapportionable, most states will conclude Seashore Pipeline can assign, subdivide, or apportion its rights in a commercial easement in gross so long as the total use does not overburden the servient estate. A court would be more sympathetic to Seashore Pipeline in this situation because the pipeline itself limits the amount of usage that can be made of the easement, and Debbie would be additionally compensated for each additional pipeline. The partial assignment to Triton Company is valid. No new pipeline was added so Debbie is not entitled to extra compensation. Triton's use did not cause a surcharge or overburdening of the easement since total volume of use is circumscribed by the size of the pipeline in place.

(b) Debbie granted Seashore two nonexclusive easements in gross to place pipelines through her property. Seashore cannot subdivide or apportion a nonexclusive easement, but it can assign the easement. Seashore owns two easements and can assign each independent of the other. The assignment of the easement and the 12-inch pipeline was valid. Triton Company owns the easement.

A second issue is whether Triton Company can expand the size of the pipeline in the easement from a 12-inch pipeline to a 20-inch pipeline. The grant for the easement stipulated a 12-inch pipeline. That stipulation established the scope of the easement. Triton's attempt to enlarge the pipeline is a misuse of the easement. Debbie can enjoin Triton from putting in the 20-inch pipeline. If Triton Company wants a 20-inch pipeline through Debbie's property, it must negotiate with Debbie for the right to an easement for that purpose. Debbie prevails.

Cable Ready Easement

3. (a) While the overall picture is still fuzzy, it's coming into clearer focus. In the case on which the Example is based, Marcus Cable Associates, L.P. v. Krohn, 90 S.W.3d 687 (Tex 2002), the Texas Supreme Court ruled the easement was for electrical transmission only: cable use exceeded the scope of the easement. The court contrasted the easement in its case with those for telegraph or television, which they thought involved communication. The cable company argued cable is just a technological development that did not exist when the easement was granted and the phrase should include cable today as a natural development. The cable company also argued the court should favor extension of cable services as a public benefit. The Texas Supreme Court rejected those arguments, but other courts have found them persuasive. Ruling for servient landowners.

   (b) Courts usually extend easement for transmitting "messages" and "communications" to include cable. Once that issue has been resolved, courts address whether the easement holder, Statewide Telephone Company in the Example, can apportion its easement. The courts typically find the easement is a commercial easement in gross, which is assignable; and the easement is exclusive, giving the easement holder the power to apportion the easement as long as the easement is not overburdened. Since the cables attach to existing poles, courts conclude the additional cable does not overburden the easement. Ruling for cable company.

   (c) This is an issue of serious economic consequence. One issue that arises is whether the grant of right of way to the railroad was an easement or a fee simple interest. If a railroad owns a fee simple estate, it can freely grant easements to lay cable. The Example posits an easement, however, which leads to more issues.

   Current litigation (as of 2007) in most cable-in-railroad-easement cases centers on class certification of servient estate owners, and not on the true substantive issue. One addressing the merits was Kershaw Sunnyside Ranches, Inc. v. Yakima Interurban Lines, 126 P.3d 16 (Wash. 2006). The court first concluded the railroad owned an easement and not a fee simple. The court sidestepped what should be a major issue in these cases related to 'incidental uses' by resorting to a state statute requiring railroad companies to allow telecommunications companies post their wires and cables on railroad corridors but only if they secure the right from landowners by eminent domain as provided by law — a victory for the servient estate owner.

In other jurisdictions, the cases could turn on whether optical cable is an incidental use. Incidental use is a scope of an easement issue. As background, a railroad historically could use its right of way for railroad purposes, which included not only the actual tracks but any incidental use that facilitated the railroad's business. A major benefit of the incidental use rule was that a railroad could string telegraph wires along the tracks because communication between stations was important for railroad operations. Some states limited the incidental use justification to uses that primarily benefited the railroad. Use of the telegraph to serve the public was allowed as long as the telegraph was operated primarily for the railroad's benefit. Other states, seeing how difficult it would be to monitor how much the public benefited, allowed even full business operations unrelated to the railroad as long as the railroad could show some incidental benefit to the railroad operations. Other states went even further and allowed as an incidental use any use that did not interfere with the railroad's operations. Railroads and cable companies argue optical cable is similar to telegraph services and should be an incidental use of the easement. Landowners claim railroads don't need cable to operate so that even the elemental connection is missing. How a state will rule depends on what standard of incidental use it adopts.

The Use and Misuse Truce

4. (a) Asphalt prevails. Asphalt had an easement appurtenant for the benefit of Parcel II. As owner of the dominant estate, Asphalt can make such use of the easement as is reasonably necessary for the full enjoyment of the dominant estate as long as the use does not unreasonably burden the servient estate. In evaluating reasonableness of both the use and the burden, the original parties' intent is presumed to accommodate normal development of the property in the general vicinity. Not much has changed since the easement was granted.

The parcels seemingly have been suited for industrial uses. Caminiti operated a construction company on Parcel I. Bagwell stored pipes on Parcel II. Asphalt operated its asphalt business for ten to twenty years before the case came to trial Even if the truck use exceeded the scope of the original reservation, Asphalt may have gained the expanded scope by prescription. The number of trucks traversing the easement seems to be a normal development of industrial use over the five-acre tract. The trucks traveling over Parcel I are not an unreasonable use or burden.

The dust might be another matter. A person must use an easement in a manner not to unreasonably burden the easement or the servient estate. Asphalt's continuing to stir up dust seems to be an unreasonable interference with the servient estate owner's use and enjoyment of his land, especially since the dust can be controlled by repairing the road, which the parties apparently agreed should be done.

(b) Caminiti is correct. While an easement holder can use the easement for the general benefit of the dominant estate, the holder's use the easement for the benefit of any nondominant land even if the same person owns both properties and even if, as is the case here, the two properties are used as an integrated unit is a misuse of the easement.

Trucks going to the asphalt plant located on Parcel III cannot go over Parcel I. Asphalt, therefore, must find another way for its trucks to get to the asphalt plant. The facts say Parcel III is not landlocked, so finding a new entrance and exit may not be a problem (though it may be inconvenient and it may increase by a few miles how far trucks must travel to get from the asphalt plant to work sites). If all trucks go to the asphalt plant, which is possible, then all or virtually all truck traffic over Parcel I must end. Caminiti may get his dream result: no trucks at all.

(c) Asphalt will retain its easement. A court will terminate an easement for misuse of the easement, but termination for misuse is not favored. A complete impossibility of use, or evidence the dominant estate holder will intentionally continue misusing the easement, or some like circumstance is crucial before a court will terminate an easement for misuse. Nothing in the facts indicates any reason to terminate the easement.

(d) The speed barriers must go. A servient estate owner cannot interfere with the dominant estate owner's use of the easement. The court may direct Asphalt, the dominant estate owner, to control the trucks' speed by putting up speed barriers or by enforcing a speed policy for its employees and contractors, but self-help by Caminiti, the servient estate owner, is inappropriate.

(e) Since Asphalt's trucks are causing the dust and Asphalt is the main user of the easement, Asphalt should pay to rebuild the road. Similarly, the persons using the easement have a duty to maintain the easement and any improvements they make to the easement. Asphalt Road Graders should maintain the road. The costs of rebuilding and maintaining the road will be allocated between Caminiti and Asphalt based on each one's percentage of their total use.

The End of Easements

5. (a) No. The easement continues. While the strict necessity ends, the easement still serves a purpose of getting to Clampett Cove Road. (The only time an easement ends when the strict necessity ends is when the easement was implied by strict necessity for egress and ingress. Heather's easement was an express easement, not an implied easement by necessity.) The mere existence of an alternate route over Heather's other property will not terminate the easement over Lot 24.

(b) No. The easement continues. Even though Heather has a road in front of her house that she probably will use most of the time, the easement across Wilbur's land remains valid. It still serves a purpose of getting to Clampett Cove Road, and will as long as there is a Clampett Cove Road.

(c) No. The easement continues. Heather seemingly stopped using the easement. The fence certainly makes it inconvenient for her to use the easement and indicates she does not intend to use the easement, but for the easement to terminate a court must conclude Heather abandoned the easement. Nothing in Heather's putting up the fence unambiguously signals her intent to abandon the easement. Mere nonuse does not amount to an abandonment. If need be, Heather can remove the fence and drive over the easement.

(d) The easement continues. A hedge adds an extra dimension of nonuse and difficulty to Heather's reopening the way, but in and of themselves planting the hedge and building the fence do not amount to an abandonment of the easement. See (c), supra.

(e) The easement continues. The shed would block Heather's use of the easement if she tried to drive on the easement. Under the facts, however, Heather has not tried to use the easement. Wilbur has the right to use his property any way he wishes as long as he does not interfere with Heather's using her easement. Until Heather tries to use the easement, Wilbur's putting a shed there is not hostile enough to start the running of the ten-year prescription period.

(f) No. The easement is terminated. As soon as Heather bought Lot 24, she became the owner of both the dominant estate and the servient estate. Since a person cannot have an easement over her own property, the easement merged into the fee simple. Once the easement was terminated, it disappeared. The easement does not spring up again when Heather sells her original home to Dante Wilbur.

(g) The easement would continue. Since Heather never owned both lots simultaneously, the easement did not merge into the fee simple.

The easement is an easement appurtenant and runs with the land. Dante Wilbur owns the dominant estate and would have an easement over Lot 24.

(h) Heather's easement would have ended by the terms of the grant as soon as she bought the adjoining Lot 35 with frontage on Drysdale Avenue (or as soon as Heather cleared a way to the street). At the latest, the easement would have terminated as soon as the county built the road in front of Heather's home.

CHAPTER 30

Real Covenants and Equitable Servitudes: Running with the Land

INTRODUCTION

Landowners always could contract between and among themselves as to the use or nonuse of their properties, and courts would enforce the contracts as between the original parties to the contract. At one time, however, neither contract rights nor obligations could be assigned to third parties. Courts would enforce contracts only if there was **privity of contract** between the parties (i.e., both parties were principals to the agreement). A person could **assume** the obligations by executing an assumption agreement or a new contract, but he could not become liable solely by purchasing the affected property.

Courts in the late eighteenth and early nineteenth centuries sought (1) to give a subsequent purchaser of property, who was not a party to the original agreement, **standing** to enforce an agreement against the other landowners who were parties to the agreement, and (2) to obligate subsequent purchasers, who were not parties to the original agreement, to honor the obligations affecting their property. Building on the concept of **privity of estate**, see Chapter 16, supra, the **courts of law** established the elements for **real covenants** or **covenants that run with the land** that made some contracts or promises affecting property bind and benefit subsequent owners of the affected properties. Later, the **courts of equity** expanded the number of subsequent purchasers who would be bound and burdened under the theory of **equitable servitudes**. There is a lot of overlap, and some critical differences, between real covenants and equitable servitudes.

527

TERMINOLOGY

Real covenants and *equitable servitudes* are agreements, promises, or deed provisions that relate to real property (land and improvements to land) and that bound or benefit subsequent owners of the respective properties solely because they own the property. Real covenants and equitable servitudes, because they benefit and obligate subsequent landowners, are said to **run with the land** (though legal purists say real covenants burden estates in land, not the land itself, and equitable servitudes bind subsequent owners but do not run with the land). The objective of the law of real covenants and equitable servitudes is to distinguish those covenants that run to subsequent or remote grantees from covenants benefiting or obligating only the original promisors.

The property whose owner **benefits** from a covenant or servitude in any controversy is called the **benefited** estate or property. The property whose owner is bound by a covenant to act or not act is called the **burdened** estate or property. A covenant often will both benefit and burden a piece of property. Whether the property is labeled the benefited or burdened property in any controversy depends on whether the property owner is trying to enforce a covenant against another landowner, or other persons are trying to enforce the covenant against the property owner.

> *Example:*   Every deed conveying lots in a subdivision contains a covenant providing that only "a two story home can be built on the property." Chris owns a lot in the subdivision. If Chris wants to prevent a neighbor from building a single-story house, Chris owns the **benefited estate** and the other person owns the **burdened property**. If, on the other hand, Chris plans to build a single-story house, Chris' lot is the burdened estate, and the neighboring lots are the benefited estates.

Covenants can be **affirmative** or **negative** (negative covenants are commonly called **restrictive covenants**). Affirmative covenants and negative covenants indicate the type of **burden** binding the landowner. **Affirmative covenants** require the owner of the burdened estate to perform some act or to pay money. Affirmative covenants include the duty to maintain a wall or a dam, for example. **Negative covenants** restrict or prohibit the uses that can be made of the burdened property. Negative covenants or restrictive covenants include, among many other possibilities, covenants restricting property to single-family residences, covenants prohibiting farm animals on the property, and covenants prohibiting the sale of alcohol on the property. Sometimes it is difficult to tell the difference between an affirmative and a restrictive covenant. Today both affirmative covenants and negative covenants may be enforced both as either real covenants or equitable servitudes if their respective elements are proved.

IDENTIFYING REAL COVENANTS AND EQUITABLE SERVITUDES

Real covenants and equitable servitudes are interests in land. Like all interests in land, the creation of the real covenant or equitable servitude must satisfy the Statute of Frauds — i.e., the covenant must be expressly created in a writing, usually a deed. The Part Performance doctrine and the equitable estoppel exceptions, Chapter 22, supra, apply here as well. Like other interests in land, real covenants and equitable servitudes to be binding on subsequent bona fide purchasers must comply with the state's recording statute. See Chapter 26, supra. Notwithstanding the Statute of Frauds, courts will imply equitable servitudes in certain situations.

The following elements are necessary for a real covenant or an equitable servitude to bind and benefit subsequent owners:

Real Covenant	**Equitable Servitude**
1. Intent to Bind Successors	1. Intent to Bind Successors
2. Touch and Concern	2. Touch and Concern

3. Privity of Estate
   a) Horizontal Privity
   b) Vertical Privity
	3. Notice

Two elements — **intent to bind successors** and **touch and concern** — are the same for real covenants and equitable servitudes. The two theories diverge significantly in their respective third elements. The **notice** requirement for **equitable servitudes** is easier to satisfy since all it requires is that the successor owner of the **burdened property** have actual, constructive, or inquiry notice of the covenant. The **privity of estate** requirements for real covenants that run with the land, particularly the **horizontal privity** element, on the other hand, have narrow technical meanings. Generally, a covenant that meets the real covenant's privity of estate requirement also satisfies the equitable servitudes' notice requirement (especially in conjunction with the recording statutes). The reverse is not true, however. Only a fraction of the covenants meeting the notice requirement for an equitable servitude also will satisfy the privity of estate element necessary in most states for a real covenant to run with the land.

Classification as a real covenant or an equitable servitude matters, especially as to permitted remedies. Today in many states monetary damages and injunctive relief are available remedies for breaches of **real covenants**, but only injunctive relief is available for breaches of **equitable servitudes**. Fortunately, most plaintiffs only care to enjoin prohibited uses and activities and are not interested in monetary damages. The more easily proved equitable servitude action serves their purposes.

Even if an element for a real covenant or an equitable servitude is not satisfied, the covenant remains enforceable and binding on the original parties to the agreement. The whole purpose of the "running with the land" issue is whether **subsequent purchasers** can enforce or be obligated to honor the covenant, not whether the covenant constitutes a valid contract between the original parties.

INTENT TO BIND AND BENEFIT SUCCESSORS

For a covenant to run with the land, the original parties must **intend** the covenant benefit and/or burden subsequent purchasers rather than the covenant merely being a personal agreement between the original parties. The intent that the covenant will run with the land must be ascertainable from the deed setting out the covenant. Intent is the easiest of the three elements to prove for real covenants to run with the land.

Several magic words serve as rebuttable presumptions of the parties' intent to burden and benefit successors. First, the parties may stipulate that a promisor agrees for himself, his heirs and assigns to be bound by the covenant. The courts interpret the "heirs and assigns" language as proving the requisite intent (absent evidence to the contrary). A common and seemingly straightforward sentence such as "This covenant shall run with the land" also shows intent. So does a statement that "The covenant is appurtenant to the land" conveyed or retained.

The covenant often is included in a deed, and the intent for the burden to run is made clear by one of the methods listed in the above paragraph. Sometimes the deed also states who can enforce the benefit (i.e., whether it is personal to the promisee or whether it runs to the owner of promisee's nearby land or to subsequent owners of the nearby land).

Unfortunately, in many cases the deed stipulates only that the burden runs with the land. An issue still remaining is whether the benefit runs with some other property or whether it is enforceable only by the original promisee. An inference arises that the benefit will run with the land if the promisee owns neighboring property. Conversely, the benefit will be considered personal to the promisee (even if the burden runs with the land) if the promisee retains no land near the burdened estate. If the promisee is subdividing land, a presumption arises that the benefit is to run with all properties in the subdivision still owned by the promisee (see Chapter 32, infra).

As the above discussion indicates, the running of the *benefit* must be analyzed separately from the running of the *burden*. One may run while the other does not. A separate analysis is required for all elements as well.

TOUCH AND CONCERN

Real covenants and equitable servitudes must **touch and concern** the **burdened property** before a court will enforce the covenant against subsequent purchasers. There are many views of the role touch and concern plays in evaluating covenants. Touch and concern at one time may have meant literally touch and concern property, but no more. Many covenants do physically touch and concern land, such as limiting the property to single-family residences, prohibiting improvements from being built closer than five feet from the property line, or requiring all structures to have brick exteriors. Other agreements such as a covenant to pay a homeowners fee or a covenant not to compete against the seller's nearby business may not physically touch the property, yet legally still will "touch and concern" the property.

"Touch and concern" is a public policy complement to the "intent" requirement. The "intent" requirement assures the court the original parties intended the covenant to run with the land. The "touch and concern" element asks whether a reasonable person upon calm reflection and hindsight (knowing what has transpired since the original promise) would have intended the covenant to run with the land. Thus it focuses on the reasonableness of having the covenant bind successors. That reasonableness is often indicated when the subject of the covenant under review is so connected to the use of the land that the original parties must have wanted it to run.

(a) Burdens that Touch and Concern Land (or Don't)

The best way to master the "touch and concern" element is to see how courts apply the doctrine to concrete situations. The frequently encountered covenant restricting the land to residential uses, for example, touches and concerns the burdened estate. As another example, a covenant that the grantee not operate a business that competes with the grantor's nearby business for five years touches and concerns the burdened estate.[1]

---

1. A court may invalidate a covenant not to compete as being an **unreasonable restraint on competition** just as it might refuse to enforce any agreement not to compete. If a court invalidates the noncompete agreement, the agreement is not enforceable against the original promisor, either. Generally, noncompete agreements must not endure for more than a reasonable period of time; the restriction must be limited to a reasonable geographic area; and the agreement must be narrowly tailored to reach its legitimate purposes. Selling a

Generally, a covenant for the payment of money does not touch and concern the burdened property. A covenant that a named management company will manage the property for a percentage of rentals, for example, does not touch and concern the land. Covenants providing that the seller will build a house on the lot, for his normal fee, when the buyer decides what kind of house to build does not touch and concern land; subsequent purchasers will not be forced to use the seller as their builder. Likewise, a contract that the seller would deliver water for a fixed price does not touch and concern the land (the burdened property's owner can as easily dig a well). Finally, a covenant promising to support (or not oppose) a rezoning application does not touch and concern the land (the right to appear in an administrative proceeding is too important).

A major exception to the general rule that payment of money does not touch and concern land is a contractual requirement that the burdened property owner pay money to a homeowners association, which will be upheld as touching and concerning the land because the money will be spent to maintain the property or a common area. Since a covenant requiring the landowner to pave parking areas, maintain shrubs, etc., would touch and concern the property, the required homeowners fee used to pave driveways, maintain shrubs, etc., also touches and concerns the land. Even if, in the case of a homeowners association, the money is used to maintain common areas, such as roads, parks, pools, and parking areas, and not the burdened property itself, courts conclude that members have undivided interests in the common areas or that the common areas make the burdened property more enjoyable. Moreover, observe many courts, the homeowners are paying the money to themselves in the guise of the homeowners association. Whatever the courts' legal rationale, homeowners fees to a homeowners association controlled by the homeowners touch and concern the land.

A covenant to keep the improvements on the land insured is taken, by most courts, to touch and concern it. True, when a claim on the insurance is payable, the proceeds are money, not the improvement, but any required application of the proceeds to rebuilding the improvement is a sufficient connection to the land for most courts considering the matter. They find that a reasonable implication of the covenant's requiring insurance is that the proceeds will be used on the land to rebuild, keeping the improvements in a condition similar to the way they were when the original promise was made.

---

business or protecting an ongoing business has been held to be a legitimate purpose as long as the noncompete agreement does not prevent competition for too long a time. To illustrate, if Pizza Man sells a lot on the same block as his popular pizza parlor, he might include a covenant the transferred lot could not be used to operate a pizza parlor for five years. A court would find the covenant touches and concerns the transferred burdened land and touches and concerns the retained benefited land.

Several possible rationales justify the courts finding these **money obligations** do not touch and concern the burdened property. First, at one time courts did not allow **affirmative covenants** to run at all because they feared covenants would encumber title so much no purchaser would buy the land. Although all courts recognize affirmative covenants today, the courts remain more wary of affirmative covenants than they do of restrictive covenants. Second, courts dislike covenants that are open-ended, in the sense that they impose costly, uncertain, and unforeseen financial burdens. For example, a court may look for a time limit on affirmative covenants requiring subsequent owners to pay money (although homeowner associations may escape the intense scrutiny imposed on other payees). Third, original landowners entering into the covenant and subsequent purchasers may not have the sophistication or take the time to appreciate the long-term consequences of a promise. A covenant that runs with the land, unlike the typical contract, does not give a subsequent landowner an opportunity to rectify her predecessor's mistakes since covenants may continue indefinitely. Finally, many affirmative covenants calling for burdened property owners to purchase goods or services from the promisee are little more than ingenious marketing tools for the promisee's business and as such might be considered unreasonable restraints of trade.

(b) Benefits that Touch and Concern Land (or Don't)

The preceding paragraphs discussed whether the covenant or servitude touched and concerned the **burdened property**. Not addressed was whether the covenant touched and concerned the **benefited property**. Recall that the burden side of a covenant and the benefit side of a covenant must be analyzed separately. The covenant must touch and concern the benefited property for the benefit to run with the land, no matter whether the burden is personal to the promisor or is a real covenant or equitable servitude running with burdened property.

Example: O owns two adjoining lots. O transfers one of the two lots to P, the purchaser. The deed restricts the transferred land to single-family residences and provides that the restriction shall run with the land. O then sells his retained lot to T, another purchaser. P attempts to build a grocery store. The issue is who can enforce the single-family residence covenant: T, the subsequent and current owner of the adjoining lot; or O, who no longer owns any property in the area. The answer depends on whether the covenant **touches and concerns** T's land. If the benefit touches and concerns T's land, T can enforce the covenant. If, on the other hand, the benefit does not touch and concern T's land, O (but not T) can enforce the covenant. In this Example all courts would hold the covenant touches and concerns the benefited property. T (but not O) can enforce the covenant.

Whether T, the subsequent purchaser in the Example can enforce the covenant against P depends on the meaning of "touch and concern." A requirement the covenant actually produces a physical presence on the land will lead to a conclusion the covenant does not touch and concern the benefited property. The suggested approach that courts under the rubric of "touch and concern" determine whether a reasonable person upon reflection and hindsight would have intended the benefit to run, leads to the correct conclusion that the legitimate purpose of the restriction on P's property is to improve the use and enjoyment of the second lot, whether O, other, or some person owned the lot. Guaranteeing nearby property will continue its residential character furthers a property owner's enjoyment of the benefited property. Once O sold the second lot, his interest in maintaining the residential nature ended. The person who would have an interest in maintaining the residential character would be the current owner of the second lot (T in our Example). The benefit touches and concerns the second lot.

This is not to say all residential restrictions are appurtenant to some land. If, for example, O initially owned and sold only the first lot and his nearest property was five miles from the lot, the nexus of benefit dissipates. The benefit in this situation would be personal to O.

In the other Examples discussed above in "Burdens that Touch and Concern (or Don't)," the noncompete covenant could touch and concern benefited land. The homeowners association fee would touch the benefited land since the money must be spent for the upkeep of the property. A court probably would find the management contract covenant is a personal benefit. The benefit of a construction contract in nearly all cases likewise will be personal. The benefit of the water supply contract may touch and concern specific property if the contract stipulated the water was to come solely from identified land.

In some states, a covenant does not touch and concern purported burdened property unless the covenant also touches and concerns some benefited property (or, alternatively, the court will hold the covenant will not run even if it does touch and concern the burdened property). In these states, once the benefit of the covenant is found to be personal, the burden will not be binding on subsequent purchasers.

Not only do courts disagree as to the better rule, so do commentators, although most seem to favor a rule that a burden that touches and concerns land can run even if the benefit is personal. The courts seem to follow one of four approaches:

1. The burden may run even if the benefit is personal or touches and concerns benefited property.

2. The burden will not run unless the covenant touches and concerns both burdened and benefited land.

3. The burden will not run as a real covenant unless the covenant touches and concerns both burdened and benefited land, but an equitable servitude will be enforced even if the benefit is personal as long as the burden touches and concerns the burdened land.

4. The burden will not run as a real covenant unless the covenant touches and concerns both burdened and benefited land, but an equitable servitude will be enforced even if the benefit is personal as long as the burden touches and concerns the land and either of the original parties would be a defendant or plaintiff in a lawsuit to enforce the covenant. See, e.g., Runyon v. Paley, 416 S.E.2d 177, 189 (N.C. 1992).

REAL COVENANTS AND THE PRIVITY OF ESTATE

The elements for real covenants and equitable servitude share the first two elements, intent and touch and concern. They diverge on the third element. In many states, the benefited party must prove there was **privity of estate** before a **real covenant** will bind the subsequent owners of the burdened property. Two separate privities of estate must exist before a court in these states will find privity of estate: horizontal privity and vertical privity. Despite the similarity of the names, vertical and horizontal privity are evaluated under different rules.

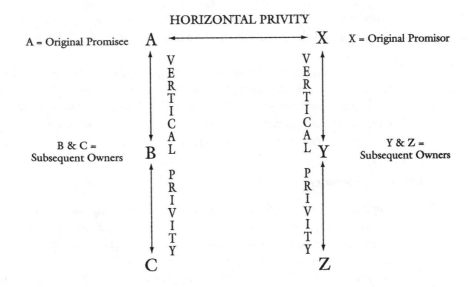

HORIZONTAL PRIVITY

A = Original Promisee   A ⟷ X   X = Original Promisor

VERTICAL PRIVITY

B & C = Subsequent Owners   B   Y   Y & Z = Subsequent Owners

VERTICAL PRIVITY

C   Z

(a) Terminology

(1) Original Promisee

The **original promisee** is an original party to the agreement creating the covenant. The original *promisee* can enforce the covenant (assuming another person is bound), either because the benefit is personal to the promisee or because it is appurtenant to the promisee's property. A person can be both a promisee and a promisor under a covenant; that is, a covenant, such as a residential-use-only covenant, may both benefit a person (so the person is the promisee) and burden the same person (so the person is the promisor).

(2) Original Promisor

The **original promisor** is an original party to the agreement creating the covenant. The original *promisor* is always *bound* by the covenant (assuming another person is benefited), either because the burden is personal to the promisor or because the burden is appurtenant to the original promisor's land.

(3) Subsequent Owners

Subsequent owners (also known as subsequent purchasers, remote purchasers or owners, assigns, or successors in interest) are those persons who were not original parties to the contract, but who now own property that may be benefited or burdened by a covenant entered into by a previous owner (the original promisee or original promisor) if the covenant runs with the land. Since a subsequent owner cannot be bound or benefited under the traditional **privity of contract** theory, the subsequent owner will benefit or be bound only if the benefit or burden runs with the land (i.e., is appurtenant to the land).

A subsequent purchaser can enter into a new contract and be bound by the new contract, of course, but the issue in real covenants that run with the land and equitable servitudes is whether the subsequent purchaser can enforce or be bound by a predecessor's deed covenant even if the subsequent purchaser does not enter into the new contract.

(4) Horizontal Privity

Horizontal privity refers to the necessary relationship between the original parties to the agreement for the covenant to run with the land (i.e., to bind and/or burden subsequent owners of the property). Horizontal privity is not necessary for the covenant to be enforced between the original parties. No "privity of estate" is needed since the original parties are bound and benefited by "privity of contract." States have evolved three different standards for horizontal privity of estate, as developed in "(b) Horizontal Privity," below. All three are narrow, technical standards. The principles for each standard are not hard to understand, although all exclude more covenants that you would have expected before you studied this matter.

There is nothing analytical about the adjective "horizontal." It merely signifies the relationship between the original promisee and the original promisor. *A* and X in the diagram are in horizontal privity.

(5) Vertical Privity

Vertical privity refers to that relationship between an original party to the contract and those subsequent purchasers tracing their interests in the benefited or burdened property back to the original party. Typically, vertical privity is found on sales, gifts, devises, and inheritances of real estate. Although vertical privity can cause some analytical problems, vertical privity is a bit more logical than horizontal privity of estate.

(b) Horizontal Privity

In the majority of states retaining the horizontal privity element, **horizontal privity** will be found *only* if the covenant is created when one original party transfers an interest in land (other than the covenant itself) to another original party. Generally horizontal privity can be created only in conjunction with grants of easements, leases, and freehold estates (such as a fee simple or a life estate). In most jurisdictions, horizontal privity will be found only when the covenant is included in a grant of a fee estate, a life estate, an easement, or a leasehold. The transfer of the property and the creation of the covenant must arise simultaneously.

Example 1: Abbott and Costello are neighbors and execute a document limiting their respective properties to single-family residential use. There is no horizontal privity because the document, even if it is a deed, does not transfer a fee, a life estate, an easement, or a leasehold. Abbott and Costello may have intended the covenant to run and the covenant does touch and concern both properties, but Abbott and Costello already owned their respective properties when they made the agreement. Thus, there could be no horizontal privity of estate. Consequently, the covenant will not run to successors in interest.

Example 2: Abbott, owning two adjoining lots, transfers one lot to Costello, incorporating a covenant limiting both lots to single-family residential use only. Here horizontal privity of estate exists because the covenant was included in a transfer of a fee interest.

Example 3: Abbott, owning two adjoining lots, transfers one to Costello, the deed containing no covenants. Six months later Abbott and Costello each give the other a deed restricting their respective lots to single-family residential use. There is no horizontal privity because the restrictions were not created in conjunction with the initial transfer of a lot to Costello.

Massachusetts, and as far as we know only Massachusetts, has a narrower rule. Horizontal privity of estate will be found by a Massachusetts court only when the covenant is created in the grant of an easement or a leasehold interest. Under this rule, none of the residential-use-only covenants in the three Abbott-Costello Examples would run to successors since in none of the three scenarios was there horizontal privity, not even where the covenant was included in the deed from Abbott to Costello.

A growing number of states are dropping the horizontal privity of estate altogether on the theory horizontal privity no longer serves a purpose. States dropping the horizontal privity of estate demand the burdened party have actual, constructive, or inquiry notice of the covenant. This approach merges the real covenant and equitable servitude theories into a single theory of servitudes that run with the land, an idea popular with many commentators.

A few states require horizontal privity for the *burden* to run but not for the *benefit* to run. In these states, the original promisor would be burdened no matter if the original promisee or a subsequent owner enforced the covenant, but horizontal privity would be necessary to enforce the covenant against subsequent purchasers of the burdened property.

(c) Vertical Privity

Vertical privity denotes the relationship between an original party to the covenant and her successors in interest. All the vertical privity element requires is that the subsequent property owner must succeed to an original party's entire estate in the property, either directly from an original party or through persons who can trace their interests back to an original party to the covenant.

Example: In the Abbott-Costello Examples above, Costello sells his land to Gracie. Costello and Gracie are in vertical privity.

Many courts distinguish slightly what constitutes vertical privity for a *burden* to run and what constitutes vertical privity for a *benefit* to run. For a *burden* to run to a successor or remote party, the party must have succeeded to the original promisor's **entire estate** or **ownership interest**. The "entire estate" requirement means **lessees** are not in vertical privity with their lessors.

On the other hand, all that is required for a *benefit* to run is that a remote or subsequent purchaser have a **possessory interest** in the property. For our purposes, **lessees** are in vertical privity if they wish to enforce or benefit from the real covenant. Lessees do not take the original party's entire estate, but they do have physical use and possession of the land, and can enforce the benefit of a covenant.

Adverse possession defeats the running of both benefits and burdens completely since the adverse possessor does not succeed to any party's interest. The adverse possessor starts a new chain of title, hence is not in vertical privity with an original party to the covenant. A rule just as sensibly might conclude the adverse possessor dispossessed the true owner but not the rights and obligations consistent with the adverse possessor's use of the property.

EQUITABLE SERVITUDES AND THE NOTICE REQUIREMENT

The third element for an **equitable servitude** (as opposed to a real covenant) to be binding on a subsequent or remote purchaser is for the purchaser to have **notice** of the covenant when he or she buys the **burdened property**. The rationale underlying equitable servitudes is that a subsequent landowner should be bound by a covenant, maybe not for damages, but at least for injunctive relief, if the original parties intended the burden to run, the covenant "touches and concerns" the land, and the person to be bound knows about the covenant when he or she buys. As with the recording statutes, **notice** as an element of equitable servitudes can be either actual notice, constructive notice gathered from the deed records, or inquiry notice gathered from viewing the premises and surrounding properties. We return to inquiry notice in the next chapter in the discussion of subdivisions and common schemes.

The notice requirement applies only to the burdens not to the benefits. **Benefited owners** do not have to take with notice of the servitude. As long as the intent and "touch and concern" elements are present, a benefited subsequent owner can enforce an equitable servitude whether or not he had notice of the covenant when he purchased the land.

The fundamental sense of justice underlying the equitable servitude theory, based as it is on intent and notice, is a major reason commentators favor dispensing with the horizontal privity of estate as a necessary requirement for a real covenant to run. States abolishing the horizontal privity of estate requirement rely on the **recording acts** to give **notice** to subsequent purchasers or to protect subsequent purchasers from covenants in deeds not properly recorded. A person held bound by a real covenant must have taken the deed with actual, constructive, or inquiry notice of a previously recorded document incorporating the real covenant. See Chapter 26, supra.

THE RESTATEMENT (THIRD) OF PROPERTY: SERVITUDES

The Restatement (Third) of Property: Servitudes, published by the American Law Institute in 2000, advocates replacing most of what is presented in this chapter with a unified approach to servitudes on land. It is unclear what impact the Restatement (Third) will have on the law of servitudes.

The Restatement (Third) attempts to simplify the law of covenants and servitudes by discarding historic labels such as restrictive covenants, affirmative covenants, real covenants, equitable servitudes, and negative easements. A single term — servitudes — encompasses them all.

The Restatement (Third) eliminates the horizontal privity element, the vertical privity requirement, the in gross and appurtenant designations, and the touch and concern requirement. While technically abolishing the touch and concern element, the Restatement instates a functionally equivalent concept whereby a court can declare a covenant invalid as illegal, unconstitutional or against public policy.

Under the Restatement (Third), courts would honor any covenant creating a servitude as long as the covenant was in writing to satisfy the Statute of Frauds, the beneficiaries are those intended to be benefited by the contracting parties, and the servitude is not illegal, unconstitutional, or against public policy. Under the Restatement, all servitudes are presumed to be assignable and divisible unless a contrary intent is discernible. Covenants are interpreted based on the parties' intent rather than favoring free use of land. A person enforcing a servitude may seek both monetary damages and equitable relief.

The Restatement gives more unilateral latitude to a servient estate owner to relocate an easement, at his own expense, as long as he does not hinder or prevent the use of the easement. The Restatement also encourages affirmative covenants such as historic preservation and conservation servitudes. It also approves of creating rights in strangers to the deed. Similarly, special rules apply to life tenants, lessees, and adverse possessors, who may be subject to servitudes and be able to enforce them in certain cases.

Examples

Running Through the Elements

1. David owned two lots on Airport Boulevard, a heavily traveled industrial road. David sold one lot to Austin by a deed containing a covenant prohibiting the sale of beer, wine, and intoxicating liquor on the lot. Later David sold the second lot to Tyler, the deed also containing a covenant prohibiting the sale of beer, wine, and intoxicating liquors. Both deeds provided the alcohol ban would be binding on the purchasers

(Austin and Tyler respectively), their heirs and assigns. David inserted the covenant into the deeds because he staunchly opposes alcohol consumption. All deeds were properly recorded. Austin sold his lot to Orlando, who wanted to open a convenience store and sell beer and wine in the store.

(a) Is the benefit personal to David or appurtenant to Tyler's lot?

(b) If David chooses not to enforce the covenant, does Tyler have standing to enforce the covenant?

(c) If Tyler chooses not to enforce the covenant, does David have standing to enforce the covenant?

(d) Does the burden of the covenant bind Orlando?

(e) Would your answer to (d) change under the following facts: David included the covenant in the deed to Austin because David operated a bar and grill on the second lot and did not want Austin or anyone else selling beer and alcohol in competition with David's bar. David later sold the bar and grill to Tyler by a deed that did not contain the covenant.

(f) Assume, instead of inserting a covenant prohibiting the sale of beer, wine, and alcoholic beverages, the deed conveyed the lot to "Austin, his heirs and assigns, as long as no beer, wine, or alcoholic beverages are sold on the premises," and David deeded the second lot to Tyler with the same restriction. Austin sells to Orlando, who wants to operate a convenience store that sells beer and wine. What result?

Home Sweet Mobile Home

2. Judy and Camille owned adjoining lots. They entered into an agreement that their lots would be restricted to single-family residential use only and that no mobile homes would be located on either lot. The agreement provided, "The covenants will run with the land." The agreement was properly recorded in the local deed records. Judy subsequently sold her lot to Tai Bohenek, the deed restricting the lot to single-family residential use only and prohibiting mobile homes on the lot. Camille sold her lot to Curtis, the deed containing the same two restrictions. Curtis bulldozed all the trees on the lot and moved six mobile homes onto his lot. When Curtis cut the trees and situated the mobile homes, the value of Tai's lot dropped $10,000. Tai brought suit against Curtis seeking $10,000 in damages and an injunction requiring Curtis to remove the six mobile homes. What result?

A Construction Setback

3. Terrell owned two adjoining lots. Terrell's house was situated on Lot 1 except his house encroached one foot onto Lot 2. Terrell contracted to sell Lot 1 to Gerard. Gerard was concerned about the one-foot encroachment. To allay Gerard's apprehension, at closing Terrell executed a "Declaration of

Restriction" providing no improvements be made on Lot 2 within three yards of the house on Lot 1. Terrell was the named grantor in the declaration, but the declaration named no grantee. At the same meeting, Terrell executed and delivered a deed conveying Lot 1 to Gerard, the deed being made subject to and including all rights accruing from all recorded conditions, restrictions, covenants, and easements affecting the property conveyed. Both documents were recorded in the local deed records that same day.

Two years later Terrell sold Lot 2 to Kim, the deed being made subject to "easements, covenants, and conditions of record." Kim contracted with House Builder, Inc. to construct a house on her lot. When Gerard saw the house was going to be built within one yard of his home, he brought a lawsuit to enjoin the construction as a violation of the three-yard setback in the Declaration of Restriction.

In the case on which the Example is based, Sonoma Development, Inc. v. Miller, 515 S.E.2d 577 (Va. 1999), Gerard would not succeed on an equitable servitude theory. The case turned on whether the Declaration of Restriction was a real covenant running with the land. Was it?

Colonel Catsup's Right of First Refusal

4. Guy owned 400 acres. He sold 150 of the acres to Colonel Catsup. The sales contract, but not the deed, stated, "Guy covenants he will offer Colonel Catsup a right of first refusal for all or part of the remaining 250 acres owned by Guy should Guy receive an offer for the sale of the land." Colonel Catsup filed a memorandum of the right of first refusal in the local deed records.

Guy received an offer from Holt Investments for the remaining 250 acres. Guy notified Colonel Catsup of the offer. Colonel Catsup declined to exercise the right of first refusal.

Five years later Holt Investments sold 100 acres (out of the 250 acres) to Timber Paper Co. Six months later Colonel Catsup filed a suit alleging Holt Investments' sale to Timber Paper Co. was made in violation of his right of first refusal. Who prevails?

Explanations

Running Through the Elements

1. (a) The deed does not say the benefit runs with the land, but that is not unusual and has not prevented courts from finding the benefit runs with the land. A court might resort to the rebuttable presumption that the benefit is appurtenant if the promisee owns nearby land that could be benefited. David owns the adjoining lot.

    It seems that, on the facts, the presumption will be rebutted. When David later sold the adjoining lot, the deed included the same covenant, and David owned no more land at that time. It appears David did not insert the covenant into either deed to benefit his retained land, but for reasons personal to him (i.e., his staunchly prohibitionist convictions). The land, moreover, is on Airport Boulevard, a "heavily traveled industrial road," which seems to indicate David did not intend to benefit Tyler's lot by burdening Austin's lot. Under this interpretation, the benefit is personal to David.

(b) If the benefit of the covenant is personal to David, Tyler would not have standing to enforce the covenant.

On the other hand, if the analysis in (a) is incorrect, and the benefit is appurtenant to Tyler's land, Tyler would have standing to enforce the covenant. The intent to run would be implied since David owned property when he burdened Austin's lot. Horizontal privity existed because David inserted the covenant into the deed transferring the lot to Austin. Vertical privity existed since Tyler acquired David's entire interest in the lot. Touch and concern may be a problem, but not much of one. A court probably would hold the benefit touched and concerned Tyler's lot since the restriction affects the enjoyment of the benefited land and is a commonly encountered restriction.

(c) Again the answer depends on the answer in Explanation (a) above. Only one person, David or Tyler, has standing to enforce the covenant. If the benefit is personal to David, he can enforce the covenant against Orlando in most jurisdictions. In some states, however, the burden will not touch and concern the burdened property (or at least the burden will not run with the land) unless the benefit also touches and concerns benefited property. In those states, since David asserts the benefit is personal to him and not appurtenant to Tyler's land, the burden will not run to Orlando at all. Thus, even though David has standing, there is no covenant to enforce. If the conclusion in (a) is incorrect, and the benefit is appurtenant to Tyler's land, David would not have standing to enforce the burden.

(d) This Explanation also depends on Explanation (a) above and the law of the jurisdiction. For the burden to run, the original parties must have intended the burden to run. The intent to run element is met: the deed provided the covenant would bind Austin, his heirs and assigns. Also required for the burden to run are horizontal and vertical privity. In all states except Massachusetts, the horizontal privity of estate element is satisfied since the covenant was created in a deed transferring the property from David to Austin. Since Austin transferred his interest to Orlando, vertical privity of estate exists, too. Normally a covenant prohibiting the sale of alcohol would touch and concern the burdened land, and so a majority of courts would find. Thus, in a majority of states the burden runs with the land and is binding on Orlando. The notice requirement for the equitable servitude also is met since Orlando at a minimum had constructive notice of the restriction in a recorded deed in his chain of title.

In a few states, however, if the benefit was personal to David rather than appurtenant to Tyler's property, a court might refuse to enforce the burden against subsequent purchasers. (See Explanation (c) above.) If the benefit was appurtenant to Tyler's property, the burden would run with Orlando's land in all states.

(e) The new facts simplify the analysis. All the elements for the burden to run are met as in Explanation (d). More importantly, the new facts lend credence that the covenant was for the benefit of the retained lot, protecting David's bar and grill operations. Thus, a court would find the benefit was appurtenant to the lot now owned by Tyler. Since the burden and benefit touched and concerned adjoining properties, the burden ran with Orlando's land and would be binding on Orlando.

(f) The Example explores the difference between a **covenant** studied in this chapter, and a **condition** studied in Chapters 9 and 10, supra. David in Example (f) did not give Austin a fee simple absolute subject to a covenant. Instead, he granted Austin a fee simple determinable. David retained a possibility of reverter. The condition subsequent is the sale of beer, wine, or alcoholic beverages on the premises. If alcohol is sold on the premises, Austin (or his heirs or assigns: Orlando in our case) loses all interest in the land, and the property automatically reverts to David or his heirs. Tyler as the owner of the adjoining lot has no rights to Orlando's land.

In contrast, the sale of alcohol on the premises under the original facts would breach a covenant. Orlando still would own the land. David (if the benefit was personal to him) or Tyler (if the benefit was appurtenant to his land) could enjoin the sales or seek monetary damages. The important point is that the consequences flowing from a violation of a condition are much more draconian than the consequences resulting from the breach of a covenant. Today the condition is imposed only in specialized situations, usually having to do with family support, charity, or oil and gas leases. Most restrictions on use today are expressed as covenants. Purchasers understandably are not willing to purchase property subject to conditions subsequent.

Home Sweet Mobile Home

2. For Tai to collect damages, she must prove a real covenant ran with the land so as to burden Curtis. Tai cannot do this. For a real covenant to run in this case, the original parties must intend the covenant to run, the

covenant must touch and concern Curtis' property for the burden to run, the covenant must touch and concern Tai's land for the benefit to run, and there must be horizontal and vertical privity. The intent to run is easily satisfied since the agreement stipulated, "The covenants will run with the land." Touch and concern also is met. The burden definitely touches and concerns Curtis' land since the land can be used only for single-family residences, and no mobile homes can be located on the lot. The benefit touches and concerns Tai's land since the restriction on Curtis' land makes Tai's use of her property more enjoyable. A court, moreover, would conclude the covenant is the kind reasonable landowners would impress upon their property and intend to bind remote purchasers. Vertical privity of estate is met in both cases as Tai succeeded to Judy's estate and Curtis succeeded to Camille's estate.

Unfortunately for Tai, the horizontal privity of estate element fails in most jurisdictions. In most states, horizontal privity will be found only when the covenant is included in a deed transferring the property, in a lease, or in a grant of easement. In this case, the lots were separately owned when Judy and Camille agreed to restrict their two lots. Thus, courts in most states will find there was no horizontal privity of estate. A few states require horizontal privity only for the burden to run. Even in these states, however, since Curtis was a remote purchaser, there must be horizontal privity for Curtis to be burdened; and, as just noted, there was no horizontal privity in this case.

The only hope Tai has to enforce the covenant as a real covenant is if she lives in one of the few states that has dropped the horizontal privity of estate requirement altogether. Tai would prevail in these states since Curtis had notice of the restrictive covenant (it was in his deed) and all other elements for a real covenant to run could be proved.

All is not lost for Tai, however. While Tai's claim for damages is doomed in most jurisdictions because she cannot prove the horizontal privity necessary to enforce a real covenant, she will prevail in her quest for injunctive relief. To get injunctive relief, Tai needs only to prove the elements for an equitable servitude. As discussed above, the intent to run and the touch and concern elements, common to real covenants and equitable servitudes, are met. Horizontal privity of estate is not necessary for an equitable servitude to bind remote purchasers. Since the first two elements can be proved, the equitable servitude will be enforced against Curtis if he had notice of the restriction. The notice could be actual, constructive, or inquiry notice. Whether or not Curtis had actual or inquiry notice, he definitely had constructive notice. The restriction was in his deed and in the original agreement, which was recorded. Curtis must remove the mobile homes.

Curtis does not have to plant new trees, however, since no covenant addressed trees on the properties. Mere loss in value does not entitle a landowner to damages or injunctive relief unless the defendant was under a legal or contractual duty not to cause the injury.

A Construction Setback

3. The court held the Declaration of Restriction was a real covenant binding Kim. To enforce a real covenant, Gerard must prove the following elements: The original parties intended the covenant would run with the land, horizontal privity, vertical privity, the covenant touched and concerned the burdened land, and the covenant was in a writing that satisfied the Statute of Frauds. Kim in the actual case conceded all elements except horizontal privity. According to Kim, the covenant was not included in the deed and Terrell attempted to burden his own land, which cannot constitute horizontal privity. The court rejected that argument, concluding horizontal privity is established when a restriction is created in connection with the conveyance of an estate in land. There is no requirement the restriction be incorporated into the deed itself. The Declaration of Restriction was executed in connection with the overall conveyance of Lot 1 to Gerard. That was enough. Gerard prevails.

   As an editorial insert, the court may have reached a contrary result if Terrell had not recorded the Declaration of Restrictions. Even though notice is not an element for real covenants, Kim's having notice of the restriction must have played a part in the court's decision. Either that or the court trusted the state's recording statute would invalidate an unrecorded Declaration of Restriction.

Colonel Catsup's Right of First Refusal

4. Timber Paper Co. prevails. Horizontal and vertical privity are met. So is the notice element. Holt Investments had constructive notice of the right of first refusal during the activity surrounding its own purchase of the 250 acres.

   Not so clear are the intent to run and the touch and concern elements. The court in the actual case on which the Example is based, Ricketson v. Bankers First Savings Bank, FSB, 503 S.E.2d 297 (Ga. Ct. App. 1998), concluded the burden did not touch and concern the 250 acres because the covenant did not affect the nature, quality, use, enjoyment, or value of the property. As such, the agreement in the sales contract was collateral to the land and did not touch and concern the land. Since the right of first refusal did not touch and concern the land, it was a personal covenant binding on the original promisor, Guy, but not on subsequent purchasers.

Under the public policy approach to touch and concern proposed in the overview, the right of first refusal is not the type of restriction that should be allowed to continue indefinitely. To do so would violate the common law Rule Against Perpetuities. Moreover, the Restatement (Third) of Property (Servitudes) gives courts the option to declare that the covenant does not run or to limit its running to a reasonable time. Its duration might then be limited at least to the period of time permitted in gross — 21 years — by the Rule or to some shorter period.

It appears the right of first refusal was personal to Colonel Catsup rather than appurtenant to the 150 acres. In some states, a burden will not run with the land unless the benefit also touches and concerns land. In these states, the burden of the covenant would not run with land.

Moreover, nothing in the documents indicates the right of first refusal was to bind any person other than Guy, the original promisor. The court, therefore, could find the original parties had not intended the covenant to run with the land in the first place.

Real Covenants and Equitable Servitudes: Common Schemes and Termination

The previous chapter covered the essential elements necessary for benefits and burdens of a covenant to run with the land to subsequent owners of property. This chapter develops common schemes in subdivisions and termination of covenants.

THE COMMON SCHEME AND SUBDIVISIONS

Just as the Industrial Revolution spurred courts to develop the theories of real covenants and later equitable servitudes, the urbanization and, more critically, suburbanization of America have added a major new wrinkle: the **subdivision** and other commonly developed properties, such as condominiums. Our focus will be on subdivisions, but the discussion could apply to other residential or commercial developments.

The subdivision usually results from a **common owner** subdividing a large parcel of land, often in accordance with local subdivision ordinances, and selling lots to individuals or builders. The common owner sometimes builds roads, sewers and drainage systems and works with utility companies to insure each lot has access to essential services. The subdivider may build homes on each lot before selling, or may sell unimproved lots to individuals or builders.

The developer may incorporate covenants into deeds to promote residential use, maintain value, preserve aesthetics, promote safety, and for other purposes the subdivider believes purchasers will desire. Invariably, problems arise. Some deeds, for example, may not incorporate all or any of the covenants, the covenants might vary from one deed to another, or the developer may try to sell some retained land for a purpose inconsistent with the use (typically residential) being made of the sold properties.

Courts adapted the law of equitable servitudes for subdivision covenant schemes. As a result, the courts have resorted to rules for a **common scheme** or **general plan of development** to impose burdens and grant standing to enforce the servitudes.

THE COMMON SCHEME AND STANDING TO ENFORCE A SERVITUDE

Let's first review by Examples the rules affecting subdivisions based on traditional real covenant and equitable servitude analyses.

Example 1: Developer owns Blackacre and deeds one of its lots subject to a restrictive covenant to Bailey. Bailey's property is the burdened estate. If Bailey breaches the covenant, Developer can enjoin the violation. Whether any subsequent purchaser of Developer's retained land can enjoin Bailey's breach depends on whether the benefit of the covenant is personal to Developer or is appurtenant to the subsequent purchaser's land. If the covenant is appurtenant and not personal to Developer, Developer's remaining land in the larger parcel is the benefited property. Each lot sold later by Developer remains benefited, and all new owners have standing to enforce the covenant against Bailey.

Example 2: A year after selling the lot to Bailey, Developer sells another lot in Blackacre to Cricket, the deed subject to the same restrictive covenants included in Bailey's deed. Cricket breaches a covenant in her deed. Bailey seeks to enjoin Cricket's breach of the covenant. Sadly, under traditional analysis, Bailey cannot enforce the covenant against Cricket (or any other subsequent purchaser) even if Cricket's deed included the covenant. Bailey cannot overcome two obstacles. First, the covenant in Bailey's deed burdened Bailey's land. It did not burden Developer's remaining property, including the lot later transferred to Cricket. Second, most states have strict laws prohibiting a grantor (like Developer) from granting the benefit of covenants to strangers to the deed, and Bailey would be a stranger to the deed transferring the lot to Cricket. Thus, even if Developer inserted the same covenant in Cricket's deed, under a traditional analysis, neither Bailey nor any subsequent owner of Bailey's property could enforce the covenant against Cricket (no intent to run and no privity of estate).

Example 3: The covenant in all the deeds out from Developer restricted each lot to single-family residential use. Fargo, the purchaser of the last lot, wants to build a gas station on his lot. Developer either waives the restriction in a writing or orally assures Fargo he can build the gas station. Bailey, Cricket, and the other landowners want to stop the gas station. Under traditional servitude law, they have no standing to prevent the gas station from being built, however. First, the benefit is personal to Developer since he owned no other property to which the benefit might become appurtenant; and Developer has indicated he will not enforce the covenant. Second, all previous purchasers are now strangers to the deed to Fargo. Under traditional servitude analysis, Bailey, Cricket, and the other landowners cannot stop Fargo from building the gas station.

Overcoming legal obstacles, courts reached the correct result in those cases. A **common scheme** or **general plan of development** concept overcame most of the legal niceties in those situations to give all subdivision owners **standing** to enforce the **benefit** of the covenant. Once a court finds a common scheme, the court will conclude that the common owner, Developer in our Example, intended to impose the identical covenant in all parcels from the time the common scheme began. Thus the entire tract became **burdened** and **benefited** as soon as the **common owner** sold the first lot as part of the **common scheme**. The entire tract is both benefited and burdened, and each landowner, from Developer to Bailey to the last person to buy, enjoys the benefit and has standing to enforce the common servitude against all landowners in the subdivision, no matter who bought in what order.

The implied burden and benefit are often labeled **implied reciprocal negative easements** or **restrictions**. ("Easement" is a misnomer.) The rationale is that by creating a substantially uniform set of covenants that permit similar uses and impose similar restrictions on every lot owner, all of them are benefited and burdened in equal measure. Additional rationales are that (1) each owner, upon buying the lot, may have been put on *constructive* notice through the recording acts that covenants were uniformly or substantially applicable — thus, taking delivery of the deed was presumed acceptance of the scheme; and (2) if the subdivision had assumed its land use character by the time the owners bought, they were on *inquiry* notice of the covenants that required that the subdivision look the way it did — houses uniformly set back from the street, all being built in the same architectural style, and so on. These latter rationales are explored more in the next section.

By applying this common plan concept to the Examples, the finding of a common scheme results in holding the **benefit appurtenant** to all lots in the subdivision rather than **personal** to the Developer. In addition, all purchasers, including Bailey and Cricket, have a right to enforce the servitude against the owner of any property subject to the common scheme, including the last purchaser. The order of purchase does not matter.

THE COMMON SCHEME AND NOTICE FOR RECORDING ACTS AND EQUITABLE SERVITUDES

Most courts will impose the burden on all land in the common scheme once they find a common scheme exists. The imposed burden is not automatic, however, since many courts fear that implying the burden weakens the integrity of the **recording systems** and the elements of **equitable servitudes**. The **recording acts** require a bona fide purchaser for value have **notice** of the burden before a court will subject the subsequent purchaser to the burden. Likewise, the critical element in **equitable servitudes** is **notice**.

Example: Building on our prior Examples, Developer deeded property to Bailey, Cricket, and others incorporating the same covenant into most of the deeds. For reasons unknown, Developer's deed to Jones omitted the covenant. Jones later conveyed his lot to Rochester, the deed omitting the covenant. Rochester wants to do some act that would breach the covenant if the covenant burdened him and his land. Can Developer, Bailey, Cricket, or any other landowner enforce the covenant against Rochester?

While Developer and maybe others have standing to enforce any covenant, the threshold issue is not whether anyone has standing to sue, but whether Rochester is subject to the covenant at all. When the title searchers searched the deed records they would not have found the restriction in the Developer-to-Jones-to-Rochester chain. Because nothing in Jones' deed mentioned the covenant, Rochester would prevail under traditional analysis in pure notice or race-notice states as a bona fide purchaser for value without notice. Hence he would be protected under the recording statutes unless a common scheme somehow gives constructive notice.

Similarly, under our facts, Rochester, the subsequent bona fide purchaser for value, did not have the **notice** necessary for the covenant to be enforced as an **equitable servitude**. Rochester probably had no **actual notice** of the covenant because he had no contact with the developer and may not have seen or heard of any plat or covenant. Since the covenant was not in any deeds in the subsequent purchaser's chain of title, he did not have **constructive notice** in the usual manner of a recorded deed. Some states require title searchers to search deeds out from a common owner. Most states do not, however. See Chapter 26, supra. A state that required searchers to read deeds out from a common owner could find the subsequent purchaser had inquiry notice.

While finding a common scheme a century ago was a challenge, today most jurisdictions have adopted subdivision ordinances. Subdivision ordinances require that a subdivider file documents including a map or "plat." The plat looks like a combination of an engineer's and a surveyor's view' of the subdivision. It contains the metes and bounds of each lot. It assigns each lot a number that may thereafter be used to transfer the title to that lot. On it usually appears a reference to the deed book and page at which a declaration of the covenants in the scheme has been filed in the recorder's office. Sometimes the plat itself may show the dimensions of any express easements affecting the subdivision, and it may even incorporate phrases with the gist of the major provisions of covenants in the declaration. Most courts hold this **recorded subdivision plat** constitutes the **notice** necessary to satisfy the notice requirement for an equitable servitude and to deny the subsequent purchaser any protection under the **recording statutes**. The notice is either **constructive notice** if the recorded subdivision plat details the covenants, or **inquiry notice** that uniform covenants may apply to all lots, including the purchaser's lot.

In older cases, before subdivision ordinances required formal approval and recording of subdivision plats, courts found the notice needed to overcome recording acts and equitable servitude obstacles by concluding uniform neighborhood characteristics gave the subsequent purchaser **inquiry notice** of the covenant. Obligating purchasers to inquire about observable conditions to gain knowledge of restrictions serves nicely to imply residential use only covenants, setback requirements, height limitations, a brick exterior requirement, and prohibitions against mobile homes and farm animals. Other covenants may not be such that a reasonable person would have inquired about them. Examples might be covenants requiring that a house have a minimum square footage or maximum number of bedrooms or occupants per square foot. If a reasonable person would not have inquired, the purchaser did not have inquiry notice of the covenant.

Furthermore, if the subsequent purchaser bought early enough, before neighboring lots were developed, the subsequent purchaser may not have had inquiry notice of the omitted covenant at all.

THE COMMON SCHEME AND THE STATUTE OF FRAUDS

Servitudes are interests in land and, as such, must be created in a writing to satisfy the Statute of Frauds. See Chapter 22, supra. The normal exceptions to the Statute of Frauds for part performance and estoppel apply. Id.

The courts welcome any hint of a writing or exception to the Statute of Frauds when subdivision covenants are at issue. A few courts straightforwardly hold a covenant established pursuant to a general scheme of development constitutes an exception to the Statute of Frauds. More courts hold that once it can be shown that the common owner indicated the land was to be restricted, either orally or by showing the prospective purchaser a plat, the purchaser has notice of the general scheme and the covenant, and will be estopped to deny its existence.

Other states, such as California, demand some writing to satisfy the Statute of Frauds. A developer's recording a subdivision plat constitutes an acceptable writing, however, even if nothing is inserted into the purchaser's deed. See Citizens for Covenant Compliance v. Anderson, 906 P.2d 1314 (Cal. 1995). In all these situations, the covenant burdens the purchaser just as though it were included in the original deed.

Still other states, such as Massachusetts, refuse to resort to the common scheme theory to impose restrictions at all. In these states, the purchaser with no covenant in his deed is not bound by the covenant.

WHAT CONSTITUTES A COMMON SCHEME

(a) Common Covenants

The sections on the effect of a common scheme on the running of benefits or the implication of a burden assumed a common scheme. Determining what the common scheme is, which lots are included in the scheme, and when the common scheme began, however, can be tricky. The **common scheme** may be found if a suitable percentage of lots in the subdivision are subject to a **common covenant**. A variation in the terms or incidence of the covenants may indicate a common owner did not intend a common scheme. How many lots or what percentage of lots must be burdened is a facts-and-circumstances inquiry.

> ***Example:*** In Sanborn v. McLean, 206 N.W. 496 (Mich. 1925), 53 of 91 lots were restricted to residential-use only and all lots on the street, including the 38 lots not expressly restricted to single-family residential use, were single-family residences. That was enough for the court to find a common scheme in 1925. Depending on the specific facts of the controversy, some courts may demand a higher (or lower) percentage of burdened lots to infer an intent to establish a common scheme.

(b) When a Common Scheme Begins

A second issue concerns the exact **point in time** when the common scheme begins. A common owner may own a tract and sell lots from it before the common plan is developed. Since these lots were sold before the common scheme of development began, they are not part of the common scheme. Consequently, covenants not included in their deeds will not be implied, nor will the owner of those lots have standing to enforce any later burdened properties that are part of the development scheme.

(c) Geographic Boundaries of Common Schemes

A third issue concerns the **geographic boundaries** of the area being developed as a common scheme. A developer, for example, may own multiple tracts and treat each tract separately. Similarly, the common owner may own just one tract, but intend to develop only part of the tract under the common scheme. A common scheme on part of the tract will not burden the land not made a part of the common scheme. Finally, a common owner may intend to develop an entire tract, but put different covenants on different parts of the tract: e.g., some single-family residences, some apartments, some retail shops, some commercial ventures, etc.

No hard and fast rule applies as to deciding what commonly owned land belongs to a common scheme. A court will evaluate all the facts and circumstances.

Example: In Snow v. Van Dam, 197 N.E. 224 (Mass. 1935), a developer owned a tract of land. The northernmost part of the property, constituting approximately 10 percent of the property, was separated from the rest of the tract by a major road. In addition, the land north of the road was swampy. The developer subdivided and sold lots south of the road, but not north of the road. After selling all lots south of the road, the developer sold the land north of the road by a deed containing the same restrictions as contained in the deeds to the southern lots. The new owner of the northern land wanted to operate a commercial business in violation of the covenant. Owners of the lots south of the road sought to enjoin the business. The case turned on whether the northern lots were in the same scheme as the southern lots. The court concluded both northern and southern lots were part of the same common scheme, explaining its analysis of the facts and circumstances as follows:

> [The northern land] lies at the gateway of the whole development. One must pass it to visit any part of [the subdivision]. The use made of that lot tends strongly to fix the character of the entire tract. It is true, that the land north of Thatcher Road was not divided into lots until 1919, but it was shown on all the plans from the beginning. The failure to divide it sooner was apparently due to a belief that it could not be sold, not to an intent to reserve it for other than residential purposes. We think that the scheme from the beginning contemplated that no part of the [northern property] should be used for commercial purposes. When the lot of the defendant was restricted in 1923, the restriction was in pursuance of the original scheme and gave rights to earlier as well as to later purchasers.

Snow, 197 N.E. at 228.

THE RESTATEMENT (THIRD) OF PROPERTY (SERVITUDES)

The American Law Institute published the Restatement (Third) of Property (Servitudes) in 2000. As explained in Chapter 30, supra, the Restatement seeks to formulate a law of servitudes unhindered by the common law technicalities. The Restatement, for example, eliminates the horizontal and vertical privity elements, as well as the touch and concern element. See Chapter 30, supra.

Importantly, for owners of land in subdivisions, the Restatement favors creating rights in strangers to the deed, which would eliminate many of the problems discussed in this chapter. Instead, the Restatement would allow any person who has a legitimate interest in enforcing a servitude to have standing. The Restatement relies on common scheme or general plan to create benefits and burdens, similar to the common law.

TERMINATION OF COVENANTS AND SERVITUDES

Covenants and servitudes can be terminated. Here are 12 commonly mentioned theories of how covenants terminate:

1. **By the Terms of the Covenant.** Many covenants by their terms continue for a specific number of years or until the occurrence of some event. The deed creating the covenant stipulates the event that causes the covenant to automatically terminate.
2. **Merger.** Since a real covenant or an equitable servitude envisions rights and obligations between landowners, once a common owner acquires the benefited property and the burdened property (and no one else owns benefited or burdened property), the covenant or servitude terminates through merger. The covenant disappears and will not be revived even if the common owner subsequent sells part of property.
3. **Release.** Covenants and servitudes are interests in property. As such, owners of the benefited property can grant a written release to the owner of the burdened state. Like other grants of property interests, the release should be recorded in the local deed records. If more than one lot is benefited, all benefited lot owners must join the release to effectively terminate the covenant (though those landowners signing a release may be *estopped* from enforcing the covenant later).

4. **Rescission.** As with releases, landowners can execute a document rescinding the covenant so that the covenant no longer binds any property. The rescission is effective only if all persons with standing to enforce the covenant join in executing the document. The most common use of the rescission is by a developer when all purchasers to that date ask or agree that a covenant is not appropriate for the subdivision and should be rescinded.

5. **Unclean Hands.** Courts will not allow a landowner to violate a covenant and at the same time to enjoin another landowner from violating the same covenant. Stated colloquially, the plaintiff cannot enforce the covenant if he has unclean hands. A plaintiff's relatively minor infraction, however, will not foreclose an action against a neighbor's more egregious violation of the same covenant.

6. **Acquiescence.** Acquiescence results when a plaintiff property owner passively endures multiple violations of the covenant by many lots in the community. The plaintiff landowner, even though she might not be violating the covenant herself, by her acquiescence in the others' violations may be *estopped* from enforcing the covenant against yet another violator. Acquiescence envisions such a pattern of violation has occurred that enforcing the covenant in this one instance would serve no purpose. In many ways, landowners' acquiescing in too many violations of a covenant approaches abandonment (discussed next). Acquiescence in the violation of one covenant will not prevent a landowner from enforcing other covenants, however.

7. **Abandonment.** Similar to acquiescence, abandonment occurs when such a high number of landowners in an area violate the common covenant that between their unclean hands and acquiescence, the covenant becomes unenforceable by any benefited landowners. Generally, for a court to find an abandonment, the violations have caused such a substantial change in the neighborhood that the original purpose of the covenants has been subverted. Minor changes in the use of the benefited or burdened land will not amount to an abandonment.

8. **Laches.** Laches occurs when a person having a right to enforce a covenant waits so long to bring suit to enjoin a violation that the breaching defendant is unduly harmed by the delay itself. The delay must be an unreasonably long delay under the circumstances. Laches does not actually terminate a covenant. It merely prohibits the enforcement against the defendant for a specific breach. The plaintiff is free to enforce subsequent breaches of the same covenant. Laches is one of those theories seemingly always argued by defendants and virtually never granted by courts. Since the

defendant's argument must be that plaintiff waited too long to bring suit even though plaintiff brought the suit within the statute of limitations period, the facts must be egregious, and the theory probably amounts to no more than a variation of equitable estoppel.

9. **Changed Conditions.** Covenants can be terminated if the conditions in the neighborhood have so changed that the covenant no longer serves its intended purpose. The majority of courts consider only changes occurring within the subdivision. Conditions on land outside the neighborhood (known as external conditions or external changes) are irrelevant even when the external conditions make some "border" lots poorly suited for their allowed uses. The border lots remain a buffer, preventing gradual encroachment of outside development into the subdivision. Note the similarities between changed conditions, abandonment, and acquiescence.

10. **Relative Hardship.** Related to the doctrine of "changed conditions," and considered a subset of "changed conditions" by some courts and commentators, is the doctrine of "relative hardship." Courts adopting the doctrine of relative hardship balance the benefits to the neighboring property from maintaining the covenant against the harm to the burdened property if the restriction remains. If the harm to the burdened property is disproportionately great compared to the benefit to the neighboring properties, a court in equity might choose not to enforce the covenant. While theoretically the doctrine of relative hardship applies to all lots in a subdivision, courts are more likely to apply the doctrine to release a border lot from a restriction. Courts not considering changes external to the subdivision in evaluating changed conditions will not adopt the doctrine of relative hardship, either.

11. **Recording Acts.** Real covenants and equitable servitudes are interests in land and are subject to the recording acts. A subsequent bona fide purchaser who takes without actual, constructive, or inquiry notice is not bound by the covenant.

12. **Eminent Domain.** Federal, state, and local governments through eminent domain or condemnation can force landowners to sell their property to the government as long as the government pays for the property. See Takings, Chapter 35, infra. When the government buys burdened property, the covenant burdening the land is extinguished.

Courts disagree whether the government must compensate owners of benefited property for the loss of their right to enforce the covenant against the government in its use of the formerly burdened lot. A majority of courts, viewing the benefit as a property right, will find a "taking" of the benefit, thus requiring the government to compensate the owners of the benefited lots. A significant minority of states, in contrast, conclude the benefit is too attenuated, the covenant was never intended to apply to governments, the covenant was a contract right, not a property right, or that the payment is against public policy. Courts reaching any of these conclusions will hold the government owes no compensation to the formerly benefited landowners.

Examples

Common Scheme Developments

1. John owned a plot of land on a hillside overlooking a bay. He subdivided the land into 12 lots, six lots (Lots 1-6) on the uphill side of Bay View Road, and six lots (Lots 7-12) on the downhill side of Bay View Road. John filed a subdivision map with the county clearly setting forth a 15-foot setback but containing no height restrictions to any lot. Because the lots are on a hill, Lots 1-6 are on a higher elevation than Lots 7-12.

   John sold Lot 4 by a recorded deed on January 24, 1974, to Frances. The deed contained the following covenant: "That at no time shall any building or structure be erected or placed or allowed to remain on Lot 4 within 15 feet of the property line bordering on Bay View Road. This covenant shall run with the land." Deeds to all twelve lots carried some version of this 15-foot setback restriction. The deed did not mention any height or view restrictions. On September 1, 2004, Frances conveyed Lot 4 to Dale (the plaintiff).

   On June 26, 1975, John conveyed Lot 11 to Lucille. Lot 11 was the first of the lower-slope lots to be sold. The deed contained the following covenants:

   1. At no time shall any building or structure be erected or placed or allowed to remain on Lot 11 of more than one (1) story in height, nor shall any building be located within fifteen feet of the property boundary line on Bay View Road.
   2. The foregoing covenant shall run with the land hereby conveyed and shall be equally binding on all subsequent owners.

   Within the year, John sold Lots 7-10 and Lot 12 by deeds containing the same restrictions contained in the deed for Lot 11.

   Lucille conveyed Lot 11 to Connie, the deed stating the conveyance was subject to the covenants in Lucille's deed. Connie in 2005 deeded Lot 11 to Vestavia "subject to all grants, easements, covenants, restrictions, liens, and encumbrances of record." Vestavia began building a two-story home on Lot 11 in January 2008. Dale was dismayed the house would interfere with his panoramic view of the bay. The owner of Lot 10 in casual conversation mentioned to Dale her deed contained a one-story restriction, and so Vestavia's house might be "too high." Researching the deed records, Dale discovered the one-story restriction on Lot 11. Dale brought an action seeking to enjoin Vestavia from constructing the two-story house.

(a) Who prevails if there is no common scheme?

(b) Who prevails if there is a common scheme?

(c) Is there a common scheme?

(d) If there is a common scheme, when did the scheme begin?

(e) Lot 11 was the last lot to be improved. Two-story homes have been built on Lots 1, 5, and 7. Single-story homes have been built on the remaining lots. Assuming the one-story restriction applied to Lot 11, does the existence of the three two-story homes result in the termination of the one-story height restrictions?

Victoria's Secret Plan

2. Victoria owned 100 acres of land. Beginning in 1997, Victoria began selling portions of the 100-acre parcel. Although no formal subdivision plan or map was ever filed, about half of the parcels contained a covenant requiring grantees not to use their property for commercial development. Some of these deeds contained a covenant that specifically ran with the land conveyed. Some deeds did not state the covenant ran with the land. About half of the deeds contained no restriction whatsoever.

Plaintiff Sherry purchased a lot from Victoria in 2005, the deed containing a covenant prohibiting commercial use of the lot. In 2007, Sherry purchased an adjoining parcel from Victoria, the deed containing a restrictive covenant prohibiting Sherry and any future grantees from using the parcel for commercial purposes.

On the same day in 2007, Victoria conveyed a lot to Wallace (who, as we shall soon see, is defendant's predecessor in title). The deed contained no restrictions on commercial use. Elwood purchased the parcel from Wallace on May 2, 2009, the deed containing no restrictive covenants. Elwood opened a restaurant on his land. Sherry brings an action to enjoin Elwood from operating the restaurant. What result?

Zoning-Covenant Conflict

3. Suburban Builders, Inc., has owned 50 acres of land for ten years, expecting someday to subdivide the land into lots for residential use. The 50 acres are subject to covenants limiting the property to single-family residential use only. The city recently annexed the 50 acres, and zoned the land "R-3, Retail." Property zoned "R-3, Retail" can be used for retail shops, small offices, restaurants, gas stations, banks, apartments, duplexes, and single-family residences. (In "R-1, Residential," by contrast, only single-family residences are permitted.) Suburban Builders,

Inc. submitted a subdivision plat, which the city approved, that calls for retail shops along the two sides of the subdivision bordering on major roads adjoining the land, with a transition area dedicated to apartments, and the remaining 70 percent of the land to be used solely for single-family residences, a park, and an elementary school.

Daniel, who has standing to enforce the original covenant, sues to enjoin Suburban Builders' development scheme. Suburban Builder claims the city's annexing the property, zoning the land "R-3, Retail," and approving the subdivision plat resulted in the residential use only covenant being terminated or superseded. What result?

Banking on a Covenant Termination

4. Henry owned a 15-acre strip of land. Between March and December 1975, Henry sold five three-acre parcels (Tracts A, B, C, D, and E), each deed containing the following restriction:

   Grantees, their heirs or assigns, agree not to erect on the property any building intended for any purpose except as a single-family private residence containing a minimum of 2,000 square feet, exclusive of garages.

   The purchasers of Tract A and Tract B built homes, currently valued between $500,000 and $600,000. Tract C remains unimproved. Tracts A, B, and C are heavily wooded, and egress and interest to them is by way of a private road.

   The State Highway Commission in 1987, through an eminent domain action, purchased Tract D pursuant to its plan to build Clarkson Road, a four-lane highway. Clarkson Road now runs across Tract D and intersects Highway 40 less than one-eighth of a mile north of Tract D.

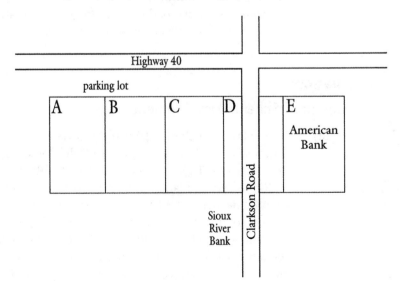

The year Clarkson Road opened for traffic, the owners of Tract E sold Tract E to American Bank. The deed expressly released Tract E from the single-family residence-only covenant. The owners of Tract A, Tract B, and Tract C likewise executed releases from the covenant to American Bank.

In 1975, the five tracts were part of a rural, agricultural community. No commercial or retail businesses operated in the surrounding area. Only a small number of homes dotted the area. The opening of Clarkson Road began a period of rapid commercial development.

Today a mall, several large office buildings, and a condominium development are all within a half-mile of the five tracts. American Bank operates a bank on Tract E. The increase in volume of traffic and commercial activity caused a substantial increase in the noise levels on Tracts A, B, and C. The county, moreover, has plans to widen Highway 40. A parking lot for an office building abuts Tracts A and B.

Tessie bought Tract C in 2000. Sioux River Bank plans to build an office building on Clarkson Road on land abutting Tract C. The bank approached Tessie about leasing or purchasing her land to construct a **paved parking lot** on Tract C, to be used by tenants and customers of the new bank (no part of the bank building would be built on Tract C). The transaction is contingent on Sioux River Bank's being able to construct a parking lot on Tract C. Tessie brings this action. Tessie makes three arguments. Please evaluate the following three theories.

(a) Tessie argues the other tract owners have waived or abandoned their right to enforce the covenant.

(b) Tessie argues the covenant is unenforceable due to changed conditions within and without the 15 acres.

(c) Tessie argues a surface parking lot would not violate the restrictive covenant even if the covenant is enforceable.

Explanations

Common Scheme Developments

1. (a) Assuming Dale is the only plaintiff, Vestavia will prevail if there is no common scheme. John sold Lot 4 to Dale's predecessor in interest, Frances, in 1974. There was no one-story height restriction on Lot 4 or on John's retained land. John no longer owned any interest in Lot 4 when he deeded Lot 11 to Lucille on June 26, 1975. When John burdened Lot 11, he benefited the lots he still owned on that date, but not the lots he had already sold. In most jurisdictions, he could not benefit the owner of Lot 4 since the owner of Lot 4 was a stranger to the deed. See discussion of "stranger to the deed" in Chapter 28,

supra. No owner of Lot 4, in particular Dale, therefore, has standing to enforce the one-story height restriction.

(b) Dale prevails if there was a common scheme with the one-story height restriction in effect when John sold Lot 4 to Frances in 1974. For the covenant to run, the intent, touch and concern, horizontal privity, and vertical privity elements must be met. The intent for the burden to run was found in the deed itself. A bit more uncertain is who was to be benefited by the covenant. The topography strongly suggests the height restriction was to protect the upslope homeowners' (including the owner of Lot 4) view of the bay.

The burden and benefit of the covenant easily touched and concerned the separate properties since only one-story homes could be built on Lot 11, and the view from Lot 4 is preserved by the covenant. With a common scheme, all lots are benefited and burdened by the covenant from the start of the scheme. The benefit of the restriction is appurtenant to all lots within the scheme transferred from John to the new owners, including John's transfer of Lot 4 to Frances.

Horizontal privity existed on the transfer from John to Frances. Vertical privity can be linked from Frances to Dale, and from John to Vestavia.

Since the elements of a real covenant are satisfied, Dale could enforce the covenant as a real covenant if the state permits injunctive relief for breaches of real covenants. Moreover, since Vestavia had constructive and maybe actual notice of the one story only restriction, and the other elements for an equitable servitude are met, Dale can enjoin the building of the two-story home on Lot 11 if the restriction was part of the common scheme.

(c) This is a close factual question. You could justify a finding of a common scheme or of no common scheme. Definitely, there was a scheme of development as evidenced by the subdivision map and John's selling the lots within a relatively short time period. Included in the common scheme is the 15-foot setback requirement. The tougher issue — and the critical one here — is whether the one-story height covenant was part of a common scheme. Since all the lower slope lots were subject to the one-story height restriction, and there seems to be no reason to have inserted a similar covenant in the deeds to upper slope lots, it appears John intended a common scheme of restricting the lower slope lots to one-story homes.

In the case on which this Example is loosely based, only three of the lower slope lots were restricted (rather than all six lower slope lots as in the Example). An appellate court nonetheless concluded a common scheme existed burdening the lower slope lots for the benefit of the upper slope lots. See Fong v. Hashimoto, 994 P.2d 569 (Haw. Ct. App. 1998). The appellate court felt no restriction was needed or appropriate to the upper slope lots since they did not block any other subdivision lots' view of the bay. The test, according to the appellate court, was whether "lots of like character or similarly situated property" were burdened. Since half of the lower slope lots were burdened, the appellate court found a common scheme. Id. The Hawaii Supreme Court disagreed, however, concluding three restricted lots were an insufficient number to support a conclusion that a common scheme existed. The Supreme Court noted the piecemeal restrictions in the conveyances plus John's not including the height restriction on the subdivision map indicated Fogarty did not intend a common height scheme. See Fong v. Hashimoto, 994 P.2d 500 (Haw. 2000).

The facts of the Example are more favorable to finding a common scheme existed since all lower slope lots were similarly restricted and John had no reason to place height restrictions on the upper lots. But then again, in neither the actual facts nor the facts of the Example did John include the height restriction of the subdivision map. Either a conclusion of common scheme or no common scheme is correct in the Example as long as you support your conclusion with facts and reasoning.

(d) The issue is critical. Only if a common scheme was in effect before John sold both Lots 4 and 11 will Dale be able to enforce the height restriction against Vestavia. Clearly, the common scheme with the fifteen foot setback was established before John sold his first lot. Not so obvious is whether the height restriction was part of the original scheme or whether John began a second scheme of development that imposed the height restriction to the lots in that second scheme. If the height restriction was part of the second scheme and not part of the initial scheme, the critical second scheme began after John sold Lot 4 to Frances (Dale's predecessor in interest), so Dale would not have standing to enjoin Vestavia's building a two-story home.

The appellate court in *Fong* concluded the height restriction was part of the initial scheme from the start notwithstanding its not being included in the subdivision plat. The court felt John intended to preserve the upslope lots' view of the bay all along and his waiting to sell the first downslope lot before incorporating the height restriction into a deed was consistent with that intent. The Supreme Court in *Fong* concluded, under the facts there, no common scheme existed; hence, it did not need to determine when the common scheme began.

(e) The one-story height covenant has not been terminated. The actual parties in *Fong* argued the theories of acquiescence and abandonment.

The court rejected both theories. Of the three lots with two-story houses, only the deed to Lot 7 actually was burdened with the one story only restriction. *Acquiescence* did not apply since the house on Lot 7 did not block the view from Lot 4. The covenant had not lost its purpose. Similarly, the abandonment theory failed because the Lot 7 violation had not worked such a substantial change in the subdivision that the purpose of the covenant has been subverted. The covenant remains valid and Dale can enjoin the building of the two-story house.

Victoria's Secret Plan

2. Elwood can operate the restaurant. The deed to Elwood did not prohibit commercial activities on his lot. The only way Elwood's lot could be burdened is if Victoria's land had been restricted; and if the benefit of the prohibition against commercial use ran to Sherry. Sherry can prove both matters only if Victoria's land was restricted pursuant to a common scheme. The problem is that Victoria's course of conduct does not establish an intent to establish a common scheme. Some deeds contained the non-commercial use restriction, but many did not. Even those that limited commercial uses imposed varying restrictions, some restricting only the original purchasers and some purporting to run with the land. Given the absence of uniform covenants, there seems to be insufficient evidence to support a finding that a common scheme existed. Without a common scheme, Sherry has no case. Judgment for Elwood.

Zoning-Covenant Conflict

3. Daniel can enjoin Suburban Builders' development scheme. Deed covenants and zoning ordinances both regulate land use. Private parties use covenants. Governments regulate through zoning laws. The landowner is subject to both. The landowner must honor the more restrictive of the two. In the Example the deed covenants permit only single-family residential use. Restaurants and retail shops are not allowed. Zoning laws do not overrule or terminate the covenants.

Banking on a Covenant Termination

4. (a) Tessie's best argument that the other owners waived or abandoned the single-family-residential-use-only covenant is that they expressly released Tract E from the covenant so American Bank could build its bank; and they did not object to the State Highway Commission's acquiring Tract D for the purpose of constructing the four-lane Clarkson Road. Her arguments are not good enough.

A court will find a waiver or an abandonment only when the violations are so pervasive as to indicate an intent to abandon the restriction. The facts here do not indicate the requisite intent to abandon. The landowners cannot prevent a state's condemning property to be used for public purposes. The State Highway Commission's purchasing the property in an eminent domain action or under a threat of an eminent dominant action extinguished the covenant on Tract D. The other landowners could do nothing about it. The state's taking Tract D for road purposes will not terminate the covenant as to the remaining lots.

The release of Tract E from the covenant will not constitute an abandonment of the covenant as it affects Tracts A, B, and C, either. Once the state builds Clarkson Road, separating Tract E from the rest of the affected lots, as a practical matter whether a business or residence sat on Tract E, became irrelevant to the beneficial uses made of Tracts A, B, and C. The four-lane highway had so separated Tract E, the owners of the four lots reasonably could conclude it no longer shared an identity with the remaining three lots. The release of Tract E under the circumstances was not an abandonment of the covenant as to the remaining three tracts.

(b) For a covenant to be terminated or unenforceable by reason of changed conditions, the changes must be so radical as to defeat the essential purposes of the covenant. If the covenant retained some substantial value to the landowners, a court will enforce the covenant even though some landowner, Tessie in our Example, suffered a hardship from the covenant's continued vitality. Here the changed conditions occurred on Tracts D and E, but those two tracts could be effectively severed from the remaining three tracts, which remained primarily wooded and residential. The substantial changes on the surrounding lands transformed the area from rural and peaceful to a commercial clutter. Yet the changes to the surrounding area were external changes, and external changes usually will not justify terminating a covenant. The affected three tracts retain their essential character. The covenant, in fact, may be more important now than ever to preserve the essential character of the land from further commercial intrusions. The covenant remains enforceable.

(c) Tessie is correct. Courts strictly interpret restrictive covenants. A court will not rewrite a covenant to say something the covenant does not itself say. The covenant in the Example prohibited the erection of "any building intended for any purpose except a one family private residence." A paved surface parking lot is not a "building." The court in the case from which the facts are drawn, Dierberg v. Willis, 700 S.W.2d 461 (Mo. Ct. App. 1985), concluded the parking lot would not violate the covenant since a parking lot is not a building and the covenant only prohibited commercial "buildings." None-theless, some courts have precluded the use of a parking lot that serves a non-residential use in contexts similar to this one on the theory the parking lot as an ancillary use to the dominant use must further a permitted dominant use before the parking lot was allowed (in our Example the parking lot would further a nonpermitted use and thus not be permitted in those states).

Public Land Use Controls

PART VI

Constitutional and Statutory Constraints on Zoning

INTRODUCTION

Recognizing that real covenants, equitable servitudes, and nuisance law cannot solve all problems associated with multiple incompatible uses of property, governments coordinate land uses through laws and ordinances. Cities and counties control land use through building codes, road construction, and utility services. The federal and state environmental protection acts, historical preservation statutes, and aesthetic regulations are yet other forms of land use control. The most wide reaching laws affecting land use are zoning ordinances.

Early ordinances controlled **nuisances**, such as stables, slaughterhouses, and pool halls, and promoted fire safety. By the 1920s, municipalities were enacting **comprehensive** zoning laws, regulating land use throughout the city. Comprehensive zoning laws regulate all uses within a zone, not just those that may be nuisances. Zoning ordinances, moreover, impose restrictions on buildings other than use restrictions. The most common such other restrictions relate to **height, bulk, area**, and **exterior design** of structures.

AN INTRODUCTION TO CONSTITUTIONAL LAW

The state constitutions grant powers to the state government officials. Most state constitutions specifically grant or have been interpreted to grant the

571

states the power to regulate activities that affect the "public health, safety, morals, or general welfare." Collectively, these regulatory powers are known as the **police power**, and, as you should have gathered, only coincidentally do they have anything to do with the power of the police.

In practice, political subdivisions such as cities and counties have only the power delegated to them by a state constitution or by legislation. Any activity that political subdivisions undertake must be either expressly delegated in a state statute, or be reasonably necessary for achieving an expressly delegated activity, or be essential to the express purposes of the statute. This rule is often called **Dillon's Rule**, named after its nineteenth-century author, an Iowa judge. In all states, the authority to zone is entrusted to city, county, regional, or statewide agencies. Most if not all state legislatures delegate the zoning authority to cities and counties through an **enabling act**. In other states, the cities' and counties' power can be found in a **home rule** provision in the state constitution.

The federal and state governments' power to regulate is limited by the U.S. Constitution and the respective state constitutions. Most first-year Property cases focus on the protections afforded landowners by the U.S. Constitution, but state constitutions can and often do offer greater or additional protections. The U.S. Constitution provisions invoked to void zoning laws are the substantive due process clause, the procedural due process clause, the takings clause, the equal protection clause, the free speech clause, the freedom of association clause, and the freedom of religion clause. Note, however, that the Takings Clause, which requires governments to compensate landowners when the government "takes" property, has been the center of recent judicial development. Most Property casebooks devote entire chapters to takings issues. (As do we. See Chapter 35, infra.)

THE STANDARD STATE ZONING ENABLING ACT

The U.S. Department of Commerce in 1922, drafted a **Standard State Zoning Enabling Act** (Standard Act). Remarkably, the Standard Act has retained its vitality into the twenty-first century, which is a tribute to the original drafters. The Standard Act makes cities or counties the primary zoning authorities. The **zoning authority** (the city council, the county commission, or other zoning authority) develops a **comprehensive plan** establishing the goals the zoning regulation should strive to achieve, such as preserving the character of the district, maintaining property values, determining the suitability of each district for various purposes, promoting health, safety, morals, and general welfare, etc. The zoning authority divides the city or county into districts or zones. The zoning authority adopts procedures for enacting, enforcing, and amending the zoning ordinances.

The Standard Act grants the local governments powers to enforce the zoning ordinance. Further, the Act recognizes that enforcement officials may make errors or will not have the authorization to adjust for unusual cases. Thus the Standard Act offers a system of appeals to an administrative body, known variously as the **board of appeals**, **board of zoning adjustment**, or **board of zoning appeals**, that allows landowners to petition the board for redress.

A right to appeal occurs if the landowner challenges an official's refusal to grant the landowner a building permit. The Standard Act also grants the administrative board of zoning adjustment (board of appeals) the power, after a hearing is afforded to all interested parties, to grant a landowner a variance. A **variance** excuses a landowner from some provision of the zoning ordinance if compliance with the ordinance would cause the landowner **unnecessary hardship**.

The board of adjustment also has the power to grant special exceptions. **Special exceptions** are permitted uses allowed in a district only if certain conditions expressed in the ordinance are met. The zoning ordinance permits some otherwise unpermitted use in the district if the board finds the use meets all the conditions for a special exception listed in the zoning ordinance. A special exception, for example, may be granted for a library, private school, hospital, church, gas station, apartment, funeral parlor or private club to locate in a district zoned for single-family residences.

Since the board of appeals (board of zoning adjustment) is an administrative body, a landowner unsatisfied with a board's ruling may appeal its decision to a court. The reviewing court will not give as much deference to the board of adjustment as it would to a city council or county commission, whose ordinances are accorded a presumption of validity. See, generally, this chapter, infra.

CUMULATIVE AND NONCUMULATIVE ZONING

In Village of Euclid v. Ambler Realty Co., 272 U.S. 365 (1926), the Supreme Court upheld the Village of Euclid's zoning ordinance against a challenge the zoning law violated the **Due Process Clause** and the **Equal Protection Clause** of the U.S. Constitution. Because of the case's posture, the Supreme Court was not called upon to decide whether the zoning ordinance constituted a "taking" of Ambler Realty's property, which may have required the Village of Euclid to compensate every landowner who was harmed by the zoning ordinance.

Euclid reviewed a simple but typical zoning ordinance, which consisted of two documents — a zoning map and the text of the ordinance. The Euclid ordinance divided the village into districts. This resulted in a zoning map, which showed the boundaries of each district. Then in the text of the ordinance, each district was restricted based on three factors. First, each district was limited to certain **uses**. Oversimplified, U-1 was limited to single-family residences. U-2 added duplexes, so single-family residences and duplexes were permitted in U-2. U-3 added apartments, hotels, schools, churches, libraries, museums, and government buildings. U-4 permitted, in addition to the above uses, retail establishments such as banks, restaurants, law offices, theaters, stores, gas stations, skating rinks, newspaper printers, garages, and police and fire stations. U-5 allowed all of the above plus billboards, warehouses, light manufacturing, stables, laundries, and bottling operations. U-6 allowed heavy industrial plants, cemeteries, prisons, a junkyard, and gasoline storage facilities. U-7 listed uses prohibited in the Village of Euclid altogether.

A similar classification scheme restricted building **heights**; and another classification scheme required minimum lot sizes (**area** restrictions). In addition to these three major classification schemes — use, height, and area — the ordinance contained other restrictions dealing with lot width, setbacks, etc. Because of this case, zoning by districts is called **Euclidean zoning**.

The particular zoning plan used in Euclid is known as **cumulative zoning**. Under cumulative zoning ordinances, the different zones or districts are ranked in a hierarchy. The districts limited to residential uses are known as the "higher districts" or "higher zones." Districts allowing multifamily and business uses are "lower districts" or "lower zones." Uses allowed in a higher zone are allowed in all lower zones, but no use can be located in a higher zone than the zone in which it is first listed. A person can build a single-family residence in all zones, including a retail district and even in the heavy industrial district; whereas retail shops and heavy industrial uses are strictly prohibited from locating in the "higher" zones. Likewise, no department store, restaurant, gas station, or stable can locate in the higher zone such as U-1, Single-Family Residential. The cumulative zoning idea applies to height and area restrictions as well. Buildings in the least restrictive area can be any height allowed in the city whereas a ten-story structure, as an example, cannot be located in an area restricted to two and one-half stories.

As an alternative to cumulative zoning, some jurisdictions adopt **noncumulative** or **exclusive** zoning, especially in industrial areas. Exclusive zoning recognizes that a single-family residence or an apartment may be just as incompatible with the activities in a warehouse, industrial, or commercial district as a manufacturing plant would be in a residential area. The exclusive zoning ordinance, therefore, permits only authorized activities in each district. Under a noncumulative zoning ordinance, a person could not locate a single-family residence in a retail or industrial district.

THE CONSTITUTIONAL LAW IN *EUCLID*

Euclid confronts constitutional issues arising under the Due Process Clause. The U.S. Constitution is the premier legal document in our country. No law can contravene it.

In Euclid v. Ambler Realty, the landowner claimed the Village of Euclid's enactment of the zoning ordinance ran afoul of the due process clause of the Fifth Amendment, which guarantees that no person shall "be deprived of life, liberty, or property, without due process of law . . . ," U.S. Const. amend. V, and of the Fourteenth Amendment, which reads in part, "nor shall any State deprive any person of life, liberty, or property, without due process of law. . . ." U.S. Const. amend XIV, § 1. The harm Ambler Realty suffered was substantial loss of its land's value and loss of the right to use its land for otherwise legal purposes.

The two references to "due process of law" are known as the **Due Process Clause**. Invoked in *Euclid* was **substantive due process**, which addresses whether the federal or state government can restrict individual rights through the law or action at issue.[1] A court will review a law challenged as unconstitutional under a substantive due process argument through several identifiable steps. First, the law must advance the public health, safety, morals, or general welfare. Stated otherwise, a state in enacting a law must be trying to promote a **legitimate state interest**. Unless the law infringes upon a constitutionally protected right, once the state shows it is attempting to further a legitimate state interest, the law will be upheld if the **means** chosen to achieve the legitimate state interest is **rationally related** to the legitimate state interest. A court would declare the statute unconstitutional only if the provision is **clearly arbitrary and capricious**, having no relation to the promotion of the claimed legitimate state interest. To summarize, a court will uphold a law if the state shows (1) the state's goal in enacting the law is the promotion of a legitimate state interest, and (2) the law (i.e., the **means**) is rationally related to the promotion of the legitimate state interest. As a practical matter, almost all laws pass this **rational relationship** test.

Once a law infringes upon an individual's **fundamental** constitutional right, however, the burden on the state increases dramatically. The state then must convince a court the state's interest outweighs the individual's fundamental right. Usually, to prevail, the state must show it is trying to advance a **compelling state interest**. If the state cannot show the state's interest outweighs the individual's fundamental right, a court will strike the statute down as being unconstitutional. The state may enact another statute to further its legitimate state interest, but a successful statute cannot infringe upon any constitutionally protected rights.

Even if the state's interest outweighs the infringement upon an individual's fundamental right, the statute must be **narrowly tailored** to achieve the state's compelling state interest while infringing as little as possible upon the

---

1. A second aspect of the Due Process Clause is **procedural due process**, which requires government to give notice and an opportunity to be heard on any administrative matter uniquely affecting an individual before the government can deny or revoke the person's rights or privileges. Procedural due rights form a cornerstone of American law and, as will be developed later, play a major role in implementing zoning ordinances.

individual's constitutionally protected right. The following series of Examples develop this concept in a nonzoning situation.

Example 1:   City Council wants to reduce the costs of removing litter from the city streets. Pursuant to the above analysis the first question is, does the city have a legitimate interest in reducing the cost of cleaning litter from the streets? The answer is yes, a city has a legitimate interest in preventing litter and saving taxpayers' money.

Example 2:   Now assume City Council passes an ordinance making it illegal to distribute leaflets on city streets and sidewalks. The council was reacting to evidence that substantial litter results when persons receiving the pamphlets drop or toss them on the sidewalks or streets. The next question is: Is the ordinance rationally related to reducing the cost of removing the litter? Again, the answer must be yes it is.

Example 3:   Police ticket a person for distributing leaflets. The person challenges the ordinance as unconstitutional. What result? The antilitter ordinance infringes upon the individual's right to free speech and freedom of the press. The distribution of leaflets is protected by the First Amendment. Because the antilitter ordinance infringes on an individual's constitutionally protected right of free speech and freedom of the press, and the city can offer only a legitimate interest and not a compelling interest to justify the ordinance, under the approach developed above, a court will hold the antilitter statute is unconstitutional.

Example 4:   Same facts as in Examples 2 and 3. Can City Council enact any antilitter ordinance? Sure it can. Only City Council must try another tact. City Council might enact an ordinance making the throwing of leaflets on the pavement illegal, or it could place trash baskets on the sidewalks. The city just cannot prohibit the distribution of leaflets in the first instance.

In *Euclid*, Ambler Realty argued the Euclid zoning ordinance's depriving Ambler Realty and other property owners of their right to use their property as they desired and decreasing their property's value greatly amounted to an impermissible interference or "deprivation" of the individual's constitutional right of property ownership. In response, the Supreme Court in *Euclid* enumerated several **legitimate state interests** furthered by zoning ordinances: zoning promotes safety and security, reduces street accidents, decreases noise, preserves an environment in which to raise children, and aids in fire prevention. The Court then likened zoning ordinances to nuisance control statutes (which were constitutional) and declared the ordinance was **rationally related** to the furtherance of legitimate state goals. The Court next concluded the ordinance did not implicate any fundamental constitutional right. Thus only a rational relationship between the ends to be achieved (the legitimate state interest) and the means chosen to achieve those ends (the zoning law is the means) is all that is required to uphold the law under a substantive due process inquiry.

UNCONSTITUTIONAL *ON ITS FACE* AND UNCONSTITUTIONAL *AS APPLIED*

Substantive due process has two aspects. The Supreme Court in Euclid v. Ambler Realty considered only whether the statue was constitutional **on its face**. A court evaluates a statute for its "facial validity" based on the statute's operation in most cases. In *Euclid*, once the Court found the zoning ordinance was a rational means to achieve a legitimate state interest, and no other specific constitutional right was implicated, the Court found the ordinance on its face did not violate the U.S. Constitution.

Because Ambler Realty challenged the zoning ordinance on its face and not as applied to any specific development on its land, the Supreme Court did not need to address whether the zoning ordinance **as applied** to Ambler Realty's land was unconstitutional:

> It is true that when, if ever, the provisions set forth in the ordinance in tedious and minute detail, come to be concretely applied to particular premises, including those of the appellee, or to particular conditions, or to be considered in connection with specific complaints, some of them, or even many of them, may be found to be clearly arbitrary and unreasonable.

Euclid, 272 U.S. at 395.

Two years after *Euclid*, the Supreme Court in Nectow v. City of Cambridge, 277 U.S. 183 (1928), concluded the zoning ordinance **as applied** to plaintiff's property was unconstitutional. The plaintiff in *Nectow* owned a large tract of land. Land on the opposite side of an adjoining street was used for residential purposes. Land on plaintiff's side of the street was used for (or intended to be used for) industrial purposes. The city included in a residential zone a 100-foot-wide strip of land (65 feet wide after expected road expansion) that was a small part of plaintiff's larger tract. The rest of plaintiff's tract was zoned industrial.

The Supreme Court recited two facts found at trial. The first was that no practical use could be made of the 100-foot strip of land in question for residential purposes because, among other reasons, plaintiff could not earn an adequate return on any development of the property. The second finding was that placing the plaintiff's 100-foot strip of land in a residential district would not promote the health, safety, convenience, and general welfare of the inhabitants of that part of the city, taking into account the natural development of the land, the character of the district, and the resulting benefit that would accrue to the whole city.

After reciting the two fact findings, the Court relied on *Euclid* for a substantive due process argument that the zoning ordinance in *Nectow* failed as a means to promote a legitimate state interest. Specifically, the Court held that a zoning regulation "cannot be imposed if it does not bear a **substantial relation** to the public health, safety, morals, or general welfare." Since zoning the 100-foot strip of land would not promote any legitimate state interest, and the invasion was serious and highly injurious, the zoning ordinance was unconstitutional **as applied** to the 100-foot strip.

NONCONFORMING USES

Uncertain about the constitutionality of demanding a landowner stop any **existing use** of land or to tear down any **structure** not in conformity with a newly enacted zoning ordinance or amendment, or unwilling to destroy established businesses, city councils routinely adopted ordinances allowing existing nonconforming uses to continue. **Nonconforming uses** are those legal uses in place when an ordinance takes effect and that, except for already being in the district, would not be permitted in that district under the newly enacted zoning ordinance.

Example: A grocery store is located in a district the city council zones residential use only. The grocery store is a nonconforming use. Absent the nonconforming use principle, the grocery store would be forced to relocate outside the single-family residential-only district.

The nonconforming use must exist at the time the ordinance takes effect. Mere ownership of land or having a plan to use the property for a nonconforming use is insufficient. Many jurisdictions by ordinance or judicial decree in equity will grant a person an equitable or vested right to build an already planned nonconforming use under certain circumstances. Generally, for a court to grant equitable relief, the claimant must have acted in good faith, meaning the claimant has no good reason to believe the ordinance would be enacted or amended to prohibit the intended use. In addition, the claimant, before the ordinance was enacted, must have made or committed to make substantial expenditures toward building or operating the nonconforming use. In addition, courts must find that the claimant in good faith had received a building permit for any nonconforming improvements.

The right to a nonconforming use runs with the land. The mere change of ownership does not end the nonconforming use status. Once a landowner abandons a nonconforming use, however, the right to use property for a nonconforming use ends, and neither the owner nor any subsequent owner can resume the nonconforming use. Often litigated at one time was whether a landowner had abandoned a nonconforming use. Today, instead of a facts-and-circumstances test as to whether the owner has abandoned a nonconforming use, most ordinances stipulate a period of nonuse — ranging from 60 days to one year — as presumptive of abandonment.

The right to a nonconforming use is limited to the nonconforming use in place when the ordinance goes into effect. A landowner cannot change one nonconforming use to another type of nonconforming use. Thus a nonconforming doctor's office in a residential-use-only district could not be turned into a lawyer's office or a beauty parlor. But while many zoning ordinances prohibit any changes in use, other ordinances allow a change to a more restrictive use. In these latter jurisdictions, a person could change the use of a building from a grocery store to a law office, for example, but cannot change the use from a law office to a grocery store.

In most jurisdictions, increasing the volume of business through natural growth usually is allowed, but increased uses through modifications to the structures or methods of operation by the landowner are forbidden. A landowner may be prohibited from increasing the hours or days a week the business is open, or change from a seasonal business to year-round operations, for example. Similarly, a tavern may not add live entertainment.

Some jurisdictions limit the nonconforming uses to the original land it used. Others allow expansion to other parts of the same tract of land owned at the time the ordinance went into effect, especially if no new structures are needed.

Most jurisdictions prohibit a landowner's expanding the nonconforming use by increasing the size or number of buildings. Nonetheless, in most jurisdictions a landowner can replace old equipment or substitute more efficient equipment as long as the landowner does not increase the nonconforming use.

Predictably, an owner of a nonconforming structure can engage in normal maintenance and repairs. A few states even allow replacement of a nonconforming building as long as the new building does not increase nonconforming uses. Other jurisdictions, with an eye to eliminating nonconforming uses, do not allow landowners to replace or substantially alter nonconforming buildings, even if destroyed by fire. Other ordinances restrict the cost of alterations to one-fourth or one-half the value of the current structure's fair market value (not cost), for example, or limit alterations to those needed for safety or to meet health or building code standards.

AMORTIZATION

Legislatures and courts hoped nonconforming uses would end of their own accord. That was not often the case. After realizing that nonconforming uses did not end through natural attrition or as quickly as would be desired, many states or local zoning bodies enacted amortization provisions that allow nonconforming uses to continue only for a specified maximum period of time, after which the nonconforming use will no longer be permitted in the district. The period of use allowed usually is based on the time necessary for the owner to recoup the cost of improvements made to the property. Depending on the type of improvements and the jurisdiction, the amortization period may range from a few months or years up to more than 50 years.

Courts have reacted differently to constitutional challenges made against amortization provisions. A minority of courts hold the amortization provision to be unconstitutional on its face, or per se unconstitutional, under the U.S. Constitution or, more likely by a state court, under its state constitution.[2] These courts liken the amortization provision to a "taking" of the property for public use at the end of the amortization period, and thus a variation of a direct "taking" requiring compensation. Under the **Takings** Clause of the U.S. Constitution or state constitution, governments can "take" or force the landowner to sell the property to the government for public purposes, but the government must pay just compensation to the landowner. In states declaring amortization provisions per se unconstitutional, a court presumably would approve the amortization provision if the provision incorporated an obligation for the state to compensate the landowner for the loss of the nonconforming use.

The large majority of state courts uphold reasonable amortization provisions as legitimate regulatory tools that do not implicate the takings clause. These courts place amortization in the same category as provisions that prohibit the expansion of nonconforming uses or that prohibit the renewal of abandoned uses. The reasonableness of an amortization provision is based on the time needed for the landowner to recoup the investment for structures and any loss of value of the property itself through the nonconforming-use prohibition. Courts tolerate a shorter amortization period for a nonconforming use than for a nonconforming structure.

---

2. Just as the U.S. Supreme Court is the final arbiter of U.S. Constitution issues, a state supreme court has the final word on its state's constitution. State constitutions can grant their citizens greater rights than the U.S. Constitution does. Thus a state constitution may be interpreted to give an individual rights even though an identically worded provision would not give the individual any rights under the U.S. Constitution. A state constitution cannot deprive an individual of his or her U.S. Constitution rights, however. If a state court interprets the state constitution as giving the individual fewer rights than does the U.S. Constitution, the individual would still have the greater rights guaranteed by the U.S. Constitution.

Courts are particularly sensitive to protecting individuals' constitutional rights where a city amends a zoning ordinance to rid the city of undesirable yet legal activities (such as adult bookstores or billboards) by establishing a blatantly short amortization period (90 days, for example), and often will strike the ordinance down as unconstitutional.

In a few states, courts declare amortization provisions unenforceable as contrary to, prohibited by, or not authorized by the state's enabling statute. The state legislature in these states can amend the law to authorize amortization of nonconforming uses (of course the amortization provision remains open to a state constitutional challenge).

Examples

Zoned Out

1. (a) Logan bought four lots in the city of Sugar Creek. The Sugar Creek city council passed a zoning ordinance five years later. Logan's four lots were zoned B-Business allowing all legal businesses. Logan then leased the four lots to Die-Cast Manufacturing, a die-casting company. The Sugar Creek city council later rezoned the four lots to CB-Central Business, restricting the district to retail establishments. Manufacturing concerns were not permitted. Will Die-Cast Manufacturing now be forced to relocate outside the district?

   (b) The Sugar Creek city council once more amended its zoning ordinance. This time the four lots were zoned R-3, Residential and Entertainment, which allows residential uses (houses, apartments, etc.) and less intensive commercial uses such as pool halls, nightclubs, gasoline stations, motels and hotels, parking lots, taverns, and theaters. The city council for the first time provided that a "nonconforming use may be continued but may not be changed to another nonconforming use." Assuming Die-Cast Manufacturing still operated its manufacturing plant on the four lots both before and after the prior amendments, will it be forced to relocate after the most recent amendments?

   (c) Die-Cast Manufacturing continued operating its plant on the four lots. In August of last year, Die-Cast notified Logan it intended to terminate its lease. Die-Cast Manufacturing vacated the premises on September 30 of last year. Logan began remodeling the building on all four lots in anticipation of opening his own automobile sales and service business. In March of this year, Logan opened his automobile dealership and service shop. Will Logan be forced to relocate his automobile sales and service business?

A Concrete Example

2. Minnesota Concrete built and began operating a ready-mix concrete plant in Frozen Lake twenty (20) years ago. Last year Frozen Lake amended its zoning ordinance to no longer permit concrete plants to operate within the town limits. The town council rezoned the property on which Minnesota Concrete operated to R-4, Multifamily Residential, to provide space for high-density, low-income housing. Under the ordinance, the city council could set reasonable amortization periods for nonconforming uses on a property-by-property basis. Pursuant to the ordinance, the city council in setting a reasonable amortization period was to consider the height of structures used; the nature of the use; the surrounding land uses; the character of the neighborhood; the cost of the property and of any improvements; any benefit to the public if the use continued or ended; the burden on the property owner who is required to terminate the nonconforming use; and the length of time the use has existed.

   After a public hearing, the Frozen Lake city council issued a ruling that Minnesota Concrete be given a two-year amortization. At the conclusion of the two-year amortization period, Minnesota Concrete's ready-mix concrete operation was to cease to operate within the district. A major factor in the council's decision was the company's having used the concrete plant for nearly 20 years. The council felt 20 years was long enough for Minnesota Concrete to recoup its original investment.

   (a) Minnesota Concrete challenges the exclusion of concrete plants from all locations in Frozen Lake. Does Frozen Lake have a legitimate state interest in excluding concrete plants from the city?

   (b) Is the zoning ordinance rationally related to the promotion of any claimed legitimate state interest?

   (c) Was the two-year amortization period constitutional as applied to Minnesota Concrete?

   (d) Is the two-year amortization period reasonable?

Explanations

Zoned Out

1. (a) Die-Cast Manufacturing may continue its die-cast operations on the four lots. Since Die-Cast was in operation before the more restrictive zoning ordinances became effective, it may continue its die-cast operations as a nonconforming use. The fact that Die-Cast is merely a tenant and not the landowner is irrelevant. The nonconforming-use status applies to use and structures, not to the specific owners at the time the ordinance was enacted. A tenant as well as the owner (as well as future lessees and owners in most states) can continue the nonconforming use.

(b) Die-Cast Manufacturing can continue as a nonconforming use even though all manufacturing and most retail establishments no longer are allowed in the district. The status as a nonconforming use is one of timing, not of the variance between the actual use and the permitted uses. Since the die-cast operations were in effect on the date of the rezoning, Die-Cast Manufacturing can continue its operations as a nonconforming use.

(c) The automobile sales and service business is not permitted in R-3, Residential and Entertainment. Logan must shut down his automobile dealership at that location. If he wants to continue the business, he must relocate it to a district allowing automobile sales and service.

The 1990 amendments specifically provided that nonconforming uses could not be changed to another nonconforming use. Under the current ordinance, Logan cannot change the use of the four lots from one nonconforming use (die-cast operations) to another nonconforming use (the automobile sales and service business).

Logan can make arguments the current ordinance does not apply to him, but he loses. One losing argument sometimes made is that because Logan owned the four lots before the amendments (or before the original ordinance for that matter), the stipulation that a landowner cannot change one nonconforming use to another does not apply to him. In effect, Logan argues his right to change from one nonconforming use to other nonconforming uses, like the nonconforming use itself, is a vested right since he owned the land before the city adopted or amended the ordinance. This argument fails because the zoning ordinance applies to the property in all regards except to the extent the use or structure violated the ordinance on the effective date of the ordinance or amendment. Future violations are not permitted.

Logan also might argue his automobile sales and service business is a higher use (i.e., less intensive use) than the die-cast manufacturing operations existing before it. That being so, continues the theory, his less intensive use should be allowed. This theory fails since the statute prohibits all changes to other nonconforming uses, not just to uses of equal or greater intensity.

Logan also could argue that his nonconforming use was leasing the property, and that he continues that role, except that he now in effect leases to himself. His error is that the nonconforming use envisioned is the primary use of the land, not the use of the landowner as lessor. The landowner could not claim the benefit of the nonconforming use, for example, if he had leased the property to a tenant who planned to operate an automobile dealership. It is the use made of the property on the effective date of the zoning ordinance (or amendment) and not who owns the property that matters. The only use qualifying for nonconforming-use status is the die-cast operations.

A Concrete Example

2. (a) Frozen Lake can offer several legitimate state interests. Any goal that promotes the public welfare (health, safety, morals, or general welfare) qualifies as a legitimate state interest. Finding a legitimate state interest for state action, including zoning, usually is an easy task, as it is in this Example. One legitimate goal was to remove the source of dust and other air pollution associated with concrete plants. Similarly, trucks to and from the plant may cause dangerous traffic conditions.

   (b) Zoning is the means to achieve the state's legitimate ends. Rezoning to prohibit the operation of the concrete plant within the city is rationally related to health (cleaner air) and safety (safer traffic conditions). Banning concrete plants also may be rationally related to the other goals, such as increasing the property tax base. For the same reasons, the amortization provision also is a means rationally related to the promotion of the legitimate state interests.

   (c) The two-year amortization period is constitutional as applied to Minnesota Concrete. To prevail, Minnesota Concrete must show the two-year amortization period is not rationally related to the promotion of any legitimate state interest or that the ordinance will deprive Minnesota Concrete of all practical use of its property. As discussed above, the two-year amortization period is directly related to the promotion of the health, safety, convenience, and general welfare of the town's citizens. Although a possibility exists Minnesota Concrete might show that no practical use of the property would remain or that Minnesota Concrete could not earn a reasonable return on the investment, it appears the land is usable for other purposes. The fact that the only use Minnesota Concrete would consider making would be the prohibited ready-mix concrete plant is irrelevant to whether some practical use could be made of the property, and would be relevant to the issue of return on investment only if the company could not sell the land to someone else.

   (d) This Example is a variation of Example (c). The court in AVR, Inc. v. City of St. Louis Park, 585 N.W.2d 411 (Minn. Ct. App. 1998), concluded a two-year amortization period was reasonable on the facts. Since Minnesota Concrete had owned and operated the concrete plant for nearly 20 years, the Frozen Lake city council (based on facts not in the problem that the plant was fully depreciated for income tax purposes and that Minnesota Concrete's return on its investment already had exceeded the plant's cost) determined Minnesota Concrete already had recouped its investment. After reaching that conclusion, the other factors set out in the statute led the council to give Minnesota Concrete two years to relocate.

The concrete company in *AVR, Inc.*, argued the useful life and the amount of the investment to be recouped should be determined as of the effective date of the zoning amendment rather than on the plant's original cost and the useful life on the day the company acquired the plant. The court rejected the cement company's claims that the city must use the fair market value or replacement cost and the remaining useful life as of the effective date of the amendment. While the city can choose to base investment on fair market value as of the ordinance's effective date, the court concluded the Constitution requires only that the owner has an opportunity to recoup its original investment (and not the fair market value on the effective date of the ordinance). Under the facts, concluded the court, Minnesota Concrete had more than recouped its original investment over the past 20 years. Hence it needed no more time to recoup its investment. The two-year amortization period gave Minnesota Concrete adequate time to locate and purchase new land outside Frozen Lake, and to construct a new cement plant on the land. Under these facts, the two-year amortization period was reasonable.

33

Variances, Special Exceptions, and Zoning Amendments

Flexibility is added to zoning ordinances through variances, special exceptions, and zoning amendments.

VARIANCES

Zoning ordinances permit the board of adjustment to grant variances. A *variance*, if granted, allows a landowner to build on land or use the land in a manner otherwise not permitted by the local zoning ordinance. The variance is an administrative order waiving application of the zoning ordinance in order to keep the ordinance from denying a landowner all reasonable use of his property. It also serves as a safety valve that prevents the city or county from being held liable under the Takings Clause of the Constitution, or the zoning ordinance from being declared unconstitutional under the substantive Due Process Clause of the Constitution.[1]

Variances are categorized as either **use variances** or **area or dimensional variances. Use variances** permit a **use** otherwise prohibited in the district. A few states prohibit use variances altogether. Even in the majority of states

---

1. The Supreme Court in Nectow v. City of Cambridge, 277 U.S. 183 (1928), cited *Euclid* for the proposition that a zoning regulation "cannot be imposed if it does not bear a substantial relation to the public health, safety, morals, or general welfare." Since the zoning of the 100-foot strip of land would not promote any legitimate state interest, and the invasion was serious and highly injurious, the zoning ordinance was unconstitutional as applied. A variance could have resolved the problem at the administrative level.

that recognize use variances, boards of adjustment (and courts) are less willing to grant use variances than to grant dimensional variances. **Dimensional variances** permit deviations from area, bulk, setback, street frontage, floor space, and height and other nonuse requirements of the zoning ordinance. Boards of adjustment (and courts) are more receptive to dimensional variances since dimensional variances usually do not change the district's essential character.

Zoning ordinances authorize variances by a provision similar to § 7 of the Standard State Zoning Enabling Act,[2] which authorizes the board of adjustment to permit such variance from the terms of the ordinance as will not be contrary to the public interest, where, owing to special conditions, a literal enforcement of the provisions of the ordinance will result in unnecessary hardship, and so that the spirit of the ordinance shall be observed and substantial justice done.

A board of adjustment will grant a variance only if there is substantial evidence that the following elements are met:

1. The variance would not be substantially incompatible with the comprehensive zoning plan;
2. The landowner suffers a **unique hardship** in the use of the land because of some zoning provision;
3. The landowner suffers an **unnecessary hardship** in the use of the land if the variance is denied (some courts substitute a **practical difficulties** standard for dimensional variances); and
4. The grant of the variance will not be detrimental to the public welfare.

The first requirement — that the variance would not be substantially incompatible with the comprehensive zoning plan — guarantees the variance will not be inconsistent with the zoning ordinance's overall plan. Moreover, too great a variance looks like an **amendment** to the zoning plan itself. Boards of adjustment have only the powers given them by the ordinance; they do not have the legislative power or authority to amend the zoning ordinance. Amending a zoning plan is the province of the city council, county commissioners, or other legislative or quasi-legislative body.

The second prerequisite is that the landowner would suffer a unique hardship in the use of the land in question if the variance is not granted. The hardship usually is identified with some unique physical condition of the lot, but the hardship could result from circumstances such as the lot bordering on a different zoning district such that the lot is unsuited for the purposes for which it is zoned. "Unique" does not mean the lot is absolutely

---

2. The Standard State Zoning Enabling Act is explained in Chapter 32, supra.

the only lot in the zone suffering from the hardship, but the hardship cannot be one generally characteristic of lots in the district. Its uniqueness will involve some peculiar condition that justifies treating it differently from other land in the district. If many lots suffer from the same disabling condition, a **zoning amendment** rather than a **variance** is the proper remedy.

Third, the hardship suffered must be an undue or unnecessary hardship. **Undue or unnecessary hardship** is a condition of the lot such that the owner could not make effective use or make a reasonable profit from owning the lot unless a variance is granted. Many states apply a **strict unnecessary hardship** standard in evaluating petitions for **use** variances. In these states, a more lenient standard, the **practical difficulty** standard is used to evaluate petitions for a **dimensional** variance (area, setbacks, frontage, etc.). The hardship suffered must go to the use of the land. A mere decrease in value of the property will not justify a variance. The unnecessary hardship, moreover, must relate to the reasonable use of the property. A landowner is not entitled to the most profitable use of the land.

Not all hardships are unnecessary hardships. A hardship, for example, will not be considered an unnecessary hardship if the hardship was **self-created**, meaning self-imposed. In other words, the hardship cannot be the result of some action by a landowner (or predecessor in interest) knowing of the zoning ordinance. In some jurisdictions, it is the landowner applying for the variance who bears the burden of proof on this point — in which case it becomes another element necessary for granting a variance; in others, it is a "defense" to an order granting the variance, meaning that the self-created nature of the hardship or difficulty will be raised by neighbors opposing the application. Still other jurisdictions require that the applicant make an effort to eliminate the hardship or difficulty before applying for the variance. If no such effort is made, the applicant then runs the risk of the board's finding that the variance is self-created. (Often the effort involved is an attempt to buy enough neighboring land to bring the lot into compliance with the ordinance.)

Example 1: A local zoning ordinance requires a 60-foot frontage before a lot can be improved. (Frontage is the amount of feet bordering on the street in front of the property. A 60-foot frontage requirement means the lot must be at least 60 feet wide at the street. A person could build on a lot having a frontage of 60 feet or more, but could not build if the frontage was 59 feet or less.) The original subdivider sold a lot with a 40-foot frontage to a landowner before the city enacted the zoning ordinance. Since the lot has a 40-foot frontage and not the 60-foot frontage necessary to improve a lot under the ordinance, the landowner suffers a hardship, which likely would be considered an **unnecessary hardship** on these facts.

Example 2: The zoning ordinance requiring a 60-foot frontage is in effect and the landowner owns a lot with a 100-foot frontage. The landowner sells part of the lot to a third party. The transferred lot has a 60-foot frontage while the retained portion has a 40-foot frontage. Having a lot with a 40-foot frontage creates a hardship for the landowner since he cannot improve the lot under the zoning ordinance. The landowner here suffers a unique hardship because of the 60-foot frontage requirement, but will not be considered to suffer an unnecessary hardship since the hardship was **self-induced** or **self-imposed** (i.e., the landowner created his own hardship by subdividing and selling part of his lot).

Similarly, a person cannot intentionally construct some improvement in violation of the ordinance or build before securing a building permit and subsequently seek a variance claiming destruction of the structure would be an unnecessary hardship. The hardship was self-created. A court might consider a variance if the person erroneously believed he built in compliance with the ordinance. Even then the landowner's innocence will be only a factor and not determinative.

The fourth element in securing a variance is to show the grant of a variance would not be detrimental to the public welfare. In general, this means the variance would not harm the use and enjoyment of neighboring properties, would not detract from the character of the neighborhood, and otherwise would not be contrary to the public health or safety of the area. Considered a harm to neighboring lands for this element, in addition to aesthetic, safety, environmental, or traffic concerns, is the decrease in value of any adjacent property.

Any variance granted may deviate from the zoning ordinance only so much as is necessary to make the affected property usable or reasonably profitable. In addition, most zoning ordinances give the board of adjustment the power to impose conditions on the use of the property in return for the variance. The conditions must be reasonably related to the promotion of the objectives of the zoning ordinance. See Contract Zoning and Conditional Zoning, infra. Commonly imposed conditions include building fences or planting hedges to preserve the aesthetics of the area, or making sewer, drainage, or flood control improvements.

SPECIAL EXCEPTIONS

The board of adjustment also authorizes **special exceptions** (also known as **special uses**, **special use permits**, and **conditional uses**). The uses qualifying for a special exception usually serve the people living or working in the district. The uses are not listed as permitted uses as of right. Instead, they are permitted only conditionally, usually because their size and the potential harmful effects associated with traffic, pollution, or other safety or health concerns demand they be sparingly permitted or permitted only under certain conditions. In contrast to the variance, which permits deviation from provisions of the ordinance for **uses** and more frequently for **dimensions**, the zoning ordinance lists as *special exceptions* those uses that may be located in the district. For example, the zoning ordinance may authorize churches to be located in a single-family residential-use-only district. The uses often listed as permitted special exceptions include parking lots, social clubs, private schools, churches, hospitals, nursing homes, gasoline stations, and funeral parlors.

The board of adjustment can approve only those uses mentioned in the ordinance. Recognizing that permitted uses are not suitable under all circumstances and in all locations within the district, city councils and county commissioners enact ordinances that authorize special exceptions only if the board of adjustment concludes the particular use meets the standards and conditions set out in the ordinance. These express standards can be quite specific on occasion, involving such things as fences, set-back lines, minimum number of occupants, and the maximum percentage of the lot covered by the specially permitted use. These specific standards are then followed in the ordinance by a general standard, e.g., that the use has "no adverse impact on surrounding lots." Such a general standard provides the board with some administrative discretion to grant or deny the application after considering such things as the number of similar uses already permitted in the neighborhood and the benefit of permitting the use relative to the adverse impact it would create in, say, extra traffic or pollution.

To qualify for a special exception, the landowner does not have to show unnecessary hardship (or any hardship at all for that matter). Instead, the landowner needs to show (a) the ordinance lists the use as a special exception; (b) the use will meet all standards and conditions set out in the ordinance; and (c) the special exception will not detract from the area's health, safety, and public convenience beyond that inherent in the normal conduct of the activity itself.

JUDICIAL REVIEW OF VARIANCES AND SPECIAL EXCEPTIONS

The board of adjustment is an administrative body consisting of appointed members. The members are not elected. The significance of these facts is easily overlooked. The board of adjustment cannot pass laws. The board can only carry out its administrative functions. The zoning ordinance (or the state enabling act) sets out the standards and conditions needed for all variances and special exceptions, and the board of adjustment's function is to determine whether the conditions and standards have been met. Once the board concludes the standards and conditions have been met, the board must grant the variance or special exception. If the conditions are not met, the board must deny the application for the variance or special exception.

Parties disappointed by the board of adjustment's decision may appeal to a court. A court will review the record developed at the administrative level to ensure the board's decision was based on standards set out in the zoning ordinance. For this to occur, several preliminary matters must have occurred. First, the zoning ordinance (or the state enabling act) must enumerate the standards and conditions controlling the board's discretion. Generally this is no problem with variances since courts hold the unnecessary hardship and not contrary to public interest language in the ordinance provides adequate guidance.

Some courts, however, have had trouble with the standards for the **special exception**. An ordinance either may not give any standards, which makes it impossible for courts to know what standards to apply to the board's decision; or one or more of the standards, in the court's judgment, give the board of adjustment too much discretion. If the board has too much discretion, some courts hold those provisions giving the board unbridled discretion to be an **unconstitutional delegation of legislative power**. Those provisions giving too much power to the board are then struck from the ordinance, and the court evaluates the board's findings without the excluded provision. The modern trend is for courts to find the ordinance has given adequate guidance, either through specific standards for the grant or denial of the special exception in the ordinance or through general statements in the preamble stating the goals of the ordinance.

A second preliminary matter and as a matter of procedural due process, persons (including neighboring landowners and the general public) interested in the decision of the board of adjustment must be given an **opportunity to be heard** and an **opportunity to present and rebut evidence**. The board of adjustment must keep a **written record** of its findings of fact and an explanation of its decision in every case. A court will not review a board of adjustment's decision unless the court has before it a written record including findings of fact and the reason for the board's decision. A court will not uphold a board's decision without a written record, and will remand the matter back to the board of adjustment to prepare a written record. A decision based on a factor not included in the written record is per se **arbitrary and capricious** and likely will result in a reversal of the board's ruling.

If a court is satisfied it has a complete written record, the court begins with the presumption the board of adjustment's decision is correct, and will reverse the verdict only (a) if the ordinance is unconstitutional; (b) if the board's finding of facts are clearly erroneous; (c) if the court finds the board of adjustment did not adhere to the procedures and guidelines contained in the ordinance or its own operating procedures; or (d) the board's decision was arbitrary, capricious, or discriminatory or was not supported by substantial evidence.

AMENDING THE ZONING ORDINANCE

Local zoning authorities (city councils or county commissioners) must follow procedures for enacting and amending zoning ordinances under the state's enabling legislation. State enabling acts require local zoning authorities give notice and conduct hearings before enacting or amending a zoning ordinance. Since the local zoning authorities in enacting or amending a zoning ordinance are acting in a legislative capacity, no formal written record of findings is necessary. However, the legislative body must make the enacted ordinances available to the general public.

Most enabling acts require that the zoning ordinances be "in accordance with" a master plan or comprehensive plan of development. Despite this, some zoning authorities do not develop a master plan or comprehensive plan of development. Nonetheless, courts in many cases overlook the zoning authorities' failure to adopt a comprehensive plan, accepting the zoning ordinance itself and the decisions made under it as a "plan." If, however, a zoning authority has adopted a comprehensive plan, many courts require zoning ordinances and amendments to conform to the comprehensive plan.

Courts will void a zoning ordinance (or specific provision thereof) or amendments thereto only (a) if the ordinance, provision, or amendment is not enacted pursuant to the state's enabling act or the local zoning authority's comprehensive plan of development; (b) if the ordinance, provision, or amendment is arbitrary, capricious, or discriminatory; or (c) if the ordinance, provision, or amendment violates some provision of the federal or a state constitution or statute. In a few states, an ordinance can be amended only if a mistake in the original ordinance or changed conditions since the enactment of the original ordinance justify the amendment.

THE PROBLEM OF SPOT ZONING

Even though courts grant local legislative zoning ordinances a presumption of validity, courts have struck down some zoning ordinances or amendments when the court felt the amendment amounted to **spot zoning**. Spot zoning occurs when the zoning authority rezones a lot or larger parcel into a more intensive or less restrictive use; the property is rezoned for the benefit of the owner of the property and not for the public welfare; nearby similarly situated property is not similarly rezoned; and the rezoning is incompatible with the comprehensive plan. Amending the ordinance this way is commonly also a violation of the requirement of the Standard State Zoning Enabling Act's provision that use districts "shall be uniform for each kind or class of building throughout each district." A violation of this uniformity provision invokes a legal analysis that, like equal protection analysis in constitutional law, requires that any classifications made in a law be reasonable.

Courts are wary that a zoning authority will rezone property for the property owner's benefit rather than for the public welfare. If the court feels the zoning amendment favors a landowner at the expense of surrounding property owners or is detrimental to the integrity of the comprehensive plan of development, the court will invalidate the zoning amendment as spot zoning.

Courts' analytical approaches vary. Some courts evaluate the situation and, finding the rezoning of a plot of land runs afoul of relevant standards, invalidate the rezoning as illegal spot zoning. Spot zoning in these jurisdictions is the conclusion. All spot zoning under this approach is illegal. In other jurisdictions, spot zoning merely identifies a rezoning of a plot of land within a district to a more intensive use. Courts in these jurisdictions then review the relevant factors to decide whether the spot zoning is legal.

No single factor determines whether a zoning amendment constitutes illegal spot zoning, but several factors are commonly found in spot zoning cases. One telling factor is whether the land to be rezoned is owned by one person or one group of persons. Other factors indicating spot zoning has occurred include a relatively small lot size or property area to be rezoned and the similarity of the rezoned land to surrounding properties. Generally, each of these factors is given equal weight, and no combination of them is likely to be dispositive.

Analytically, courts evaluate alleged spot zoning violations by answering one or more of the following three questions:

1. **Is the zoning amendment in accord with the comprehensive zoning plan?** Failure of the amendment to conform to the comprehensive zoning plan if the city or county in fact has adopted a comprehensive zoning plan often results in a court invalidating the rezoning. Conversely, courts are prone to defer to the zoning authority's discretion if the amendment conforms to the comprehensive zoning plan. Some courts will look at other factors, especially if the court feels the amendment was for the benefit of one landowner or to the detriment of the community welfare.

2. **Is the rezoned use compatible with uses in the surrounding area?** This test is useful when no comprehensive zoning plan exists, or to aid a court in evaluating whether the rezoning is in conformity with the comprehensive plan of development. The more incompatible the

uses, the more likely a court will strike down the zoning amendment as spot zoning. Not all different or more intensive uses are incompatible, however. Land in a single-family residential use only zone under the right facts may benefit the residential users by being rezoned to retail or multifamily uses, for example.

Example: Landowners own a corner lot in a residential neighborhood one mile from the business district. All lots for five blocks in any direction are used for single-family residences. Landowners petition the town council to rezone the corner lot from single-family residential use only to commercial use so landowners can open an ice-cream parlor. Since the single corner lot is in the middle of a residential district and surrounded completely by homes, the court should invalidate the rezoning as illegal spot zoning. See Eden v. Town Planning and Zoning Committee, 89 A.2d 746 (Conn. 1952).

3. **Does the rezoning serve the public welfare or does it merely confer a benefit to the rezoned property's owner?** A court will balance the public welfare benefit of the proposed zoning amendment against the harm to neighboring lands and to the community in general. A court will scrutinize a zoning amendment closely if the amendment primarily benefits the owner of the rezoned property, especially if there is no ascertainable public benefit and neighboring property owners are harmed. In reviewing a zoning amendment for spot zoning, look for the benefit to the rezoned land's owner, the benefit to the community at large, and the harm to the neighboring property. The most important of these is the benefit to the community. If the benefit to the community is great, such as where the community is underserved by some function, or where significant jobs may be created by the rezoning, complaints by neighboring landowners more likely will fall on deaf ears at trial. On the other hand, if the benefit to the community is negligible, the protesting neighbors are likely to prevail (and the zoning amendment invalidated as spot zoning).

Example: Landowner owns undeveloped property originally zoned residential use only. The property is bounded by a railroad, commercial property, a state highway, and a U.S. highway. Assuming rezoning the property to commercial would not materially benefit the community or harm the community, the fact that the property is surrounded by busy roads and commercial activity favors the landowner in her rezoning effort. Likely no court would find a rezoning from residential to commercial on these facts constitutes spot zoning. To prevail, protesting landowners must identify some harm significant enough for a court to override the local zoning authority's discretion in rezoning the property from residential to commercial.

INITIATIVE AND REFERENDUM

Initiative and referendum refer to actions by citizens through voting. As applied to zoning, an **initiative** describes the process through which citizens petition to have a proposed zoning amendment placed on a ballot, and voters adopt or reject the zoning amendment. A **referendum** occurs after the local zoning authority enacts or amends an ordinance. Either the local zoning authority or a citizens group by a petition containing a required number of signatures has the ordinance or a specific provision placed on the ballot; and the voters decide whether to ratify or repeal the ordinance or provision. The U.S. Supreme Court upheld zoning by initiative and referendum against charges the initiative and referendum constituted an unconstitutional delegation of legislative power. See City of East Lake v. Forest City Enterprises, Inc., 426 U.S. 668 (1976). In contrast, several state constitutions have been interpreted to prohibit zonings by initiative and referendum. Zoning by initiative or by referendum, though constitutional as a process for amending a zoning ordinance, remains subject to the same constitutional challenges as would any zoning action.

CONTRACT AND CONDITIONAL ZONING

Sometimes a local zoning authority sees merit in a landowner's petition to have her property rezoned, but the zoning authority either wishes to limit potential uses of the property or to place some affirmative obligation on the landowner to protect owners of surrounding property. The zoning authority might demand a landowner comply with **conditions** as part of the rezoning. The landowner, for example, may be required to build a fence or plant hedges, to accept increased setbacks, to reduce the building-footage-to-lot-size ratio, or to limit the property to certain uses such as a grocery store. While most courts approve these conditions to a rezoning as an exercise of the police power, some courts reject conditions completely and invalidate some rezonings or some imposed conditions.

While most jurisdictions approve the use of conditions, a few states reject all conditions to a rezoning, and yet other states reject **contract zoning** but permit **conditional zoning**. Under **contract zoning**, the local zoning authority agrees to rezone property if the landowner agrees to certain conditions. Courts distinguishing between contract zoning and conditional zoning invalidate **contract zoning** because the government body by contract has attempted to bargain away its legislative power, which it cannot do. Under **conditional zoning**, on the other hand, the local zoning authority does not consider a rezoning petition until the landowner has recorded some specified affirmative or negative covenants on the use of the property or, alternatively, the zoning authority incorporates the restrictions into the zoning amendment. Technically, the zoning authority is not legally bound to rezone even if the landowner records the stipulated covenants. Courts distinguishing between contract zoning and conditional zoning approve conditional zoning.

Conditional zoning (and contract zoning where acceptable) also faces attack on the basis of being illegal **spot zoning**. See the discussion of spot zoning above. All the considerations discussed under spot zoning, supra, apply: The zoning amendment must conform to the comprehensive plan of development; the rezoned use must be compatible with the uses being made of surrounding property; and the zoning amendment must benefit the district or community rather than the property owner.

FLOATING ZONES, CLUSTER ZONES, AND PUDS

As land-use planners became more sophisticated, they developed new zoning techniques. One current tool is the floating zone. A **floating zone** is a zoning district authorized in a zoning ordinance (where standards for its use are expressly set out) but not located on the zoning map, so that it does not yet encompass any land. The local zoning authority uses its power to locate the zone long after the text of the ordinance is enacted as the need arises and when the proper location becomes more apparent. Thus, the floating zone is the host for a variety of flexible use districts. It is particularly useful for things like garden apartments and commercial office parks. It is more responsive to market forces than the comprehensive planning process, allows both for legislative reflection about the location of a use on the zoning map and for site planning that is thoughtful in ways a more hastily enacted ordinance might not foresee, is not inconsistent with most state enabling acts, and enjoys the presumption of validity accorded legislative actions. On these grounds, most courts considering the validity of floating zones have approved them. The floating zone is a sensible idea, but is fraught with the opportunity for abuse or favoritism. Hence, **spot zoning** analysis must be applied when the floating zone is located.

Cluster zoning is another option sometimes used. **Cluster zoning** allows a developer to overdevelop some land within a larger parcel, increasing the density beyond that allowed in the district, while underdeveloping or dedicating other land in the parcel to parks or leaving it in its natural undeveloped state such that the density for the parcel as a whole stays within the zoning ordinance standards.

The **planned unit development (PUD)** is an extension of cluster zoning that also allows a range of varying uses within a large tract of land. The developer can coordinate single-family and multi-family uses with commercial uses to meet the needs of the residences. Zoning ordinance provisions authorizing PUDs may incorporate density flexibility similar to those allowed under cluster zoning, but the PUD's main attraction is the flexibility of **uses** allowed on the tract. This technique is used mostly for large parcels of land, converting them into very large subdivisions or even new towns.

Examples

Doctor, Lawyer, Insurance Salesman

1. Lisa, a doctor, owned a 1.5-acre lot located in an R-1 Residential zone. A house and a large barn sat on the lot. The local zoning ordinance authorizes professional offices as **special exceptions** in the R-1 Residential district if (1) the professional office will not increase traffic substantially; (2) the users and visitors of the office will not necessitate the expansion of the existing parking area; and (3) the professional office would not result in a devaluation of surrounding property values. The zoning ordinance defines a professional office as "an office maintained by a physician, surgeon, dentist, podiatrist, lawyer, clergyman, architect, professional engineer, landscape architect, artist, teacher, or musician."

    The zoning ordinance specifically excluded from the residential district all "limited business offices" and all "business offices." The ordinance defined limited business offices as including "real estate offices, accounting firms, insurance offices, travel agencies, and similar businesses." The ordinance defined business office as "an activity, other than a professional office, conducted for gain and to which the public is invited or expected to visit in the conduct of the activity." The ordinance authorized the board of adjustment to grant **variances** from the terms of the ordinance "as will not be contrary to the public interest, where, owing to special conditions, a literal enforcement of the provisions of the ordinance will result in unnecessary hardship, and so that the spirit of the ordinance shall be observed and substantial justice done."

    (a) Lisa wants to remodel the barn and use it as her medical office. Will Lisa apply for a special exception or a variance? Will Lisa be allowed to remodel the barn and use it in her medical practice?

    (b) Five years later, Lisa wanted to remodel the top part of the barn and lease the space to Elinor, Attorney at Law, to use as her law office. Would Lisa be able to remodel the top part of the barn and lease it to Elinor? Would Elinor be able to conduct her legal practice in the remodeled barn?

    (c) Five years later, Elinor relocated her law office to another building in town. Lisa's husband, Alec, wanted to use the office for his insurance business. Will Alec be able to conduct his insurance business in the barn?

Three Dimensional Variances

2. Country Living, LLC, owns 60 acres of property zoned RR-80, a zoning district that permits single-family residences on two-acre or larger lots. Country Living plans to subdivide the 60 acres into 5 lots ranging from 8 acres to 15 acres each. Under the proposed subdivision plan, three of the five lots lack the frontage on a public street that the zoning ordinance requires. Under Country Living's plan, the three lots needing access to a public road would share one common road to reach a public road. The planning commission granted preliminary approval to Country Living's subdivision proposal.

   Country Living applied for, and the Town Zoning Board unanimously granted, dimensional variances allowing owners of the three lots to use the common private road instead of having each of the lots front on a public road. Of significance to the Town Zoning Board, Country Living submitted an alternate development plan entailing a much more intensive development scheme that would comply with the frontage requirements. Country Living and the Town Zoning Board favored the five-lot proposal needing the variances because it preserved the rural character of the area. The Town Zoning Board conditioned the grant of the variance on Country Living's placing a deed restriction prohibiting Lot 1 from ever being subdivided.

   Neighboring landowners who did not want the common private road to exit next to their lands challenge the variance, claiming the Zoning Board acted contrary to the ordinance. The challengers claim Country Living could reconfigure the lots to front on a public road and use an adjacent street for egress and ingress into the 60 acres. Under the neighboring landowners' option, Country Living would have to spend money to build or upgrade the public road.

   (a) What is a dimensional variance?
   (b) What is the standard of review when a court reviews a zoning board of appeals grant of a dimensional variance?
   (c) The State Zoning Enabling Act mandates the evidence satisfy the following standards:

   > In granting a variance, the zoning board of appeals shall require that evidence to the satisfaction of the following standards be entered into the record of the proceedings:
   > 1. That the hardship from which the applicant seeks relief is due to the unique characteristics of the subject land or structure and not to the general characteristics of the surrounding area; and is not due to physical or economic disability of the applicant;
   > 2. That the hardship is not the result of any prior action of the applicant and does not result primarily from the desire of the applicant to realize greater financial gain;

3. That the granting of the requested variance will not alter the general character of the surrounding area or impair the intent or purpose of the Ordinance or the Comprehensive Plan upon which the Ordinance is based; and

4. That the relief to be granted is the least relief necessary. [In addition, the Town Zoning Board must satisfy] the following restriction prior to granting a dimensional variance:

The zoning board of review shall, in addition to the above standards, require that the evidence be entered into the record of the proceedings showing that: . . .

In granting a dimensional variance, that the hardship that will be suffered by the owner of the subject property if the dimensional variance is not granted shall amount to more than a mere inconvenience, which shall mean that there is no other reasonable alternative to enjoy a legally permitted beneficial use of one's property. The fact that a use may be more profitable or that a structure may be more valuable after the relief is granted shall not be grounds for relief.

Do the above provisions give the Town Zoning Board adequate guidance, or will a court strike the provision as an unconstitutional delegation of legislative authority?

(d) Assuming the above provision passes constitutional muster, and procedural due process requirements of notice, opportunity to be heard, and a decision based on the facts and reasoning set out in a written record are met, what result on the challengers' suit in court?

School Zone

3. A church plans to build a high school on 18 acres of vacant land it owns in Chatsworth. The school will accommodate 1200-1500 pupils. The school building will occupy 5 percent of the 18 acres, two-thirds of the land will be undeveloped, and the rest will be used for parking and recreational purposes. Events such as football games will take place elsewhere.

The high school is to be located on Royal Avenue. All traffic to and from the school must travel on Royal Avenue. All roads accessing Royal Avenue are two-lane roads serving residential neighborhoods. To accommodate the traffic, the Town of Chatsworth must widen Royal Avenue and build sidewalks and add street lights. The church will build enough off-street parking spaces on the 18 acres for all student and faculty parking.

The 18 acres are in a residential area developed entirely for country or suburban residential living. The high school will change the residential character of the neighborhood and have a slightly depressing effect on real-estate values in the neighborhood. There is a borderline of trees surrounding the 18 acres, however, which will serve as a natural screen to insulate adjoining homeowners from the school.

The city's current sanitary sewer system is adequate to service the increased burden the school would place on it, but the school's construction will increase the runoff of surface water from the land. Consequently, the city may be required to improve its storm sewers.

The 18 acres are located in a district zoned AA-Residential. In addition to residences, the zoning ordinance permits the following uses: "Public utility buildings, a telephone central office, municipal buildings, railway passenger stations, and educational, religious, or philanthropic institutions, with the approval of the Board of Adjustment, excluding hospitals, sanitariums, rest homes, or correctional institutions." The Chatsworth Zoning Ordinance provides that the Board of Adjustment in ruling on variances and special exceptions shall promote the health, safety, morals, and general welfare of the town and citizens of Chatsworth.

(a) The church is applying for a permit to build the high school. Is the church seeking a variance or a special exception?

(b) Should the board of adjustment permit the church to build the high school on the 18 acres?

(c) The church owns a 26-acre tract that according to experts is more suitable for the location of a high school. Does this fact affect the answer to (b)?

Bad Spot on the Road

4. Langum is a growing community. Much of the growth occurs along Pleasant Road, which is the main city road to the town of Thomley. Bill Anderson bought 11 lots on Pleasant Road in an area that has been zoned SR_Single-Family Residential for 17 years. The 11 lots together have a frontage of 1500 feet on Pleasant Road and have a depth of 300 feet. All land on Pleasant Road is used for single-family homes except for a small area near the Thomley town line (about a mile west of the 11 lots). Bill bought the 11 lots intending to move his automobile showroom there to take advantage of the population growth in both Langum and Thomley. Bill applied to the Langum city council to have the 11 lots rezoned from SR–Single-Family Residential to CD-Commercial, which would allow his automobile showroom. The Langum city council after required hearings amended the zoning ordinance to place the 11 lots in a CD-Commercial district. Patsy, a landowner in the district, petitioned the court to invalidate the zoning amendment.

(a) What is the standard of review when a court reviews a zoning amendment?

(b) Should the court uphold or invalidate the zoning amendment?

Explanations

Doctor, Lawyer, Insurance Salesman

1. (a) Lisa's barn is located in an R-1 Residential district. Nonetheless she should be able to remodel the barn and conduct her medical practice by applying to the local board of adjustment (or board of appeals) for a special exception. Professional offices are allowed in the R-1 Residential district as long as the landowner can convince the board of adjustment her use of the barn as a medical office would not increase traffic substantially, she would not expand the parking area, and her medical practice would not affect the value of neighboring properties. Professional offices include medical offices. Lisa should be able to satisfy the other conditions.

   (b) A lawyer's office is a professional office under the ordinance, so Lisa could apply to the board of adjustment for a special exception to allow the upper part of the barn to be used for a law office. Once more Lisa must show the added law office would not increase traffic substantially, she would not expand the parking area, and the surrounding properties' value would not be negatively affected.

   Without more details, it appears the most troublesome element would be the prohibition against expanding the parking areas. Assuming Lisa and Elinor can conduct their respective practices without adding extra parking, the board of adjustment likely will authorize Elinor's law practice as a special exception.

   (c) Alec will not be able to use the barn to conduct his insurance business. While the barn was legally used as a law office and as a medical office as special exceptions, the special exception category does not include business offices or limited business offices. An insurance office is a limited business office under the ordinance. Insurance offices therefore are not permitted as special exceptions in the district. The board of adjustment has no power to authorize Alec's insurance business as a special exception.

   Alec and Lisa could apply for a use variance but it is unlikely the board of adjustment would grant them the use variance. Even though an insurance office seems similar to a medical or law office as to compatibility with the neighborhood and the barn is already remodeled, Lisa and Alec cannot show the unique hardship essential to the grant of a variance.

   An insurance office will be allowed in the district as a use variance only if the landowner suffers a unique hardship in the use of the land and the landowner will suffer an unnecessary hardship if the variance is denied. The only hardship suffered here is that Lisa and Alec cannot use the property for a use prohibited by the local zoning ordinance. The hardship is one that is generally suffered by all land-owners in the district. The hardship (if it even be that) is not unique to them, nor is there some special condition of the property justifying a variance. Lisa and Alec in fact are making effective use of the land. Their personal residence and Lisa's medical practice are located on the land. Lisa can rent out the top half of the barn to another qualified "professional." Thus, it appears that Lisa and Alec are making tremendous use of the land and have suffered no unique hardship at all. Since they suffer no unique hardship, they do not need a variance to ameliorate an unnecessary hardship. Alec cannot operate his insurance office in the barn.

Three Dimensional Variances

2. (a) Dimensional variances are variances related to area, setbacks, street frontage, height, square footage, etc. Dimensional variances are to be contrasted with use variances, which allow a landowner to make some use of the property otherwise impermissible in the district. Zoning boards are more willing to grant, and courts are more willing to approve, dimensional variances than use variances.

   (b) The following standard of review given by the court in Quattrochi v. Finney, 1999 WL 1096064 (Super. Ct. R.I. 1999), the case on which the Example is based, is representative (citations and quotation marks omitted):

> The court shall not substitute its judgment for that of the zoning board of appeals as to the weight of the evidence on questions of fact.
>
> The court may affirm the decision of the zoning board of appeals or remand the case for further proceedings, or may reverse or modify the decision if substantial rights of the appellant have been prejudiced because of findings, inferences, conclusions or decisions which are:
>
> (1) In violation of constitutional, statutory or ordinance provisions;
> (2) In excess of the authority granted to the zoning board of appeals by statute or ordinance;
> (3) Affected by other error of law;
> (4) Clearly erroneous in view of the reliable, probative, and substantial evidence of the whole record; or
> (5) Arbitrary or capricious or characterized by abuse of discretion or clearly unwarranted exercise of discretion.
>
> The essential function of the Zoning Board is to weigh the evidence presented at the hearing, and it has the discretion to either accept or reject any or all of the evidence. This Court must examine and review the entire record to determine whether substantial evidence exists to support the findings of the Zoning Board. Substantial evidence as used

in this context means such relevant evidence that a reasonable mind might accept as adequate to support a conclusion and means an amount more that a scintilla but less than a preponderance. Furthermore, this Court may not substitute its judgment for that of the Zoning Board if it can conscientiously find that the board's decision was supported by substantial evidence in the whole record.

(c) The guidelines easily pass constitutional muster. Courts are more critical of the board's discretion in special exception determinations than for variance grants or denials. Even so, the standards listed in the ordinance — unique hardship, hardship not self-induced, the variance does not impair the purpose of the zoning ordinance or alter the general character of the surrounding area, a hardship more than mere inconvenience but less than a strict necessity standard in determining hardship [a common standard for dimensional variances; a strict necessity standard for use variances is the norm] — are adequate guidelines.

(d) The challengers contended no feature of the property was so unique as to warrant a dimensional variance. The challengers argued Country Living sought the variance mainly to realize a greater financial gain by not having to pay money for an upgraded road. Furthermore, the challengers correctly observed a variance was not needed. Reconfiguring the lots and upgrading an adjacent road was an acceptable alternative, and could be accomplished without a variance. To the challengers, the dimensional variance might make the use more convenient for the landowners; but mere convenience is not a practical difficulty justifying a dimensional variance.

Despite these legitimate concerns, the court refused to find the Board's grant of a dimensional variance was clearly erroneous or arbitrary, an abuse of discretion, or clearly unwarranted. The court was persuaded by Country Living's desire not to alter the general rural character of the area, that the size and shape of the property required the common private road variance for access to the back part of the 60 acres, and that the other option (in which the road improvements would have been made) meant a more intensive development that would detract from the area's rural character. The zoning board concluded the development scheme that the variance made possible promoted rather than impaired the purpose of the zoning ordinance. All things considered, the court could not conclude the Board had erred.

School Zone

3. (a) The church seeks a special exception. Educational institutions are specifically authorized in the district if the Board of Adjustment

approves the use. The approval requirement does not give the Board unfettered discretion. The Board's approval is limited to a determination the applicant satisfies the requirements for a special exception set out in the ordinance.

(b) In re O'Hara, 131 A.2d 587 (Pa. 1957), concluded the Board must authorize the church to build the high school.

The court first concluded the ordinance was not an unconstitutional delegation of legislative authority to the Board. The provision concerning the promotion of health, safety, morals, and general welfare of the town and citizens of Chatsworth "provides sufficient appropriate conditions and safeguards controlling the board's discretion." Id. at 594.

The ordinance specifically allows educational uses in the AA-Residential district. As for the increased traffic, the court noted persuasively that the zoning authorities must have known the use of land would result in increased traffic when they approved educational uses and other uses as special uses in the district. Considering other special exceptions allowed in the district including utility buildings, a telephone central office, a municipal building, and a railway passenger station also would increase traffic with all its attendant noise, dust, dangers, and hazards, the court viewed these consequences as the "inevitable accompaniments of suburban progress and of our constantly expanding population which, standing alone, does not constitute a sufficient reason to refuse a property owner the legitimate use of his land." Id. at 596. For the Board to refuse a special use permit for a use, the anticipated increase in traffic must be so great as to indicate a high degree of probability the traffic will affect the safety and health of the community, not the mere possibility of such effects.

The court similarly minimized the effect on the quiet residential character and on the real estate values. Schools are permitted in the district. Nothing about the use of the site for a high school would change the character of the neighborhood or affect the land values any more than the establishment of any school or church.

In the same vein, the court noted the town in enacting the zoning ordinance anticipated growth and the problems (including added costs) of growth. Among these foreseeable problems and costs was the necessity of the city's improving roads, sewers, and other city services. These additional costs on the city bear no relationship to the health, safety, morals, and general welfare factors that guide the Board in granting or denying the church a special use permit to build the high school. The Board must permit the high school as a special exception in the district.

(c) To quote the Pennsylvania Supreme Court,

> The fact that [the church] owns another site, which in the [Board's or the court's] opinion is more suitable is irrelevant. No court is empowered to substitute its judgment for that of the multiple site owner and, in effect, direct which of several sites is to be used by him for a particular purpose.

Id. at 597. In addition, which is a better site falls outside the considerations listed in the ordinance. The board does not have unfettered discretion to choose its own factors.

Bad Spot on the Road

4. (a) The city council is a legislative body and courts are quite deferential to zoning enactments and amendments. Notwithstanding the deference afforded the city council in zoning matters, a court will invalidate a zoning ordinance or amendment if the ordinance or amendment is arbitrary, capricious, or discriminatory. Of importance in the Example, a rezoning for the benefit of an individual landowner rather than for the public benefit, especially when the amendment is detrimental to the comprehensive plan or harmful to surrounding properties, will be struck down as spot zoning.

   (b) Hines v. City of Attleboro, 244 N.E.2d 316 (Mass. 1969), invalidated this zoning amendment as illegal spot zoning. The area is essentially residential. Nothing about the 11 lots differentiates the 11 lots so much from the surrounding lands that would warrant the zoning amendment.

34

Selected Challenges to Zoning Ordinances

Zoning ordinances sometimes are challenged on constitutional grounds other than those based on the Due Process, see Chapters 32 and 33, supra, and Takings Clauses, see Chapter 35 infra. This chapter discusses some frequently encountered disputes.

AESTHETIC REGULATION

Local governments often regulate on **aesthetic** grounds. This section reviews challenges to government's attempts to regulate signs and billboards, architectural design, and historic districts.

(a) Signs and Billboards

Local zoning authorities have tried to ban or restrict the use and placement of signs and billboards through local ordinances. Ordinances regulating signs and billboards have been challenged on **substantive due process** and on **First Amendment free speech** grounds. Early cases generally invalidated all ordinances regulating aesthetics and signs on **substantive due process** grounds because the state had only the authority to regulate matters that impaired the public "health, safety, and morals." Only if a specific sign or billboard became a nuisance could a government take action against the sign owner. After Village of Euclid v. Ambler Realty Co., 272 U.S. 365 (1926), which justified zoning laws on the broader **general welfare** standard, local zoning authorities justified sign regulation as promoting the general welfare. Aesthetics standing alone was found an insufficient basis for such regulation.

Today courts generally justify sign regulations as aiding the economic well-being of the city by **promoting tourism** or by **preserving the values** of neighboring properties. Other sign regulations are justified as necessary to solve **traffic problems** (sign and billboards are distractions and block drivers' views of pedestrians and other vehicles) or **safety** concerns (criminals could hide behind signs and pounce on unsuspecting victims). A state could, and usually did, complement the economic justifications with a secondary aesthetic appeal. Most courts accepted the aesthetic considerations as long as the aesthetic purpose was a subordinate factor in approving sign regulations, but continued to invalidate ordinances based exclusively on "aesthetics." Today 25 to 30 states permit zoning based solely on aesthetics, about 10 states considering aesthetics permissible as a supplemental factor to bolster other factors such as economic or traffic goals, and about 10 states still reject aesthetics as a legitimate concern of local zoning authorities.

Permitting local zoning authorities to regulate signs and billboards shifted the constitutional argument from substantive due process to the First Amendment **freedom of speech**. As developed more fully in Chapter 32, supra, all laws and ordinances must be the **means** to promote a **legitimate state interest**. A court will uphold an ordinance if the regulation **rationally relates** to the accomplishment of the stated legitimate purpose unless the law or ordinance infringes upon a constitutionally protected right. If the ordinance infringes on a constitutionally protected right of free speech, the state must show (1) the interest it is trying to achieve is a **compelling state interest**, and (2) the ordinance is **narrowly tailored** to **substantially advance** the state's compelling state interest, while (3) infringing as little as possible on the free speech rights.

Five factors are important:

1. Whether the ordinance regulates **commercial speech** or **noncommercial speech**. Noncommercial speech receives great protection whereas commercial speech is afforded only "intermediate" protection.
2. Whether the signs and billboards all are **on-site** (on-premise) or **off-site** (off-premise). On-site signs promote or refer to some activity conducted on the premises where the sign is located. A sign identifying a business conducted on the premises is an on-site sign. Signs located on another's land or along the street or highway promoting a business located elsewhere is an off-site sign. On-site signs (even commercial on-site signs) receive more protection than off-site signs.

3. Whether the regulation is **content-based** or **content-neutral**. Content-based statutes aim at or affect the topic or impact of the sign's message. Courts are much more likely to invalidate content-based ordinances than content-neutral ordinances. Content-neutral regulations aim at location, size, height, or other aspect having nothing to do with the message conveyed by the sign.
4. Whether the sign is located on a **residential** lot. The most protected signs are noncommercial signs on a residential lot.
5. Whether the state is attempting merely to regulate the time, place, or manner of sign placement, or whether the state is attempting to ban a category of signs or billboards.

An ordinance that aims at the content of a sign's message will be struck down as unconstitutional. In contrast, an ordinance that regulates land use (time, place, and manner regulation) will be upheld as constitutional if the regulation is unrelated to the suppression of the speech involved.

Laws regulating commercial use of signs and billboards, including absolute bans on certain types of signs, will be upheld if the government offers a legitimate state interest; and the law **substantially advances** the legitimate state interest. The required means/end relation is more demanding than the typical rational relationship test, however. The distinction between the "rational relationship" and the "substantially advances" standards puts a greater onus on the government to show it has not overregulated the placement or physical appearance of commercial signs.

While a state can differentiate between different types of **commercial signs**, courts will scrutinize more closely those ordinances aimed at commercial speech that appear to be **content-based** rather than **content-neutral**. Courts guard against a state's "rationalization of an impermissible purpose." For example, courts have struck down ordinances ostensibly for aesthetic or safety reasons that really attempt to fight adult bookstores or to stop "white flight."

Judicial scrutiny increases dramatically when the ordinance infringes upon **noncommercial speech**. Noncommercial speech includes political speech, which is afforded absolute or near absolute protection. The first question concerning ordinances that infringe on noncommercial speech is whether the statute or ordinance at issue is a content-based or a content-neutral regulation. Courts invalidate content-based regulations that are not narrowly tailored to promote a compelling state interest. Aesthetic, traffic safety, and mere economic concerns do not qualify as compelling state interests. In effect, courts declare nearly all content-based regulations of noncommercial speech to be unconstitutional.

Example: City, citing traffic safety and aesthetic reasons, enacts an ordinance prohibiting all outdoor commercial and noncommercial signs. The ordinance exempts all on-site commercial signs that relate to the activities conducted on the property from the prohibition. Upon judicial review, a court will hold City can ban all off-site commercial signs, but cannot ban on-site or off-site noncommercial signs. See Metromedia, Inc. v. City of San Diego, 453 U.S. 490, 514 (1981).

On the other hand, a court will uphold a content-neutral regulation, even one that infringes on free speech or free expression, if (a) the ordinance promotes a substantial state interest unrelated to the sign's message; (b) the ordinance is narrowly tailored so as to minimally affect the individual's free speech rights, and (c) other reasonable methods of communicating the same information are available. Aesthetic, traffic, safety, and economic concerns qualify as substantial state interests.

Noncommercial signs on residential property receive near absolute protection. The Supreme Court in City of Ladue v. Gilleo, 512 U.S. 43 (1994), invalidated a content-neutral ordinance that banned almost all signs on residential property. The Court used such phrases as "special respect for individual liberty in the home" and "venerable means of communication that is both unique and important," and stressed the uniqueness and affordability of noncommercial signs on residential property to conclude the city could not ban residential signs. No adequate substitute exists for noncommercial residential signs.

(b) Architectural Controls

Architectural design ordinances require that a proposed structure conform to minimum architectural design standards before a city will grant the landowner a building permit. Usually the proposed structure's external appearance and function must not be so at variance with other structures in the district or neighborhood as to cause a substantial depreciation in values of neighboring properties. While a few architectural design ordinances mandate a variety of architectural plans to prevent a monotonous sameness of homes, most architectural ordinances promote conformity of appearance and function. Critics charge the architectural design ordinances suppress innovation, expression, and creativity.

Challengers to the ordinances make predictable arguments. First, the landowner might argue the state enabling act does not authorize an aesthetic standard. Usually the enabling statute does authorize an aesthetic standard. Second, the landowner might claim the ordinance does not set out sufficient standards to guide the administrative board and thus is an unconstitutional delegation of legislative authority. This argument is sometimes successful in the proper fact situation. A third argument is that the standards in the ordinance are too vague. Homeowners sometimes, but only rarely, prevail on this argument.

Finally, an argument that courts have not yet accepted is that the external architectural design of a home or any structure should be protected under the First Amendment as freedom of speech (broadly construed as freedom of expression). If courts were to treat architectural design as protected free speech or free expression, an analysis comparable to that described above relating to regulation of signs and billboards would severely restrict the power of architectural boards to consider aesthetics. Most likely, architectural boards would be limited to a review of architectural designs for safety, fire hazard, or under other standards unrelated to how the structure compares with those in the surrounding area. Maintaining conformity and aesthetics then would be left to restrictions between private landowners. See generally Chapter 31, supra.

(c) Historic Districts

A specialized form of architectural design ordinance concerns historic districts. Historic district ordinances predate the more general community-wide architectural design ordinances. Governments pass historic district ordinances to preserve the exterior appearance of historical or architecturally significant buildings, monuments, and districts. The ordinances also prohibit demolition of structures in the historic district and may restrict landowners' attempts to build new buildings in the district. Preservation of historic districts for aesthetics, historic, cultural, and tourism reasons is a legitimate state interest.

Historic district ordinances are constitutional. The main constitutional challenge, usually unsuccessful, is that the administrative board reviewing and approving (or disapproving) all plans for demolition, construction, and remodeling in the district constitutes an unconstitutional delegation of legislative power to the administrative body.

Denial of permits to demolish or improve structures in an historic district may result in a claim the denial resulted in a **taking** of the property by the government. Usually the takings claims fail in historic district cases. Takings are developed further in the next chapter.

ADULT ENTERTAINMENT

Adult entertainment facilities include movie houses; adult bookstores; adult video stores; strip, nude, and topless clubs; massage parlors; and escort services. The Supreme Court has held that the First Amendment protects adult entertainment as free speech or freedom of expression. Hence an outright ban on adult entertainment establishments because city leaders oppose adult entertainment is unconstitutional. The constitutional analysis to be applied in the regulation of adult entertainment establishments parallels the analysis set out above on the regulation of signs and billboards. Supreme Court guidance, however, is inconsistent, and we will cover only the essential factors here.

Some elements are basic. An ordinance that aims at the content (pornography) will be struck down as unconstitutional. An ordinance that regulates land use (time, place, and manner regulation) will be upheld as constitutional if the regulation is unrelated to the suppression of the speech involved. Specifically, (1) the state must be trying to promote a **substantial state interest** (higher than a mere legitimate state interest) unrelated to the suppression of the speech; (2) the means chosen (the ordinance) must advance the substantial state interest; (3) the ordinance must be **narrowly tailored** to achieving the substantial state interest, infringing as little as possible freedom of speech or expression.

Substantial state interests include minimizing the problems associated with traffic, parking, prostitution, crime, juvenile delinquency, vagrancy, depreciation of property values, and deterioration of retail areas. For example, the Supreme Court accepts "quality of urban life" as a legitimate goal in regulating adult entertainment facilities. One complicating factor is that a state has a legitimate interest in combating obscenity. Obscenity is illegal, and the state has the power and right to prohibit obscenity. What is obscenity is beyond the scope of your Property course, but the fact that obscene materials and acts are illegal results in some leeway for states to monitor and regulate adult establishments. See generally City of Erie v. Pap's A.M. dba Kandyland, 529 U.S. 277 (2000). Another complicating factor is that legitimate (and substantial) state interests include the promotion of health, safety, morals, and the general welfare. States can pass laws to combat prostitution, for example. The morals aspect includes public decency standards. Courts will uphold long-standing decency laws of general application as long as the laws are not aimed at adult establishments alone.[1]

The second element — that the ordinance advance a substantial state interest unrelated to suppression of free speech — prevents officials from rationalizing a law actually aimed at the content of adult entertainment rather than at its secondary consequences. It permits courts to determine the officials' predominant purpose in enacting the ordinance despite their stated purpose.

Similarly, courts will invoke the narrowly-tailored element to invalidate vague or overbroad ordinances. Vague and overbroad laws are those that

---

1. As another avenue to regulate adult establishments, the Twenty-First Amendment gives states the right to regulate the sale of alcoholic beverages. The states enjoy great latitude in regulating the sale of alcoholic beverages. Many states use this power to regulate the sale of alcohol, to prohibit the sale of alcoholic beverages in adult establishments, or to put restrictions on the entertainment offered in the establishment as a condition of receiving a license to serve alcohol.

have a "chilling" effect on free speech, free expression or other constitutional right. Laws that have a chilling effect on the exercise of fundamental rights like free speech and free expression will be struck down. Ordinances that give too much discretion to a licensing authority will be struck down either for vagueness or as an unconstitutional delegation of legislative power to an administrative body.

Courts approve many ordinances regulating adult entertainment. The Supreme Court, for example, has approved ordinances that disperse adult entertainment businesses to minimize the harm to any one part of town. The opposite stratagem, requiring all adult entertainment businesses to concentrate into one (or one of several) locations (referred to as "combat zones") also have been approved. On the other hand, an ordinance that prohibits all live entertainment but which is enforced only against adult entertainment establishments is unconstitutional. See Schad v. Mount Ephraim, 452 U.S. 61 (1981).

The Supreme Court has approved ordinances that ban all public nudity including nude dancing in a nude dancing cabaret. Barnes v. Glen Theatre, Inc., 501 U.S. 560 (1991). *Barnes* resulted in four separate opinions. Three justices called the ordinance one of general application promoting the public decency. The ordinance was enacted before the advent of nude dancing clubs so regulating nude dancing clubs could not have been a predominant purpose of the statute when it was enacted. Justice Scalia said nude dancing is not speech or expression protected by the First Amendment. Justice Souter said nudity is a condition not the expression. To Justice Souter, it is the dance that is the protected expression not the condition of being nude. The dissenting justices constituted the largest number of justices to agree on any view. They concluded, alternatively, that nude dancing deserves First Amendment protection, or, under the regulation at issue, nude dancing inside a club is not public nudity.

The Supreme Court's tendency to treat adult entertainment as a lower class of speech deserving a lesser degree of protection and allowing cities to regulate such establishments is reflected in the City of Renton v. Playtime Theatre, Inc., 475 U.S. 41 (1986). The ordinance in *City of Renton* prohibited the location of adult movie theaters within 1000 feet of all residential areas (including apartments), churches, and parks, and prohibited locating an adult theater within one mile of any school, ostensibly to offset the negative secondary effects of adult movie theaters. The Court approved the ordinance as a reasonable time, place, and manner regulation. That the ordinance effectively restricted the movie theater to about 5% of the area of the town and that the available areas were not viable locations for the theaters was irrelevant said the Court. The Court said 5% of the town's land (or 520 acres in the case) was enough locations to allow reasonable alternative avenues of communication.

HOUSEHOLD COMPOSITION OF SINGLE-FAMILY RESIDENCES

The highest zone or district in cumulative zoning ordinances is the single-family residential use only district. Of critical importance in many cases is the meaning or definition of "single-family residence." Certainly the definition excludes apartments, boarding houses, and other multifamily residential uses, and obviously excludes retail and other commercial activities. The term could also describe the type of structure being used for noncommercial purposes. Most ordinances, however, define single-family residences in terms of the number of people and the legal relationships of those persons as constituting a "single family." Often the ordinance limits the term to persons related by blood or marriage, or to a maximum of three or four persons unrelated by blood or marriage. The issue is the extent to which the state may regulate the composition of households as "single families."

(a) Village of Belle Terre v. Boraas

Two Supreme Court cases consider constitutional due process limitations. In the first, Village of Belle Terre v. Boraas, 416 U.S. 1 (1974), the Supreme Court approved as constitutional an ordinance that defined "family" as follows:

> [O]ne or more persons related by blood, adoption, or marriage, living and cooking together as a single housekeeping unit, exclusive of household servants. A number of persons but not exceeding two (2) living and cooking together as a single housekeeping unit though not related by blood, adoption, or marriage shall be deemed to constitute a family.

The landowner in *Belle Terre* rented a home to six unrelated college students. The village ordered the landlord to comply with a single-family residential ordinance. Instead, the landlord and three of the tenants challenged the ordinance. The majority opinion at the Supreme Court found a legitimate state interest in controlling noise, traffic, and parking, and in promoting quiet seclusion, clean air, family values, and youth values. The means chosen, the definition of "family," was rationally related to the promotion of the legitimate state interests. Critically, the majority found no infringement on a fundamental constitutional right, nor was the categorization based on blood and legal relationships a violation of the Equal Protection Clause of the Constitution (unrelated persons are not a "suspect" class).

Justice Thurgood Marshall in an oft-printed dissent argued the zoning ordinance unnecessarily burdened the tenants' First Amendment freedom of association rights and the constitutional rights to privacy and of liberty. The right of association, according to Justice Marshall, extends to selection of living companions, and not just who can visit. Justice Marshall further believed that all matters related to establishing a home, including choice of household companions, implicates the right of privacy and of liberty.

(b) Moore v. City of East Cleveland

The Supreme Court returned to the definition of family in Moore v. City of East Cleveland, 431 U.S. 494 (1977). East Cleveland's ordinance defined family in "single-family" to include a head of the household and spouse and all their unmarried children who did not themselves have any children living with them. The ordinance then provided that one dependent married child and his spouse and their children or an unmarried child and his or her children also could live in the home.

Living with Mrs. Moore were one of her sons and his son (Mrs. Moore's first grandson), which the ordinance permitted. Mrs. Moore had a second son, who was a single parent. The son went out of town to find work, leaving his son (Mrs. Moore's second grandson) to live with Mrs. Moore. This violated the ordinance. The city issued an "illegal occupant" notice to Mrs. Moore, and when she did not send her second grandson away, the city brought criminal charges against Mrs. Moore. She was convicted and sentenced to five days in jail and fined $25.

The Supreme Court plurality held "the Constitution protects the sanctity of the family." The family includes persons related by blood and marriage and extends at least to uncles and grandchildren.

In summary, Belle Terre permits zoning authorities to limit the number of unrelated persons that may live in a house as a single family. Moore, on the other hand, prohibits the zoning authorities from limiting the number of related persons that can constitute a family (but see (d) below: Ordinance can establish maximum number of people who may live in home, whether the persons are related or not).

(c) State Constitutional and Statutory Law

As Belle Terre signifies, local governments enjoy wide latitude under the U.S. Constitution to restrict the composition of "family" as long as the government does not limit the number of persons related by blood, marriage, or adoption from being a "family." Some state constitutions and state statutory laws offer more protections in this area. Some state courts, for example, have interpreted their own constitutions to prohibit the ordinance approved in *Belle Terre.*

(d) Fair Housing Act and Group Homes

Congress enacted the Fair Housing Act, 42 U.S.C. §§ 3602 et seq., to prohibit discrimination in the sale or renting of property on the basis of race, color, religion, sex, handicap, familial status, or national origin. **Familial status** means parents or a parent with dependent children under age 18. One of the groups protected by the Fair Housing Act includes the handicapped. **Handicap** means, with respect to a person, (1) a physical or mental impairment which substantially limits one or more of such person's major life activities; (2) a record of having such impairment; or (3) being regarded as having such impairment; but the term does not include current, illegal use of or addiction to a controlled substance.

One particular area of litigation involves the Fair Housing Act's effect has on group homes. **Group homes** refer to houses where a relatively small number of people with some common attribute live together instead of living in a larger institution. It helps the residents maintain or adjust to a normal life in the community. Group homes generally house foster children, juvenile offenders, recovering drug addicts, alcoholics, disabled persons, and criminals ready for release (halfway homes). As you may suspect, group homes often are not welcome additions to a neighborhood.

Although the Fair Housing Act applies to all state and local government, the Act itself specifically exempts "any reasonable local, State, or Federal restrictions regarding the maximum number of occupants permitted to occupy a dwelling." 42 U.S.C. § 3607(b)(1). The prohibited "discrimination" is not only active discrimination, but also "a refusal to make reasonable accommodations in rules, policies, practices, or services, when such accommodations may be necessary to afford such persons equal opportunity to use and enjoy a dwelling." 42 U.S.C. § 3604(f)(3)(B) (1999).

The Supreme Court interpreted the Fair Housing Act to prohibit cities from passing zoning ordinances that discriminate against group homes housing protected individuals. See City of Edmonds v. Oxford House, Inc., 514 U.S. 725 (1995). In *Oxford House*, the City of Edmonds defined "family" as "an individual or two or more persons related by genetics, adoption, or marriage, or group of five or fewer persons who are not related by genetics, adoption, or marriage." Oxford House opened a group home for adults recovering from alcoholism and drug addiction. The number of residents ranged from ten to twelve people at any given time. Since ten to twelve people was greater than the five unrelated occupants permitted under the local ordinance, the City of Edmonds issued a criminal citation to Oxford House. Oxford House countered, claiming the city must accommodate the group home under the Fair Housing Act. The city countered, citing § 3607(b)(1)'s exemption for "any reasonable local . . . restriction regarding the maximum number of occupants permitted to occupy a building." The Supreme Court addressed only whether the city's "five unmarried persons to a family" language was exempt from Fair Housing Act coverage. The Supreme Court said the Fair Housing Act § 3607 exemption did not protect the city. According to the majority, the city adopted the maximum-of-five-unrelated-persons language to preserve the family character of the neighborhood. The Court concluded the city could not by subterfuge restrict the number of unrelated handicapped persons in a household, who were protected under the Fair Housing Act, while imposing no similar restriction on families.

According to the Supreme Court, the § 3607 exemption includes provisions that cap the number of persons who may occupy a dwelling, whether or not related. The provisions are usually correlated with square footage or number of bedrooms.

The City of Edmonds, therefore, was required to accommodate group homes for persons in the protected classes under the Fair Housing Act. The city still could limit all homes of a certain size to a maximum number of bedrooms, number of people, or square footage (which it did elsewhere in the ordinance). It also could enforce the five-unrelated-persons ordinance against persons who are not part of a protected class. Fraternity and sorority houses, for example, are not protected. So the six students in *Belle Terre* discussed above would not be protected either.

EXCLUSIONARY ZONING

Zoning is an exercise in separation. A city can and does exclude many activities and structures from the various districts or zones. In *Ambler Realty*, for example, the Supreme Court favored the separation of apartment dwellers from families living in houses. Many ordinances also exclude mobile homes from single-family residential districts. Because of the socioeconomic status of the persons differ among persons likely to live in houses, apartments, and mobile homes, zoning on these bases segregates classes of people. How far may a community go to exclude people rather than structures and uses from the city or zones within the community?

An ordinance based on a **suspect class** (race, color, religion, or national origin) will be struck down as unconstitutional on equal protection or substantive due process ground, or as illegal on a statutory basis. Subtle racial discrimination provisions and ordinances may be invalidated as unconstitutional if the aggrieved person proves the city acted with a **discriminatory intent** or **purpose**. See Village of Arlington Heights v. Metropolitan

Housing Development Corp., 429 U.S. 252 (1977). A plaintiff class may submit statements of political leaders or associations with past discrimination practices as evidence of the leaders' discriminatory intent or purpose. A mere **discriminatory impact** or **effect**, however, does not warrant constitutional relief.

Most actions today are brought under the Fair Housing Act or state laws. Courts hold aggrieved plaintiffs may prevail under the Fair Housing Act by showing **discriminatory impact** or **effect** rather than the harder to prove **discriminatory intent**. Likewise, some state courts interpret their state constitution or state statutes such that discriminatory impact or effect, especially if the ordinance continues past discriminatory practices, will be enough to violate the state's constitution or statute.

A growing issue revolves around cities' struggle to offer services while keeping taxes low. Most local governments try to offer the highest quality of life and governmental services at the lowest cost to the citizen taxpayers. The ideal mix is a high property tax base from clean industry coupled with a low need for public services. Education is a major expense for local communities. A major portion of local government's budget must be allocated to schools and the education system. A local government can reduce taxes and maintain lower taxes on property owners by keeping the number of school-age children low.

To achieve an optimal mix of high-income citizens needing a minimum of municipal services, a city ordinance may specify larger-than-needed minimum lot sizes and minimum floor area for all new homes. These zoning standards increase the cost of land and buildings, making moving to the community viable only for people of moderate or high income or wealth. Thus the persons living in the community more likely will pay enough property taxes to cover the costs of educating their children. Prohibiting mobile homes and apartments also serves to exclude poorer families, who probably do not pay even close to enough taxes to fund the costs of educating their children. Local zoning authorities usually can justify (critics say "rationalize") these provisions as serving some legitimate state interests.

Socioeconomic class (or being poor) is not a suspect class, so the federal Constitution's Equal Protection Clause does not prohibit zoning ordinances that disfavor the poor. Neither does the Fair Housing Act protect the poor from exclusionary zoning practices. Four or five states, mainly in the Northeast, have found their state constitutions or state zoning enabling acts impose a duty to provide opportunity for all citizens to live in every community.

The most famous of this series of cases started with a review of a Mt. Laurel, New Jersey, ordinance. See Southern Burlington County NAACP v. Township of Mount Laurel, 336 A.2d 713 (N.J. 1975). Mount Laurel is a small bedroom community whose community leaders were worried about urban sprawl from Camden, New Jersey. The zoning ordinance aimed at keeping government expenditures low and the value of land high. The city imposed minimum lot sizes, minimum lot widths, and minimum floor area for houses so that as a practical matter only middle- and upper-income families could afford the homes (low- and moderate-income families could not afford to live in Mount Laurel).[2] Developers were required to dedicate 15 percent to 25 percent of all developed land to public uses, such as schools, parks, public buildings, etc., as required by the planning board. Apartments and other multi-family units were allowed in a few areas. With an eye to keeping the number of school-age children to a minimum (to save on education expenses), the city limited apartments to one and two bedrooms; no school-age children could live in a one-bedroom apartment; and no more than two school-age children could live in a two-bedroom apartment. In an intriguing provision, if for a multi-family complex an average of more than a certain number of schoolchildren attended the town's schools in a year, the *developer* had to pay the tuition and expenses attributable to the excess number of children. There were other provisions, but their net effect was to force developers to raise the price of land sold, thereby limiting purchasers to upper- and middle-income persons who had no more than a certain number of school-age children.

The New Jersey Supreme Court concluded New Jersey's zoning enabling act and its state constitution both required zoning laws to promote the general welfare. The "welfare" contemplated was of all citizens and areas of the region, not just those within the township's boundaries. Mount Laurel's exclusionary ordinance affected other cities and towns in the area. Once enough facts were introduced to show an ordinance's "presumptive invalidity" by not serving the general welfare, the burden shifted to the township to justify its zoning practices. Mere fiscal reasons would not serve to justify the exclusionary practice. Mount Laurel offered ecological and environmental justifications, which the court brushed aside under the facts of the case (but which the court said could be a legitimate consideration in some cases). As a remedy, Mount Laurel was required to take appropriate action to fulfill "its fair share of the regional need for low and moderate income housing."

Exclusionary zoning remedies are many and various. First, plaintiff home builders are often given a "builder's remedy" — that is, the right to build as they proposed. Such a remedy is preferable to invalidating the zoning and remitting the builder once more to a balky legislative process, and it is aimed at giving plaintiffs an incentive to challenge exclusionary ordinance provisions. Second, the beneficiaries of the remedy must be defined — typically,

---

2. The minimum sizes were not outrageously large, and to those of you from the South and West, they will sound sensible or even downright small. The minimum floor area, for example, was 1,100 square feet for a house. The minimum lot size in the most restricted area was one half acre (smaller lots were allowed in other zones).

these are (besides the plaintiff) the would-be purchasers of "affordable housing" excluded by ordinance provisions that raise the cost of housing beyond what they can afford. Affordable housing is not least-cost housing or low-income housing; it is generally a stripped-down version of what the builder would otherwise construct. Third, remedies often impose mandatory duties on political subdivisions to rezone land for affordable housing — adding, say, a townhouse-use district to a single-family residential community. In order to impose such duties, however, a court first has to figure out how many townhouses fulfill the defendant community's obligation to provide its "fair share" of the regional need for them. Its share might be figured on the basis of a whole metropolitan region, or on the basis of the land available in urbanizing areas of the region, or on the basis of the land available within commuting distance of the jobs that persons able to afford such housing might hold. These are complex issues, and though they may be triggered by a court case or the denial of a rezoning involving affordable housing, the task of resolving them often winds up as an administrative matter handled by a state urban planning department.

Examples

Protest Signs

1. Maui quarreled with his neighbor for several years concerning the neighbor's dog (which was always on the verge of attacking Maui) and the neighbor's wood-burning stove (which, as operated, polluted the air). Maui finally brought a nuisance action to force the neighbor to get rid of the dog and the wood-burning stove. The court dismissed both complaints.

    Maui posted signs in his front yard to protest the court's decision and to condemn his neighbor's failure to control his dog and his neighbor's wood-burning stove. The signs read: "Warning: Town Justice Allows Neighbor's Biting Dog to Run Loose!!"; "Tie up Your Biting Dog"; "Poison Your Own Air, Not Ours!"; "Stop the Smoke Pollution"; "God Will Not Forsake Us"; "Let the Truth Be Known"; and "Neighbors and Town Want to Do Away with Our Freedom of Speech and Our Right to Protest!" The Town's building inspector issued an Order to Remedy to Maui to remove the signs for violating the local zoning ordinance. The zoning ordinance permitted several types of signs without a permit, including all on-site advertising, address signs, identification signs for hotels and non-dwelling buildings, and for sale and rental signs. A section of the ordinance also allowed signs and billboards

    > in the interest of public information and convenience, [if] the Building Inspector upon approval of the Zoning Board of Appeals, issues a temporary

permit for a period to be designated by said Board. Such temporary signs shall be completely removed by the property owner at the termination of the permit.

Maui applied for seven permits for each of seven signs he wished to keep in his front yard. At a full hearing before the zoning board of appeals, several neighbors opposed the application because they believed Maui's signs were dangerous and could cause accidents. The zoning board of appeals granted Maui a temporary permit allowing him to post the seven signs for two weeks. The two-week period was not acceptable to Maui. Maui filed this suit seeking a restraining order to prevent the city from enforcing the ordinance against him.

Was the sign ordinance constitutional as applied to Maui?

More Protest Signs

2. As the case from Example 1 came to trial, the town replaced the original sign ordinance with the following ordinance:

A. Purpose. The Town's ability to attract economic development activity is accomplished in part by the enforcement of regulations that maintain an attractive community and streetscape, of which signs are a contributing element. A multiplicity of signs clutter the overall appearance of the Town, detracts from its visual quality, and shall be discouraged.

B. Permit Required. Except for signs erected for the identification of the occupant of a single-family or two-family dwelling, no sign shall be erected or installed upon any structure or upon any land, nor shall existing signs be changed, until a sign permit has been obtained from the Building Inspector. No sign shall be erected for any development requiring site development plan or subdivision approval by the Planning Board, without sign plan approval by the Planning Board.

Town Code § 199-15.

Further, the amended ordinance provided a list of exempted signs for which no permit was required. Exempted signs included signs required by government bodies; traffic control signs; government flags; emblems and banners or name and meeting-place signs of civic, philanthropic, educational, or religious organizations or institutions; signs relating to the tenant's membership in a professional or civic organization; temporary signs pertaining to campaigns, drives, or events of civic, philanthropic, educational, or religious institutions, provided the signs are not erected more than three weeks prior to the event, and are removed not later than two weeks after the event; memorial plaques; signs required to be posted by law; signs indicating the name or address of occupant; sale or rental signs; temporary construction signs; signs announcing a change in the status of a business; signs not visible outside a building; signs displayed in a window indicating a public telephone or notary; holiday decorations in season; temporary signs for garage sales; and "No Trespassing" signs.

Of relevance to Maui, § 199-15(B) authorizes, among others, the following signs without a permit:

> (18) Signs setting forth matters of public information and convenience (i.e., statements of personal opinion), including statements of protest other than temporary signs referred [to elsewhere]; and provided that the size of such sign does not exceed twelve (12) square feet, not more than two (2) signs are placed upon any property, unless such property fronts upon more than one (1) street, in which event two (2) more signs may be erected in each additional frontage, subject to the size requirements established in this paragraph.

Town Code § 199-15(B)(18).

The town offered on the first day of trial to allow Maui to post two signs in accordance with the new ordinance. Maui is unwilling to accept the town's offer; and seeks a declaration the new ordinance is unconstitutional. Is the amended sign ordinance constitutional as applied to Maui?

The Bosom of Democracy

3. Plaintiffs planned to open an adult cabaret featuring topless dancing. Plaintiffs bought land located 500 feet from a private, family-oriented campground and 500 feet from the town's only public park. Local citizen groups actively opposed the cabaret. After three public meetings, the town council adopted an ordinance prohibiting all persons from operating an adult cabaret (defined as a nightclub, bar, restaurant, or similar establishment in which persons appear in a state of nudity) without a valid permit. The council could deny a permit application if the cabaret violated any zoning ordinance. The council also enacted an ordinance that "No adult cabaret shall be established or operated on a parcel of real estate within 1,000 feet of the boundaries of any other parcel of real estate having situated on it . . . a public playground or township park, including campgrounds, public or private." Because plaintiffs' proposed adult cabaret was to be located within 1000 feet of both a campground and a township park, the town council denied plaintiffs' permit application. Plaintiffs filed suit seeking declaratory relief that the council must grant plaintiffs a permit.
   (a) What is plaintiffs' theory they should receive the permit?
   (b) Is the ordinance content-based or content-neutral? What is the significance of this determination?

(c) Is the state interest being furthered a substantial state interest unrelated to the suppression of speech or expression?

(d) Assuming you found a substantial state interest unrelated to the suppression of speech or expression in (c), does the regulation advance that interest?

(e) Is the ordinance narrowly tailored to promote the substantial state interest, infringing as little as possible on the freedom of speech or expression?

Family Values

4. (a) Bedford's local zoning ordinance limits occupancy of homes and apartments. There must be a minimum of 200 square feet of habitable space for the first occupant and 150 additional square feet for each additional occupant. Thus, for four occupants, a house or apartment must have 650 square feet of habitable floor space. Bedford passed the ordinance in part due to residents' concern that too many people living in one apartment, unsupervised children, children playing in unsafe environments (e.g., balconies, parking lots, hallways, elevators), noise, and overcrowding were dangerous and unhealthy conditions. Bedford also has a good school system and too many people moved to Bedford specifically because of the schools. There is some indication some people favored the ordinance to stop an influx of people who wanted to live in Bedford for the schools, but that was not the town's main stated reason for enacting the ordinance.

    A group challenges Bedford's ordinance as violating the Fair Housing Act prohibition against discriminating against tenants and purchasers based on familial status. Bedford defends, citing the Fair Housing Act § 3607 exemption discussed in (d) Fair Housing Act and Group Homes, supra. Does § 3607 of the Fair Housing Act serve as a defense for Bedford?

   (b) The Building Officials and Code Administrators (BOCA) (BOCA is a national organization of housing experts) has adopted a model code that sets forth the following minimum occupancy standards: A minimum of 70 square feet of habitable space per person in a *bedroom* for the first occupant and 120 square feet of habitable space in a bedroom sleeping more than one person. Thus a four-occupant house or apartment must have 240, 260, or 280 square feet of habitable space in bedrooms to meet the BOCA model code (dependent on the number of people to a bedroom). In addition, under the BOCA model code, a dwelling with three or four occupants must have a minimum of 100 square feet in a living room, 80 square feet in a dining-room, and 50 square feet in the kitchen. Other

623

national organizations propose occupancy standards based on the maximum number of persons permitted per bedroom (usually two persons to a bedroom) rather than any square footage standards for either the bedroom or for the dwelling unit as a whole. Does the BOCA model code change your answer to Example (a)?

Explanations

Protest Signs

1. The ordinance is unconstitutional. The Supreme Court has said noncommercial residential signs are entitled to the highest protection afforded by the Constitution. While a city can regulate the size of residential signs and otherwise can regulate signs if the regulation is content-neutral, the ordinance in the case distinguishes signs based on content. The ordinance allows on-site advertising, for sale signs, etc., without a permit, whereas other signs, such as Maui's political speech signs, are subject to regulation. The ordinance, therefore, is content-based and not content-neutral. A court will evaluate the content-based ordinance under a strict scrutiny standard.

   Since the regulation is content-based, the ordinance is presumptively invalid. To prevail, the city must show the ordinance serves a compelling state interest (and not just a substantial state interest) and the ordinance is narrowly tailored to achieve the compelling state interest. The facts do not give the reason for the ordinance, but aesthetics and maybe traffic and safety concerns seem viable state interests here. These are substantial state interests; but they are not compelling state interests. Moreover, the ordinance is not narrowly tailored to achieve aesthetics, traffic, or safety concerns.

   In addition, the ordinance allows some commercial signs to be permanent whereas noncommercial signs "in the public interest" are only allowed temporarily and then only if the board of zoning appeals in its discretion allows the signs. The board of zoning appeals' unbridled discretion also may constitute an unconstitutional delegation of legislative authority to an administrative body.

More Protest Signs

2. The district court in Knoeffler v. Town of Mamakating, 87 F. Supp. 2d 322 (S.D.N.Y. 2000), held the amended ordinance was unconstitutional, also. First, the ordinance was content-based rather than content-neutral. While requiring a license for all signs, commercial and noncommercial, the ordinance exempted some signs from the license requirement based on the type of message conveyed by the sign, and commercial signs were

treated more favorably than noncommercial signs. The regulation of content-based signs is subject to a strict scrutiny analysis. The town must show a compelling state interest and show the regulation is narrowly tailored to achieve the compelling state interest. Aesthetics, traffic, and safety are not compelling state interests (they are substantial state interests but not compelling state interests).

Here, the town justified the sign ordinance as a means to attract economic development activity to the town. The court specifically refused to decide whether attracting business to the town was a compelling state interest on the facts, but concluded instead that even if attracting business was a compelling state interest, the sign ordinance was not narrowly tailored to achieve that end. Moreover, the court did not believe that state interest was compelling enough to outweigh the "uniquely valuable and important mode of communication" that is the residential sign. The court concluded with the following explanation:

> [The town's] laudable efforts to preserve the attractiveness of the town's residential areas, enhance the homeowners' enjoyment of their property, attract new residents and maintain property values deserve all the support the courts can properly give. There is less inherent sympathy for a homeowner who undermines those efforts by erecting a small forest of unsightly signs on his property. But where the municipality permits signs of any kind on private property, it cannot discriminate against comparable signs publicizing real or imagined grievances against one's neighbors or the town administration. Indeed, this form of speech affords the speaker considerable "bang for the buck." Plaintiff in this case has undeniably received great notoriety for his messages with a minimal monetary outlay. Others might wish he had chosen a less obtrusive mode of expression, but the true freedom of speech assures the speaker not only control of the content of his message but also a reasonable choice of delivery media, including all those available for messages of less controversial content.

Id. at 333.

The Bosom of Democracy

3. (a) Plaintiffs claim the regulation of topless dancing infringes on the First Amendment right of free speech or free expression.
   (b) The court said the ordinance was content-neutral. The federal district court in Harris v. Fitchville Township Trustees, 99 F. Supp.2d 837 (N.D. Ohio 2000), concluded the ordinance regulated conduct— i.e., persons in a state of nudity—regardless of whether that nudity was accompanied by any expressive activity. The significance of this determination that the ordinance is content-neutral is that the court

will not apply a strict scrutiny analysis. Instead a more relaxed standard of review applies, asking whether the regulation furthers an important or substantial state interest unrelated to the suppression of the speech or expression; whether the regulation advances the substantial state interest; and whether the regulation is narrowly tailored to infringe as little as possible on free speech or free expression.

(c) Yes, the ordinance attempts to further an important or substantial state interest unrelated to the suppression of speech or expression. But be careful here. The suppression of nude or topless dancing cannot be the substantial state interest. The substantial state interests in this case are the negative or adverse secondary effects of fighting crime and neighborhood blight. In a similar type case, a plurality of the U.S. Supreme Court wrote:

> Put another way, the ordinance does not attempt to regulate the primary effects of the expression, i.e., the effect on the audience of watching nude erotic dancing, but rather the secondary effects, such as the impacts on public health, safety, and welfare, which we have previously recognized are "caused by the presence of even one such" establishment.

City of Erie v. Pap's A.M., 529 U.S. 277, 291 (2000) (state interest was morals and prohibiting public nudity).

(d) The court in the actual case summarily concluded the town council reasonably believed the ordinance advanced the substantial state interest of reducing crime and neighborhood blight. The plurality Supreme Court opinion in *Pap's A.M.* reasoned since crime and other public health and safety problems are caused by the mere presence of nude dancing establishments, a bar on such nude dancing or topless dancing would further the substantial state interest in preventing such secondary effects. The court recognized that "requiring dancers to wear pasties and G-strings may not greatly reduce these secondary effects, but [the Constitution] requires only that the regulation further the interest in combating such effects." *Pap's A.M.*, 529 U.S. at 300.

(e) The district court in *Harris* said the ordinance was narrowly tailored. First, adequate alternative avenues of communication existed. There were locations in Fitchville where the adult cabaret could locate. Second, dancers could still express themselves as long as they wore pasties and a G-string.

The district court in *Fitchville Township Trustees* approved the regulation, as did the United States Supreme Court for a similar regulation in *Pap's A.M.* Nonetheless, in *Pap's A.M.*, a minority of the justices voiced strong reservations that the government's proclaimed state interests were not the true motivations for enacting the ordinance. The minority did not believe the city could prohibit nude dancing completely; nor did the minority believe the ordinance was the most narrowly tailored remedy available.

Family Values

4. (a) The Fair Housing Act prohibits discrimination based on familial status, meaning no person, including the town of Bedford, can discriminate in the sale, rental, or regulation of dwellings based on the occupancy of dependent children under the age of 18. Plaintiffs must have contended the occupancy requirements force parents with children to pay for larger units than if they had no children or than they would have had the ordinance not been in effect. Larger units are more expensive, and the difference in price could force some or many parents, especially lower income parents, to seek housing elsewhere.

Section 3607 of the Fair Housing Act exempts "any reasonable local . . . restriction regarding the maximum number of occupants permitted to occupy a building." Section 3607 thus requires (a) a reasonable (b) ordinance (c) regarding the maximum number of occupants permitted to occupy a building. Bedford enacted an ordinance and the ordinance regulates the number of people allowed to occupy a building. Hence elements (b) and (c) are met.

City of Edmonds established that cities could not use the § 3607 exemption as a subterfuge to discriminate. As to the subterfuge issue, the Supreme Court noted Congress meant the exemption to apply to ordinances that limit the number of persons who may occupy a dwelling based on the number of persons per square footage or per number of bedrooms. The Bedford ordinance limited the number of persons entitled to live in a dwelling based on the square footage of the dwelling. Thus facially the ordinance falls precisely within the exemption.

Section 3607, however, by its express terms demands the restriction be "reasonable." The Bedford restrictions seem reasonable. The stated purposes of protecting health and safety by preventing overcrowding are legitimate state interests and the means chosen are rationally related to achieving those ends. The restrictions, moreover, apply to all persons, related or not, which gives further credence to the occupancy limits being geared to achieve legitimate ends and not to discriminate against any group based on familial status. The court found the ordinance reasonable in these respects. The ordinance, therefore, was valid.

Plaintiffs also argued Bedford adopted the square footage with the intent to discriminate against families; or at lease the ordinance had a discriminatory impact or effect since a consequence of the ordinance was a reversal of population trends such that, instead of growing, Bedford's population decreased after the city enacted the ordinance. All the plaintiffs must show under the Fair Housing Act is discriminatory effect or impact, not the stricter discriminatory intent required under the federal Constitution. The court ruled against the plaintiffs on their discriminatory intent or impact claims, however, reasoning that the ordinance was facially neutral, and that plaintiffs needed more proof that the ordinance caused the decrease in families living in Bedford. Finally, the court rejected all Constitutional arguments since families are not protected classes under the Constitution (though some are under the Fair Housing Act). Nothing in the Constitution or the Fair Housing Act grants an unlimited number of family members to live together in one dwelling.

(b) Plaintiffs in Fair Housing Advocates Association, Inc. v. City of Richmond Heights, 209 F.3d 626 (6th Cir. 2000), contended Bedford's not adopting the BOCA square footage *per bedroom* or the two persons *per bedroom* standard was per se unreasonable. The Sixth Circuit disagreed, saying there is no national standard, and cities are free to choose whatever standard seems most appropriate for that particular city.

CHAPTER 35

Takings

Federal, state, and local governments can buy private property. They may buy whole lots, strips of land, or partial interests such as easements. Unlike private persons who must find a willing seller, governments can force unwilling persons to sell private property to the government. The power to force persons to transfer private property to the government is called **eminent domain.** This eminent domain power to **take** private property is so well established the framers of the Constitution assumed it was an inherent right of government. The Fifth Amendment's **Takings Clause** simply states, "nor shall private property be taken for public use, without just compensation" (applicable to the states through the Fourteenth Amendment). The Takings Clause mandates **reasonable compensation** be paid when the government takes private property. While the power to take private property for public purposes is called eminent domain, the normal process by which the property is taken and compensation paid is called **condemnation**.

This chapter introduces takings issues associated with **conventional condemnation** — i.e., when the state admits it is taking private property. The chapter then moves to **inverse condemnation** issues that arise when a state occupies or invades private property before initiating a condemnation proceeding. The major inverse condemnation takings discussions in the chapter concern **regulatory takings** — those takings that occur when a government's regulation of private property "goes too far." Finally, the chapter reviews **exactions**, a particular type of regulatory action occurring when a government imposes a condition or exaction on a private landowner in return for issuing a building permit.

CONVENTIONAL CONDEMNATION

In the conventional condemnation process the government identifies the desired property and begins the condemnation process. Often the government and the property owner agree on a price such that the transaction resembles a private sale and purchase. At other times, the government carries the condemnation process to trial, especially if the parties disagree over the amount the government will pay for the taken property.

(a) Public Use

The U.S. Constitution provides, "nor shall private property be taken for public use, without just compensation." The **public use** requirement prohibits the government from taking property for **private use or benefit**. On its face, the term "public use" seems to mean the taken property must be used by the government for some governmental function. But the U.S. Supreme Court, in Hawaii Housing Authority v. Midkiff, 467 U.S. 229 (1984), interpreted public use as equivalent to the achievement of a public purpose under a substantive due process analysis. See Chapter 32, supra. Condemnation is merely the means to accomplish a legitimate state purpose. Once the state identifies a legitimate state interest or purpose, the state has the power to take private property if taking the property is rationally related to the furtherance of the legitimate purpose. Courts will not substitute their judgment for a legislature's determination unless the stated purpose is "palpably without reasonable foundation" or the taking is not rationally related to the promotion of any legitimate purpose. In Midkiff, the Supreme Court concluded the State of Hawaii could condemn land and immediately transfer the land to private citizens to use as private residences. Even though the land would be used by private persons for private uses, the state had a legitimate state interest in diversifying land holdings in Hawaii and condemnation was a legitimate means to accomplish that goal.

The Supreme Court ruled that a government's taking and transferring private property to private third parties as part of an urban development project of a blighted area of Washington, D.C., was a constitutional means to effect a "public use." Berman v. Parker, 348 U.S. 26 (1954). The government had a legitimate interest in making the community healthy, spacious, aesthetic, clean, sanitary, or well-balanced. Id. at 33. Taking and transferring the property to private parties was a rational means to advance the legitimate state interest.

Fifty years later, the Supreme Court held legitimate public uses or public purposes includes promoting economic development and increasing tax revenue. Kelo v. City of New London, 545 U.S. 469 (2005). The government body can take property, even property that in no wise approximates a blight, and transfer the property to private developers to achieve the legitimate public purpose. Federal courts, moreover, are very deferential to state and local political leaders discerning public needs.

In *Kelo*, the City of New London condemned 115 privately-owned properties and transferred them to a private nonprofit entity that planned to build a new coordinated "village," a conference center, a marina, a pedestrian river-walk, 80 new residences with walking trails, office spaces, restaurants, and retail shops. The legitimate state interest was to revitalize the waterfront area, to attract tourists and businesses, to create jobs, and to increase tax revenues.

The *Kelo* opinion evoked widespread alarm among the general population. Most state courts have interpreted their state constitutions in accordance with the *Kelo* decision. A few states, however, interpret their state constitution "public use" requirement as requiring use by the public or by the government. Others allow a transfer to private citizens only when something about the property at issue justifies the taking, with "blight" most commonly used as an example. In a backlash to the *Kelo* opinion, several states passed laws prohibiting condemnation for purely economic reasons.

Example 1: Mayor Blundergus convinces the city council that the mayor should live in a city-owned mansion to host dignitaries on behalf of the city. He proposes that the city acquire a suitable home to be used by himself and all succeeding mayors to be used in part for entertaining or meeting persons doing business with the city. The city council agrees and the city begins condemnation proceedings to acquire the most stately mansion within five miles of city hall. The mansion's owner challenges the city's right to take his house. The city can force the current owner to sell the mansion since the mansion will serve a legitimate purpose of providing a home for the current and future mayors to use for city needs.

Example 2: Ten years later, Mayor Blundergus decides not to run for reelection. He tells the city council he would like to retire to a particular house on the seventh hole of a private golf course. The city council agrees to use its eminent domain power to acquire the house and sell it to Mayor Blundergus. The homeowner challenges the city's right to take his home. The homeowner prevails since the city cannot use its eminent domain powers to take property for private use. Here the city tried to acquire the house strictly to benefit the mayor in his private life.

(b) Just Compensation

The Fifth Amendment provides, "nor shall private property be taken for public use, without just compensation." Thus, even if the state has the power to take private property for public use (or for a public purpose), the state must pay the current owner just compensation. The **just compensation** that must be paid is the property's fair market value. If only a portion of the property is taken, the state must compensate the owner for the fair market value of the property taken.

INVERSE CONDEMNATION

In contrast to the conventional condemnation process where the governmental body identifies property and begins proceedings to acquire the property, paying just compensation before putting the property to public use, **inverse condemnation** occurs when a landowner claims the government has physically occupied or taken some property right from the landowner without compensation and without initiating the condemnation process, or has regulated the property is such a way that the government has constructively taken the property. Whereas in a conventional condemnation proceeding the government initiates the action, in an inverse condemnation action the landowner brings the action against the government, claiming the government has taken the landowner's property and must compensate the landowner.

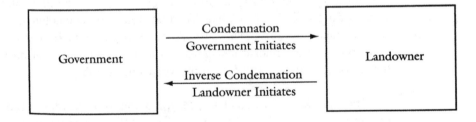

A landowner must have standing to bring an inverse condemnation against a government entity. Most often, the landowner when the regulation is passed is the person with standing to bring the inverse condemnation action. Sometimes, however, a subsequent owner can bring suit. In Palazzolo v. Rhode Island, 533 U.S. 606 (2001), the U.S. Supreme Court decided that a purchaser or successive title holder, even one who purchases with notice of a regulation enacted earlier, is not barred from challenging a regulation as a taking. The State argued the purchaser in that case (and in most similar situations) bought with full knowledge of the regulation, and as to the purchaser, the regulation was "a principle of state law." The Supreme Court rejected that logic. Otherwise, a government entity could create a windfall for itself since a challenge to the regulation could take years, leaving a landowner with unacceptable options: hold the property for years until litigation resolves the issue, or sell the property to a purchaser who would not have standing to challenge the regulation. The Supreme Court refused to permit an unconstitutional regulatory takings to become "transformed into a background principle of the State's law by mere virtue of the passage of title." Id. at 630.

CATEGORICAL OR PER SE REGULATORY TAKINGS

(a) Physical Invasions

The inverse condemnation situation that is easiest to identify occurs when the government physically invades or occupies private property, or by statute or regulation authorizes a third party's physical invasion or occupation of private property. Most **physical invasion** and **occupation** cases are **categorical** or **per se takings**. The government has no legal defense for the invasion. Once a landowner shows his property has been physically invaded or occupied by a government body or by a private party under authority of a government, the landowner can maintain a successful categorical takings claim against the government.

Example 1: State bought a strip of land from the record title owner to construct a new road. State was unaware that Britt had gained ownership of the land through adverse possession several years before State purchased the property. Britt and his family returned from a two-week vacation to find his backyard had been dug out and dirt removed to within ten feet of the back of Britt's home. His house remained untouched. Because State physically invaded Britt's property, State is liable to Britt for taking a large part of Britt's backyard. A categorical physical invasion taking by the government is similar to a trespass action if a private party had invaded Britt's property (though the remedies may differ since the landowner may not be able to eject or oust the government).

Example 2: Causby raised chickens on three acres. An airport runway ends 2,200 feet from Causby's house and her chicken shack. U.S. government planes approaching an airfield fly 83 feet over Causby's house and 20 feet over the highest tree in her yard. The planes blow leaves off trees and create loud noises. Chickens get so frightened they kill themselves flying into walls. The Causby family members are sleep-deprived from the noise and are nervous from worrying that planes might crash on them (though no plane accidents have occurred on the Causby land). Because of the low-flying planes, Causby no longer can raise chickens. In addition, Causby's land has depreciated in value since the government planes began flying so low.

The U.S. government has "taken" an easement by physical invasion. While airspace well above the immediate reaches of the land is part of the public domain, an intrusion so close to the ground intrudes upon and affects the normal use of the property. Even though the invasion or occupancy is of airspace and the planes never touch the ground, trees, or buildings, the continuous and recurring invasion affects the use and value of the land. That the planes never touch the soil is immaterial in this case. The invasion is in the same category as telephone wires that overhang property where no wires or poles actually touch the land. Causby has a legitimate takings claim against the U.S. government for the physical invasion. See United States v. Causby, 328 U.S. 256 (1946). (Note the similarity to a trespass claim if the planes had belonged to a private person.)

Example 3: A state law provides that a landlord must permit a cable television company to install its cable facilities on and in rental units. Pursuant to this law, a cable company installs a cable slightly less than one-half inch in diameter across the rooftop of Jean Loretto's five-story apartment building, installs cable boxes and directional taps on the rooftop, and strings cable down the side of the apartment building to tenants subscribing to the cable service. A taking occurred because the cable and boxes were compelled permanent physical invasions. A permanent physical invasion by or under the authority of the state is a *per se* taking (a categorical taking). In this Example, the state authorized the third-party cable company to occupy part of Jean Loretto's apartment building. See Loretto v. Teleprompter Manhattan CATV Corp., 458 U.S. 419 (1982).

The cable access law itself is constitutional, however, and can be enforced. The availability of cable television to all persons is valuable for its educational community benefits. Encouraging access to cable television, therefore, is a legitimate state interest. Laws allowing cable companies to string their cable is rationally related to the accomplishment of the legitimate goal. The law therefore is constitutional. That issue, however, is separate from whether the government must compensate the aggrieved owner for the "taking." A state willing to compensate all landlords can continue the law. Alternatively, a state may choose to revoke the law or amend the law to require the cable companies to pay the just compensation on behalf of the state.

In these three Examples, the good faith or the public benefit derived from the governmental action makes no difference. There is no balancing of private injuries against the public benefits involved; there is no such thing as degrees of invasion or a permitted decrease in fair market value. A taking occurs, or it does not. A related consequence of this all-or-nothing analysis is that no matter how small the damage to the property invaded, just compensation must be paid. A further consequence is that just compensation is payable, no matter that the landowner whose property is invaded is also benefited, as Jean Loretto undoubtedly was in Example 3: The fact that she was able to offer apartments with cable hookups (presumably for a higher rent than for apartments without them) did not offset her compensation under the Takings Clause.

There is long-running precedent for compensating physical invasions in this way. If property is a metaphorical bundle of sticks, a physical invasion doesn't just remove one stick from the bundle; instead it shortens each of them. With a physical invasion, the government has, pro tanto, taken away the right to possess, denied the right of use, and decreased the right to sell — hence the justification for the per se rule for analysis of physical takings (as outlined in the preceding paragraph). Finally, the per se rule presents few problems of proof and can be black lettered and easily understood — further justifying its unique status in the law of takings. When the government enters an owner's premises, the government must pay for the privilege.

(b) No Economically Viable Use

A per se or categorical taking also occurs when a government regulation prohibits all economically beneficial or productive use of private land. See Lucas v. South Carolina Coastal Council, 505 U.S. 1003 (1992). In *Lucas*, for example, a state law forbade the construction of all new permanent buildings on some beachfront lots. In one stroke of a pen, two lots costing nearly $1 million were rendered valueless or near valueless. The Supreme Court concluded such a complete loss of value amounted to a taking requiring compensation.

A prima facie takings occurs if a regulation renders property valueless or prohibits all economically viable or beneficial use. The categorical "no economically viable use taking" is subject to two exceptions. First, all laws and regulations that duplicate results reached under common law as to the regulation of nuisances, see Chapter 27, supra, do not amount to a taking.

Example I: Kathleen owns land on which is located a large part of a lake. Kathleen decides to fill in the lake bed on her property. Filling in the lake will cause other lakefront lots to flood. A government law, regulation, or administrative decision that denies Kathleen's request for a landfill permit or forbids landfill operations on lakes and rivers that might cause flooding on others' lands will not amount to a taking. See *Lucas*, 505 U.S. at 1029.

Example 2: Third Eye Nuclear Power Plant is located on an earthquake fault. The state can order the plant be shut down and the state will not have to compensate Third Eye Nuclear Power Plant even if shutting down the plant eliminates the land's only economically productive use because the state did "not proscribe a productive use that was previously permissible under relevant property and nuisance principles." Id. Building the plant on the fault was a nuisance to begin with. Thus it can be removed completely from the get-go.

A second exception to the categorical "no economically viable use taking" arises when a regulation or restriction, even one that eliminates all economically viable use, "inheres in the title itself, in the restrictions that background principles of the State's law of property . . . already place upon land ownership." Id. It would seem adverse possession, prescription, implied easements, recording acts, riparian rights, and executory interests in favor of a government fall into this exception to takings, as might the historic right of governments to destroy private property to help control the spread of fire. The exact contours of the exception are yet to be developed.

(c) Nuisance Control (Not a Taking)

Laws and regulations that control or restrict nuisances generally do not result in takings. Nuisance control is a traditional function of government to protect the health, safety, and welfare of the community. Hence early ordinances prohibited stables in certain parts of town; or barred brick manufacturing plants from residential areas, Hadacheck v. Sebastian, 239 U.S. 394 (1915). The state may regulate traditional public and private nuisances.

REGULATORY TAKINGS — THE *PENN CENTRAL* AD HOC FACTORS

Inverse condemnation jurisprudence today centers on **regulatory takings**. Governments constitutionally regulate land use. Regulations affect land values (increases as well as decreases land values). Regulations, moreover, prohibit some or all uses of particular pieces of property. Two sentences from Pennsylvania Coal Co. v. Mahon, 260 U.S. 393 (1922), sum up the conflict: "Government hardly could go on if to some extent values incident to property could not be diminished without paying for every such change in the general law" and "The general rule at least is, that while property may be regulated to a certain extent, if the regulation goes too far it will be recognized as a taking." The fact-based inquiry in most regulatory takings cases is whether the regulation at issue under the facts of the case has gone "too far." Because the inquiry is regarded as factual, inverse condemnation issues of takings and compensation can be tried before a jury.

When no per se or categorical takings occurs, courts conduct an ad hoc factual inquiry based on two broad factors first enunciated in Penn Central Transportation Co. v. New York City, 438 U.S. 104 (1978). One of the *Penn Central* factors focuses on the character of the government's action. The other focuses on the effect the regulation has on the remaining use and the value of the regulated property. These are the factors:

(a) The character of the government action.
(b) The economic impact of the regulation on the landowner and, particularly, "the extent to which the regulation has interfered with distinct investment-backed expectations."

The key inquiry is the severity and burden the government imposes upon private property rights. See Lingle v. Chevron U.S.A., Inc., 544 U.S. 528 (2005). A court will focus on the magnitude or character of the burden a regulation imposes on property rights, and how any regulatory burden is distributed among property owners. Id. at 542.

(a) Character of the Government Action

As to **the character of the government action**, as noted above, government invasions and occupations are categorical takings. A regulation noticeably affecting one or a few lots to the landowners' detriment that results in a benefit to the state or surrounding landowners is a factor weighing in favor of finding a taking occurred. Some people should not in fairness be forced to bear a burden or confer a benefit that should be borne or paid for by the public at large. This is the oft-identified "fairness rationale" for the Takings Clause. This is a fact determination, however, and the government's actions must be evaluated considering the purpose to be achieved and the economic effect the regulation has on the claimant property owner. Thus, the phrase invites an analysis balancing various factors. If no physical invasion is involved, the inquiry asks whether the regulation broadly confers a public benefit, or one extracted from only a few.

If a government body misuses the regulatory process to benefit the government's later use or acquisition of the land, a landowner can assert a takings claim. For example, if the government, intending to condemn land, denies its owner public services in the hope of decreasing its fair market value in advance of paying just compensation, a taking occurs. If the government proposes to condemn an owner's land for a park, but finds its parkland plans too expensive and then restricts the owner's land to "parkland uses" in its zoning ordinance, a taking also occurs. If the government proposes a park, but abandons its plans in an on-again, off-again manner that goes on for a decade, a temporary taking occurs during the time that the owner cannot use or sell the land because of the uncertainty of governmental action.

Example: In City of Monterrey v. Del Monte Dunes at Monterrey, Ltd., 526 U.S. 687 (1999), the city denied the landowner permits and repeatedly demanded additional concessions because of the city's long-time interest in acquiring the property for public use rather than for its stated purposes of protecting the environment, providing public access to a public beach, or protecting the habitat of the Blue Butterfly. In the case, the landowner over a five-year period submitted nineteen plans, most of them drafted to meet the city's demands, while the city rejected every application and added new demands. The Supreme Court accepted the landowner's theory that the city's acting in bad faith and failing to follow its own zoning ordinances and policies could amount to a temporary taking. See *Del Monte Dunes*, 526 U.S. at 722.

(b) Economic Impact and Investment-Backed Expectations

The second *Penn Central* factor — **the economic impact** of **the regulation** — takes into consideration the economic loss to the landowner. The Supreme Court often mentions "use" and "value" interchangeably. The loss of "use" often correlates with the loss of "value." Courts look at whether a "reasonable number of uses" are left an owner after a regulation is imposed. Generally, no regulatory taking occurs if the landowner can make economic use of the property with the regulation in place.

The diminution in value must be great — indeed, it must be a complete loss of value. See "No Economically Viable Use" supra. For example, the zoning ordinance in Village of Euclid v. Ambler Realty Co., 272 U.S. 365 (1926), see Chapter 32, supra, decreased Ambler Realty's property value 75 percent (i.e., its property after the zoning was worth only 25 percent of its pre-zoning value). Yet no compensable takings occurred. See also Hadacheck v. Sebastian, 239 U.S. 394 (1915) (92.5 percent diminution in value did not result in a taking).

The analysis becomes more landowner friendly once the landowner adds improvements to the land — thereby creating investment-backed expectations. As to a given property, The Supreme Court in *Penn Central* said a regulation may be deemed a taking if the regulation interferes with the landowner's *distinct* **investment-backed expectations**. Courts quickly changed the word "distinct" to "reasonable" investment-backed expectations. Once a person improves property in justifiable reliance on regulations in effect at the time the improvements were made, the person must have the opportunity to recoup the cost of the improvements. A regulation that interferes with an owner's reasonable investment-backed expectations may be a taking. But if an owner after the regulation is imposed still can use the property as he used it before the regulation, there is no taking.

CONCEPTUAL SEVERANCE

The economic impact and interference with investment-backed expectations analysis assumes courts know what the "property" is. A major challenge in many situations is identifying the property claimed to have been taken. More specifically, the issue is whether the property can be conceptually severed in part. Often this issue is phrased as determining the denominator in the fraction to calculate whether the property has been regulated too far or invaded. Property theoretically might be severed in different ways.

(a) The Surface as Denominator

Property can be conceptually severed based on how much of the surface is affected. This usually happens in eminent domain actions when a state wants to acquire only a strip of land at the edge of a larger parcel to build or widen a road. Because the state will permanently occupy the land, the state will purchase the strip, leaving the landowner with the remaining land. The state acquires the strip's surface, subsurface, and air rights. Alternatively, the state may pass a law or ordinance restricting the use of part of the parcel. The taking analyses differ dramatically depending on whether a physical occupation or mere regulation is anticipated, as the following Examples illustrate.

Example 1: City intends to widen White Oak Street. City plans to use a 20-foot strip across the front of Morrison's lot for the expansion. City must compensate Morrison for the land because City intends to permanently occupy the 20-foot strip. City must compensate Morrison even though Morrison retains 90 percent of the original lot, and even if Morrison's retained land becomes more valuable because of the widened street.

Example 2: City passes an ordinance prohibiting all improvements within 20 feet of White Oak Street. Morrison will not receive any compensation. Even though Morrison cannot use the 20-foot strip of his property adjoining White Oak Street, and as a practical matter the 20-foot strip's value approaches zero since no one can develop it for any purpose, a court will evaluate the regulation's impact on Morrison's entire lot and not just on the 20-foot setback. The lesson here is that the surface area will not be considered severed in evaluating regulations. Instead, the economic impact analysis will be applied to a lot as a whole.

As a caveat, the landowner in Palazzolo v. Rhode Island, 533 U.S. 606 (2001), argued to the Supreme Court his property should be severed into the small portion, which he could develop under the state wetland regulations, and a much larger portion, which he could not develop because of state wetland regulations. The Supreme Court acknowledged the severability issue, but refused to address it since the landowner did not present it as an issue in the petition for certiorari. The Court said its cases indicate the parcel is treated as a whole but the Court "at times expressed discomfort with the logic of this rule." 533 U.S. at 631. The following year, in Tahoe-Sierra Preservation Council, Inc. v. Tahoe Regional Planning Agency, 535 U.S. 302 (2002), the Court emphasized that in regulatory cases the focus is on the parcel as a whole.

(b) Airspace, Surface, and Mineral Rights as Separate Interests

Property can be conceptually severed into airspace, surface area, and subsurface or mineral interests. Once severed, the surface, mineral, and air rights can be considered separate properties. As a generalization, courts in a regulatory taking analysis will sever a person's interests in these interests only in unique cases. As a rule of thumb, surface rights are critical. The regulation that prohibits all use of surface rights, fully allowing mineral extraction, likely will constitute a taking. In contrast, a restriction on mineral production that permits full surface use likely will not amount to a taking unless either (a) the property owner has made substantial improvements to extract the minerals and can claim he was deprived of his investment backed expectations, (b) the surface is unusable and the regulation makes the mineral estate valueless, or (c) the property owner holds only the mineral interest and the regulation makes the mineral interest valueless. Severance is only an issue in regulatory takings analysis. A physical invasion into any of the three is a per se taking.

Example 1: A government aircraft landing approach to an airport carries planes to within 80 feet of a private house. This is a physical invasion of *airspace* affecting a landowner's use of her surface area and thus constitutes a taking. See United States v. Causby, 328 U.S. 256 (1946).

Example 2: City passed a landmark preservation ordinance prohibiting substantial changes to the exterior of historical buildings. Pursuant to the ordinance the owner of a railway terminal could not construct an office tower in the airspace above the terminal. The law does not effect a taking because the terminal owner can continue operating the terminal and receive a reasonable return on its investment in the terminal. The airspace above the terminal is not a separate property interest. The whole property (airspace, surface use, and subsurface use) is one property for taking analysis. See Penn Central Transportation Co. v. City of New York, 438 U.S. 104 (1978).

Example 3: In State A, persons owning mineral rights in land often are not the persons owning the surface rights. State A enacts a subsidence law requiring coal mine operators to keep up to 50 percent of the coal in place to prevent land subsidence, protect the environment, insure the state's economic future, and safeguard its citizens' well-being. The law will not effect a taking since the coal that must remain in place cannot be conceptually severed from all the coal in the ground. See Keystone Bituminous Coal Association v. DeBenedictis, 480 U.S. 470 (1987). If, however, the law as applied to any particular coal operator reduces the value of extractable coal to zero, a taking will be found unless the coal operator also owns the surface rights.

Example 4: In State B, persons owning mineral rights often are not persons owning the surface rights. In addition, State B's law traditionally recognizes a separate property interest called the support estate. State B enacts a law prohibiting coal owners from removing coal in the support estate within 150 feet of any improved property belonging to another person. The prohibition applies whether or not the owner of the mineral estate owns the support estate. The Supreme Court held this law effected a taking. According to the Court, the State B law in many cases made the coal in the support estate valueless and, contrary to the state's contract and property law, took the support estate from the coal operator and gave it to the surface owner. Even assuming the law served a public purpose, the transferring of the full support estate from one private citizen to another was a taking. See Pennsylvania Coal Co. v. Mahon, 260 U.S. 393 (1922).

The majority opinion in *Keystone Bituminous Coal Association* attempted to distinguish the law applied in Examples 3 and 4. The majority said the government action in Example 3 was to "arrest what [the state] perceived to be a significant threat to the common welfare" (a legitimate state interest) whereas in Example 4 the law "merely involve[d] the balancing of private economic interests of coal companies against private interests of the surface owner" (and thus subject to a takings claim). In addition, the Court noted the coal companies in Example 3 continued profitable operations while the coal companies in Example 4 could not profitably engage in coal mining operations and thus there was "undue interference with their investment-backed expectations." To be valid this last observation requires a conceptual severance of the mineral and support estate in Example 4 while refusing to accept the same reasoning in Example 3. These two Examples are not easily reconciled; perhaps Examples 3 and 4 both should have been a taking or not a taking.

(c) Temporal Severance

(1) Permanent Takings

Property can be conceptually severed on a timeline. If a state takes land for a highway, for example, and the property is owned by a life tenant and a remainderman in fee simple, the purchase price would be allocated between the owners of the two interests. Likewise, a regulation that permanently reduced the property's value to zero would be compensable in part to each owner.

(2) Temporary Takings

In Loretto v. Teleprompter Manhattan CATV Corp., 458 U.S. 419 (1982), the Supreme Court concluded a **permanent** physical invasion constituted a categorical taking. Five years later the Supreme Court specifically held the government can be liable in damages for a **temporary** regulatory takings as well. See First English Evangelical Lutheran Church of Glendale v. County of Los Angeles, 482 U.S. 304 (1987). While a permanent taking is akin to a purchase, the temporary taking is more like a lease or an option, with just compensation measured accordingly. The temporary taking may result from a physical occupancy or from a complete denial of use as was alleged in First English.

A temporary taking, moreover, can result from bad faith abuse of the regulation or licensing process. See City of Monterey v. Del Monte Dunes at Monterey, Ltd., 526 U.S. 687 (1999). The city in Del Monte Dunes repeatedly denied the landowner development permits, ostensibly because the city was interested in buying the land at issue, and not because the landowner failed to meet all requirements for the permit. The city owed the landowner just compensation for this temporary taking.

Not all temporary deprivations of use of property due to government action are temporary takings, however. In Tahoe-Sierra Preservation Council, Inc. v. Tahoe Regional Planning Agency, 535 U.S. 302 (2002), for example, the U.S. Supreme Court decided that a 32-month moratorium on development around Lake Tahoe while the agency formulated a comprehensive plan for property abutting the lake was not a taking. The Court held that the validity of the moratorium is best evaluated using a fact-based ad hoc *Penn Central* regulatory takings analysis, not a categorical takings analysis, considering the nature of the government action and the impact of the regulation on the landowner, with particular attention to the landowner's reasonable investment-backed expectations. This was not to hold that a moratorium never effects a taking, but to hold that the purposes, length, and effects of a moratorium should be balanced within *Penn Central's* analytical framework. Normal administrative and other understandable governmental delays do not constitute a temporary taking.

EXACTIONS

Exactions are conditions imposed by a government that a landowner or developer must meet before the government will issue the landowner or developer a subdivision or building permit. The exaction may be a dedication of land to public purposes, a restriction on development, a required improvement, or a payment of money. A city, for example, may require a developer when subdividing a parcel to dedicate land for a school, road, or park; or a developer may be required to incorporate flood control measures, connect the property's streets to public streets, or furnish sufficient parking when applying for a building permit.

Other actions, in contrast, are attempts by the government to implement some government plan without paying just compensation. An exaction must further a legitimate state interest, and cannot be a pretext or subterfuge to avoid the Takings Clause compensation requirement.

As a starting point in determining which exactions constitute a taking and which do not, recall the familiar substantive due process mandate that government laws, regulations, and ordinances must serve a legitimate state interest. Exactions can be the means to achieve a legitimate state interest. The **essential nexus** or relationship between the end to be achieved (the legitimate state interest) and the means chosen to achieve that end (the exaction) must be close enough so that the exaction **substantially advances** the legitimate state interest. Nollan v. California Coastal Commission, 483 U.S. 825 (1987) (involving a beach house renovation and enlargement).

Two Supreme Court cases developed the line between legitimate government exactions and an exaction that constitutes a taking. In Nollan v. California Coastal Commission, 483 U.S. 825 (1987), the Nollans bought and sought to demolish a beach home and replace it with a larger, more modern home. The property was located on the Pacific coast on a strip of land between two public beaches. The California Coastal Commission conditioned the grant of a building permit on the Nollans' granting the state an easement for the public to walk on the Nollans' property to go from one park to the other.

The Supreme Court concluded the exactions "utterly fail[ed] to further the end advanced." Id. at 837. The California Coastal Commission's stipulated state interest in Nollan was guaranteeing persons driving along the coastal highway were able to see (have "visual access" to) the beach. The U.S. Supreme Court accepted the visual access goal as a legitimate state interest. The Coastal Commission, however, chose to guarantee the public's visual access by conditioning the building permit on the Nollans' granting the state an easement for the public to walk along the beach along the Nollans' property. The Court quickly homed in on the logical flaw here. The Court said there must be a nexus (relationship) between the legitimate state interest and the means (the exaction demanded). In Nollan the Coastal Commission could not show this "essential nexus." The Court saw no nexus or relationship between the easement along the beach and visual access from the highway. Instead, the Court saw the exactions as a preconceived attempt to gain easements for the public from all landowners on the beach without the state's having to compensate the landowners. The Court found a taking had occurred.

Two questions left open in Nollan involved the definition of an exaction and what degree of connection must exist between the demanded exaction and the impact of the proposed development. To date, the U.S. Supreme Court has not found a taking for an exaction beyond physical dedications or physical intrusions as conditions of development to public use. See Del Monte Dunes (dicta), discussed supra. There the Court said that the law of exactions was not readily applicable to and was not designed for situations involving nondedicatory fees and "money exactions." Many exactions are appropriate to address legitimate state concerns about developable property.

The overall concern with exactions is that government might cite a legitimate fault with the landowner's proposed use of his property to exact an excessive concession that does more than necessary to mitigate the harm caused by the landowner's development. The Court felt some test must be imposed on government to protect citizens against a government's overreaching. In Dolan v. City of Tigard, 512 U.S. 374 (1994), which involved the expansion of a hardware store, the Supreme Court adopted a **rough proportionality** test that demands the government agency make "some sort of individualized determination that the required dedication is related both in nature and extent to the impact of the proposed development." Id. at 391.

Thus, after Dolan, courts analyze exactions under a two-step process:

1. Courts determine whether the **essential nexus** exists between the legitimate state interest and the condition exacted (Nollan).

2. If the essential nexus exists, courts determine whether there is a **rough proportionality** between the condition exacted and the projected impact of the landowner's proposed development (Dolan).

To illustrate, Dolan's development contributed to potential flooding in a nearby creek and increased traffic on local streets. The city conditioned Dolan's building permit on Dolan's dedicating land in a floodplain along the creek to the city so the city could improve its storm drainage system along the creek. In addition, the city conditioned the grant of a permit on Dolan's dedicating 15 more feet of its land outside the floodplain to the city so the city could build a pedestrian/bicycle path to help reduce the automobile traffic on nearby streets. Both the drainage system and the bicycle path had already been included in a master plan developed well before the Dolan applied for her building permit.

The Supreme Court first concluded the **essential nexus** existed between the dedication of the floodplain land and the flood control; and the Court also found the **essential nexus** existed between the dedication of the additional 15 feet of land for the pedestrian/bicycle path and the reduction of traffic congestion problems. The Supreme Court then concluded the demanded exactions failed the **rough proportionality** test.

As to the floodplain dedication, the Court, citing the importance of a landowner's right to exclude others from his property, felt that there was no reason for the city to demand a public access greenway as opposed to a private greenway to serve its legitimate state interests. The landowner's right to exclude others and monitor her property was not being regulated, said the Court; it was eviscerated! In addition, the Court believed the city could achieve its aims by forbidding Mrs. Dolan from building on the floodplain.

As to the pedestrian/bicycle path, the Court noted that dedications for streets, sidewalks, and other public ways generally are reasonable exactions to avoid excessive congestion resulting from the development. Nonetheless, on the record before the Court, the city had not met its burden of demonstrating that increased traffic usage to be generated by the landowner's development was roughly proportional to the city's requirement of the dedication of land for a pedestrian/bicycle path easement. How many customers, after all, bike to a hardware store to shop?

REMEDIES

At one time, the standard remedy in inverse condemnation cases was invalidation of the law, ordinance, or regulation. Today, courts award money damages once a court finds a taking. Once a court rules a government action constitutes a taking, the government has the option of compensating the landowner for the loss associated with the taking, or of revoking the law, ordinance, or regulation. If the government revokes the regulation, it still must pay compensation for the time the government action constituted a taking. That is, the government must pay for this temporary taking.

Examples

Plane Examples

1. (a) Government drug enforcement officers decide to use remote unproductive land owned by a private citizen to store, fuel, and repair airplanes used to search out drug smuggling activities along the border. On any given day over a two-year period an average of four planes land on the makeshift airstrip. Trucks are used to supply fuel, food, and supplies. Can the private landowner bring a successful takings claim?

   (b) An airplane engaged in government drug enforcement operations along the border developed engine trouble and was forced to land on remote unproductive land owned by a private citizen. Government employees using government vehicles drove onto the private property to repair the aircraft. When repaired, the airplane resumed its flight and the government vehicles left the farm. Can the private landowner bring a successful takings claim?

A Contaminated Example

2. Gladys owned 250 acres of land adjoining the federal government's Rolling Ridge Technical Research Facility (Rolling Ridge), a nuclear research and production facility. Gladys operated a clay mine on the 250 acres. Gladys granted the surface rights to the 250 acres to the federal government to use as a buffer zone surrounding Rolling Ridge. Gladys expressly reserved the mineral interest.

   Unbeknownst to Gladys, the federal government periodically sprayed waste from Rolling Ridge onto 100 acres of the 250 acres. Five years ago the Department of Energy (DOE) tested soil samples from the 100 acres. After viewing the test results, the government designated the 100 acres as a "hazardous substance site." To study the land for contamination more thoroughly, the government drilled several monitoring wells on the 100 acres without seeking Gladys's consent. The government also sent a letter to the State Mining Department, demanding that the state halt Gladys's mining operations until the federal government cleared any contamination on the 100 acres. The state after a hearing withdrew the 100 acres from Gladys's mining permit. Gladys could not mine the 100 acres until the federal government gave its approval. She could continue mining the remaining 150 acres, however.

After four years of study, the federal government concluded no remedial action was needed, and that Gladys could begin mining the 100 acres again without posing a significant threat to human health or to the environment.

Gladys brings three inverse condemnation claims against the federal government. (QUERY: Without looking below, can you identify three possible takings claims?) Please evaluate the following:

(a) Gladys claims the government's spraying the effluence on the 100 acres contaminated her mineral estate and that contamination constituted a taking.

(b) Gladys claims the installation of groundwater monitoring wells that extended into her mineral estate constituted a taking.

(c) Gladys claims the state's reduction of the area of the mining permit, instigated by the federal government, was a regulatory taking.

Rails to Trails

3. Congress through the National Trails System Act provided that abandoned railway easements or determinable fees shall be used as trails for walking and bicycling. Tri-State Railroad filed documents with the ICC to abandon railway easements in a 50-mile stretch of land. The government began converting the easements into hike and bike trails. The owners of the land over which the easements ran brought suit alleging a taking. See Glosemeyer v. United States, 45 Fed. Cl. 771 (2000). What result?

Services Please

4. Corwin owned 30 contiguous unimproved lots in the New Harmony. Ten years later, in anticipation of developing the 30 lots, Corwin asked the town of New Harmony to bring streets, water, sewers, and gas to each of the 30 lots. The city attorney wrote back to Corwin that New Harmony would provide streets, water, sewer, and gas to the 30 lots if Corwin agreed in advance to be assessed for the full cost of the expansion of the services to the lots. Corwin had not intended to pay for the improvements himself, however, and he put his development plans on hold.

Three public roads bordered Corwin's 30 lots, but none of the roads entered into Corwin's land. Corwin can enter or leave his land by any of the three roads, however. One of the three paved roads dead-ended on the west side of Corwin's 30 lots. A year after Corwin asked the city to expand services to his lots, neighbors complained to the town council that cars, trucks, and motorcycles were speeding on and off the paved road from and onto a dirt path on Corwin's land, tearing up the dirt, posing a safety risk, and disturbing the neighbors. In response, the town put a chain across the paved road right at Corwin's property line.

Corwin countered by filing an inverse condemnation suit against the town of New Harmony. Please evaluate Corwin's takings claims:

(a) A taking occurred when New Harmony placed the chain across the dead-end road entering Corwin's land.

(b) New Harmony's refusal to extend essential services to Corwin's 30 lots at the town's sole expense, effectively depriving Corwin of all economically viable use of his property, constituted a taking.

Access Denied

5. The State Highway Department purchased a 200-foot-wide strip off the west side of Grubb's farm. The deed from Grubb to the State Highway Department reserved an easement for access to the highway to be built on the 200-foot-wide strip. Grubb used the easement at the location specified in the deed for a dirt road to access the highway for the next 39 years. Two years ago the state condemned another strip of Grubb's land to widen the highway further.

At about the same time, Grubb applied for a permit to construct a concrete access road to the highway where the current dirt road was located. The state denied Grubb's permit application, citing public safety concerns. In addition, the state denied Grubb access to the highway over the dirt road, digging a ditch to prevent Grubb from entering the highway from his land. Grubb could access the highway by traveling over county roads that ran by his land. Grubb sued the state, alleging inverse condemnation from being denied the permit. What result?

The Fun Part of Town

6. Breyer owned 150 acres of land. She operated a private golf course on 110 of the acres for decades. The other 40 acres surrounded were unimproved. The golf course was located in a district zoned "Residential," but in which golf courses were permitted. Breyer hired a firm to plan a residential development on the 40 acres surrounding the golf course and submitted her plans to develop the 40 acres to the town board. The town board requested certain revisions, which Breyer incorporated into her plans.

While Breyer was making her plans to develop the 40 acres, the town hired a private planning firm to help formulate a comprehensive plan taking into account the town's growth patterns. The firm made three observations that affected Breyer's golf course and remaining

40 acres. First, urbanization had resulted in overdevelopment of the town, reducing the open space in the town's watershed below acceptable levels. Second, additional residential development could lead to increased flooding. Finally, because of current overdevelopment, the town needed to preserve recreational opportunities for area residents. Based on these findings, the town rezoned Breyer's golf course, including the 40 acres surrounding the golf course, from "Residential" to "Solely Recreational Use" (as it did three other golf courses in the town).

The town refused to issue building permits to Breyer because the 40 acres were zoned Solely Recreational Use. Breyer brings an action against the town alleging an unconstitutional taking of her property without just compensation. What result?

The Law Is a Rough Proportionality

7. Refined Oil Co. owned an automobile service station at the corner of Hard Road and Easy Street in Poplar Heights. Because of Poplar Heights' growth, many roads, including the intersection of Hard Road and Easy Street, experienced above-capacity traffic during the morning and afternoon rush hours. Because of the increased traffic flow and anticipated growth of Poplar Heights, the town leaders decided to widen Hard Road and Easy Street by adding extra lanes of through traffic as well as dual left-turn and right-turn lanes at the Hard Road and Easy Street intersection.

Meanwhile, Refined Oil Co. wanted to modernize its service station. The current station is classified as a Type A station and is qualified to operate in the B-2 General Retail Business District, which is where it is currently located. If improved (including adding a food store), the station would be classified as a Type C station. To operate a Type C station in the B-2 General Retail Business district would necessitate Refined Oil Co.'s getting a special use permit from Poplar Heights.

Poplar Heights agreed to issue a special use permit under guidelines set out in the zoning ordinance if and on the condition that Refined Oil Co. dedicate a 40-foot by 40-foot triangular piece of land at the corner of Hard Road and Easy street (about 20 percent of the property's total footage) to Poplar Heights. Studies indicate the improved station would increase traffic less than 0.4 percent. The need to widen the roads existed before Refined Oil Co. proposed its improvements. Poplar Heights' policy was to require dedications along congested roadways as a condition of land use permits without regard to whether the exactions related to the intended use of the property.

Refined Oil Co. brings a takings claim against Poplar Heights. What result?

Explanations

Plane Examples

1. (a) The government has effected a taking and will be liable to the land-owner in an inverse condemnation suit. The facts indicate an intended physical invasion of private property occurred. The taking was temporary. Damages are allowed for temporary takings. The amount of the damages should approximate a fair rental amount of the land plus the cost of repairing the land. The government here acted as a trespasser. (b) No taking. Just as common law recognizes an exception to trespass actions in emergencies, a government's temporary invasion of private property because of an emergency should not amount to the intentional action characterized as a taking. Nonetheless, the government should still be liable for any damages its invasion actually caused on the private property.

A Contaminated Example

2. (a) Gladys loses. A surface estate owner can use the surface in any legal manner that does not harm the mineral estate owner's enjoyment of her estate. While the government's contamination of Gladys's mineral estate likely would be a taking, the ultimate conclusion that the mineral estate was never contaminated defeats the action. Fear of contamination is not the same as contamination.

   (b) Whether the drilling of monitoring wells constituted a taking depends on whether, under state law, the surface owner has the implied right to drill wells to benefit his use of the surface estate; and, if so, whether wells drilled to determine the extent of any contamination is a normal incident of the beneficial use of the surface. The court in McKay v. United States, 199 F.3d 1376 (Fed. Cir. 1999) (the case on which this Example is based), concluded under the state law the surface estate owner could not drill multiple exploratory wells extending into the mineral estate. The wells, therefore, were physical invasions into Gladys's mineral estate. A physical invasion is a categorical taking. The government is liable to Gladys even though the wells are now closed. The federal government owes damages for a temporary physical occupation.

   (c) The court in McKay, as a preliminary matter, concluded the state in revoking Gladys's mining privileges as to the 100 acres was acting as an agent for the federal government. Hence, if a regulatory taking occurred, the federal government would be liable as the principal. Gladys could claim a regulatory taking occurred since she was prohibited for at least four years from mining the 100 acres. She could claim the regulatory action denied her all economically beneficial or productive use of her mineral estate in the 100 acres during those four years. The *McKay* court remanded the case without deciding the issue. It appears the issue will turn on whether the mineral interest in the 100 acres can be severed analytically from Gladys's mineral interest in her remaining 150 acres. If the 100-acre interest is severable from the remaining 150 acres, Gladys might prevail on her complete loss of economically beneficial use theory. If, as is likely, the mineral estate is not severable, Gladys cannot prevail on the complete loss of economically beneficial use.[1] Alternatively, Gladys could claim, under an ad hoc factual inquiry, the government regulation took her property based on the circumstances of her case. The inquiry would consider the character of the government action — the prohibition of all mining was a direct result of the government's spraying on the surface estate — and the economic effect on Gladys as the landowner. Gladys may prevail. Normally, a regulation of this type would not be a taking since a primary purpose of government is to safeguard the health and safety of people and the environment. The government's acting for safety concerns ordinarily would defeat a takings claim in this situation if not for the overriding character of the government's action in this case. The spraying was risky; and the effluence did seep into the mineral estate, potentially contaminating Gladys's mineral estate. Even though the ultimate conclusion was that no contamination occurred, the possibility of contamination was enough for the state to revoke Gladys's mining privileges. While a court (and you) might disagree with us, we would hold the government liable to Gladys under the facts for the four years' loss of mining privileges.

Rails to Trails

3. Tri-State Railroad abandoned the easements and determinable fees. The easements should revert to the owners of the underlying fee. Hike and bike trails are not railroad purposes. Since the government Act denies fee owners their expectation of having their lands returned to them, there was a taking. The taking is a physical taking. The government plans to allow members of the public to use the surface.

   The federal government has the right and power to continue the easements as hike and bike trails, however. The National Trails System Act is constitutional under a substantive due process analysis. But under the Takings Clause, the government must compensate the landowners for the value of the easements taken.

---

1. The mineral interest in the 10 acres is severable from the surface estate since the two estates are owned by different persons.

Services Please

4. (a) No taking occurred. Under most states' common law, a person has a right to access a public road if necessary for ingress and egress to his property. Closing one alternative does not amount to a violation of the common law as long as the landowner has an alternative route off his land. The town's closing the road did not deprive Corwin of any legal right, so no taking occurred.

   (b) Corwin loses again. Corwin must allege a regulatory taking resulted. Corwin asserts he lost all economically viable use of his land. That is not true. He could sell the land, or pay for the improvements. Corwin cannot win on the "no economically viable use" categorical taking theory.

   Alternatively, Corwin might insist he should be compensated based on an ad hoc factual inquiry focusing on the character of the government action and on the economic impact of the refusal on Corwin, particularly on the economic impact of the government's refusal on Corwin's reasonable investment-backed expectations. Unfortunately for Corwin, he had no reasonable investment-backed expectations. He owned unimproved land. He bought the land knowing the lots needed essential services and that he would have to work with the town to get them.

   Also weighing against Corwin is the character of the government action. The government did not invade Corwin's property. Historically, cities often make assessments against landowners whose property benefits from sidewalks, sewers, streets, and other improvements. As the Fourth Circuit Court of Appeals maintained, "[W]e can see absolutely no warrant for the proposition that where the government does not affirmatively prohibit the realization of investment-backed expectations, but merely refuses to enhance the value of real property, a compensable taking has occurred." See Front Royal IPC v. Town of Front Royal, 135 F.3d 275, 285 (4th Cir. 1998).

   The town acted appropriately. No taking occurred.

Access Denied

5. The state is liable to Grubb. Generally, a landowner has a common law right of access to a public road. (See Explanation 4(a) above.) A state can deny that access, however, if the landowner has other access off the property to another public road. The state in the case on which the facts of this Example are based argued alternatively that the state could deny Grubb all access to the highway because it was prudent for the state to deny Grubb's access for safety reasons and because Grubb had reasonable alternative access to a public road. See State v. Hanson, 987 P.2d 538 (Or. Ct. App. 1999).

Neither argument is relevant. Grubb was not relying on his common law right to access, but on an express reservation of an easement in the deed granting land to the state decades earlier. An easement is a property right. The state took the easement without compensating the Grubbs. The result was a taking.

As a review, the state has the right and power to deny Grubb access to the highway. The state has a legitimate state interest in safe driving conditions on public highways. Denying an individual landowner's private access to the highway is *rationally related* to the promotion of the *legitimate state interest* of public safety. Refusing to permit the continuation of an easement to the highway also is rationally related to achieving the legitimate state interest of safe driving conditions on the public highway. Whether the state has the power to deny Grubb access to the highway is a different issue, however, from whether the state must compensate Grubb. As discussed above, the state must compensate Grubb for taking his easement.

The Fun Part of Town

6. A zoning law or amendment effects a regulatory taking if the regulation is not related to a legitimate state purpose. Here the rezoning furthered at least three legitimate purposes: density control, flood control, and recreational opportunities.

A zoning law also can effect a taking if it denies the owner all economically viable use of her property. This rule does not help Breyer since she still can use her property for entrepreneurial recreational activities (i.e., a golf course and other activities).

Breyer might prevail under an ad hoc factual inquiry that considers the character of the government action and the economic effect of the regulation on the owner, particularly the owner's reasonable investment-backed expectations. The character of the government's action does not aid Breyer. The government will not physically invade her land nor authorize third parties to enter the land. Moreover, zoning through comprehensive planning is not a taking.

The effect on Breyer's use of her property does not aid her, either. Her reasonable investment-backed expectations center on the improvements made to operate the golf course. The zoning ordinance anticipates the golf course's ongoing operations. Breyer suffers no loss of investment-backed expectations on the golf course itself.

Breyer's real loss is on the 40 acres not directly related to the golf course. She has expended money in anticipation of building homes but has not built any yet. Unfortunately, that is not enough for Breyer to have investment-backed expectations in the 40 acres. The town's refusal to grant Breyer a building permit may have reduced the value of the

40 acres, but the land still has value. Mere diminution in value does not constitute a taking. Even if the 40 acres are valueless (which is unlikely), Breyer could prevail only if the court conceptually severs the 40 acres from the 110-acre golf course. A court most likely would not vertically sever the acreages. If the 150 acres are evaluated as one large parcel, a court likely would conclude Breyer can make a reasonable return on the full 150 acres by operating the golf course. The rezoning does not amount to a taking of Breyer's property.

The Law Is a Rough Proportionality

7. The dedication requirement is an exaction or condition for a special use permit. An exaction may constitute a taking if the exaction bears little or no relationship to the harm caused by the proposed development. Exactions review entails two steps. First there must be an essential nexus between the exaction and a legitimate state interest. The dedication of land to help reduce traffic problems is logically related to ameliorating increased traffic resulting from a larger service station (with a food store). Hence, the first element favors Poplar Heights.

Poplar Heights loses on the critical second analytical step, however. Under the second step, once the essential nexus is found, a court must decide if there is a rough proportionality between the condition exacted and the development's projected impact on the area. In this case, Poplar Heights had a policy of conditioning grants of special permits along Hard Road and Easy Street (and other places) on dedication of land for roadway expansion. The fortuitous increase in traffic by less than 0.4 percent does not justify dedication of 20 percent of the service station's land to the city, especially when, as would occur here, the city and the public would physically invade property formerly owned by Refined Oil even though only a small percentage of the travelers were there because of Refined Oil's service station. Finally, the city must lose because the city demanded the exaction as part of a program of required dedications rather than as an individualized determination the dedication related both in nature and extent to the increased traffic resulting from the remodeled service station.

Table of Cases

655

Table of Cases

Index

Index

Index

Index

Index